The

Concordia Pulpit

for 1963

Volume XXXIV

CONCORDIA PUBLISHING HOUSE -:- Saint Louis, Missouri

1962

CONTRIBUTORS

Vernold W. Aurich
Ann Arbor, Mich.

Robert O. Bannon
Port Huron, Mich.

Walter J. Bartling
Fort Wayne, Ind.

John H. Baumgaertner
Milwaukee, Wis.

Max G. Beck
Roosevelt Roads, Porto Rico

Charles R. Birner
Tulsa, Okla.

A. Karl Boehmke
Birmingham, Mich.

Armin W. Born
Detroit, Mich.

William H. Bornemann
Torrington, Wyo.

Norman Brandt
Milwaukee, Wis.

Henry W. Brill
El Paso, Tex.

Alfred M. Buls
Granite City, Ill.

Richard R. Caemmerer
St. Louis, Mo.

Robert H. Clausen
Athens, Ga.

John Daniel
Bethlehem, Pa.

Richard P. Deffner
Athens, Ga.

Robert L. Dorow
St. Joseph, Mich.

Paul J. Foust
Detroit, Mich.

Philip Fry
Beatrice, Nebr.

Carl A. Gaertner
Dallas, Tex.

Wilbert E. Griesse
Fort Smith, Ark.

Kurt V. Grotheer
Itasca, Ill.

Paul G. Hansen
Denver, Colo.

Henry W. Hartenberger
Toledo, Ohio

Raymond C. Hohenstein
Washington, D. C.

George W. Hoyer
St. Louis, Mo.

Harry N. Huxhold
Minneapolis, Minn.

Emil G. Jaech
Seattle, Wash.

Enno E. Klammer
North Highlands, Calif.

Clarence W. Knippa
Tulsa, Okla.

Alfred W. Koehler
Oakland, Calif.

Leonard W. Koehler
Winnipeg, Man., Can.

Walter E. Kraemer
Oakland, Calif.

Arne P. Kristo
Valparaiso, Ind.

Ottomar Krueger
Akron, Ohio

Henry A. Loeber
Fair Lawn, N. J.

F. Dean Lueking
River Forest, Ill.

Elmer O. Luessenhop
Sioux Falls, S. Dak.

Arlin A. Maas
Whitestone, N. Y.

Walter A. Maier, Jr.
Milwaukee, Wis.

Martin E. Mayer, Jr.
Wausau, Wis.

Richard P. Meibohm
Tucson, Ariz.

Robert K. Menzel
Portland, Oreg.

Arnold F. Meyer
Minneapolis, Minn.

Lothar K. Meyer
Niagara Falls, N.Y.

Ewald H. Mueller
Ridgewood, N.J.

Gerhard H. Mundinger
Los Angeles, Calif.

William H. Mundinger
Sebewaing, Mich.

Lewis C. Niemoeller
Springfield, Ill.

Gilbert T. Otte
Detroit, Mich.

Harold G. Parsch
Shawano, Wis.

Clarence H. Pauling
Minneapolis, Minn.

Arthur Carl Piepkorn
St. Louis, Mo.

Edwin E. Pieplow
Fort Worth, Tex.

Albert F. Pollex
Toronto, Ont., Can.

Rudolph F. Rehmer
West Lafayette, Ind.

Waldemar A. Rook
Baltimore, Md.

Robert H. Rosenkoetter
Manhattan, Kans.

Samuel J. Roth
Ferguson, Mo.

Edgar G. Runge
Charlotte, N.C.

Martin W. Rupprecht
St. Petersburg, Fla.

Clemonce Sabourin
New York, N.Y.

Herman C. Scherer
St. Louis, Mo.

G. Walter Schoedel
Midland, Mich.

Kenneth R. Schueler
Forest Park, Ill.

John F. Schutt
Port Colborne, Ont., Can.

Roland H. A. Seboldt
Oak Lawn, Ill.

Alfred C. Seltz
Thief River Falls, Minn.

Robert C. Seltz
Ann Arbor, Mich.

George H. Sommermeyer
St. Louis, Mo.

Paul G. Stephan
Des Moines, Iowa

Omar T. Stuenkel
Denver, Colo.

Carl H. Toelke
Chicago, Ill.

Arnold T. Wangerin
Kirkwood, Mo.

Walter J. Warneck
University City, Mo.

William F. Wedig
New Orleans, La.

Earl E. Weis
Hammond, Ind.

Arthur O. Werfelmann
Libby, Mont.

Roland P. Wiederaenders
Corpus Christi, Tex.

George W. Wittmer
St. Louis, Mo.

Henry C. Wolk, Jr.
San Francisco, Calif.

Theodore A. Zeile
Flint, Mich.

Edwin C. Zschoche
Portland, Oreg.

PRINTED IN U.S A

Themes and Authors of Sermons

IV

Special Series

INDEX OF SCRIPTURE TEXTS TREATED

Sermons
Based on the
Synodical Conference
Alternate Gospel Series

A Deathless Promise at the Birth of a Year

By Edwin C. Zschoche

(The First Sunday in Advent)

And when He was demanded of the Pharisees when the kingdom of God should come, He answered them and said, The kingdom of God cometh not with observation. Neither shall they say, Lo here! or Lo there! For behold, the kingdom of God is within you. And He said unto the disciples, The days will come when ye shall desire to see one of the days of the Son of man, and ye shall not see it. And they shall say to you, See here, or See there. Go not after them, nor follow them. For as the lightning that lighteneth out of the one part under heaven shineth unto the other part under heaven, so shall also the Son of man be in His day. But first must He suffer many things and be rejected of this generation. — *Luke 17:20-25*

We have met today, on this first Sunday in Advent, to usher in, by God's grace, a new church year. At the beginning of a year the various trades and occupations customarily make predictions concerning the year ahead. Some of these are optimistic, some pessimistic, some alarming. We Christians are human, too, and at the beginning of a new church year many questions fill our minds — questions to which we wish we knew the answers. We look to the Lord of the church for help and guidance, but somehow we also wish there were some way we could gauge our success in advance. We are in sympathy with the Pharisees as they ask when the kingdom of God is coming. We, too, would like a sign of some kind from the Lord in the year of grace ahead.

Nor is such a request, rightly asked, something offensive to our Lord. He Himself once invited Abraham to count the stars to show him how countless his seed would be. Gideon was given a sign of the truth of God's promises through the fleece which remained dry while all the earth was wet. The angel on Christmas Eve gave the shepherds a definite identification concerning the newly born Jesus when he declared, "This shall be a sign unto you: Ye shall find the Babe wrapped in swaddling clothes, lying in a manger." But God does not always provide visible signs, nor the exact signs we desire. On this side of eternity our work by and large is a work of faith, which rests on things unseen. Only when we stand before our Lord in glory shall we hold results and fruit in abundance.

Yet the loving Jesus does not leave us without promise concerning our work. Our text is well timed to bring out His faith-strengthening lesson in regard to this matter at the very beginning of a new church year. May it inspire us to greater effort than ever before. May its promises thrill us in the day of fulfillment.

This deathless assurance at the birth of a new church year reads:

"The Kingdom of God Is Within You"

These words of Jesus were addressed to a group of Pharisees who had asked Jesus for a definite statement concerning the appearance of God's kingdom. They were neither the first nor the last to ask about a special appearance of the Kingdom. Some of those who asked, asked in ridicule, some in puzzlement, some in scorn, some in honest concern. There is nothing in the text to indicate that the questioners were attempting to trap Jesus, and His answer is simply that the Kingdom is within you. This is a deathless promise. It was first made when God had every reason to withdraw His love from man, back in the Garden of Eden, when man had exchanged the beauty of the promise of God for the ashes of Satan's lies and delusions. It was there that the merciful God first promised His love to the man and his wife cowering in shame behind their hastily fashioned garments of fig leaves. In that hour the Lord promised an overthrow of the devil, to whom they had foolishly sold themselves. He promised to conquer Satan through His Son, whom He would give the woman. And in the hearts of Adam and Eve were born new hope and faith and forgiveness. This moment was the birthday of the kingdom of God as we sinners know it; for when God through the Gospel offers His love to sinners, that is the kingdom of God.

Every Generation Has Heard It

Every generation since then has heard this promise. It came to Abraham, to Isaac, and to Jacob. Moses and Aaron heard it, as did David and his seed. In every generation we have evidences of the working of God's love in human hearts. There was Mother Eve, to whom the very first promise was given, calling her very first son Cain, because she believed the woman's Seed promised of God would be her firstborn. There was Joseph, the prime minister of Egypt, happy and content in his adopted country, who on his deathbed commanded that his bones should not be buried in Egypt, but that he be laid to rest in Canaan, in the country God had promised to the patriarchs, the country whence Jesus would come. There was Job, who, in the very midst of the troubles which beset him, declared his faith in the promises of the coming Messiah by confessing, "I know that my Redeemer liveth." It was this kingdom of God within which prompted David to write: "The Lord is my Shepherd; I shall not want." It is this kingdom which Isaiah (ch. 53) pictures so beautifully.

There were times, to be sure, when the promises of Christ's advent in the flesh seemed to be without a single receptive, believing heart. Such days occurred before the Flood, when the wickedness of men caused God to say, "I will destroy man, whom I have created, from the face of the earth." Another such time, it is recorded, took place in Israel when Elijah the Prophet had exposed and destroyed the prophets of Baal and the reaction was far different from what Elijah had hoped; for in her anger Jezebel, the Baal-worshiping queen, vowed to avenge their lives by killing Elijah. We read that this man of God asked the Lord to let him die because his ministry was completely without fruit. Or again, think of the day when Nebuchadnezzar, who had taken the Jews captive, made a decree that anyone found worshiping anybody besides the huge image of gold would be thrown into a fiery furnace. How could the kingdom of God survive under such conditions?

But to each generation God's promise "The kingdom of God is within you" was kept. Noah and his sons carried the promise into the ark during the Flood, in which all flesh was destroyed; Elijah was assured that 7,000 Israelites had not worshiped Baal; Nebuchadnezzar's threats could not drive the Kingdom from the hearts of Shadrach, Meshach, and Abednego. Every generation, faithless or faithful, had this assurance. Even among the proud Pharisees there were those whose hearts accepted Christ as the Messiah, and such stood before Him during the interview pictured to us in Luke 17.

It seems strange that there should be such a misunderstanding of the Kingdom in the days of Jesus. John the Baptist had under God prepared the way, had pointed out the Christ as the Lamb of God. By deed and word Jesus had painstakingly pointed out that everything was in fulfillment of Scripture, that this was Kingdom work. Perhaps it was not so strange after all that the meaning of the Kingdom was not grasped. We often accept as true what we like to hear. Certain childhood customs linger with us even after we learn differently. It was somewhat like that with the Jews of Jesus' time. They recalled that Scripture spoke of Jesus as David's Son. David to them was a man of God, but they recalled him more as a fearless king who made their nation a world power. Their popular thinking made the coming Christ more and more a king of power. This picture was especially winsome because the hated Romans had overrun their country and made it a province. So when John the Baptist proclaimed the advent of the Kingdom, and when Jesus Himself spoke of it, they were satisfied that this was the Messiah; but they were impatient and wanted Jesus to "get down to business." They wanted action. They wanted Him to assert His influence in driving out the Romans. After several miracles, especially after He fed the 5,000, they thought His hour had come — or rather, their hour of deliverance. Their sins did not trouble them as much as their Roman lords; conquest over Satan did not seem as important as triumph over Caesar Augustus.

So the Jews sent representatives to Jesus repeatedly, as here in the text.

In repeating to them, "The kingdom of God is within you," Jesus laid upon their hearts once again the truth that the kingdom of God is the gentle rule of the Lord through the Holy Spirit in the hearts of the believers, won for them by His sacrifice on the cross, and mediated through the means of grace, the Word and the Sacraments. Those who become members of this Kingdom are those whom we call the holy Christian church, or as Luther calls them in his Smalcald Articles, "the holy believers and lambs who hear the voice of their Shepherd." According to v. 25, Jesus states that the establishment or fulfillment of all the Kingdom promises hinges on His Passion. To this every Christian subscribes, but there are times — and there will also be such in the new church year — when our flesh will be weak and our work will seem uphill and without special blessing of the Lord. It was because our Lord knew of this that He turned to His disciples after his interview with the Pharisees and told them they would pass through trials (vv. 22, 23) and that there would come times when they would be almost at the point of despair for desiring proof of His kingdom. In those days it would stand them in good stead to remember this promise: It is within you. My Word will never change. My love will never cool. My promises will never fail. Others, He told them, will try to see Christ's revelation in occurrences aside from the Word. "Go not after them," Jesus says, "nor follow them."

"See Here"; "See There!"

This business of looking for Jesus apart from His express Word and promise is a favorite trick of Satan since the very beginning. Sometimes subtly, sometimes brazenly, he has gone about his lying task. Sometimes successfully, sometimes without result, he has approached every generation. To Adam and Eve he spoke: "Not within you is the kingdom of God but in the fruit of this tree. Here you will become like God Himself. Here you will receive wisdom and power you do not now have." At the side of Lot's wife, as she fled from the burning city of Sodom, he whispered, "Not in tiny, unknown Zoar lies your happiness but in the city from which you are fleeing. Turn around, and see what I mean." To Joseph, a slave in Egypt, he came through his master's wife: "Why try to serve the God of your father Jacob? What but unhappiness has that brought you? What reward is there in that? Behold what manner of pleasure is yours if you but heed the invitation of the temptress!" To the Children of Israel he came in the pessimistic report of the twelve spies: "Your future does not lie in Canaan with its high-walled cities, its giants, and its terrain.

All this means only hard work. Nay, turn back to Egypt, with its fish, and melons, and cucumbers, and leeks, and onions, and garlic. Appoint you a general to take you back."

Satan even had the audacity to try the same tactics on Jesus Himself. It was right after His Baptism and God's calling Him My beloved Son that the devil came to Jesus and showed and offered Him all the kingdoms of the world. The clear implication was that, if He was really the Son of God, He deserved more than the mere word God had spoken.

"Go Not After Them"

"Lo here!" and "Lo there!" Thus Satan still tempts. No doubt until the end of time these words will resound because it is so human to look for tangible results. There is danger that the church will lose its proper perspective when we stress visible results at the expense of sowing the Word of God. Such matters as social reforms, integration, anticommunist campaigns, blue laws, housing regulations, and even the attainment of synodical goals, may be things to which every Christian may subscribe; but when the impression is given that only such as are actively engaged in such activities are the true Christians even though they do not in their hearts love the Lord and serve Him with their talents and means, that is certainly not teaching that "the kingdom of God is within you."

Our task is to make sure that we are sowing the Gospel seed in human hearts. Without this, there can be no harvest such as God promises. This matter of sowing the seed is largely a matter of doctrine, proclaimed especially by those who are called to declare the will of God — the preachers. That was one reason why the disciples and other Christians of Christ's time had difficulty in grasping the truth of the Kingdom. Their priests and religious leaders did not teach it correctly. Remember how one time Jesus asked His disciples, "Whom do men say that I, the Son of man, am?" He received a number of answers. Some thought he was a prophet, some Elias, and some even thought He was a devil. It was then that Peter declared, "Thou art the Christ, the Son of the living God." And Jesus did not correct him. He called him blessed.

Suppose Jesus had said, "Peter, you must not go contrary to what the religious teachers of this age are saying. They are very learned. They should know." The devil has ever used so-called prophets to say, "Lo here!" and "Lo there!" to mislead the simple. Think what would have happened had Noah listened to these pseudo prophets while he was building the ark! What would have happened if Isaiah and Jeremiah had been taken in by what the theologians were saying in their day? What would have happened to Luther and the Reformation if he had permitted himself to be influenced by popular theological trends of his day? How could The Lutheran Church — Missouri Synod ever have come to life if Dr. Walther and his brethren had been content to live under the rationalistic influence of 19th-century theologians of Germany?

This is a danger which ever challenges the church. We can become influenced by what theologians are thinking in our generation. With their learning, their "new" style, their findings, their studies, they begin to make myths of Scripture, and they weaken the infallible Word of God by asserting that God actually did not inspire His Word, but that in condescension He used witnesses who spoke in a way which agreed with legends and religious theories. Thus they can tear down the authority of Scripture and teach another way of salvation, not *the* Way. This also is a "Lo here! Lo there!" of the devil. Let us be on our guard. Let us continue to confess with the fathers:

> God's Word and Luther's doctrine pure,
> Shall to eternity endure.

"My Word Shall Not Return unto Me Void"

And so we constantly sow the seed, firmly believing that God will provide us with a harvest. At times we may feel tempted to underrate the means of grace as the means by which God wants to build His kingdom. Then we need to remind ourselves of texts like this: "As the rain cometh down, and the snow from heaven . . . so shall My Word be that goeth forth out of My mouth; it shall not return unto Me void, but it shall accomplish that which I please, and it shall prosper in the thing whereto I sent it." (Is. 55:10, 11)

This Kingdom Is Within Me?

"The kingdom of God is within you." This means, since by the grace of God I am a Christian, it is within me. It means that this body of mine has become God's temple, my heart has become His throne, and my intellect and members are now first and foremost the servants and handmaids of my King. That is what I read in 1 Cor. 6:19, 20: "Know ye not that your body is the temple of the Holy Ghost, which is in you, which ye have of God, and ye are not your own? For ye are bought with a price; therefore glorify God in your body and in your spirit, which are God's."

But this can't be true, can it? When the Lord on the night of His betrayal told His disciples that one of them would betray Him, they in doubt and shame asked, "Lord, is it I?" They could not believe this possible. So my weak flesh asks here, "Lord, is it true that Thy glorious kingdom of love is within me?" And God's Holy Spirit, whispering of Christ's forgiving love to my soul, as demonstrated on Calvary, assures me it is true — gloriously, wonderfully true. Then, like the centurion, I say, "Lord, I am not worthy that Thou shouldest come under my roof." What does God want in my heart? Could He not find better hearts than mine, more brilliant minds than mine, more talented and better educated people, for the promotion and advancement of His kingdom? But God in His mercy chose me as certainly as He chose Mount Ararat as a place for His ark to settle, as certainly as He chose a virgin named Mary to mother His only-begotten Son. And with this promise in my heart, I can face the new year joyfully.

If I Lose This, I Lose All

A prominent painting shows a man rowing steadily through a heavy sea. The air is storm-laden; all about are glowering clouds and darkness and winds of gale velocity. In the sky near the horizon is a lone star to guide him. The caption of the picture is: "If I lose this, I lose all." Never has the ark of our beloved church been launched at the birth of a new year under circumstances more fearful, more uncertain, than those which usher in this year. But here we have a divine promise, and it guides our souls in the darkest night: "The kingdom of God is within you." This is a comfort which nothing devised by the world, Satan, or even our frail flesh can take from us. This is the promise of which Luther sang:

> And take they our life,
> Goods, fame, child, and wife,
> Let these all be gone,
> They yet have nothing won;
> The Kingdom ours remaineth.

My soul, ponder this. Advent is upon thee. Again thou wilt hear the story of how Jesus was not ashamed of the manger — neither the one in Bethlehem nor the one within thy bosom. Surely thine eyes must light as the star over little Bethlehem if thou art certain of His desire to dwell with thee. And thy lips must join the voices of the Christmas angels, for this is a sign unto thee: "The kingdom of God is within thee." This deathless promise, my soul, is thine, at the birth of this new church year. Bless the Lord, O my soul!

The Message of Advent

By Earl E. Weis

(The Second Sunday in Advent)

And his father Zacharias was filled with the Holy Ghost and prophesied, saying: Blessed be the Lord God of Israel; for He hath visited and redeemed His people and hath raised up an Horn of salvation for us in the house of His servant David, as He spake by the mouth of His holy prophets, which have been since the world began: that we should be saved from our enemies and from the hand of all that hate us; to perform the mercy promised to our fathers and to remember His holy covenant, the oath which He sware to our father Abraham, that He would grant unto us that we, being delivered out of the hand of our enemies, might serve Him without fear, in holiness and righteousness before Him, all the days of our life. And thou, child, shalt be called the prophet of the Highest; for thou shalt go before the face of the Lord to prepare His ways; to give knowledge of salvation unto His people by the remission of their sins, through the tender mercy of our God, whereby the Day-spring from on high hath visited us, to give light to them that sit in darkness and in the shadow of death, to guide our feet into the way of peace. And the child grew, and waxed strong in spirit, and was in the deserts till the day of his showing unto Israel. — *Luke 1:67-80*

The Message of Advent

A baby was born in the hill country of Judah almost 20 centuries ago. The child's name was John. This fact, isolated from its rich context, would be devoid of either interest or significance to posterity. However, certain factors contributed to the great importance of this event recorded by Luke as God inspired him to write it.

This boy John, born to aged Elizabeth and her husband Zacharias, was a child of promise. God's angel Gabriel had announced the coming of John to Zacharias, revealing to him the fact that the son yet unborn would one day be filled with the Holy Ghost. At this announcement Zacharias should have responded with a song of praise. Because of his disbelief, however, the father-to-be was rendered dumb, that is, temporarily speechless, until the angel's promise should be fulfilled.

When in due time the child was born, Zacharias disappointed the relatives, who wanted the boy to be named after his father, by announcing in writing that the baby's name was John. Thereupon God loosed the tongue of the happy father so that the pent-up stream of prophecy could flow forth from his mouth in a rhythmic hymn of praise. His words, the Benedictus, constitute the essence of our text for this Advent Sunday. As we examine them, let us draw from them through God's Holy Spirit.

The Message of Advent

I

The Nature of the Message

"Zacharias was filled with the Holy Ghost and prophesied." When he spoke, parental joy was swallowed up by zeal for God and religious fervor. The song he sang was a song of rejoicing in redemption for fallen and lost mankind. His was a song that earth could neither comprehend nor properly appreciate. Zacharias' hymn was born in heaven to tell of earth's redemption.

A Content of Deep Significance

Without a doubt, the apparent joy evidenced in the words of Zacharias issued from a heart filled to overflowing with fervent faith. Once he had doubted divine omnipotence, but now his eyes were opened. He was confronted with the eternal faithfulness of divine promise. He recognized God's Word as altogether true, even as He is true. In the face of current skepticism and unmasked doubt the unwavering faith of God's holy prophet is both refreshing and encouraging.

Zacharias' Advent message proclaims the good news that "God hath visited and redeemed His people." Not that God for a time had forgotten and ignored His people, cutting off from them His eternal concern or the stream of His mercy. The everlasting arms of the Lord were upholding His chosen ones as always, and God was still looking upon His children with an active concern. But now the fullness of the time was come. All things were now ready that the prophecies of old should be fulfilled and revealed in Christ the Lord.

So clearly did God reveal the approaching birth of Jesus to Zacharias that he said of the Covenant God of Israel, "He *hath* visited and redeemed His people." To him the advent was already an accomplished fact. Zacharias took his imagery from the prophecies of the Old Testament, but his lucid words gave evidence of the rising light of the New.

God's purpose in visiting His people was spelled out most plainly by Zacharias when he explained that it was to *redeem* them. His entire prophecy has aptly been described as a "Song of Redemption." Zacharias was fully aware of the spiritual bondage and the disastrous plight of the whole human race. He knew full well that sin had come into the world and death by sin. He, too, had to say with the psalmist, "I acknowledge my transgressions, and my sin is ever before me" (Ps. 51:3). As a priest of God of the course of Abia he had doubtlessly brought numerous sin offerings to the Lord in behalf of his people. No wonder he could sing of redemption in such a soul-stirring way!

The Message of Redemption

When God's people sing of redemption today, do they always capture the full scope and significance of the term? Do they always rejoice in a complete realization of what this word should mean to them? If the present Advent season brings into sharper focus for us the glorious purpose of God's coming down in Christ Jesus to this sin-sick, death-infested earth to save us, it shall once again have served a most worthy purpose. By visiting us with His salvation, sending His Son to redeem us, our loving Father has visited us with His mercy. Christ Jesus, by His supreme sacrifice has purchased and won us from the bondage of sin and from the power of death and the devil. Now we need no longer be afraid of God — afraid of either the past, present, or future. We need not fear death itself, for Jesus came to be our Savior. Since all have sinned, all men who would be released from sin's bondage need the world's only Savior. Thanks be to God, redemption is all-embracing! Zacharias rejoiced because God had visited and redeemed the people Israel. However, this does not preclude His forgiveness and peace for the Gentile nations. Jesus came to be the Savior of all the world. When He lauded the faith of one particular Gentile, the centurion of Capernaum, He added, "I say unto you that many shall come from the east and west and shall sit down with Abraham and Isaac and Jacob in the kingdom of heaven" (Matt. 8:11). Today we Christians of the Western world rejoice in God's redemption. We now are dedicated to share our Savior with all men of every race and land and clime.

Zacharias holds another picture before us when he describes the Redeemer as "an Horn of salvation." The horn had long been viewed as a symbol of power and strength. David had already praised God as his Fortress and Deliverer, his Strength and Buckler, "the Horn of my salvation, and my high Tower" (Ps. 18:2). Such symbols of strength may seem incompatible with the products of present-day scientists and engineers. Nuclear devices with explosive power measured in ratio to dynamite by the megaton obviously are capable of producing destruction beyond the wildest expectation of scientists of not too many years ago. But the Coming One described in our text exerts a greater strength. The whole world is in His hands. He is Lord of the heavens and the earth. His name is called Wonderful, Counselor, the mighty God!

Serving Without Fear

Through the redemption long foretold and subsequently unfolded to him by special revelation, Zacharias knew "that we should be saved from our enemies and from the hand of all that hate us." The Children of Israel in Zacharias' day cherished the hope of emancipation from the Roman tyranny. It is impossible to say how much hope for national, political, and social deliverance Zacharias may have included in his own thought. The enemies to which he referred in our text, however, are the enemies against which Christ proved Himself a "Horn of salvation" namely, Satan and all the powers of darkness. He came to deliver us from the devil, the world, and our own sinful flesh.

Zacharias' Advent message also reminds us that God's redemptive work is not carried out because we deserve any degree of favor or consideration from Him. Mankind since the fateful fall of Adam and Eve in Paradise has been devoid of righteousness. Mankind has been languishing in the miserable, wretched plight of sin. So loathsome is man's status by nature that it has evoked the pity of God, who is Love. Our text explains that God has sent His Horn of salvation "to perform the mercy promised to our fathers." All the mercy of God manifested or promised during the Old Testament dispensation pointed to the one great act of mercy that He would show to His people by sending forth His Son. Out of His constant cognizance of man's need and His promise to save him came this action of remembering His holy covenant.

The redemption that God planned by the blood of Jesus was not a new or a sudden solution on His part to remove the calamity of man's sin with its eternally disastrous consequences. Rather this had all been foretold "as He spake by the mouth of His holy prophets, which have been since the world began." As a case in point, Zacharias makes reference to "the oath which He sware to our father Abraham, that He would grant unto us, that we, being delivered out of the hand of our enemies, might serve Him without fear, in holiness and righteousness before Him, all the days of our life." Christ's true disciples, delivered from sin, death, and the devil by His atoning sacrifice, ought always to serve God without fear even in the face of trial and persecution. When Jesus sent out His disciples, He included these words in His admonition: "Fear not them which kill the body but are not able to kill the soul; but rather fear Him which is able to destroy both soul and body in hell" (Matt. 10:28). All of us who profess to be children of the heavenly Father ought to give evidence of our trust in Him by maintaining a calm, collected spirit even when beset by adversity. One of the gravest menaces to the body of Christ today is atheistic communism. When its haughty advocates cajole, threaten, and attempt every sort of intimidation, even proposing to "bury" us, we Christians should remember the promise of the Lord that we are indeed delivered from the hand of all our enemies. Let us trust in Him who says, "Be not afraid, neither be thou dismayed, for the Lord, thy God, is with thee whithersoever thou goest" (Joshua 1:9). Let us be strong and of good courage, always ready to serve the Lord with gladness.

A Reflection of Happiness

Zacharias' prophecy does not cater to mere earthly gratification. In our day of crass materialism, with all of its alluring enticements, it is becoming an increasingly difficult challenge really to serve God as a people distinctly set apart. Beset as we are with the concepts of mass production and big business, we are under constant pressure to rationalize ourselves into the compromising position of worshiping at the false shrine of conformity. The young child already persists in various absurd demands for the profound reason that "everybody in school does it." And the father comes home a little worse for wear after a "few drinks with the boys" because somebody laughed at his naïveté when he declined last week. But genuine satisfaction cannot be discovered in the crowd.

Neither can it be purchased with gold. While Americans gave some $2 billion to the Lord in recent years, they spent 5 billion for tobacco, over 9 billion for vacations, and about 17 billion for recreation and sports. But where is the calm serenity and peaceful satisfaction that men seek? Not in the ways of the world, to be sure. Lasting happiness is reflected on the face of that man, that woman, and that child only who rejoices with Zacharias because God has raised up the Horn of salvation "that we should be saved from our enemies," that we might serve Him without fear.

II

The Deep Meaning of the Message

After Zacharias had poured out from his heart the expression of a rich measure of love for God in his eloquent song of praise, he proceeded with a brief description in prophecy of the part his own son should play in the great saving work of God. "And thou, child, shalt be called the prophet of the Highest; for thou shalt go before the face of the Lord to prepare His ways." Gabriel had revealed to Zacharias already at the announcement of John's birth that many should rejoice at his birth, "for he shall be great in the sight of the Lord . . . and he shall be filled with the Holy Ghost, even from his mother's womb. And many of the children of Israel shall he turn to the Lord, their God" (Luke 1: 15, 16). The angel's message was corroborated by a statement from the lips of Jesus in His testimony concerning John: "Verily I say unto you, Among them that are born of women there hath not risen a greater than John the Baptist" (Matt. 11: 11). Still the Baptist showed no sign of conceit. It was he who sensed unworthiness even to loose the Master's shoes. His humility was prompted by the same knowledge revealed to his father, that Jesus Christ is Lord. John was to be the greatest of the prophets destined to "go before the face of the Lord to prepare His ways." How proud Zacharias must have been! Nonetheless, he showed his humble spirit and his vision of the glory of the Lord. For rather than dwell on the divine favor bestowed upon his own son, he once again stressed the deep meaning of the Messianic gift. It was John's appointed purpose to prepare the way of the Lord, to make straight in the desert a highway for our God, "to give knowledge of salvation unto His people by the remission of their sins." Here Zacharias pointed to the central teaching of the Bible: salvation by the remission of sins. For Christ's sake, on account of His atoning sacrifice, the Father declares those righteous who accept His precious gift.

Darkness Turned to Light

The world, having fallen from God and turned against Him, found itself bogged down in an unenviable predicament. Our text describes the world as sitting in darkness and in the shadow of death. Physical darkness is bad enough. Close your eyes for a few moments only, and try to move about. You immediately have a small concept of what blindness can mean. Picture a lost caravan trudging across a hot desert through the darkness of night. What a sensation of utter hopelessness and despair! Many a child has an exaggerated fear of darkness developed by someone who has prompted his fright. Most adults have some rather definite misgivings about walking alone along some dark street in the blackness of the night. Spiritual darkness is worse by far! By his sinful nature, man is blind, dead, and an enemy of God. He is walking in the shadow of death. Death is so near to him that its dreary shadow falls over his helpless form. This deplorable condition was not peculiar to the generation to which Christ came. It applies today in the very heart of Christendom wherever men refuse to let Christ's light shine.

Jesus came to bring light to this dreary world darkened by sin. He is the Dayspring from on high promised in the prophecy of Zacharias. In Him we see Malachi's "Sun of righteousness . . . with healing in His wings" (Mal. 4:2). He is our bright and morning Star, as John aptly describes Him in his Revelation. He sends light and hope to shine brightly into the night. When instruments fail the pilot flying aimlessly through the night, what sight could be more welcome to him than that of a beacon to guide him on his course? By means of the piercing light of Christ we who follow Him can see. First we see but darkly, as those who enter a dim room from one that is very bright. Then, after some time, our eyes become adjusted. As God's Holy Spirit enters our hearts through the light of the Gospel, we are enveloped more and more with His pure brightness. If we keep our eyes focused on Christ, one day our eyes will be completely opened in heaven, where we shall enjoy perfect vision forever.

Christ Guides Our Steps to Heaven

In the closing words of the Benedictus, Zacharias gives the assurance that Christ would "guide our feet into the way of peace." Natural man has no inborn radar to guide him to heaven. On the contrary, the world is pointed to hell; "the wages of sin is death" (Rom. 6:23). Each of us must confess, "I know that in me (that is, in my flesh) dwelleth no good thing" (Rom. 7:18). "I believe that I cannot by my own reason or strength believe in Jesus Christ, my Lord, or come to Him." Natural man, by virtue of his perverse nature, is in the hand of his enemies, says the holy writer. Science has unfolded many mysteries today. But it still has discovered no alloy against sin, and it never will. Only Jesus offers hope. He alone is the Bringer of salvation. Oh, may every one of us dedicate himself forever to Him that he may walk in the way of peace, the condition of harmony between God and us through Christ Jesus!

For all Christ has done for us and our salvation we owe Him much, we owe Him everything. Let us consecrate our lives to Him. We are weak, but in Him we shall be strong. May the Advent season help us properly to prepare to receive Him who guides our steps to heaven!

> Redeemer, come! I open wide
> My heart to Thee; here, Lord, abide!
> Let me Thine inner presence feel,
> Thy grace and love in me reveal;
> Thy Holy Spirit guide us on
> Until our glorious goal is won.
> Eternal praise and fame
> We offer to Thy name.

An Advent Service in the Wilderness

By G. WALTER SCHOEDEL

(The Third Sunday in Advent)

And He came into all the country about Jordan, preaching the Baptism of repentance for the remission of sins, as it is written in the book of the words of Esaias the Prophet, saying: The voice of one crying in the wilderness, Prepare ye the way of the Lord, make His paths straight. Every valley shall be filled, and every mountain and hill shall be brought low, and the crooked shall be made straight, and the rough ways shall be made smooth, and all flesh shall see the salvation of God. Then said he to the multitude that came forth to be baptized of him, O generation of vipers, who hath warned you to flee from the wrath to come? Bring forth therefore fruits worthy of repentance, and begin not to say within yourselves, We have Abraham to our father. For I say unto you that God is able of these stones to raise up children unto Abraham. And now also the ax is laid unto the root of the trees. Every tree therefore which bringeth not forth good fruit is hewn down and cast into the fire. And the people asked him, saying, What shall we do, then? He answered and saith unto them, He that hath two coats, let him impart to him that hath none, and he that hath meat, let him do likewise. Then came also publicans to be baptized and said unto him, Master, what shall we do? And he said unto them, Exact no more than that which is appointed you. And the soldiers likewise demanded of him, saying, And what shall we do? And he said unto them, Do violence to no man, neither accuse any falsely; and be content with your wages. — Luke 3:3-14

"WE're ready for Christmas," say the department store advertisements; "are YOU?" The shelves of these establishments are filled with merchandise. The public is urged to buy so that all may have a so-called merry Christmas. The streets and homes of our cities have been decorated with lights and trees and tinsel. Everywhere people are preparing for the big day.

The church, too, is ready. During the Advent season it proclaims its message to all who will listen. From countless pulpits we hear again the many Old Testament prophecies concerning the coming of the Messiah. We sense something of the intense longing of God's ancient people to experience the fulfillment of these promises. We rejoice in the knowledge that the prophecies have been fulfilled.

The church is ready, but are *you*? In the midst of all your preparation for Christmas, do not forget the true significance of Christ's birth for you and for all mankind. Let God make ready your hearts so that the Savior may enter and dwell there. The Advent season should help you appreciate more fully what God has done for you. It would be difficult to find a better preparation than that afforded by a service held some 1,900 years ago near the river Jordan. Let us in spirit attend

An Advent Service in the Wilderness

I

The Congregation

The holy writers tell us that multitudes came to the first Advent service. We mingle with the crowds who have come out from the city of Jerusalem, from the towns and villages of Judea, from all the region about Jordan. The word has gone out that a most remarkable preacher is attracting large numbers to hear his stirring messages. We look about us and notice priests and Levites, soldiers, publicans, Pharisees, Sadducees, and people from all walks of life. Many of this throng have come merely out of curiosity, others are here because they always follow the crowds, and still others are present because they want to give the impression that they are exceptionally holy. But there are also those who feel a real and desperate spiritual need. They hope to hear or learn something that will supply the answers to the problems of their souls.

Again this Christmas we may expect crowded churches throughout our land. Unfortunately many people will come only because John or Mary will have a "piece" to recite during the children's service. Others will follow their usual custom of attending church on special occasions. Thank God, however, that there will be many devoted Christians who never tire of hearing the Christmas Gospel. They are happy for the opportunity afforded them to worship the Christ Child and in thanksgiving and praise to join their voices with those of fellow Christians.

II

The Advent Preacher

The Advént preacher at the Jordan River is John the Baptist. Where could you find a more qualified person to conduct this service? Who is this extraordinary man? He is one of the most popular and successful preachers of all time! The historian Luke says very simply of him: "The Word of God came unto John, the son of Zacharias, in the wilderness. And he came into all the country about Jordan, preaching the Baptism of repentance for the remission of sins."

His coming had been prophesied by Isaiah, saying, "The voice of one crying in the wilderness, Prepare ye the way of the Lord, make his paths straight." His father, the aged priest, had made this prediction concerning him, "And thou, child, shalt be called the prophet of the Highest, for thou shalt go before the face of the Lord to prepare His ways, to give knowledge of salvation unto His people by the remission of their sins." (Luke 1: 76, 77)

Many have wondered how John spent his years from infancy to manhood. The Scriptures do not tell us. Presumably many of these years were devoted to study, meditation, and waiting for the day when he should emerge from the desert to make ready the way for the Messiah. God was preparing him for his appointed task. The same Lord who revealed Himself to Moses at the burning bush, to Ezekiel at the river Chebar, to prophets and apostles by inspiration of the Holy Spirit, in some way made His Word and His will known to John in the wilderness. And when he was fully prepared he came out of seclusion to begin his public ministry.

His Appearance

The evangelists describe our Advent preacher as one leading an austere life. His food was locusts and wild honey. His raiment was of camel's hair. He wore a leather girdle about his loins. His very appearance and manner of life presented the image of a man intent on a holy and serious mission.

His Zeal

What impresses you most about this man is his fiery zeal. He reminds you of Elijah, who was zealous to bring his people back to the God of Israel. With scathing denunciations he lashes out against cruelty and injustice. He is so dedicated to this task of being Christ's herald that later when the crowds leave him and follow Jesus, he will watch them go and say, "He must increase, but I must decrease." Christ said of him, "Among them that are born of woman there hath not risen a greater than John the Baptist." The followers of Christ have held his name and work in such high regard that while the church usually celebrates the festivals of the saints on the days of their death, it honors John by observing the festival of his birth. It is interesting to note that the feast of the nativity of our Lord is celebrated on December 25 at the time of year when the days begin to lengthen. The nativity of John the Baptist, on the other hand, is observed on June 24, at the time of year when the days begin to shorten. What a striking illustration of the fact that when the influence of John began to diminish that of Christ began to increase!

His Example for Pastors

The zeal and preaching of John serve as outstanding examples for Christ's messengers today. The Epistle for this Sunday bids all pastors to be faithful and trustworthy stewards of the mysteries of God. As modern ministers of the King they prepare Christ's people for a proper observance of Christmas. Faithful ministers always seek to imitate the forerunner by saying, in effect: "Don't look at me; look to Christ. It does not matter what happens to me. What really matters is that Christ's name be honored, that His kingdom be established in the hearts of people everywhere, and that all who are called by His name will not live to themselves but to Him who died for them and rose again."

His Example for All Christians

All Christians may learn from John to put aside trivial matters and to give God first place in their lives. Have you ever thought what tremendous claims God makes upon you? Your very soul belongs to Him. He says, "Behold, all souls are Mine" (Ezek. 18:4). He bids you, "Seek ye *first* the kingdom of God and His righteousness" (Matt. 6:33). He wants you to put "first things first." He teaches you to pray, "Not my will but Thine be done" (Luke 22:42). When you face the problems and duties of life, do you ask, "What does God want me to do?" And as Christmas draws near, do you really put first things first? God forgive us if we at this time think only of feasting and merriment and miss the holy joy which should be ours because on that first Christmas our Savior was born.

III
The Advent Message

The Advent preacher had an important and timely message for the crowds that had come to hear him. Since he was fulfilling the prophecy of Isaiah "to prepare the way of the Lord," it was necessary, first of all, to convict his hearers of sin.

Conviction of Sin

John knew about the wickedness and graft and duplicity of the worldly Romans and of the proud religious leaders. He did not hesitate to tell Herod that it was not lawful for him to have his brother Philip's wife. He applied the Law of God in such a telling way that there was a great deal of heart-searching among cruel and dissatisfied soldiers, dishonest tax collectors, and people who were unloving and uncharitable. He minced no words when he addressed the insincere and hypocritical who came with the crowd and were willing to be baptized but were not truly penitent. Hear his condemnation of those who relied on the fact that they were descendants of Abraham, "Begin not to say within yourselves, We have Abraham to our father; for I say unto you that God is able of these stones to raise up children unto Abraham."

Judgment

But more needs to be said. When sinners refuse to repent there is nothing left but wrath and judgment. In v. 9 of our text we read: "And now also the ax is laid unto the root of the trees. Every tree therefore which bringeth not forth good fruit is hewn down and cast into the fire." This is the inevitable consequence of transgression. Since sin is rebellion against a holy and just God, the sinner deserves nothing but punishment. It is still true that "the wages of sin is death" (Rom. 6:23). And it is also true that "your iniquities have separated between you and your God." (Is. 59:2)

The World of Our Day

Our astronauts tell us that as they go into outer space the heavens above and the world below appear very beautiful. We look up to the heavens and are moved to agree with them. "The heavens declare the glory of God, and the firmament showeth His handiwork" (Ps. 19:1). The world about us, too, contains so much that is lovely and awe-inspiring. We are saddened, however, when we observe so many things that are not good, are not beautiful. We are shocked and distressed when we read in our newspapers about the crimes, the graft, and the wanton wickedness in the world. There is so much that is downright sordid.

In our own lives there is evidence enough that we fall short of what we ought to be. Low desires, lack of love to God, lack of charity to our fellowman, pride, indifference — these sins and many more attest to the truth that "there is not a just man upon earth that doeth good and sinneth not" (Eccl. 7:20). Many who claim to be Christian are quite satisfied, as were the Pharisees at Jordan, to rely on outward connection with God's people. The true Christian takes his faith seriously. He knows that sin is ugly and repulsive no matter where it shows itself. He is sensitive to the demands of God's Law. He realizes that when he sins he is "letting his Lord down" and that if it were not for the mercy and love of God he, too, would be under condemnation.

Call to Repentance and Faith

John's Advent message would not have been complete if he had spoken only about sin and judgment. He had been sent to preach the Baptism of repentance for the remission of sins. "Every valley shall be filled, and every mountain and hill shall be brought low, and the crooked shall be made straight, and the rough ways shall be made smooth." We think immediately of the extensive road-building operations of our times. Modern turnpikes and throughways have made travel to many parts of our country comparatively simple. Engineers have filled up the low places, cut down hills, removed obstacles, and created magnificent highways which afford quick and easy access to many places that in former years were reached only by driving over tortuous and dangerous roads.

The fearless forerunner of Christ demanded repentance, a complete change of mind and heart. The way of God must be properly prepared. Pride and self-righteousness must give way to humbleness. Wrongs must be righted. Obstacles to holy living must be removed. Evils must be corrected. The insincere must turn to a genuine acceptance of God's ways. Depressed souls must be guided to the help which only God can give. And therefore John, who had come to make the Lord's paths straight, directed his hearers to Jesus, who alone could give forgiveness and comfort.

Convinced of a Savior

It was through Christ Jesus that the world should be freed from sin and its awful consequences. Isaiah had prophecied, "All flesh shall see the salvation of God." Soon after the birth of Jesus, Simeon said, "Mine eyes have seen Thy salvation." Of John the Baptist we read that he "came for a witness, to bear witness of the Light, that all men through Him might believe" (John 1:7). He bore this witness by pointing to Jesus and saying, "Behold the Lamb of God, which taketh away the sin of the world." (John 1:29b)

After Dannecker, the noted sculptor, had worked two years on a marble statue of Christ, he invited a little girl into his studio, directed her attention to the statue and asked her, "Who is that?"

She replied, "A great man." Disheartened the sculptor started over again. After several years another child was invited to see the completed figure. This time he was not disappointed. In answer to his question, "Who is that?" the girl quoted the words of Jesus, "Suffer the little children to come unto Me." He now knew that the added years of labor had not been wasted. Dannecker wanted to have Christ stand out. Something like this took place in the life of John the Baptist. He wanted people to see Jesus. His ministry was a very brief one, lasting probably not more than a year and a half. But during this short time he was able to accomplish what he had been commissioned to do. He directed penitent sinners to the Lamb of God. He had not lived in vain.

Significance of Christ's Coming

Advent will have very little spiritual significance for you if you merely wax sentimental about the birth of a child in Bethlehem. It will mean something unutterably great if you look beyond the manger to the cross of Calvary. It will be a source of undying comfort to you if you will remember that the Child was called Jesus because He would save His people from their sins.

The words "salvation" and "forgiveness" ought to give you the real thrill of this season. Perhaps you feel that life has treated you unfairly. Like many others you may be worried about your health and your children and family. You may be much concerned about your business and your future. You may be deeply aware of the smart which sin has caused in your life. You may be deeply ashamed of things which have happened and of which you know that they should not have happened.

Your disappointments, your discouragements, your fears, your doubts, your feelings of guilt and shame — all these can be removed. To accomplish this the Son of God was made flesh. He was wounded for your transgressions and bruised for your iniquities, and with His stripes you are healed.

> When sinners see their lost condition
> And feel the pressing load of sin,
> And Jesus cometh on His mission
> To heal the sin-sick heart within,
> All grief must flee before His grace,
> And joy divine will take its place.

All our lives, pray God, we shall be grateful that He has called us into His kingdom. We shall never cease speaking of Him as the greatest Teacher of all times. We shall direct others to Him as the only perfect Example. We shall preach about His compassion for those in need and trouble. We shall recommend Him as the only Physician who never lost a case. We shall never forget that He made it possible for us to pray without fear or doubting to the

Father in heaven. Above all, however, we shall continue to talk and preach and sing about the amazing love of Him who brought us peace with God and a blessed assurance of life everlasting.

Counsel for Believers

Let us return once more to the Advent service on the banks of the river Jordan. John demanded "fruits worthy of repentance." He wanted his hearers to prove true repentance. He stood ready to serve as counselor to those who inquired as to how they could demonstrate sincere repentance in their lives. All were told that they should be willing to share their bounty with those in need. "He that hath two coats, let him impart to him that hath none; and he that hath meat, let him do likewise." The tax collectors were counseled not to collect more than the law prescribed. The soldiers were urged not to push people around, not to bring false charges, and to be satisfied with their pay.

Genuine repentance always strives to express itself in a God-pleasing manner. It is impossible to think of a Christian who does not have the desire to perform good deeds. And Christians of our day have a distinct advantage over the crowds at Jordan. They possess a much clearer understanding of all that Jesus came to do. They have accepted Him as their Savior. The Spirit of God dwells in their hearts. Impelled by this Spirit and motivated by love and gratitude, they also ask, "What shall we do?" John's counsel and advice still holds good. It is as relevant and up-to-date as anything could be.

As Christians we know that faith without works is dead. We should, for instance, be much concerned about the millions of people in many parts of the world who are slowly dying of starvation and lack sufficient clothing and adequate shelter. Think about how bountifully God has blesesd us in this fair land of ours. Let us share with others and be generous in our support of the relief agencies which have been established to alleviate some of the distress in the world.

Less than one third of the estimated three billion people in the world confess Jesus as God and Savior. Let us pray and witness and give so that many more may see the salvation of God.

God does not ask you to give up your lawful occupation, but He does want you to be honest and fair in your dealings with others. He does not demand that you give up your business, but He does ask you to dedicate it to His service. God does not condemn military service, but He does expect men and women in the armed forces to be a credit to their families, their church, and their country.

God's Word gives direction for every station or calling. Resolve that with His help you will be a pious husband, a devoted wife, a Christian parent, a dutiful son or daughter, a serious and earnest student, a responsible leader, a good citizen, a trustworthy employee, a faithful friend and neighbor.

Give evidence of the sincerity of your repentance and your faith in Christ by being rich in good works. "Let your light so shine before men that they may see your good works and glorify your Father which is in heaven." (Matt. 5:16)

Are *you* ready for Christmas? Why not make this your Advent prayer:

> Redeemer, come! I open wide
> My heart to Thee; here, Lord, abide!
> Let me Thine inner presence feel,
> Thy grace and love in me reveal;
> Thy Holy Spirit guide us on
> Until our glorious goal is won.
> Eternal praise and fame
> We offer to Thy name.

The Witness of a Voice

By Gerhard H. Mundinger

(The Fourth Sunday in Advent)

The next day John seeth Jesus coming unto him and saith, Behold the Lamb of God, which taketh away the sin of the world! This is He of whom I said, After me cometh a Man which is preferred before me; for He was before me. And I knew Him not; but that He should be made manifest to Israel, therefore am I come baptizing with water. And John bare record, saying, I saw the Spirit descending from heaven like a dove, and It abode upon Him. And I knew Him not; but He that sent me to baptize with water, the same said unto me, Upon whom thou shalt see the Spirit descending and remaining on Him, the same is He which baptizeth with the Holy Ghost. And I saw, and bare record that this is the Son of God. — *John 1:29-34*

The advent of Jesus Christ in the flesh — the happiest news that mankind has ever heard — is inevitably related to the saddest event in human history: the death of the holy, innocent Son of God. It is for this reason that the season of Advent, with all its joyous overtones, is designated by the church as a season of repentance. These first weeks of the new church year, filled as they are with expectation and wonder at the coming of Christ, are also weeks of somber self-examination, in which we remind ourselves of our share in the responsibility for His suffering and death. As we look to the Babe in Bethlehem, we must also see "the Lamb of God, which taketh away the sin of the world." For unless we repent and confess that "it was my transgression that brought this woe on Thee," we shall miss the meaning and purpose and the true joy of Christmas.

The Gospel for the day is the story of a delegation sent by Jewish priests to John the Baptist to find out who he was: the Christ, Elias, or "that prophet" whose coming was expected in fulfillment of ancient prophecy. There was good and sufficient evidence that John might be any one of the three. But he disavowed every claim to the name or status of any and all of them. He was a voice, he said, "the voice of one crying in the wilderness: Make straight the way of the Lord." And now, the day after this testimony about himself, John, seeing Jesus coming to him, identified this unknown rabbi whom he had recently baptized as the Messiah who was to come.

John the Baptist's witness to the advent of Christ contains three astonishing assertions: (1) That Jesus is the Lamb of God, who takes away the sin of the entire world; (2) That Jesus is the One who baptizes with the Holy Spirit; and (3) That Jesus is the Son of God. Each of these has special significance for us as we prepare for the coming of our Lord into our hearts and into the world.

The Witness of a Voice

I

Jesus Is the Lamb of God, Who Takes Away the Sin of the Entire World

The exodus experience of the Children of Israel, the high point of history under the Old Covenant, was an object lesson in the role of the coming Redeemer as "the Lamb of God." On the eve of the rescue from bondage in Egypt, in every household of Israel a lamb without blemish gave its blood to save those within from the angel of death. "When I see blood, I will pass over you," the Lord had said. On that day, some 1,500 years before the birth of Christ, the shedding of the blood of the lamb became identified with the rescue of God's people, from the Land of Egypt in the first instance, but more importantly from the land of sin and death and all the terrible consequences of man's separation from God.

The Lamb of God as the means of salvation for the people of God was subsequently incorporated in the tabernacle and temple worship of Israel. Atonement for sin and reconciliation with the Lord God was, by the command and ordinance of Jehovah, dependent upon the shedding of blood in the sacrifice of animals — the calf, the bullock, the goat, the ram, the dove, and the lamb without blemish and without spot.

In the days of the prophet Isaiah, by further revelation God had made it unmistakably clear that the salvation of the world would not be accomplished without an immeasurably greater sacrifice, the suffering and death of the Son of God, no less. The Holy

One of Israel, who was to redeem God's people, would one day be brought as a "lamb to the slaughter" and as a sheep to its shearers. He was to bear the "sins of many," and His soul was destined to become "an offering for sin."

And so, by degrees of increasing clarity, God's plan for the salvation of mankind identified the Messiah as the Holy One of God, but also as the Suffering Servant, whose advent in the flesh would lead directly to His sacrifice and death. That is why the witness of the voice hailed Him as "the Lamb of God, which taketh away the sin of the world!"

II

Jesus Is the One Who Baptizes with the Holy Spirit

The witness of the voice preparing the way for the coming of our Lord Jesus included a distinctive, outward, visible act: the rite of baptism. The word of the Lord which came to John, the son of Zacharias, in the wilderness instructed him to preach "the baptism of repentance for the remission of sins." More than the traditional and symbolic washing of vessels and parts of the body, the baptism of John was essentially related to the coming of Christ. Without repentance the advent of Christ was impossible; He could become the Lamb of God which takes away the sin of the world only if the world confessed its sin and turned from its own evil ways to the way of the one, true God.

For John the baptism ritual also became a means of recognizing Jesus. And on the testimony of God Himself he saw in Jesus the One "who baptizes with the Holy Spirit." Contrasted with John's baptism with water, a prophetic, symbolic act of cleansing, the baptism of Jesus with the Holy Spirit brings about a radical transformation of the whole person. In this baptism we are "buried with Him . . . into death: that like as Christ was raised up from the dead by the glory of the Father, even so we also should walk in newness of life." This is "a washing of regeneration and renewal of the Holy Spirit," as St. Paul describes it in his letter to Titus.

By this means of grace we are not only led to repentance, but our sins are actually taken away. We are not only prepared for the advent of Christ, but we actually receive Him into our hearts as we are changed from death into life. In Holy Baptism we receive the Holy Spirit, by whom we are called, gathered, enlightened, sanctified, and kept with Jesus Christ in the one, true faith.

This is the witness of the voice crying in the wilderness: that the Lamb of God which takes away the sin of the world also imparts, in Holy Baptism, the Holy Spirit, the Author and Finisher of our faith. What a great comfort our baptism is in these days of Advent! This little Child, whose birth we shall be celebrating again this week, has in the sacrament of Holy Baptism provided for us a guarantee that our faith will not be in vain and that no one can take this precious heritage from us. John the Baptist knew that the baptism of Jesus was "not simple water only." It was fire and Spirit and life. And so in announcing Jesus to the world he declared, "He that sent me to baptize with water, the same said unto me, Upon whom thou shalt see the Spirit descending and remaining upon Him, the same is He which baptizeth with the Holy Ghost."

III

Jesus Is the Son of God

Perhaps the most astonishing part of the witness of the voice was the declaration that Jesus the Lamb of God was also Jesus the Son of God. Old Testament predecessors of the latter-day prophet had described the Messiah as a son, but not specifically as the Son of God. They had stated that He would be a prophet who would speak in the name of the Lord. As the Messiah He would be the one anointed to rule over Israel in a kingdom that was to last forever. But it wasn't until the Father's voice was heard at the baptism of Jesus that He was revealed in the fullness of truth as the very Son of God. "This is My beloved Son, with whom I am well pleased." (RSV)

Here at the beginning of the public ministry of Jesus our heavenly Father places divine approval upon the incarnate Son. This is the Name above all names! Not only does it provide revelation of the divine nature, it is also a guarantee that the atonement of Jesus as Lamb of God was sufficient to take away the sin of the whole world. Only the perfect Son of God could possibly accomplish the salvation of all mankind.

Ironically, it was precisely this claim — that He was the Son of God — which became the focal point of the attack by His enemies and which ultimately led to Christ's death. For Caiaphas, the high priest, and his council this claim of Jesus was utter heresy. "He hath spoken blasphemy! . . . He is guilty of death! . . . What need we any further witness?"

On this Fourth Sunday in Advent we are grateful to God and praise Him for the witness of the voice in the wilderness at the beginning of the earthly ministry of Jesus, a witness that declared for all the world to know and for all the ages to come that Jesus Christ, born in Bethlehem, the Son of Joseph and Mary, was also (1) the Lamb of God that taketh away the sin of the world; (2) the One who baptizes with the Holy Spirit; and (3) the only-begotten Son of God.

Even so, come, Lord Jesus!

Oh, Come, Let Us Adore Him!

By E. G. JAECH

(Christmas)

In the beginning was the Word, and the Word was with God, and the Word was God. The same was in the beginning with God. All things were made by Him; and without Him was not anything made that was made. In Him was life, and the life was the light of men. And the light shineth in darkness, and the darkness comprehended it not. There was a man sent from God, whose name was John. The same came for a witness, to bear witness of the Light, that all men through Him might believe. He was not that Light, but was sent to bear witness of that Light. That was the true Light, which lighteth every man, that cometh into the world. He was in the world, and the world was made by Him, and the world knew Him not. He came unto His own, and His own received Him not. But as many as received Him, to them gave He power to become the sons of God, even to them that believe on His name; which were born, not of blood, nor of the will of the flesh, nor of the will of man, but of God. And the Word was made flesh, and dwelt among us, and we beheld His glory, the glory as of the Only-Begotten of the Father, full of grace and truth. — *John 1:1-14*

The name of Jesus has been in the hearts and on the lips of Christian people during this Christmas season more than at any other time of the year. Christmas carols, hymns, recitations, and greetings are familiar to us all. The impressive words of St. Luke's second chapter have been repeated in one form or another over radio, television, and by the printed page. The story of our Lord's birth is so familiar that for many its familiarity almost breeds contempt. Said a saleswoman whose counter for weeks on end daily reechoed with department store Christmas music, "I never want to hear a Christmas carol again." What a tragedy if the observance of Christ's birthday should become so commonplace that we lose our love and respect for Him and for His Word! There is need for us to pray: Dear Lord, teach us to reverence Thy Son as Thou didst teach Moses to stand in awe of Him before the burning bush. Teach us, dear Father, to reverence Thy Son as Isaiah gave reverence to Thee when in a vision he beheld Thee upon Thy throne. Give us, O Lord, the mind of the shepherds and the Wise Men, who came solemnly to kneel and to adore.

Because this is our Savior's birthday it is certainly a joyous occasion. Nevertheless it is one that should be observed by us with a holy awe and a solemn rejoicing. Even though Jesus Christ was born a man, we dare not presume to treat Him like a man. He is so much more than that. Indeed, as this text from St. John's Gospel so eloquently sets forth, He is worthy of the highest honor and our most devout adoration. On this festal day, therefore:

Oh, Come, Let Us Adore Him!

I

This Jesus Is the Mighty God

John, the evangelist, calls Jesus by a strange name. He calls Him "the Word." You will notice that the Bible translators write this name with a capital "W." In other words, John is not telling us about a spoken word, or a printed word, but a living Word. He is giving us a message about the great God Himself. This becomes very clear in the first verse: "In the beginning was the Word, and the Word was with God, and the Word was God." Verse 14 reads: "And the Word was made flesh, and dwelt among us, and we beheld His glory, the glory as of the Only-begotten of the Father, full of grace and truth." There is no question in the mind of John about the identity of this Word. He is telling us about God Himself. The Word is one of the names for God, and when he says that the Word was made flesh, he is saying that God was born a man. God became flesh of our flesh. That is what happened when Jesus was born in Bethlehem.

John identifies this Word made flesh with the great work of creation. "All things were made by Him, and without Him was not anything made that was made." In the beginning of time when the Father brought this vast universe into being, and the Spirit of God moved upon the face of the waters, this Jesus, who was made flesh in Bethlehem, shared in that mighty work of creation. Together with the Father and the Holy Spirit, He spoke, "Let there be!" and lo, all that exists came to be. And now, wonder of wonders, this eternal Son of God and Creator of the universe Himself becomes a creature, flesh of our flesh. How mysterious and exciting! St. Paul thought so, too, when he wrote, "Great is the mystery of godliness, God was manifest in the flesh" (1 Tim. 3:16). So let us drop to our knees with prophets and apostles! Fall down and worship with shepherds and wise men! Speak His name with loving awe and reverence! This Word made flesh is God who has become man.

But Why Is He Called the Word?

But why does John call Him the Word? Why does he not simply say, "In the beginning was God's Son, and God's Son was with God, and God's Son was God"? The Holy Spirit has His reasons for telling John what to write. We may never fully understand what those reasons are, but we may observe that this is not the only place in Scripture where Jesus is so named. In the opening verses of his First Epistle, John used this name for

Jesus. Again his Book of Revelation (19:13) reads: "His name is called the Word of God." From this we learn that Jesus is actually a living Bible. In the life and teachings of Jesus we learn to know our God.

This name of Jesus was the subject of a discussion in one of our Bible classes one day, and a member of the class offered an illustration which had been helpful to him. He told us about a medical missionary who was fighting an epidemic raging in the remote territory where he worked. People were dying every day. His supplies were running short, and help was desperately needed to care for the sick. He sent an urgent message to his headquarters for aid, and the reply came, "Do the best you can. Supplies and helpers are on the way." It was an encouraging message, but the days went by, and nothing happened. Finally, after many days, a plane touched down in a nearby field and brought the hoped-for relief. Now the message that had promised help became a reality. The word was made flesh when the plane discharged the long-awaited helpers and supplies. In somewhat the same way God had promised His chosen people in Old Testament times that a Savior would come and bring them deliverance from the dreadful scourge of sin and death. When Christ was born that promise was realized. That Word was made flesh! What an appropriate name for Him who came as God's answer to the greatest needs of man. The Word, the mighty God, was made flesh and dwelt among us. Oh, come, let us adore Him!

II

This Jesus Is the Life of Men

The text now leads us to a deeper understanding of this "Word made flesh." It says that "in Him was life." At first glance this seems to be so obvious. Surely no one would suspect that the Son of God, born in Bethlehem, would be a dead Christ. But John is not telling us the obvious. He is speaking about a different kind of life than just that He was alive. Our newborn children, for example, are physically alive, but in them there is also death. The Bible informs us that in our natural birth we are all dead in trespasses and sins. Jesus said, "That which is born of the flesh is flesh. . . . Marvel not that I said unto thee, Ye must be born again" (John 3:6, 7). The new little baby is alive in its flesh and blood, but it is dead as far as its spirit is concerned. It needs to be born anew in Holy Baptism. Jesus, however, was not only alive in the flesh, but "in Him was life," the life of God which is full, complete, and eternal. He came into the world to give this spiritual, this complete, this eternal life to those who were dead in trespasses and sins. Jesus says: "I am come that they might have life, and that they might have it more abundantly" (John 10:10). This is God's Christmas gift to the whole world, and as many as receive Him, to them He gives power to become the sons of God. Oh, come, let us adore Him!

He Gives Us Power to Believe

Let us take note that "the Word made flesh" also gives the power to believe. "As many as received Him, to them gave He power to become the sons of God." Here again we are reminded of the dreadful and destructive scourge of sin. Not only are we by birth full of sin, but we are incapable of coming to our God or of believing in His mercy. St. Paul says that man judges the good news about Jesus Christ to be foolishness. This accounts for the fact that so many people ignore and reject Christ. They have no power to come to Him and believe. Faith is a gift of God, even as Christ Himself is a gift of God. Wherever this Jesus, the living Word, moves among men the power to believe goes forth from Him. John tells us that all who believe in Christ are born "not of blood, nor of the will of the flesh, nor of the will of man, but of God." What a remarkable gift God has given us in His Son who was made flesh! We who have come to worship Him on His birthday are able to do this only because He has given us the power to believe. And believing, we know that we have eternal life. Oh, come, let us adore Him!

III

This Jesus Is the True Light of Men

The evangelist continues: "In Him was life, and the life was the light of men." He explains: "That was the true Light, which lighteth every man that cometh into the world." Light and life belong together. Christ is the Life, and He is also the Light. But what does that mean? It means that He disperses the darkness that had engulfed us and replaces it with light. The words which stand in sharp contrast here are "darkness" and "light." In Scripture darkness is identified with sin. It says that "everyone that doeth evil hateth the light, neither cometh to the light lest his deeds should be reproved" (John 3:20). It also says that "God is Light, and in Him is no darkness at all" (1 John 1:5). There is no sin in Jesus Christ at all. The Bible says that "He is holy, blameless, unstained, separated from sinners" (Heb. 7:26 RSV). He is all Light, no darkness, no sin. That is why the Christmas season is observed in a setting of brilliance and light. We place colorful lights on our trees, both indoor and out. We decorate our churches, homes, and places of business with many lights and colorful ornaments. We present gifts to one another in gay and colorful wrappings. This is one way in which we declare with joy that the Jesus whose birth we celebrate is not associated with the darkness of sin, but is instead the holy, the blameless, the unstained Light of the World. That's what John is so anxious for us to know and remember.

He Floods the World with Light

Not only is Christ the Light within Himself, but He also floods the world with His light. The text reads: "He is the true Light, which lighteth every man, that cometh into the world." The Lord foretold this in the prophecy of Isaiah: "I will bring the blind by a way that they know not; I will lead them in paths that they have not known. I will make darkness light before them and crooked things straight" (Is. 42:16). Christ's purpose in becoming man, flesh of our flesh, was to deliver poor sinners from the darkness of sin and death, and to restore them to the eternal light and life in His kingdom. Jesus said: "I am the Light of the world; he that followeth Me shall not walk in darkness, but shall have the light of life" (John 8:12). Jesus flooded us with His light when He perfectly fulfilled the holy Law of God for us and canceled the damning power of our sin. He flooded us with His light when He paid the enormous debt of our sin by His suffering, death, and resurrection. Our sins are gone. Death is vanquished. Hell is conquered. How wonderfully Old and New Testaments fit together! How marvelously God fulfilled the word which He long since had spoken! Isaiah might have been kneeling with the shepherds or with the Wise Men when he penned those sublime words in his 60th chapter: "Arise, shine, for thy Light is come, and the glory of the Lord is risen upon thee. For, behold, the darkness shall cover the earth, and gross darkness the people; but the Lord shall arise upon thee, and His glory shall be seen upon thee. And the Gentiles shall come to thy light, and kings to the brightness of thy rising" (Is. 60:1, 2). Oh, come, let us adore Him!

This Light Shines on Us

How good it is to know that this same Light of the Lord Jesus Christ is still shining today and that He shines on us. This light shines on us whenever Christ comes to us by His Word and the sacraments. This light shines within us when we believe His Word and trust in the good news that God "hath made us meet to be partakers of the inheritance of the saints in light; who hath delivered us from the power of darkness and hath translated us into the kingdom of His dear Son, in whom we have redemption through His blood, even the forgiveness of sins" (Col. 1:12, 13).

How wonderfully blessed we are that this very day as we hear the Christmas message this light of Christ is shining on us, and He is right now giving us the power to believe in Him, to love God, and to have eternal life in His name.

Many millions of people are born into the world and die again without ever having this blessed light shine on them. God has been so very good to you and me. He has brought Christ to us and us to Christ. If there is anyone among us who still lives in the darkness of sin and unbelief it surely is not because the light of Christ has not been shining on him, but because he is ignoring and rejecting that light. For you and me the ancient prophecy is now fulfilled: "The people that walked in darkness have seen a great light; they that dwell in the land of the shadow of death, upon them hath the light shined" (Is. 9:2). This is our great Christmas joy. This is our greatest of all Christmas gifts. God has given His only Son to become flesh of our flesh that we might become spirit of His Spirit. He is our Life. He is our Light. By Him and through Him we, who of ourselves are lost and condemned creatures, are now the redeemed children of God, made holy and righteous by His grace. God loves us! His beloved Son has come to us! Oh, come, let us adore Him, Christ, the Lord!

Did You Receive the Greatest Christmas Gift?

By LEWIS C. NIEMOELLER

(Second Christmas Day)

John bare witness of Him, and cried, saying, This was He of whom I spake, He that cometh after me is preferred before me; for He was before me. And of His fulness have all we received, and grace for grace. For the Law was given by Moses, but grace and truth came by Jesus Christ. No man hath seen God at any time; the only-begotten Son, which is in the bosom of the Father, He hath declared Him. — *John 1: 15-18*

Did you receive the gifts you expected for Christmas? What each of us expected varied according to our age and according to our wants and desires. Perhaps some of you children were disappointed, perhaps others of you were agreeably surprised. The same situation quite likely exists in the lives of many others.

Did you receive the greatest Christmas gift? Did you receive that gift that enabled you to sing with joy the Christmas carols in spite of the ache of sorrow in your heart, that enabled you to greet your friends with a "Merry Christmas" in spite of the troubles and difficulties that plague your life? There was such a Christmas gift available for each and every one of us.

Did You Receive the Greatest Christmas Gift?

This day after Christmas we are going to look at the greatest Christmas gift in order that we may yet receive it, if we have not counted it among our gifts, and that we may treasure it the more, if we have come to enjoy it. This gift to which we refer is the greatest gift because it is the gift of God's only-begotten Son, because it gives us the grace we need, because it gives us a knowledge of God and His ways.

The Gift of God's Son

Did you receive the gift of God's Son for Christmas? The person whose birthday we celebrated yesterday, the historical individual called Jesus is more than a human being. True as it is that He is true man, just as true it is that He is true God. Note how John the Baptist speaks of Him as recorded by the apostle John in his Gospel: "John bare witness of Him, and cried, saying, This was He of whom I spake, He that cometh after me is preferred before me, for He was before me" (v. 15). John the Baptist in these words pointed out to some of the Pharisees that Jesus was indeed born later than John but is nevertheless before him in point of time. This is possible only if Jesus is both man and God. Note furthermore how the apostle John refers to Jesus in the words: "No man hath seen God at any time; the only-begotten Son, which is in the bosom of the Father, He hath declared Him" (v. 18). As we read the words that precede our text, we know that the apostle John is writing of Jesus. These words are a clear statement that Jesus is the only-begotten Son of God, who is in the bosom of the Father and who is more than man because He knows God and can give knowledge of God.

The witness of the two Johns testifies that to receive the gift of Christ at Christmas is to receive the greatest gift, for the Christ is the Son of God, true God with the Father and the Holy Spirit. You will agree that this gift far surpasses any other present that we could possibly receive during the Christmas season.

The Devil Would Keep This Gift Away

The devil and all the forces of evil are very happy that we forget about the deity of the Baby whose birth we celebrated yesterday. They would have us remember Jesus only as a human being. In a sense the devil can spend a happier Christmas season if more and more people fail to receive this greatest gift. The devil would be very happy to see Jesus Christ, the Son of God as well as the Son of man, completely left out of Christmas. The devil would be well satisfied to have people praise Christmas as the festival of peace and of good will and love if these same people will forget about the truth that Jesus is the Son of God. If the Christ of Christmas is only a human being in the minds and hearts of men and women and children, then the Christ of Christmas is no more an enemy of the devil than is Santa Claus. The devil will spend a happy Second Christmas Day if you and I keep busy with all the external things of Christmas and forget about the Christ, who is the eternal Son of God. The devil knows that the greatest Christmas you and I can receive is the gift of Jesus as the Son of God, our Savior.

Was Christ, the Son of God, among the gifts you received? Or did you permit the trimmings of Christmas to rob you of the greatest Christmas gift?

The Gift of God's Grace

The gift of God's Son is the greatest gift because Jesus gives us the grace we need. All of us need the grace of God, which is God's undeserved love, God's unmerited favor.

The Gift Needed

As soon as we look at our actions in the past, we come to realize how much we need God's grace. Across all our thinking, all our speaking, all our doing we must write the judgment "failure to measure up to God's standard." The Lord God, who has created us and taken care of us, who has redeemed and provided forgiveness for us, who has called us into His kingdom, we have not kept first and foremost in our lives. His honor and position we have often given to others. The name of God, the Word of God, which alone can give us a faith in the love and redemption of God, we have misused. The worship of the gracious Lord, who draws near to us with His blessings, we have again and again neglected. The gifts of parents and of life and of earthly possessions we have failed to appreciate and to treasure and use in keeping God's will. This failure that characterizes all our actions has marred our entire life. If the Lord would judge us on the basis of our holiness and righteousness, each and every one of us would be doomed to destruction. That we can point to someone who is perhaps worse than we are helps in no way to keep us from being eternally separated from God. If we are to know happiness and hope, God must not deal with us on the basis of what we deserve, but He must deal with us according to His grace and unmerited favor.

In Christ Is the Gift

In the gift of God's Son we receive the grace we need. The apostle John writes of Jesus: "And of His fullness have all we received, and grace for grace" (v. 16), and "Grace and truth came by Jesus Christ" (v. 17). Jesus, the Christ of Christmas, brings us the grace we need, the forgiveness for our sins, the righteousness for our lives, the holiness for our daily tasks. The phrase "grace for grace" points to the fact that for every need in our lives there is grace doubled and tripled, so that we may have hope in life's dark hours, strength in life's weak moments, guidance on life's pathways, cleansing in life's sinfulness.

The Christ is able to give this grace because He is also the Christ of Good Friday and of Easter. The person whose birth was the occasion of making holiday yesterday walked on this earth for 33 years as He lived the perfect life for us and as He died the vicarious death for us on the cross on Calvary. For us He took on Himself all the sin and guilt, all the wrath and condemnation we had deserved. For us He gained the victory over sin and death and has won for us free and full forgiveness for all our sins. Truly "grace and truth came by Jesus Christ."

The Law Cannot Give the Gift

Some have sought to argue that we do not need the grace that came by the death and resurrection of Christ. These would have us believe that the solution to all of our wrongs and ills lies in following the great teacher of the Old Testament or in following the law of love in the New Testament. The Pharisees of Christ's day thought that following Moses brought happiness. There are many who would likewise point to such passages as "Thou shalt love thy neighbor as thyself" (Matt. 22:39), and "What doth the Lord require of thee, but to do justly, and to love mercy, and to walk humbly with thy God?" (Micah 6:8) and declare that here is the way to happiness. Even though they appeal to such a passage as "Pure religion and undefiled before God and the Father is this, to visit the fatherless and widows in their affliction and to keep himself unspotted from the world" (James 1:27), the truth remains: "The Law was given by Moses, but grace and truth came by Jesus Christ" (v. 17). Only in Jesus Christ, God's gift at Christmas, do we receive the grace and love we need for the removal of our sins and transgressions and for the ability to follow the paths of pure religion.

Did you receive this greatest gift among all the other presents that came to you? If you did, you discovered that it lifted your Christmas celebration above a simple emotional thrill that disappears faster than the Christmas decorations in most stores.

The Gift of the Knowledge of God

The gift of the Son of God as our Savior at Christmas is the greatest gift we can receive because He is the gift of the revelation of God and His ways.

It would seem that man is born with a feeling that there is a god who rules over him and to whom he is accountable. I know of no instance in the history of the world of any nation or tribe that knew nothing of the concept of God. The most uncivilized of people still believe in a god. Only the man who has wholly corrupted himself in all manner of sin and immorality tries to convince himself that there is no god. He tries to excuse himself by declaring there is no god. But in spite of the feeling that there is a god, and the general acceptance of the idea of god in the history of mankind, nevertheless our text states the truth in the words: "No man hath seen God at any time" (v. 18). No one has ever been able to discover God in the test tube of the research laboratories. The Russian astronaut spoke truthfully when he declared that he did not see God as he made his trip around the earth in space.

Only Christ Gives the Knowledge of God

The only way you and I can ever learn to know God is the way of God's revealing Himself to us. The Lord God must come to us in some way and give to us a knowledge of Himself. The way the Lord has used we have in the words: "The only-begotten Son, which is in the bosom of the Father, He hath declared Him" (v. 18). What man could not accomplish in his own imagination and research, the Lord Jesus has done, namely, given us a knowledge of the Lord God.

The God whom the Christ reveals is in a class by Himself. He is not simply the heroic personification of a great human being, with all the faults and frailties of the human race. He is the holy, yet loving Lord, who is concerned about the plight and condition of man, who is ready and willing to bring to man the help man needs because of his own sinfulness and corruption. This God is not just a type of Santa Claus who never punishes but indulgently brings gifts to all. He is a God who must condemn sin but who in love brought about a way of escape from condemnation for man in the life and work of Jesus Christ. The Lord is indeed the infinite God, far beyond all our comprehension; yet He is the gracious God, nearer than the reach of our hand. The Lord is indeed the only one God, but always the three Persons in the one God — Father, Son, and Holy Spirit.

Jesus Christ is able to give a revelation of the true God and of the traits and qualities of the true God, because He is the only-begotten Son of God, who is in the bosom of the Father. As we listen to the words of Jesus, as we study the life of Jesus, as we meditate on the death and resurrection of Jesus, we have a knowledge of God that makes us the children of God and heirs of salvation.

In giving us a knowledge of the true God, Jesus gives the knowledge of the truth in religion. In the multiplicity of religions, in the labyrinth of claims and counter claims in religion, we may wonder whether we can ever know the truth about God and about religious beliefs. In the gift of Christ at Christmas we have the gift of the knowledge of the truth in religion. No longer need we guess or surmise, reason or philosophize, about the truth. We have the truth in the Lord Jesus. No wonder Christ is the greatest Christmas gift.

Did you receive this gift?

Is there one among you who had to reply with a no? Before this service is over, will you accept the gift? This is one Christmas gift that is free. This gift will not put you into debt, rather it takes away your debt of sin and guilt. This gift brings with it the victory over all that is evil. This gift gives the joy and the peace about which you have heard so much during the past days. Accept the Lord Jesus as your Savior, own the greatest Christmas gift.

Surely most of you can rejoice with me in declaring that we have received the greatest Christmas gift. You have enjoyed Jesus as your divine Savior from sin, you have received the grace He so lovingly bestows, you have known the revelation which He has given of the Father and of His love. Hold fast to that gift.

As you leave the service, as you hold fast to the greatest Christmas gift, will you also give it to someone else so that he will rejoice with you in the Savior, in the grace He gives and in the knowledge of the true God?

All the Way with Jesus

By CARL H. TOELKE

(Sunday After Christmas)

As they were going along the road, a man said to Him, "I will follow You wherever You go." And Jesus said to him, "Foxes have holes, and birds of the air have nests, but the Son of man has nowhere to lay His head." To another he said, "Follow Me." But he said, "Lord, let me first go and bury my father." But He said to him, "Leave the dead to bury their own dead; but as for you, go and proclaim the kingdom of God." Another said, "I will follow You, Lord; but let me first say farewell to those at my home." Jesus said to him, "No one who puts his hand to the plow and looks back is fit for the kingdom of God."

Luke 9:57-62 RSV

That human nature does not change, even over a period of centuries, is demonstrated by the fact that many people enter into projects without counting the cost. Consider the fact that a congregation may embark upon a building program and incur a debt which taxes its financial capacity to the breaking point. Consider the young couple embarking upon marriage and purchasing everything they desire to furnish their new home, thus plunging themselves into debt that forces them to deny themselves any form of recreation, entertainment, or leisure-time activity. Consider the individual who becomes a member of a congregation under the impression that he is now in a position where all spiritual nourishment will be fed him, all the blessings of the church be granted, and he needs simply worship occasionally, just as occasionally drop an offering into the basket, sit back, and so to speak, relax until the angels take him to heaven.

Suddenly things change — he is asked to visit the sick and shut-ins; to make calls on mission prospects; to attend an adult Bible class (after all, he's been confirmed); to serve on the finance board, or to serve in some other capacity. In short, he learns that he neglected to count the cost of having the privilege of being a member of a congregation.

This takes us back to the days of Jesus' visible sojourn on earth when He spoke of the man building the tower only after he had considered the cost. It reminds us of the occasion when Jesus had just finished some "hard words" after which many of His disciples "drew back and no longer went about with Him" and the Savior had to ask the Twelve, "Will you also go away?"

We have just sung the praises of God's gift, the Babe of Bethlehem, in volume and enthusiasm, suggesting that nothing in our lives takes precedence over the Savior. Is our service to Jesus commensurate with our song? Do we go . . .

All the Way with Jesus

I

Doubtful Christianity

What it all adds up to is this: When we think in terms of following Jesus and living as His children, we must realize that total commitment on our part is demanded regardless of the cost. This is brought out in our text in which Jesus speaks of three types of individuals who may or may not have been able to commit themselves totally to the Lord.

The incidents mentioned by Jesus in our text are probably grouped together because of similarity. They certainly demonstrate varying attitudes of so-called Christian behavior. We can't help but get the impression that the first fellow mentioned by Jesus was rather impetuous and wanted to jump into something without realizing all of the implications of the promise he was making. When Jesus answered, "Foxes have holes, and birds of the air have nests, but the Son of man has nowhere to lay His head," He was indicating to the man that there would be no ease in a life dedicated to Jesus, that the kingdom of heaven came first, that he would have to be prepared for disappointment and disillusionment at times. In short, Jesus was indicating that He wanted no unrealistic people among His disciples, especially since Christianity looks at sin for what it is as well as salvation in all its glory.

When we look at the second fellow — the one who was simply commanded by Jesus, "Follow Me" — we find that he was unprepared for the demands that Jesus makes upon His disciples. When he requested, "Lord, let me first go and bury my father," he thereby indicated that there were other obligations in his life that must take precedence over the demands made by Jesus. This man learned the difficult truth of Jesus' pronouncement, "He that loveth father or mother more than Me is not worthy of Me, and he that loveth son or daughter more than Me is not worthy of Me." Jesus was here indicating that there was no room for sentimentalists in the kingdom of God when this sentimentality permits anyone or anything else to interfere with the imperatives of the Savior. Jesus is telling this man: Now! — You can stop for nothing!

The third man in our text learned that when one enters the discipleship of Jesus, there are to be no regrets; that one must be able to turn himself away from the world; that he must head with tenacity toward the goal which Jesus has set. When Jesus told the third man, "No one who puts his hand to the plow and looks back is fit for the kingdom of God," He is telling him that He wants undivided attention; that any regrets at having chosen the side of Christ cannot stand in the way of carrying out the purpose for which God wants him in His kingdom.

What did these three persons in our text do? Actually we do not know. What would you do if the circumstances were the same? Are we among those people who would rather join another church where the pastor doesn't have such a long course of instruction or where they aren't always asking you to do something for the church? Are we perhaps among those who are momentarily overwhelmed with a burning desire to become very active in the church and who for about one month are hustling about day and night, working on the bazaar, cooking in the church kitchen, and then like a straw fire, which burns furiously at first, die out completely and become totally inactive? Perhaps some of us are almost ready to "go all the way" if it weren't for just this one thing. "It would make my husband feel bad about this because he isn't a church member." "You know if it weren't for my family, I could be active in the church." "I can go along with everything they do in that church — except." Perhaps we are among those who, even though we do not articulate it, nevertheless, in our lives and by our behavior, say: "I am sorry I made that vow at my confirmation. I didn't realize how much I was promising then when I said I would remain true to Jesus even unto death. I wish I had known then what the cost would be." It's something to think about, isn't it?

II
Total Commitment

No one has ever made such uncompromising claims on men as has Christ. No one has ever made such demands. What a shame it is that so many of those who call themselves Christians should voluntarily weaken those demands, rationalize them, sugar-coat them, endeavor to make them palatable and plausible by saying in effect that Christ will overlook any shortcomings or any failure to live up to what He asks of His children. How difficult it is for us to understand that Jesus demands total commitment! Yes, He demands total — though imperfect — consecration. Nowhere in the Gospel do we read that Jesus is satisfied with only a part of the Christian. Nowhere are we told that Jesus is happy if He gets just a little of our time, a little of our talent, a little of our treasure. Just as Jesus demands that we accept all of Him or none of Him, so He demands every bit of us or none of us. Just as He, at the time He spoke the words of our text, had "steadfastly set His face to go to Jerusalem" to carry out unstintingly and unequivocally what His Father demanded for the redemption of mankind, so He asks of us that we steadfastly commit ourselves to His cause.

We are Christians through our commitment to Jesus. There are strong and there are weak Christians. The degree of our being strong or weak in our Christianity is in direct proportion to the degree of our commitment. Thomas Henry Huxley, in a moment of spiritual insight, wrote, "It does not take much of a man to be a Christian, but it takes all there is of him."

While on his way to his great missionary work among the Indians, St. Francis Xavier, returning from Italy, passed through Spain and came into his native country. As he and his party of travelers entered a rich and fertile valley, they saw the sun shining upon the turrets of a noble castle. "What a lovely spot!" said one of St. Francis' traveling companions. Then suddenly stopping, he exclaimed, "Why surely, Father Francis, we must be in the neighborhood close to your home! Is not that the castle of Xavier we see yonder, just visible between the trees? We must make a halt hard by in order to give you time to pay a visit to your mother and your family."

"With your permission, noble sir," returned Francis, "we will pursue our journey. My dwelling is now wherever our Lord is pleased to send me; I have given up my earthly home to Him and have no intention of revisiting it."

"But consider," resumed the other, in astonishment at such a resolution, "that you are about to depart for India, that you may probably never return, and anyhow, seeing your mothers' age, you are not likely to do so during her lifetime."

Francis smiled gently as he replied, "I thank you, noble sir, for the kindness which induces you to urge me in this matter, but pardon me for continuing steadfast in my first intention. Such a visit and such a leave taking would be productive only of useless pain and regrets. It would be like looking back after having put the hand to the plough and would tend perhaps to unnerve and unfit me for the labors which are before me, while the non-indulgence of my natural wishes is a little offering I cheerfully and gladly make to our good God."

Total commitment to Christ means that we must be separated from the world while we are in it; that we must be "different" from the children of the world in many ways; that we need not be so concerned about satisfying the demands of society, living up to worldly standards and values in order to maintain our status in life. Total commitment means that our Christianity must be much more than "one of life's optional little extras." The Christian is totally committed to worship God, to witness for Christ, to serve Him. This does not mean withdrawal from the world, but it does mean separation from those values and standards and concerns which will prevent him from worshiping and witnessing and serving to the extent that the Savior demands these things of him. Under no circumstances does the Christian have a right to rationalize: "Certainly Christ couldn't deny me a few material comforts or the right to fulfill some of the necessary obligations within my family or a few side journeys to recall some of the 'good old days.'" Christ would deny me these! That is why He says, "If any man will come after Me, let him deny himself and take up his cross and follow Me." It takes real courage to be a Christian and a follower of Jesus. Are you an "all-the-way Christian" or a "part-way Christian"?

III

Christ Makes the Difference

The question arises that if Jesus knows we are sinners, knows that we are imperfect, knows that because of the old Adam dwelling in us we can never live up to this ideal, why does He make such demands? It seems not only unfair but at first even ridiculous.

The answer, of course, is that Jesus makes the difference. Your life and mine, imperfect as they are, when totally dedicated and committed to Christ, become perfect through Him. In other words, the redemption wrought by Christ makes it possible for you and me to stand before our heavenly Father as perfect individuals because we are by grace, through faith, covered with the perfect righteousness of Christ. That is why, as the apostle Paul says, "I live, yet it is not I, but Christ lives in me, and the life which I now live in the flesh [and Paul was a sinner whose life was imperfect] I live by the faith of the Son of God, who loved me and gave Himself for me." That is why this same apostle, speaking from prison, was able to say, in spite of all his imperfections, "I can do all things in Him who strengthens me." That is why Paul, who was a persecutor of Christ and the Christians, and whose head was always weighed down, heavy with the searing recognition of what he had been, still affirms: "If anyone is in Christ, he is a new creation" — he has new power in his life. He has new motivation. He has given himself over completely to Jesus, who will take this earthen vessel, imbue it with power, make out of it, as Luther says, "a little Christ," who will fulfill the demands that Jesus makes.

What greater privilege could there be than committing oneself to Jesus? As we take time to count the cost: all our life, all our time, and all our talent, and as the thought of "going all out" in such a manner begins to overwhelm us, let us try to remember how overwhelming the love of God for sinful mankind is in making it possible through the cross to render God this perfect obedience in Christ. What a beautiful life in the service of the Savior can be rendered by those, who, rejoicing in their Christian faith, can say: "Nothing unrealistic, nothing sentimental, no regrets! Just Christ and I." Yes, the infant in the manger makes the difference.

Face the Future with Courage

By George W. Wittmer

(New Year's Day)

And I say unto you My friends, Be not afraid of them that kill the body and after that have no more that they can do. But I will forewarn you whom ye shall fear: Fear him which after he hath killed hath power to cast into hell; yea, I say unto you, Fear him. Are not five sparrows sold for two farthings, and not one of them is forgotten before God? But even the very hairs of your head are all numbered. Fear not therefore; ye are of more value than many sparrows. Also I say unto you, Whosoever shall confess Me before men, him shall the Son of man also confess before the angels of God. But he that denieth Me before men shall be denied before the angels of God. — *Luke 12:4-9*

Dear Friends in Christ, our Help in ages past, our Hope for years to come:

Last night we wrote the last words of the last paragraph of the last chapter of the old year. No repentance, no tears, no regrets can recall any day or hour that is gone into the tomb of time. As we look back, we thank and praise God for all His bountiful blessings, and we ask forgiveness of the many times we have insulted Him with our transgressions. Through Jesus Christ our sins are fully blotted out. The slate is clean.

This morning we begin a journey into the new year. This journey is different from those we customarily make for a vacation or for our profession or occupation. Ordinarily when we take a trip, we secure a map in advance and study other information about the roads on which we will travel and the country through which we will pass. We have marvelous resources for such study. Experts who have gone that way have prepared maps and descriptions and made them available to us.

On this journey into the twelve months ahead of us we have no such benefits. No man has ever gone that way before. The way is unexplored and unmapped. Although modern science has given us astonishing advances over our forefathers, man still lacks the ability and power to penetrate through the curtain that separates the present from the future. He can only wonder and wait. The experiences on the new and untrodden paths are completely hidden from him.

We cannot foretell whether the road ahead of us in the new year will be rough and rocky and narrow and twisting, or whether it will be broad and shady and sheltered and smooth. It may lead through beautiful verdant valleys and fertile plains, or it may go through dark and dangerous valleys, treacherous mountain passes, and around steep and rocky cliffs.

As we begin this journey into the new year, we need assurance and encouragement. Our Bible, with its precious pledges of our dependable God, is our source for such confidence. In our text the Lord Jesus Himself speaks to us as we take our first steps across the threshold of this new year. He tells us that we can

Face the Future with Courage

In these words Jesus gives us wise counsel and blessed encouragement.

Friends of Jesus

These words were originally spoken to the disciples who were with Him that day, but His counsel to them has been recorded in the deathless pages of the Bible and preserved by the Holy Spirit also for us.

The Lord Jesus addresses His disciples of that day and now with the term "My Friends." It is good to know that we are the friends of Jesus, the beautiful Savior. He has loved us with an everlasting love. Speaking of that love of Jesus for us, St. Paul says, "Ye know the grace [unmerited love] of our Lord Jesus Christ, that though He was rich, yet for your sakes He became poor that ye through His poverty might be rich." In the afterglow of the high and holy festival of Christmas we should see this limitless love of Jesus toward us with clear vision. His purpose for leaving the glories of heaven and coming to this earth, marred and scarred by sin, was to gain the forgiveness of all our sins. To accomplish this, He had to humble Himself and become obedient to the Law. On this day the Christian church remembers that He had to submit to the Jewish law of circumcision, that He should fulfill all ordinances for us. Then later He went to the terrible agony and humiliation of His sorrow in Gethsemane and before the courts and finally to the cruel cross on Calvary. There He handed to His Father the crimson coin of His own blood as full payment for the sins of all men. As we see all this, we are convinced of the fact that He loved us as friends. We know the truth of the words of Jesus, "Greater love hath no man than this, that a man lay down his life for his friends." This same Jesus rose again from the dead and now is in heaven to rule all things, especially to govern His church.

As we step forward into the unknown future, we are certain that we are friends of Him who now rules over all things as King of kings and Lord of lords. No matter what great forces of evil may rise in our world, to Jesus belongs all power and glory. His is the Kingdom forever and ever.

No Fear

This Friend of sinners tells us, "Be not afraid of them that kill the body and after that have no more that they can do." As we look out into the big world around us, we see many things that could make us tremble and quake. The international tensions so evident in the United Nations meetings, the bold, extravagant threats by Russia, the revelation that many nations have superbombs 2,500 times as powerful as the atom bombs dropped on Hiroshima, the development of many other nuclear explosives, guided missiles, superjets, and other materials for war and destruction, might bring trembling and fear to our hearts. The bold threats of Communism, boasting that soon the entire world will be engulfed in its orbit, might make us afraid of the dark future.

As friends of Jesus we can go forward with courage, with

a spring in our steps and a song in our hearts, in spite of the dire predictions. These enemies can do no more than God will allow them. They may have their little day on the stage of life. They may swagger and strut as they please, but when God wants to, He will raise His powerful arm and strike them down. If God in His infinite wisdom should allow them to carry out their cruel threats, they can do no more than destroy our bodies. Our souls are safe in God's all-powerful hands.

Fear of God

If there is to be any fear in our hearts as we walk forward into the uncharted future, it should be that reverent awe we feel toward God, who has told us, "I am the almighty God, walk before Me, and be perfect." He says again, "Ye shall be holy; for I, the Lord, your God, am holy." As a loving child is careful not to offend its parents, but tries to be obedient to their wishes, so a child of God carefully avoids anything that will offend His heavenly Father. His happiness consists in serving God. Therefore he prays, "Make me to walk in Thy commands, 'tis a delightful road." This fear of God is not to be a cringing terror before the power of the Almighty Lord of heaven and earth, but awe and respect and love for our God, who is also our heavenly Father. Our delight is to do His holy will.

With all the big and important events happening in the world around us, we may wonder whether God can know about our needs and desires. We may doubt the truth of His pledge, "Like as a father pitieth His children, so the Lord pitieth them that fear Him." But when we have such thoughts, we make the mistake of ascribing to God human limitations, human weaknesses and frailties. Man cannot know all the needs and wants of his friends. When he is away from his friends, man cannot know of any troubles and trials that come to them. But God is not limited as man is. He is the all-knowing God. Nothing ever escapes His all-seeing eyes.

Jesus wants us to remember that microscopic care of our heavenly Father. He directs us to look at the sparrows, the most plentiful of the birds of Palestine. They were sold in the market place for less than a cent each. Yet none of them is forgotten by God. We are worth much more than sparrows! We are God's highest creatures. He made us in His image. He gave us a rational soul. He formed man out of the dust of the ground and not as a part of the creation of a larger group. If God is concerned about sparrows, how much more will He be interested in our welfare, who are His highest creatures!

Then Jesus used what is considered by some to be an exaggeration. He said, "Even the very hairs of your head are numbered." This is no exaggeration. God's care for us is truly microscopic. Nothing, absolutely nothing, happens to us without His knowledge and permission. There are no accidents or unforeseen experiences in God's plan of our life. Everything has a purpose.

Now let us go forward another step. Assured of the love of God for us, a love that knows no limits, certain of God's constant care and His careful control of our lives, why should we ever be afraid? With David we say, "I will fear no evil, for Thou art with me." This all-knowing and loving God will allow no real harm to come to us. Nothing can happen to us without His full permission. Therefore we can conclude with St. Paul, "I know that all things work together for good to them that love God."

Surely we can walk forward with courage in this unexplored year before us. Confidence in the love of our God gives us that power. Our faith must be a power for us. Our Christianity must never be considered a burden. It is the kind of burden that sails are to a ship, that wings are to a bird, that a motor is to an airplane. God does not want to heap burdens on us, but He gives us power to bear our burdens. He tells us, "Underneath are the everlasting arms." They are *underneath* us to help us up, not *on* us to weigh us down.

This joyful truth we must share with others as we go on our way. The Lord Jesus tells us today, "Whosoever shall confess Me before men, him will the Son of man also confess before the angels of God; but he that denieth Me before men shall be denied before the angels of God."

It is said that the greatest honor and privilege shown to fighting men during the Civil War was to have their names mentioned on the floor of Congress. How much greater the honor, how much more glorious it will be, to have our names mentioned by the Lord before the angels, when He will say, "This is My friend. Here is My faithful follower."

Confess the Lord Jesus with your lips and with your life! A person who professes the Christian faith and then is wearied with worries about the future is no advertisement for his faith. But a calm and certain and trusting child of God is one who, by his very attitude of trust and confidence in the Lord's leading, calls attention to his faith and its power. Christ wants us to be such lights in the world. He tells us, "Ye are the salt of the earth." We are to be as an antiseptic keeping the world from complete corruption.

On this first day of the new year I would not try to deceive you into believing that there will be no battles for you to fight,

no enemies to conquer. You will be called upon, perhaps more
than ever, to "fight the good fight of faith." The old evil Foe,
who means deadly woe, will not lessen his attempts to lead you
to disbelief and doubt in the new year. The evil world will still
set its traps and snares. With honeyed words it will seek to entice
you and try to conceal the poison of asps that is under its tongue.
The enemy within the camp, your own sinful flesh, will continue
to try to mislead you. But in every one of these encounters with
this triple alliance of evil — the devil, the world, and your flesh —
you can conquer in the power God supplies. "Let the word of
Christ dwell in you richly in all wisdom." "Hold fast to the profession of your faith without wavering." You cannot accomplish
this by your own might and power, but you can conquer with God.

If you make any New Year's resolutions, make this one first,
"I will seek first the kingdom of God and His righteousness. I will
give highest priority to the Lord and to His church." Then I can
assure you that whatever may come, yours will be a blessed new
year. Then you can go forward with courage and confidence, with
your hand in God's, assured that He will lead you aright here on
this earth and that He will lead you to the glory of heaven in
eternity.

May God help and strengthen you to that end, for Jesus' sake.
Amen.

The Coming of Light

By ARNE P. KRISTO

(Epiphany)

Now when He heard that John had been arrested, He withdrew into
Galilee, and leaving Nazareth He went and dwelt in Capernaum by the
sea, in the territory of Zebulun and Naphtali, that what was spoken by
the prophet Isaiah might be fulfilled:

> "The land of Zebulun and the land of Naphtali,
> toward the sea, across the Jordan, Galilee of
> the Gentiles —
> the people who sat in darkness
> have seen a great light,
> and for those who sat in the region and shadow
> of death light has dawned."

From that time Jesus began to preach, saying, "Repent, for the kingdom of heaven is at hand." — *Matthew 4:12-17 RSV*

I

The Coming of Light Can Be the Sign of Judgment

"The people who sat in darkness have seen a great light. . . ."
These words were written originally by the prophet Isaiah. Their
purpose was to give the people of his day the assurance that the

Messiah was coming and also to help them understand the meaning of His coming. In this text those ancient words were quoted by St. Matthew with the same purpose. The difference is that Matthew was writing about the Messiah who had now come. It was his role to interpret the presence of Jesus Christ in the world.

In Our Own Day, the Light of the A- or H-Bomb Has Revealed Weaknesses and Forced Ultimate Decisions upon Us

But the same words are relevant to us and our circumstances. As we hear them, their meaning is brought home to us against the background of the times in which we live. There was a national and international situation against which Isaiah spoke. There was a given set of circumstances at the time of Matthew. We, too, live in a particular kind of world.

Of us it may also be said, "The people who sat in darkness have seen a great light. . . ." I think now not of the coming of Jesus Christ. I think of the coming of the atomic and space age. We have seen the bright light of the bomb. We have seen the shining surface of the space vehicle against the darkness of the night sky. We did not think we were living in darkness before the coming of the bomb. Our civilization was having problems, but they were merely temporary setbacks in the long upward sweep of man. Diseases were being conquered. Nature was being subdued and even improved. It was only a question of time, and fabulous wealth would be distributed evenly throughout the world. Man would somehow discover a way to extend the rule of law so that it would be enforceable not only within nations but also between nations.

But the light we have seen has brought us face to face with judgment. We have discovered that we were, after all, living in darkness. For now in the face of the problems of the new age, we see that all was not well. If the potentiality of man for good has been enhanced through the coming of the spage age, so also has his potentiality for evil. We are finally face to face with the moment of truth. Before the bomb, error could be handled; now it is fatal. Before the great light on the deserts of Arizona and Algeria, national ambition could be contained; now we are all crowded into the small elevator that the world has become. Before the space age, selfishness was more of a personal tragedy; now it is not only a personal tragedy but a national and world cancer.

Yet the light is there, and light can be good. The atomic era could be the beginning of unprecedented well-being for all men. It is within the physical power of man to plan programs of assistance that would benefit staggering numbers of people. The imagi-

nation could run riot with ways of raising the living standard
of the entire world's population.

Thus have we been brought to judgment by a light. The coming of the light of nuclear reaction has revealed the fission of
our souls. There is nothing wrong with our science. We discover
that it is we who are in darkness.

The Coming of Jesus Christ into the World Is Also the Sign of God's Judgment upon Us

This is what God told us years ago. He did it then through
the coming of Light. Jesus Christ is the Light of whom Isaiah
wrote. The brightness of His coming is so piercing that He reveals
all men as sitting in darkness and in the shadow of death.

His coming is like the sudden appearing of the noonday sun
at midnight. In the beams of this Light, we discover that we have
been living in the penitentiary of sin. This Light, on the penitentiary walls, shows us that it is impossible for us to escape our
imprisonment through our own powers. The walls are too high.
The doors are securely locked.

The coming of Jesus Christ is a bright light shining on the
movie screen of our life, disclosing to us that we have not been
living in reality, that reality is to be found elsewhere. In this
light we discover that we have been living a sham existence if we
have been living apart from Jesus Christ. In Him we know that
to be without Him is to be without hope and life in God. We know
that we have been living in the shadow of death.

The power of this Light is such that it searches into the
depths of our being. Paul says, ". . . the Lord comes, who will
bring to light the things now hidden in darkness and will disclose
the purposes of the heart." (1 Cor. 4:5 RSV)

This is no candle shining gracefully and peacefully on a dinner
table in a semidarkened room. This is not the calm glow of a camp-
fire on a moonlit night. Malachi the Prophet said,

> . . . behold, He is coming, says the Lord of hosts. But
> who can endure the day of His coming, and who can stand
> when He appears? For He is like a refiner's fire and like
> fullers' soap; He will sit as a refiner and purifier of silver.
> . . . For behold, the day comes, burning like an oven, when
> all the arrogant and all evildoers will be stubble; the day
> that comes shall burn them up, says the Lord of hosts . . .
> (Mal. 3:1-3; 4:1 RSV)

It is a frightening thing to find yourself suddenly standing
in a bright light when you have been in darkness. Is it the light

of the secret police come to haul you to Siberia? Is it, perhaps, the falling of the bomb? It is judgment.

The words of the prophets have been fulfilled. Jesus Christ came. The Light of the world appeared in the world. Judgment has come.

II

But the Coming of Light Has Another Alternative

But the words of the prophets did not take into consideration the dimension of time. The atomic or space age has dawned. Life can never be the same once we are aware of the new era. We are under judgment now. Nevertheless the catastrophic event, which is potential, has not yet become actual.

It is the same way with the Messianic age, started when the King of kings came into His world. Things can never be the same. The kingdom of heaven has come. Just as the question confronting us in the world is, "What shall we do with the new potential in our hands?" so the question confronting all men is, "What shall we do with Jesus Christ?" Whether we like it or not, the space age must be faced, and our response to it is ultimate. So Jesus Christ, the Light of the world, must be faced, and our response to Him is ultimate.

In the case of the bomb, we deal with an inanimate object. The response to the bomb takes the form of hiding in a shelter or of wearing tinted glasses. But Jesus Christ is a living person. And this makes a great difference. This means that He, too, has purposes. The brightness of His coming is more than the rising of the sun or of the falling of a bomb. It is the coming of a person with the purposes of a person.

Jesus Christ Came to Establish the Kingdom of God and to Invite Us into It

His purpose is not to burn and destroy us. He came with the intent of healing. He came to bring us light so that we might be in the light instead of in darkness. He came to bring us life so that we might rise from the death of our sin.

Our Lord went to the spiritual reactor of Calvary. There He permitted Himself to be smashed. The first Adam had been smashed by Satan years before. The result of this was that man was divided from God and united with Satan. Now the Second Adam, Jesus Christ, placed Himself into the reactor, the cross. Heaven and earth were shaken at this event. The Second Adam was smashed. He, too, was separated temporarily from the Author and Giver of life. But there was more power in the Second Adam than had ever before or since been seen in this universe. He restored Himself to wholeness.

Out of that event has come forth the healing power of God.
The smashing of the Son was a unique event. It is not repeated.
Yet its values are duplicated. They are intended to be duplicated.
They are intended to be duplicated in the lives of people in such
a way that they, too, become as Christ is — able to withstand the
bright light of God's judgment and the fury of Satan.

This is what Jesus meant when He said, "Repent, for the kingdom of heaven is at hand." From the point of view of the ancient
prophet the entire history of Christ was treated as though it took
place in a moment.

But from our persepective, it is not so. From where we
stand, we hear the words of Christ, "Repent, for the kingdom of
heaven is at hand." The coming of Jesus Christ into the world calls
forth from us a response to His purpose. We do not respond to
a natural light. We react to God's purpose.

There is no question about His purpose. His purpose was
to establish the kingdom of heaven and to invite men to enter it.
He purposed to bring us to repentance. He intended that the
experience of His being smashed in the divine reactor, the cross,
would be applied to us that we would be prepared for the final
Day of Judgment. The response we are urged to make is to see
that we cannot face that Day without the power of the cross behind
us and in us.

He Continues to Offer Us the Power of His Coming
Through Word and Sacrament

Now that man has discovered the great powers in nature,
he continues to make withdrawals from that store of power. We
build atomic plants. We build weapons. Thus, in the continuing
march of history, we are continuously under judgment in the use
of this power.

Our Lord has dealt with His power in the same way. He has
established safe and peaceful use of His power. But He has also
reserved one final event which will not be peaceful for all men.

He has placed the soothing and healing power of His Gospel
into His Word and sacraments. The full force of Calvary is chan-
neled to us in the Word, in Holy Communion, and in our Baptism.
Through these means something happens that can happen in no
other way — we are separated from sin, death, and Satan; and we
are united to God the Father, Son, and Holy Spirit.

III

We Who Have Seen This Light Now Have
Not Only a Gift but Also a Responsibility

This union with God is both a gift and a responsibility. It is
a gift because it brings us into the kingdom of God, the new era.

Our Allegiance Is Now with Him Who Is the Light of the World

But it is a responsibility because it immediately attached us to the forces of light in this world. We awaken to the fact that there is a dreadful battle between the powers of darkness and the powers of light. And we cannot be neutral. In fact, we have gone from one side to the other — from darkness to light. And as in all cases where there has been a change of allegiance during wartime, the former associates are now personally committed to our destruction. If we are to fulfill our role in this struggle, we must regularly replenish our strength from the source, the Word and the Sacraments.

We Must Participate with Our Fellow Christians in Bringing This Light to Bear upon the Lives of People

And we must also realize our participation in the battle with our fellow Christians. We cannot exist alone. We must associate with our brothers and sisters in the faith. Our witness should join with others to help bring the Light of Christ into the lives which are still in darkness and in the shadow of death.

We cannot afford the luxury of indolent Christians. We cannot afford the luxury of lazy congregations. No sociological, economic, national, cultural, educational, racial, or personal barriers should impede the bringing of the power of Christ into the hearts of all men. We are engaged in deadly in-fighting. The enemy does not sleep.

This Responsibility Will Continue

It will continue in this fashion until God Himself changes the situation through the reappearing of Christ in the world for the final Judgment.

One day God will establish a permanent coexistence. At that time the words of Malachi will be finally fulfilled.

God will set apart the kingdom of darkness forever. Those who have not heeded the brightness of His coming now will have to face it then. But God will also open to His people the everlasting kingdom of heaven. Then we shall experience fully the true purpose for the coming of the Great Light, Jesus Christ. The Light will shine, but it will not burn. Death and darkness will have disappeared.

We have not yet reached the day of the ending of the cosmic cold war. We are still living in the day of the Epiphany of our Lord. Like the Wise Men of old we can heed the shining bright light of the Gospel and enter into the kingdom of heaven. We can do our part in the battle against darkness. We can say to the world around us, "Repent, for the kingdom of heaven is at hand."

The Hazard of a Christian Life

By OMAR T. STUENKEL

(The First Sunday After Epiphany)

Whosoever therefore shall confess Me before men, him will I confess also before My Father which is in heaven. But whosoever shall deny Me before men, him will I also deny before My Father which is in heaven. Think not that I am come to send peace on earth; I came not to send peace but a sword. For I am come to set a man at variance against his father, and the daughter against her mother, and the daughter-in-law against her mother-in-law. And a man's foes shall be they of his own household. He that loveth father or mother more than Me is not worthy of Me, and he that loveth son or daughter more than Me is not worthy of Me. And he that taketh not his cross and followeth after Me is not worthy of Me. He that findeth his life shall lose it, and he that loseth his life for My sake shall find it. — *Matthew 10:32-39*

Safe Christianity

Plaster saints are often referred to as illustrating a weak and sentimental religious attitude. Ornate churches do not necessarily come as a result of vigorous, robust concern for the primary needs of men or the true glory of a forgiving God. The realistic words of a sharp, stinging confessing litany may be used as an evasion because a less incisive and repentant response would result from a person-to-person confrontation with the Word of God. We are, perhaps, too often unwilling to let our faith live in the hurly-burly of ambitious activity of daily life and the temptation of an obnoxious routine. We sometimes try to surround faith only with the peaceful sound of proper responses and stifle the discussion doubt wants to raise instead of dealing frankly with it on the basis of God's Word. In doing so we show more spiritual insecurity than steadfast Christian faith.

At the same time we know also that vigorous Christian faith is not expressed by violent insistence that nothing is certain. The forceful, rugged, unyielding convictions which put principle before expediency, right before popularity, and decency before advancement are needed in our Christian circles as well as in the world about us.

Not Peace at Any Price

The Christmas song of the angels which heralded Jesus' birth as ushering in "peace on earth" is not to be understood as calling His followers to a program of "peace at any price." To see Jesus as the Prince of Peace (Is. 9:6) does not mean that we forget Him as the resolute Champion whose bitter struggle against sin and Satan ended in the triumph of the Easter resurrection. His summons to us is not to a life of indolent enjoyment but to a stern battle against considerable satanic odds. The victorious outcome of this struggle is assured us only as long as we faithfully follow our divine Champion.

We need to take heart and be prepared for conflict in our day. Military preparedness is considered essential for safety and for success in war. Spiritual preparedness is essential too. Too many Christians have been made to think that they must come to terms with the world. Religious appeasement has been chosen rather than conflict with the world which might result in material losses. Spiritual convictions have been adapted to the phrases current in other fields of learning of our day, and all too often the Bible truths themselves have been made to yield by the very men who should have been their most stalwart defenders.

An Example

The simple story of the uncomplicated faith of Polycarp, an aged bishop of the early church, may be passé in our day, but it reflects the kind of steadfastness Christians need still. This old man was being asked to renounce his faith or be put to death by fire. The magistrate urged him: "Swear the oath, and I will release thee; revile the Christ." Polycarp replied, "Fourscore and six six years have I been His servant, and He hath done me no wrong. How, then, can I blaspheme my King who saved me?" And thus he went to his death.

Jesus' stirring call to steadfastness and courage (v. 28) needs to be heard by the listless, compromising Christians of our day and can serve equally well to renew the hearts of the steadfast. Jesus said, "Fear not them which kill the body, but are not able to kill the soul but rather fear Him which is able to destroy both soul and body in hell."

Our text once more lays before us the glorious call of Jesus to a steadfast, heroic Christian life, and so we consider

The Hazard of a Christian Life

I

Boldly Identify Yourself with Christ (vv. 32, 33)

The Hazard

In our country being a Christian is not generally considered a hazard either to one's position in life or to one's personal fulfillment. Most people respect Christian virtues and even think highly of moderate participation in church worship and responsibility. The hazard that should exist often disappears not because the world has grown soft toward basic Christian commitment but, sad to say, because the church and the individual Christian have grown soft toward the ideals and habits of the world.

Too often we feel apologetic in insisting on the uniqueness of Christ as Savior when we are confronted with the contention that faithful followers of non-Christian religions can scarcely be peremptorily read out of heaven. Only the clear words of Christ "I am the Way, the Truth, and the Life; no man cometh unto the Father but by Me" (John 14:6) and similar statements compel our consciences to hold, almost reluctantly, to the doctrine that salvation comes only through Christ. We need renewed strength so that the commendable compassion we may feel for those outside Christ may move us to zeal in publishing the good news of forgiveness.

Identify Yourself with Christ

In clear, simple, concise words Jesus urges in our text that we openly and boldly identify ourselves with Him. He states it in terms of the consequence that results, on the one hand, from outspoken, sincere confession of faith in Him and, on the other hand, from cowardly or unbelieving denial. If we boldly stand with Him now, He will recognize us as His own in heaven. The alternative reminds us of another of Jesus' statements: "Many will say to Me in that day, Lord, Lord, have we not prophesied in Thy name? and in Thy name have cast out devils? and in Thy name done many wonderful works? And then will I profess unto them, I never knew you, depart from Me, ye that work iniquity" (Matt. 7:22, 23). Our confession of faith in Christ must be sincerely meant and steadfastly adhered to.

Before Men

One of the very interesting points of our text that give it individuality in comparison with similar texts is the stress that here falls on the words "before men." Many people feel that religion is something entirely between the individual and God. The stress that we need no human intermediary between us and God is wholesome, for Christ has made us all priests who may go to God directly. This stress, however, should not blind us to the fact that Christian faith also concerns us and our fellowmen. Nor is this true only in its welfare implications and its moral laws. It is true also in the deeply personal aspects of confessing our faults one to another (James 5:16), warning the straying (Ezek. 33:8), comforting one another (1 Thess. 4:18), and rebuking the erring (Titus 1:13).

Secret Disciples

We read of secret disciples of Jesus in the New Testament in whom finally the weak flicker of faith grew strong enough to bring them to an open stand for Christ. Jesus does not deal in our text with the question whether secret faith is possible. In the words before us He rather points to the blessedness of an open confession of faith and the disastrous consequences of a denial. From this it is certainly clear that Jesus wants us to take an open stand for Him. We need the courage to be Christians wherever we are. For the danger is always that our motive for being disciples is so weak, almost selfish, that it endangers the very existence of faith. It is certainly not an admirable picture of believing when, for example, we read: "Nevertheless, among the chief rulers also many believed on Him, but because of the Pharisees they did not confess Him, lest they should be put out of the synagog; for they loved the praise of men more than the praise of God." (John 12: 42, 43)

Christ in Home and Church

Confess Christ boldly. Start at home. Of a famous American some generations ago the story is told that he came home elated and excited. He had just come to the conviction that Christ was his Savior. He told his wife, a Christian woman, and asked her to kneel with him at once in a prayer of thanksgiving. She said, "But hadn't we better wait? There are some very important guests waiting to see you in the other room." "No, we won't wait," the man replied, "I have kept Jesus Christ out of my heart and home long enough."

How sad as well as shocking to think that the only religious words some children hear from the lips of their parents are words of profanity! If we cannot and do not speak freely of Christ in the Christian home and unite our hearts in prayer there, where will we do so?

Not only, however, in the castle of our home should we openly be Christ's, but with full energy, consistent zeal, and continuing faithfulness we should support the cause of Christ as part of the congregation of believers. Any effort which moves forward in the name of Christ within that church should receive our careful attention and such willing effort as we are capable of.

Confessing Before Men

If we restrict our confessing of Christ only to what we can do among family and Christian friends, we still have not fully confessed before men. Opportunities come which each may use in his own way to confess Christ. I do not think that all could do well what I know one Christian of my acquaintance did. As the argument in an important union meeting in a certain town grew more bitter and profane during a lengthy strike, this man asked for the floor. He said: "I've sat here and listened to the kind of talk that's going on and wondered why we can't resolve this strike.

I think the whole spirit of this union would change if we asked that one to come in whom many of us shut out from anything like this. I'm referring to Jesus Christ." That man saw an opportunity he felt he needed to grasp and was able to take hold of to confess Christ. The effect was in the hand of God.

II

Accept the Inevitable Earthly Consequences (vv. 34-37)

Religion for Heroes

Our text calls on us not only to confess Christ openly but also to be prepared for some unpleasant consequences. Now we must certainly be careful not to demand that another Christian must do what we would do in the same circumstance. Two Christians, both sincere confessors of Christ, might not confess Him in the same way even in the same situation. We must depend on the Holy Spirit to guide us. But Jesus does state in our text that faithfully following and confessing Him can and will throw us into conflict at times even with those who are dear to us by blood or friendship.

One famous English bishop said, "The trouble is, Christianity is a religion for heroes, and we are just ordinary people who want everybody to have a good time." Unfortunately, the sting of that remark applies to many comfort- and security-seeking Christians in our day who often consider anyone taking heaven and hell seriously something of a fanatic.

Primary Allegiance

Jesus sets the claim before us that our allegiance to Him is *the* primary one. Nothing is right, no matter what favor it accomplishes for friend or family, if it contradicts or precedes our love and devotion to Him. The choice between friend and Christ, family and Christ, advancement and Christ, popularity and Christ, must frequently be made. Perhaps none feel the choice so keenly as the young who think that to make the choice for Christ is to lose all earthly happiness. They imagine that their efforts to establish earthly security are thereby threatened. Of this danger they were always aware.

So vital to us is the new life which becomes ours by faith in Christ that we dare not risk losing it for the sake of anything else. God's place is preeminent. He will tolerate no competitor, and to give Him second place in your life is to give Him no place at all. There can be only one God in your life. What He has done for you through the sacrificial death and the victorious resurrection of Christ calls for your supreme allegiance.

Of His Own Household

Making Christ preeminent in our daily life can create difficulties for us. In that sense Jesus brings not peace but a sword. Inevitably our allegiance to Christ raises problems with conflicting claims. The claims may be valid and good in their place, but their place is not first place. That place belongs to Christ.

We know that one of the problems of mission work among the Japanese, Chinese, certain Hindus, and especially the Muslims, is that the Christian convert is thrown into violent conflict with his own family. His experiences are reminiscent of the words of Jesus in our text: "And a man's foes shall be they of his own household." The fact that similar conflicts do not ensue in our own land is a cause for thanksgiving to God for the country in which we live. But it may sometimes be an indictment of the casualness of our Christian faith, which lacks contrast with the fruits of unbelief.

False Hazards

No one should understand Jesus to say that whoever is persecuted or has a hard time of it and claims to be Christian is therefore beyond doubt a true Christian. Those who seek martyrdom in order to have assurance of salvation regardless of their life deserve the sarcasm G. B. Shaw heaps on them in one of the characters of the play *Androcles and the Lion*.

Few things are more repulsive than the person who clothes his self-righteousness with self-pity and claims to be martyred because of his faith. Christian people surely are not to seek antagonism or invite it by being obnoxious. Anyone who has sincerely repented of sin and gratefully received the forgiveness Christ obtained for him will scarcely be inclined to self-righteously plead martyrdom as long as that forgiveness holds meaning for him. Real martyrdom, in the truest sense, may indeed descend on him. For this Christ's words in our text prepare us.

The Sword

Be faithful in your loyalty to Christ, your desire to forgive others, your concern for their welfare, your self-sacrifice, your uprightness of heart, and you will encounter "the sword" of which Christ speaks. Recall the words of the apostle Paul "All that will live godly in Christ Jesus shall suffer persecution" (2 Tim. 3:12). Even friends and relatives may desert you and misunderstand or misrepresent your motives.

Because they were following the Lord and sharing what He suffered, Paul and other apostles found it possible to rejoice even in tribulations. The apostle James says, "Count it all joy, my brethren, when you meet various trials, for you know that the testing of your faith produces steadfastness." (James 1:2, 3 RSV)

III

Deliberately Use Your Life in Self-Sacrifice as Jesus Did (vv. 38, 39)

Ready for Hazards

The Christian life is a hazard. The very fact that it rests for its assurance on faith already makes it seem a hazard. Because many people trust neither the outcome on which Christian faith depends nor the means it relies on to achieve it, the hazard seems tremendous. Paul pointed to this apparent hazard when he said, "If in this life only we have hope in Christ, we are of all men most miserable."

Only the conviction that He who valued not His own life or His unique place in heaven so highly that He could not be touched by our needs convinces us and holds us steadfast to our Christian hope. Jesus Christ summons us in our text with the words: "He that taketh not His cross and followeth after Me is not worthy of Me." In the perspective of His self-sacrifice on the cross, His assuming the burden of our guilt when He Himself was guiltless, and His triumphant resurrection as Lord of death and Conquerer of hell, that summons stirs us to carefree abandon even in the face of frightening opposition. The call to you today is to deliberately use your life in self-sacrifice as Jesus did. Because God has forgiven you your sins for Jesus' sake, you are free to choose to serve Him in gratitude and praise. Even the burden and heat of the day spent in His service will be satisfying, even the trials, misunderstandings, and persecutions you can count but joy because you are identified with Him.

The Cross

Taking one's cross to follow Jesus is not the same as bearing one's cross. Bearing one's cross, the peculiar and particular burden that afflicts Christians but does not afflict unbelievers, is part of the Christian life too. In taking up our cross daily we are not to let each day's cares and toils prevent us from glorifying Christ. Rather we should use them as opportunities to express, defend, and spread our faith. Take your cross and follow Jesus. Where will it lead you? Where did it lead Him? To sorrows, pain, suffering for the Gospel's sake, but finally to eternal glory. This is the only "success" that really counts.

Risking One's Life

Along the same line of thought but with a slightly different emphasis Jesus follows the summons just quoted from our text with another. He says: "He that findeth his life shall lose it, and he that loseth his life for my sake shall find it." Jesus does not ask us here to throw our life away. He rather asks us to consider Him and what He means to us and then live our life in such a way that it seems to the worldly-minded that we are throwing it away, but really we are finding that "success" which counts. Too many Christians are living lives that are too filled with care for the security the world offers. Risk all on your faith in Christ. Only if He is true (of which, praise God, there is no doubt) will your life count for anything in the measure of eternity. The hazard of a Christian life is only an apparent hazard. Its outcome rests secure in the promises of Almighty God.

Romance of Discovering and Following Jesus

By RICHARD P. MEIBOHM

(The Second Sunday After Epiphany)

Again the next day after, John stood and two of his disciples. And looking upon Jesus as He walked, he saith, Behold the Lamb of God. And the two disciples heard him speak, and they followed Jesus. Then Jesus turned and saw them following and saith unto them, What seek ye? They said unto Him, Rabbi (which is to say, being interpreted, Master), where dwellest Thou? He saith unto them, Come and see. They came and saw where He dwelt and abode with Him that day, for it was about the tenth hour. One of the two which heard John speak and followed Him was Andrew, Simon Peter's brother. He first findeth his own brother Simon and saith unto him, We have found the Messias, which is, being interpreted, the Christ. And he brought him to Jesus. And when Jesus beheld him, He said, Thou art Simon, the son of Jona; thou shalt be called Cephas, which is by interpretation a stone. — *John 1:35-42*

Vast as the Christian church is now, there was a time when it consisted of only two weak members. It all came about this way: Jesus had just returned from His victorious conflict with Satan in the wilderness when He presented Himself before John the Baptist, His "way preparer," in the presence of an official Jewish delegation from Jerusalem, for a witness and evidence that He was really the long-promised Messiah.

For three days in succession, days memorable in the history of the Christian church, this last great prophet pointed out Jesus and introduced Him publicly to all the world.

On the first day he made a solemn declaration before a deputation from the Sanhedrin. "The Messiah is present," he declared. "He is among you" (v. 26). This announcement no doubt thrilled the hearts of those who were looking forward to His coming, but we are not told of any who followed Him at this time.

The next day the forerunner, pointing out Jesus, added to what he had said the day before, declaring: "There He is! 'Behold the Lamb of God, which taketh away the sin of the world'" (v. 29).

And on this second day John further testified concerning the occasion of Jesus' baptism: "I saw the Spirit coming down from heaven like a dove and resting upon Him. I did not know Him, but He who sent me to baptize in water had told me, When you see the Spirit coming down upon someone and resting upon him, you will know that this is He who is to baptize with the Holy Spirit. I saw it myself. . . . This is God's Chosen One. . . . This is the Son of God." (NEB)

Finally on the third day, the Sabbath day . . . the Holy Day (Edersheim, I, 345) John repeated his words of the day before and said to two of his disciples, "Follow Him."

These great testimonies of John lead us to think of the

Romance of Discovering and Following Jesus

What John is saying in effect here is: I have told you before about this Lamb of God and now you see Him. Here He is. He is the Master. He baptizes with the Holy Spirit and with fire.

Now, when John's disciples, plain and pious men, heard their teacher say, "This is the Lamb of God," they believed him and followed Jesus. Note the humility of John who encouraged his own prize pupils to leave him and follow Jesus. Why would any men be willing to do a thing like this? I submit that it was because John himself had discovered who Jesus really was and believed that He was the heaven-sent Messiah, whom all must follow, that he did not want these men to follow him, but wanted them to follow the One for whom he was only the "way preparer." You see, John the Baptist was, as he himself said, only a voice crying in the wilderness, only a "way preparer," but, praise God, he was a voice that knew what to cry — "Behold the Lamb" . . . the very heart of the Gospel of salvation, and as a "way preparer" he did not set himself up as a Messiah but pointed out the way to Him.

Follow Jesus

This is the first great lesson of our text that we — to whom the prophet of the Old Testament cries out, "Prepare ye the way of the Lord" —by our preaching and witnessing do not lead people to become disciples of ours or of our congregations but followers of the Lord Jesus.

I believe that to lift up Christ is the work of all Christian preachers and teachers; as far as they can, to hide themselves behind Jesus Christ, or at the most to let themselves appear, just as the old painters used to let their own likenesses appear in their great altar pieces . . . a little kneeling figure there, away in a dark corner of the background. Present Christ. He Himself is the mightiest proof of Christianity.

What Seek Ye?

Jesus' first word to these disciples of the "way preparer," as He turned and directed His attention to them, was the question, "What seek ye?"

We cannot doubt that our Lord knew perfectly well the hearts and motives of these two disciples. In asking this question, therefore, He spoke partly for their encouragement and partly to stir them up to self-inquiry. "What seek ye?" Is there anything that I can do for you, any truth that I can teach you, any burden that I can take away? If so, speak, and be not afraid. "What seek ye?"

That's a good and timely question, isn't it? "What seek ye?" What is your goal? What are you looking for? What is your object in life? I suppose that most men and women and young people have never really answered that question. And I am not only thinking of that question on the level that some adults put it on when they ask John or Jane, "What are you going to be when you grow up?" I am asking you the very basic question, "What are you living for?" because some people have never asked, or at least never answered this question for themselves. They are saying, "Oh, what's the use of living?" Or when they are faced with reverses in business or sickness, we hear them say, "I give up; it's no use!"

Some of us might well be ashamed if we were faced with having to answer this question of the Savior. There are in us all plenty of shabby low answers that cannot stand to be brought out into the light of day. Then, of course, if we don't dare to put our life's object into words, the question is: "Should it be our life's object at all?"

But if we do not hedge or turn away but take time to examine ourselves and to determine honestly our life's goal, then we shall not make so many silly mistakes in regard to the places where we look for the things we are seeking. We should know where to go and find them. Perhaps someone or the other is having a little difficulty in determining what he is seeking. Do you want me to help you, to tell you what you are seeking? You are seeking for peace of heart and mind. You are seeking for truth unchanging, for a clean heart and a right spirit. Isn't that true? You are seeking for all these things, which can be found only in one place . . . rather, in one Person. The psalmist calls Jesus the Fountain of life. Each man that goes with his empty cup to Him gets it filled . . . filled according to his inmost need. What do you seek? Wisdom . . . true wisdom comes from Him who knoweth all. What do you seek? Love, peace, self-control, comfort for sorrow, hope? He says, "Come unto Me" . . . "seek and ye shall find."

Come and See

That's what Jesus says to these disciples of John, "Come and see!" They were perhaps about to answer, "Some other time," as many people answer today when invited to "taste and see that the Lord is good." Some other time.

He says to them, Come now. They ask Him, "Where dwellest Thou?" But the answer to this question was not important. The place did not matter. The manger-born Babe had no place to call His own though He was Lord of all. So pick any place — the woods on a summer day with your Testament in hand. Yes, He dwells there. The forest is His; He made the trees that spread above you. Or your private room at home at night upon your pillow . . . "darkness and light are both alike" to Him whether at 4 P. M., as here, or at 4 A. M. Yes, He dwells there. But He dwells especially in His house and especially when the congregation is present. Wherever His Word and sacraments are offered, there He dwells.

Come, Lord Jesus, be our Guest. They came and dwelt with Him in quiet confidential fellowship. They had a good long talk and visit. We don't have a record of that talk, but you know how it was with those other private communications of Jesus with the woman at the well at noon, with Nicodemus at midnight, with the disciples on the way to Emmaus. They got to the very root of the question, and "their hearts burned within them as He opened to them the Scriptures." Yes, that's the key to dwelling with Him. He is in His Word. Stay close to the Word, and you stay close to Jesus. He said: "If ye continue in My Word, then are ye My disciples indeed, and ye shall know the truth!"

Tell Someone About It

One evening at a mission station in the Belgian Congo a converted native prayed: "Lord Jesus, Thou art the Needle, and I am the cotton. To the missionary this seemed strange language, and so he asked the man what he meant by his unusual words. It turned out that the native had visited the mission school that day and watched the girls sewing. What interested him most was the fact that the thread always followed the needle. Just so he wanted to follow Jesus wherever He led. When Jesus tells us "Follow Me," He wants to have us so close to Him at all times, so completely yielded to Him, that we follow Him as directly and dependently as the thread follows the needle.

From these words of John's Gospel we somehow get the conviction that when a man has found Jesus he has an unmistakable impulse to tell someone else about it. When an ancient Greek discovered a law of physics he cried "Eureka!" That is, "I have found it!" When Dr. Salk discovered the vaccine for poliomyelitis, he readily and joyfully made it known to all mankind. So Andrew, after finding Jesus, "first findeth his own brother Simon." No one had to say to Andrew, "Now go look for your brother, and bring him." As soon as it dawned on him that the man standing before him was the Messiah, he hurried off to find his brother.

Everywhere in life we hear people shouting their convictions all around us. Over television and radio they say, "This is the best toothpaste. This is the best automobile, the best place to live," and the like. In fact, I believe that it is a laudable thing that people have such courage of their convictions, whether it be in selling breakfast cereal or in sharing the discovery of Christ, their Savior. But, incidentally, there is a brave logic beneath all this. If it is natural for a person with convictions to speak about what he is convinced of. If you do not speak of your convictions of faith, you may quite naturally ask "How strong are my convictions?" This man Andrew, before he was a day old as a disciple, had brought another to his Lord. Now some of you have been disciples for many years. Has there perhaps been too much silence on your part?

With your conclusions as to the ultimate purpose and goal of your life in mind, you may now ask yourself a question like this: "Why has God led me to live here in Tucson, Ariz. . . . and on this particular street with these particular neighbors?" And remember, if you as a Christian living in the midst of worldly, nonreligious people, do not influence them for good, they will surely influence you. But you say, "I can't." From the lesson of this story I say, "You can if you yourself have made this discovery." It's an adventure, a romance. Love cannot be hid. The lover wants to shout his love from the housetops. His eyes sparkle with it, and his joy is written, as we say, all over his face. If you have found Christ you can say that you have. Never mind how. That's not important anyhow. Only say it!

A New Name

Now look at this new follower of Christ who came as the result of Andrew's enthusiastic report of discovery of the Messiah. Jesus met him with a look, and you know what volumes He could speak by a tender glance. "You are Simon," Jesus said to Andrew's brother. You are Simon, the son of John. You shall be called Peter, a Rock. In the next chapter of his Gospel John says that Jesus "knew all men." Isn't that wonderful? That's how He knows you. This of course can be a terrifying thought to many men. But it is a blessed thought when I realize my Jesus knows me better than I know myself in all my weaknesses and my sins, and still He loves me.

If it be asked why our Lord gave Simon this new name, the best answer appears to be that it was given with special reference to the change which He was to work in Simon's heart. Naturally impulsive, unstable, and unsteady, he was finally to become a firm, solid stone in the church of Christ and to attest his unshaken adherence to Christ by suffering martyrdom.

Jesus said, "You are Simon, the son of John. You shall be called Cephas [Peter, the Rock]." Jesus gave him a new reason to live, a new name to live up to. Always, whatever he might do, this would be the name he had been given, perhaps as a warning as in the day of his triple denial. If he was moved to pride as a leader in the church, he could well remember that he was a rock, even though only a little rock, and there was after all that greater Rock from which he had been hewn.

What name does the Savior give you? Some of you may have the name Christ, Christine, Christopher, Christian. But we all hear the name of Christ as we sing, "I was made a Christian when my name was given." Let us also bear this name with humble pride, remembering our royal lineage when we are tempted to what is mean or low, not becoming to sons or daughters of God, to brothers or sisters of Christ. If you are despondent and forlorn, recall that this name of Christian entitles you to a large inheritance, for we are joint heirs with Christ of mansions eternal in the heavens.

One other question remains to be answered as we read this record of John. You noted that the evangelist said that there were two disciples and that one was Andrew. Now who, pray tell, was the other? All who study this record agree that the other disciple must be John himself, the writer of this gospel, who modestly omits his name throughout his gospel. But from the way he records that "Andrew first went and found his brother" we gather that John also very likely at this time went and found his brother James and brought him to Jesus. Note that John is so impressed by the events of that first afternoon interview with Jesus that he remembers the very hour when he first went with his brother, Andrew, and heard Him whose teaching he was to feast on and live by so completely for the rest of his life; whose last word he was to hear from the cross (19:30); and whom he was the first to recognize after the resurrection (21:7), and from whom, in apocalyptic vision, he was to hear words of wondrous power (Rev. 1:17-20).

Is not the first meeting of the Savior with all His true disciples, when they recognize and acknowledge Him as the "Sent of God" and their "Beautiful Savior," to be cherished in memory. We cannot all point out the exact day or hour as John did, but we can point to many occasions that highlight our life as Christians: the prayers we learned at our mother's knees, our first vacation Bible school or Sunday school, our Confirmation day, our first Communion, a glorious Easter service with the assurance of our own resurrection unto life. So we say again as we meditate on the Gospel text:

> Savior, I long to walk Closer with Thee;
> Led by Thy guiding hand, Ever to be
> Constantly near Thy side, Quickened and purified,
> Living for Him who died Freely for me.

Does Living Water Intrigue You Too?

By WILBERT E. GRIESSE

(The Third Sunday After Epiphany)

When therefore the Lord knew how the Pharisees had heard that Jesus made and baptized more disciples than John (though Jesus Himself baptized not, but His disciples), He left Judea and departed again into Galilee. And He must needs go through Samaria. Then cometh He to a city of Samaria which is called Sychar, near to the parcel of ground that Jacob gave to his son Joseph. Now Jacob's well was there. Jesus therefore, being wearied with His journey, sat thus on the well, and it was about the sixth hour. There cometh a woman of Samaria to draw water. Jesus saith unto her, Give Me to drink. (For His disciples were gone away unto the city to buy meat.) Then saith the woman of Samaria unto Him, How is it that Thou, being a Jew, asketh drink of me, which am a woman of Samaria? For the Jews have no dealings with the Samaritans. Jesus answered and said unto her, If thou knewest the gift of God, and who it is that saith to thee, Give Me to drink, thou wouldest have asked of Him, and He would have given thee living water. The woman saith unto Him, Sir, Thou hast nothing to draw with, and the well is deep. From whence, then, hast Thou that living water? Art Thou greater than our father Jacob, which gave us the well and drank thereof himself, and his children, and his cattle? Jesus answered and said unto her, Whosoever drinketh of this water shall thirst again. But whosoever drinketh of the water that I shall give him shall never thirst, but the water that I shall give him shall be in him a well of water springing up into everlasting life. — *John 4:1-14*

It is characteristic of the Lord Jesus that He used the commonplace and the natural thing in order to illustrate the great and profound truths of the love of God and to relate them to the lives of men. Relationships that were found so normally in nature were used by Him to indicate and symbolize relationships between God and man.

In the instance of our text He used the very common and very natural item of water. Water is so common to us, and its use is so natural that we tend to take it for granted. In fact, it is usually only when its use is denied us, or when we have it specially called to our attention by our acute need or by another's suggestion, that we notice it at all or reflect upon its wholesome and happy uses.

Still, water appeals to us. You are at the oceanside, and you wonder at the vast expanse of it and the might of it and constant motion of it. You are in a woody glen, and you listen to the chatter of it. You are drawn to it to sit by its side and watch it tumbling prettily over the rocks and rushing to the serenity of the lovely pool.

Perhaps it is a little difficult for us, who only need to turn the tap whenever we want water, to capture the deep satisfaction of drawing water from a well, pulling on the chain until the bucket comes into view, and then watching its fresh and clear contents sometimes spilling abundantly over the side as the vessel is made secure.

Jesus was sitting at the well of Jacob about the noon hour on His trip back to Galilee, and His thoughts must have been on water: the drawing of it and the use of it and its relationship to life. And, of course, He would also consider the spiritual relationship, thinking that as water refreshes and enlivens and cleanses, so the water of life does the same for the soul. And when the woman comes, He speaks to her about her spiritual needs and what living water can do for her. The woman was intrigued by the possibilities.

Does Living Water Intrigue You Too?

I

Do You Recognize It?

One of the problems that confront the church of today is that its members are not sufficiently familiar with the living water they possess. In some instances they are not even aware that they possess it. Like the disciples we should very likely be so interested in our going into the city to buy bread that we, too, should register surprise if the Savior said to us, "I have meat to eat that ye know not of." And we would be just as perturbed that the Lord Jesus had taken this particular route back from Jerusalem to Galilee. And to make matters worse, instead of hurrying on to His destination, He has lingered here in this abominable place and exposed them to all the uncleanness that abounds among these uncouth people. That they, the disciples, should also be intrigued with this unusual living water, as the woman was, somehow escaped them, and somehow it tends to escape us too.

All of us seem to be attracted to lively water that tumbles over the rocks in a stream, but we fail to recognize the Living Water that tumbled over rocks of sorrow and into pools of suffering for us that we might be redeemed.

We may imagine that the woman came to the well that day

engrossed in thoughts that related to her personal life and her troubles. Was it a sudden unforeseen need of water that sent her to the well at the unusual hour of noon? Or was it that she preferred this hour to get her normal supply in order that she might not need to hear the contemptuous and derisive remarks of her fellow villagers?

Whatever the reason, she is here to draw water, and her chore does not seem to be made lighter by the presence of the Stranger at the well. She would have preferred to come up unnoticed, draw her necessary water, and make her return without incident. But there He is, and He accosts her. Well for her that He did, because otherwise she would never have been intrigued as she was.

He asks for a drink, and she questions the propriety of His action. He perplexes her by suggesting a better water than she can get from Jacob's well. And while she is concerned with the mechanics and with her prejudices, He refers to the deeper needs and to the more important satisfactions.

Life hasn't changed much basically from that time to this, even though the methods of drawing water have been made more convenient. We let ourselves get engrossed in our activities and our business and social relationships to the point where they glaze our lives with a coating that protects the deep-seated trouble within. And even when we do the things that make us think we are religious, do we sometimes also unconsciously slur over something we should discuss with our Father in prayer and omit from our confessions an embarrassing moment or two? Are we sometimes unconsciously looking for loneliness when we worship, and do we hurry back home before we can become too involved in the family life of the church? Worse yet, when we go to draw our water, are we distressed to see Reality Himself sitting there when reality was what we were unthinkingly trying to avoid? And does it bother us when He asks us those pesky questions which have their purpose in shifting our focus and our desires from what *we* think is proper and important to what *He* wants us to consider and do?

It develops, then, that we are a little more like the woman than we imagined ourselves to be. We, too, need higher aims and motives. Our defenses need to be penetrated, and the underlying trouble needs to be laid bare. We need to recognize the living water and be intrigued by it and use it for our cleansing and for our refreshment.

II

Are You Refreshed by It?

Far from being hesitant and withdrawn about coming into contact with and recognizing this living water, we should realize that it is the only life-giving and satisfying and truly refreshing substance that we can find in this world. Jesus says, "Whosoever drinketh of the water that I shall give him shall never thirst."

Intriguing, isn't it? Once the woman recognized that this water was something special, her practical mind could conjure up all sorts of uses for this liquid. Perhaps there could be a quality to this water by which physical thirst could be permanently satisfied. Then she wouldn't need to draw so often and so laboriously. Maybe this water had magical cleansing powers that could materially lessen her washing needs. Oh, there were so many good things that could be obtained if only this water would respond the way she wanted it to.

It's odd that she should be so right about the satisfying and cleansing powers of this water but so wrong about their applications.

Really her mistake lay partly in the sequence of the application. She thought first of her material and physical needs and placed these ahead of her spiritual needs. This will never work out. Spiritual refreshment, implanted by God, always develops from within, and faith must always first work spiritual health before it spreads to our physical well-being and blessing.

Thinking primarily of our own creature comforts, we tend today to emphasize the social effect of the Gospel, and we are desirous that this should be effected irrespective of our primary spiritual needs of forgiveness, strengthening of faith, and peace with God. We tend to want the words of the Savior "I am come that they might have life and that they might have it more abundantly" to mean earthly prosperity and happiness for all. But God would rather give us prosperity of faith, and happiness of spirit, and refreshment for our souls first. Then our lives will be in balance before Him, and He can then allow us all the physical blessings that His love will bestow.

> I heard the voice of Jesus say,
> "Behold, I freely give
> The living water; thirsty one,
> Stoop down and drink and live."
> I came to Jesus, and I drank
> Of that life-giving stream.
> My thirst was quenched, my soul revived,
> And now I live in Him.

It is significant that this must be experienced and lived through before it can be properly understood and appreciated. One can imagine that this woman, reflecting later upon what had happened to her, would wonder how she could ever have counted herself happy, let alone continue with day-to-day living.

And where do *we* seek our refreshment? Do we sometimes let earthly refreshments take precedence over our receiving spiritual refreshment? It is so easy to satisfy our bodily wants and our recreational desires before we partake of the living water for our souls, simply because our physical needs make their demands known so effectively. In the area of spiritual need, constant attention and practice is required to develop the taste for this living water.

"Oh, taste and see that the Lord is good!" recommends the psalmist (34: 8). And St. Peter has the same idea, though he changes the picture slightly: "As newborn babes, desire the sincere milk of the Word that ye may grow thereby, if so be ye have tasted that the Lord is gracious. (1 Peter 2: 2, 3)

Can anything be more satisfactory and more refreshing than to put our whole trust in the precious promises of salvation? To know that "God was in Christ, reconciling the world unto Himself," that you can "cast all your care upon Him, for He careth for you," that "all things work together for good to them that love God," that you can be of good cheer because your sins are forgiven you — for one to know this and believe it and put one's trust in it — is to be refreshed by the living water that Christ provides. This refreshment is ours by faith, and it becomes ours the more surely, the more we share this refreshment with others.

III

Do You Share It?

Jesus continues in His dialog with the woman, "But the water that I shall give him shall be in him a well of water springing up into eternal life." In these words the Lord Jesus refers to the symbolism of the well of Jacob. Its founder had used the water, but its use did not stop with Him. Down through the ages the people continued to use the wholesome water and were refreshed by it.

People who partake of living water become both users and transmitters of the blessed substance. Isn't it intriguing? And it is so important that we do both — use and transmit — but in the proper sequence. You can't transmit unless you yourself are a user, and to use the water without sharing it doesn't quite fit the picture that Jesus proposes: that it shall be in *you* a well of water springing up into everlasting life.

We know that the woman understood it that way. She shared her newfound living water almost as soon as she discovered it, and with considerable success. The townspeople said (v. 42), "We know that this is indeed the Christ, the Savior of the world." They, too, drank of the living water and were refreshed by it.

So we come to the important matter of sharing our living water with the thirsty, dying world today. God wants us to be associated with Him in the spiritual refreshment of the world, to serve with Him and for Him as springing wells that give the water of life to the thirsty world.

Could it be that the reason we share so little is that we *use* the living water so little? Does our sparse use reflect itself in the lack of sharing?

It would be so wonderful and so pleasing to God if we should become more ardent in the use of the Word, recognizing it as the living water that Christ provides, using it abundantly as we refresh our souls with its coolness, and really sharing this life-giving treasure.

Jesus planned His way into the hearts of this Samaritan community. Perhaps it would take a little more ingenuity on our part, and a little more love, and a lot more use of the water of life for ourselves, but if we were to give the whole world this living water, only God could tell what would happen to His kingdom. Wouldn't it be intriguing and blessed and profitable to find out? Let's do it for the sake of Him who gave the living water in His great love for us and for the world! Amen.

The God We Worship

By R. H. A. SEBOLDT

(The Fourth Sunday After Epiphany)

The woman said to Him, "Sir, give me this water, that I may not thirst nor come here to draw." Jesus said to her, "Go, call your husband and come here." The woman answered Him, "I have no husband." Jesus said to her, "You are right in saying, 'I have no husband'; for you have had five husbands, and he whom you now have is not your husband; this you said truly." The woman said to Him, "Sir, I perceive that You are a prophet. Our fathers worshiped on this mountain; and you say that in Jerusalem is the place where men ought to worship." Jesus said to her, "Woman, believe Me, the hour is coming when neither on this mountain nor in Jerusalem will you worship the Father. You worship what you do not know; we worship what we know, for salvation is from the Jews. But the hour is coming, and now is, when the true worshipers will worship the Father in spirit and truth, for such the Father seeks to worship Him. God is spirit, and those who worship Him must worship in spirit and truth." The woman said to Him, "I know that Messiah is coming (He who is called Christ); when He comes, He will show us all things." Jesus said to her, "I who speak to you am He." — *John 4:15-26 RSV*

Who is God, and how do we worship Him?

This is the question of mankind in every civilization. The religious curiosity of the human creature leads him to seek some answer.

Even when we have received the answer, we still find questions arising. Many of us in our assembly today have found doubts arising. How do we know that our God, the Father, Son, and Holy Ghost, is the only true God? How can we be sure that our worship is correct?

St. John relates an account of Jesus meeting a woman at Jacob's Well. In this account we have revealed

The God We Worship

St. John informs us that Jesus was traveling from Judea to Galilee. His journey took Him through Samaria. He sat down at Jacob's Well in Sychar, a town in Samaria, to rest from His travels. While the disciples were in the village to buy food, a woman came out to draw water. Jesus made a request of her: "Give Me a drink."

This surprised the Samaritan woman. She said, "How is it that You, a Jew, ask a drink of me, a woman of Samaria?" Her surprise is not unusual. St. John explains, "The Jews have no dealing with the Samaritans." The Jews were the covenant people of God, who accepted all 39 books of the Old Testament. They worshiped at the temple in Jerusalem. Therefore they had no sympathy for the Samaritans, a mixed people, who accepted only the first five books of the Old Testament and who worshiped on another mountain.

Jesus replies to the surprised Samaritan. He speaks of the living water which springs up into everlasting life. The words of our text follow, in which we hear God revealing the shallowness of some half-worship of a vague God. We also hear the Word about the true God and our worship of Him.

A Vague God

Sometimes we find a vague notion of God. When we do not know God as He is, a Person of grace and love in Christ, we may have a false picture. One who has a vague notion of God may desire to use God for personal satisfaction. This becomes apparent in the woman at the well. After Jesus speaks about the living water of everlasting life, the woman says, "Sir, give me this water, that I may not thirst nor come here to draw." She did not understand His reference to the water of eternal life. She thought of the work in trudging to the well to carry water to her house. The thought of having one's physical thirst quenched forever appealed to her. Her notion of God and His help led her to try for personal satisfaction without the full thought of who God is and what His will desires.

Using God as Our Servant

Our experience in life is often similar to that of the Samaritan woman. We hear the promises of God, offering the abundant life. We gain the impression that God is around to satisfy our personal wishes. This vague notion of God may lead us to use God for satisfying our own desires. We may use God to be successful by material standards, to be healthy so we feel good, to have God around for any emergency or accident in the conduct of our life. The tendency to make God our servant and to turn ourselves into the god we worship is prevalent in the Western civilizations, who too glibly claim for themselves the name "Christian."

Another result of a vague notion of God is to view Him as a prophet. Jesus asked the woman to call her husband. When she confessed that she had no husband, Jesus says that she has had five husbands. To this she responds, "I perceive that You are a prophet." She was attracted by His ability to know her life.

Some are inclined to look on God as a mighty ruler who knows all the answers. He seems to be a kind of heavenly policeman, who keeps account of our crime record. Others think of God and the Bible as ways of foretelling the events of world history. This view is partially true. If God is only One who knows as a prophet, we see no more than His knowledge, wrath, and judgment. We miss the truth of His love. We miss the God of history who lives and guides human life according to His gracious plan.

A God Without Christ

A vague notion of God results in an indefinite hope for the Messiah. For the Samaritan woman, the Messiah was one to show all things. He would be a kind of magician, who would reveal mysteries and satisfy curiosities of the human mind. She had an idea of the Messiah, but she did not have the faith to hope for a redeemer who would overcome evil and return sinners to God.

We can see the same results in our time. A general idea of God may express itself in the motto on American coins, "In God we trust." We may add "under God" to our pledge of allegiance. Yet this does not make a clear confession of the redemption by God in Christ. A vague God results in a vague Christ. Many think only of the ethical laws of Christ. They look on Christianity as a way of setting goals for a higher life, urging man to strive harder for noble ideals. Such a view misses the Gospel which Christ Jesus announces and achieves by His own life, that man is made new and rescued from evil and death.

Half-Worship of God

A vague notion results in a kind of half-worship of God. An attempt to worship is made when we cling to ourselves and still try to reach out to God. The woman at the well talked about worshiping God here, yet she lived in adultery. On the one hand, she lived in self-satisfaction, in sinful violation of God's will. At the same time she claimed to be interested in the worship of God. This is a kind of half-worship, a split between satisfying self and recognizing God. It is really no worship at all, for we cannot come to God while we are clinging to ourselves.

In our life today, the pleasures of self result in disobeying God for personal advantage. One who talks of prayer to God while living in sin is not worshiping. Being guilty of deceit, unfaithfulness, dishonesty, and pride while still trying to think of worshiping God is to be a split personality. God is worshiped only through complete confession of our sinfulness and a total dependence on His mercy in Christ.

Missing God in Concern for Details

A vague notion of God may lead us to be concerned more with place and methods than about facing God in His presence.

The Samaritan woman talked about the difference in worship between her people and the Jews. People of Samaria chose the mountain. Jews praised God in the temple of Jerusalem. The big issue seemed to be the place and the method. In this conflict of traditions, God in His Person was forgotten. To be more concerned with place and method than about God in His reality is to engage in half-worship. This is none at all!

When the power and presence of the Person of God are overlooked, confusion reigns in our own time. Some places are considered more sacred than others. Pilgrimages to historic places are valued more highly than prayers and praises in the congregation's chapel. Relics of historic heroes are viewed with high respect. Methods of worshiping may be elevated to a place higher than the God whom they are to honor. Works of music, art, and liturgy are helpful as a language of worship when used to awaken the response of God's people to praise and thank Him. They may not replace the concern with adoring God, but are used as expressions of adoration.

God Shut in a Box

A vague notion of God and a pretended worship may result from our failure to communicate clearly. Are we sharing Christ Jesus and God's purpose through Him to people of our day? In his play, "Cry Dawn in Dark Babylon," P. W. Turner has one of his characters say:

> For everyday Jones whose capable hands
> Tighten the nuts of a rattle-trap globe,
> The corpse-Christ is an enemy alien
> And God is shut in a box.

God is shut in a box, removed from the hurt of a bereaved parent and the disillusionment of a man in a confused world. There is a long distance between the God of the Scriptures and the daily situation. The God of childhood is the only kind many adults know. The infant picture of God seems to put Him in the same class with Santa Claus, someone who is nice for the kiddies to believe in, but ready to be shelved in childhood reveries when the adult realities begin.

We ask ourselves:

Have we a vague notion of God? Have we slipped into a pretended worship of God? Are we guilty of adding to the vagueness of God in others by our unclear witness in word and life?

God Revealed in Jesus Christ

The true God reveals Himself. We see this in our text from St. John.

God is very clear as He reveals Himself in Jesus Christ. This Jesus who speaks to the Samaritan woman is God incarnate! To the woman who has a vague idea of the Messiah Jesus says, "I who speak to you am He!" This tired Traveler is the Word of God made flesh. He is the eternal Son of God, living among men. He is God, revealing Himself in assuming the full scope of human life.

He is born of the Virgin Mary.
He lives a boyhood life in Nazareth.
He obeys the will of His Father as He moves around in Galilee, Samaria, Judea.
He suffers poverty and opposition.
He accepts the death of a common criminal on a cross.
He endures the pain and punishment of sinners.
He is a Servant, who sets aside His Lordship to undergo our burden of guilt and death.
He rises triumphant from death to live as our Lord.

This is God revealing Himself. God is clear, giving us a sharp image of Himself as a forgiving, merciful God in the person of Christ. The Holy Scriptures give us the account of His revelation in Christ.

The God of Grace

In Christ, God reveals the Gospel of grace. All of God's mercy is embodied in the life and person of Jesus Christ. In Christ we are delivered from vague notions of God as a mere principle of nature. We are freed from the vision of God as a sentimental old man. In Christ we see God as a Person who sees our needs. He acts to redeem us. He daily provides His love for us. He is the waiting Father, who has love for the youth who rebel and feel rejected by adults who do not seem to understand. He is the patient Father, waiting for the juvenile adult who still wants to make his own decisions in defiance of God's will. He is the reaching Father, who sends sincere witnesses to those who call every Christian a hypocrite. He is the compassionate Father, touching the life of this adulterous woman at the well to lead her to repentance and reunion with God.

The Holy Spirit

God sends the Holy Spirit to work true, saving faith in the hearts of men. In our story, Jesus reaches out with the power and grace of God. He works to reclaim, to redeem, and to restore an insecure, sinful woman. In our time, Jesus has sent the Holy Spirit to be His power in our lives. The Holy Spirit filled Peter and the other apostles to proclaim Christ at any cost. The Spirit of God converted Saul to become an apostle to the world. The Holy Spirit worked through Christians, dispersed into many lands by persecution. The same Spirit of God now brings clear testimony to the revelation of God in Christ to men. He uses people, ordinary people like us, to share the Gospel with others.

We Worship the God of the Gospel

This is the God of the Gospel. This is our God, who was made man in Jesus Christ, to be Savior and Lord. This is our God, who acts upon us by His Holy Spirit through the Word and the sacraments. We do not ask how God can be Three-in-One. We cannot solve the mystery of His Being. But we do believe God, who has revealed Himself to us.

We believe Him, and we worship God. In the words of Jesus, "We worship what we know." We worship a personal God, whom we know by faith. Ours is not an "unknown god" as that of the Greeks on Mars' Hill in Athens. We do not indulge in the worship life of the agnostic who says, "Dear God, if there is a God, please forgive me, if there is forgiveness." We worship a God whom we know! The Holy Spirit has made Him real to us. By Baptism we have died with Christ, and we have risen with Him. In the Gospel, by words and Holy Communion, we know Him as our forgiving God.

We worship the God whom we know in spirit and in truth. People who know the God revealed in Jesus Christ also have a clear expression of their worship. To worship God is to give complete acknowledgment to Him. To worship is to give Him all honor, praise, and glory. In great reverence we see God as the Absolute, the One and Only, who is above all else. He alone is Giver of life. In Him all things find their existence.

Worship in the Assembly

We worship God in the formal sense when we gather for the assembly of His people. We hear and receive the Word of the Gospel. We celebrate the redeeming acts of Christ in the Sacra-

ment. We confess our sins to God and to one another. We rejoice
in the forgiveness of Jesus Christ. We use all the gifts of worship
in art, music, building, and liturgy to respond to the coming of
God's grace in Christ. In the gathering of Christians we help one
another to praise God, to live in His forgiveness, to gain strength,
and to be His strong witnesses.

Worship in Daily Witness

We worship God not only as we praise Him in public services.
We worship God as we serve and acknowledge Him in life. From
this conversation of Jesus and the Samaritan woman we gain the
emphasis that we worship God as we share Him. Our worship is
not complete after the final prayer of the worship service. It is
completed as we move out into daily life to witness to people of
God's grace in Christ. We are the witnessing, worshiping people
of God as we talk to the members of our family about the Gospel
of Christ; as we include Christian sharing in our neighborhood
conversations; as we share Christ in the office and at the shop;
as we honor God in the car pool on the way to work.

Who is God and how do we worship Him?

God is the Creator of life, who has revealed His grace in Jesus
Christ, and who acts upon us by His Holy Spirit.

We worship as we respond to His forgiving grace in words
and in life.

Bibliography

Turner, P. W. *Cry Dawn in Dark Babylon.* (London: S. P. C. K.,
1961), p. 32.

Outer Space or Inner Space

By PAUL G. HANSEN

(Septuagesima Sunday)

Now as they went on their way, He entered a village, and a woman
named Martha received Him into her house. And she had a sister called
Mary, who sat at the Lord's feet and listened to His teaching. But Martha
was distracted with much serving, and she went to Him and said, "Lord,
do You not care that my sister has left me to serve alone? Tell her, then,
to help me." But the Lord answered her, "Martha, Martha, you are
anxious and troubled about many things; one thing is needful. Mary
has chosen the good portion, which shall not be taken away from her. —
Luke 10:38-42 RSV

A science-fiction writer penned a story once about a pedestrian
in the coming mechanical age. He told of a man going out for
a walk in the fashion of today. A robot police car eased up beside
him, demanding to know why he was walking. "To breathe some
air," was the answer. And the robot said mechanically, "But you've
got an air conditioner." "I wanted to see things," the man said.

"But you've got a television set," replied the robot — and the police hurried the pedestrian off to an insane asylum.*

Probably none of us is looking forward to anything like the mechanical age pictured by science fiction, the *Brave New World* of Aldous Huxley or the "1984" of George Orwell. We realize how lacking in love and tenderness and beauty and warmth any such period would be. We agree that the worship of material things can lead to ultimate hopelessness. But while we admit to all such arguments, we sometimes contribute directly toward the mechanistic age by the way we live and act. We are more concerned about an air conditioner than about the conditioning of the soul. We are more interested in seeing the funny side of life on television than in seeing the reality of human need around us. We certainly will have no one to blame but ourselves if the whole world is eventually run by robots and mechanical brains and our activity is confined to pushing buttons and twirling dials.

And so we come today to the beginning of a season of penitence and prayer in the church. What better way to begin such a season than to sit down and take stock of where we are really going with our lives? As a nation we have become more and more interested in outer space. The days are full of surprises, and no one knows what may be the next achievement in space exploration. And yet there is tremendous danger that in being concerned about science and invention and space travel and planetary discoveries we have failed to be concerned about God and His grace and our souls and their eternal destiny. We might say that much of the tragedy which exists in the world today is there because men have thought more of material than of spiritual things, more of outer space than of inner space, more of the heavens above us than of the heart within, more of the solar system than of the soul system, more of research in science than of real search in Scripture.

I
God Approves Concern for "Outer Space"

Until the last few years I am quite sure no one would ever have thought of the story of Mary and Martha in relation to any kind of space. Possibly it still seems strange to connect that peaceful little scene in Bethany with Cape Canaveral or the ICBMs which may either lead to thrilling exploration or thunderous extinction in global warfare. But really, if we just stop and think for a moment of the principle involved in what Martha did, what Mary did, and what Jesus said, the whole connection becomes clear.

---

* J. Carter Swaim, *Body, Soul and Spirit* (New York: Thos. Nelson and Sons, 1957), p. 111.

Martha was concerned with material things. Only as a Jewish housekeeper her concern was with meat and vegetables and bread and wine and a table with dishes. Homemakers today have many of the same worries. But what essentially is the difference between Martha's interest in being a good hostess and any modern attention to business, politics, science, or the host of material interests which vie for our attention?

One of the main things our text shows us, of course, is that *God approves of Marthas* — of human efforts toward a better world. These things are not wrong in themselves. In fact, Jesus would probably have been very much disappointed if Martha had made no effort at all to provide a meal for Him. And I am quite sure He appreciated tremendously the work she did and the sacrifices she made. There is no excuse in Christianity for the lazy good-for-nothing who says that he is being "religious" by wasting his life. The story of Mary and Martha gives no one an excuse for failing to get a good education, for a lack of ambition on the job, for showing no interest in government or political programs, or for failing to serve and defend one's country. In fact, any season of penitence and prayer is a time for honest soul searching in regard to what we have done with the opportunities God has given us for making this world a better place for Jesus to visit in, a place where His message can be more easily spread, and a place where people can see evidences of the power of believing. Part of the trouble in our world is directly due to the fact that we haven't had enough Marthas in the Christian church, people who have really let the Christian influence be felt in business, politics, science, and the arts, but instead have thought that all Jesus ever wanted was some one to sit at His feet and hear His Word.

Marthas are needed also in the church. Congregations are full of people who justify their failure to attend voters' meetings by saying, "First things first," as though that meant one should never get around to the second things. They won't serve on boards or committees; they grumble about overorganization; they want no part of financial campaigns; and they excuse their neglect by saying that the church should "stick to its business of saving souls." These are the people, too, who never bother to attend a congregational social, because they don't see any sense in Christians drinking coffee and eating doughnuts together. "First things first!" they always say. But somehow they never seem to get past the first things, and it is rather doubtful that they even take care of those. They are simply fugitives from the order of Martha. Whether God does or does not approve of man's explorations in outer space may be unimportant. I for one think He does. But the main point of our text so far is that God approves the best use of our abilities, whatever they may be, as a fitting and very necessary result of those things Jesus called "needful."

Believe me, we Christians might not be faced with the threat of global war if we had, in some respects at least, been *better Marthas for Jesus.* No amount of our sitting at the feet of Jesus, without action, is going to convince a godless Communist that Christianity is concerned about the poor. No amount of mere listening to the Word is going to show the Negro that the whites are not prejudiced against him. No amount of nothing but quiet meditation is going to heal the diseases of natives in far-off lands. No devotional exercises alone are going to put better men in political office or preserve the Christian influence in a community's police force. All of this we can call "outer space" — the area outside of the person himself. And it's all related to the very same kind of activity which may eventually lead man to explore the moon and the planets. The Christian influence must be felt in all walks of life if Christianity is to be what Jesus said it should be, "the salt of the earth" and "the light of the world."

But of course we have missed the whole point of the story unless we realize *the true nature of Martha's problem.* It wasn't what she was doing for Jesus that was wrong. In fact, what she did was very right and very worthwhile. She was *"distracted"* with much serving, says the text, and Jesus said to her, "Martha, Martha, you are *anxious* and *troubled* about many things." She had permitted her concern for outward activities to distract her attention from the inner needs of her soul. She was like the space traveler who has lost his contact with earth. She was like a ship that has lost its moorings in a storm. In many respects she was like you and me when we worry about what's going to come of our world and get all shaken up over Russian tanks in Berlin and 50 megaton bombs exploding over Siberia. She was like you and me if we start paying so much attention to the outward organization of our church and its administrative and financial problems that we lose all track of its real purpose and what really makes it worthwhile. God forgive us for the way we have failed to be Marthas at all — or for the way we have been Marthas without first being Marys.

II

God Wants "Inner Space" to Come First

"Inner space" has to come before *"outer space."* One is not an excuse for neglecting the other. Moffatt translates our text: "Mary has chosen the best dish, and she is not to be dragged away from it." Here we can see that Jesus is really not making a comparison at all between Martha's activities and Mary's. He is not

contrasting Christian service with Christian knowledge. He is really asking: "What is more important toward serving God — food for the body or food for the soul?" Martha wanted to hurry up the dinner, because she was sure everyone was hungry. Mary was willing to have the "devotions" first, because she was sure spiritual food was more important. Jesus agreed with her. Mary had the "best dish." The decision isn't between "inner space and outer space." Both are important. The question is: "What inner space is more important — body or soul?" "What is more important to really worthwhile activity — food or faith?"

"A man has to eat" is the excuse so often given for failure to make sacrifices for the kingdom of God. Jesus does not deny the need of human sustenance. But He is saying that if the choice becomes necessary, *food for the soul is more important than food for the body.* The most brilliant scientist can play havoc with his own life and with the world (witness what is happening in Russia today) if he has not first of all taken care of his soul. And the most consecrated church worker can create turmoil in congregational life and hinder the spread of the Gospel if his own inner peace is not first of all assured. Mary was not merely getting "pearls of wisdom" from the lips of Jesus. She would not have found the "best dish" if Jesus was to her merely a great philosopher expounding on the meaning of life. To Mary Jesus was what He must be to everyone who is really going to care for the "inner space" of the soul. He was her God and her Savior, One who could forgive her sins and cleanse her conscience and sanctify her soul. He was the "Son of man who came not to be ministered unto but to minister and to give His life a ransom for many." As the apostle Paul put it: "Being justified by faith, we have peace with God through our Lord Jesus Christ." That is truly caring for inner space.

The text does not say that Mary did nothing toward preparing the meal. Perhaps she had been as active as Martha, but merely sat down for a moment of devotion with Jesus before the meal was put on the table. So let's not confuse the picture by saying we should be like Martha in one respect and like Mary in another. Let's merely say that we would all be better servants of God and man if like Mary we first permitted the Lord Jesus to satisfy our souls. In fact, that is the only way we can really serve at all. Jesus is not with us in visible form so that we may sit at His feet and hear His Word, but we have our Bible for daily reading and meditation, our church services for receiving instruction and inspiration, Bible classes for deeper insights and the Sacrament for spiritual power. We have so many wonderful ways in which the inner space of the soul can be filled with good things. How can we ever leave it empty? The coming Lenten season will give additional opportunities for discovering what the "one thing needful" can do for our lives.

Wasn't it Sir James Simpson, the man whose research in the field of anesthesia relieved untold suffering, who was once asked what he considered his greatest discovery? He replied: "The greatest discovery I have ever made is that I am a sinner and Jesus Christ is my Savior." That's taking care of "inner space." With that discovery "outer space" has no terror. The future is an exciting adventure with God.

The Church Invincible

By ARLIN A. MAAS

(Sexagesima Sunday)

When Jesus came into the coasts of Caesarea Philippi, He asked His disciples, saying, Whom do men say that I, the Son of Man, am? And they said, Some say that Thou art John the Baptist; some, Elias; and others, Jeremias or one of the prophets. He saith unto them, But whom say ye that I am? And Simon Peter answered and said, Thou art the Christ, the Son of the living God. And Jesus answered and said, Blessed art thou, Simon Barjona, for flesh and blood hath not revealed it unto thee, but My Father, which is in heaven. And I say also unto thee, That thou art Peter, and upon this rock I will build My church; and the gates of hell shall not prevail against it. And I will give unto thee the keys of the kingdom of heaven; and whatsoever thou shalt bind on earth shall be bound in heaven; and whatsoever thou shalt loose on earth shall be loosed in heaven. Then charged He His disciples that they should tell no man that He was Jesus the Christ. — *Matthew 16:13-20*

It was England's darkest hour when the reins of government were given over to another Prime Minister, whose name has already gone down in history as a mighty leader of his people. The British had just suffered a humiliating defeat at Trondheim, Norway. Their expeditionary forces in Holland and France were being pushed back into the sea, and the debacle of Dunkirk was only three weeks away. It was during these first few weeks that the stature of the new Prime Minister, Winston Churchill, was revealed. Addressing his first meeting of Parliament, he minced no words, but stated frankly, "I have nothing to offer but blood, toil, sweat, and tears." Three weeks later the arms of the empire lay scattered on the beaches of Dunkirk, and its battered army was rescued from total annihilation only by a superhuman effort on the part of its navy and air force, plus a thousand civilians operating every vessel they could lay hands on. The Prime Minister did not hesitate to inform his people of the terrible threat that now hung over them of invasion from the continent, but, he said, "We shall fight on the seas and the oceans, we shall fight in the air,

we shall defend our island whatever the cost may be, we shall
fight on the beaches, we shall fight on the landing grounds, we shall
fight in the fields and in the streets, we shall fight in the hills, we
shall never surrender. Our aim is victory — victory at all costs,
victory in spite of all terror, victory, however long and hard the
road may be." It was these assurances more than anything else
which gave hope and strength to the grieving and bewildered
people of England in their darkest hour.

An even more dismal hour of darkness was about to come
upon the disciples of Jesus as He spoke the words of our text.
From Caesarea Philippi they would turn south and go to Jerusalem. Before beginning this journey back, Jesus would reveal to
them that "He must suffer many things of the elders and chief
priests and scribes, and be killed" (Matt. 16:21). And they, too,
He said, will have to deny themselves and take up their cross
if they would be His disciples. However, while He paints a dark
picture of the terrible things that are to come, at the same time
He also gives the assurance of victory by picturing to them

The Church Invincible

I

The Church's Strength

The strength of a building is determined by its foundation.
All skyscrapers built and being built in New York City go several
stories underground for the simple reason that the site must be
excavated down to bedrock. More tons of material are removed
from the plot of land than the total weight of the completed building. The church's strength, too, lies in the fact that it rests upon
bedrock.

Christ the Rock

The church which Christ was constructing stone by stone must
likewise have a solid foundation if it was to stand up against the
devil-driven winds and waves with which he would, if it were
possible, destroy even the Builder Himself. It could therefore not
be built on sand or on crumbling stone, but on nothing less than
rock — bedrock. He Himself became that Bedrock, the sturdy
Foundation of the church, "for other foundation can no man lay
than that is laid, which is Jesus Christ." (1 Cor. 3:11)

But is He the man to make the church a solid and lasting
structure? "Is not this the carpenter's son?" His hearers ask one
another. "Is not His mother called Mary? And His brethren, James
and Joses and Simon and Judas?" (Matt. 13:55). Others comment,
"Shall Christ come out of Galilee? . . . Out of Galilee ariseth no
prophet" (John 7:41, 52). Still others were somewhat more kindly

disposed toward Him, as Jesus learned from His disciples, when one day He asked them: "Whom do men say that I, the Son of Man, am?" They tell Him: "Some say that Thou art John the Baptist; some, Elias; and others Jeremias or one of the prophets." Now these were all good men, men of God, even great men of God, but they were still only men. They were men who themselves needed a solid foundation, a Redeemer and Savior, whose task it was to point the people to the One whom God would anoint to this office. All were now dead and buried and were awaiting the resurrection of the dead. Good men as they were, and strong as they might have been, if this is all that Christ were, a strong and lasting church could not be built.

But now Jesus turns again to the disciples and asks, "But whom say ye that I am?" to which Simon Peter answers, "Thou art the Christ, the Son of the living God." Here, now, was a foundation which no other man could lay — a living foundation which neither time nor tide could destroy, a mighty foundation begotten of the almighty God Himself, a foundation that was chosen by God from all eternity and anointed by Him to be the Rock upon which His church should rest and therefore endure. "Upon this rock I will build My church," said Jesus upon the response of Peter.

Rocklike Men

A building, however, consists of more than a foundation. Jesus was building the church, or as we also call it in the Apostles' Creed, "the communion of saints." This communion of saints, this family of God, in Jesus' day was woefully small. It had been decimated during previous centuries because of idolatry, wicked kings, and more recently because of teachers whom Jesus called hypocrites and whited sepulchers. The last prophet of God, John the Baptist, had succeeded in calling some to repentance, thereby preparing them to follow the Christ. For some three years Jesus Himself had been traveling the length and breadth of the land where lived God's people to whom the Savior was promised first. On the way He had called into His intimate company men who recognized His prophetic office. These now numbered twelve. Among them were at least four fishermen, one former publican, and others of similar background. Though none were distinguished for their education or culture, it was these ordinary men whom He was preparing to take up the ministry which He must soon interrupt in order to complete the work for which He had been sent as the Anointed of the Father. But would these men be effective ministers of His church? Would they stand up under the storms and conflicts that the prince of darkness would unleash against Christ and His church? Would they be rocklike men? Would they be solid stones in the church?

Built on the Rock

That would depend. It would depend on what they believed and the conviction they had regarding Jesus. It mattered not what others believed Him to be, whether a John the Baptist or an Elijah or a Jeremiah. What mattered was that they, His disciples, believed. Therefore He asks them the crucial question: "Whom say ye that I am?" placing emphasis upon the "ye." Peter as usual picks up the question, though it was directed to all the disciples, and answers: "Thou art the Christ, the Son of the living God."

Here was not simply opinion, but conviction; not simply the result of observation, but faith. There was no doubt or question in the mind of Peter, nor for that matter of any of the other disciples, as to who this was standing before him. Jesus was not just a prophet or even simply a great prophet or even the greatest of the prophets returned from the dead — a John the Baptist; but the Christ, the very Anointed of God whom all the other prophets proclaimed, yes, the very Son of the living God Himself. Here was solid conviction built upon a solid foundation. This is what changes men and gives them strength beyond their own.

Our American forefathers had conviction when they laid the foundations for our country. They were convinced "that all men are created equal; that they are endowed by their Creator with certain inalienable rights; that among these are life, liberty, and the pursuit of happiness." Their conviction gave strength to their arms and victory over a mighty empire.

God-given Conviction

Peter's conviction, as also that of the other disciples, was not, however, derived from education or from reason. When he had answered Jesus, the Lord said to him: "Blessed art thou, Simon Barjona, for flesh and blood hath not revealed it unto thee, but My Father, which is in heaven." He calls him Simon Barjona, the name given him by his parents. He is Simon, the fisherman's son, a man of coarse language and rough manners; the Simon of flesh and blood whom Jesus must call a Satan in the very next dialog; Simon, the boaster and coward who would flee from danger and who would deny his Lord. The kind of conviction the Lord would need with which to build His church could not come from flesh and blood. It must be a conviction given by the Father in heaven. And fortunate indeed is that man who sees beyond what flesh and blood can reveal; who sees beyond observation and reason, but is given the eyes of faith, eyes which are not cast down upon things of the earth, but are lifted up to heaven. These are the rocklike men with which His church is built; not a Simon Barjona, but a Peter, a rock, by which name Jesus now addresses him,

saying: "And I say also unto thee, Thou art Peter." "Even as you
said to Me that I am not an Elias or a Jeremiah, but the Christ,
the Son of the living God, so also do I say to you, you are not
a Simon Barjona, but Peter, the rock, made so not by flesh and
blood, but by My Father, which is in heaven." Peter, the rock,
because his faith rests upon the Rock, upon Christ as the Son
of the living God. "Upon this rock I will build My church." It is to
this that St. Paul later on points when he encourages the Ephesian
Christians to remain steadfast and says: "You are built on the
foundation of the apostles and prophets, Jesus Christ Himself being
the chief Cornerstone." (Eph. 2:20)

We Are Strong by Faith

It was this firm conviction, that Jesus of Nazareth was the
Christ, that is, the Messiah, the Son of the living God, which made
simple fishermen the mighty heralds of God; it was this which
drove a physically afflicted Paul to exhaust himself in a lifetime
of missionary journeys to proclaim the good news in Christ; it was
this which gave strength to the lowly monk of Wittenberg when
he lifted up his voice so that his Christ might be glorified.

We, the church which Christ built, so often underestimate the
strength that is ours. In a world that seems to be dedicated to
bigness in men or in money, we sometimes find ourselves wondering whether the church can withstand the power that is arrayed
against it. Let us remember that it is not numbers or wealth
which gives strength to the church, but the fact that it rests upon
a solid foundation: Christ the Son of the living God; and furthermore, that it is built with men of conviction — men who truly
believe with Peter and Paul and Luther that Jesus of Nazareth
is this Christ, the promised Messiah, the Son of the living God,
the only Savior of mankind, the Lord of heaven and earth. Let
this be the rock upon which we continue to build the church that
Christ has established, and let this be the conviction wherewith we
labor. Built on this rock, the church is truly invincible.

II

Its Victory

It is significant that Jesus elicited this confession when He
did, for in the very next words He reveals to His disciples the
shocking things that would be happening to Him. Not many weeks
hence the disciples would see the object of their faith and hope
taken captive as a common thief, questioned as an inveterate liar,
ridiculed as an utter fool, slapped and whipped as a worthless slave,
and crucified as a despicable criminal. They must then remember
that He is not just another prophet, but the Christ; not simply

another teacher whom the people have put to death, but the Son of the living God, who would arise again from the dead. With this faith they would endure the days of affliction that would come to the Lord, and, yes, as He warned, also to them. As long as they remembered their confession and held fast to their conviction that He is indeed the Christ, the true Messiah, these events would yet terminate in victory. It is this assurance that He now gives them when He says, "The gates of hell shall not prevail against it." Built upon this rock, the church will always be victorious.

The Church Afflicted

The prince of hell will try — he will try mightily to destroy the church which Christ has established, because he knows its victory will mean his own destruction. He wasted no time. No sooner did the Lord's Anointed arrive, than with the sword of Herod he sought to slay Him. He did not prevail. He tried again during the Lord's sojourn of 40 days in the wilderness, again in the Garden, and once again during the hours of agony on the cross. For a time he seemed to have prevailed, but on the third day his intended Victim arose again from the dead. When the Lord returned to glory, the prince of hell shifted his attack to the church. He afflicted the church of the Lord's Anointed with persecutions which began within weeks in Jerusalem and did not end until some 300 years later in Rome. He succeeded, however, only in making the blood of martyrs become the seed of the church. The experience of the church was the experience of Israel in Egypt, of whom it was said: "The more they were afflicted, the more they multiplied and grew." (Ex. 1:20)

The prince of hell now changed his tactics and instead of persecution used the corrupting influence which wealth and power and glory often bring. His intent was to make the church forget its mission, that is, the mission of proclaiming Jesus as the Christ, the Son of the living God and only Savior of mankind. When during this darkest period of the church's life Thomas Aquinas visited Rome, he was told, "The church in our day cannot say: 'Silver and gold have I none!'" To this Aquinas replied, "No, neither can it say, 'In the name of Jesus Christ of Nazareth, rise up and walk.'" Though the church of Christ suffered as it did in the days of Elijah, who thought he was the only one still faithful to God, there were still thousands who had not as yet bowed their knees to Baal. In Italy there was a Savonarola; in Bohemia a Huss; in England a Wycliffe; and in Germany a Luther. With such men of firm faith and loyal conviction in the Christ, the Son of the living God, the gates of hell could not prevail. Once again persecution of the faithful succeeded only in giving renewed strength and health to the church of Christ.

The Afflictions Continue

Do not think that the prince of hell ever becomes exhausted. He will afflict the church as long as the world shall stand. In over half the world today the intimidation and persecution of the church has become public policy; in the other half the worship of power and riches is being urged upon its people. Some there are who would give up the struggle and say the church cannot stand. To all who are becoming tired of the struggle, to all who are bewildered and discouraged in their afflictions, hear again the promise of our Lord: "The gates of hell shall not prevail." We say with St. Paul: "Who shall separate us from the love of Christ? Shall tribulation or distress or persecution or famine or nakedness or peril or sword? . . . Nay, in all these things we are more than conquerors through Him that loved us. For I am sure that neither death nor life, nor angels nor principalities, nor things present nor things to come, nor powers nor height nor depth, nor anything else in all creation will be able to separate us from the love of God in Christ Jesus, our Lord" (Rom. 8:35, 37; 37-39 RSV). In Him the church is invincible.

The Key to Heaven

All this, however, is simply defensive action. An army always on the defensive will never win the war. Christ gives to His spiritual army, the church, not only an impregnable fortress to keep hell out, but also a key with which to open heaven itself. "I will give unto thee the keys of the kingdom of heaven," He promises Peter. "Whatsoever thou shalt bind on earth shall be bound in heaven; and whatsoever thou shalt loose on earth shall be loosed in heaven." Again, it is not only to Peter that He gives this promise, but, as we read in the 18th chapter of Matthew, also to the other disciples, whose confession was the same as Peter's. They were His church, trained and commissioned to carry on His ministry. Therefore even as Jesus spoke to them the Word that forgives and opens heaven, so they, too, shall speak the Word that looses men from sin and opens heaven to them. What they speak by faith in Christ is spoken by Christ Himself, "for where two or three are gathered together in My name, there am I in the midst of them" (Matt. 18:20). And also, contrariwise, whatever judgment they speak in faith, that word of judgment also binds in heaven. This is indeed victory, for an army that can command the enemy to loose the bands that tie the friend, and bind the hands of the foe, shows itself thereby to be the victor. Yes, this is the church invincible, the church against which hell cannot prevail and for which the gates of heaven are opened.

The battle of Britain of which Winston Churchill spoke so eloquently has long since ended in victory for his people. The

church's final victory against the prince of darkness must await the
day of the Lord. Until then his afflictions continue and the war
goes on. Already many of our brethren are feeling this heavy hand
of affliction. To them it must seem as though the Lord were sleeping; as though He had hidden His face and forgotten them in their
affliction. Their cry goes up, "O Lord, how long?" "Our soul is
bowed down to the dust; arise for our help and redeem us"
(Introit). "Let the nations know that Thy name is Jehovah; Thou
alone art the Most High over all the earth" (Gradual). Our
Savior gives us our answer. The church of Jesus Christ is invincible! Its foundation is Christ; its strength is in faith; its victory is assured.

> Crowns and thrones may perish
> Kingdoms rise and wane,
> But the church of Jesus
> Constant will remain.
> Gates of hell can never
> 'Gainst that church prevail;
> We have Christ's own promise,
> And that cannot fail.

God's Point of View and Man's Point of View Are Contradictory

By A. O. WERFELMANN

(Quinquagesima)

From that time forth began Jesus to show unto His disciples how
that He must go unto Jerusalem and suffer many things of the elders
and chief priests and scribes and be killed and be raised again the third
day. Then Peter took Him and began to rebuke Him, saying, Be it far
from Thee, Lord; this shall not be unto Thee. But He turned and said
unto Peter, Get thee behind Me, Satan. Thou art an offense unto Me,
for thou savorest not the things that be of God but those that be of men.
Then said Jesus unto His disciples, If any man will come after Me, let
him deny himself and take up his cross and follow Me. For whosoever
will save his life shall lose it, and whosoever will lose his life for My
sake shall find it. For what is a man profited if he shall gain the whole
world and lose his own soul? Or what shall a man give in exchange
for his soul? For the Son of man shall come in the glory of His Father
with His angels, and then He shall reward every man according to his
works. — *Matthew 16:21-27*

When something different or unusual or unexpected is announced, it invariably is met with doubt, unbelief, or an "I know
better" attitude and reaction. Adventurers, explorers, inventors,
and enterprisers of one kind or another have always experienced
this. Think of men's reaction to the first crossing of the Atlantic
by ship, or the first time wireless communication was proposed,
or travel by aircraft was suggested, or travel to the moon was

declared possible. People listened in doubt and disbelief, and they listened only because of the novelty of the announcement. After they became accustomed to the practical feasibility and reality of these things, they increasingly took them for granted and either reacted with indifference or with a self-satisfied take-it-or-leave-it attitude.

Unfortunately, something similar is to be noted in man's reaction to the great announcements that God has made in the course of human history concerning His plan for man's redemption. Down through the ages these have invariably aroused doubt, unbelief, or an "I know better" attitude and reaction on man's part. They sounded incredible, or irrelevant, or simply contradictory from man's point of view. Even the immediate circle of our Lord's disciples was no exception. Though they had been exposed to an explanation of the meaning of those grand announcements which God had made to Adam and Eve in the Garden of Eden, and to Abram at Haran and Canaan, and to Isaiah and Zacharias in the temple in Jerusalem, and to Mary and Joseph in Nazareth, to the shepherds in the fields of Bethlehem, and to many others concerning His plan of redemption, they found it most difficult to accept God's point of view and to reconcile it with their own opinion of what had to be done so that the world of men might have eternal life. People in all ages have had the same difficulty of understanding God's plan of salvation through Christ and the impact which this plan must have on man's views concerning life. And no one is ever completely immune to this sort of thing, because the devil will to the end of time try to confuse and confound men on these vital issues.

That's why we need the Lenten season — a time each year when we can through special spiritual devotions and Bible study sharpen our spiritual insights and intensify our Christian convictions and refresh our personal feelings about the most important thing in the world and in our own personal life, which is our redemption through Christ and our commitment to Christ. Our text shows us how necessary this is because, from a practical standpoint, we know how often

God's Point of View and Man's Point of View Are Contradictory

I

On the Subject of Man's Salvation

When the words of our text were first spoken, Jesus and His disciples were on their last journey together before Jesus brought

God's plan of redemption to fulfillment by His suffering and death
and by His rising again on the third day. They were on their
way to celebrate a Passover Festival in Jerusalem that was unique
and that was the climax of all the other Passover Festivals that
had been observed very religiously by the Jews for 1,500 years.
As they walked along, Jesus and His disciples had different
thoughts on their minds. The disciples were doubtless thinking
about the superficial things of their immediate experiences in life.
They hoped to be "big shots" in Christ's kingdom and to enjoy
a reflected glory from their association with Him. Jesus obviously
had on His mind and heart the deep, basic, and eternally important
aspects of life and history.

To get them to give thought to "first things first," He referred
to a matter that He had increasingly told them they would have
to think seriously about — His own sacrificial suffering and death
for the sins of the world, by which their faith and hope in Him
would receive a solid foundation. What's more, a proper understanding of this great truth they must recognize as basic to their
whole life and work. With His divine wisdom He foresaw the
terrible treatment He would receive from His fellow Jews when
God laid upon Him the iniquity of the whole human race. He
foreknew the terrible role that Judas and Peter and all the rest
of the disciples would play in His Passion history — the anguish
and misery He would experience when Judas betrayed Him and
Peter denied Him and they all forsook Him and fled into the night.
He could envision the terrible crucifixion scene on the hill of
a skull, where He would experience a humiliation and pains of
body and soul that defied human description. He could understand that His lifeless body would be laid into Joseph's tomb
and that after three days He would rise triumphantly from death
and the grave. Yes, He knew the divine necessity of all these
things, because, after all, He was God and, furthermore, as a man
He knew and believed the Scriptures which had predicted in so
many prophecies the details of His life and work and death. As
a perfect human being His will was in complete harmony with
God's will in all things, and so He did not try to contradict what
God deemed absolutely necessary for man's salvation.

The disciples, on the other hand, could not reconcile their
hearts and minds to His predictions of things to come. Because
their viewpoint was distorted by emotion, sentiment, and human
reason, they insisted that they knew better than God in such matters as man's salvation, and this threw them off course when it
came to their thinking concerning life's purpose and life's values.
It wasn't long before Jesus proved to them what fools these mortals
are. Peter as usual vocalized the thinking of doubtless all the dis-

ciples when he said: "No, Lord, this shall not happen." By insisting upon their own human way of thinking about things, the disciples were unwittingly identifying themselves and their thoughts with those of the devil, who had always fought the wisdom of God because it spelled his own downfall. Ever since the Garden of Eden the devil had known the divine necessity of Christ's suffering and death, because God had predicted it in terms he could understand. But he had consistently tried to prevent it because he knew it involved at the same time his own destruction. He had tried to persuade Christ at the very beginning of His public ministry to attempt to become the Savior of the world in other ways than by suffering and dying, but he had miserably failed to dislodge the Lord from that course in His life which He knew to be absolutely necessary and mandatory if God was to be glorified and His purposes accomplished. When he could not divert Christ in His purpose to go through with God's plan for His life, he tried to confuse the whole matter in the minds of men, and he did not even hesitate to enlist Christ's own disciples to his way of thinking. Because Christ at once saw the fact that Peter was playing into the hands of Satan when he suggested that Christ should not go up to Jerusalem to suffer the many things that were necessary for man's salvation, He rebuked him in no uncertain terms. He then proceeded to explain that the disciples' mistaken ideas about salvation had also distorted their views when it came to the matter of understanding life's purpose.

II

On the Matter of Life's Purpose

It was, of course, a strange view which Jesus expressed concerning the purpose of men's lives when He suggested the paradoxical idea: "If any person wants to be My follower, he must deny himself and become a crossbearer. In fact, God's idea of saving one's life involves losing it for the sake of Christ." Here again was a viewpoint that immediately clashed with what the disciples had always been thinking about their life and discipleship. They were not looking for crossbearing and suffering and self-denial. They expected a life of ease and prestige and those things which cater to the "lust of the flesh and the lust of the eyes and the pride of life." They had as little taste for the life that Jesus was here suggesting as the apostle Paul had for it before his conversion. Until his experience with Christ on the road to Damascus, Paul had always thought of life in terms of saving his own hide at all costs, playing his cards right so that he could stand on the sidelines and reap glory by having other people rather than himself experience suffering and death. Man so often thinks that his life's purpose is accomplished by the superficial things of life rather than by something deep down inside himself. He thinks it consists of externals rather than of an internal relationship with Christ. He fails to see that a proper perspective in life must always begin with a proper evaluation of what Christ has done for him by His suffering, death, and resurrection. Yes, when people are confused on the matter of their salvation, they are also going to be necessarily confused on the matter of their life's purpose. Paul did not come to realize that for him "to live was Christ" until after he realized that Christ had delivered him from a body of sin and death that hung about his neck like a millstone and was dragging him down and drowning him in everlasting destruction and perdition.

God always sees willful man putting himself rather than God into the heart and center of his life. He sees man's self-will and self-love and self-sufficiency daring him to believe that he can reach his own self-chosen carnal goals in life by his own strength. Yes, when man does not recognize his own hopeless predicament apart from Christ to accomplish life's basic purpose, which is to glorify God and to live with Him forever, he tries by devious ways to settle for lesser goals in life. He persuades himself to think that getting money or fame or power or complete independence is a worthy goal in life. When man refuses to accept his role as a creature of God and as a son in the heavenly Father's family and as a disciple in the Savior's kingdom — when he sets himself up as the planner of his own destiny or as the determiner of his own way or as the savior of his own life — then he misses entirely the purpose for which God created him and redeemed him. My life has not been given me for that purpose. Through Christ I have a new relationship with God and a new chance to accomplish what God would fulfill through me. I am in the world for Christ and for God, and my aim must be to identify myself wholly and completely with the life I have with God through Christ. To do so, I must, if necessary, be willing to deny myself those creature benefits which pass away in order to lay hold of those spiritual treasures that are eternal. I must fall in love with Jesus as I am by nature in love with myself. I must realize that God sent His only Son into the world, so that I might have life, the truly abundant life, through Him. I must act upon the truth that Christ "died for all that they which live should not henceforth live for themselves but for Him which died for them and rose again." Yes, there cannot even be any hesitancy on my part to suffer and sacrifice for Christ and His cause once I agree with God on the purpose of my life. This presupposes, of course, that I have a proper understanding of life's values.

III
On the Question of Life's Values

Jesus says in our text that the person who builds his life on the abundance of the things which he possesses, who is materialistic rather than spiritual in his outlook on life, will simply strike a fool's bargain when all is said and done. "For what is a man profited if he shall gain the whole world, and lose his own soul? Or what shall a man give in exchange for his soul? For the Son of man shall come in the glory of His Father with His angels, and then He shall reward every man according to his works." The rich young ruler who came to Jesus with great possessions which he prized above everything else, or the rich farmer who kept building larger barns so that he could store his material possessions here on earth, or the prodigal son who wanted his material inheritance so that he could do as he pleased — these men all had a false sense of life's values. Their idea of life was distorted by their emphasis on material things at the expense of spiritual values in their life. They failed to remember that man's soul is what gives man real value in the eyes of God and in the eternal scheme of things, and ultimately it is the state of the soul that will determine man's eternal weal or woe. When men stand before the judgment throne of God, they will not be saved on the basis of their wealth or popularity or power or social position in this world, but they will be judged solely on the basis of their faith in Christ and the life of faith they lived in Christ. This is the only thing that finally counts — whether I have treasured what Christ has done for my salvation and have sought those heavenly treasures through a life of faith in Christ and service to Christ, whether I have lived my life on this earth with my eye on the goal of heaven and have evaluated everything in this life in terms of this goal.

The disciples of our Lord found it difficult to agree with God on the matter of their life's purpose and what was really important for them to get out of their life on this earth. They looked for a life of ease and prestige in this world as a result of their association with Christ, the Messiah. They needed to realize that there was no crown without a cross, no glory without a shame. They needed to learn that the Christian life calls for effort and suffering and self-sacrifice, that they would have to get an entirely different perspective of life than their own carnal minds suggested to them. They would actually have to be willing to lose their physical life in order not to lose their spiritual and eternal well-being. Their life as followers of Christ would involve them in the disagreeable experience of crossbearing. But in this very kind of life they would discover experiences and values which would more than compen-

sate for any physical sacrifices they made. They would find that
the soul is more important than the body, that eternity is more
lasting than time, and that salvation in Christ is life's pearl of
great price for which they could gladly afford to sacrifice everything else. All of these things were brought to their attention as
they walked with Christ along that path that led ultimately to
His suffering and death.

These are also thoughts and truths that we all need to have
brought to our attention again and again, so that our spiritual
insights will always be clear and sharp, our Christian convictions
will always be intense, and our personal feelings about Christ
and salvation may be fresh and strong. That's why Christians
traditionally observe the six weeks of Lent with a greater than
usual spiritual emphasis. This coming Wednesday, known as Ash
Wednesday, the startling announcement of Jesus to His disciples
will be sounded throughout the Christian world: "Behold, we go
up to Jerusalem, and all things that are written concerning the
Son of man shall be accomplished." Yes, the most startling announcement ever made by God about man's redemption will be
sounded wherever men have ears to hear and hearts to believe
the message of redemption. But will men stop in their mad rush
and hear and listen? Some doubtless will, for during Lent the
church customarily enjoys her largest church attendance. But they
will listen with varying degrees of personal interest. Since some
church people have heard the same announcement many times in
their lives, at the beginning of many a Lenten season, they may
be inclined to hear something more novel, like "Behold, we go
up to the moon, and all things that have been predicted by nuclear
scientists and space experts shall be accomplished. There will be
green cheese aplenty to eat, and man will be involved in life's
greatest adventure." Nothing could be farther from the truth. We
can do nothing better during these weeks before Lent than to be
eyewitnesses and earwitnesses of those tremendous happenings in
Jerusalem 2,000 years ago, by which our eternal salvation was
secured and our purpose in life was revealed and the values of
life were determined. Let us permit nothing to interfere with
this spiritual opportunity to get a clearer understanding of God's
plan of redemption and a sharper insight into life's purpose and
values. Where but at the foot of the cross can we better understand
our salvation, our life's purpose, and the true values that abide
forever?

Love: When Duty Becomes Joy

By Richard P. Deffner

(Invocavit)

As the Father hath loved Me, so have I loved you; continue ye in My love. If ye keep My commandments, ye shall abide in My love, even as I have kept My Father's commandments and abide in His love. These things have I spoken unto you that My joy might remain in you and that your joy might be full. This is My commandment, that ye love one another as I have loved you. Greater love hath no man than this, that a man lay down his life for his friends. Ye are My friends if ye do whatsoever I command you. Henceforth I call you not servants, for the servant knoweth not what his lord doeth. But I have called you friends, for all things that I have heard of My Father I have made known unto you. Ye have not chosen Me, but I have chosen you and ordained you that ye should go and bring forth fruit and that your fruit should remain; that whatsoever ye shall ask of the Father in My Name, He may give it you. These things I command you, that ye love one another.

John 15:9-17

This text confronts us with a number of similar statements — commands — from the lips of the Lord: "continue ye in My love" (v. 9); "This is My commandment, That ye love one another as I have loved you" (v. 12); "These things I command you, that ye love one another" (v. 17). Five times the word "command" or "commandment" appears, and even in the first reading it becomes quite clear that the Master is laying on the hearts of His disciples a matter of deep concern which is basic to their mutual relationship.

It is particularly significant in the light of the setting of these words. We recognize this chapter in St. John's Gospel as being a part of the farewell discourses of our Lord. The time is Maundy Thursday. The place is the Upper Room, where Jesus has arranged a supper meeting with His intimate ones. The days immediately ahead would not allow the time or occasion for such instruction. The nature of the events to follow were such that a great deal of preparation was necessary and advisable.

Up to this time the disciples had been repeatedly told what was to come. The unusual mission of the Savior had been outlined in relation to the prophecies of His redemptive work. True, it had not been fully understood or accepted. The disciples had gone so far as to try to talk Him out of it. But it was not as if they hadn't been informed. And here was one more attempt to fit them for future hours.

On this First Sunday in Lent it should not be difficult for us to walk into the Upper Room and identify ourselves with the disciples, hearing Him who is about to launch the intense program of His Passion. Of course, it isn't exactly the same. We've been on this road before — in the sense that we have annually reviewed in detail the happenings of Holy Week. And yet what we bring to this place each year is not the same. We come with old sins and new sins, old failures and new failures, old resolves and new resolves. We come because we, too, need to be fitted for the hours and days ahead. We sit at the Master's feet and learn from Him what Lent is all about. For in so doing we learn what life is all about.

Here is the Christian life: "As the Father hath loved Me, so have I loved you; continue ye in My love" (v. 9). It begins and ends in love, and it starts with the Father's love. "As the Father hath loved Me." We know a lot about the Father's love for the world. It strikes us every time we recite the passage "For God so loved the world that He gave . . ." (John 3:16). This same Father love was always evident in the life of our Savior. Jesus lived in His Father's love. His bearing was constantly expressive of His intimate relationship with His loving Father. Every revelation of the words He addressed to His Father are like a symphony based on the theme "God is Love." To know Jesus is to know the Father's love.

By this time we should also know a lot about Jesus' love for us. "So have I loved you" (v. 9). In fact, it is almost embarrassing that we should have to be reminded of His love for us. "Greater love hath no man than this, that a man lay down His life for his friends" (v. 13). We are surrounded by reminders — crosses, crucifixes — reminders of His love. Every aspect of the Passion of our Lord in this season touches on the love of our Savior for all sinners. No service omits this central fact of our redemption. We partake of the blessed Sacrament of the Altar — of the body "given for you" and of the blood "shed for you" (Luke 22:19, 20). There is His love right in front of you. But He still finds it necessary to remind us: "Greater love hath no man than this, that a man lay down his life for his friends." (V. 13)

Obviously we need it. Somehow even we forget the simple truth that God loves us. These words may help us bite our tongues when we are all prepared to say, "God has forgotten me," "He let me down." "Sometimes I wonder if even God understands me." Even if we don't say it, there are times when we think it. We literally question God's love.

What's wrong? Hasn't God done enough? What does He have to do to convince us? What more can He do than give Himself? As a matter of fact, He has done more. He continues to give His love in spite of the fact that we are so unlovable. "But God commendeth His love toward us in that, while we were yet sinners, Christ died for us" (Rom. 5:8). And while we are yet sinners, He continues His loving care and forgiveness to us. St. John introduced this scene of our text in the Upper Room: "Now before the feast of Passover, when Jesus knew that His hour was come that He should depart out of this world unto the Father, having loved His own which were in the world, He loved them unto the end." (Ch. 13:1)

It should therefore not be surprising that Christ tells His disciples of then and now to do the same: "This is My commandment, that ye love one another as I have loved you" (v. 12). You know, and I know, that we also need this reminder. Too often our love amounts to no more than it does in a tennis score. It sounds nice, but it stands for nothing.

Is it really necessary to illustrate our lack of love to one another? You can do it better than I. Think back to yesterday. You saw it there — in others. Perhaps by now you've forgotten, but you noticed it also in yourself. I am speaking not only of hatred but also, and especially, of the lack of love — indifference, unconcern. No wonder our Lord and His apostle John had so much to say about love.

Surely this should be and is the identifying mark of Christians. And we do well to ask ourselves: Is our Christianity known to others by our love? Do we have such a reputation for loving one another that others may learn the love of God through us? What is the honest measure of our love?

Without a doubt our love has been weighed and found wanting. This is evident when we consider the love Christ is talking about — not just any kind of love but "as I have loved you" (v. 12). He commands that our love, like His, be a life-giving love — a love which reveals by its very nature that it comes from God. Yet, too often, what love we do show is quite foreign to His.

What do we do about it? Shrug our shoulders and say this is the best we can do? Beg off with the remark that we're satisfied, thank you, and God should be too? Are we satisfied? We can't fool ourselves. Especially on those rare occasions when we take an honest look at ourselves and examine ourselves under the exposure of God's Law, we look dangerously like the unmerciful servant in our Lord's parable. And we know, as surely as we know anything, that our love — if it is to be love at all — is to have the same quality as that of our merciful Lord.

And here we have the secret of such a life: "As the Father hath loved Me, so have I loved you; continue ye in My love" (v. 9). He doesn't ask or expect us to manufacture within ourselves a love that looks like His. Rather He provides the conditions, the atmosphere, under which our love can really work: "Continue ye in My love" (v. 9). Continue in the enjoyment and possession of My love. The absence of love in our own lives betrays what empty

hands we have. But He fills them with His love. We are first
of all recipients; we can do nothing but receive. And God is the
Giver — the Giver of life, the Giver of forgiveness, the Giver of
salvation — and this is the way He gives us His love.

Through Word and Sacrament we receive His love. He lives
in us, and we in Him, so that we literally become inhabitants of His
love. This is the kind of relationship which we can and should
enjoy as God's very own. But it is also a mutual relationship. Continuing in God's love, receiving His love, means participating in it.
"If ye keep My commandments, ye shall abide in My love, even
as I have kept My Father's commandments and abide in His
love." (V. 10)

We hear the words, "This is My commandment," and we shudder. Something else to do. Another demand on my time. Another
burden to pile on top of this life already complex. Well, that isn't
exactly what Christ had in mind. His is the kind of giving that
brings — not fatigue — but joy, even when He gives a commandment. He explains: "These things have I spoken unto you that
My joy might remain in you and that your joy might be full."
(V. 11)

We are not usually inclined to associate duty with joy. Perhaps
this is one of the reasons we know as little about joy as we do.
Christ knew from personal experience the importance of His words:
"This is My commandment, that ye love one another as I have
loved you" (v. 12). The Author of the new commandment lays
down this precept for the purpose of joy, not to make us cringe.
He was not speaking with tongue in cheek, for this was He "who
for the joy that was set before Him endured the cross, despising
the shame. . . ." (Heb. 12: 2)

This joy began at Christmas with the announcement of the
angel: "Behold, I bring you good tidings of great joy . . ." (Luke
2: 10). And this same joy continued after His ascension, when the
disciples "returned to Jerusalem with great joy" (Luke 24: 52).
Always it was associated with purpose. Christ approached His
life's work with joy, and continually out of its fulfillment there
came joy.

And you and I have every reason to approach our life's work
with joy. For the joy that is set before us we have the high and
holy privilege of walking in His commandments, especially the command to love one another, even when it is not the easiest or most
convenient thing to do. For He has demonstrated this almost incredible truth that there is joy in the duty to love.

He not only demonstrated it during His days in the flesh centuries ago but also continues to make it known in the lives of men

and women and boys and girls today. The joy of duty for you and me is the warm association which our Lord chooses to call friendship. "Ye are My friends if ye do whatsoever I command you" (v. 14). This is why He can say that His command is a reason for and an instrument of joy. It is the duty not of a servant but of a friend. "Henceforth I call you not servants, for the servant knoweth not what his lord doeth. But I have called you friends, for all things that I have heard of My Father I have made known unto you." (V. 15)

Friends have no secrets from one another. If we were to ask for the definition of a friend, one answer would undoubtedly be: "Someone you can trust." And so we chant in the tract for Invocavit: "I will say of the Lord, He is my Refuge and my Fortress, my God; in Him will I trust. He shall cover thee with His feathers, and under His wings shalt thou trust." (Ps. 91: 2, 4)

Into this wonderful, loving, trusting relationship He calls us. He makes us His friends, not of our own choosing, but His. "Ye have not chosen Me, but I have chosen you and ordained you that ye should go and bring forth fruit and that your fruit should remain . . ." (v. 16). And we, His friends, who are called for the purpose of love, are granted the additional promise of friendship: ". . . that whatsoever ye shall ask of the Father in My name, He may give it you" (v. 16). This same promise we voiced in the antiphon of today's Introit: "He shall call upon Me, and I will answer Him. I will deliver him and honor him. With long life will I satisfy him and show him My salvation." (Ps. 91: 15, 16)

Christ's command is not a burden of life but a way of life. Paul introduces his famous chapter on love (1 Cor. 13), like this: "And yet show I unto you a more excellent way" (1 Cor. 12: 31). Our Christ, in word and deed, showed us that "more excellent way" of love. And now He invites us to call God Father and to know Him as Friend. Living in His love, our love can be what He really intended it to be: our duty and our joy.

The Attitude of the World Toward Christians

By R. WIEDERAENDERS

(Reminiscere)

If the world hate you, ye know that it hated Me before it hated you. If ye were of the world, the world would love his own. But because ye are not of the world, but I have chosen you out of the world, therefore the world hateth you. Remember the word that I said unto you, The servant is not greater than his lord. If they have persecuted Me, they will also persecute you; if they have kept My saying, they will keep yours also. But all these things will they do unto you for My name's sake, because they know not Him that sent Me. If I had not come and spoken unto them, they had not had sin; but now they have no cloak for their sin. He that hateth Me hateth My Father also. If I had not done among them the works which none other man did, they had not had sin; but now have they both seen and hated both Me and My Father. But this is come to pass that the word might be fulfilled that is written in their Law, They hated Me without a cause. — *John 15:18-25*

In the early verses of John 15 we read a winsome discourse of our Savior on the subject of love. The Lord Jesus says unto His disciples, "As the Father hath loved Me, so have I loved you." Then He develops this thought by adding, "This is My commandment, that ye love one another, as I have loved you."

After this beautiful discourse on love, we are a bit jarred when we read in the closing verses of the chapter that though we bask in our Savior's love, though our great aim in life should be to reflect our Savior's love for us by loving one another, we shall be hated. Immediately a number of questions come to mind: Who will hate us? Why will we be hated? What is our defense against this hatred?

These are questions which the Savior answers for our instruction and comfort as He speaks to us about

The Attitude of the World Toward Christians

In the Word which lies before us for study He explains this attitude of the world toward Christians by emphasizing three thoughts:

I

The World Hates Christians

The Lord Jesus "pulls no punches" when He speaks about the world's attitude toward Christians. In verse 19 He puts it bluntly: "Therefore the world hateth you." Originally the Lord adressed these words to His disciples of that distant day, but these words apply to us in our day with equal force.

"The world hateth you," says Jesus to you and to me. Before we consider the dimensions of this hate, let us learn what the Lord means by "the world." Does He mean the world of nature, the world of field and forest, of river and lake, of seed time and harvest? That world is not meant. That world is beautiful, and under the benediction of a gracious God pours out its bountiful blessings upon us season after season. When the Lord says, "The world hateth you," He is speaking about people — not Christian people, but wicked people who refuse to humble themselves in the presence of God, self-righteous people who in their pride imagine themselves to be as good and as great as God, proud people who resent it with fury when the mask of their hypocrisy is ripped from their faces and they are compelled to take a good look at the ugliness of their sin. This is the world Jesus had in mind when He said to His disciples, "The world hateth you."

We are cautious, reluctant to jump to conclusions; therefore we ask: How does this saying of Jesus square with history? Is it true that the world hated the disciples of Jesus? The answer is written with bold letters on practically every page of the Book of Acts, which tells the story of the early Christians at work in the world of their day.

On the day of Pentecost, as the children of the world heard the disciples tell "the wonderful works of God" in many different languages, they showed their hatred toward the disciples by mocking them and saying, "These men are full of new wine" (Acts 2:13). When Peter and John refused to remain silent but boldly witnessed to the resurrection of Jesus Christ, the children of the world were indignant, laid hands on them, and cast them into prison (Acts 5:17, 18). When Stephen rebuked the children of this world for resisting the Holy Ghost, they "gnashed on him with their teeth . . . cast him out of the city, and stoned him" (Acts 7:54, 58). When Paul commanded an unclean spirit "in the name of Jesus Christ" to come out of a damsel in the city of Philippi, the children of the world took Paul and his companion Silas, "rent off their clothes . . . laid many stripes upon them . . . thrust them into the inner prison, and made their feet fast in the stocks" (Acts 16:22-24). In Athens the hate of the children of the world did not express itself through physical violence, but it expressed itself nonetheless. As the apostle Paul preached his classic sermon on Mars' hill, his hearers remained attentive until he spoke about the resurrection of the dead, but then they mocked him. (Acts 17)

To these examples of hatred many others recorded in the New Testament could be added. And what the disciples of Jesus experienced at the hands of the world all Christians experienced down through the ages. For a moment we think of the bloody persecutions suffered by the Christians during the early centuries, when they were cast to wild beasts in the Roman arena, when they were crucified, when they were painted with pitch and set afire to become living torches for the amusement of the children of the world. Yes, the words which Jesus addressed to His disciples, "The world hateth you," square with history over and over again.

But all of that is past, one or the other may argue. Let us therefore look about and see what is happening in the world today.

Over half of the world has yielded to the iron fist of atheistic communism. Look at what has happened and what continues to

happen to the Christians living in lands given to this curse. The
hatred of the communistic world against Christianity is always red-
hot and razor-sharp. Except for a remnant, Christianity has disappeared under the crushing heel of sickle-and-hammer hatred.
Communism has no love for Christianity. It has nothing but scald-
ing-hot hatred. How true the words of Jesus, "The world hateth
you."

And let us not imagine that only the communistic world hates
the Christian religion. This hatred is found everywhere in our
day. In our universities learned men of the world show great
love for fantastic theories which glorify the so-called inherent
goodness and greatness of man together with his progressive
achievements. However, the same learned men of the world ridicule
the Bible teaching that all men are sinners, that all men need
a Savior, that Jesus Christ, true God and true man, is the Savior
all men need. These proud teachers of the world find little
difficulty believing that the universe in which we live is millions,
even billions, of years old, but they smile in ridicule and derision
at the Bible truth that in the beginning God created the heavens
and the earth in six days of morning and evening. These are just
a few examples setting forth how the world shows its hatred toward
Christianity today. These examples could be multiplied many
times.

Thus, with fire and sword, with contempt and derision, the
world continues to give expression to its hatred against the followers of Jesus Christ.

II

The World Hates Christians Because It Hates Christ

This raises the question, Why? Why does the world hate the
Christians? Jesus answers, "If the world hate you, ye know that
it hated Me before it hated you. If ye were of the world, the world
would love his own. But because ye are not of the world, but
I have chosen you out of the world, therefore the world hateth
you" (vv. 18, 19). Accordingly, the world hates Christians because
the world hates Christ.

How bitter and intense was the hatred of the world against
Christ during His sojourn here on earth. When He was a tiny
Baby, Herod sought to kill Him. Throughout the years of His
ministry His enemies of the world rejected Him, mocked Him,
ridiculed Him, said that He had a devil, said that He was Beelzebub,
the chief of the devils. Time and again the children of the world
sought to put Him to death. Finally they succeeded to bind Him
and lead Him away captive. In a mock trial they declared Him
guilty of death. They gave vent to their hatred by spitting on Him.

They scourged Him, crowned Him with thorns, led Him to Calvary where they nailed Him to an accursed cross. Even while He was suffering and dying, nailed to the cross as their Savior for their redemption, they poured out the venom of their hatred against Him by saying, "He saved others, Himself He cannot save. He trusted in God; let Him deliver Him now, if He will have Him." (Matt. 27:42)

This hatred of the world against Jesus becomes all the more terrible to behold when we remember that the world had no cause to hate Him. Throughout His life Jesus did nothing but good. He never raised His hands to hurt but only to help and to heal. He never moved His lips to curse but only to speak words of peace and life. To the multitudes which came to Him He said:

Give Me your rags, and I shall give you My riches,
Give Me your ugliness, and I shall give you My holiness,
Give Me your nakedness, and I shall give you My robe of
righteousness,
Give Me your poverty, and I shall give you My wealth,
Give Me your weakness, and I shall give you My strength,
Give Me your death, and I shall give you My life.
Christian Giving: An Act of Worship, by M. L. Koehneke

May we ever remember with faith and joy that this is the Savior's message to the world today. And yet the world keeps right on hating Jesus. The world prefers its darkness to the light Jesus offers. The world would rather continue to live in its sin than to humble itself and accept the salvation which Christ accomplished through His life and death.

And because the world hates Christ, the world hates Christians. Jesus says, "If they [the children of the world] have persecuted Me, they will also persecute you but all these things will they do unto you for My name's sake." (Vv. 20, 21)

Christians do not deserve to be hated and persecuted by the world. True, Christians daily commit sin. Their lives are far from perfect. However, out of gratitude to their Savior, who daily forgives their sins, they earnestly seek to live lives which reflect the love of their Savior, lives laden with beautiful fruits of righteousness. It is largely because of Christian influence and financial support that we have hospitals dedicated to the healing of the sick, that we have homes for the aged, that orphans are not abandoned. Trace any movement motivated by mercy and compassion, and you will find that it flows from the mercy and compassion of Christ reflected in the lives of Christians.

Why, then, does the world hate the Christians? Jesus answers, "If ye were of the world, the world would love his own. But because ye are not of the world, but I have chosen you out of the world, therefore the world hateth you" (v. 19). The world hates Christians because Christians refuse to walk the wicked ways of the world. Thus the lives of Christians are a rebuke to the sinfulness of the world. This rebuke stings the world and is therefore resented with caustic bitterness. This is a reason why the world seizes every opportunity to express its hatred against Christians.

III
In the Midst of This Hatred There Is Comfort for Christians

It was to prepare and to fortify the disicples of old and the Christians of today against this hatred of the world that Christ spoke the words we here study. Therefore let us learn from these words not only the reason why the world hates us but let us also learn where to find comfort and strength courageously to bear the hatred of the world without rebellion or bitterness. How good and comforting it is for Jesus to bid us remember His saying, "The servant is not greater than his lord. If they have persecuted Me, they will also persecute you." (V. 20)

When the hatred of the world hurts us and through such hurt we are tempted to forsake Christ, our Savior, let us remember that the world first hated Christ. Therefore Christ understands our hurt. He knows exactly how we feel. Not only that, but in His Word He has given us many promises to comfort and to strengthen us. When we feel helpless in the face of the world's hatred, He says, "Be still, and know that I am God." I am your "Refuge and Strength, a very present Help in trouble" (Ps. 46). When we feel downcast and discouraged because of the world's hatred, He bids us cast all our care on Him and He promises to care for us (1 Peter 5:7). When we are heartsick because of the hatred of the world, Jesus whispers near, "Let not your heart be troubled; ye believe in God, believe also in Me. In My Father's house are many mansions. . . . I go to prepare a place for you. . . . I will come again and receive you unto Myself that where I am, there ye may be also" (John 14:1-3). With these assurances of Jesus to give us comfort and strength we are able to bear the hatred of the world with a smile of confidence and a heart filled with hope.

Furthermore, in Jesus our Master we His servants learn how to overcome the hatred of the world. Jesus did not permit the hatred of the world to fill Him with bitterness or to turn Him aside from doing the will of His Father or to hinder Him from accomplishing His great mission on earth, namely, the redemption of sinful mankind. Similarly, remembering that "the servant is not greater than his lord" (v. 20), let us not permit the hatred of the world to dampen the joy of our salvation or to hinder us henceforth to live for Christ or to dull our earnest desire to destroy the hatred of the world by winning the world for Christ and His kingdom.

As we take leave from the words of our Savior, written for our instruction, let us remember these thoughts: The world hates Christians because it hates Christ. However, this hatred of the world should not discourage us from boldly confessing and living our faith in Christ. Rather this hatred of the world should convince us of how desperately the world needs to repent of its wickedness and to look to the Lord Jesus Christ for pardon. Thus this hatred of the world will stir our hearts to greater zeal in the work of missions, to the preaching and teaching of the Gospel of Christ, which is not only the power of God unto salvation but in addition the only power powerful enough to change the hatred of the world into love for Christ and His cause.

Pride and Envy Do Not Agree with Genuine Christianity

By OTTOMAR KRUEGER

(Oculi)

And James and John, the sons of Zebedee, come unto Him, saying, Master, we would that Thou shouldest do for us whatsoever we shall desire. And He said unto them, What would ye that I should do for you? They said unto Him, Grant unto us that we may sit, one on Thy right hand and the other on Thy left hand, in Thy glory. But Jesus said unto them, Ye know not what ye ask. Can ye drink of the cup that I drink of and be baptized with the baptism that I am baptized with? And they said unto Him, We can. And Jesus said unto them, Ye shall indeed drink of the cup that I drink of, and with the baptism that I am baptized withal shall ye be baptized. But to sit on My right hand and on My left hand is not Mine to give, but it shall be given to them for whom it is prepared. And when the ten heard it, they began to be much displeased with James and John. But Jesus called them to Him and saith unto them, Ye know that they which are accounted to rule over the Gentiles exercise lordship over them, and their great ones exercise authority upon them. But so shall it not be among you; but whosoever will be great among you shall be your minister. And whosoever of you will be the chiefest shall be servant of all. For even the Son of man came not to be ministered unto but to minister and to give His life a ransom for many. — Mark 10:35-45

The 20th century has been and is the century of superlatives. People have grown accustomed to such words as *greatest, strongest, mightiest, wealthiest, grandest,* and similar words. These are constantly being dinned in our ears and printed in our daily newspapers and other journals, and the small children on the street use terms of which they have no conception at all. Hollywood thrills with its announcements of new pictures which are stupendous, phenomenal, epoch-making, etc. Countries are vying with one another to be considered the strongest and greatest among the nations, and each is constantly striving to get ahead of the other.

One question seems to bother many people today, as it did in the day of our Lord Jesus, and that is: "Who is the greatest in the kingdom of heaven?" We recall the incident recorded in Matt. 18. The disciples came to the Savior with this very question, and Jesus set them back on their heels by calling a small child to Himself and telling them that unless they would become as this little child, they would not enter into the kingdom of heaven. This indicated that they needed a spiritual change of heart. They needed conversion and to have the spirit of the little ones — meekness and humility.

What causes people to be so concerned about the places of honor in the Lord's kingdom? It ought to be sufficient for us to know that we, through the grace of God and by the love of our Savior and Redeemer, have entered the holy Christian church. The question of the relative importance of people, of being greatest or having particular honors in the church on earth and in heaven, stems from pride and envy in the heart. It calls for conversion and repentance, as the Lord Jesus stated.

This morning we shall make our theme:

Pride and Envy Do Not Agree with Genuine Christianity

I

The Disciples Were Prone to Such Evils and So Are We Today

The Reason for Christ's Words

James and John, two of the Lord's disciples, were intimate friends of our Savior. They loved Him, and He loved them. Jesus likewise loved their mother, Salome, and their father, Zebedee. The fact is that John calls himself the disciple whom Jesus loved, which indicates that he was very close to the Lord. The mother is referred to in Matt. 20 in this connection. These brothers came to the Savior with a petition that He might do for them what they desired in their hearts. The Lord agreed. So they said: "Grant unto us that we may sit, one on Thy right hand and the other on Thy left hand, in Thy kingdom." Matthew refers to the fact that the mother joined with them in this petition. The fond mother, proud of her sons, seconded this strange desire. Certainly this was a very foolish notion and indicated a certain amount of pride in their hearts and in the heart of the mother.

Application to Us

This section of our text must call us to halt a moment and reflect upon some of the senseless, inept prayers that we have spoken and which the Lord did not answer according to our liking. In fact, the Lord ignored these petitions entirely, knowing that they were foolish or even harmful thoughts.

Effect on Other Disciples

We are interested to note the reaction of the rest of the Twelve to this request of James and John. They evidently heard what their fellow disciples and the mother, Salome, had asked. This disturbed them greatly. They were irritated. Immediately they became envious and jealous of these two who thought that they should receive preferential treatment. The words used in the original indicate that they were filled with anger toward them. This all seems to us a natural reaction, one to be expected.

Illustration

This reminds us of another incident that occurred, according to John 21, when Jesus met with seven disciples after His resurrection. You remember how He spoke with Peter, instructed him concerning his duties in the future, and indicated to him that he would die a martyr's death. Then Peter, noticing John, asked Christ what would happen to him, and Jesus answered rather brusquely: "What is this to thee? Follow thou Me. This is none of your business. Just serve Me, and do not be jealous of John or anyone else."

Nature of Envy

Envy, jealousy, and pride are not Christian emotions but emotions contrary to genuine Christianity. They are affections of our sinful flesh and blood. They are the work of Satan, who takes special delight in seeing them fostered within us. Implanted also in our sinful flesh and blood, they are inclined to flare up occasionally. Yes, they crop up constantly in this 20th century, even as they did in the first century of the Christian church. (1 Cor. 13:4; 1 John 2:16; Prov. 16:18; Prov. 28:25; Luke 18:11)

In the Family

They exhibit themselves frequently in the family circle, probably in a child who feels itself repulsed or neglected. He becomes peevish, dissatisfied with everyone and everything. The other members of the family, even the parents, cannot seem to do anything to satisfy him. He enjoys being demanding, insolent; he wants to tyrannize others and have them dance to his whistling. In his heart there is probably envy of some other child in the family, a feeling of inferiority and insecurity.

In the Congregation

This same jealousy and envy can also be found occasionally in a Christian congregation and can become a very disrupting and disturbing factor. Sometimes such jealousy causes the onlookers to wonder whether there is any real Christianity in the congregation at all. St. Paul found some of this spirit in the congregation at Corinth. There were factions jealous of one another, trying to lord it over one another. If there was trouble among 12 disciples, each thinking of who the greatest might be and hoping that the Lord would mention his name, certainly such feelings will arise more easily in a large group.

Who is the greatest in the kingdom of heaven? No doubt, we shall be surprised on Judgment Day to find some unknown, quiet Christian person receiving the honor rather than many who on earth thought that they must certainly be scheduled to receive the prime honors.

II
How Jesus Lovingly Set Them Straight, and Us Too

The Solution

How did the Lord Jesus resolve the problem of James and John? Neither did he give them a direct answer nor did He mention any names, but He set certain conditions for them to fulfill. Jesus did not say, "James, you will be the first of the Twelve to die a martyr's death; therefore you are the greatest." Nor did He say, "John, you are such a lovable character; you will live to a ripe old age and be beloved by your disciples. Hence you are the greatest in My kingdom." But He asked them a question. Would they be able to drink the cup He would have to drink and would they be willing to be baptized with the baptism He would be baptized with? This was, of course, a reference to the cup of sorrows of which He later complained in the garden, and it referred to the baptism of death which He was to experience shortly. They assured Him that they could. Then Jesus declared that they assuredly would have to drink of that cup of suffering. However, sitting at the right hand of God in the Kingdom would be something for the Father to decide.

Jesus Converts the Ten

Then Jesus spoke to the 10 disciples who had become envious and angry at James and John and sets them straight in His Christlike manner. Jesus called them aside as a father would call his child when he wished to correct the child, and spoke to them in all friendliness. He said: "You know that in the world the recognized rulers lord it over their subjects and their great men make them feel the weight of authority. That is not the way with you; among you, whoever wants to be great must be your servant, and whoever wants to be first must be willing to be the slave of all." (Quoted from the New English Bible.) He points out that in His kingdom there prevails an entirely different philosophy — service to our fellowmen and especially to our fellow church members. True greatness in Christ's eyes is not wielding the big stick and exercising authority but serving one another in great lowliness and humility. That is Christian, whereas selfishness, envy and jealousy, is the very opposite; it is heathenish.

Application

This must have caused the disciples to take stock of themselves and their attitude of heart. They were probably very much disappointed and ashamed of themselves for having had such ambitious thoughts. They were put in their place very definitely, but with all love and concern for their own welfare and for their salvation.

The Climax of His Answer

Now comes what might in modern language be called the punchline. The Lord Jesus calls attention to His shining example in words that are golden and treasured by all His children. "For even the Son of man came not to be ministered unto but to minister and to give His life a ransom for many." This is the important thing in our lives as it was in the lives of the Twelve, and He impresses this upon them and us. Look at our Savior. What was His highest ambition, what was His purpose in life, what mattered to Him? It was to do the will of His heavenly Father, to serve mankind for the redemption and salvation of men, and to give Himself — not to carry away honors among men.

Conclusion

To minister means to serve. Think of how the Son of man, the Son of God, served. He came to this sinful earth and lived among sinful men, to whom He daily brought the Word of life, the Gospel. Think how He went about preaching and teaching individuals and multitudes. He must have been rather exhausted at times, but He was always ready to break the bread of life to anyone who needed it, or be helpful with His miracles upon the suffering. Think how helpful and sympathetic He was toward suffering mankind, how the humblest call for help caused Him to turn in love and readiness to heal and help. Think what menial services He rendered, even washing the disciples' feet.

The noblest, greatest service, however, that the Son of man rendered was that of His holy Passion and death for sinful man-

kind, for you and me. His noblest service was paying the price
of our redemption, which St. Paul describes in Phil. 2. "He humbled Himself and became obedient unto death, even the death on
the cross." He became the most miserable and lowly of us all
in order that we might have eternal glory and happiness. Jesus
said that He gave His soul a ransom for many, and this "many,"
as we see from the Bible, means all. "He died for all," we read,
and again, "God was in Christ reconciling the world unto Himself,
not imputing their trespasses unto them, and hath committed unto
us the Word of reconciliation." If an ancient king of Austria
could take as his motto the words "I serve," how much more
fittingly could this be applied to our Savior. Who could serve
as Jesus served, of whom it is written, "The zeal of Thine house
hath eaten Me up"? Then and now His illustrious example should
therefore teach His disciples lowliness and humility and a devout
willingness to serve Him in responsive love. Thanks be to God
for our Savior, who served us to the point of dying for us.

Should you and I, then, ever complain about someone else's
position or honor in the Kingdom? Should you and I ever be
jealous of each other? Should you and I ever wonder who will
be greatest in the Kingdom? Should you and I ever become
peevish because we think someone else is being honored and we
being slighted? No, rather let us thank God for His abounding
mercy and grace that found us when we sought Him not, and
in His dear Son chose us to be His own from eternity.

The question is not, "Who is the greatest in the kingdom?"
but "Are we in it?"

The Glory of the Cross

By WALTER J. BARTLING

(Laetare)

These words spake Jesus and lifted up His eyes to heaven and said:
Father, the hour is come; glorify Thy Son that Thy Son also may glorify
Thee, As Thou hast given Him power over all flesh, that He should give
eternal life to as many as Thou hast given Him. And this is life eternal,
that they might know Thee, the only true God, and Jesus Christ, whom
Thou hast sent. I have glorified Thee on the earth; I have finished the
work which Thou gavest Me to do. And now, O Father, glorify Thou
Me with Thine own self with the glory which I had with Thee before
the world was. I have manifested Thy name unto the men which Thou
gavest Me out of the world. Thine they were, and Thou gavest them
Me, and they have kept Thy Word. Now they have known that all things
whatsoever Thou hast given Me are of Thee. For I have given unto them
the words which Thou gavest Me, and they have received them and
have known surely that I came out from Thee, and they have believed
that Thou didst send Me. I pray for them. I pray not for the world but
for them which Thou hast given Me, for they are Thine. And all Mine
are Thine, and Thine are Mine, and I am glorified in them. And now

I am no more in the world, but these are in the world, and I come to Thee. Holy Father, keep through Thine own name those whom Thou hast given Me, that they may be one, as We are. While I was with them in the world, I kept them in Thy name; those that Thou gavest Me I have kept, and none of them is lost but the son of perdition, that the Scripture might be fulfilled. And now come I to Thee, and these things I speak in the world, that they might have My joy fulfilled in themselves. I have given them Thy Word, and the world hath hated them because they are not of the world, even as I am not of the world. I pray not that Thou shouldest take them out of the world, but that Thou shouldest keep them from evil. They are not of the world, even as I am not of the world.

John 17:1-16

The text we have dared to choose for our sermon this morning has been called the "most sacred passage even in the four Gospels" (William Temple). Philip Melanchthon's last lecture shortly before his death was based on this prayer, this prayer which is in a special sense the *Lord's* prayer, this prayer which only He can pray. "There is no voice," said Melanchthon, "which has ever been heard, either in heaven or in earth, more exalted, more holy, more fruitful, more sublime, than this prayer offered up by the Son of God Himself." This voice was heard both in heaven and right here on our earth. It was heard, and it was remembered by those who heard our Lord pray in the Upper Room on that night when He was betrayed. It was heard, and it was recorded for our good.

A mistaken reverence might suggest the choice of a text more suited to the abyss of our ignorance and the shallows of our spiritual understanding. True reverence suggests that, admitting both ignorance and shallow spirituality, we frame a prayer of our own and approach the Holy of holies with the joy of an expectant faith:

Holy Father, glorify Thyself among us this day in answer to the prayer of Thy Son, Jesus Christ, our Lord. Amen.

As we read our text the concept of glory and glorification strikes us with repeated emphasis, and it is of this that we shall speak this morning. To this concept of glory, however, we shall relate a second word which does not occur a single time in our text. Our theme, you see, is:

The Glory of the Cross

There is in our text not a single word that ordinarily means "to die," or "to kill," or "to crucify." This is remarkable; surprise is heightened to wonder when we note that in all those long chapters of discourse which begin with the foot washing in chapter 13 and end with the prayer of our text, there is only one expression which would normally be understood as meaning "to die," "to kill," or "to crucify." Once Jesus speaks of "laying down"

His life, in a context which clearly suggests death. Otherwise He uses alternate expressions which mean "to go away," "to depart," "to leave the world," "to go to the Father," "to return to the Father." All these expressions can be equated with the word of our text, "to be glorified," and all of them alike are ambiguous. They may all be applied to the cross, and they may all, with equal validity, be applied to the ascension and glorification of our Lord. "The hour is come," Jesus says. The foot washing, the discourses, the prayer — everything that took place from the night in which He was betrayed until He was received up into glory — took place within the hour of fulfillment. In a real sense it is already the risen and ascended Christ who speaks. He has overcome the world. He has finished His work. But if we may speak of one moment within the hour of fulfillment as central, it is the moment which in the literal sense of historic progression immediately followed the prayer of our text. That central moment was the cross. If there is glory at all, it is not just that there is a glory after the cross, or a glory because of, or through the cross. Of all this, too, one may properly speak. Today, conscious that our terms appear to be contradictory, we witness to the glory *of* the cross.

I

The glory of the cross is the glory of Christ's completed task of redeeming the world. "I have glorified Thee on earth. I have finished the work which Thou gavest Me to do. And now, O Father, glorify Thou Me" (vv. 4, 5). Jesus is praying for the cross as the death which will fittingly illuminate His entire life.

The world has always marked with special honor the man who dies nobly for what he perceives to be a noble goal. There is a glory which can be won only in death. Achilles, the hero in Homer's telling of the Trojan war, is offered the choice between a long and safe life in his homeland, far from the scene of the Trojan combat, or a brief life of glory and the endless renown gained through a hero's death on the battlefield. Achilles chose to die fighting, and his name still shines in undimmed splendor in the memory of man. His is the glory which can be won only in death.

Is this the glory for which our Lord prays, the glory of a hero's death? The cross has, indeed, often been heralded as a deed of heroism, and such we may concede it was. The cross, we may say, was the glory of Jesus because He was never more majestic than in the hour of His death. But having said that, what have we said that would lend to the death of Jesus a greater, or even a different, value than attaches to the death of Achilles? Who could even honestly dispute that Achilles's death in the raging offensive of hand-to-hand combat was not more manifestly heroic, more grandly glorious than the death of a passive victim, immobilized on a cross? We must seek the essential glory of the cross in some other dimension.

Achilles was concerned about the one shining deed which would set him apart from the generations of mortals who pass away unheralded into the oblivion of death. Jesus' death is no isolated act. It is all of a piece with His whole life on earth. John himself best summarizes the motive power of Jesus' life in the verse which introduces the farewell discourses, which culminate in the prayer of our text. "Now before the feast of the Passover, when Jesus knew that His hour was come that He should depart out of this world unto the Father, having loved His own which were in the world, He loved them unto the end." The climactic hour has struck, the hour in which Jesus will illuminate His purpose of love in the decisive act of the cross. But the love there revealed was active from the first.

The love that was always perfect — perfect in the manger, in the home, in the carpenter shop, in the works of mercy, in the words of life — "now reaches its culmination in the absolute self-abnegation of love undimmed — nay, victoriously intensified — by agony and death. . . . It is not the cross as an isolated episode which is thus the focus of the eternal glory; it is the cross as the culmination of the life of love, as the achievement of the purpose of the incarnation, as the projection of divine light across the spaces of the world's darkness." (William Temple)

"I have finished My work." This is not, then, the sigh of a world-weary and disappointed pessimist who courts death as a relief from boredom or pain. This is the bold affirmation of the only Man who has ever been able to welcome death with the sense of life totally fulfilled. "We are none of us complete," an aging saint once confessed to me. No shining deed, no heroic death, can hide the frustrated purposes which lie before: the wasted energies, the misspent years, the impure motives, the sullied and imperfect ideals only imperfectly realized. "I have finished My work." Thank God that those words could be spoken of the work of redemption! *The glory of the cross is the glory of Christ's completed task of redeeming the world.*

II

Yet have we really passed beyond a superficial evaluation of the glory of the cross? We require a further dimension, the full divine dimension. Shall we add that dimension? *The glory of the cross, in the completed work of Christ, is the glory of God Himself in the revelation of His love.* All that we adore in Christ is the glory of the Father shining through Him. The glory of the cross is God Himself revealed.

This is the real burden of Christ's prayer, that the Father may now through the cross glorify Himself. It is not a self-chosen work that Christ has completed. "I have finished the work which Thou gavest Me to do." Jesus is willingly fulfilling a mission as one sent by God Himself. The prayer repeatedly suggests this and no less than five times says so explicitly: "I have come from Thee" (v. 8); "Thou hast sent Me into the world" (v. 18); again, "Thou hast sent Me" (v. 21); and again, "Thou hast sent Me" (v. 23); and yet again, "Thou hast sent Me" (v. 25). This is the climax of the prayer which our Lord prays in the climactic moment of His life. "The hour is come," the moment of fulfillment. "Glorify Thy Son, that Thy Son also may glorify Thee." Henceforth men shall judge the Sender by Him who has been sent, the commissioning Lord by the commissioned Servant, the King by His Messenger, the Father by the Son.

Glory is an imposing word, a heavy word. Indeed, the Hebrew word for glory means literally something which is heavy, weighty, and is therefore, in given relationships, imposing. What is there about God that imposes itself upon us? What has God revealed of Himself? In other words, what is His glory? Some of the answers to that question suggested by the Old Testament are not reassuring. There is, for example, the repeated illustration of the glory of God drawn from some of the more impressive phenomena of nature in storm and fury:

> Clouds and darkness are round about Him; righteousness and judgment are the habitation of His throne. A fire goeth before Him and burneth up His enemies round about. His lightnings enlightened the world; the earth saw and trembled. The hills melted like wax at the presence of the Lord, at the presence of the Lord of the whole earth. The heavens declare His righteousness, and all the people see His glory. (Ps. 97:2-6)

A very wise man once stated that if he were given one question to ask of the Sphinx he would ask, "Is the universe friendly?" Far more poignant is the cry that a passage such as I have just read should evoke: "Is God ultimately friendly?" It is not accidental that it was the face of God turned toward him in a physical storm that aroused the crisis in Luther's soul which sent him into the monastery in search of an answer to this very question: "Is God friendly?" God's glory, in at least some aspects, is thus the expression of His essential distance from us in His majesty and power.

But that is not all, even in the Old Testament. Especially illuminating is the account in which Moses, after witnessing the apostasy of Israel in the worship of the golden calf, begs to see the glory of God. Listen carefully as I read the remarkable passage:

> And he said, I beseech Thee, shew me Thy glory. And He said, I will make all My goodness pass before thee, and I will proclaim the name of the Lord before thee, and will be gracious to whom I will be gracious and will shew mercy on whom I will shew mercy. And He said, Thou canst not see My face, for there shall no man see Me and live. And the Lord said, Behold, there is a place by Me, and thou shalt stand upon a rock. And it shall come to pass, while My glory passeth by, that I will put thee in a cleft of the rock and will cover thee with My hand while I pass by. And I will take away Mine hand, and thou shalt see My back parts, but My face shall not be seen. (Ex. 33:18-23)

Wonderful is the way in which the glory of God is related to His goodness. Equally notable is the fact that the glory of God, in the very revelation of His goodness, is here still an expression of His essential distance. Even when God turns toward man in His goodness, man must turn aside his own glance or die. Man can endure to see only the back of the glorious God; God's face no man may see and live.

In Jesus God has turned His face toward us in such a way that we not only may look into His face but also are actually invited to look, and to look precisely that we may live. John never tires of this emphasis. It is announced as the major theme in the prologue to the Gospel: "And the Word was made flesh and dwelt among us, and we beheld His glory, the glory as of the Only-Begotten of the Father, full of grace and truth" (1:14).

Here is another verse from the prologue which is a direct but transforming echo of the Old Testament emphasis upon the hiddenness and distance of God: "No man hath seen God at any time; the only-begotten Son, which is in the bosom of the Father, He hath declared Him" (1:18) Perhaps the most striking statement of this theme is found in Paul: "God, who commanded the light to shine out of darkness, has shined in our hearts to give the light of the knowledge of the glory of God in the face of Jesus Christ" (2 Cor. 4:6). The glory of God can at last be seen full front — but only "in the face of Jesus Christ."

Now surely we have passed beyond superficiality into the heart of the Christian Gospel. Simply to state that God is Love, however, could still be trite and superficial. Love may be "a many-splendored thing"; it is also a thing of many meanings, not all splendid. Here from a recent book is an interesting collection of some of love's meanings:

> Love is, of course, by no means limited to love between the sexes. The same word designates the feeling of fathers and mothers for their sons and for their daughters, of sons and daughters for their fathers and mothers, of boys for their sisters, of girls for their brothers, grandparents for grandchildren, grandchildren for grandparents, nuns for Christ, some men for

God, few for their neighbors, 17-year-olds for 17-year-olds,
70-year-olds for 70-year-olds, men for their country, women
for the fatherland, both for Beethoven, girls for pink, boys for
the bow, girls for a beau, readers for some books, writers for
their work, and not quite everybody for himself. (Walter Kauf-
mann)

We may note that the love of God for man is not included in the
list. It is a fortunate omission. To affirm the love of God in
such a context would be to say something trite and superficial.
I can almost convince myself that it would be to say something
blasphemous. God is Love, but not just any kind of love, not
just one love in a series of possible loves. God is Love in the
revelation of Himself in Jesus Christ. That love, we must insist,
is simply incomparable.

Nevertheless, Jesus' prayer suggests one human comparison
in the address of "Father," repeated six times. But that we might
not contaminate our view of God as Father with sentimental
associations drawn from our imperfect human relationships, Jesus
once addresses God as "holy Father" and once as "righteous
Father." The cross, which proclaims the love of God, at the same
time and in the same act proclaims God's continued distance from
those who refuse to submit to the condemnation which the cross
itself pronounces upon all unholiness and unrighteousness. Yet
Father He would be. And Father He is to *you* when through
His grace you yield yourself completely to the forgiving love
which the cross alone reveals and promises.

The small child may know little about his father. His father's
profession, his pursuits throughout the long day, his many social
contacts, his life out there beyond the home — the child knows
nothing of all this. The child knows his father only at those few
places and in those few relationships in the busy day at which
their lives intersect. Yet who is to say that the child does not
know his father better than anyone else does? He knows that
his father loves him, and he has the unspoken, unreflective conviction that everything that his father does out there in the secret
and mysterious world away from home is somehow related to
that love. Everything that father does is for him. And what
father would call that child wrong?

Can you give yourself this assurance about God? Much about
God is still distant to our understanding and to our experience.
There are mysteries still in His governing of the world and in
His secret guidance of your life. But once He came close enough
to convince you that He is essentially a being of love. In the
cross His life has intersected yours at the point of your greatest
need. And what you have seen there is love.

That you might see that love and, in seeing it, recognize the true glory of God is the first and central petition of Jesus' prayer. "Father, glorify Thy Son, that Thy Son also may glorify Thee." "I have glorified Thee on earth." "I have manifested Thy name." And that is but another way of saying, "I have glorified Thee," for the name of God, like the glory of God, is God Himself in His self-revelation. "I have glorified Thee on earth." That is: "I have made Thee known as a God who is Love, in all My life of loving service and obedience. I would now make Thee known in the ultimate act of My self-giving. I would show men that Thy love for them in Me will stop at nothing. Never wilt Thou say, 'Thus far and no further.' Father, make Thyself gloriously known now in the glory of My cross."

Yes, *the glory of the cross, in the completed work of Christ, is the glory of God Himself in the revelation of His love.*

III

Our text contains another sermon on the glory of the cross, a sermon that wants very much to be preached. It is a long sermon with as many parts as there are worshipers in my congregation this morning. It is the sermon each of us must preach as we live our lives under the cross to the glory of God. Let me briefly sketch the outlines of that sermon as we add one final dimension to the glory of the cross: *the glory of the cross, in the revelation of God's love through the completed work of Christ, is the glory of men as they share in the divine life of glory.*

The family of the redeemed, as the object of Christ's redemptive work, is never far removed from the Savior's mind as He prays: "I have manifested Thy name to the men which Thou gavest Me out of the world. Thine they were, and Thou gavest them Me. . . . I pray for them . . . for they are Thine And all Mine are Thine, and Thine are Mine, and I am glorified in them." "We feel," said a grand preacher of the last century, "as if we could dwell on that sentence and never weary of the wonderful theme it presents to us" (Rainsford). "I am glorified in them." Angelic power cannot reveal Christ's strength as does our weakness; the wealth of heaven cannot display Christ's riches as does our poverty; the holiness of archangels cannot speak His praise as much as does the covering of our unrighteousness; the anthems of the heavenly choirs cannot utter His praises as do the songs of the redeemed; and not all the worship of the heavenly hosts can render Him so grateful an offering, or crown Him with so rich a crown as does the love of His people. "I am glorified in them."

But there is more to the sermon you are to preach than the heart's grateful response to the glory of the cross. Accept this

now! You are actually taken up into and made a part of the
divine glory as you share in the life of the glorified Son and of
the Father, whose life the Son shares and whose intimate being
of love He has revealed. This is that eternal life of which our
Lord speaks, that eternal life which He equates with the knowledge of God: "Father . . . glorify Thy Son, that Thy Son also
may glorify Thee . . . that He should give eternal life to as many
as Thou hast given Him. And this is life eternal, that they might
know Thee, the only true God, and Jesus Christ, whom Thou
hast sent." Observe, eternal life is not won through knowledge,
and it is not given to knowledge; eternal life *is* knowledge.
To know God *is* eternal life, for this is not the knowledge of
mere intellectual recognition. This is the knowledge of mutual
affection and of intimate relationship, in which knower and known
are united in love. God's knowledge of me in Christ is love, and
my knowledge of Him is love. So to know God in the cross is to
glorify Christ by sharing in the glory which He had with the
Father before the world was, the glory of mutual indwelling in
perfect love.

And see, we are to reflect that glory! Christ's work was
completed in the death of the cross; He has been received up
into glory. But He has left us in the world as witnesses to His
love. "I pray for them," He said (and He says it still!), "I pray
for them. I pray not for the world but for them which Thou hast
given Me." And what is His prayer for us? Surely that through
us that very world which He excludes from this intimate family
prayer may be brought home to the Father. He prays that we
may be one, even as He and the Father are One, in order that
our brotherly unity may witness to God's purpose of reconciling
love. He prays that we may be kept from the Evil One and from
the hatred of the world, so that our witness may not be silenced.
He prays that we may live in the world, not as those who are
of the world but as those who even now share the eternal life
of glory and as such are God's enduring testimony to the glory
of the cross.

The glory of the cross — confess it now! — *the glory of the
cross, in the revelation of God's love through the completed work
of Christ, is the glory of men as they share in the divine life
of glory.*

> I take, O Cross, thy shadow
> For my abiding-place;
> I ask no other sunshine than
> The sunshine of His face;
> Content to let the world go by,
> To know no gain nor loss,
> My sinful self my only shame,
> My glory all the cross.

Jerusalem — Old and New

By Vernold Aurich

(Judica)

Wherefore, behold, I send unto you prophets and wise men and scribes, and some of them ye shall kill and crucify, and some of them shall ye scourge in your synagogs and persecute them from city to city, that upon you may come all the righteous blood shed upon the earth, from the blood of righteous Abel unto the blood of Zacharias, son of Barachias, whom ye slew between the temple and the altar. Verily I say unto you, All these things shall come upon this generation. O Jerusalem, Jerusalem, thou that killest the prophets and stonest them which are sent unto thee, how often would I have gathered thy children together, even as a hen gathereth her chickens under her wings, and ye would not! Behold, your house is left unto you desolate. For I say unto you, Ye shall not see Me henceforth till ye shall say, Blessed is He that cometh in the name of the Lord. — *Matthew 23:34-39*

Beneath the discerning eye of God's Son, Jerusalem was a naked city. Though to human view its sin disguised itself behind the cloak of righteousness, to God the garments of disguise were lifted away to reveal a willful rejection of its only hope and rescue. This was the cause of the painful lament on the part of Him who Himself was the Hope of Jerusalem and of all men, the only-begotten Son of the Father.

The Jerusalem over which Jesus spoke His words of lament is the old Jerusalem. Not old in point of time, though it was old in years, but old in the way that St. Paul spoke of the old man "which is corrupt according to the deceitful lusts" (Eph. 4:22b). The old man for Paul is the sinful, corrupt flesh, centered in sin and rejection. The Jerusalem over which Jesus passes judgment is an old Jerusalem, old because it chose to live in the terrible condition of the "flesh" and, what is worse, chose to remain there. It was the "old" Jerusalem because its people were dominated by their old Adam, corrupt in willful unbelief and self-satisfied hardness. And so it rejected its Savior, and its Savior was forced to reject it. Such was the situation that occasioned our Lord's lament over the Jerusalem He loved.

But the name Jerusalem is a name too long associated with the people of God to pass from usage because of its corrupt inhabitants. Though the "old" Jerusalem of sin could only be condemned because of its sin, God saw a "new" Jerusalem, one "which after God is created in righteousness and true holiness" (Eph. 4:24b). As the "new man" actuates him to whom God has won through with His forgiving grace, so we hear of another Jerusalem, a "new" Jerusalem which would be citizened with the saints, the total number of true believers. This "new" Jerusalem was another name for heaven, the heaven which the cleansing work of Christ assured those who would accept Him in faith.

While this Jerusalem is not mentioned in our text, it lies at the basis of Jesus lament. His disappointment derived from this, that the "old" Jerusalem would not be part of the "new." It is still so today that whenever men choose to remain part of the "old" Jerusalem through unbelief, the Savior laments, for by His death He showed His desire to have us all become part of the "new." For all of us, then, there is here both a warning and a promise. To each let us hearken.

Jerusalem — Old and New

I

The Old Jerusalem

City of Guilt

What was the character of the "old" Jerusalem? What kind of city was it that caused our Savior's lament?

It was first of all a city of guilt. Jerusalem was the favored city of a favored land. It was the political and spiritual capital of a nation chosen to bear the world's Savior. David the Psalmist sang of God's goodness within her walls, and David the King raised her to a city of fortune. Isaiah and Jeremiah taught and prophesied within her streets. On her holy hill of Zion Solomon raised the most magnificent temple ever to be erected. And finally it received its greatest honor by Christ Himself entering it midst loud hosannas.

All of this causes her guilt to stand out in bold relief. In a way Jerusalem excelled in guilt because she excelled in favor and rejected it. The Savior's words, "How often would I have gathered thy children together, even as a hen gathereth her chickens under her wings!" expressed the uncountable opportunity that was hers. But though many of her own had been saved, though some of her history reveals a warm response to God's grace, yet so often, and especially here, she can only stand condemned in her guilt, the guilt of going her own way. Though God wanted her, she did not want God. Though the Savior came unto her, she thrust Him away. Though Christ would still forgive, she chose to remain self-righteous. She is stained with the guilt of rejecting the God she claimed to worship and climaxes her guilt by delivering up her Christ to death.

City of Stubborn Will

She was also a city of a stubborn will. Though she had abundant opportunity, she willfully set her feet in the path of death. Thus she manifests a hardness which is both surprising and unique: surprising because it is beyond what one would expect, and unique because unlike any other. She did not just turn her back on God but also killed the prophets and stoned those that were sent to her.

God did not leave her without witness. God chastened her, invited her, witnessed to her, but she responded with exaggerated hate.

This had been characteristic of Jerusalem and all Israel for much of her history. The "how often" of Christ's lament reaches back to the slaying of righteous Abel and an Old Testament prophet named Zacharias, son of Barachias, two victims of the stubborn treatment accorded God's messengers. "Ye serpents, ye generation of vipers," Jesus calls them (v. 33). John the Baptist had called them the same, and Stephen, another man whom they slew, said: "Ye stiff-necked and uncircumcised in heart and ears, ye do always resist the Holy Ghost. As your fathers did, so do ye. Which of the prophets have not your fathers persecuted? And they have slain them which shewed before the coming of the Just One, of whom ye have been now the betrayers and murderers" (Acts 7:51, 52). As were the fathers, so were the children, hardened fast in their stubborn hatred of God.

City of Doom

Thus a just God could do nothing but proclaim doom upon Jerusalem. By sending more messengers he would confirm her in her hardness. Even yet He would act in mercy. The Word would still be proclaimed, and opportunity for repentance would be granted. Yet in His omniscience He knew that the stubborn rejection would not cease. Therefore the future sending of His messengers would only increase the guilt of the Jews. The message of peace would be to them not life but death because they would reject it. Their hardness would make of Christ a stumbling block, causing them, instead of returning to God, to shun Him more.

It seems there is no stopping it. There can't be, for God's justice must take its course. They had inherited the guilt of their ancestors, and that accumulated evil had hardened their hearts into stone. As God hardened the heart of Pharaoh, who first hardened his own, so now He sent His messengers to the hardened Pharisees that they might be hardened further. This intensified hostility would lead them to deeper guilt. Soon they would murder God's Son and in their obdurate condition willingly cry, "His blood be on us and our children." Not only His blood but also all the righteous blood shed by their fathers would be this generation's to suffer.

Already one can begin to hear the thundering Roman Legions who in A. D. 70 leveled this city so that no stone remained upon another. But this judgment, already recorded in history, is small in comparison with the greater judgment to follow, the eternal judgment of death. Then they will finally know that Jesus is the Christ and will say on the Day of Judgment as they see Him come to judge, though only in terror, not in faith, "Blessed is He that cometh in the name of the Lord."

City Which Caused the Savior's Lament

Yet, in spite of this, we hear from our Lord words of divine pity. The Lord had wept over Jerusalem. Now again His heart yearns with compassion for the city that He loved. Regardless of their stubborn rejection He still has a desire for their return. Again and again He preached to them. Again and again He warned them. Again and again He prayed for them. And finally He would die for them that they might escape the wrath to come. Their hardened hearts did not deter His desire. His love, though disappointed, still wanted them for His own.

City That Still Exists Today

Was Jerusalem destroyed? Does the "old" Jerusalem still exist today?

Yes, Jerusalem of old was destroyed in A. D. 70, but the "old" Jerusalem still exists today. It exists wherever there are those who reject the Word, turn their backs on God, and harden their hearts against Him. We can claim no exemption from the number of those who choose their own way. We too have been citizens of the "old" Jerusalem, and if our hearts are hardened stubbornly against Him, ours too will be the fate of eternal death. And overlooking our lives is the same compassionate Savior, lamenting our fate, wanting us to repent, pleading through His Word for our hearts that we might be citizens of that other Jerusalem, the "new" Jerusalem, which is heaven.

II

The New Jerusalem

A City Eternal

If you therefore are willing to renounce citizenship in the "old" Jerusalem, you can be assured that there is another Jerusalem to receive you. It is the "new" Jerusalem, new because it is inhabited by new men in Christ who wear the crown of life. Throughout its streets are holiness and righteousness, and among its people reign harmony, bliss, and hearts full of worship. With one voice they praise the Lamb that was slain and gather round His throne to give Him glory and honor and praise. It is the eternal city, world without end, the heavenly home which Christ even now prepares for those who love Him.

Its name is to signify that it is God's city, citizened with His people even as the Jerusalem of old was to have been but seldom was. It is the city of the future scheduled to begin when time ends and saints with glorified bodies ascend on high. Its builder and maker is God (Heb. 11:10). It will be partially inhabited by an "innumerable company of angels" (Heb. 12:22). It will be holy and thus free of all sin and hate and sorrow. (Rev. 7:17).

A City Founded in Suffering

But the existence of this city does not depend upon its inhabitants. Rather it depends upon the Son of God, whose complete sacrifice opened the door of heavenly citizenship for those who love Him. It *exists* because of the Lamb of God, who took away the sin of the world. We are now "fellow citizens with the saints" (Eph. 2:19). We who are saved will occupy a place in the "new" city, not by works of righteousness which we have done, but only by the mercy of God, who sent His only-begotten Son to pay the price of redemption, of citizenship in the "new" Jerusalem. That price was not paid with "corruptible things, as silver, and gold . . . but with the precious blood of Christ as of a Lamb without blemish and without spot" (1 Peter 1:18, 19). And they who enter will be those alone who "have washed their robes and made them white in the blood of the Lamb" (Rev. 7:14), by faith in the forgiving grace of God.

It is to this "new" Jerusalem that all new men in Christ look forward. They live each day in the hope of eternal life, which is to say, in the sure confidence that they will inhabit the "new" Jerusalem. As they wait, they are gathered under the Savior's protecting wings, strengthened daily in the sure knowledge that heaven is their home and that, because their Lord arose from the dead, they too shall arise to enter the heavenly Jerusalem, where "God shall wipe away all tears from their eyes." (Rev. 17:17)

For those who possess this hope there is rejoicing in heaven. For them the Savior does not lament. Therefore let us cast off the stubborn rejection of Christ, which is characteristic of the "old" Jerusalem, and in faith accept the precious blood of Christ for the forgiveness of our sins and citizenship in the Jerusalem that is "new".

This Holy Week — Something in Time

By George W. Hoyer

(Palm Sunday)

Six days before the Passover, Jesus came to Bethany, where Lazarus was, whom Jesus had raised from the dead. There they made Him a supper; Martha served, but Lazarus was one of those at table with Him. Mary took a pound of costly ointment of pure nard and anointed the feet of Jesus and wiped His feet with her hair; and the house was filled with the fragrance of the ointment. But Judas Iscariot, one of His disciples (he who was to betray Him), said: "Why was this ointment not sold for three hundred denarii and given to the poor?" This he said, not that he cared for the poor but because he was a thief, and as he had the money box he used to take what was put into it. Jesus said, "Let her alone, let her keep it for the day of My burial. The poor you always have with you, but you do not always have Me!"

When the great crowd of the Jews learned that He was there, they came, not only on account of Jesus but also to see Lazarus, whom He had raised from the dead. So the chief priests planned to put Lazarus also to death, because on account of him many of the Jews were going away and believing in Jesus. — *John 12:1-11 RSV*

"Were the whole realm of nature mine, that were a tribute far too small" for "love so amazing, so divine." It will always be too little, what we "render unto the Lord for all His benefits toward us," always too little — but need it always be too late? It certainly need not be so!

Most of them were not aware of it, but for many of the people in this text this was the last chance to do something in time for the Lord Jesus Christ. The Epistle for the day urges, "Have this mind among yourselves, which you have in Christ Jesus," that we "do nothing from selfishness or conceit, but in humility count others better than ourselves," that "each of you look not only to his own interests but also to the interests of others." For them it was the last chance to do something in time before God would "highly exalt Him." How many more days do you have to do something in time for the Lord?

Supper was served for Christ "six days before the Passover." On Friday morning Jesus, after a night spent at the home of Zacchaeus, the publican, walked on to Bethany and arrived there in the afternoon. The Sabbath, which began at dusk, was kept by Jesus with His friends in Bethany. Then as the dusk of Saturday and the end of the Sabbath arrived, His friends prepared Him a supper.

"Of all sad words," you remember, "of tongue or pen the saddest are these, 'It might have been!' " By the following Friday night it would be finished. Our Lord Himself would have said so. "The strife o'er, the battle done," the Lord in His grave, and people in their homes not only contemplating the events of Good Friday but also remembering the last opportunities they had had to do something for Him — in time.

Which ones were at peace on Good Friday? Was it enough to have known Him? To have been there when they crucified the Lord? Even to have trusted that it was indeed He who would redeem Israel? The great peace which *passes* understanding is a free gift of God's grace with the forgiveness and life He gives in His Son. But the peace which we can *understand* is never ours unless we "have done whatsoever we could" for our Lord, something in time.

I asked the members of a Christian study group: "If your time were to come tonight, if this night God should tell you your soul was required of you, would you be sure that God would take you home to His eternal peace?" One of the members said hesitantly, "Well, maybe not tonight — but give me a week." Never in a week, never in all time, could we do enough to earn *His* peace. This must ever be God's gift in Christ; but given a week, can we not do for Him something in time that will give us as well a human sense of peace, a peace that though it was too little, yet it was not too late; not enough, but something — in time.

Take this week, then, with the men and women in the text, the week God's grace seems to be giving again this year, and make it your Holy Week. Think of what they did or failed to do and of what you can do — mindful of the Lord's desire, spoken with tears, "Would that even today you knew the things that make for peace!" (Luke 19: 42)

I

Was Martha at Peace on Good Friday?

Obviously we cannot compare the peace past understanding which we know with her peace, for we understand the significance of our Lord's entry into Jerusalem and can sing, "Blessed is He." We realize why "He humbled Himself and became obedient unto death, even death on a cross," and we know how on the third day "He rose again for our justification." But even assuming that she knew on Good Friday what she discovered on Easter, was Mary at peace on Good Friday?

"Martha served." She did what she could do best, and she did it well — for Him. Would she ever have been quite at peace if her last service had been the one when she "was distracted with much serving and went to Him and said, 'Lord, do You not care that my sister has left me to serve alone? Tell her, then, to help me'" (Luke 10: 40). But she served the Lord again and served Him well — in time.

The Lord's friends got together to give a great supper for this Friend. They had it at the home of Simon the Leper. He had a house but not much help. So Martha served. And Mary wasn't helping again, it seems. And Lazarus, her brother, "was one of those at table with Him." So Martha served. But this time it was "a good part," "chosen" — for Him. She did what she could do best — for Him — and did it in time.

There will be many dinners cooked and served by mothers, and by grown-up girls whose mothers are ill or away, in this parish this week. And there will be chores of another kind done by boys in yards and men in offices and by secretaries and teachers and doctors and carpenters. "What thou doest" do well, and "do quickly" — for Him — something in time, in time to make this a holy week, to know peace in Holy Week.

II
Was Mary at Peace on Good Friday?

If, like us, she had known all about Good Friday's finishing
of the problem of sin, and Easter's victory over death and devil,
would she have been at peace on Good Friday?

"Mary took a pound of costly ointment of pure nard and
anointed the feet of Jesus and wiped His feet with her hair, and
the house was filled with the fragrance of the ointment." She
looked for something special to do — and did it — for Him, in time.
There was criticism. She knew she could expect this. And Judas
did not let her be disappointed. But the Lord said, "Let her alone,
let her keep it for the day of My burial." "Why do you trouble
the woman? For she has done a beautiful thing to Me. . . . In pouring this ointment on My body she has done it to prepare Me for
burial. Truly, I say to you, wherever this Gospel is preached in the
whole world, what she has done will be told in memory of her."
(Matthew 26: 10, 12, 13)

It need not be that this was only an interpretation which the
Lord placed upon her act. Did she perhaps believe what she saw,
the Lord's face set steadfastly to go to Jerusalem? Did she believe
what the Lord had said quite plainly, that "the Son of man will
be delivered into the hands of men, and they will kill Him: and
when He is killed, after three days He will rise?" (Mark 9: 31). And
did she realize that this would be the only chance to anoint His
body for burial — time at the end only for a hasty mixture of spices
dusted into the winding sheet and a hasty procession to the sepulcher, and no time even "very early in the morning on the first day
of the week," for He would not be there, He would be risen?

This much for sure: She hit upon something special to do for
Him, and she did it — in time.

"The poor you always have with you." Do you believe what
the Lord said to you? Look about you. Let your mind travel
at least as far as jets can take you in 18 hours. The *world* is hungry.
"Truly, I say to you," He said, "as you did it to one of the least
of these My brethren, you did it to Me" (Matt. 25: 40). Are you
realizing this? There is time before Good Friday to plan something
special to do for Him — and to *do* it. There will be Judas' voices
around you to urge you to bank your money (and forget to add
"where moth and rust consume and where thieves break in and
steal," Matt. 5: 19), and your own anxious voice asking, "What shall
I eat?" or "What shall I wear?" But if now you are thinking of
something special to do for Him — do it! Do it in time — to make
this a holy week.

Do you believe our Lord meant it when He said, "Take heed

to yourselves, for they will deliver you up to councils: and you will be beaten in synagogs, and you will stand before governors and kings for My sake, to bear testimony before them. And the Gospel must first be preached to all nations" (Mark 13:9, 10). And do you understand He did not mean, "Take heed so that you can avoid all this," but "Take heed to yourselves that nothing thwart your testimony in the most difficult situations?" Now can you think of something special to do for those who go for you and for Christ into danger? Then do it — do it in time for Him. And think now of something special *you* can do, somewhere special you can go — nothing as spectacular as testimony before kings, perhaps; after all, Mary was among friends when she unbound her hair and wiped His feet. But some of her best friends thought it was indecent, and you could hear their murmurs telling her so. The special thing you can do may be just as embarrassing — bearing testimony to the Lord in the barber chair as you get your Easter haircut, with every man in the shop suddenly quiet and your voice plunging on to say, "Crucified, dead, and buried . . . *is my Lord!*"

That special thing to do, do it in time — for the Lord, to make this a holy week, to know peace in Holy Week.

Will contrast help make clear the point of our peace in Holy Week?

III

Was Judas at Peace on Good Friday?

Never — not all day; not from the time he betrayed the Son of man with a kiss; not when he flung down the 30 pieces of silver on the temple floor; no, not when he hanged himself. And, oh; so dreadful to think, to say — not ever, not ever again, forever and ever.

But eternal disquiet, hell, began so rationally. Couldn't you agree that money given to the poor is better spent than for a perfume that fills the Lord's house with fragrance and then is gone? Couldn't you be persuaded that Christians don't have to walk into suffering ("God forbid, Lord! This shall never happen." . . .), that there can be some kind of peaceful coexistence? (The Lord said a "Get behind Me, Satan!" to this. "You are a hindrance to Me, for you are not on the side of God but of men," Matt. 16: 22, 23.)

Other evangelists say that some of the disciples were caught up in Judas' objection, and we can so easily be. But can there be peace in Holy Week if we "count ourselves out" from doing something for our Lord — in time? Only tears, when it is too late, only tears and bitter regret.

IV

Or Take the Chief Priests — Were They at Peace on Good Friday?

Already they were figuring out what to say to Pilate: "Sir, we remember how that imposter said while He was still alive, 'After three days I will rise again.' Therefore order the sepulcher to be made secure . . ." (Matt. 27:63, 64). No peace for those who have known Jesus Christ, who He is, and have tried "to think better" of their conviction instead of thinking better of their Savior. For them only the dubious peace of a man with a millstone tied about his neck drifting down to the depths of the sea, for opposition to Christ leads to offense against His people. It was not enough to oppose Christ, they "planned to put Lazarus also to death because on account of him many of the Jews were . . . believing in Jesus." A millstone's peace is better than what is in store for those whose neglect of the Christ causes little ones to stumble, whose discounting of the claim of the Christ on their lives and the lives of their families keeps boys and girls from growing up to the fullness of the stature of Christ. No peace in Holy Week — no peace at the last — for them.

V

Or Take the Crowd — Could Any of Those People Be at Peace on Good Friday?

Not those who came "not only on account of Jesus but also to see Lazarus, whom He had raised from the dead," who came out of curiosity and who left and just as curiously simply disappear in the shuffle. Were some of them in the crowd that cried, "Crucify Him?" When He was crucified, what peace to realize, "This man has done nothing amiss"; "Truly, this was the Son of God?"

In each case — the crowd who left, the chief priests, and Judas — there was no peace on Good Friday because they resisted all the love which God had brought to a focus on them personally at a given point in time. See it in the life of Judas. God's own Son was "born of a woman, born under the Law to redeem them that were under the Law." He was born in Judas' country, chose Judas to be a follower, camped with Judas, talked with Judas, laughed with Judas, trusted Judas, warned Judas, pleaded with Judas, in heartbreak received a kiss from Judas — and yet Judas said, "Hail, Master," only in betrayal.

Now, in this point of time, the love of God is focused upon you. "The saying is sure and worthy of full acceptance, that Christ Jesus came into the world to save sinners." And you and I are "the foremost of sinners" (1 Tim. 1:15). "Will you also go away?"

There is no peace in Holy Week if you do . . . unless you go away, *believing.* Many of the crowd did, you know. Because they had seen the Christ and had seen His miraculous power in that Lazarus who had been dead, but was alive, "many of the Jews were going away and believing in Jesus."

VI

Was Jesus at Peace on Good Friday?

Our Lord was — at peace because the awful agony was over. The tearing muscles and the screaming nerves were still in death. The eyes were closed that had looked upon the very people He had come to save surrounding His cross, jeering and mocking. "It is finished." What peace!

Our Lord was — at peace because He had finished the work the Father had given Him to do. A very satisfactory day's work — or a terrible day's very satisfactory work — a Good Friday's good work! He had secured salvation, guaranteed forgiveness, pardon, a life of blessedness on earth and in eternity for every man, woman, and child that was, had been, would be, and is. "It is finished!" What peace!

But, understandably, the peace that passes understanding is offered in vain to such as refuse to accept it. Our Lord's full peace, like the joy of angels in heaven, awaits the sinner's repentance — your repentance and mine. Give Him His peace — take your peace from Him — now, in time. Your confession "My Lord and My God" and His "Go in peace and sin no more" make this a holy week.

VII

Lazarus Was at Peace on Good Friday

And since he was a man who had been dead and was made alive again, you can identify yourself with him. For God has quickened you who were dead in trespasses and sins, God has given you new life in Holy Baptism, empowered you from this Scripture, fed you with food not only believable but given also to eat and to drink — the body and blood of His Son. Your peace this Holy Week can be as real as that of Lazarus, and, in time, just as much in time as his, and just as certain in eternity!

What does it take to disturb a man who has been dead and is alive again? Can the threat of death? Can death frighten a man who has heard the voice of God say, "Lazarus, come forth"? We know Him who has brought life and immortality to light, and we have no fear of death's darkness any time.

Can we be moved by men who threaten our Lord and His cause? A man who has seen the other side of time, who has been where God lives and reigns, where "He who sits in the heavens laughs" at "kings of the earth [who] set themselves, and rulers [who] take counsel together, against the Lord and His anointed" (Psalm 2:2), such a man knows peace in time and forever. Lazarus was taken across the great divide and saw, while God Himself crossed over into time and *showed* us these things so that we believe. In either case we have seen — and in time. "Who shall separate us from the love of Christ? Shall tribulation, or distress, or persecution, or famine, or nakedness, or peril, or sword? . . . No, in all these things we are more than conquerors through Him who loved us." (Rom. 8:35-37)

Lazarus "understood" by faith the peace that passes understanding. But don't you think that Lazarus also knew the peace that we can understand, the peace that comes from doing something in time for our Lord? Wasn't he a part of Martha's serving, urging her to do what she did best, to do it well — for Him, in time? Didn't he know of Mary's plan to do something special for the Lord, and didn't he encourage her and urge her on to do it, in time? And can't we find a part in the usual things and the special things to do for Him this week — something in time? And can't we be a part of the usual things and the special things our family and our church undertakes in these days? Here was a man who was dead and, behold, he lived. And here are we who were dead and, behold, *we* live. We can have the peace that *passes* understanding and know the peace that we *can* understand this Holy Week! Always too little, what we can do, but this Holy Week is not too late for something for the Lord — something in time.

The Last Passover — The First Communion

By J. H. BAUMGAERTNER

(Maundy Thursday)

Then came the day of Unleavened Bread, on which the Passover lamb had to be sacrificed. So Jesus sent Peter and John, saying, "Go and prepare the passover for us that we may eat it." They said to Him, "Where will you have us prepare it?" He said to them: "Behold, when you have entered the city, a man carrying a jar of water will meet you. Follow him into the house which he enters, and tell the householder, The Teacher says to you, 'Where is the guestroom where I am to eat the passover with My disciples?' And he will show you a large upper room furnished; there make ready." And they went and found it as He had told them, and they prepared the passover. And when the hour came, He sat at table, and the apostles with Him. And He said to them, "I have earnestly desired to eat this passover with you before I suffer, for I tell you I shall not eat it until it is fulfilled in the kingdom of God." And He took a cup, and when He had given thanks, He said, "Take this, and divide it among yourselves; for I tell you that from now on I shall not drink of the fruit of the vine until the kingdom of God comes." And He took bread, and when He had given thanks He broke it and gave it to them, saying, "This is My body, which is given for you. Do this in remembrance of Me. And likewise the cup after supper, saying, "This cup, which is poured out for you, is the new covenant in My blood." — *Luke 22:7-20 RSV*

The words just read to you tell a dramatic story of tremendous significance, the story of the last Passover and the first Communion.

As we gather in our churches on Maundy Thursday of Holy Week to receive the blessed sacrament, our Jewish friends and neighbors are making their Passover preparations.

You know, of course, that there is a connection between the two. In fact, the story we have heard again from the inspired record of Luke, the beloved physician, tells us how the one ended and the other began. It is the story of an ending that was really a beginning, this story of the last Passover and the first Communion.

I

The Last Passover

As religious people, as intelligent churchgoers, as members of a church which finds all its teachings in the Bible we ought to know the meaning of that word *Passover* and the significance of the ancient festival which is still observed by our Jewish friends.

"Passover" actually means a great deal more to us than it does to those who still observe the feast. Just as the name *Messiah* means a great deal more to us than it does to them, so the word "Passover" has a fuller and richer meaning for Christians than it does for Jews. We know that Jesus Christ was, and is, the Messiah, while they are still waiting for a Messiah or some vague Messianic manifestation yet to come. We know that Christ is our Passover Lamb, while they are still slaughtering and eating the Passover lamb of which He was, and is, the personal fulfillment.

Passover. What does it mean? Perhaps we should refresh our memories. What passed over? Who passed over? When did it happen?

The Historic Fact

It happened on that historic night when the people of Israel, who had sojourned in Egypt for more than 400 years, were delivered from bondage and slavery and began their great migration to the Promised Land.

Nine plagues had been visited upon the people of Egypt, and still Pharaoh had not let God's people go. And now God's patience was at an end. It was time for the 10th and last and most dreadful visitation.

Carefully the Children of Israel were instructed to prepare

for sudden flight. They were to eat one more meal in Egypt. In each home a lamb was to be slain, and the blood of it was to be painted on the doorposts of each Israelite house.

That night, the Scripture says, the angel of the Lord came and struck all the firstborn in the land of Egypt, but he *passed over* the houses whose doors had the paschal lamb's blood on them. In the resulting clamor and confusion the people of Israel swept out of the land of Egypt and began the long and dreary desert wandering that led to freedom and glory.

The Blessed Remembrance

Every year thereafter they kept the Passover in commemoration of that historic event. It was one of the highest and most sacred celebrations of the year and began with the slaying, roasting, and eating of a perfect young lamb, entirely without blemish, in the Passover meal. It lasted one entire week.

It was, so to speak, their Fourth of July, commemorating their independence from the yoke of Egyptian bondage, reminding them of God's deliverance in the great hour of their national peril and need. This is the Passover which our Jewish friends observe to this very day.

The Hopeful Anticipation

It was a festival that looked back to that glorious day in their nation's history. But it was also a festival that looked forward, in hopeful anticipation of the paschal Lamb who would be offered up for the sins of them all and by the shedding of His blood would atone for the transgressions of His people. In other words, there was a *Messianic* importance to the Passover feast. The promised Messiah, the Deliverer, the Savior, who was to come, would also be the final Passover Lamb, whose sacrifice upon the altar of God's wrath would deliver them from the slavery of sin and the bondage of death and hell. Just as every sacrifice which was offered on their bloody, smoking altars pointed forward to the coming of the Lamb of God, who would take away the sins of the world, so did the lamb that was slain and eaten at the beginning of the Passover celebration look forward to the coming of Him who by His death would lead His people out of their spiritual Egypt into the Promised Land of heaven.

II

The First Communion

Our neighbors of the Hebrew race have not accepted Jesus as their Messiah. So they continue to observe the ancient Passover because they have not accepted Christ as their Passover Lamb. Our Jewish friends are still living in the Old Testament. For them the New Testament has not yet begun.

One Age Ends — Another Begins

You and I know that it has. We know that the old testament ends with Jesus and that with Him the *new* testament begins.

"Testament" means covenant, or promise. The old covenant, the old promise, was the promise of the Savior who was to come. And when He did come, it was the end of the old covenant and the beginning of the new promise that those who believe in the Savior, who has come, who has appeared, shall have forgiveness of sins and everlasting life.

Today we live in the New Testament. We are members of the New Testament church, the church which is built upon that promise.

All history divides itself here. This is by far the most significant turning point in all the story of man. We reckon every event which has ever happened in its relationship to the appearance of the Messiah. It happened, we say, whatever it was, it happened either before or after Christ.

The Exact Moment

Knowing that the old testament ended and the new testament began with Christ, have you ever wondered just when it took place, at what exact moment in the 33 years that God's own Son was living here on earth? Was it Christmas, Good Friday, Easter? Did the age of the new promise begin with His ascension into heaven?

The answer is in our text. It happened on Maundy Thursday, in Jerusalem's Upper Room, on the night in which He was betrayed, the night before He died.

That night, for the last time, Jesus kept the Passover with His disciples, and then, as a mark that the old Passover had now been completely fulfilled, instituted the holy sacrament of His body and blood to take its place. That night in the Upper Room, the old testament turned its last page and faded into history. That night, in the eternal wisdom and love of God, the new testament began. That night Jesus said to His own, "I have earnestly desired to eat this passover with you before I suffer; for I tell you I shall never eat it again until it is fulfilled in the kingdom of God." That night He said to them, as He offered them the chalice of Passover wine, "This cup is the *new* testament in My blood, which is shed for you."

The Unfolding of the Scene

How did God set the stage for this dramatic announcement?

Scholars who have tried to reconstruct for us the events of Holy Week point out that there is a great silence between Tuesday night and Thursday morning, a silence of some 36 hours in which

His disciples were forced to ponder something they were quite unable to grasp — that things were coming to an end. It was evident from everything that Jesus said and did that a great crisis was approaching.

Expected Preparations

Then, early on Thursday morning, Jesus calmly gave orders to prepare for the celebration of the Passover, for it was the "day of Unleavened Bread, on which the Passover lamb had to be sacrificed." This was something that Jesus had always done, so they were not surprised. It was no more than they expected. Perhaps they wondered why He had not spoken of it sooner. All Jewry was in a frenzy of preparation, just as we are at Christmastime.

An Unexpected Miracle

But the unexpected happened, too, as it did so often in the life of our Lord. This Christ was Son of God and King of kings, yet He had no place of His own where He could meet with His disciples for one last Passover meal, no place of His own where He could give them for all time, His final testament of love, no place of His own where He could end one age and begin another, where He could stop all of the clocks and calendars of time and reset them all. Someday all men everywhere would remember this moment and would have to reckon with it, whether they believed in Him or not, for He was about to announce the new covenant, the new promise, which would change everything. But Jesus had no place of His own. From someone whose very name is unknown to us He had to borrow the setting and the scene for one of history's most significant events.

To us it is all very strange, as it must have been to the disciples, for we have here a strange and wonderful mingling of poverty and power. Jesus has to depend on the kindness and generosity of an unnamed friend chosen and pointed out to His disciples by a miracle of foreknowledge which must have been startling even to them. They were still outside the walls of Jerusalem when Jesus singled out Peter and John and said to them: "Go into the city. You will meet a man carrying a pitcher of water. Follow him to the house that he will enter. Tell the owner of the house that I need a place for the celebration of the Passover. He will show you to a large upper room. There prepare the Passover lamb." And it happened just as He had said.

The Approaching Destiny

Jesus knew that He was about to die. It was only a matter of hours now. The perfect life that He was living on earth in order to be able to present it to God for us was coming to an end. How well they remind us, these very last moments, that His obedience to the divine Law, which He was keeping for us, was a perfect obedience. For these few remaining hours the old testament was still in effect. The Passover in its ancient form, still valid, was still pointing forward to Him who was come and now sojourned among them.

The Lamb and *the* Lamb

So He entered the Upper Room in the twilight of the old testament's last day. There, to be received once, and only once more, is the Passover lamb, its blood running dark and red. And there, beside it, is the Lamb of God, about to shed His blood for the sins of all the world. We see the bleeding carcass of a lamb, the visual embodiment of promise and prophecy; we see Christ, whose blood will soon be staining the soil of Calvary, and we know that this is fulfillment.

So they ate together, Jesus knowing, knowing full well, and the disciples wondering. "This is the last time," He said to them, knowing that before another sunset His bruised and broken body would be hanging in death's collapse on Calvary's cross while His spirit would be home with God. The Passover lamb of which they ate was a bitter reminder of the road that must still be trod, of the journey that must still be made, before He would know the peace and the joy of return and reunion.

Through Death to Life

For now He was that Lamb who would die so that the angel of death would ever pass over those who by faith, through grace, would be His own. Now He was about to be offered. In just a matter of moments His own flesh would be raised to the altar of sacrifice, His own spirit would know the forsakenness of hell and the agony of death, and then, at last, He would be free, and all His own would be free with Him, free because their sins for once and for all would be atoned for and forgiven, free to pass through the portals of death into the everlasting joys of heaven. It is a shout of triumph that goes up from the apostle in the Easter Epistle: "Christ, our Passover, is sacrificed for us!" This, too, must have been in the heart and mind of Jesus there in the Upper Room. He was about to be offered for the sins of the world. But His death would purchase salvation. The giving of His life would bring life and immortality to light for all time.

To Be Remembered Forever

This was something, He knew, that the world must never be permitted to forget. This dying as man's Substitute, this vicarious death, this blessed atonement for all the guilt of guilty men, must be remembered till the end of time. Should men forget and go their way without Him, they would walk in darkness and die in their sins. If that would happen, then all that He had done, all that He had suffered, all the love that He had poured out for all the children of men — it was all in vain.

A New Covenant — a New Feast

So it was that when the last Passover meal was eaten there in the Upper Room, when prophecy became fulfillment and type had become reality, when the old testament had turned its last page, Jesus announced the beginning of a new testament, a new covenant, in the sacrament of His body and blood. It is often called the *Last* Supper but it is really the *first*, the first of countless millions of commemorative celebrations in which His believers, through the changing ages, have been reminded of the Lamb that was slain and have received, in a sacramental miracle, the very body and blood once given and shed for their sins.

How simply and beautifully the Holy Scripture describes that moving scene!

"He took bread, and when He had given thanks, He brake it and gave it to His disciples and said: 'Take, eat. This is My body, which is given for you. This do in remembrance of Me.' After the same manner also He took the cup, when He had supped, gave thanks and gave it to them, saying: 'Take, drink ye all of it. This cup is the *new testament* in My blood, which is shed for you for the remission of sins. This do ye, as oft as ye drink it, in remembrance of Me.' "

There was a time, now past, when the slaying of the Passover lamb reminded the faithful among God's people of the divine love which permitted the angel of death to pass over their homes in Egypt, and looked forward to the coming of the sacrificial Lamb of God.

Now the blessed sacrament is our Passover meal, a constant reminder of the blood that was shed and the life that was given for our salvation, a continual strengthening of our faith in Christ, who is our Passover, having been sacrificed for us.

Is Christ truly *your* Passover? Do you believe it in your heart of hearts?

Have you shown in your daily life that you believe it?

Never Love Like This!

By Paul G. Stephan

(Good Friday)

And He, bearing His cross, went forth into a place called the place of a skull, which is called in the Hebrew Golgotha, where they crucified Him and two others with Him, on either side one and Jesus in the midst. And Pilate wrote a title and put it on the cross. And the writing was, JESUS OF NAZARETH, THE KING OF THE JEWS. This title then read many of the Jews, for the place where Jesus was crucified was nigh to the city, and it was written in Hebrew and Greek and Latin. Then said the chief priests of the Jews to Pilate, Write not, The King of the Jews but that He said, I am King of the Jews. Pilate answered, What I have written I have written. Then the soldiers, when they had crucified Jesus, took His garments and made four parts, to every soldier a part, and also His coat. Now the coat was without seam, woven from the top throughout. They said therefore among themselves, Let us not rend it but cast lots for it, whose it shall be, that the Scripture might be fulfilled which saith, They parted My raiment among them, and for My vesture they did cast lots. These things therefore the soldiers did. Now there stood by the cross of Jesus His mother, and His mother's sister, Mary, the wife of Cleophas, and Mary Magdalene. When Jesus therefore saw His mother and the disciple standing by whom He loved, He saith unto His mother, Woman, behold thy son! Then saith He to the disciple, Behold Thy mother! And from that hour that disciple took her unto his own home. After this, Jesus knowing that all things were now accomplished that the Scripture might be fulfilled, saith, I thirst. Now there was set a vessel full of vinegar, and they filled a sponge with vinegar and put it upon hyssop and put it to His mouth. When Jesus therefore had received the vinegar, He said, It is finished, and He bowed His head and gave up the ghost.

John 19:17-30

Good Friday, the cross, and the Christian are indissolubly linked. On Good Friday the Christian turns to the cross with a deeper, holier feeling, a more penitent heart, a more sincere love for Christ, than on any other occasion. The full impact of the Savior's suffering and torturesome death weighs more heavily upon the Christian's heart and mind; the full import of Christ's sacrificial death comes into sharper focus on Black Friday, or Good Friday, than at any other time in the calendar of the Christian church year. I do not feel that this is only, or primarily, an emotional experience, a matter of maudlin sentimentality, but I really believe that the majority of Christian people, if not all of them, are prompted by penitence and love to approach the cross for pardon, peace, and spiritual renewal.

Black Friday

The day of the cross is sometimes called Black Friday, possibly because of an early church custom to drape the crucifix in black on Christ's death day and to place black paraments upon the altar, pulpit, and lectern. In some churches not even the candles upon the altar were lighted; the bell in the church tower was only tolled. The worshipers were particularly mindful of the solemnity of the service in God's house. On Good Friday no one so much as whispered to another! Christ was given, at least, the same respect that we extend to our departed loved ones.

The Central Figure in Church and Life — the Cross

In his book *Preaching Unashamed* Dr. Joseph R. Sizoo states:

> It is the Cross which stands central in the faith of Christendom. . . . The early Church was held together by keeping that Cross central. What a strange and complex group it was! These early Christians represented different nationalities with different languages, different traditions, different types of organizations and with different creedal statements. You come upon the fickle Galatians; there were the wayward Romans; you meet the warmhearted Philippians; there were the unpredictable and unstable Thessalonians. And yet, all these differing groups with their different patterns were held together in one great fellowship because their common gospel was, "He loved me and gave Himself for me!" "God forbid that I should glory save in the Cross of our Lord Jesus Christ!"
>
> That is still so today. The areas of estrangement and tension in Christendom are always in the direction of creeds. The increasing sense of oneness is always in the direction of the Cross. Wherever the Cross ceases to be central, Christendom has become weak, quarrelsome, and divided. The way back to oneness is by kneeling again in reverence and confession before the Cross.

The cross is the emblem of our Savior's highest and deepest love. Good Friday commemorates the endless, limitless, self-giving love of Jesus. The Christian accepts this forgiving love with a believing heart.

With these thoughts in mind we want to consider this appropriate Good Friday text as I group my thoughts around the theme:

Never Love Like This!

I

Love Constrained Christ to Bear the Cross and to Suffer and Die Willingly

"And He, *bearing His cross,* went forth," the sacred writer begins. There never was a love like that which compelled Jesus to go to Calvary. He stumbled along the Street of Sorrows, "bearing His cross," not because He was under the compulsion of Roman law, not because of Pilate's verdict, not because He was driven by the whip and the lash of the heartless soldiers, but because His love for you and for me and for all the world of sinners drove Him to endure all this and the cross.

He Bore His Cross, an Emblem of Shame

The cross in His day, it hardly need be said, was an object of contempt, derision, scorn; it was the most despised of all repulsive objects. Death by crucifixion was the most shameful form, reserved for the most vile criminals and the most hated public enemies. Christ's death upon the two jagged timbers, and between two thugs, was an added infamy. So horrible, loathsome, and terrifying was this form of execution upon the two rugged and ugly crosspieces that Cicero wrote concerning the cross and crucifixion, "Let it never come near the body of a Roman citizen, nay, not even near his thought or eyes or ears." The fact that today the cross is worn proudly by Christian people; the fact that Christ's people today are willing to sing, "In the cross of Christ I glory," is only because of Jesus, who hung upon it and thus made it an object of grace and blessing. But when Jesus "went forth" "bearing His cross" He stumbled along in weariness and sorrow, not only because of His sinking weakness, not only because the cobblestones were rough and uneven, not only because the log on which He was to die was crushingly heavy, but because of the disgrace and shame He was enduring. Never was there love like this!

He Went Forth — Love the Only Compulsion

"And He, bearing His cross, *went forth.*" He went forth willingly, courageously, determinedly. Long before the actual ordeal in the Garden, with its blood-stained sweat, the sniveling betrayal, the unjust arrest, the mock trials, Jesus "set His face to go to Jerusalem." He wanted to suffer. "No man taketh it [My life] from Me," He once said, "but I lay it down of Myself" (John 10:18). He "went forth" because His love for you and for me and for all the rebellious sons and daughters of men was so indescribably all-inclusive and compelling that He willingly, yes, even gladly, "went forth" to be "delivered for our offenses and raised again for our justification." This He did for us sinners. Never was there love like this!

He Bore His Cross to Skull Hill — a Repulsive Place!

"And He, bearing His cross, went forth," the holy writer continues, "into a place called the place of a skull, which is called in the Hebrew Golgotha." Skull hill, as Jerome, the ancient church father, called it, was the place for federal executions. It was so named, both because of its shape and because it reeked with the remains of previous executions. All of this, detestable and unthinkable in its filth and crudity, only added insult to injury. But Jesus, the Lord of all, bore it — for you and for me! Never was there love like this!

II

Love Helped Him Endure the Crucifixion, Disdain, Disrespect, and Indifference

The Crucifixion — Cold, Callous, Cruel

When the death march halted on Calvary's crude crest, the hardened soldiers ruthlessly ripped the robe from the shoulders of Jesus, ordered Him and the other victims to lie down upon the cross-beams, and then perfunctorily proceeded to spike each one to his cross. That done, the crosses were raised, thumped into the holes quickly dug, with Jesus in the middle and two malefactors on each side of Him, and then the earth was scraped back into the holes around the base of the crosses with a spade, and packed firmly with the feet — all in a day's work! And then the soldiers sat down in complete apathy, stolid indifference, and by gambling began to while away the time until their captives died. Someone got the idea that it would be better not to tear the upper garment or coat that Jesus wore into equal parts but rather to roll the dice for it and the lucky number would win the whole garment. We can well imagine that this was a shocking scene of vulgarity, revelry, carousing, cheap comedy, idle jests, and indecent conduct. It is hard to understand how these soldiers could remain so completely untouched and indifferent to the groans and moans of the dying men and so inattentive to the seven sacred utterances that fell from the divine lips of Him who languished on that central cross. Think of it! Just a little above their heads the holy Man of God was enduring unspeakable pain, disdain, disrespect, and this revolting indifference, and included them in His prayer for His heavenly Father's forgiveness. Never was there love like this!

Shocking Indifference

We shudder at the indifference of the soldiers, but, really, is it very much worse than the indifference that meets our eyes in modern history? How many people are there who live within the shadow of a Christian church who never think of entering it to worship! Perhaps the only time the church has meaning for them is to get out of the rain. Perhaps the only time some will ever enter a church is when the hearse leads the way — if then! How great is the number of those who just never think of attending divine services on a Sunday morning, not because they hate preachers, or church people, or the Bible, or things sacred, but because it never occurred to them to worship. The things of this world have a greater attraction for them, an all-absorbing interest. They just don't care!

The Title of Truth

No sooner was Jesus suspended between the earth that had rejected Him and the heaven that frowned upon Him than Pilate wrote a superscription in three languages and commanded it to be tacked to the cross of Jesus Christ, so that all the people of that day who were able to read, and who passed that way, would know that He who was dying on that center cross was "Jesus of Nazareth, the King of the Jews." Pilate meticulously had the title printed or engraved in the three outstanding languages of the day, the Hebrew, which most of the people spoke, and in which the Sacred Scrolls were written, the Greek, the language of the intelligent, and the Latin, the language of business and legal documents, so that it would have widespread publicity.

Apparently Pontius Pilate, who had had no end of trouble with the annoying people He governed, and to whose whims he had to give in, wrote this title as a last gesture to prove to them that he still thought Jesus was innocent, telling them in effect, "You have put this Galilean to death, but He is still your King!" Or it may be that he intended this to be a sarcastic taunt, the ridicule of the ages, as though he were saying: "This emaciated, agonized, writhing crusader for truth, this visionary, this wilderness preacher, is your King!" But unwittingly he spoke the truth. And when the leaders of the Jewish people came to him with the demand that he change this to read: "He said, 'I am the King of the Jews,'" the Roman governor was adamant, firm, peremptorily refusing to change what he had written. And thereby, under God's direction, he proclaimed the greatest truth of all time, that Jesus Christ was in very truth the promised Messiah, the King of the Jews, who would pay with His lifeblood on the cross the price for the sins of all the world, so that all might be saved from every land and language by their faith in Him. Never was there love like this!

III

Love Moved Him to Forget Self and to Think of Others

A Home for His Mother — Care for Us

St. John, the author of this text, is about ready to conclude this portion of the narrative, but he cannot pass on without mentioning an incident which was of great significance to him, that virtually changed his life. He refers, of course, to the honor Jesus gave him by asking him to take His mother into his home. This little story within the entire Passion narrative has meaning also for all mothers, fathers, and children today and for all time. It begins by stating that the mother of Jesus and several other Marys, some of whom were, no doubt, relatives, were standing at the foot of the cross keeping watch, giving Him their moral support. And when Jesus saw His mother and John, He then spoke the two words which brought them together in a mother-and-son relationship for the rest of their lives.

This tender scene touches our hearts deeply, not only because Jesus was moved with compassion to provide a home for His mother but also because He did so at an hour when no one would have blamed Him if He had not done so, in the midst of excruciating pain, unendurable anguish, suffering, bleeding, dying, for the sins of all men. And yet He forgot His own sorrows and troubles and thought of others.

We Are His Concern

What an Example for us! What assurance that Jesus thinks of us today! He has the whole world in His care, yet He is not so occupied in carrying out the affairs of the universe for the good of all and the glory of God that He cannot think about you and me as individuals. Our home life concerns Him; our business life concerns Him; our problems concern Him; our joys and our sorrows, our wants and our needs, concern Him. He who foresees the future has also provided for it. There is no need at all for any anxiety or worry on our part about anything. "He that spared not His own Son, but delivered Him up for us all, how shall He not with Him also freely give us all things?" and again: "Seek ye first the kingdom of God and His righteousness, and all these things shall be added unto you." Never was there love like this!

The Thirsting Savior

The succeeding events must have passed in quick succession. When Jesus was forsaken of His Father, left alone to suffer the torments of the damned, to battle the viciousness and the villainy of Satan, our Savior touched the deepest depths of our redemption. He got the victory, and Satan slinked away crippled and conquered forever. His spiritual battle and agony had passed. And now, only after everyone else had been helped, did He have time to think of Himself, and so He uttered a cry of personal pain and want. This cry, "I thirst!" showed the reality of His physical suffering, for no pain is as intense, as terrible, as thirst. It reminds us also of His perfect humanity, that even to this day "He is touched with a feeling of our infirmity"; He understands. His cry is also indicative of His thirst for the souls of men, a deep, spiritual longing that men should be willing to receive His "so great salvation," which He had purchased with His own precious blood. Never was there love like this!

IV
Love Bowed His Head into Triumphant Death

When the soldiers heard Him cry, "I thirst," they took a sponge, soaked it in a stupefying potion, and fastened this on a pole or reed, and put it to His mouth, intending thereby to deaden His senses and to ease His pain. But Jesus refused this because He wanted to suffer everything until that bitter, dismal, merciless end of suffering. And then, and only when His hour had come, knowing that He had perfectly fulfilled His mission, the redemption of the human race, by His suffering, the shedding of His blood, and His death, He cried the greatest word that has ever been uttered, "It is finished!" This was His cry of victory, of triumph. The word in Greek and also in the language in which it was most likely spoken is but one word — a word which means "a thing matured, brought to perfection." It was not a thing merely brought to an end, but something brought to a *successful* completion. It was indeed a shout of triumph! And having given His cry of victory, which to this day keeps reechoing down through all the corridors of time, love closed His eyes and bowed His head into death.

Never was there love like this! May God grant that as we look upon the Lamb of God for sinners slain, we may not only be moved to deeper appreciation, but also compelled by our gratitude to live our lives dedicated to Him, to testify to His far-reaching, world-encircling love, to speak to others about the love that would not let us go, a love that compelled Him and constrained Him to bear our sins upon His own back on the accursed tree, to endure the vilest mockery ever hurled at anyone, to forget Himself, and to think only of others, and then when our redemption had been completely and unreservedly won, to bow His head into death, only to rise again on the glorious third day as our once-crucified but now ever-living Lord. May this Good Friday help us understand a little better that there never was love like the love with which the Lord Jesus loved us.

The Meaning of Easter

By Kenneth R. Schueler

(Easter — Pericope for Easter Monday)

But Mary stood without at the sepulcher weeping. And as she wept, she stooped down, and looked into the sepulcher, and seeth two angels in white sitting, the one at the head and the other at the feet, where the body of Jesus had lain. And they said unto her, Woman, why weepest thou? She saith unto them, Because they have taken away

my Lord, and I know not where they have laid Him. And when she
had thus said, she turned herself back, and saw Jesus standing and
knew not that it was Jesus. Jesus saith unto her, Woman, why weepest
thou? Whom seekest thou? She, supposing Him to be the gardener,
saith unto Him, Sir, if thou have borne Him hence, tell me where thou
hast laid Him, and I will take Him away. Jesus saith unto her, Mary.
She turned herself and saith unto Him, Rabboni, which is to say, Master.
Jesus saith unto her, Touch Me not, for I am not yet ascended to My
Father, but go to My brethren, and say unto them, I ascend unto My
Father and your Father, and to My God and your God. Mary Magdalene
came and told the disciple that she had seen the Lord and that He
had spoken these things unto her. — *John 20:11-18*

If the story of Easter has any meaning, its meaning will be
perceived first by sad people. The broken in heart, the lonely
and frightened in life, the desperate — these must be the first to
be transformed by Jesus' resurrection from the dead. If this
truth escapes us or we disbelieve it, we have missed all there
is to Easter. What is more, we have not understood Good Friday
either. For the events of these two days form a unity of meaning
which cannot be separated. Without Easter we should have no
reason to remember the Friday preceding or to call it good.
And without the brutal facts of Jesus' crucifixion and death, the
first day of the week would speak no message of joy or hope.
Mary's experience is a dramatic illustration that Jesus is the
Savior of those whom life has killed. He is the Lord of life
because He is the Lord of death!

So closely does Mary's story correspond to the universal facts
of human experience that no writer could have invented it. Told
by the evangelist in a totally artless way, the story is yet moving
in its very simplicity. Mary was weeping over the death of One
she loved with all her heart. What is more common in life than
tears in a cemetery? But for all its commonness, what is more
precious and costly than the love thus expressed? Friendship and
affection may be known the world over, but never does love
come cheap. Finally, the price of love must be measured by the
vast emptiness and hurt it creates when it is gone. In Joseph's
Garden that Sunday morning long ago Mary knew the cost of
love as she never knew it before. The very violence and abrupt-
ness with which love had been torn from her magnified her
loneliness and deepened her wound.

The last meeting with Jesus had been three days before at
His public execution. She had stood by His cross then, one of
only a few who knew the meaning of compassion at Golgotha.
Yet she could not help Him; she was compelled to watch Him
die alone. The world of kindness and dignity which had grown
up briefly between them — the only world of real humanity she
had ever known — was over and done when she helped lay Jesus'
body in the grave.

Those who have stood where Mary stood before the tomb in the garden — and who has not stood in her place or will not do so? — must know the reason for her crying: "They have taken away my Lord. . . ." This is the way everything in life ends. It is snatched away, and we do not know where to find it. Eventually the grave mocks all the "busyness" of life, extinguishes every flame of human aspiration and devotion, laughs at happiness, joy, and goodness — and calls it all insignificant and empty. It is no use to think life ever ends differently. You may pretend it does, but death puts an end to all pretentions concerning life, whether of the wise man or fool, king or beggar, lover or criminal. In his *History of the World* Sir Walter Raleigh wrote:

> O eloquent, just and mighty Death, whom none could advise, thou hast persuaded; what none hath dared thou hast done; and whom all the world hath flattered, thou only hast cast out of the world and despised. Thou hast drawn together all the far-stretched greatness, all the pride, cruelty, and ambition of man, and covered it all over with these two narrow words, *Hic jacet.*

The last word to life will be spoken by death; there is no appeal from its judgment, no replying to it. That is why Mary was weeping, and there is not a man, woman, or child who does not weep for the same reason. Death comes equally to us all and makes us all equal when it comes. "Dust thou art," it says to every man, "and unto dust shalt thou return." Hear it well, all young men and maidens; know it, old men wise and women rich in years, you are as substantial as a puff of smoke in the wind, as durable as a sand house before the tide, as abiding as snow under the sun of spring! In your beginning is your end!

It is true, life was made for better things. Sundays were not made for weeping, nor Fridays for dying. Mary was not made for being crushed, and Jesus was not made for being forsaken. Crowns were not made to be of thorns, nor trees and nails for crucifying. You and I were not made for the ash heap. All things — time and love, breath and atoms, freedom and utility — all things were made good by God and for man. Above all, man was made for the joy and praise of God. "Thou hast made us for Thyself," wrote St. Augustine, "and our heart is restless till it rests in Thee."

But so long as death remains, there is no rest for anyone; no Father's gracious heart to turn to and find gladness and life; no form that is permanent; no tenderness or beauty that stays the same. All is gone quickly, for death is a robber who knows the way to every man's house of life and takes what is precious in it. He takes affection from Mary; makes it necessary for the Redeemer to give up His spirit — the only thing He still possesses — and abandons Jesus' naked self to the grave. Death is man's first and last enemy, the rapacious intruder in God's world. He is Satan's ultimate weapon, the cutting edge of sin. For if sin separates man from the goodness, love, and power of his Creator, death, if it remains in control, makes the cut deep and final. Until a power greater than Satan, sin, and death appears, Mary must go on weeping, and the whole sinful world must weep with her.

But He who is greater than death, Satan's Lord and sin's Conqueror, has come to Mary and to us all. Heavenly messengers could not convince Mary, and angels may not impress us to dry our tears. Only the voice of Him who was dead and is alive forevermore can speak to our sad mortality and quicken us to hope and new being. It was enough that Jesus called Mary by name; the sound of His word was power. For this was the voice of Him who made heaven and earth, and He was also Mary's Lord and Savior. On Sunday in the garden she knew the meaning of His love as she had not know it before.

When He hung on the cross she had seen Him as an object of her love and as a hapless, helpless victim of death. What she did not understand on Friday was that both in life and in death she was the object of His love. Jesus was God's elect, suffering Servant, of whom it had been prophesied: ". . . He was cut off out of the land of the living; for the transgressions of my people was He stricken. And He made His grave with the wicked, and with the rich in His death, because He had done no violence, neither was any deceit in His mouth." Yes, that is the reason for His death: ". . . for the transgressions of my people was He stricken." No victim of death is He, nor helpless on the cross. He is the true Son of man appointed by God to fulfill all righteousness in our stead. Joyfully and freely He is obedient to the Father's will even when this means dying for the unrighteous and disobedient. In God's foreordained plan the cross redeems the world from sin. There Jesus is revealed as God's Christ, the Victor, who destroys sin by atoning for it. He covers the past ages of mankind's defiance of God with his life and death, and so He breaks Satan's power to accuse man before God.

The last enemy to be overcome is death. With sin forgiven and Satan cast down, death, too, must lose its venomous sting. It cannot separate the Son from His Father. On Sunday the Father commands, and the chains of death are loosed from Jesus' body in the grave, and He takes up His life. First He must go to proclaim God's victorious and saving deed to those who do not know it. Thus He comes to Mary, who sits literally in the shadow of death at the graveside. She who believed in death must be first to believe in the resurrection and life.

Shall we believe the truth of the resurrection and life less than she did? Is not our need to believe the Word of the risen Lord Christ more than hers? Almost 21 centuries of sinning have been added to mankind's guilt since she wept in the garden. The long ages of evil have left their mark deep and cumulative upon us and our world. Though our sophisticated generation would like to deny it, we have more reason than any previous one in history to recognize the presence of demonic elements that seek to dominate and possess life. And where there are devils, there will be sin and death. The facts are so patent that one does not have to be a professional historian to substantiate the claim.

Depressing as are the facts of life and history at this time, the Easter story breaks upon our world as the living Word of God, reminding us that this very year and these very circumstances are redeemed by the Lordship of Christ. It is not without reason that we call all time since He appeared the year of our Lord. Mary's story is divine revelation calling us to believe that the sign of the cross still exorcises all evil spirits. The power of evil is broken and defeated by Jesus. D-day has happened at Golgotha, and the decisive battle has been won. The crucified and risen Christ is Lord of life because He has overcome death. God is for us; who can be against us? Christ lives and intercedes for us; who can accuse us?

Why do we sit today in the world's graveyard fearing that death will rob us of what is precious in life? weeping because death will bury us? Have we not already been buried with Christ by Baptism into his death? Then we have died to sin. Now let us also rise with him in joy. The past is finished and gone. Its sins are forgiven, and we are justified. Everything has become fresh and new. The end for the child of God is really his beginning.

The new age is upon us, and blind and faithless we are if we do not read the signs of the times. The evil spirits of our time will and must disappear before the presence of the Holy One of God. With the Gospel of Good Friday and Easter He will slay the enemies, and He will reign forever and ever. Take heart, all sad ones, all who are anxious, live in fear, and dread before death, know that your sins are forgiven. You are alive with God's life and breath, which cannot be taken from you. By faith in Christ you are the firstfruits of God's new heaven and new earth. Then live as new creatures, for He has come who calls you by name and promises: "I am the Resurrection and the Life. He that believeth in Me, though he were dead, yet shall he live; and whosoever liveth and believeth in Me shall never die."

Truly, Christ, our Passover, is sacrificed for us. Let us keep the eternal feast of Easter, not with the old leaven of death working fear and trembling in us. But let us draw near, our heart assured by grace, eat and be filled with the living Bread that came from heaven. Let us raise high the cup filled with the blood of our Lord and say, "I will take the cup of salvation and call upon the name of the Lord."

For all things are ours — whether the world, or life, or death, or things present, or things to come — all are ours — because we are Christ's, and Christ is God's.

For out of darkness shall come dawn, out of winter shall come spring, out of striving shall come peace, out of death shall come life — not by our power, but by the power of God.

Unnecessary Tears

By WALTER J. WARNECK

(Easter Monday)

But Mary stood without at the sepulchre weeping; and as she wept, she stooped down, and looked into the sepulchre, And seeth two angels in white sitting, the one at the head, and the other at the feet, where the body of Jesus had lain. And they say unto her, Woman, why weepest thou? She saith unto them, Because they have taken away my Lord, and I know not where they have laid Him. And when she had thus said, she turned herself back, and saw Jesus standing, and knew not that it was Jesus. Jesus saith unto her, Woman, why weepest thou? whom seekest thou? She, supposing Him to be the gardener, saith unto Him, Sir, if thou have borne Him hence, tell me where thou hast laid Him, and I will take Him away. Jesus saith unto her, Mary. She turned herself, and saith unto Him, Rabboni; which is to say, Master. Jesus saith unto her, Touch Me not; for I am not yet ascended to My Father; but go to My brethren, and say unto them, I ascend unto My Father, and your Father, and to My God, and your God. Mary Magdalene came and told the disciples that she had seen the Lord, and that He had spoken these things unto her. — *John 20:11-18*

Our blessed Lord in accordance with His omniscient and there- fore unerring wisdom in various places in the Holy Scriptures describes our present place of habitation as a veritable vale of tears. Of course, as always, He is correct, because if there has ever been anything that every person on earth has done at some time or other in his life, it is to cry. According to every hope and wish of parents and attendants, a newborn babe is expected to cry. As a matter of fact, if this is not spontaneous the physician will take measures to see to it that it occurs. A little child sitting on the living-room floor and playing with a balloon will suddenly prick the rubber with its sharp little fingernails; the balloon will burst with a resounding noise; and the child will cry. Indeed, there are tears of various types: tears of joy, tears of sadness, tears of pain, and tears of a broken heart; there are a thousand and one causes for tears. The psalmist often cried out to God for grief because of his sins. Simon Peter wept because of his denials. Jesus wept over Jerusalem. There is simply no end to the shedding of tears in this world.

But there are some tears that are unnecessary. There are some for which there is no sufficient basis or cause. Indeed, there are some tears shed for sorrow which should really be tears shed for joy. And this is the sort which we observe in our text. Jesus here declares that Mary Magdalene was weeping

Unnecessary Tears

I

The Occasion for Her Tears

It was early on resurrection day when Mary cried. And you and I who are able to look back upon almost 2,000 years of New Testament history know there was no real reason for Mary Magdalene to cry. But she was not aware of this. She had been one of those women who had gone in that early dawn to the sepulchre expecting to do for Jesus' body the final kindness of preparing it for its "repose," as we say, "in the bosom of the earth." But they found the grave had been opened, and the body of Jesus was not there. She had rushed back to the city of Jerusalem to tell His disciples Peter and John. These two faithful followers had run to the grave and found it as she had said. Indeed, they had looked into the tomb and seen the grave clothes lying there and the napkin that had been wound about His head neatly folded and placed in the corner of the sepulchre. Angels, moreover, had told the women that the Lord Jesus was risen again from the dead.

But Mary was too confused and saddened to be able to grasp the full import of their wondrous pronouncement. After reporting to the disciples she began to run back to the sepulchre with them. She apparently was not able to keep up with them. By the time she arrived they had already left. Mary now broke down and cried. She laid her head against the cold stone wall and poured out her distress in tears. For because the grave was empty, the whole world was empty for her too. She was unable to concentrate on the words of the angels. They had spoken to her and said, "Woman, why weepest thou?" But her grief was so great she could not respond even to the fact that they were angels. At first we hear that the women, including Mary Magdalene, when they saw the angels of the Lord, were affrighted. But Jesus' devoted follower now was beyond that. All she could feel was grief. The dead Christ was more to her than a living world.

In answer to the angels she said, "Because they have taken away my Lord and I know not where they have laid Him" (v. 13). When she previously had reported to the disciples she had said, "They have taken away *the* Lord out of the sepulchre, and *we* know not where they have laid Him" (v. 2). But now her sorrow is more personal and intense for she is alone and she significantly changes the pronouns and says, "*my* Lord," and "*I* know not where they have laid Him." The whole great wide world could forget Him. Yes, even the disciples could leave the sepulchre, but not she. She returned, as love will do, to seek and to seek and to search once again. She went from one place to another. She looked first here and then there. And finally she came back to the place where she had searched before. She simply could not reconcile herself to a loss so total that she would not again be able to regain His presence in any way. And so she said, "they have taken away *my* Lord," as if no one could feel the bereavement that she did.

II

The Folly of Her Grief

But that grief (as sometimes our grief in this world too) was unnecessary, because now a magnificent awakening occurred. Jesus appeared to her. Precious Savior that He is, He could not have kept himself away from her any more than He could have kept Himself from His heavenly Father for whom He also had an exceedingly great love. Indeed, He would look for and find her even though she could not find Him. She had been looking for a dead Christ. And for this reason she could not find Him. But He could find her. And this He did. He stood behind her. And in His first recorded words after His resurrection He said to her, "Woman, why weepest thou? Whom seekest thou?" (V. 15.) And although she had sensed that someone stood behind her, as we often do, yet she did not recognize Him. She thought He was the gardener and said (not in answer to His question, but as if she thought He should know what she was looking for, because who could look for anything else?), "Sir, if thou have borne Him hence, tell me where thou hast laid Him and I will take Him away" (v. 15). That is, she would remove the precious body which they could not let rest. She would relieve them of the responsibility of caring for it. Yes, she would do for Christ what she thought no one else would. And so Jesus addressed her with that one single word, "Mary" — that one personally directed and recognizable name — *her* name. And Mary now immediately recognized Jesus. She bounded forward and cried, "Rabonni, which is to say, Master" (v. 16). She clutched for His garments to hold on to Him, not to let Him go again. She supposed she could cling to Him and no one would ever again cause her such grief.

While she was standing at the sepulchre she no doubt had wondered, as oftentimes people of our day also do, why she had ever been so foolish, so heartless, and so inconsiderate and lacking in love that she had left the tomb at all; why had she allowed herself to become separated from Christ for even a few hours. She no doubt thought that if she had been present perhaps she could have prevented the tomb from being emptied. But she had failed. And she could not fill it again. The body of Jesus had disappeared. And her grief had mounted higher and higher.

Mary, a Type of Believers Today

But what a picture we have of ourselves in Mary! We see how we often look for a dead Christ, too, and are not able to find Him. And how we drift away from Him because we fail to see that He lives for us. The Christ we confess, we feel is a Christ who lived so many, many centuries ago. Oh, to be sure, He was a wonderful Jesus. The record of what He did, what He taught, what He said, and how He suffered moves us and impresses us very deeply. In spirit we have again stood before the cross on Calvary; we saw His awful and willing giving of Himself to the shame of crucifixion for our sins. We were moved to a great and true repentance for our guilt and our transgressions. We may even have decided that we would serve Him as we have never served Him before. But that is where our grief oftentimes stops. We do not realize that He is alive. We know He promised to be with His disciples even to the end of the world. But we forget Him. The pressure of living, our job, our recreation, our pleasure, our chores are not shared with Christ. On the contrary some are shared rather with the devil. And so sometimes we fall into grief and despair.

How a person must feel who has not kept in close communion with our heavenly Father and with Jesus Christ our Savior! He may have lost a dear one in death, let us say, and he realizes that he did not do all in his power to bring that poor soul to Christ. He may once have regularly given himself to quiet hours of contemplation, to prayers, and to services that were devoted to Jesus, but these for a long period of time have been left to lie as empty as the cold and pale forms of those linen clothes that were left lying in Jesus' sepulchre. In short, such a one once may have been a true child of God, but he began to drift. And now his grief, like Mary's, is intense and he has to weep because he fears he has lost Christ.

Mary's Error Corrected

But this is not necessary and these tears are needless because Jesus is alive. He says to Mary, "Touch Me not." That is, hold Me not, prevent Me not. "For I am not yet ascended to My Father; but go to My brethren, and say unto them, I ascend unto My Father, and unto your Father; and to My God, and your God" (v. 17). To be sure Jesus did not in these words rebuke His loving follower for wishing to cling to Him. He doesn't say, "You wicked person, get away from Me." No, for she was doing this without a clear understanding of how He could be with her and with us now. She thought He could visibly be present again from then on.

All sorts of conjectures, of course, have been offered as to the purpose for which our dear Lord spoke these words, "Touch Me not." Some have said that He objected to her touch because it would have been indecorous. That is, that it would have been shocking to the world for her to take Him into her arms. But Jesus did not raise this objection when at a dinner table a woman kissed His feet, scandalizing the guests and provoking the suspicions of the host. Some say she wished to assure herself by touch of the reality of His appearance and they object to this. But this was surely not necessary, for she could see Him. Nor did Jesus object to touch for this reason, because in the case of the other disciples such as Thomas and the rest, He actually wished it and encouraged it saying, "Handle Me and see; for a spirit hath not flesh and bones, as ye see Me have" (Luke 24: 39). Nor did He speak these words, as some have maintained, because this embrace would have disturbed the process of glorification of His body.

No, but Jesus very likely said these words, "Touch Me not," because Mary had made a mistake. She thought she could keep Him with her just as He was; that the "little while" of which Jesus had spoken had come to an end and that she could now keep Him with her in His physical and visible presence as He had been before. But Jesus tells her this cannot be, for He must ascend to His Father. That is, He must go to the Lord, and we who love Him on earth must learn to live without the actual seeing, touching, and hearing of our well-known Master. We may no more kiss His feet and anoint His head with oil and serve Him with food and the like. There must be no more sitting at His feet, as the sister of Martha did, to hang on His every spoken word. No, this can come again only when we sit down with Him in the kingdom of heaven. But there is an homage of a deeper sort — we should trust and believe in Him whether we are able to see Him or not. This is what Jesus wanted to teach Mary and us.

III

Our Tears of Joy, a Reason for Service

And if these words of Jesus at first seem sort of hard for us
to bear, if it seems to us that it could have been otherwise and
that Jesus should have stayed with us visibly on earth so we
could believe — if we cry for this reason, then let us remember
that even these tears are needless, because Mary did not feel
that way. No, she left immediately as one who had a message
to tell, as one who had something to do for her weak, doubtful,
and sinful fellow human beings. Jesus had said to her, "Go to
my brethren, and say unto them, I ascend unto My Father and
to your Father and to My God and your God" (v. 17). And Mary
was willing to carry out this command. She left the sepulchre
and our Savior as hastily now and surely even more excitedly
than she had before, because this time she had a different message
to bring. Indeed, it was a message of joy and of happiness and
not of tears. She had the message that you and I should bring
to a grieving, confused, and dying world, too.

And what is that message? Why, it is that God is not a God
and a Father of Jesus Christ only, but that He is a God and
Father of us, too; that through this risen and now ascended Lord
Jesus we are made the children of God and heirs of God's
kingdom of heaven; that there is a reconciliation for us before God
and that one day we shall be reunited with our Savior visibly
in the realm where with glorified bodies and eyes we shall see
Him. This is what He means. Jesus' love binds us as strongly
to Him as His rights carry Him to the Father. And He can
abandon us as little as God the Father could refuse to own Him
as His Son. All this Jesus means to say when He declares,
"Touch Me not, for I am not yet ascended unto My Father,
but go and tell My brethren," etc.

Mary's joy can easily be understood. Once before by the
smile of Jesus she had been awakened out of the foul pit into
which the evil spirits which possessed her had cast her. And
now the precious presence of Jesus had again awakened her to
His Savior love. Therefore she is not only joyful but eager to
tell of her Lord. And has this not happened to us? How deeply
into degradation and sin have we fallen; how bitter and hot
have been our tears as we once again during the past season of
Lent saw the evils we have done. But the Lord Jesus lives.
He has removed our sins and transgressions from us. He arose
from the dead. Our heavenly Father was willing to receive Him.
And we are the happiest people in the world. Yes, He has
called us by our names. He has said, Mary, John, Jim, Jane,

can you not see Me? When we are deeply burdened by grief, by sin, by illness, or even by a death, Jesus brings us the assurance that all is not ended, but that He will make our joy to be full. He says, "I shall go before you into Galilee, too."

Let us not ever leave this true and personal relationship with Christ. Let us not become so busy with the things of this world, so preoccupied with life and so devoted to sin that we cannot hear our name called. No, like Mary, when Jesus does call us may it be necessary for Him to call but once. And let us recognize Him. Yes, let us go even as she did and tell the brethren. Let us be active in the work of the kingdom of God. And let us shed no more tears because we despair of Christ's presence. No, let us realize that all such tears are needless tears indeed, because Jesus our Savior lives.

Fishing on the Right Side

By CLARENCE H. PAULING

(Quasimodogeniti)

After these things Jesus showed Himself again to the disciples at the sea of Tiberias; and on this wise showed He Himself. There were together Simon Peter, and Thomas called Didymus, and Nathanael of Cana in Galilee, and the sons of Zebedee, and two other of His disciples. Simon Peter saith unto them, I go a fishing. They say unto him, We also go with thee. They went forth, and entered into a ship immediately; and that night they caught nothing. But when the morning was now come, Jesus stood on the shore; but the disciples knew not that it was Jesus. Then Jesus saith unto them, Children, have ye any meat? They answered him, No. And He said unto them, Cast the net on the right side of the ship, and ye shall find. They cast therefore, and now they were not able to draw it for the multitude of fishes. Therefore that disciple whom Jesus loved saith unto Peter, It is the Lord. Now when Simon Peter heard that it was the Lord, he gird his fisher's coat unto him (for he was naked), and did cast himself into the sea. And the other disciples came in a little ship (for they were not far from land, but as it were two hundred cubits), dragging the net with fishes. As soon then as they were come to land, they saw a fire of coals there, and fish laid thereon, and bread. Jesus saith unto them, Bring of the fish which ye have now caught. Simon Peter went up, and drew the net to land full of great fishes, an hundred and fifty and three; and for all there were so many, yet was not the net broken. Jesus saith unto them, Come and dine. And none of the disciples durst ask Him, Who art Thou? knowing that it was the Lord. Jesus then cometh, and taketh bread, and giveth them, and fish likewise. This is now the third time that Jesus showed Himself to His disciples, after that He was risen from the dead. — *John 21:1-14*

I'm glad that John did not lay away his "pen" after he had finished chapter 20 of his Gospel. He might have, because he had come to the climax of his message to posterity after he had substantiated the resurrection of Jesus by reporting the personal appearances of Jesus, which had satisfied even the profound doubt of Thomas. The concluding two verses of chapter 20 even sound like a summary. (Read vv. 30 and 31.) See? John had proved his point, for he, like all the witnesses for Christ in their endeavors, also aimed to establish that Jesus was the Son of God and Savior of mankind. But as stated before, I'm glad that John added what some like to call a "postscript", a "P. S.", to his story, because it is so rich in instruction and comfort for any follower of Christ. It gives us vital information about after-Easter living. You see, just as the Gospel of John does not end with the proof that Jesus is God and Lord, so the Christians' Easter experience does not end with the conviction of the mind that the resurrection of Jesus is well documented, but the thought must permeate their lives and make them think and act and behave like people who are sure that Jesus rose from the dead; this conviction is to be completely mixed into all their experiences and activities.

In order to connect this thought with the story of our text, we would like to title our message

Fishing on the Right Side

Bill and Tom are trying to keep warm as they carefully watch the bobber on their fishing line in the hole cut into the ice of the lake. They are about 300 feet from shore in front of Bill's uncle's cabin at a spot where during the summer they had fabulous success in fishing. But now it is quite different! Tom is discouraged after freezing out there several hours with not even a nibble. Just then a resort owner comes by and asks the embarrassing question, "Any luck?" Upon Tom's disgusted "Naw," the stranger says that they are fishing on the wrong side of the lake. "In winter," he says, "the fish are way on the other side; where you see those fish houses." After thanking the man, the boys pick up their gear and start out for the other side. They are delighted to find that their luck changes; they catch fish because now they are *fishing on the right side*.

I

As It Pertained to the Disciples

Their Resolve to Go Fishing

Peter was a man of *action*. He hated to sit around doing nothing. That's why he whipped out his sword when he thought Jesus needed defending in the Garden. That's why he dared to step on the waves of Lake Galilee when he recognized Jesus walking on the water. He was always quick to speak, and usually just as quick to act. "I'm going fishing," he announces to his friends. They do not hesitate to agree, "We'll go with you."

Their Secret Thoughts

It's interesting, and harmless in this case, to speculate what the thoughts of Peter and the disciples were at this time. Their spirits had been on a "roller-coaster" these past three weeks. They were up in the clouds while they were with Jesus, heard His inspiring messages, and saw His amazing miracles. Then on Maundy Thursday night their faith "hit the skids," so to speak, and by Good Friday night it had hit the bottom of the "slough of despond." Jesus was dead, and so were their hopes and aspirations. But the smoking flax began to flicker again when reports came to their ears about the Lord's resurrection. The spark became a flame when they saw Jesus in person. But Jesus left them again, even after His second appearance to the group; although He made a formal appointment with them for some later indefinite time, the common opinion among them was that He would soon leave them altogether. Jesus had encouraged them to pray and wait. But even followers of Jesus sometimes get tired of just praying and waiting. At least Peter's patience was too short. Whether it was an attempt to dispel his discouragement, or to break his boredom, or just to be a good steward of time and earn a few dollars while waiting for clear directions, Peter decided to do something on his own. The plan and program of Jesus was a puzzle to him. But he did know something about fishing. So away he went to resume his former trade, at least temporarily; six of his friends went along.

Failure Versus Success

Impatience led them to failure. In spite of strenuous effort their nets remained empty. In their hands they had only blisters for their hard work. They were fishing on the wrong side, because their work was not yet Christ-directed. They were not even cognizant of the Lord's invisible presence. Their embarrassment is intensified by the solicitous question of a stranger on shore. "Boys, did you catch anything?" he asks. In one emphatic word they admit their failure. "No! . . . ." But the stranger has a word of advice even for these expert fishermen. It's simple but effective. "Fish on the *right* side." It takes humility for them to follow such simple advice. . . . It was hard for Naaman to swallow his pride and wash in the waters of Jordan upon the advice of Elisha. . . . However, the results were rewarding. So also the result of the disciples' humble obedience was fruitful beyond all expectations. They make a miraculous catch of fish; without breaking their nets they land 153 "great" fish, which meant food for their mouths and money in their purse. Best of all, prompted by John, they recognize Christ, and their response is joyous. Peter, man of action, impatient, impetuous, jumps into the water and swims to shore.

The rest immediately pull to shore. All of them are breakfast guests of the Savior, who demonstrates His provident care and love for them, and while stilling the hunger of their bodies soon lifts their drooping spirits and strengthens their faltering faith by His hospitality, His magnetic presence, and His stimulating conversation. The fog and clouds of gloom and failure suddenly are lifted and the morning is bright with the joy of success and security in the holy presence of the abiding, living Savior. All this — and more, because they had fished on the right side, where Jesus had directed them to fish. What they learned during this thrilling visit with the risen Lord helped sustain their faith and restore their trust in the Lord until they were completely filled with the Holy Spirit on Pentecost.

II

As It Pertains to Us

EASTER MORNING

This is the beauty of our Easter morning:
In Him humanity may now arise
Out of the grave of self, all baseness scorning;
The holy radiance of His glorious eyes
Illumines everywhere uplifted faces,
Touches the earthly with a heavenly glow,
And in that blessed light all human graces
Into divine beatitudes must grow.   Lucy Larcom

Our Proneness to Fruitless Fishing

The inspirations and thrills of Lent, Good Friday, and Easter notwithstanding, our faith often rides on a "merry-go-round" too. We nod willing approval to all the ponderous truths we have heard. We deny any doubt in the Resurrection and in the Savior's presence in our hearts and lives, but — we still talk and act as though Jesus were still in the grave. Easter morning is bright and thrilling for us too, in that it fills us with the glorious determination to show that the old man within us has been drowned and that there has been a resurrection, a rising to new life within our souls. But alas, the night of gloom, indifference, and careless living settles upon us all too soon. We forget the message of the risen Christ so quickly. We lose the consciousness of His almighty presence so easily. How can there be gloom in the presence of a victorious Lord and Redeemer? How can there be apathy in the loving presence of Him, who cared so much that He died to rescue us from our souls' most frightening fate, damnation! Yet we are prone to cast our spiritual nets in the wrong places and on the wrong side. Therefore our nets are empty. More than that! Our nets are often worse than empty, because they are filled with soul parasites, such as discouragement, worry, fretfulness, unkindness, dishonesty, impurity, and disloyalty. Without the assurance and consciousness of the Lord's presence it is a long, dark, miserable night of unhappy, fruitless living.

A Voice of Encouragement

So this morning, by the grace of God, the Master stands on the shore of our lives and asks, "Boys, girls, how's fishing? Any luck?" He means, "Are you really getting anything worthwhile out of life as you are living it?" He reminds us that He has come that we might have life — not a life of sin and disappointment, but the abundant life. Once our heart admits that we have tried to live our lives as directed by ourselves instead of as directed by Christ, and that this has been the cause of our failure, the Savior through His Word will show us where to cast the net for the blessings He has provided for us through His redemptive life, death, and resurrection. He says, "Cast the net where I tell you."

Abundant Blessings

What a difference it makes when the living Christ enters our troubled hearts and trembling souls to stay. What a difference when our spirits realize that Jesus has taken over, that He stands on the shore directing, watching our weatherbeaten craft as it struggles and tosses on "life's tempestuous sea," and that He is waiting for us to be His grateful guests and to partake of heavenly provisions, which He has Himself prepared. Humbly obedient we will then cast our nets on the *other* side, not where we think, but where He commands; and things really begin to happen.

Our nets are no longer empty, life is no longer boring, or meaningless, or burdensome. Each moment of it will reveal a blessing. The delectable meat of faith, purity, kindness, honesty, happiness, courage, hope, and peace, all that our nets can hold, will show His blessings upon us. With overwhelming joy our souls will cry, "It is the Lord!" With John we will love Him more than ever before; with Peter, we will want to get closer to Him than ever before; with all the disciples, we will not have to ask, "Who art Thou?" We know now that He lives and is with us always. Life takes a new turn. We surrender it to the pierced hand of our Savior. We never forget the misery and failure that were ours when we were "fishing" on the wrong side, without Christ, and our heart says, "From this day on I will fish where He directs me." That will change everything in our lives — our personal relationship with God, our relationship with our fellowmen, our relationship with the Lord's kingdom.

Do you ask "How does 'fishing on the right side' affect these areas of my life?" Good, I'm glad you asked. The Lord wants this message to be of practical value to you.

Keeping Our Values Straight

Whether you think so or not, your soul's relationship to God, the way you feel in your heart toward your God, is the most important part of your life. Oh, it's hard to accept that, particularly since we are more and more surrounded and infiltrated by secularism and materialism. The one tries to get us to rule God out of our lives altogether and the other tends to make us ascribe greater value to the tangible and visible things of this world than to the invisible things that pertain to God and our soul. The more we listen to the false philosophies of the world, the more surely we are "fishing on the wrong side," and the more futile and fruitless our life becomes.

"Fishing on the Wrong Side" in Soul Relationship with God

Test yourself, my friend. Ask yourself a few frank questions. Just how much does God mean to you? How important is it really to you that Jesus was born, that He died, and that He rose again? It depends on how well you know God and yourself. If you don't recognize yourself as a lost sinner, and therefore do not recognize Jesus as your Savior, you are fishing on the wrong side. Jesus might just as well still be buried. If you are still conceited enough to think that your own efforts and virtues and intentions contribute to your salvation, and Jesus is not your ONLY hope for heaven's glory, you are dragging your net through empty waters. If you bristle every time your sins are pointed out to you, and you think you are better than other people, or if you think your sin is not serious and that damnation is not real you are not living a Christ-directed life. If you don't take God's Word seriously (each one of the Ten Commandments, and every promise of the Gospel); if you think that you can eat from the fleshpots of lust and sinful pleasures and still have Christ as your Bread of life; and if you think that you need not surrender to Christ completely, but expect Him to be satisfied with the dregs of your service while you offer the full cup of yourself, your time, talents, and treasure in service to the world and its fiendish prince, your soul is still shrouded in night and death.

Success Upon Changing Sides

Jesus confronts you with the startling question: "Friend, any luck in worthwhile living?" "Try fishing on the right side where I direct!" You do this and your soul says with sincerity, "I was lost, but Jesus found me; I was filthy with sin, but Jesus cleansed me; I believe that Jesus is my only hope, and the only way to eternal life is through His cross; I believe He is my Savior; His promises are true, every one of them, and if I make Him my Lord and surrender myself, body and soul, to Him, He will take me

to Heaven, because He loves me." Friend, your soul is fishing
on the right side when you follow unfailingly wise directions. Your
net will be filled with every good, peace, hope, assurance, and
joy in godly living.

"Fishing on the Wrong Side" in Family Relationships

Think of your relationship with your fellowmen, at home,
at work, and at play. If your marriage and home are built and
maintained on a shaky foundation, without Christ as the cornerstone (and by that I mean that God's Word has no prominent
place); when there is no family altar, no grace at meals; when
children are religiously given their "shots" and vitamins for the
body, but little concern is shown for the needs of their souls; when
Santa and Huckleberry Hound and Dennis the Menace are given
more prominence than Jesus; when the house is littered with
much-read comics and sensational and off-color literature, but
the Bible lies dusty on the shelf and Christian literature remains
unread — then the net of life will very likely be filled with the
rough fish of hatred, dishonesty, unfaithfulness, drunkenness, cursing, selfishness, worry, and disgrace. Actually the net is empty,
because the life is fruitless and Christ's living, cleansing presence
is not felt.

"Fishing on the Wrong and Right Sides" in Other Social Relationships

The same sterility and fruitlessness will characterize your relationship with other people, at work, at play, and in society in general. Oh, you may make good money, rise high in status, have
fun, and be considered successful by men, but God will pronounce
you a failure unless you follow *Christian* principles, which glorify
the Father and add to your own spiritual stature.

(Elaborate, or adapt to needs.) If your life is not a witness
to the power of Christ dwelling in you, you can be sure, you are
fishing on the wrong side. "Cast your net on the right side," says
your risen Master today, "and you shall find." Make it plain to all
who hear or see you that it is always Easter morning in your soul
and that your soul has seen the risen Christ. Your life will be one
brilliant reflection of your Savior's *love.*

Empty Nets in Church Life

Our post-Easter living should also influence our relationship
with our church and her work. Evidences of fishing on the right
side in this realm are shown in various ways. If our church attendance has priority listing on Sundays instead of being forced to give
way to interests which God would never accept as valid substitutes;
if we are aggravated by the demands Kingdom work makes upon

our time, talents, and treasure, instead of offering them cheerfully
and gratefully for the Lord's use, we are ignoring the living Christ
standing on the shore, anxious to direct us. Should we belong
to that increasing multitude, who consider the church's function
important only for three contacts in life (as Readers Digest once
put it, when one is "hatched, matched, and dispatched"), and consider a church member's function primarily that of putting the
church on the map of the world rather than putting Christ into the
hearts of people, we are casting our nets in wrong places and can
expect to gather only such worthless things as bickering, distrust,
doubt, and careless living. Even with all the lights on, the risen
Christ is not seen or heard or even wanted in His own house.

The Net Filled

Christ exalted pleads with us today, "Follow my direction and
you shall reap fruit a hundredfold." He bids us be aware and
appreciative that we are members of the body of Christ and that
as such we accept Him as our Head joyfully, do His bidding un-
questioningly, serve Him unstintingly, and love Him immeasurably.
Such lives will yield to Him a soul repentant, a heart faithful,
a service consecrated.

FOR RESURRECTION LIVING

For resurrection living
There is resurrection power,
And the praise and prayer of trusting
May glorify each hour.
For common days are holy,
And years an Eastertide
To those who with the living Lord
In living faith abide.   — Author Unknown

The Disciples Satisfied

The text states that having drawn their richly filled nets to
shore, the disciples enjoyed the comforts which Jesus had provided.
There was fire to warm them, food to still their hunger, comfort
and rest in His presence for their weary minds and hearts.

We Shall Be Satisfied

So also after our term of fishing on the Lord's side is done, and
we have joyfully drawn our nets, laden with soul-blessings, to
eternity's shore, Christ will be there to offer the warmth of His
love to us weary pilgrims at Heaven's sacred fires. Our hunger
will be stilled at the Bridegroom's wedding feast, and our burdens
lifted as we rest in His bosom.

We have felt His presence while living here; there we shall
see Him always, face to face, because there will be no longer
a "wrong side." Hallelujah.

The Work of Christ for Our Salvation Stands Divinely Approved

By GILBERT T. OTTE

(Misericordias Domini)

Therefore doth My Father love Me, because I lay down My life that I might take it again. No man taketh it from Me, but I lay it down of Myself. I have power to lay it down, and I have power to take it again. This commandment have I received of My Father. There was a division therefore again among the Jews for these sayings. And many of them said, He hath a devil and is mad; why hear ye Him? Others said, These are not the words of him that hath a devil. Can a devil open the eyes of the blind? — *John 10:17-21*

In a letter written to his son at Oxford University, Archbishop Temple referred to the poet Coleridge's speculations about the Holy Trinity: "I am obliged to confess that from 15 to 17 I indulged largely in such speculations. But I felt all along like a swimmer who sees no shore before him after long swimming, and at last allows himself to be picked up by a ship that seems to be going his way. My passing ship was St. John's Gospel."

There are many who have similarly found the fourth gospel in the New Testament to take hold of them as no other portion of the New Testament has done. Or from the words of the first chapter: "We beheld His glory, the glory as of the Only-Begotten of the Father, full of grace and truth" the conviction grows on the open-minded reader that Jesus Christ is truly God. Ponder His majestic words about His being the Bread of Life come down from heaven, or His being the Light, which lighteth every man that cometh into the world! Ponder His manifestation of superhuman power at the grave of Lazarus. All Christ's words and works recorded in the Gospel According to St. John impel us to declare of our blesesd Savior:

> Thou art the King of glory, O Christ.
> Thou art the everlasting Son of the Father.

Yes, sure conviction, blessed assurance, come into our hearts and minds as we absorb more and more of this Word of life. Particularly those sublime truths dealing with the facts of Good Friday and of Easter, which cast their healing and enlightening beams over us during this season of the Christian year, become all the more true and unshakable to us: Christ Crucified and Risen *is* our perfect, divine Savior from sin. He *is* the winner of our eternal salvation. That fact should make us thoroughly happy and unafraid. It should give us an enduringly joyous religion.

Our text from the glorious Gospel According to St. John guarantees that

The Work of Christ for Our Salvation Stands Divinely Approved

I

It Is the Work Not of a Mere Man but of the Eternal Son of God

Our text concludes the utterance of our Lord following His miraculous restoration of sight to the man born blind, the beggar who had sat for so long at the temple gate asking alms. Because this man gratefully confessed Christ as Savior and Benefactor before the leaders of the Jewish church he was forthwith excommunicated. In his distress he turned to Christ for spiritual refuge and direction. In a spiritual as well as physical sense the man could say "One thing I know, that, whereas I was blind, NOW I SEE!" (John 9:25)

We have just come through the high, holy days of Lent, Holy Week, and Easter. Again and again there have been occasions to observe that some churchmen are still as perplexed as Pilate: "What shall I do with Jesus?" The golden opportunity which this sacred season provides them to search the Scriptures and to set forth its Christ as the very Son of God and Redeemer of all sinners is so tragically muffed. Hundreds of attendants at noonday or evening Lenten services come away wondering what Lent is all about and what significance Christ has for the modern world. Alas, that from so many pulpits and altars the testimony is not given as it should be to the Christ who emphatically taught His own deity and proved it, who stood up to His gainsayers that were about to have Him crucified and said they would never be able to kill Him if He did not allow them to, that His life was His to lay down and to take back as He wished. Who but God could say such a thing? Yet there are countless churches that keep on silencing this basic truth, that undermine the validity of Christ's word and work by making of Him only a good man, a social reformer, an example. This relegates Him to the hall of fame of the world's great men along with philosophers, scientists, inventors, statesmen; this ranks the sayings of Jesus with the meditations of Marcus Aurelius, the sensual fancies of Mohammed, and the plays of Shakespeare.

Oh, it may be popular to water down the doctrine of Holy Writ that Christ is the Son of God and that His Word is the divine truth, all of it; that He was no mere victim of circumstances when He was nailed to the cross of Calvary but the very Savior of the world by determinate foreknowledge and providence of God; that because the blood He shed on Calvary was the blood of the Son of God it has the divine authority and power to cleanse us from all sins; that somehow the continuous witness to the Savior by the evangelists, apostles, and martyrs is to be ignored as an ecstatic overstatement. But with such satanic perversion we do not go along. Let the world go on spurning our divine Lord and Savior as did the blaspheming Jews who said, "He hath a devil and is mad; why hear ye Him?" Christ is the incarnate God-man; Christ is the only Savior and Mediator for all men. That remains our confession.

> There was no other good enough
> To pay the price of sin,
> He only could unlock the gate
> Of heaven and let us in.

II

It Was Carried Through to Completion by Christ Under Direct Commission of His Heavenly Father

If Christ our dear Lord were not what the inspired and inerrant Scriptures present Him to be, the divine Savior, who effected a perfect redemption, then Christianity would be a fraud, and all the faith of centuries of believers in the Gospel would be in vain. But this whole matter of His incarnation for the express purpose of redeeming the world from sin was no accident or a theory of men. "Christ Jesus came into this world to save sinners." In our text Jesus plainly states that His heavenly Father destined Him to become the Savior of men, that He was to give His life for men and take it back again, die as the Bearer of all men's guilt and punishment but rise again to prove that God the Father recognized His death as full atonement, as securing reconciliation forever between God and man. Christ's giving His life and His taking it again, His death and resurrection, give us a certified Christianity, an accredited salvation. With these two basic facts Christianity stands or falls.

Christ was either the Son of God and the Savior of the world as He claimed to be or a base deceiver. But in the latter case God would surely not have raised Him to life again and helped perpetuate a fraud. What hopeless creatures we would be if Christ had not laid down His life for us and had not taken it again. Above all else we wish to have the assurance that our account with God has been settled, that in Jesus we do have THE Savior, who wholly atoned for all of our sins, winning God's forgiveness of them all and with that our eternal life and salvation. Precisely this is what Holy Scripture assures us of. This is the very plan of God for our salvation, the plan that God carried through.

III

It Was All Done by Christ Voluntarily to the Full Satisfaction of the Father

This blessed assurance that we are saved through Him who loved us and gave Himself for us comes with even greater force when we consider that Christ's work for our salvation was all done voluntarily to the full satisfaction of His heavenly Father.

We know that God looks at the heart, at the motive of men, not merely at the outward act. We know that from the fear and love of God the fulfilling of the Commandments should flow. So then, if our doing God's will must be voluntary, based just on love to Him, certainly Christ's work must have no lesser motive.

Now, what gleams and sparkles in all of Christ's life and work if not His great love to His Father, to us, and to all other sinners? "My meat," He said, "is to do the will of Him that sent Me and to finish His work. I came not to do Mine own will but the will of Him that sent Me. Therefore doth My Father love Me, because I lay down My life that I might take it again." God loved the world and wished to save it from sin and damnation. Christ presented Himself to His heavenly Father to accomplish this total task of salvation. Therefore out of the open heaven God called down to men and said of Jesus: "This is My beloved Son, in whom I am well pleased; hear ye Him."

Yes, because our blessed Savior willingly and lovingly endured the bitter cross for our redemption from sin and hell, God the Father loves Him dearly and now showers His love upon us, taking us one by one into His blessed presence in the heaven Christ won for us. The fact that God raised up Jesus from the dead proves we are redeemed. By that act of resurrection God established for eternity Christ's work as valid, and on and on it has been set forth by faithful witnesses winning more and more souls for heaven. The world and a corrupted church may reject the gospel of Christ's atoning death and resurrection, but we know it is valid, it is the power of God unto salvation. By it God is continually building up His true church of believers.

It is for us to accept this Christ come from God as our Savior and Lord, to become sheep of the flock of this Good Shepherd, to manifest in our lives that we belong to Him. The one thing in life that matters is our relationship to Christ. To accept Him as He is — the Savior God provided for us — this will mean for us everlasting blessedness.

> Thine forever, God of love!
> Hear us from Thy throne above;
> Thine forever may we be
> Here and in eternity!

Affliction and the Kingdom

By R. H. Rosenkoetter

(Jubilate)

Now a certain man was sick, named Lazarus, of Bethany, the town of Mary and her sister Martha. (It was that Mary which anointed the Lord with ointment and wiped His feet with her hair, whose brother Lazarus was sick.) Therefore his sisters sent unto Him, saying, Lord, behold, he whom Thou lovest is sick. When Jesus heard that, He said, This sickness is not unto death, but for the glory of God, that the Son of God might be glorified thereby. Now Jesus loved Martha and her sister and Lazarus. When He had heard therefore that he was sick, He abode two days still in the same place where He was. Then after that saith He to His disciples, Let us go into Judea again. His disciples say unto Him, Master, the Jews of late sought to stone Thee; and goest Thou thither again? Jesus answered, Are there not twelve hours in the day? If any man walk in the day, he stumbleth not, because he seeth the light of this world. But if a man walk in the night, he stumbleth, because there is no light in him. These things said He; and after that He saith unto them, Our friend Lazarus sleepeth; but I go that I may awake him out of sleep. Then said His disciples, Lord, if he sleep, he shall do well. Howbeit Jesus spake of his death; but they thought that He had spoken of taking of rest in sleep. Then said Jesus unto them plainly, Lazarus is dead. And I am glad for your sakes that I was not there, to the intent ye may believe; nevertheless let us go unto him. Then said Thomas, which is called Didymus, unto his fellow disciples, Let us also go, that we may die with Him. — *John 11:1-16*

The words of this text tell us about affliction and the Kingdom.

Until now we have celebrated Easter. We felt as though we were in the clouds. We could have cried with Peter, "It is good for us to be here." We forgot, with the good news of victory over sin, death, devil, and hell, that we were still on earth. But the church is not so unrealistic that it would keep its people in the clouds. The fact is that the church is very realistic. The Epistle for today reminds us that the Christian is to be conscious of the "little while" that he walks on earth. The Gospel reminds us that the way — through suffering to glory — which Christ walked is also our way. So the church's preaching, its message to itself, leads us back today into the crude everyday life of pain and misery and suffering. At the same time it reminds us that the Christian sufferer's posture is one of faith and hope and joy.

Affliction and the Kingdom

I

In the Kingdom There Is No Escape from It

Affliction Comes to Christian Homes

This Gospel confronts us not merely with a house of mourning, but with a Christian house of mourning. Christ and His Gospel message of redeeming work, done to rescue men from sin, death, and hell, was known in this household. Lazarus and his two sisters believed in Christ, and Christ loved them dearly. And yet affliction comes. Lazarus falls ill. The sisters are distressed. Lazarus even dies. The hopes and prayers of the sisters remain unanswered. Even the Jews, when they saw the tears of Jesus, questioned, "Could not this man which opened the eyes of the blind have caused that this man should not have died?"

That's the way it is with affliction. We like to escape it, evade it when it comes. We may close our eyes to it and tell ourselves that it isn't happening. We may try to get rid of it as quickly and as easily as possible. But still it comes. It comes with great weight, and sometimes it remains indefinitely.

Did you expect it to be otherwise when you stepped into the kingdom of God? Maybe by stepping in you thought that you were doing something nice and good, doing God a favor, putting Him under obligation to yourself. Or maybe you thought you ought to escape sickness and suffering and death because you are a friend of Jesus. You're a privileged character! Isn't that what we have in mind when we complain and sigh, "Why do I have to suffer? Why does God let this pain and misery come into my life? After all, He tells me that He loves me."

It is very possible because of the close and intimate association which Jesus had with this family that they more or less thought of themselves as privileged characters. Jesus had spoken highly of Mary's anointing Him. John refers to it in our Gospel lesson. Jesus was on intimate terms with the family as the sisters imply when they say, "The one whom You love is sick." "Your friend is sick," they mean to say. Jesus had made it quite clear that He prized their love, their friendliness, their home. But now the glamour of it all disappears. Lazarus gets sick. He grows worse. Jesus does not come. Lazarus dies. And with him, they now bury the last vestige of their pride. Affliction does come to God's people. We're not privileged characters.

Christians Share the Burden of Affliction

Did you expect to escape affliction by coming into God's kingdom? When you stepped into the community of believers, you didn't get away from pain and affliction. You just added to your pain and woe. At the same time, of course, you lightened your load of pain and misery. When you stepped into this community, you became a member of Christ's body on earth. If a member of your body is not functioning properly, the other members of your body cannot disregard the pain of the sick member or behave as though it made no difference! Each member of the body shares

in the sickness and the health of all the members of the body.
And that's the way it is in the Kingdom. Paul says, "And whether
one member suffer, all the members suffer with it; or one member
be honored, all the members rejoice with it. Now ye are the body
of Christ and members in particular." Jesus says, "Our friend
Lazarus." In the Kingdom "any friend of Jesus is a friend of mine,"
and we share in the sickness and the health of all our friends
in the Kingdom.

Jesus Suffered and Died

In the Kingdom, Jesus could not escape affliction and tribulation either. He could have said to His disciples, "Let's go to Bethany
to awake Lazarus out of sleep," thus trying to avoid the thought
for Himself and His disciples that suffering and death lay ahead.
Instead He says, "Let us go into Judea," making it quite clear that
He knew that He was stepping into enemy territory on his way
to the cross and the grave.

Please understand; we are not suggesting, at this point, a sort
of fatalistic viewpoint about suffering and the kingdom of God,
a sort of "What comes, comes" attitude. We are not suggesting
that you say, "There is no rhyme or reason to anything that happens." Not at all.

II

In the Kingdom There Is a Purpose in It

Jesus Suffered and Died with a Purpose

It is true that in the Kingdom you cannot escape affliction.
Jesus couldn't escape suffering and death. But this suffering and
death had a purpose. Jesus went into the grave and out of it on
the third day. He died and rose again. And that fact marks the
beginning of the end of death and misery and affliction. One day
you will live in a world that is completely devoid of these miseries.
Do you believe that? Your guarantee is the fact that Jesus went
into the grave and out of it again. He met death and conquered
it. He lives now in the world without pain and death; and so
will you.

Our Affliction Has a Purpose

But Lazarus still died. The sisters had to suffer the pain of
losing a loved one. Affliction, death, and misery are still with us,
but now it's different. In the Kingdom there is a purpose in it.
John in recording this wonderful chapter says, "Now Jesus loved
Martha and her sister and Lazarus." This love is a purposeful
love. It rises above mere affection and personal attachment. This
love has not only the physical, but also the spiritual and eternal
welfare of this little family at heart. This love is concerned not
merely about the health of their brother, but also about their

spiritual health. This love has as its goal to help them stand in the posture of faith, hope, and joy — and to be able to do this in the midst of affliction.

Out of this love of Christ for Mary, Martha, and Lazarus come all the actions which follow. At first glance they are difficult to understand. He sends the messenger back with a message, "This sickness is not unto death, but for the glory of God, that the Son of God might be glorified thereby." The whole family hears the message. But Lazarus grows worse. He dies. Then we are told that Jesus "waited"; that it wasn't until the fourth day after Lazarus's death that Jesus came to Bethany. Just what was going through their minds is evident when they meet Jesus and say, "Master, if Thou hadst been here, our brother had not died."

To be a friend of Jesus, to be embraced in His tender affection and yet to lie sick, to grow worse, and finally die, as if Jesus our friend had forgotten. How can that be?

Know God's Love

The answer lies in the words "Jesus loved Martha and her sister and Lazarus." God implies that these actions flow out of Jesus' love and concern for this family, not merely as their Friend, but as their Lord and Savior. This was the proof of His love: "Whom the Lord loves, He chastens." Would you like to live in a world where there is no evidence of God's love for you? Then treasure this suffering and affliction in your life. It's the mark of God's love.

Grow in Faith

Affliction and misery in the Kingdom is God's school where we not only learn to know His love for us, but also where we grow in faith. Affliction helps us to look away from ourselves, our goods, our loved ones, or some supposed privileged status. It serves to strengthen our reliance on Christ, to deepen it, to strengthen our hold on His love, to be more patient and trustful of His power, to be more certain and joyous in our hope. In suffering, our faith is made more precious. Again and again in this chapter Jesus indicates that what He does, He does "to the intent that ye might believe."

For the Glory of God

And Jesus says, "In the Kingdom this sickness is for the glory of God." One of God's people sick, and that's for the glory of God? Yes, it is. When people are led to believe in Him as their Lord and Savior, as the Resurrection and the Life, that's to the glory of God. When people learn to know the love of God in Christ for them, that's to the glory of God. When people learn to stand in the posture of faith and hope and joy, that's to the glory of God. And that's what happened here. Mary and Martha and many others came to this confession. They confessed that Jesus died and rose for them and cleared the way through death to endless life and joy for them.

III

In the Kingdom There Is Deliverance from It

And this story teaches us, too, that in the Kingdom there is deliverance from affliction. As far as this Gospel lesson goes for today, it hardly seems that there is deliverance. In Bethany all is still dark. In the sisters' hearts were questions and doubts and disappointments. They struggle to hold fast the hope in the words of Jesus sent by the messenger. There seems to be no deliverance.

Jesus' Death Puts an End to Dying

But it only seems that way. On the other side of the Jordan the sun is already shining. Deliverance is on the way. Jesus says, "I go to awake him out of sleep." That word "sleep" suggests the resurrection from the dead; for those who sleep have the hope of rising again.

Yes, Jesus was on His way to make that hint of resurrection to endless life a reality. His activity at Bethany led to his suffering and death and resurrection. Deliverance from affliction and death is now a reality. Jesus' calling Lazarus out of the sepulcher, His own death and resurrection a short time later mark the beginning of the end of our world of affliction and pain and death. Jesus' death and resurrection are the guarantee that one day we'll live in a world without pain and death. You want to stand even now with Mary and Martha in the posture of this faith and hope and joy? Then ponder again the fact that Christ went into the sepulcher and out of it again to clear the way for you to endless life and joy. Ponder again the fact that Christ closed His eyes in death for the three days and then opened them on the third day so that we need not close our eyes in eternal death, but open them to an endless life of joy and bliss in the presence of God.

Jesus Comforts Mourning Friends

By WILLIAM F. WEDIG

(Cantate)

Then when Jesus came, He found that he had lain in the grave four days already. Now Bethany was nigh unto Jerusalem, about fifteen furlongs off. And many of the Jews came to Martha and Mary to comfort them concerning their brother. Then Martha, as soon as she heard that Jesus was coming, went and met Him, but Mary sat still in the house. Then said Martha unto Jesus, Lord, if Thou hadst been here, my brother had not died. But I know that even now, whatsoever Thou wilt ask of God, God will give it Thee. Jesus saith unto her, Thy brother shall rise again. Martha saith unto Him, I know that he shall rise again in the resurrection at the Last Day. Jesus said unto her: I am the Resurrection and the Life; he that believeth in Me, though he were dead, yet shall he live. And whosoever liveth and believeth in Me shall never die. Believest thou this? She saith unto Him, Yea, Lord, I believe that Thou art the Christ, the Son of God, which should come into the world.

John 11:17-27

People often feel very inadequate on the occasions when they go to offer sympathy to friends who have lost a dear one to the coldness of death. On the way we think ahead of the words we wish to say, and we worry that they will not sound natural or that they will be a bit hackneyed. We are sure that they will be completely insufficient to convey the earnestness of the sympathy we feel, but just can't quite express. Everybody who has ever been to a wake or a funeral has at some time suffered this feeling.

We go today to visit a funeral in the company of Jesus, who was calling on mourners who were precious friends. Tears streamed down His face as He later recalled the loving acquaintance which He shared with him who now was so stiff silent and still. He felt all the loss that we feel at a wake, for He was such a man as was fully "touched with the feeling of our infirmities" (Heb. 4:15). Our distress at seeing a fellowman lose the prized gift of life — that He too must have felt. However, when we see Jesus calling on Martha and Mary four days after the funeral of their brother, Jesus' friend, Lazarus, we hear Him speak words of reassuring sympathy that *were* fully adequate and helpful to the mourning sisters. We find help in listening to the words that were spoken.

I
Conversation with a Mourner
Three Texts from John 11

Possibly most of you recognized the text as being Part II of a story that we began last Sunday; Part III next Sunday will complete our study of John 11. Today we are past halfway in the five-week period following Easter, a time when we have been reassured that Christ truly rose from His grace, proving our redemption, and a time that guarantees to us that our Lord thereby did something about human death.

Jesus was away from the home of the dear friends at Bethany, Lazarus, Martha, and Mary, when the distressing news came that the brother was seriously ill. Jesus had confidently said that the sickness would not be fatal, but two days later He announced, through miraculous knowledge, that Lazarus was dead. "Let us go to him," Jesus said to the disciples.

Martha's Troubled "If"

The two sisters' worst fears had materialized into reality four days before Jesus arrived. Lazarus died, and they buried him, probably the same day, following the usual Jewish funeral custom. Out of the thick cloud of gloom that still hung over the home there constantly came the heart-tearing, booming thunder of *if*. It rumbled again as Martha ran from the house to meet Jesus, choking between her sobs, "Lord, *if Thou hadst been here,* my brother had not died."

It must have been the echo of a hundred conversations she and Mary had with each other and with friends. When Lazarus fell sick — "If only Jesus were here!" Then when his condition became critical, "Oh, if only Jesus were here!" They had sent word to Him in Perea and anguished together, "If Jesus would only come!" But He had not, and sickness quickly took its victim. Before the funeral, and after the burial, and in the four days since then, when friends came to call and express their sympathy, the conversation would always turn to that awful "If." They had confidence that Jesus *could* have healed Lazarus, for He had cured many others. They were sure that Jesus *would* have restored Lazarus, for he was a close friend whom Jesus loved. Everything would have been so different — if.

Martha earnestly told Jesus what troubled her heart. "Lazarus' life would have been saved if only You had been here!" Let's not understand these words as a gentle complaint that Jesus had not come when they notified Him that Lazarus was ill. While He had delayed for two days after word came, Lazarus would have been two days buried upon Jesus' arrival, even if He had set out at once. Rather than being a rebuke, Martha's words reveal her reliance on the love of Jesus and on His power. She was sure that He would have gotten a foot in before death's door slammed shut on the man of their house.

Consolation That Did Not Comfort

In your funeral-home visits to mourning Christian friends I hope that you have used the same comforting assurance that Jesus gave to mourning Martha: "Thy brother shall rise again." Those are words that *must* be spoken if the death of a dear one is not to crush our hearts completely, though they be cut to the quick. They are words that can be spoken at the death of every believer — spoken with the full confidence of Christian faith and with the solid ring of reliable truth.

Jesus' comfort missed the mark with Martha. "Thy brother shall rise again." This could mean two things, could it not? It did mean two things. It predicted Lazarus' bodily restoration to life in the unknown future of the great day of the Lord. It also predicted Lazarus' resurrection to life within the short span that was measured in the minutes that it took them to walk out to the cemetery. We easily see both meanings in Jesus' word, but we must not find fault with Martha for her failure to understand. Jesus had not yet worked His miracle of which we have read. There was only one focus for her comprehension, clouded and blurred as it was by grief. She thought Jesus spoke of Lazarus coming alive again on the Last Day. "I know that he shall rise again in the resurrection at the Last Day," she said. Hope for then, yes; for now — hardly. Jesus had raised others, but none who had been dead so long as this one.

II

Full Comfort for a Mourner

"I Am the Resurrection and the Life"

Jesus' consoling conversation with Martha did not fully comfort her. "Thy brother shall rise . . ." missed its mark. His next words did not. He told the weeping woman, "I am the Resurrection and the Life."

Christ that day clarified for Martha what had been true at the beginning of days, "In the beginning . . . in Him was life" (John 1:1, 4). To have life it is necessary to come unto Him (John 5: 39, 40). "God hath given unto us eternal life, and this life is in His Son" (1 John 5:11). He, as God, was the Originator of life. Having ordained life, He distributed it as He chose to His creatures, giving to mankind life in its highest form, a life to last forever. Having done this, He could also give life back again when life had been lost.

Do you see how here Christ was drawing Martha's sight close, away from the far horizon of Judgment Day? He was also lifting her eyes up and away from the corpse so close by — doing both in order that she might clearly look at the issue that is more important: life itself. There was a truth more vital than the distant day and more essential than the death of one man — even a brother. She must realize that Life was here now, not someday — that Resurrection had come already! "I am the Resurrection and the Life. They are present in Me! I have the power to produce them now!"

Believers Live

"He that believeth in Me, though he were dead, yet shall he live. Whosoever liveth and believeth in Me shall never die." A believer, Lazarus, had died four days earlier; "He shall yet live." Two believers, Martha and Mary, still living, mourned for him; "they shall never die." This is Christ's wonderful answer to the fearful problem of death.

Few people then believed that there was an answer to the fearful specter death. Still fewer believed that Christ had power over death. Many today still do not know it, or do not believe it. Yet here is assurance both of the possibility and of the fact that life ends *in life,* not just in death. Christ exclusively has the answer, and has it for those who believe in Him. Ask those who follow Shinto or Tao or Hindu, and they offer no comparable assurance. The Buddhist will show you how to get *away from* life and from the world, but knows nothing encouraging about the *end* of life. The Mohammedan simply resigns himself to death, saying, "Allah wills it." Confucius could do no more than encourage you to be a little more philosophical about both life and death.

But contrast Christ's positive facts: "I am Life! I am Resurrection! I made life, putting man together from the dust, and I make man alive again after he dies, simply putting his dust back together again. This is not at all at issue — Can I, or will I do so?"

Faith Is Needful

Can you, will you, believe it? "Believest Thou this?" Jesus asked Martha. "She saith unto Him: Yes, Lord. I believe that Thou art the Christ, the Son of God, which should come into the world." The need is to search your own soul — not to search the Savior's power.

Martha's confession had three clauses: You are Christ, You are God's Son, You are the One who was to come. Although she did not directly answer the question Jesus asked, "Can you believe that I am the Resurrection, the Life, and that believers live though dead," Martha's faith *did* have a broad base. "The Coming One, the Christ," was her way, and the way of all believing Jews, of speaking of the Savior they expected God to send. They called Him the Anointed One. As such He would be the Bringer of truth. He had just shown her the truth that He was Resurrection and Life; she believed that. We should not believe that Martha was always in the kitchen when Mary was sitting at Jesus' feet; she too believed the words which He had spoken on happier visits to their home. Believing Him to be the Anointed One, she expected that He would also sacrifice for sin, dim as her understanding might then have been of this saving event of the future. As the Anointed One, Jesus was also her Master. Lord she called Him — Ruler. She accepted both His divine origin and His divine nature. "Thou art . . . the Son of God." This was a broad faith!

Even now it was broadening. She made no claim to understand the "how" of His resurrection or the "when" of the life which He called Himself. Yet she believed it as a part of her Messianic hope. She heard His words speak hope for her brother's life and peace for her own soul. Not everything was clear, but this much was certain, "I know that even now, whatsoever Thou wilt ask of God, God will give it Thee." She was ready for more. He once had said, "The hour is coming, and now is, when the dead shall hear the voice of the Son of God, and they that hear shall live." (John 5:25)

Martha's broad and constantly broadening faith had an immediate reward. They went from there to the cemetery, and very soon Lazarus was called from his tomb, the family reunited, and peace had come again where only tears had flowed so shortly before.

III

Comfort for All

There is a reward also for us who shared with Jesus this visit to believing mourners.

Life Has Come

I am sure that Christ wanted this death and mourning to show *us* that life is here with us *now*. Death frightens and grieves us today as much as it did then, even though medical knowledge has moved the mileposts a bit farther down the road. We need no convincing about the reality of funerals, wakes, and cemeteries.

We *do* need to understand always better the source of death — sin. All the flowers of a funeral must not overcome for us the smell of death that clings to every sinner. Every misdeed, every act of hand or heart, every thought or thoughtlessness, that cannot be stamped "Holy" — this is a stench to the sensitive holiness of our all-perfect God. It deserves, and gets from Him, not only the sorrow of a bodily death that ends our years; it also destines us to the suffering separation in hell for all the years that never end.

We need stronger saving belief in Jesus, whose words were, "I am the Resurrection and the Life. . . . Believers in Me shall never die." We must trust Him, our Savior from sin, in whom it is possible for us someday to be "blessed . . . dead which die *in the Lord.*" As Christ, the Son of God, His life was without spot or blemish — a perfection and holiness that God has imputed to us. His death, the result of no sin of His, but the punishment of our sins, which were charged against Him, provides for us the life He promised in Himself. His Easter resurrection switches power over to us against our own grave, so that like Lazarus we shall heed His call to "come forth" to live eternally. Jesus, Resurrection and Life, by His atonement, gives ability to us for holy living in His sight.

Help Has Come

Life and resurrection have come in Christ to remove the problem of death and damnation. But in Christ there is also help for us with the many problems that still remain to man during our earthly days.

We too have the worries that were so upsetting to Martha even thought we do trust Christ, as God and Lord, as Savior. Belief we have, saving belief, but so many details of life escape our understanding.

Death still hurts when it comes. We believe, but not the full 100 percent of our heart and mind is able always to believe. So Jesus uses the convincing power of His Holy Spirit to tell us again that *life* comes through death, a death died believing in Him as Savior. Though this life ends always in death, death is the way to start the life that is for us all that God wanted us to have in living. Death only *changes* life — for the better. The grave is only the transfer point on life's route — not life's terminal.

Who of us has not often been bothered too with the troublesome "if" that rumbled around in Martha's heart? Who has not thought of what might have been — if? — If you had chosen another career — if you had invested when you did not — if a different school, if some good opportunity, if better health care. To a questioning Christian the Lord may give no direct answer, even as He did not answer Martha when she so lamented. But to every if-asking Christian God says: "That's all useless. *My* will is always done. What you did is exactly what I directed." God can even chide us for asking too many "ifs." "All you did at My directing — that *was* the best, and not the things you now think of with the hindsight which you consider so clear." He ". . . is able to do exceeding abundantly *above* all that we ask or think, according to the power *that worketh* in us." (Eph. 3:20)

Such thoughts point up the need that we too have for a broad and steadily broadening faith. "Believest thou?" Jesus asked Martha. "Yes, some things," was her approximate answer, shortened a bit. That belief grew through hearing Jesus' words, and who would doubt that in the days ahead both these sisters sat often at Jesus' feet? More belief, stronger faith, is available also to you, through the hearing of God's Word, by receiving Jesus' Sacrament. God gave us Word and Sacrament to be the pipline to us for life-giving faith. He gives us His church to be the pumping station for these means of grace. If we fail to understand some of His ways with us, if we cannot hear His voice speaking through some event in life, it could be from not having listened to His voice often enough. Not to understand some of the "ifs" of life can result from not having heard the Lord explain all the "whys" which He has clearly revealed.

Our God took special care so that one of the frettings of the two sisters would not burden their lives — their complaint "If Jesus *had* been here. . . ." He *is* here with us, His people. Here with *special* grace in sorrow or suffering, He assures of His presence also when we may not so sharply feel the need for Him. He *is* here when we are burdened and also when we feel richly blessed; not only in sorrow but also in sunshine; in times that test and in times that thrill.

"Believest thou this? She saith unto Him, Yea, Lord, I believe that Thou art the Christ, the Son of God, which should come into the world." A casket will not change a child of this world into a child of God, nor will a shroud switch a sinner into a saint. So it is that now is the time to be building a faith.

O Dead, Come Forth

By MARTIN W. RUPPRECHT

(Rogate)

And when she had so said, she went her way and called Mary, her sister, secretly, saying, The Master is come and calleth for thee. As soon as she heard that, she arose quickly and came unto Him. Now Jesus was not yet come into the town, but was in that place where Martha met Him. The Jews then which were with her in the house and comforted her, when they saw Mary, that she rose up hastily and went out, followed her, saying, She goeth unto the grave to weep there. Then when Mary was come where Jesus was and saw Him, she fell down at His feet, saying unto Him, Lord, if Thou hadst been here, my brother had not died. When Jesus therefore saw her weeping, and the Jews also weeping which came with her, He groaned in the spirit and was troubled and said, Where have ye laid him? They said unto Him, Lord, come and see. Jesus wept. Then said the Jews, Behold how He loved him! And some of them said, Could not this man, which opened the eyes of the blind, have caused that even this man should not have died? Jesus therefore again groaning in Himself cometh to the grave. It was a cave, and a stone lay upon it. Jesus said, Take ye away the stone. Martha, the sister of him that was dead, saith unto Him, Lord, by this time he stinketh, for he hath been dead four days. Jesus saith unto her, Said I not unto thee that if thou wouldest believe thou shouldest see the glory of God? Then they took away the stone from the place where the dead was laid. And Jesus lifted up His eyes and said, Father, I thank Thee that Thou hast heard Me. And I knew that Thou hearest Me always; but because of the people which stand by I said it, that they may believe that Thou hast sent Me. And when He thus had spoken, He cried with a loud voice, Lazarus, come forth. And he that was dead came forth bound hand and foot with graveclothes, and his face was bound about with a napkin. Jesus saith unto them, Loose him, and let him go. Then many of the Jews which came to Mary, and had seen the things which Jesus did, believed on Him. — *John 11:28-45*

In the calendar of the Christian church this is the fifth and last Sunday after Easter. During these Sundays we have been studying lessons about the great Easter miracle of the resurrection

of our blessed Lord from the dead or lessons from the life and
teachings of our everliving and ever-loving Savior.

The text for this last Sunday after Easter deals once more with
Jesus and with the subject of death. In fact, our text records the
second greatest miracle which Jesus performed. The greatest miracle of course was His raising Himself from the dead, thereby proving that He is indeed the only-begotten Son of God and the Savior
who was to come into the world. To be sure, the other miracles of
Jesus were impressive too. For instance, when He fed 5,000 with
a few loaves and a few fish; when He changed water into wine;
when He stilled the storm, so that His own disciples had to say,
as we would word it today: "What a man!" Still greater miracles
were performed when He raised the widow's son at Nain and the
daughter of Jairus from the dead. But this miracle of our text
is greater than all those because Lazarus, whom Jesus raised from
the dead, had been dead four days already; his body was in a state
of decomposition. Yet even death and decay in such an advanced
state had to yield to Christ's almighty word.

For our spiritual edification we shall today study this word
from the mouth of our blessed Lord:

O Dead, Come Forth

I

As It Was Spoken to Lazarus

The account of Lazarus' sickness and death and resurrection
covers 45 verses of John 11. Our text contains only 18 verses of
this entire account. And so it might be well for us to review briefly
what preceded our text.

Jesus was an intimate friend of Lazarus and his two sisters,
Martha and Mary, who lived in Bethany. Lazarus on one occasion
became seriously ill. Jesus was in Perea at the time, on the other
side of the Jordan River. Somehow the sisters got word to Jesus
that their brother was sick. This, by the way, is the first thing we
ought to do when a loved one falls ill — tell it to Jesus; talk to
Him in prayer; call the pastor, so that he might comfort and
strengthen the patient.

Upon hearing the news Jesus purposely delayed His coming
until Lazarus had died; then He went to Bethany. When He
arrived, Martha went out to meet Him, and Jesus had her call her
sister to come to Him also. Martha "called Mary, her sister, secretly,
saying, The Master is come and calleth for thee." Mary promptly
left the friends who had come to comfort her. It was a Jewish
custom for friends to come and mourn with the bereaved for
seven days.

Poor Comforters

We pause for a moment in our account to reflect what poor comforters many are at the time of death. We often hear empty, comfortless expressions, such as "Too bad, but we all got to go sometime," or "He sure was a good man!" How much better, fellow Christians, it is to comfort the mourners with the words of Jesus "Thy brother shall rise again" (v. 23). Or say: "May you comfort yourself with the words of Jesus 'I am the Resurrection and the Life. He that believeth in Me, though he were dead, yet shall he live. And whosoever liveth and believeth in Me shall never die.'" The Lord's command to hearers as well as to pastors is "Comfort ye, comfort ye My people." This calls for more than just a parrot-like repetition of meaningless funeral-parlor expressions or just "paying one's respects."

Returning to our account, we are told: "Then when Mary was come where Jesus was, she fell down at His feet." At Jesus' feet — that was the place where Mary delighted to be. Remember how at a previous visit of Jesus Martha served while Mary sat at Jesus' feet and listened to His message of salvation. And that is a good place for us to be, too — at Jesus' feet.

Jesus Wept

When Jesus saw His friends weeping over their loss, the account reports, "Jesus wept" (v. 35). This is the shortest verse in the Bible. But it is not short in meaning. It proves the human nature of Christ. It shows how near Jesus is to every mourner. It shows us how terrible an enemy death must be. The Scriptures speak of the tears of Jesus only on three occasions: when He wept over Jerusalem because of their unbelief, when He wept in the Garden of Gethsemane, and when He wept over Lazarus' death.

Applying this to ourselves, we note that it certainly is not sinful to weep at the departure of a loved one. Don't be ashamed of your tears at such a time; you thereby resemble the human Christ. Tears are the natural and universal language of deep sorrow. Our tears do not help the dead, but they reveal our sympathy.

However, excessive grieving is sinful and shows a lack of trust in God. In the case of Jesus it was silent weeping rather than explosive sobbing. Within bounds weeping is sacred; out of bounds it is harmful. It is the consensus of funeral directors that those who make a show of weeping generally forget soonest. We are not to sorrow "as others which have no hope" (1 Thess. 4). Those whose loved ones died without faith in Christ have a double reason to mourn. But mourning for a departed believer should always have a sweet undertone of joy at the loved one's going home. Any survivor who for months and years remains melancholy and morose is showing an attitude displeasing to the Lord of life and death and to the God of all comfort.

Criticism

Some of the Jews now criticized Jesus. "Could not this man," they said, "which opened the eyes of the blind, have caused that even this man should not have died?" Perhaps these were the same critics who later, when Jesus hung on the cross, said, "He saved others; Himself He cannot save. If He be the King of Israel, let Him now come down from the cross."

Many today question God's ways, especially in time of death, and say: "Why? Why did this have to happen to us? Why did our loved one have to die so soon?" Oh, if people would only let God be God! He has His purposes in all that He does. Our attitude is to be one of submission and resignation to His will, which is always best. Has He not assured us: "My thoughts are not your thoughts, neither are your ways My ways, saith the Lord. For as the heavens are higher than the earth, so are My ways higher than your ways and My thoughts than your thoughts"? To illustrate how wrong these critics of Jesus were, let us assert that we thank God that He did not come down from the cross. If He had, our salvation would not have been accomplished. And preventing the death of Lazarus, we can be sure, would likewise have been a mistake.

Reasons for Lazarus' Death

Why did Lazarus have to die? 1. That his sister Martha might grow in faith and rise to making this beautiful confession: "I believe that Thou art the Christ, the Son of God, which should come into the world." (V. 27)

2. That Jesus' own disciples might come to greater faith in Him, as Jesus Himself said "I am glad for your sakes that I was not there, to the intent ye may believe." (V. 15)

3. That others might through the miracle of raising Lazarus from the dead come to faith in Christ, which did happen, as the last verse of our text reports: "Then many of the Jews . . . believed on Him."

4. That we might come to faith in Christ or have our faith in Christ as the true and only-begotten Son of God strengthened. This was the purpose of all of Christ's miracles. "And many other signs truly did Jesus in the presence of His disciples, which are not written in this book. But these are written that ye might believe that Jesus is the Christ, the Son of God and that, believing, ye might have life through His name." So, child of God, never, never question God's purposes, even when He allows sorrows to

come into your life. Rather learn submissively to say, Lord, "not My will but Thine be done."

Returning to our account, we find Jesus with Lazarus' sister now arriving at the grave. The Jews normally buried in a cave or sepulcher scooped horizontally into the rock. The entrance was closed by a stone in order to exclude beasts which might prey upon dead bodies.

"Take Away the Stone!"

Jesus now gave the command "Take ye away the stone." He could have removed the stone Himself. But what others can do He lets them do — reserving for Himself what only He as God can do: raise Lazarus from the dead. Similarly, the Lord of the church uses us as His instruments in building His kingdom. We are to preach and teach, invite others, give and serve, but only God the Holy Spirit can convert souls.

Martha objected to the opening of the tomb with these words: "Lord, by this time he stinketh, for he hath been dead four days." In other words: "No use, Lord; You can't help now. Brother Lazarus has been dead four days, and his body is in a bad state of decomposition." But after Jesus had gently chided Martha, the stone was removed. Then Jesus prayed to His Father and thanked Him in advance for answering Him (we should also thank God, knowing beforehand that God will answer the prayers of the righteous, according to His will). After this, Jesus cried with a loud voice, "Lazarus, come forth!" Incidentally, an unbeliever criticized this account by saying, "Since Jesus was standing right at the tomb of Lazarus, why did He mention Lazarus' name in the demand?" A believing Christian replied, "Because of Jesus' almighty word; if He had not specified Lazarus, all the dead might have answered the command."

The Miracle Performed

Lazarus' soul was far away from that rock cave, for we know that the soul upon death is immediately separated from the body. Nevertheless Lazarus heard the voice; he knew the voice; he obeyed the voice. He was made alive again. He arose from the tomb.

St. John now breaks off the narrative. He does not tell of the happiness of the sisters or the celebration of the citizens of Bethany. We have to imagine this. St. John just hastens to conclude his account by telling us of something more important: "Then many of the Jews which came to Mary, and had seen the things which Jesus did, believed on Him." They had previously witnessed miracles of Christ, but they had stubbornly refused to believe in Him. Now they believed. As for us Jesus says, "Blessed are they that have not seen and yet have believed!"

II
As It Will Be Spoken to You and to Me Someday

Now we want to think for a while about Jesus' command "O dead, come forth!" as it will be spoken someday to you and to me.

Death must come to all men as it came to Lazarus. It will also come to us. But for us Christians death is only a momentary shadow preceding a life that is far, far better. Without Christ the grave is dark, very dark. But for believers there is life and hope and peace even in the grave.

And on Judgment Day all who have ever lived and died will also hear the command "Come forth!" — wherever you are. Don't doubt God's ability to do this! It is an easy thing for Him to do who created the world and formed man of the dust of the ground. And to show His ability as well as His willingness to raise the dead, Jesus did raise three persons from the dead during His earthly sojourn. Our Lord, who is Truth, assures us in His Word: "The hour is coming in which all that are in the graves shall hear His voice and shall come forth. They that have done good, unto the resurrection of life, and they that have done evil, unto the resurrection of damnation." So join Job in his statement of faith: "I know that my Redeemer liveth and that He shall stand at the latter day upon the earth. And though after my skin worms destroy this body, yet in my flesh shall I see God, whom I shall see for myself, and mine eyes shall behold, and not another." He who called Lazarus by name, He who calls the stars by their names, certainly knows the names of all His believers sleeping in the dust of the earth. Don't worry, He will lose none of them.

There are two resurrections to which Christ's voice will awaken men: the resurrection to life and the resurrection to condemnation. You, too, will hear that voice. Decide whether you will now follow the Holy Spirit's promptings to faith and godliness, so that when the Son of man calls you on that great day, you will by grace be able to answer joyfully, "Lord, here am I"; or whether you will rise reluctantly and repeat what Scripture has prophesied about the lost: "Then shall they begin to say to the mountains, Fall on us, and to the hills, Cover us." Oh, why risk this terrible, eternal fate by now stuffing your ears with so much clay and worldliness and sin and forgetfulness of God that the call of the Gospel cannot get through to your heart?

"What Must I Do?"

Let us rather ask: What must I do to be saved? There is only one way: faith in Christ as the only-begotten Son of God and as man's only Savior from sin, who by His death on Calvary's cross won forgiveness of all our sins and opened heaven's door for us. Those will be raised to life eternal who can from the heart echo the sound and sure confession of Martha in the verse preceding our text: "Lord, I believe that Thou art the Christ, the Son of God, which should come into the world."

But we must hasten to add that the faith which assures our resurrection to life is not a dead but rather an active faith, a faith that gives evidence of its genuineness by acts of love and service to God and man.

True, saving faith spells obedience to God. Whatever He asks us to do, you will do it; whatever He forbids, you will avoid. If He calls you to service, you will imitate Mary in our text. When her sister Martha announced, "The Master is come and calleth for thee," "she arose quickly and came unto Him." Faith is swift! Faith hears the Lord's call to work in His vineyard, does not grope for excuses and alibis, but welcomes the opportunity and promptly goes into action. Jesus called Mary; Mary ran. If Jesus calls you to work for Him, answer quickly: "Here am I, send me!"

True, saving faith will show itself in regular and reverent worship. We saw how being at Jesus' feet was a favorite place for Mary. That ought to be also our favorite spot each Lord's Day without fail. By our hearing of the Word of God the Holy Spirit works faith in our hearts, or strengthens our faith, or gives us the ability to resist sin and remain on the path that leads to God and heaven. So for the sake of your soul's salvation take every opportunity you can to worship your God and Savior.

Don't let Satan whisper those worn-out excuses into your ears and hearts. In this account Mary gives us a good example. She had a houseful of company who came to mourn with her. But when Jesus called for her, she just left her company so that she might fall at His feet, worship Him, and confess Him. Similarly, if company (often used as an excuse for not worshiping on the Lord's Day) is rude enough to come on Sunday, do like Mary: leave them in order that you might sit at the feet of Jesus in the divine service of your church, or better still, invite them to go with you. Nor will faith permit other excuses such as recreation, unnecessary work, the comforts of home, hurt feelings, minor illnesses, and the like, to keep us from hearing the Word and permitting the Holy Spirit to cleanse and recreate our hearts.

True, saving faith and gratitude to Christ for His having saved you will also prompt you to speak to others and to win others for Christ. The voice of Jesus that woke the dead can also waken the spiritually dead, even those who have been spiritually dead for so long that even Christians say regarding them: "No use trying to win them; they are too far gone, hopeless!" Something may just temporarily be blocking their hearts, perhaps a stone of some kind. But just as Jesus said, "Take ye away the stone" — from Lazarus' tomb, so Jesus can, through the Holy Spirit and through your instrumentality of bringing them frequently in contact with God's powerful Word, remove the stones that heretofore have been impeding faith and the Christian life. He can do it! We don't care how bad the case is. Don't sell the Almighty short. And once the stone of prejudice or misunderstanding is removed, the way to the heart is wide open for the power-packed Gospel to enter and do its God-pleasing work there. Your conversion is a miracle. Why regard such a miracle as impossible in someone else's heart and life? Your task is to pray for such, invite them, yes, more important, to bring them under the stone-hammering preaching of the Law and faith-building sound of the Gospel.

"Believest Thou This?"

We find Jesus, after instructing Martha, asking her the question: "Believest thou this?" Similarly, after instructing you this morning from God's Word, I ask you this same question. And please regard it as a very personal question, addressed to you alone, as if you were the only one sitting in this church today. "Believest thou this" — that just as Jesus raised up Lazarus from the dead, He will also raise up your body on the Last Day and that your soul will be reunited with it to live forever?

"Believest thou this" — that Jesus, the Way, the Truth, and the Life, meant what He said after He Himself arose from the dead: "Because I live, ye shall live also"?

"Believest thou this" — that you have sinned and for that reason have come short of the glory of God; that you must someday appear before the judgment seat of Christ; that if you were left to yourself, you would surely be lost forever; that if you ignore Christ and His church and hope to be saved by your own good life and your own good deeds, you are dead wrong, for Scripture plainly states, "By the works of the Law shall no flesh be justified"?

"Believest Thou this" — that a loving God does not want you to be lost and earnestly, passionately desires your salvation, and that to this end He has sent His only-begotten Son into the world, so that if you believe in Him you shall not perish but have everlasting life?

"Believest thou this" — that saving faith, while relying on Christ alone, not on works, for salvation, is nevertheless active and swift in obedience and service to God and man?

"Believest thou this" — what your crucified, risen, ascended, and everliving Savior said: "In my Father's house are many mansions: if it were not so, I would have told you. I go to prepare a place for you . . . that where I am, there ye may be also"?

"Believest thou this" — that when you die in the faith and on Judgment Day answer the call that came to Lazarus, calling you by name and saying, "Come forth," you will rise and so ever be with the Lord?

Oh, then you are truly blessed! Such a faith will survive the shock of temporal death, and on that great Day you will be translated from the land of the dying to the land of the everliving and will forever be with Him who once wept but who will then "wipe away all tears from their eyes, and there shall be no more death, neither sorrow, nor crying," nothing but joy forever with your Lord. That this experience may be yours by grace through faith in Christ is my prayer for every one of you today.

The Ascension of Our Lord

By CLARENCE W. KNIPPA

(Ascension Day)

Sanctify them through Thy truth; Thy Word is truth. As Thou hast sent Me into the world, even so have I also sent them into the world. And for their sakes I sanctify Myself that they also might be sanctified through the truth. Neither pray I for these alone, but for them also which shall believe on Me through their word, that they all may be one, as Thou, Father, art in Me, and I in Thee, that they also may be one in Us, that the world may believe that Thou hast sent Me. And the glory which Thou gavest Me I have given them, that they may be one, even as We are one, I in them, and Thou in Me, that they may be made perfect in one, and that the world may know that Thou hast sent Me, and hast loved them as Thou hast loved Me. Father, I will that they also whom Thou hast given Me be with Me where I am, that they may behold My glory, which Thou hast given Me, for Thou lovedst Me before the foundation of the world. O righteous Father, the world hath not known Thee, but I have known Thee, and these have known that Thou hast sent me. And I have declared unto them Thy name and will declare it, that the love wherewith Thou hast loved Me may be in them, and I in them. — *John 17:17-26*

Shortly before Ascension Day in 1961 Lieutenant Commander Allen Shepherd, Jr., the first American spaceman, was projected 115 miles up out into space and traveled 300 miles down range, in about 15 minutes reaching a top speed of 5,160 miles per hour. It was not merely a successful flight and a clever propaganda stunt, which the United States needed at the time. It was an historic event. It meant that a momentous milestone was passed. The recognition given it by President Kennedy in Washington was justified. This event was the culmination of months and years of research, study, and experimentation. The best that brilliant minds could produce was put into it. The spending literally of millions of dollars preceded this flight into space. It was a culmination.

When we say it was a culmination, we do not mean that it was the conclusion of a project. In fact, in the light of the effort and resources spent, if nothing more had been achieved but a single flight of 300 miles down range, it would have been the colossal failure of the ages. It was a historic event because it meant that the door had been opened to achievements yet to come. It meant that man who had hurtled obstacles to transportation on land, on sea, and in the air was now on the threshold of conquering space also. That was its significance. It was a great step toward achieving a goal, but it was not the reaching of the goal itself.

Why do we speak of this on Ascension Day in the pulpit? We are here to commemorate the ascension of our Lord. But there is a parallel.

When our Lord had completed His work here on earth, He gathered His disciples together on a mountaintop and began to ascend into heaven. After ascending a small distance, a cloud came and received Him out of sight. Jesus removed His visible presence from His disciples on earth. It, too, was a culmination, not a conclusion. It marked the climax of all that had preceded it in the life of our Lord. It signaled the return of Jesus to His Father. Approximately 33 years before, He had left His Father in heaven. He gave up the full use of His glory and majesty to come down upon earth. He was made in the form of a man, humbled Himself, and became obedient unto death, even the death of the cross. He did this that He might redeem man unto God. He suffered, died, and rose again on the third day. By His resurrection, God declared the sins of the world forgiven. The resurrection tells us plainly and definitely that Jesus is the eternal Son of God and that we through faith in Jesus Christ are the children of God. After establishing the fact of His resurrection during the 40 days after the resurrection, Jesus visibly took His leave from His disciples and ascended into heaven, there to take His place in full majesty and glory.

In a sense it was a culmination and a conclusion. It was the return to His Father. He entered the world with a mission, He was returning to His Father with the mission completed. In one sense it closed a cycle, but in another sense it was the beginning of a new cycle. Everything up to this point was only preparatory for what was to happen from this time on. Jesus' ascension into heaven meant that He now was about to assume a new role and perform a new function. He was to govern and rule His church which He had redeemed with His blood. He ascended on high to sit at the right hand of God to exercise the power and authority and majesty which was His and to govern the world, particularly His church. He ascended into heaven so that He might send forth His spirit. On Pentecost Day, with flaming tongues and the sound of rushing wind He sent the Spirit of God upon the apostles. It was the beginning of a great ministry which is continuing to this day. It is an extension of the ministry of our Lord Himself. Our Lord is active even now in the heavens as He directs His church on earth.

Continuing Ministry

It was this continuing ministry of our Lord of which He was thinking in His high-priestly prayer, of which our text is a part. On the night of His betrayal Jesus was with His disciples. On this last night His thoughts went back to past events and projected forward into the future. In this state of mind Jesus thought of His work on earth as having been completed. Before Him was Gethsemane and the empty tomb, but He viewed His work as having been completed. It was only a matter of days, and it would all be over and He would have accomplished that for which the ages had been waiting.

He now had something to say to His disciples. What He had to say is recorded in the Gospel according to St. John. But He not only spoke to His disciples, He prayed in their presence. He said, "O Father, glorify Thou Me with Thine own self with the glory which I had with Thee before the world was" (John 17:5). He thought of Himself and His relationship with His heavenly Father. He thought of the disciples whom He had gathered. He asked God not to take them out of the world, but to keep them in the world and to sanctify them in the world that they might be one, even as He and the Father were one. He wanted these disciples to have the full fellowship which He had gained for them by His holy life and by His innocent suffering and death. Then He looked beyond His disciples and began to pray also for those who would believe on Him through their word. Therefore He prayed that they might be one and have the love of God even as He had explained and demonstrated it to them and would continue to demonstrate it to them. He had given them God's name. He had shown them God's love. Now they were to have this love and to be one in this faith and fellowship. The world was to see this in them, and through them the world was to learn and to be brought to God. These were the thoughts that Jesus had in mind as He prayed that evening.

Set Apart

The key verse in our text is, "*Sanctify* them through Thy truth. Thy Word is truth." The word "sanctify" means to set apart. In the Old Testament when an object was set apart from ordinary use for sacred use, it was said to be sanctified. For instance, a lamb without spot or blemish was taken from the flock and was sacrificed to God. Because it was set apart for sacrifice to God, it was considered holy. In this way the word "set apart" came to mean sanctify, to make holy or consider holy. When Jesus said, "Sanctify them," He meant, "Set these people apart, cleanse them, purify them." On the other hand, He also said: "Do not take them out of this world. Leave them in the world, but sanctify and cleanse them and make them one in Us as I have set Myself apart. As I have set Myself apart for this cause, do Thou also set them apart."

Genuine Reality

Jesus said, "Sanctify them *through Thy truth.* Thy Word is truth." The truth of which He speaks is not merely truthfulness but reality. Occasionally people ask why preachers in their sermons do not get down to practical things in life. They complain that preachers speak much of Jesus and the things that happened back in Biblical days, when they want to hear something applicable to our day. The most practical message in the world and the message most applicable to our time is the truth to which Jesus refers in this text. Truth here does not mean simply a system of truth. Truth means reality, that is, that which is real, genuine, and without sham. It cuts through the superficial, the frills, and the transitory to get at the heart of life's great issues. In fact, if you do not have truth, you have mere husks, the nonessentials of life, and you live in a make-believe world. Jesus says, "Set these people apart in that which is genuine reality."

What is genuine reality? It is that God *is,* that He sent His Son Jesus to redeem men, that He sent His Spirit to call men into fellowship with God, that man was created and made to be at one with God and at one with other men, and that this oneness is in the Lord Jesus. There is no message more practical than this one. You can own everything under the sun, but if you do not experience this basic relationship with God through the Lord Jesus, you cannot begin to comprehend who you really are and why you are here. You live in a make-believe world until you grasp this clearly. God has called us into fellowship with Himself in and through this great reality, that He has reclaimed and made us His own through Jesus Christ.

The Oneness We Have

There are many differences separating us, countless likes and dislikes, interests so diversified that we tend to go in every direction of the globe, but in this basic reality we are one, one in our faith in the Lord Jesus and our fellowship with God through Him. In this reality God sets us apart for Himself. He does not take us out of this world but transforms us in this world. As He calls us out of darkness into light, out of sin unto holiness by the cleansing power of God's Spirit, He sets us apart for a life with God, great in its purpose and having a great cause. In this truth we find the meaning of life. In it is comfort, motivation, and goal. This is why we live.

As we are sanctified and cleansed and become one with God, others begin to believe also through us that God *is* and that He sent His Son to redeem and save us. They also enter into this unity and fellowship. In this way the church progresses and the Lord Jesus extends His power and influence over people. The world needs this influence. We need the vision of Jesus sitting in the heavens, extending His saving and sanctifying influence. We should keep the cross of Christ before us, and we should proclaim the resurrection of our Lord Jesus Christ. But we should also remember vividly the ascended Lord. We do well to remember that Jesus now rules in spite of what dictators may be doing or in spite of whatever headlines the communists may be making. One thing is sure: that the salvation of the world lies not in various ideologies but in the recognition of Jesus as Lord and Savior. Jesus is the basic Reality of life.

Our Task

The commemoration of Ascension Day gives us an occasion to lift up our eyes heavenward to see Jesus ascending on high and ruling in the heavens. Before ascending on high, Jesus said, "All power is given unto Me in heaven and in earth. Go ye therefore and make disciples of all nations . . . and lo, I am with you always even unto the end of the world" (Matt. 28:18-20). Jesus is fulfilling this promise of His presence. A great avenue of opportunity lies before us. There is much to do. We need to be consecrated, set apart for God to this task. As important as food and clothing is, more important is the task for which God has called and set us apart. Food, clothing, and shelter will be taken care of according to the promise of God if we seek first the kingdom of God and His righteousness.

Occasionally people ask, "Is the church progressing? Is the kingdom of God growing?" The answer is "Yes" and "No." Never before in the history of our denomination have as many adults been associating with the church as have been in the past few years. Never in its history has so much money been given to the cause of Christ. Never before have our missions been as successful as they have been in the last few years. But in spite of this, in Southeast Asia, for instance, annually two and one-half million people are added to the population, but the net growth of all

Christian churches in that area is about 25,000 a year. But even at this we can say more people in that area were gained for the church by our denomination in the last five years than during the first fifty years of this century. Jesus is still in the heavens.

Greater Works

Some years ago I was traveling the 300 miles from Houston to Dallas on a streamlined diesel-powered train which had just been put into service. It was the latest in rail transportation. People made reservations long in advance to assure themselves of a seat. While I was riding on this train, impressed with the tremendous advances of modern technology, one of the many sayings of our Lord became clear to me. It was the passage in the Gospel according to St. John, in which Jesus told His disciples, "He that believeth on Me, the works that I do shall he do also, and greater works than these shall he do because I go unto My Father" (John 14:12). I had been reading about missions in the South Pacific. Incidentally, in the South Pacific the 19th century wrote one of the most thrilling chapters in the history of missions of the Christian church since the days of the apostle Paul. I had been reading how missionaries had changed the lives of people in New Guinea and other countries, changed not so much their customs and mode of living as their basic orientation toward God and life. It was then that I began to understand what Jesus said, "Greater works than these shall he do." Jesus did great works of healing. We have seen great works of healing in our time. We shall see even greater works of healing in time to come, but greater works than these shall be done because Jesus went to the Father. Because Jesus completed His work here on earth, because He suffered, died, and rose again, and because He ascended on high with His mission completed and sent forth His Spirit and now governs and directs His church, His disciples will do greater works in the world than the works of miracles which He performed. What are they? They are the works being done in the name of Jesus, as the Word of God, the truth as it has been revealed in Jesus Christ, is brought to people. It is evidence of a great work done when a native Christian can begin his address to his fellow natives with these words, "My grandfather was a cannibal." Greater works are being done today because Jesus set Himself apart for His task; greater works because Jesus prayed, "Set them apart through Thy truth"; greater works because Jesus ascended into heaven to rule and govern His church.

We need the vision of the ascended Christ, holding His hand of benediction and protection over His church as He gathers, sanctifies, and sends it out for greater works.

Keep On Praying

By THEODORE A. ZEILE

(Sunday After Ascension)

And He said unto them, Which of you shall have a friend, and shall go unto him at midnight, and say unto him, Friend, lend me three loaves; for a friend of mine in his journey is come to me, and I have nothing to set before him? And he from within shall answer and say, Trouble me not; the door is now shut, and my children are with me in bed; I cannot rise and give thee. I say unto you, Though he will not rise and give him because he is his friend, yet because of his importunity he will rise and give him as many as he needeth. And I say unto you, Ask, and it shall be given you; seek, and ye shall find; knock, and it shall be opened unto you. For everyone that asketh receiveth, and he that seeketh findeth, and to him that knocketh it shall be opened. If a son shall ask bread of any of you that is a father, will he give him a stone? Or if he ask a fish, will he for a fish give him a serpent? Or if he shall ask an egg, will he offer him a scorpion? If ye, then, being evil, know how to give good gifts unto your children, how much more shall your heavenly Father give the Holy Spirit to them that ask Him?

Luke 11:5-13

One of the great Christian privileges is that of talking to God. Those who are God's children have for generations regarded this as something important and vital to their spiritual life.

Our text this morning is much more than a mere command to pray. While it is true that there are many such lessons in the Scriptures, here we have a lesson that emphasizes continuance in prayer. When our Lord spoke these words He was trying to impress on His hearers the necessity of persistence in their talking to God.

Keep on Praying

I

Advice Where It Is Needed

The Master knew that in every generation His children would be guilty of forgetting. He foresaw the many resolutions which would be made, resolutions which would be forgotten all too soon. He saw the many plans that would be made, plans that would never be carried out. So the Lord begins with this very interesting account: "Which of you shall have a friend, and shall go unto him at midnight, and say unto him, Friend, lend me three loaves; for a friend of mine in his journey is come to me, and I have nothing to set before him? And he from within shall answer and say, Trouble me not; the door is now shut, and my children are with me in bed; I cannot rise and give thee. I say unto you, Though he will not rise and give him because he is his friend, yet because of his importunity he will rise and give him as many as he needeth."

Suppose a man upon a sudden emergency goes to borrow a loaf or two of bread of a neighbor, at an unreasonable time of the night, not for himself but for his friend who came to him unexpectedly. His neighbor will be very unwilling to accommodate him, for he has awakened him with his knocking and disturbed him in his sleep. The door is shut and locked, the children are asleep and in bed in the same room with him. If he makes a noise, he will disturb them. His servants are asleep, and he cannot make them hear. In spite of everything, however, the neighbor continues to knock, continues to remind him of his request. Finally the man must give in. He will rise and give the bread to his friend because he continued with his asking.

Here is the lesson He wants us to remember. He wants us to be persistent. He wants us to be regular in our petitions and in our prayers. He wants us to realize that the full value of our prayer life can be obtained only if we keep on in our prayers. He knows, too, that this is advice, encouragement, admonition, which every son and daughter of God will need.

We are here this morning as members of the body of Christ. We have come to church with our fears, our crosses, our worries, our problems, our challenges, our failures. What a long catalog of items we could list if each one of us were given just two minutes to speak, to tell, to recall. So this morning the Master says to us: "Husbands and wives, are you having domestic problems in your home? Has something happened to your mutual understanding and love? Are you far from the high and holy ideals which God set down with regard to holy wedlock?" Then this text is for you. The Master says, "Keep on praying, keep on calling, keep on in your conversation with God." Have you come to church this morning worrying about the world situation, the continuing threats of Russia, the foreboding future? To you He says today, "Keep on praying." Remember yours is a privilege given only to God's children; use it, persist, be regular in your prayers.

You who are teen-agers — are you having trouble trying to be popular and accepted and yet somehow trying to be the upright, decent, proper young people God would want you to be? Are you wondering how you can live in our modern world and yet live for Christ? "Keep on praying," He says. Keep on bringing these petitions to your God. Boys and girls, are you having trouble with your parents? Do you find it difficult to love and honor them? Do you feel again and again that your parents just do not understand you? Jesus says to you today, "Keep on praying." Bring these individual and particular problems to God, who hears and answers every real prayer.

It is amazing how many outstanding examples of this persistent, regular praying we find in Holy Scriptures. You remember the story of Jacob, who wrestled with God, exclaiming, "I will not leave Thee except Thou bless me!" Then there was the woman of Canaan who was willing to be classified with the dogs. She kept on praying, she kept on calling, and the Lord saluted her as a woman of great faith.

A few years ago, at a reception for adult confirmands, a faithful woman came to her pastor as her husband was being welcomed into church, and she made this remark: "I think this is the happiest day in my life. You know, Pastor, I've been praying for this for 15 years — today God granted it." Scripture speaks the language of persistent prayer when the apostle admonishes us to "pray without ceasing" and again to "be instant in prayer." My friend, whether you are old or young, rich or poor, whether you have few problems or many, remember the Master speaks to you this morning and gives you the advice we all need — to keep on praying.

II
Realize What Kind of a God We Have

"If a son shall ask bread of any of you that is a father, will he give him a stone? Or if he ask a fish, will he for a fish give him a serpent? Or if he shall ask an egg, will he offer him a scorpion? If ye, then, being evil, know how to give good gifts unto your children, how much more shall your heavenly Father give the Holy Spirit to them that ask Him?" Jesus makes reference to human fathers. He speaks of the everyday man of the house, the one who works faithfully and tries to fulfill his responsibilities in the home as provider, as husband, and as father. Then, by way of contrast, He directs the reader to the heavenly Father, the same Father to whom our Lord directs His children to pray in the prayer He taught us. Here is the Father to whom He speaks this grand doxology: "Thine is the kingdom." — You are the King of kings and the Lord of lords; "Thine is the power." — In contrast to the strength and endurance of human fathers, You stand before us as the Almighty God, with whom everything is possible; "Thine is the glory." — The praise for the blessings asked does not in any way or to any extent belong to us, or to any creatures, not even the angels, but to Thee alone.

Could it be that we, you and I, fail to keep on praying, fail to be persistent, because we forget what kind of God we have? because we underestimate His goodness, new to us every morning, His love, which prompted Him to send down from heaven His best, His only-begotten Son, as our personal Savior from sin? Could it be that we fail to keep on praying because we have forgotten the great lesson of the providence of our God? This morning again He speaks to each one of us and says, "I have called you, you are Mine. I know you as a member of My family."

It happened in a coffee shop in a Chicago hotel. A clergyman was finishing his breakfast when a man slid onto the stool beside him and nervously ordered rolls and coffee. "Did you see that headline?" the stranger asked, pointing to a bold streamer across the morning paper: "Air Crash Kills Fifty-Two." "I'm supposed to catch a plane for Los Angeles this noon. Frankly, I'm scared stiff. If I didn't have to be there for a meeting in the morning, I'd cancel my ticket and take the train."

It so happened that the clergyman also had a plane reservation that very afternoon. He had a ticket for Buffalo, and he intended to use it. "Well, I guess it's all the way you look at it," mused the stranger. "When your number's up, it's up."

The minister looked at the frightened man a moment, and then replied, "Yes, I suppose so, but I happen to know the Man who puts the numbers up." The stranger was bewildered. Could the clergyman be joking, or was he really serious? But before he could bring himself to ask, the minister continued, "You see, the Man who puts the numbers up happens to be my Father." Then he went on to tell the stranger of the loving care and the protection of our Father in heaven.

Surely again today as we speak about continuing with our praying, our God wants to impress us with the fact that He is a great God, a big God, an almighty God. Indeed, we dare not underestimate or undervalue what He has done for us and what He will do for us also with regard to our praying.

How fortunate, then, how blessed, we are in contrast to those who neither have Him nor would have Him. How privileged we should feel in our faith in His only-begotten Son, our Lord and Savior, whose first mission was to redeem us and to whom we can come regularly in penitent prayer and from whom we receive the continuing assurance of mercy. Every one of us also, in our lesson on prayer, must behold Him this morning as our personal Redeemer, as not only the One to whom we speak but, above all, the One who came to give His life as a ransom for many.

III

God's Assurance in Answering Prayer

Listen: "And I say unto you, Ask, and it shall be given you; seek, and ye shall find; knock, and it shall be opened unto you." The word "ask" suggests asking humbly; it is the asking of a son or daughter addressing a superior. The work "seek" means to search for, to pursue with persistence. The word "knock" means to beat and to pound. Each verb is more intense than the preceding one. Their choice is due to the illustration which had just been used. The friend in need at first called out at his friend's house, humbly asking for bread. When he received no response, he diligently sought where the sleeper might be lying and then repeated his request. Then, obtaining no answer, he began knocking at the door until he aroused the sleeper and finally obtained his request. A threefold promise is given for those who persist. It is Christ's own promise, stated in the most positive way, "It shall be given you." Says Martin Luther:

> Prayer has hitherto upheld the church; therefore we must continue to pray. This is why Christ says: Ask, seek, knock. To begin with, we should ask. When we then begin to ask, He hides Himself somewhere and will not hear — will not let Himself be found. Therefore we must seek Him out, that is, must continue in prayer. When we seek Him, He locks Himself in a closet. If we want to go to Him, we must knock. When we knock once or twice, He acts as if He had not heard us. Finally, when we are about to overdo the knocking, He opens and says: Well, what do you want? Lord, I want this or that. Then He says: Why, then take it. In this way everyone must wake Him up. Therefore the verse: Ask, seek, knock, wants only to command: Ask, call, cry, seek, storm! And we should do this constantly, without ceasing.

For true Christians there are no unanswered prayers. Indeed, some may not be answered as we desire them to be answered, some may not be fulfilled in accord with our expectation, but make no mistake about it, they are answered. Three times the Master uses the word "shall." To everyone who hears this important verse, there is His assurance which dare not be overlooked. There is a promise which dare not be bypassed. I must keep on praying because I have a God who will answer. Furthermore, this is a truth that is repeated again and again in the Scripture. Old Testament believers and New Testament Christians know well the repeated promises which God made regarding answer to prayer.

Yes, keep on praying. Replace forgetting with remembering. Come to the Lord regularly. Also realize the kind of God we have: His greatness, His goodness. Be sure, too, that the prayers of His children, your prayers, are answered and heard. So God help you to keep on praying.

The Quickening Spirit

By Wm. H. Bornemann

(Pentecost)

Many therefore of His disciples, when they had heard this, said, This is an hard saying; who can hear it? When Jesus knew in Himself that His disciples murmured at it, He said unto them, Doth this offend you? What and if ye shall see the Son of man ascend up where He was before? It is the Spirit that quickeneth; the flesh profiteth nothing; the words that I speak unto you, they are spirit, and they are life. But there

are some of you that believe not. For Jesus knew from the beginning
who they were that believed not, and who should betray Him. And He
said, Therefore said I unto you that no man can come unto Me except
it were given unto him of My Father. From that time many of His
disciples went back and walked no more with Him. Then said Jesus
unto the Twelve, Will ye also go away? Then Simon Peter answered
Him, Lord, to whom shall we go? Thou hast the words of eternal life.
And we believe and are sure that Thou art that Christ, the Son of the
living God. Jesus answered them, Have not I chosen you Twelve, and
one of you is a devil? He spake of Judas Iscariot, the son of Simon;
for he it was that should betray Him, being one of the Twelve.

John 6:60-71

Two Miracles

The pioneers, driving their wagons over the old Oregon Trail
through western Nebraska and into Wyoming, saw vast stretches
of dry and desolate land. The traveler today, driving on Highway 26 through the same country, sees acres upon acres covered
with the lush growth of sugar beets and corn and beans. The flow
of water over the dry land, made possible through irrigation, has
made the difference! This is a miracle of nature.

So also we see a human life, barren of faith and love and works,
changed into a life full of faith and love and goodness and a wealth
of good works. The Holy Spirit, working through the Gospel of
Jesus Christ, has made the difference! This is the miracle of
Pentecost! The Holy Ghost has made a new creature out of man.
What God the Holy Ghost can do is clearly seen in the example of
Paul, who, as Saul, had been a fierce persecutor of the Christians,
and who then became one of the greatest workers for the Savior.
This miracle of Pentecost has also taken place in the hearts of all of
us who worship the Lord Jesus Christ today. In the text before
us our Savior reminds us of the fact that faith, together with all of
its fruits, is the gift of God and the work of the Holy Spirit in our
hearts and lives. He speaks of

The Quickening Spirit

I

The Quickening Spirit Works Faith
Through the Means of Grace

The Audience

A large number of people stood around our Lord on the occasion recorded in our text. The Twelve were present, as well as
many others who considered themselves to be disciples of Jesus.
These were members of the larger circle of His disciples, from
whom He on one occasion chose the Seventy, whom He then sent
out two by two to preach the Gospel. There were also others, who
had been fascinated and intrigued by the miracles of Jesus and by

His preaching, but they had not yet reached a definite decision about Him. These people had followed Jesus to Capernaum from the other side of the Sea of Galilee, where on the previous day Jesus had fed five thousand men with five loaves of barley bread and two small fish.

The Unbelief of the People

As Jesus talked to the people, He knew that many were still confused in their thinking about Him. He was also aware of the fact that some of them did not believe in Him as the promised Messiah. He knew that the miraculous feeding of the five thousand had missed its purpose and that "they sought Him not for what He was, their Savior, but for what they wanted Him to be, a bread king, now that they had eaten the loaves and enjoyed a good meal" (Fahling, *The Life of Christ*, p. 352). Therefore Jesus said to them, "This is the work of God, that ye believe on Him whom He hath sent" (v. 29). Since the miracle of the bread was still upon their minds, He compared Himself and His salvation to the Bread of Heaven, "For the bread of God is He which cometh down from heaven and giveth life unto the world" (v. 33). "I am the Bread of Life; he that cometh to Me shall never hunger; and he that believeth on Me shall never thirst." (V. 35)

The words of Jesus puzzled them. They tried to reason them out, and they came to the conclusion that they could not accept them. In fact, His words shocked and offended them. The omniscient Jesus knew this, and therefore He told them, "It is the Spirit that quickeneth; the flesh profiteth nothing." By nature man cannot accept or believe the mysteries of God. These shocked and offended people who stood around Jesus were simply bearing out the truth of the apostle Paul's inspired words: "The natural man receiveth not the things of the Spirit of God, for they are foolishness unto him; neither can he know them, because they are spiritually discerned" (1 Cor. 2:14). In all spiritual matters natural man is blind and dead. His mind is set on sinful things, and he is unable to grasp and accept the truths of God concerning our salvation in Christ Jesus. This was true of Jesus' hearers, and therefore He had to remind them that "the flesh profiteth nothing." As long as they tried to test His words through the power of their own minds, they would remain helpless and confused and unbelieving.

The Work of the Spirit

The quickening Spirit, the Holy Ghost, must give spiritual life. He is the life-giving Power. "It is the Spirit that quickeneth," said Jesus to His hearers. He also pointed out to them the manner in which the Holy Spirit comes into the hearts of men: "The words that I speak unto you, they are spirit, and they are life." Just

a little later the twelve disciples backed up His statement when
Peter answered Him, "Lord, to whom shall we go? Thou hast the
words of eternal life. And we believe and are sure that Thou art
that Christ, the Son of the living God." Through the words which
He had spoken to them they had become convinced that Jesus was
the Holy One of God. Through His life-giving words the quickening Spirit had worked faith in their hearts. So also Paul wrote to
the Christians in Corinth some years later: "In Christ Jesus I have
begotten you through the Gospel." (1 Cor. 4:15)

The Situation Today

Conditions have not changed since that day long ago when
Jesus spoke to the people at Capernaum. Man by nature is still the
lost, hopeless, and helpless sinner that he has been since that sad
day when Adam and Eve fell into sin. He is still conceived and
born in sin, as the psalmist sadly confesses (Ps. 51:5). Man still
cannot change his condition through any power or strength of his
own, because "the imagination of man's heart is evil from his
youth" (Gen. 8:21). Man cannot believe through any power of his
own that Jesus Christ is true God and his Savior. No man can
come to Jesus, except through the power that is given him by the
heavenly Father through the working of the quickening Spirit.
Lazarus could not come forth from his tomb by his own power
and strength, but his lifeless body could be quickened or made alive
only by the power of the Savior's word; so also the spiritually dead
person cannot come to Jesus by his own power and strength, but
he must be spiritually quickened by the Holy Spirit through the
Word of God.

We Should Be Thankful

How thankful we Christians should be that the Holy Ghost has
taken us — dead, lifeless, worthless, and condemned creatures that
we were by nature — and has brought us to the knowledge of our
Savior! We can take no more credit for our faith and for our
sure and joyful hope of life everlasting than could the three thousand who were converted on the first Pentecost. Jesus Christ suffered and died freely, willingly, and lovingly for all sinners, even
us, and now, through the life-giving Word of God, through the
precious means of grace, God's holy Word and the sacrament of
Holy Baptism, the quickening Spirit has led us to repent of our sins
and to accept Jesus Christ as our Savior. He has changed us and
has made new creatures out of us. Now, when we look to the
cross on Calvary, we do not see a great man dying for a noble
cause, but we see the Son of God, who as true man bears in His
holy body the sins of the whole world. We know that His holy,
precious blood, flowing from His holy wounds, has washed us
clean of every sin. Out of love and gratitude and thankfulness to

our God and Savior we now see our lives here on earth as His workmanship, created in Christ Jesus unto good works. All of this is the work of the Holy Ghost in our hearts and lives. How eagerly we should pray:

> Come, oh, come, Thou quick'ning Spirit,
> God from all eternity!
> May Thy power never fail us;
> Dwell within us constantly.

II
The Blessing of the Quickening Spirit Can Be Lost

The Work of the Holy Spirit Can Be Resisted

It is the plain teaching of God's holy Word that man cannot bring himself to Christ, but that our sanctification is entirely the work of the Holy Spirit. It is equally true, however, that man can resist the power of the Holy Ghost and lose the blessings of salvation. Note what happened when Jesus spoke to the people of His salvation. He told them plainly: "Verily, verily, I say unto you, He that believeth on Me hath everlasting life. I am that Bread of Life" (vv. 47, 48). Yet many were offended. They said, "This is an hard saying; who can hear it?" They could not grasp and understand His words, and therefore they refused to accept them. They closed their minds and refused to believe. Their unbelief resulted in one of the saddest statements of the Bible: "From that time many of His disciples went back and walked no more with Him." Their unbelief brought upon them eternal damnation in hell.

The Danger Is Always Present

Do not many in our day follow the example of the unbelieving people in our text? Just because certain teachings of Jesus seem to be unreasonable, they refuse to accept them. They refuse to accept Jesus as the Bread of Life. Their reaction is still the same as it was that day in Capernaum. "This is an hard saying; who can hear it?" They refuse to believe in spite of the fact that Jesus Christ rose from the dead and ascended into heaven. When a popular magazine published an article based on a survey and on interviews with more than one hundred young men in eight of the nation's leading divinity schools, it revealed that fewer than one half of them believed in the virgin birth of Jesus, or that Jesus ascended physically after His resurrection, and fewer than one third believed that there is a real heaven and hell. (Redbook, November 1961, pp. 52 ff.). Isn't it true that often we experience the same reaction when we speak to a neighbor or a friend or a relative about his sins and his need of Jesus Christ, his Savior? Unbelief and rejection of Jesus Christ was not limited to the people of Jesus' day, but it prevails among men today.

Unbelief may be found also among those who claim to be His disciples. Looking upon them with loving and saddened eyes, the Savior said to His twelve disciples, "Have I not chosen you Twelve, and one of you is a devil?" John adds the footnote to His account, "He spake of Judas Iscariot, the son of Simon; for he it was that should betray Him, being one of the Twelve." Membership in a church or association with Christians is in itself no guarantee that a person will always remain a disciple of Jesus Christ. A time of testing comes to every Christian, when he must decide to follow the teachings of Jesus Christ or to follow his own ideas and reasonings. When such a time comes, Jesus asks us to be on guard, and He puts the question to us: "Will ye also go away?" How will we answer His question?

The Quickening Spirit Gives Us Power

Here again we must confess that we have no power to continue to walk with Christ. This power must come from the Holy Spirit. Jesus says, "If ye continue in My Word, then are ye My disciples indeed" (John 8:31). Through the precious Gospel of Jesus Christ the quickening Spirit continues to work in our hearts the good work which He has begun. He keeps us in the faith and strengthens us. Daily He leads us to know and to repent of our sins and brings us again to our Lord Jesus Christ, in whose innocent suffering and death and holy, precious blood we find complete forgiveness of all our sins. "Ye are kept by the power of God through faith unto salvation" (1 Peter 1:5). Through the Gospel the Holy Spirit draws us ever closer to our Savior and effectually works in our hearts so that we will live unto Christ, our Savior. Each day, as we read our Bibles, as we come to God's house to hear His Word, as we partake of His Holy Supper, as we discuss the Word in our Bible classes and in our family devotions, we can feel the power of the quickening Spirit in our lives, in our thoughts, in our actions. Our minds and hearts will be filled with peace and joy and comfort. Our hearts will be filled with love to our Lord and the desire to serve Him. Our hearts will burn with zeal to bring the Gospel of salvation to others so that the Holy Spirit can perform the miracle of Pentecost in their hearts. And should we be asked, "Will ye also go away?" we will answer through the power of the quickening Spirit: "Lord, to whom shall we go? Thou hast the words of eternal life. And we believe and are sure that Thou art that Christ, the Son of the living God."

> Although all the world should forsake and forget Thee,
> In love I will follow Thee, ne'er will I quit Thee.
> Lord Jesus, both spirit and life is Thy Word;
> And is there a joy which Thou dost not afford?

The Church's Partnership with the Triune God

By Elmer O. Luessenhop

(Trinity Sunday)

Then the eleven disciples went away into Galilee, into a mountain where Jesus had appointed them. And when they saw Him, they worshiped Him; but some doubted. And Jesus came and spake unto them, saying: All power is given unto Me in heaven and in earth. Go ye therefore and teach all nations, baptizing them in the name of the Father and of the Son and of the Holy Ghost, teaching them to observe all things whatsoever I have commanded you. And, lo, I am with you alway, even unto the end of the world. Amen. — *Matthew 28:16-20*

> All praise to God, who reigns above,
> The God of all creation,
> The God of wonders, power, and love,
> The God of our salvation!

The salvation of sinful mankind is the will and work of the Triune God. It is God — the Triune God — who "will have all men to be saved and to come unto the knowledge of the truth" (1 Tim. 2:4). It is God — the Triune God — who "is not willing that any should perish, but that all should come to repentance." (2 Peter 3:9)

God the Father, out of His great love for the world, "gave His only-begotten Son, that whosoever believeth in Him should not perish but have everlasting life" (John 3:16). God the Son, out of His love for sinners, "made Himself of no reputation, and took upon Him the form of a servant, and was made in the likeness of men; and being found in fashion as a man, He humbled Himself and became obedient unto death, even the death of the cross" (Phil. 2:7, 8). God the Holy Ghost, out of the same love, makes the blessings of salvation our very own by bringing us to faith in Christ, and through such faith restores us to fellowship with God.

You see, when God first created man, He intended for him to enjoy a blessed communion and a perfect fellowship with his Creator. But man, through sin, severed this relationship. God, however, did not want to lose man. He wanted man to return to Him as His child. And God provided the way. Man could never have found his way back to God. Man the sinner could never have restored the broken fellowship. But "God was in Christ, reconciling the world unto Himself, not imputing their trespasses unto them" (2 Cor. 5:19). Through the redemptive work of Christ the barrier of sin has been removed, the fellowship has been restored, atonement has been made, man is declared at one with God.

The salvation of sinners is an accomplished fact. When dying on the cross, Jesus declared His mission completed when He said, "It is finished!" His saving work was done. But while the salvation of the world has been accomplished, the good news of that

salvation is to be proclaimed to sinners everywhere, for it is
through this good news, the Gospel, that the Holy Spirit brings
men to faith in Christ and thus makes them partakers of His
salvation.

At one time Jesus told a parable about a certain man who
prepared a sumptuous banquet. When everything was in readiness,
he sent his servant to invite the guests, "Come, for all things are
now ready" (Luke 14:17). In like manner the feast of our salvation
has been prepared. All that remains is to send forth the invitation,
"Ho, everyone that thirsteth, come ye to the waters; and he that
hath no money, come ye, buy, and eat; yea, come, buy wine and
milk without money and without price" (Is. 55:1). God, in Christ,
has reconciled the world to Himself. The only task remaining is
to proclaim to lost mankind the Word of reconciliation and to voice
the appeal, "Be ye reconciled to God" (2 Cor. 5:20). This is the
task that God has given to His church on earth, to all Christians,
to you and me.

Now here is a wondrous thing: God could have commissioned
His angels to proclaim the Gospel of salvation to this sinful
world. But He did not. He gave that charge to His church, to His
redeemed people. It was to His disciples that Jesus said, "Ye shall
be witnesses unto Me . . . unto the uttermost part of the earth."
"Go ye into all the world, and preach the Gospel to every creature."
(Acts 1:8; Mark 16:15)

What a glorious privilege! We have been called, as it were,
into partnership with God! It is our privilege to share with God
the task of saving the world. God has indeed done the saving;
but ours is the responsibility to proclaim to the world this saving truth.

May the Holy Spirit bless our meditation this Trinity Sunday
as we consider

The Church's Partnership with the Triune God

I

The Great Commission

The obligations resting upon us, as partners with the Triune
God, are expressed in the words of the Great Commission: "Go ye
therefore and make disciples of all nations, baptizing them in the
name of the Father and of the Son and of the Holy Ghost, teaching
them to observe all things whatsoever I have commanded you."

These words were spoken by Jesus to His disciples sometime
after He had risen from the dead and shortly before He ascended
into heaven. The place was a mountaintop in Galilee.

A Mountaintop Experience

It is interesting to note that many of the significant events in the ministry of Jesus occurred on mountaintops. One of His temptations took place on the top of a mountain. It was from a mountain that He preached His magnificent Sermon on the Mount. His transfiguration before Peter, James, and John occurred on a mountaintop. He was crucified on "Calvary's mournful mountain." It was from the mount called Olivet that He ascended into heaven.

So also here, the event recorded in our text took place on a mountain. It was an important occasion. It was to be a most significant meeting.

A Divine Appointment

The meeting was no accident; it had been prearranged by divine appointment. On the night of His betrayal, in the Garden of Gethsemane Jesus had said to His disciples, "All ye shall be offended because of Me this night; for it is written, I will smite the Shepherd, and the sheep of the flock shall be scattered abroad. But after I am risen again, *I will go before you into Galilee*" (Matt. 26:31, 32). And on that first Easter morning, at the empty tomb, the angel had announced to the women, "Ye seek Jesus, which was crucified. He is not here, for He is risen, as He said. Come, see the place where the Lord lay. And go quickly and tell His disciples that He is risen from the dead; and, behold, *He goeth before you into Galilee; there shall ye see Him.*" (Matt. 28:5-7)

In keeping with this divine appointment, the disciples and other followers of Jesus — perhaps as many as five hundred of them — assemble on a Galilean hillside. Suddenly Jesus appears; and when they behold His glorious visage, they prostrate themselves before Him in worship and adoration. The risen Lord steps into their midst, reassuringly, and He says, "All power is given unto Me in heaven and in earth. Go ye therefore and make disciples of all nations . . ."

The Church's Mission

In the words of this great commission Jesus spells out the church's mission. The task of the Christian church till the end of time is to go and make disciples of all nations. The church is not to stand still and wait for people to come to it, but it is to go into all the world, and having gone, it is to make disciples of people. Like a mighty army the church is to move, to advance, to invade. Our mission map has no boundaries; our divine Captain has set no limits on the conquests we are to make.

What diversity exists among the families of the earth! There are differences in race, color, nationality, language, culture, achievement; yet all have sinned and come short of the glory of God (Rom. 3:23). All are thus separated from God, in need of a Savior; all have been redeemed by the same Savior; all are to be made His disciples.

Jesus, in our text, tells us how this discipling is to be done: by baptizing and teaching. "Go ye therefore and make disciples of all nations, *baptizing* them in the name of the Father and of the Son and of the Holy Ghost, *teaching* them to observe all things whatsoever I have commanded you."

Baptize!

Jesus has commissioned His church to baptize. This sacrament is frequently administered in our midst, but how much do we really know about it? Luther tells us that "Baptism is not simple water only, but it is the water comprehended in God's command and connected with God's word." Baptism is not merely a symbolic washing as some would have it. It is a means of grace, a means of making disciples of people. It is a means of imparting the blessings of God's grace to sinners. "It works forgiveness of sins, delivers from death and the devil, and gives eternal salvation to all who believe this."

Infant Baptism

We are to make disciples of *all nations* baptizing them. . . . And so we baptize men and women, oldsters and youngsters, adults and infants. Jesus nowhere tells us that we must wait until a person reaches a certain age before we can baptize him. He wants us to make disciples of all nations; He wants the little children to be His disciples too. "Suffer the little children to come unto Me and forbid them not; for of such is the kingdom of God" (Mark 10:14). Little children are not the disciples of Jesus by nature. They are born in sin, under the wrath of God, separated from God; they, too, must be born again if they are to enter the kingdom of God. We can never sufficiently thank God that He has given us this wonderful means of grace whereby even our little infants can become disciples of Christ, children of God and heirs of heaven.

The Formula of Baptism

We are to baptize in the name of the Triune God: ". . . in the name of the Father and of the Son and of the Holy Ghost." These words are not a mere pious recital. They are the word of God which makes the water of Baptism "a gracious water of life and a washing of regeneration in the Holy Ghost." These words constitute the power of Baptism, and they convey the blessings of Baptism. Through Baptism God the Son becomes our Father; He adopts us as His children. Through Baptism God the Son becomes our Redeemer and Brother; we become members of His body; we put on Christ; His righteousness becomes our glorious dress. Through Baptism God the Holy Ghost becomes our Comforter, and we become His temple in which He deigns to dwell. Thus, through Baptism, we enter into an intimate communion with God; we are received into fellowship with Him. He becomes our God and we become His people, the sheep of His pasture.

Teach!

Jesus, further, has entrusted to His church the task of teaching all nations: ". . . teaching them to observe all things whatsoever I have commanded you." In the case of infants: we first baptize, then we teach. In the case of unbaptized adults: we first teach and then we baptize. We are to do both — baptize and teach — and through such means of grace we are to make disciples of all nations.

The Content of Our Teaching

What is it that we are to teach? Sad to say, many churches nowadays have lost sight of their teaching mission. They keep their people informed of the latest developments in current events, science, politics; they discuss with them the latest fads in philosophy, the problems and methods of psychology. But this is not the teaching task of the church. Rather, we are to teach people to observe all things whatsoever Christ has commanded us. We are to portray sin in all its heinousness; we are to declare the grace of God in all its sweetness. We are to preach Law and Gospel: the Law, to crush men's stony hearts; the Gospel, to pick up the pieces, to create new hearts in them. We are to teach the Word of God in its truth and purity, clearly enunciating each and every doctrine as it is set forth in the inspired Scripture.

"Teaching them to observe *all things* whatsoever I have commanded you," Jesus says. We have no business selecting a doctrine here and a precept there and forgetting the rest. We have no right to omit from our teaching a doctrine of the Bible which doesn't happen to agree with us, or which doesn't appeal to our reason. We are to *teach all* that Christ has commanded so that people may be led to *observe all* that He has commanded. Jesus says, "If ye continue in My Word, then are ye My disciples indeed; and ye shall know the truth, and the truth shall make you free." (John 8: 31, 32)

The Purpose of Our Teaching

This is the purpose of our teaching: to lead people to observe all that Jesus has commanded so that they may be His disciples indeed; to lead them to repentance and faith; to bring people *to* Christ, to keep them *with* Christ, and to help them grow *in* Christ. It is to make them wise unto salvation, through faith which is in Christ Jesus (2 Tim. 3:15). It has to make people true children of God who are thoroughly furnished unto all good works

(2 Tim. 3:17). It is to give them the knowledge of God, the only true God, and of Jesus Christ, whom He has sent (John 17:3). This is life eternal. And this is the ultimate goal we are striving for in the teaching mission of the church.

II

Encouragement for the Task

A tremendous challenge confronts the church. Jesus has commissioned us to make disciples of all nations. This is an urgent, formidable task.

The Urgency of Our Task

In many ways the world of today is growing smaller. Thanks to modern methods of communication and transportation, the far reaches of the earth have become almost as accessible as the house down the street. In another sense, however, our world of today is growing larger. The Great Commission concerns itself with people, and the world's population is expanding at an amazing rate.

While the Christian church is growing, it is growing relatively smaller. The Christians of the world have always been a minority group, but they are becoming more of a minority all the time. The growth of the heathen population is rapidly outstripping that of the Christian population. At the same time we must remember that no one in this world is born a Christian; everyone is born a heathen, and remains a heathen until he is made a disciple of Christ. To put it another way: Christians are reborn, not born; and the *birth* rate is far exceeding the *rebirth* rate.

Divine Backing

In view of all this we recognize the urgency of our task. It would be an impossible task were it left up to us. But it is not left up to us, nor does the successful accomplishment of the task depend upon us. We have behind us the power and authority of Jesus, the almighty Son of God. When commissioning His church, Jesus said, "All power is given unto Me in heaven and in earth. Go ye *therefore* and make disciples of all nations. . . ."

Jesus, the Lord of the church, the One who has commissioned us to disciple the nations, is the Possessor of all power and authority in heaven and earth. As true God He has had this power from all eternity; as true Man He *received* this power; this power has *been given* to Him. Just think of it: our Lord Jesus Christ has complete authority over heaven — over all the angels and archangels and all the saints in glory, over all principalities and powers and dominions and thrones. This authority extends over all the hosts of hell, for He has subdued them under His feet. This authority embraces all the earth — all the forces of nature, all living things, all nations under the sun, all human governments, all the rulers of men, all the armies and navies of the world, all atomic power.

This same Jesus, the Ruler of heaven and earth, the King of creation, the Lord of the nations, has commissioned us to go and make disciples of all nations. We are far from being helpless; the task is not impossible. We have the power and authority of Christ behind us; and no government on earth, no army, no human organization has had such resources to back it up!

Who then can withstand us? Whom need we fear? As Christians we are carrying in our hearts the credentials, and on our lips the message, of the King of kings and the Lord of lords. Our mission cannot fail. This is not to say that our efforts will always meet with success. They won't. But, as we said before, the success of our mission does not depend upon us. All Jesus asks of us is that we hold forth the Word of life to a dying world. It is still God who gives the increase. Our credentials will not always be received; our message will often fall on deaf ears. Nevertheless God has promised that His Word shall not return unto Him void, but it shall prosper in the thing whereto He has sent it. (Is. 55:11)

A Divine Companion

Our Lord offers us still another word of encouragement. As we go about our task, carrying out the Great Commission, we are not alone. Jesus has left with us the promise, "Lo, I am with you alway, even unto the end of the world."

To do the work of the Lord is often a lonely task. It is not easy for a missionary to leave home and country to go into a strange, far distant land. But he does not go alone. Jesus is with him. It is not always easy for a young man, leaving the seminary, to begin his ministry in some out-of-the-way place which he has never heard of before. But he is not alone. The Lord Jesus is with him. It is not a simple matter to walk up to the door of a strange house, push the doorbell, look into an unfamiliar, forbidding countenance, and speak of Christ. But again, we are not alone. The Lord is by our side.

To do the work of the Lord is often a dangerous task. "Behold, I send you forth as sheep in the midst of wolves" (Matt. 10:16). But we are not alone. The Shepherd is with us to sustain us with the rod of His power and the staff of His authority. "And ye shall be hated of all men for My name's sake" (Mark 13:13). But we are not alone. Jesus is with us to comfort us with His abiding love.

The work of the Lord is often discouraging. And in that work we often become sensible of our many weaknesses. But the Lord is ever present at our side. His grace is sufficient for us; for His strength is made perfect in our weakness. (2 Cor. 12:9)

On this Trinity Sunday let us lift up grateful hearts to God, praising Him for having called us into fellowship with Him, thanking Him for the privilege of being His partners; and let us pray that He will fill our hearts with zeal to do the work He has given us to do while it is day, before the night cometh when no man can work.

Fruit Required in His Kingdom

By W. H. MUNDINGER

(The First Sunday After Trinity)

I am the true Vine, and My Father is the Husbandman. Every branch in Me that beareth not fruit He taketh away; and every branch that beareth fruit, He purgeth it that it may bring forth more fruit. Now ye are clean through the Word which I have spoken unto you. Abide in Me, and I in you. As the branch cannot bear fruit of itself except it abide in the vine, no more can ye except ye abide in Me. I am the Vine, ye are the branches. He that abideth in Me, and I in him, the same bringeth much fruit, for without Me ye can do nothing. If a man abide not in Me, he is cast forth as a branch and is withered. And men gather them and cast them into the fire, and they are burned. If ye abide in Me, and My words abide in you, ye shall ask what ye will, and it shall be done unto you. Herein is My Father glorified, that ye bear much fruit; so shall ye be My disciples. — *John 15:1–8*

Agriculture and horticulture have made tremendous strides in recent years. By selective breeding and mating superior strains, our experimental farms and stations have developed improved domestic animals, fruits, grains, and vegetables. Skilled management of high-yielding varieties of plants and animals has created an abundance of food and fiber for this our favored generation.

With all the success our scientists and technicians have been achieving in the improvement of varieties, the basic principles of the laws of nature, laid down in creation, have remained unaltered. In His parables and illustrations our Lord uses the observable phenomena of nature as comparisons in teaching the truth concerning His kingdom.

In our text Christ uses the relationship of vine and branches to illustrate that a productive, fruitful life in His kingdom is possible for us only by remaining in constant contact with Him as the only Source of life and strength. He speaks of

Fruit Required in His Kingdom

This can be produced only when

I

We Remain in Him

Any observer of nature knows that a branch cannot live and thrive unless it remains intimately attached to its vine. The moment a branch is severed from its vine it must wither and die. It is utterly impossible for a detached branch to live, thrive, and bear fruit independent of its vine. All nature demonstrates the absolute dependence of a branch on its vine. There must be a constant, uninterrupted flow of life-giving nourishment from vine to branch. Throughout the growing season the sap flows continuously through vine to branch to develop and bring the fruit to perfection. Whether we comprehend the mysteries of life or not, we definitely know that the moment a severance of branch from vine occurs all further development ceases; the branch begins to wither, die, and eventually is destroyed without having accomplished its purpose.

The application to spiritual life is obvious. Without continuous nourishment through the life-giving Word from vine to branch, from Christ to Christian, there can be no fruit. "Without Me you can do nothing." Yet in spite of our Lord's unmistakable implication there are those who in their own conceit imagine themselves capable of producing independently. Having been once endowed with His gifts, they consider constant contact with their Lord unessential. They do not consider the continuing use of His Word absolutely necessary for a productive Christian life. Have they not been charged and filled with grace and knowledge of salvation? Can they not continue on the momentum once received? They consider themselves beyond the need of constantly hearing His Word. Our Lord says, "No more can ye [bring forth fruit] except ye abide in Me." Not only is it impossible for a detached believer to bear fruit, but he is doomed to eventual destruction. "He is cast forth as a branch and is withered, and men gather them and cast them into the fire."

On the other hand, remaining in connection with the vine, a branch is expected to produce. Branches of a vine are not intended to be mere ornaments. A grapevine is among the most productive of plants. It spreads its branches far out, and each branch is intended to bring forth fruit. No vine grower would be so foolish as to invest time and effort in cultivating vines merely for the foliage on its branches. He looks for results, fruits.

Even so in the kingdom of God the branches are expected to produce. That is their sole purpose and mission. We are bought with a price. Richly and daily we receive forgiveness of our sins that we may be His own, that we may serve Him, that we may bear much fruit. St. Paul spells out some of the fruits which our gracious Lord looks for in His Christians: "But the fruit of the Spirit is love, joy, peace, long-suffering, gentleness, goodness, faith, meekness, and temperance" (Gal. 5: 22, 23). What an array of abundant fruit! There is hardly a virtue conceivable that does not come under one of these categories. Pages upon pages could be written describing the far-reaching effects of each of these fruits on the life of an individual Christian and the influence they have on all that come in contact with a fruitful Christian. And all these virtues are to be brought to perfection by the constant flow of the Word to every vein and pore of the branch, the member of the body of Christ. "Without Me ye can do nothing."

Our Lord announces the eventual doom of those who do not remain in Him. Reverting to the figure of vine and branches, He says: "If a man abide not in Me, he is cast forth as a branch and is withered. And men gather them and cast them in the fire, and they are burned." Dead branches are not permitted to clutter up a vine. We've seen them cut off from the vine, gathered in piles, and burned — a perfectly logical process, which every intelligent vine-dresser follows.

Likewise branches of the body of Christ, having reverted to a death of trespasses and sins. Faith having died in his heart, the life-giving Word having been excluded, the dead branch is cut off, removed, and consigned to its everlasting doom. Thus the simile of our Lord is a dire warning that the continuance in Him through His Word is absolutely essential to a productive life of faith.

In considering a person's eternal fate human thinking frequently slips a few cogs. Men think of heinous sins as decisive in sealing a person's eternal damnation and of a tolerably decent life as being a pass to eternal life. Not so, according to the authority of our Lord. Decisive in determining our eternal fate is the matter of remaining in Christ. There is no other way to salvation than faith in Him who reconciled us to God through His own sacrificial suffering and death. To His inquiring disciple Thomas, who asked, "How can we know the way?" He answered clearly and positively: "I am the Way, the Truth, and the Life; no man cometh unto the Father but by Me" (John 14:6). This should leave no doubt in anybody's mind that there is no salvation but by remaining in Christ. St. Peter expresses it in language as clear as human tongue can make it: "for there is none other name under heaven given among men whereby we must be saved" (Acts 4:12). Remaining in Christ Jesus is therefore an absolute essential to a productive, fruitful life. This can be had only

II

When We Are Cleansed with His Word

Our Lord has a further word to say regarding those who remain attached to Him: they are made increasingly productive in their faith life. "Every branch in Me that beareth not fruit He taketh away, and every branch that beareth fruit He purgeth it that it may bring forth more fruit."

As a lad of about 10 I came home from school one mild early spring day to find an old gentleman at work on the apple trees and grapevines of our little orchard. He was known in our community as a successful grower of apples, cherries, and grapes. Today we would probably call him an amateur tree surgeon. I watched with fascinated curosity how he went about treating trees and vines. He carefully lifted branches which had become matted and tangled. He lifted them gently where they had become wedged in the trellis, to prevent injury to the delicate shoots. To my endless childish questions he patiently explained that tangled and matted branches could not bear fruit unless they were loosened and fluffed up to give them room to produce. Then he took the pruning shears and snipped off shoot after shoot. In my childish notion he seemed to be defeating his purpose, but to my objections he pointed out that the shoots he was pruning away would just be wasting life-giving nourishment flowing from vine to branches, and cutting the unproductive shoots away would give the vigorous branches additional strength to produce more and better fruit. When I saw the denuded vine from which so many shoots had been cut away I doubted the wisdom of the old gentleman, but during that growing season I watched the vine flourish, the branches growing vigorously and eventually producing so many more and better grapes that I was convinced of the skill and wisdom of the old gentleman in caring for our grapevines.

Israel of old was known for the rich production of its vineyards and its skill in cultivating and managing these products. In fact, some of our most popular brands of wine to this day are said to be produced and processed according to formulas handed down from long ago. The fruit of the vine was an important factor in the economy of Israel. The disciples would therefore readily understand the simile of our text and easily make the application.

"Now are ye clean through the Word which I have spoken unto you." They had been exposed to the influence of His Word throughout their careers as His disciples. They had been lifted up, stirred, and cleansed by His Word. At times it had been painful, as when He had chided them for the littleness of their faith, for the stupidity which they had shown whenever He had told them of His real mission to give His life as a ransom for many. It must have cut Peter to the quick when His Lord told him, "Get thee behind Me, Satan; thou art an offense unto Me" (Matt. 16:23). Then again his gentle "Peace be with you" must have lifted the disciples up out of a maze of misgivings they had become entangled in. His Word as a two-edged sword cut away the residue of the old man in them and as a hammer that breaketh the rock into pieces it broke their faults, sin, and vices. Again and again His powerful Word lifted them up, gave them further opportunity to bear fruit, to overcome their weaknesses, and made them bold, courageous witnesses, who in a few weeks were said to have filled Jerusalem with their doctrine. The cleansing Word made effective witnesses out of ignorant, timid, cowardly men, who soon turned the world upside down. They became the most productive men in the history of Christ's kingdom of grace on earth.

Such has always been the power of the cleansing Word. Through it we have been called out of darkness to His marvelous light. Through it we have been grafted as living branches into the living Vine. Abiding in Him, and His Word abiding in us, we shall ask what we will, and it shall be done unto us. Our productive potential as members of Christ's body has never been reached, much less exhausted.

May our gracious Father be glorified in us and through us that, remaining in Him, and His Word remaining in us, we shall bear much fruit and thus prove to be His disciples.

Making the Most of Our Opportunities

By ROBERT O. BANNON

(The Second Sunday After Trinity)

But whereunto shall I liken this generation? It is like unto children sitting in the markets, and calling unto their fellows, and saying, We have piped unto you, and ye have not danced; we have mourned unto you, and ye have not lamented. For John came neither eating nor drinking, and they say, He hath a devil. The Son of man came eating and drinking, and they say, Behold a man gluttonous, and a winebibber, a friend of publicans and sinners. But wisdom is justified of her children. Then began He to upbraid the cities wherein most of His mighty works were done, because they repented not. Woe unto thee, Chorazin! Woe unto thee, Bethsaida! For if the mighty works which were done in you, had been done in Tyre and Sidon, they would have repented long ago in sackcloth and ashes. But I say unto you, It will be more tolerable for Tyre and Sidon at the Day of Judgment than for you. And thou, Capernaum, which art exalted unto heaven, shalt be brought down to hell. For if the mighty works which have been done in thee had been done in Sodom, it would have remained until this day. But I say unto you, That it shall be more tolerable for the land of Sodom in the Day of Judgment than for thee. — *Matthew 11:16-24*

Pliny the Elder, a Roman scholar who lived in the days of the apostles, wrote in his 37-volume *Natural History,* "Opportunities lost can never be regained." He was only echoing the opinion of Solomon, whom a thousand years before God inspired to write, "They hated knowledge, and did not choose the fear of the Lord; they would none of His counsel; they despised all His reproof.

Therefore shall they eat of the fruit of their own way" (Prov. 1:29-31). In our text the greatest voice of all ever heard on this earth, that of Jesus Christ, God's very own Son, our Savior and Lord, also urges us to

Make the Most of Our Opportunities

Jesus is speaking particularly of our opportunities for coming to Christian faith and life. But there are other areas, too, in which we want to make the most of our opportunities.

In our wonderful country we all get a chance to learn. Fine educational establishments would expand our horizons and develop our skills — all the way from the kindergarten to the final year of postgraduate study in the great university. Between these are the elementary and high schools, the trade and business schools. The opportunity to obtain a good education has hardly any limit. All may develop the mind and talent and skill with which their Creator has endowed them.

Marvelous opportunities are present at our work. Imagination and faithfulness can bring thrilling rewards. While Eli Whitney was visiting the South a century ago, some of the cotton planters told him of their difficulty in extracting the seeds from raw cotton. If someone could only devise a machine to do that laborious work! That night Whitney lay awake thinking of the problem. Long after midnight he went to the window to get a breath of fresh air. There in the moonlight was a cat that had killed a chicken and was trying desperately to pull it out of the coop. But the space between the slats was too narrow, and every time the cat's paw came out it clutched nothing but a mass of white feathers. Whitney turned back to bed . . . and then began to think more vigorously than ever. Why not build an iron claw that would pull the cotton fibers through a fine mesh, leaving the hard seeds behind? A week later Whitney had worked out the first rough sketch of his cotton gin. Such opportunities still appear, and at other times the opportunity at our place of work depends on our loyalty and dependability.

Every marriage presents the opportunity for love and happiness and companionship. The children born to our homes are also opportunities. They can bring us laughter and joy. We can help them grow up sound and strong. Every hour of life is filled with opportunities.

Most important of all our opportunities, however, are those to which our Savior is making specific reference in our text. He speaks of man's chance of becoming a child of God through faith in Him. He is thinking about our relationship to Him and the Father.

Some people living at the time had an excellent chance to

know about Christ. They should have trusted that He was the Son of God and their only Savior. They should have loved Him and served Him. They heard John the Baptist. Jesus pronounced this man the greatest of all the prophets. They heard and observed Jesus Himself. The cities He mentions — Chorazin, Bethsaida, and Capernaum — were the scenes of much of His preaching and many of His miracles. Many of the people of Bethsaida must have witnessed His feeding of the 5,000. Capernaum was our Lord's own city. Here lived the centurion whose palsied servant Jesus healed. Here Jesus healed Peter's mother-in-law when she was stricken with a fever. Here he healed a demoniac and the son of a nobleman. All these people heard Him who spoke as never man spake. They saw the mighty works which were to give credence to His words. They watched the one perfect Man. They moved in the very presence of Him who was God in flesh. What an opportunity!

This opportunity to come to Jesus for pardon and to give yourself in grateful love to Him is also yours and mine week after week. The whole story of Jesus — as told by God's inspired penmen Matthew, Mark, Luke, and John — each of us can read whenever he desires. As members of _____ Church you hear about that Savior in every service. The emphasis is on the Gospel — the good news that you have forgiveness and eternal life — because Jesus, God's Son, came to this world, lived a perfect life in your place, and died for your transgressions. The Spirit of God works mightily on your heart as you read or hear about this Jesus. These are golden opportunities, opportunities as fine as those offered Jesus' own contemporaries. Of all life's opportunities this is the most important. Surely we will want to make the most of it. If educational opportunities and the chance to build a fine marital and family relationship are not to be neglected, how much more this is true in regard to our Christian faith and life! Ultimately all we do with our other opportunities is conditioned by this. The eternal issues of life are decided by what we do with this opportunity.

Catastrophe follows when we do not make the most of our opportunities. What a pity when we waste opportunities to learn! How discomfiting to know that you are, through no one's fault but your own, far less than what you could be and should be! Others suffer, too, when such opportunties are wasted. Human society, your family, your God are receiving something less than they deserve from you.

A carpenter had been picked for a foreman's job by his employer. One day the employer happened to be watching that carpenter when the quit-work whistle blew. At the moment the carpenter was driving a nail. He stopped hammering at the first sound of the whistle. He did not finish driving in that one nail. Then and there he lost his chance to become a foreman. Here was a lost opportunity at the man's work.

Marriage can exact appalling prices for wasted opportunity. If husband and wife fail to forgive and be patient and bestow Christlike love, divorce can follow or a most painful, obliged, cold living under the same roof. We have seen tears shed too late for neglect and failure in regard to husband or wife:

> I did not know how short your day would be!
> I had you safe, and words could wait a while —
> E'en when your eyes begged tenderness of me,
> Behind their smile.
>
> And now for you, so dark, so long, is night!
> I speak, but on my knees, unheard, alone —
> What words were these to make a short day bright!
> "If I had known! Ah, love — if I had known!"

And must we weep as did David over Absalom, "My son, my son . . ." before we recognize the opportunity each child offers as God hands it into our keeping for a little while?

Every opportunity lost is pitiful. But when it comes to the matter of faith in Christ and a life of loving devoted service to Him, words fail us. How tragically "funny" the people who would not listen to John because he was too austere and who would not listen to Jesus because He seemed to have too much love of life! Hear that sobering "Woe" of that same pleasant, kindly Jesus as He sees those cities of Chorazin, Bethsaida, and Capernaum muff their opportunity. The Son of God in their midst, earth-shaking miracles, the most sublime ethics and theology mankind would ever hear, their Savior — all this before them — and they walk on in darkness and selfishness and hate and unpardoned sin. They walk on to their place in hell.

What about us? We dare not miss our opportunity as they did. If we do not lay hold of Christ as our Savior and stay with Him, then we will forfeit the life of faith and love and hope, the abundant life, the victorious one. We will forego the peace which passes understanding — that peace which only Jesus can give, a peace only those have who know that God through Christ accepts them and cares for them. We will be giving humanity only a fragment of the love and sacrifice we would be giving if we had Christian faith.

Opportunity knocks on every hand. As alert servants of God, we want to make the most of every one of our opportunities, especially of the opportunity to be in Christ.

The Soul of Every Child Is Precious

By MARTIN E. MAYER

(The Third Sunday After Trinity)

And they brought young children to Him that He should touch them, and His disciples rebuked those that brought them. But when Jesus saw it, He was much displeased and said unto them: Suffer the little children to come unto Me, and forbid them not, for of such is the kingdom of God. Verily I say unto you, Whosoever shall not receive the kingdom of God as a little child, he shall not enter therein. And He took them up in His arms, put His hands upon them, and blessed them. — *Mark 10:13-16*

A number of years ago a young man was coming from California to visit in the East. In the Pullman car with him were three or four race-track gamblers. They were rough, hardened, godless, but somewhat interesting men, and this young man, who had wandered somewhat from the training of his mother, was attracted to them. At a town on the way a little boy was put on the car and given into the custody of the Pullman conductor.

When night came the porter made up the berth for the boy. The gamblers and the young man were sitting across the aisle from the boy's berth. Presently the boy came out in his pajamas and, first looking timidly up and down the aisle, knelt to say his prayers. At once the gamblers ceased from their loud conversation and removed their hats in respect. The young man felt a lump in his throat as he looked at the praying child. What had happened? The prayer of a child had carried them all back in time to the knees of their God-fearing mothers. The young man afterward entered the holy ministry and became a well-known preacher of the Gospel. Thus was fulfilled the saying "And a little child shall lead them." (Is. 11:6)

All of you, I am sure, have a deep love for children. I trust that to you every child represents an opportunity to carry out the command of our Savior to do it "unto one of the least of these." There is nothing more thrilling than to watch a child develop into a fine young man or woman. That is our privilege so often.

But I should like for all of you to feel a little of this joy, and for that reason I am going to speak to you in a terribly serious vein. I am going to remind you that

The Soul of Every Child Is Precious

I

We Want to Observe that This Soul Is Precious to Jesus

How do we know that Jesus loved children? Certainly the story of our text ought to be an adequate proof of this. We are

told that our dear Savior was weary after all of His efforts to show
the way to life to so many people. He needed a rest. But just
at that moment a group of mothers came with their children and
desired that Jesus should bless them. The disciples, knowing how
weary Jesus was, tried to keep the mothers from Jesus. But they,
no doubt, kept insisting that they wanted to see Jesus. At any
rate the Lord knew what was going on, and so He rebuked
His disciples and said: "Suffer the little children to come unto
Me, and forbid them not, for of such is the kingdom of God."
Then He took each one of those little ones and fondled it in
His arms.

Jesus loves the little ones? He saw that they, too, were on the
road to perdition because of their sins. But He wanted them in
heaven, and He knew that without forgiveness they could not
enter the gates of a blissful hereafter. So He suffered and died
for their sins too. Does He not therefore have a large heart of
love for them?

It was His love for the little ones that moved Him to encourage the mothers to bring them to Him. He still wants those children
brought to Him, and we have the opportunity to do this. That is
why, above all, He instituted the Sacrament of Holy Baptism,
so that we could bring our little ones to Him. We can do it also
by seeing that they learn to know about Jesus early in life.
We can tell them those beautiful stories about the Savior. We can
go with them to Sunday school, and this should begin at least when
they are three years old. All of us need to visit such a Sunday
school class that we may see how the little ones love to hear about
Jesus. The most wonderful way of bringing them to Jesus is
through the parochial school, where those little ones every day
live in close contact with their Savior, so that He actually becomes
a living part of their lives and they become as familiar with Him
as with their own parents and teachers.

But there is yet another reason why Jesus loves little children.
He knows the potential that exists in each child and He is always
aware of the need to build His kingdom. That is why He loves
children — He sees the power in a child. When you stand on the
brink of a volcano's crater, you tremble to think of the explosive
power hidden there, now asleep but one day to burst forth. But
what are those explosive powers compared with the powers for
good that God can use — or the powers for evil that the devil
can use — that are hidden in the heart of a little child!

Or on top of some mountain you rest by a spring, and you try
to realize how this little stream, as it goes down the rocky ridge,
will grow and gain power until finally it becomes a mighty river.

But what is that power again compared with the power that is lodged in the heart of every child — the power for good or evil? Jesus knows that potential, and that is why He loves children, for He would harness that power for the good of His kingdom.

II
The Soul of Every Child Is Also Precious to Parents

There is something completely wrong with these parents if this is not true. Even that mother, who in her mad frenzy slew her three little children recently, stated that she did it so that they would be sure to go to heaven. Parents love their children. They want the best for those children, but many do not know what "the best" is. They don't love their children wisely.

Parents who truly love their children are eager to bring them to Jesus. It is a lack of true love when parents delay the Baptism of their little ones, or when they do not make the effort to see that their little ones go to Sunday school. But above all, must we not say that it is a loveless mother that will not take the time to teach her child to fold his hands and pray? And isn't it a loveless father that will not take his little one on his lap and read to him the wonderful stories of Jesus? We dare not forget that we are dealing with the eternal welfare of these children and that their souls will be required at our hands.

A little child brought to Jesus, so that he in faith accepts Jesus as his Lord and Savior, has such a wonderful approach to life. He will know why the Lord has placed him here on earth. Such children will be prepared for any crisis that may arise in their lives. Their love of God and their complete trust in His mercy will give them an outlook on life that will be of value to them for time and eternity.

But while under the guidance of the Holy Spirit we are trying to develop this kind of hopeful philosophy in the heart of the child, the devil is not resting. In any way possible the devil seeks to estrange this child from the Lord Jesus. He does not want your child to have the peace and joy that comes from Christian faith. Therefore our love for our children must certainly constrain us to fortify them with the best possible Christian training and guidance. The devil does not take a day's vacation. Nor can we if we truly love our children. No sacrifice to provide the best possible religious training for them is too great.

The great writer Coleridge was once talking to a man who told him that he did not believe in giving little children any religious instruction, for in that way the child's mind would be prejudiced. He thought the child should be permitted to choose its own religious opinions for itself. Coleridge said nothing, but invited the man into his garden and then took him into a section where only weeds were growing. The man objected that this was no garden. Coleridge replied: "I did not wish to infringe upon the liberty of the garden in any way. I was just giving the garden a chance to express itself and to choose its own production." A timely parable indeed!

Parents who love their children will not only see that those children receive the proper Christian training but also provide for their children the best possible example. How can boys or girls be inspired to come and worship Jesus when their mother and father, whom they love, do not feel any need to do so?

III

The Soul of Every Child Is Precious Also to the Church

Every soul is precious, more precious, as Jesus indicated to us, than all the wealth of the world. If the annual budget of our congregation were $100,000, and if at the end of the year we could show absolutely no results but that one child had been brought to Jesus through our program, would we not all agree that we had not wasted one nickel of our money? Now we know, by the promises of Jesus, that our efforts are going to meet with much greater success than that.

Why is Christianity such a force in the world to this day? Is the answer not to be found in the attitude taken over against children by Christians in contrast to that of non-Christians? Infanticide is common in heathen countries. Girl babies are often destroyed. Parents often regard another child as a curse and so rid themselves of it. What a different attitude we have, for we regard each child as a precious heritage of God.

If Christianity, then, is to continue to be a powerful force in our world today, we as a church must take care of the little ones in the best possible way. On every level we must provide better schools in which the Christian philosophy will be emphasized. The schools that we have need to be analyzed carefully, so that we can make them the best possible agencies for our children. Only to the degree that we give our children a sound Christian education is the church going to be a power in the world. The Roman Church recognizes this. Think of the millions of dollars that it spends annually on child education.

Our theme declares the soul of each child is precious. We are also tempted to think of mass production or assembly line Christian education. But each child is to be considered individually. I must tell you a story. In a remote district of Wales a baby boy lay dangerously ill. The widowed mother walked five miles at night through a drenching rain to a doctor. The doctor hesitated for a moment. He would get no money, and the lad would grow up just to be another drain on society. But he was faithful to his doctor's duty. That little child became the great Lloyd George of England. In saving the life of that child the doctor rendered England a great service. We have no conception of what the things we do as a church for children today will mean for tomorrow. Luther, Abraham Lincoln, Dr. Walther, all were boys who had to go to school.

The Lord Jesus is looking upon us today with His loving eyes. He sees the many fine children He has given us, and He loves each one of them. He sees what we as parents are doing in fulfilling our responsibility to each one of them. He observes whether our congregation is truly concerned about our educational program, or whether we are content just to say that we have a Sunday school or a parochial school.

How precious is the soul of every child to you? Precious enough to do something concrete for the eternal welfare of that child? God help you to see the importance of this matter before it is too late.

The Christian's Faith Is Sensitive

By JOHN F. SCHUTT

(The Fourth Sunday After Trinity)

Then said He unto the disciples, It is impossible but that offenses will come; but woe unto him through whom they come! It were better for him that a millstone were hanged about his neck and he cast into the sea than that he should offend one of these little ones. Take heed to yourselves: If thy brother trespass against thee, rebuke him; and if he repent, forgive him. And if he trespass against thee seven times in a day, and seven times in a day turn again to thee, saying, I repent; thou shalt forgive him. And the apostles said unto the Lord, Increase our faith. And the Lord said, If ye had faith as a grain of mustard seed, ye might say unto this sycamine tree, Be thou plucked up by the root, and be thou planted in the sea; and it should obey you. But which of you, having a servant plowing or feeding cattle, will say unto him by and by when he is come from the field, Go and sit down to meat? And will not rather say unto him, Make ready wherewith I may sup, and gird thyself, and serve me, till I have eaten and drunken; and afterward thou shalt eat and drink? Doth he thank that servant because he did the things that were commanded him? I trow not. So likewise ye, when ye shall have done all those things which are commanded you, say, We are unprofitable servants, we have done that which was our duty to do. — *Luke 17:1-10*

How sensitive are you? How sensitive are your faculties of sight, for example? Do you walk the streets of your community and miss half the sights? Can you walk through a beautiful park and not really notice all the smaller flowers and all the delicate colors a bountiful God has painted on the petals of countless flowers? How sensitive is your touch? When you and I run our fingertips over a page of Braille type, we feel only a rough sea of dents and points. A blind person, whose fingers have been trained, runs his fingers over the same page and reads, "God so loved the world that He gave His only-begotten Son, that whosoever believeth in Him should not perish but have everlasting life." It pays to develop the sensitivity of our natural faculties.

How sensitive is your faith? Does it respond only to a few fundamental doctrines of sacred Scripture, or does it respond to every teaching which it finds in God's Word, especially in the Ten Commandments? In His Sermon on the Mount, Jesus tried to sensitize the faith of His disciples. That is behind every one of His statements, "Ye have heard — but *I say unto you.*" (Matt. 5:21; 5:27; 5:33; 5:38, etc.)

How sensitive is your faith? Does it recognize its own needs and its own defects, or is it satisfied with the *status quo*? Is it sensitive to the feelings, needs, and weaknesses of others, or does it live in utter disregard for the feelings of others?

Jesus tried to sensitize the faith of His disciples. We will have to respond to His teachings in order to meet the rigid requirements He set before a real, vibrant, growing, glowing faith. We will be richly rewarded in our Christian life if we study our text carefully, and, with God's help, endeavor to mold our faith according to His pattern. For,

The Christian's Faith Is Sensitive

It is sensitive:

    I. to the weaknesses of others

    II. to its own need.

I

The Christian Is Not Alone

The Christian is not an ostrich, hiding his head in the sand, nor a hermit, hiding away from the real world in a cave. He knows full well that he belongs to and is part of a worldwide community. As a Christian he has been called out of the darkness of unbelief into which he was helplessly born into a new community, the community of believers. That is a thrilling and challenging concept, as real as life itself, that he does belong to the communion of saints. He cannot and he has no desire to live in this community by himself. He cannot only give to this community, but he also receives so much from this community.

As a child of God he still lives in the community of an unsaved world. He is not of the world, but he definitely is still in the world — in unfriendly surroundings. A Christian is, therefore, sensitive to his surrounding and to the people around him.

He Endeavors to Live So as Not to Give Offense to Others Around Him (Vv. 1, 2)

Because he knows the weaknesses of his fellow Christians and of those who do not belong to the household of faith, he realizes how easy it is to give offense to others. He knows that by some unguarded word or by some thoughtless deed he may actually harm the faith of a Christian or hinder an unbeliever from accepting the message of free grace in Christ, the Savior. If he ever gives credence to any false teaching or lives in some known sin, he knows that some unconverted person may be strengthened in his indifference or unbelief. He is, then, extremely sensitive to the possibility of becoming a hindrance or snare to a weaker brother or sister.

He knows how true it is what Jesus says about offense — some cannot be avoided. He remembers reading in the Gospels that many people turned away from following Jesus because He told the unvarnished truth to hardened sinners. He does know that when he fearlessly confesses his faith before some people, then they will take offense and close the door to further opportunity to witness. He remembers what storms of protest St. Paul caused by his fearless witnessing to the crucified and risen Savior among the bitter Jews. He sympathizes with his pastor and with the elders of his congregation who sometimes must accept abuse from those whom they are trying to help from the paths of sin to the pathways of Christian living. He knows that it is impossible to live among people and not give offense. But this is such a serious matter to him. Because he earnestly desires to see all people brought to saving faith and to remain in the saving faith, he is so sensitive to this problem. He guards his words and discreetly watches his actions so that he may avoid giving offense needlessly and heedlessly. His faith is sensitive — not coarse and reckless and thoughtless. He has no sympathy with those Christians who recklessly treat other people with disdain and excuse themselves by saying piously, "I say what I think, and I don't care what anybody thinks about it." A sincere Christian "takes heed to himself" and really endeavors to live so as not to give offense to others. He is the salt of the earth — a wonderful person to know and to live with. He lives his faith.

He Charitably Rebukes His Erring Brother (V. 4)

But while he lives his faith, he will also meet people — many people — who are living in a soul-destroying sin and who must be rebuked and corrected. He is not a son of Cain to say, "Am I my brother's keeper?" Because these folks all belong to his community, he loves them all, because Christ loved them all

and died for all. If others do not know it, he does know that sin
separates people from God. He is not indifferent to the seriousness
of this matter. His brother may assure him that he is not worried
about this sin and that he will take his chance on Judgment Day.

Our Mr. Christian knows how fatal this reasoning is. His
faith is sensitive. He must rebuke his brother or sister in the
winsome manner in which His beloved Savior rebuked sinners.
He sees Nathan going to an impenitent David and rebuking him
with kindness and firmness. He strives to go and do likewise.
He is careful that he does not fall into the easy habit of mercilessly
scolding his brother or holding him up to scorn and contempt.
He will have nothing to do with the shameless Pharisees who
gleefully brought the woman taken in adultery into public gaze
and humiliation. He loves his brother, and so he will kindly
show him his damning sin and plead with him to forsake the sin
and to correct his life. He will not continually pick his neighbor
to pieces because he falls into sins of weakness which he is trying
to overcome. He is deeply and solicitously concerned about those
sins which will rob him of his faith. He cannot help himself.
He loves his brother, and his faith is sensitive to his danger.
He cannot stand idly by and see a brother or sister or any child
walking dangerously near the brink of the precipice without
doing something. He must point out the danger and lead to
safer ground. A sensitive faith knows that it may be rebuffed
for doing this, but it still charitably rebukes the erring brother.

He Eagerly Forgives the Penitent Sinner (Vv. 3 b, 4)

Since Mr. Christian rebukes the erring brother in order to
bring him to repentance, he naturally is happy and eager to
forgive the penitent brother. He knows that there is genuine
rejoicing in the presence of the holy angels of God over one
sinner who repents. He knows that the loving Father stands
with arms outstretched to receive the prodigal son home, regardless of where he has come from or what he has been up to.
His sensitive faith is just so thrilled to hear the penitent say,
"I am sincerely and truly sorry." He flings his arms about his
neck and forgives him in the name of Jesus Christ, whose blood
cleanses from any sin. And he does this not only once or perhaps
twice, but many times. He remembers that a merciful Father
has to forgive him the sins he commits over and over again
against better knowledge. Even when he suspects that the repentance of the professing brother is not genuine, he will yet
forgive him. Even if the repentance is not sincere, his forgiveness
must be sincere and genuine. He will not act like Jonah, who
became very angry with God because God forgave the penitent

Ninevites. He will again follow the example of Jesus, who, from the agony of the cross, pronounced forgiveness upon those who were sinning in ignorance. He will treat his penitent brother even as his own loving father and mother treated him over and over again when they forgave him every time he came and said, "I am sorry, Mother and Dad." His sensitive faith makes it easy for him to forgive the penitent sinner over and over again.

Thus his faith, by exercise, grows more sensitive all the time and thus *grows*. Such a faith is active and victorious. Such a faith almost sounds glamorous. Such a faith meets the requirements of Jesus.

II
Sensitive to Own Needs

Faith Is Not Oblivious to Self

Yet such a sensitive faith is not oblivious to self. The Christian knows full well that he must continually and prayerfully contend for the faith that has been born in him through the blessed efforts of God's Holy Spirit, using the means which He has designed and designated, namely, God's powerful Word and the efficacious sacraments. The Christian knows from bitter experience that he himself is beset with many temptations from within and from without. Not the least of the dangers which lie hidden and concealed along life's highways is a smugness and a deadening satisfaction with faith as it is. The Christian is always restless when he looks closely and sharply at his faith. He feels the need of undergirding, underpinning, and strengthening his personal faith.

Faith Cries Out for Increase (V. 5)

So faith cries out with the alerted disciples, "Lord, increase our faith." A sensitive faith looks to self-improvement. It does not look to any new gimmicks. It does not reach out for a "do-it-yourself" kit. It knows the Source of new strength and dips its bucket into the well of the living Word and drinks and revives. A sensitive faith is a growing faith. As the oak tree which stands away from other trees and takes the full brunt of the winds and storms has the deepest roots and the finest grain, so a faith which stands up to the tests of God is the strongest and the proved faith. We marvel at the faith of Abraham, which rested only on the bare promises of God, even though those promises ran counter to reason and nature. But how that faith grew to new proportions as it made the journey to Mount Moriah! Every step which father Abraham took as he climbed the hill was a test of his faith. We can almost hear the cry being wrung from his anxious heart, "Lord, increase my faith!" When Abraham descended from that mount of decision, his faith had a new glow. It had been tuned to the will of God. The reed had been bent and all was harmonious now. Thus the faith of Abraham grew and became more sensitive through trial and testing. That has often been our God's way with men. When man cries for a stronger faith, God often answers by leading us into the shadows — only to lead us refreshed into the sunlight. The ore has to be refined and subjected to terrific heat to permit the gold to settle at the bottom. The slag has to be separated from the nickel to produce the pure ingot. Thus God works with the believer in many devious ways in order to improve and strengthen his faith. If the Christian rebels against these tests of faith, he frustrates the designs of our God to increase our faith.

When we cry, "Lord, increase our faith," then we also make a solemn promise to permit God to have His way. The prayer is ours, but the answer is His. Thus we pray for a faith

That will not murmur nor complain
Beneath the chast'ning rod,
But in the hour of grief or pain
Can lean upon its God.

A faith that shines more bright and clear
When tempests rage without;
That, when in danger, knows no fear,
In darkness feels no doubt.

When the disciples realized what the Master expected of their faith, their hearts cried out, "Lord, increase our faith." When you and I, my fellow Christians, realize what kind of faith we need for such a time as this, then let us flee to the Throne of Grace and plead, "Lord, increase our faith." If we will let Him have His way, then our faith will grow and increase more and more.

Such Faith Recognizes That It Has Limitless Potentiality (V. 6)

Instead of doing anything spectacular for the disciples, our Lord turned to them and said, "If ye had faith as a grain of mustard seed, ye might say unto this sycamine tree, Be thou plucked up by the root, and be thou planted in the sea; and it should obey you." Do you think the disciples were disappointed in this response to their request? Do you think they fully understood then what Jesus was trying to say to them? We have had two thousand years to meditate upon these words of Jesus — and they still amaze us. It almost sounds as though Jesus did not understand their prayer. They had asked for an increase in the quantity of their faith, and He speaks to them about a faith as small as a mustard seed. To such a small faith Jesus ascribes limitless power. He has to correct their thinking about faith. It is not so much that they need more faith in quantity, but that they need a more genuine faith. They were to examine the essence of their faith, rather than the magnitude of their faith. If faith is genuine, it can perform seemingly impossible things, even though it is small as a mustard seed. The sincere Christian's concern, therefore, is not primarily to possess mountains of faith, but rather to possess the true seed of faith. We do not necessarily need the faith of Abraham to accomplish seemingly impossible things; but we need a faith that is genuine, born of the Holy Spirit.

Faith, then, is not only sensitive to its own weakness, but it is also sensitive to its strength. It does not bewail the fact that it is not an Abraham or a David or a Roman centurion; but it thrills to the fact that it is genuine and that it is empowered with the full power of God, upon which it can draw. It does not daydream about becoming a superman, but it realizes that it has limitless power within its grasp. Faith blushes when it realizes that it has not been flexing its muscles at all and that the impossible was possible all the time. Our faith flushes with shame to hear Jesus point out to us the latent power that was there all the time. Here we have been bewailing our weak faith and using that as an excuse for our apparent failures and impotence, and all the while we had a faith that could do the seemingly impossible.

So we shift our attention from the quantity of our faith to the quality of the same. Now we begin to understand why Jesus was so concerned about the genuineness of faith as He found it in men of His generation. Now we understand why He so vigorously condemned the sham and shallow faith of the religious leaders of His day. They seemed to be satisfied with the form of faith, without looking to see what was in that form. Jesus saw how empty that form was, even though they were displaying it for exhibition. But we are deeply concerned about our own faith now. We must be sure that it is not just a formal faith which we are carrying around in an empty box. Such a faith is impotent and can produce no real fruits. But how can we know that our faith is genuine and that it can accomplish great things? It is genuine if it rests entirely and completely on the powerful Word of God. It is genuine if it apprehends the grace of God in Christ Jesus and trusts one hundred percent on the grace of God for final salvation. Such a faith has been born through the workings of the Holy Spirit. It is a genuine faith if it exercises itself in good works.

The disciples had such faith but were not making full use of it. Jesus challenged them to use their faith and to expect great things to happen. In like manner Jesus would challenge us to exercise our faith and to permit it to accomplish seemingly impossible things. His challenge is an indictment of our weakness and impotence. Here we have a faith that could do so much, and we are not making use of it! Here we bewail our lack of a victorious faith, and all the while we have victories to claim! God has put the power into our genuine faith, and we failed to recognize and make use of the power. Fellow Christians, there are sycamine trees to be transplanted into the sea! If we would permit our faith to exercise itself in our lives, there are so many victories to be claimed in our own lives over sin, worry, doubt, and frustration. If all the members of our congregation would exercise the faith that is theirs, we would be able to accomplish so much more for the kingdom of God without stooping to methods and motivations which we have borrowed from the world. If all true believers in the world would jointly make use of the power of faith, we could change the world situation without resorting to the dreadful power of atomic warfare. It almost sounds fanatic to say so; but Jesus attributed to genuine faith the power to perform seemingly impossible things. His Word is true.

When Jesus on another occasion was teaching His disciples to make use of the power that is present in true prayer, He spoke these challenging words, "If ye then, being evil, know how to give good gifts unto your children, how much more shall your heavenly Father give the Holy Spirit to them that ask Him?" (Luke 11:13). Even as the majority of professing Christians have never exploited the power of prayer, so the majority of us have never exploited the power of the faith which God has worked in us. Because it is Spirit-born, it is also Spirit-filled. And with God nothing is impossible. Christians, let us now begin to put our faith to work, assuredly expecting it to accomplish wonderful things for us, according to the will of God.

Faith Is Sensitive to Its Own Unworthiness (Vv. 7-10)

Lest the disciples now become overcharged with conceit and pride and with the feeling of their own greatness in being able to perform such great things, Jesus tells them a short story to keep them humble. When the servant, who has been laboring in the fields all day, comes home from the fields, he does not expect the master to serve him. He remembers who he is and continues to fulfill his duties to his master. He does not feel that he has deserved a bonus because he has done what he was hired to do. So likewise, says Jesus, we should not become demanding and proud and haughty when we accomplish great things with the faith which God has bestowed. When we have rendered a great service, we should still say, "We are unprofitable servants; we have only done that which was our duty to do." We cannot claim a special worthiness because God has permitted us to do greater things than others with our faith. A sensitive faith will not despise those who have not yet learned to put faith into full action. Faith is sensitive to its own unworthiness and ascribes all glory and success to the grace of God. A sensitive faith does not blow a trumpet before it to attract attention to itself, but it attracts attention to the grace of God in Christ.

When St. Paul referred to his own life and labors as a witness to the workings of God in men, then he invariably pointed out that it was the grace of God which performed these things in him, even though he himself had once resisted the grace of God. Paul was afraid that his members might ascribe to him any glory or honor which was due only to God. How often he interrupts himself to interject, "But by the grace of God I am what I am" (1 Cor. 15:10). St. Paul was sensitive to his own unworthiness, even though the victories of his dynamic faith stand out above anything which is recorded in the New Testament. Paul would despise anyone who claims for his own person and effort the power which comes from God through a sincere faith. Likewise, Christians who have claimed the victories of a powerful faith ought not and dare not claim any honor for a "superior" faith. We are all unworthy servants. We are the caretakers of the faith which our Father has given us through the means of grace.

Let us attempt a faltering illustration. We all know that a car battery is made up of a box with plates suspended in it. Standing empty, it has no power whatever in it. A mechanic must add the acid. The chemical reaction now produces power to start a motor, which drives a car hour upon hour. When the battery is run down because of overuse or abuse or neglect, then the mechanic charges the battery by feeding a strong current into the battery. Man's faith would be empty and powerless unless God adds the divine power to it. Such faith would run out again unless God continues to charge this faith with power through the means of grace. If saving faith cannot produce bountiful fruits, then that faith is not being charged regularly by the Word and the sacraments. Then we must check our connections again and secure them! A faith that is regularly nurtured by the Word of God and the sacrament of our Lord's body and blood will be powerful and effective. It will accomplish great things if we will permit it to exercise itself. But it will still be a humble faith.

What a wonderful thing a living faith is! It will busy itself in serving all other people in the community of our world. It will be sensitive to the weaknesses of others and will try to remove these weaknesses and help replace them with the strength of Christian faith. It will carefully avoid giving offense. It will charitably rebuke the erring brother and eagerly forgive him when he repents. It will recognize its own weaknesses and short-comings and will daily charge this faith with the diligent reception of that divine power which comes from the life-giving Word of the living and powerful God. Christian, you can possess such a sensitive and victorious faith! Pray with all your heart:

"Lord, give us such a faith as this."

Our Lord, the Iconoclastic Builder

By ALBERT F. POLLEX

(The Fifth Sunday After Trinity)

So when when they had dined, Jesus saith to Simon Peter, Simon, son of Jonas, lovest thou Me more than these? He saith unto Him, Yea, Lord; Thou knowest that I love Thee. He saith unto him, Feed My lambs. He saith to him again the second time, Simon, son of Jonas, lovest thou Me? He saith unto Him, Yea, Lord; Thou knowest that I love Thee. He saith unto him, Feed My sheep. He saith unto him the third time, Simon, son of Jonas, lovest thou Me? Peter was grieved because He said unto him the third time, Lovest thou Me? And he said unto Him, Lord, Thou knowest all things; Thou knowest that I love Thee. Jesus saith unto him, Feed My sheep. Verily, verily, I say unto thee, when thou wast young, thou girdedst thyself, and walkedst whither thou wouldest; but when thou shalt be old, thou shalt stretch forth thy hands, and another shall gird thee, and carry thee whither thou wouldest not. This spake he, signifying by what death he should glorify God. And when He had spoken this, He saith unto him, Follow Me. — *John 21:15-19*

Man is a builder. Man has built. Pause and study, for example, the ancient, massive ruins in Egypt, Babylonia, and other countries, buildings now falling to pieces and buried partly in sand. We are filled with awe and amazement at the ingenuity, skill, and craftsmanship of the builders in ages past.

Look at the Sphinx, which looms above the desert sands at Giza. Or pause to look at the pyramids. The one known as the Great Pyramid, we are informed, has a base covering thirteen acres and rises to a height of four hundred and fifty feet. Man in those days had no modern machinery, but he built, and he built well.

Turn to your Bible for another outstanding example of an engineering feat and building project, Solomon's temple, one of the great wonders of the world. Listen to the description of the erection of that building. The Bible says: "The house, when it was in building, was built of stone made ready before it was brought thither, so" — note these concluding words — "that there was neither hammer nor axe nor any tool of iron heard in the house while it was in building" (1 Kings 6:7). That was an engineering feat! Man has built.

Man *is* building. He is building today, we could say, as never before in the history of mankind. As we travel, by car or by plane, through our continent, north or south, east or west, we are amazed at the many huge building projects undertaken in our age. Highways are being widened, new highways are being built; intricate cloverleaves are being constructed; throughways, superhighways, skyways, and most elaborate airports are being designed and built. Need we mention the deepening of the St. Lawrence River in the "Seaway and Hydro Project," undertaken by the two friendly countries of this continent, Canada and the United States — one of the construction marvels of the world? And above all, as we ponder the electronic brain and space age, we say: "Verily, man is building!"

Let us not, however, overlook the greatest Builder, our LORD. At this very hour, at this very moment, while we are assembled in this house of God for divine worship, another Builder is at work. That Builder is God. He uses a most unique tool in building. It is here, this Word, the Bible. He also follows a most unique method. First He destroys, He tears down, He totally dashes things to pieces; and everything seems topsy-turvy. Then He takes those broken pieces, puts them together, and makes out of them a beautiful building or vessel, a vessel of silver or a vessel of gold.

A concrete example of this building method we find in the words of our text for this Fifth Sunday after Trinity. Here we see our Lord, the Builder; and Peter, the apostle, the "material." Let us keep our eyes upon both, but especially upon the Lord, as we ponder this topic:

Our Lord, the Iconoclastic Builder

I

First He Dashes to Pieces (the idol self)

The first step in the building method of our Lord is "dashing to pieces." He takes the idol, "self," and demolishes it completely. He does this, however, in a most unusual, unobtrusive, quiet way. Look at our text. It begins with these words: "So when they had dined" (v. 15a). What? Who? When? Where? Why? What were the circumstances? What was the occasion? Who "dined"? When did they "dine"? Watch the Lord closely.

Our text is taken from the last chapter of the Gospel according to St. John. The event related took place shortly after the resurrection of Jesus. Good Friday was over. Easter was over. A short time later seven disciples of Jesus went to the Sea of Galilee to fish. They therefore got into a boat and went out on the lake. They went to work. But, a preceding verse tells us: *"that night they caught nothing"* (v. 3c). All their labors were in vain. They had toiled, they had labored, they had worked very hard, but all their combined efforts and fishermen's knowledge and acumen, all was in vain. There were no fish. Their nets were empty. Discouraged, disheartened, they pulled at their nets and ropes and oars. It was dark and cold on the water.

"But" (note the sudden change — many of you fellow Christians have personally also experienced this change), we read in the fourth verse of this chapter (our text begins at the 15th verse), "But when morning was now come, *Jesus stood on the shore.*" Jesus was there. Jesus saw them. Jesus knew their need. "But the disciples knew not that it was Jesus. Then Jesus saith unto them, Children, have ye any meat? They answered Him, No. And He said unto them, Cast the net on the right side of the ship, and ye shall find. They cast therefore, and now they were not able to draw it for the multitude of fishes" (vv. 4b-6). First emptiness; now fullness! What a sudden change! How marvelously God provides! "A multitude of fishes" — 153 in number (v. 11), should we say 1,000 pounds of fish? What a provision! What a blessing! "Therefore (v. 7) that disciple whom Jesus loved saith unto Peter, It is the Lord. Now when Simon Peter heard that it was the Lord, he girt his fisher's coat unto him (for he was naked) and did cast himself into the sea." He swam to the shore for Jesus. The other disciples came later, dragging their nets, and "dined with Jesus."

"So when they had dined," our text continues, "Jesus saith to *Simon Peter.*" He singles out one person, Peter. Thomas was there. John was there. James was there. Nathanael was there. Two other disciples were there. These six, for the time being, Jesus bypassed and took Peter individually. Jesus had an important work to perform on that disciple. Peter was the "material." Jesus wanted to "build" and "rebuild."

We all, I'm sure, know the man Peter, spoken of in our text. A few years before the event in our text took place he had been brought to Jesus by Andrew, his brother. John the Baptizer was at the Jordan preaching repentance. One day he saw Jesus among his audience. With uplifted finger he pointed to Jesus and said: "Behold the Lamb of God, which taketh away the sin of the world!" (John 1:29). When John, later on known as the evangelist, heard these words, he followed Jesus. Andrew also followed. Andrew thereupon looked for his brother Peter (personal evangelism) and said unto him, "We have found the Messiah!" And Andrew brought him, his own brother, Peter, to Jesus. That happened about three years before the event related in our text.

During these three years Peter had been highly honored by the Lord. At the raising of Jairus' daughter, Peter was there; at the transfiguration of Jesus, when Jesus went up into a mountain shortly before His great suffering and death, when "His face did shine as the sun, and His raiment was white as the light. And, behold, there appeared unto them Moses and Elias talking with Him" (Matt. 17:2b, 3) — what a heavenly view! — Peter was there; and, lastly, on that Holy Thursday night in the garden of Gethsemane, when our Savior lay prostrate on the ground in dire agony of body and soul for the sins of all mankind, only a stone's throw away, Peter was there. Verily Peter had been highly honored!

A few days ago, however, something had happened to Peter, something sad, something depressing, something terrible, something shocking! Peter, this chosen and highly honored disciple, had fallen. He had fallen deeply into sin. Within the space of a few hours he had denied his Master three times. Read Matt. 26:31-35, 69-75. Jesus looked. "And Peter went out and wept bitterly." Peter had been proud: "I," "I," "I." He had been boastful and self-reliant. He had trusted in the idol self. Now that idol was broken, demolished. Here was Peter, on the shore of the beautiful Sea of Galilee that morning, standing or lying before Jesus — Peter, like a broken vessel.

Not only the apostle Peter but *every man* by nature, as he is born, is in a greater or lesser degree proud, self-reliant, and self-righteous. He has in him the idol self. He worships this idol. He worships this idol in various ways. He works and labors spiritually, perhaps also all night, but in the end all efforts are in vain. Then one day the Lord comes to man in His Word, and the idol self is dashed to pieces. In the midst of all our proud self-evaluation God says: "They are all gone aside, they are all together become filthy; there is none that doeth good, no, not one" (Ps. 14:3). Again: "There is not a just man upon earth that doeth good and sinneth not" (Eccl. 7:20). And who does not know the words of the Epistle to the Romans where the Lord totally dashes everybody to pieces: "All have sinned and come short of the glory of God"? (Rom. 3:28)

As we stand before the Lord, when the Lord in His grace takes you and me aside like Peter, all our boasting is gone.

When the Lord spoke to Peter on that shore of Galilee that morning, we find a changed Peter. We read in our text: "So when they had dined, Jesus saith to Simon Peter, Simon, son of Jonas, lovest thou Me more than these? He saith unto Him, *Yea, Lord; Thou knowest that I love Thee.* He saith unto him, Feed My lambs. He saith to him again the second time, Simon, son of Jonas, lovest thou Me? He saith unto Him, Yea, Lord; Thou knowest that I love Thee. He saith unto him, Feed My sheep. He saith unto him the third time, Simon, son of Jonas, lovest thou Me? Peter was grieved because He said unto him the third time, Lovest thou Me? And he said unto Him, Lord, Thou knowest all things; Thou knowest that I love Thee. Jesus saith unto him, Feed My sheep" (vv. 15-17). Peter was "grieved." Peter was troubled. He had nothing whereof he could boast. Peter was broken.

As we, too, stand before the Rock of Ages, we say:

Nothing in my hand I bring,
Simply to Thy cross I cling;
Naked, come to Thee for dress;
Helpless, look to Thee for grace;
Foul, I to the fountain fly —
Wash me, Savior, or I die!

We are like Peter, broken vessels, broken in and through sin.

II

Then He Puts These Broken Pieces Together Again

Our text, however, does not end with that thought. It contains another, the second, leading thought. It is something beautiful. This beauty is described thus: "Our Lord is a Master Builder; *He puts these broken pieces together again.*" He is iconoclastic in His ways, yet not to destroy but to build and to rebuild. He is a Rebuilder. He gathers these broken pieces in His gracious hands, reassembles them, and makes of them chosen vessels in the worldwide building of His temple.

Look at the apostle Peter again. On the shore of the Sea of Galilee Jesus tells broken Peter that morning: "Feed My lambs," "Feed My sheep," "Feed My sheep." He reinstates him into the apostleship. He makes him again one of His chosen disciples. Three times he had denied his Master, and three times Jesus gives him this commission. He rebuilds him spiritually. That is something man cannot do for himself. It is totally a work of God.

We can kill. We can destroy. We can kill a bird. We can crush a worm, but we cannot remake, we cannot give life. That is God's work, not only in the physical but also, and above all, in the spiritual realm. In Luther's explanation of the Third

Article, of Sanctification, we confess: "I believe that I cannot by my own reason or strength believe in Jesus Christ, my Lord, or come to Him; but the Holy Ghost has called me by the Gospel, enlightened me with His gifts, sanctified and kept me in the true faith." That is God's work, especially when we have fallen from grace. We need God; Peter needed God.

Man can, it is true, do many things, marvelous works. He can, as in ages past, build monumental works which stand for many centuries. He can, as at the present age, split the atom, enter the airwave mysteries in radio and television, make jet-propelled planes, and even, as most recently, orbit the earth. But in spite of this outward advance man cannot make a single petal on a flower, a single blade of grass, one drop of blood, a single hair; and he can do infinitely less in soul culture. He cannot make, much less remake, a single human being. That is solely and only entirely God's work.

We all know, I'm sure, the words of the Bible: "Turn Thou me, and I shall be turned, for Thou art the Lord, my God" (Jer. 31:18). It is God who "turns" man; it is God who "turned" Peter; it is God who "turns" me. He does this miracle mediately, through His Word. "Ye are kept by the power of God through faith unto salvation." It is God's power, not man's power. Man is impotent. Man is powerless. Man is broken in sin. God must come to his rescue.

God does so in the case of fallen Peter. He not only reinstated him into the apostleship, but He foretold his future. It would be hard, but it would be a life of Christian service. Jesus foretold the manner of his death. He would stretch forth his hands on the cross and die a martyr's death. That death seemed hard. The way seemed dark. But, as the Christian poet puts it, "Behind a frowning Providence, God always hides (in Christ) a smiling face."

After the Lord had told Peter: "Feed My lambs," "Feed My sheep," and again, "Feed My sheep," He continued: "Verily, verily, I say unto thee, When thou wast young, thou girdedst thyself, and walkedst whither thou wouldest, but when thou shalt be old, thou shalt stretch forth thy hands, and another shall gird thee and carry thee whither thou wouldest not. This spake He, signifying by what death he should glorify God." The Lord was going to use him now in Christian service. We are "saved to serve."

About ten years later Herod, the king, took Peter and put him in prison (Acts 12). He was bound and chained. "Four quaternions of soldiers" kept close watch over him. He was very closely guarded. A few days before, James, his fellow

disciple, who also had been with him and the Master this morning
on the shore of the Sea of Galilee, had been beheaded by Herod,
the king. His confession of Christian faith had cost him his life.
He had been faithful unto death. "Peter," thought Herod, "will
be next. He's in prison, secure between soldiers. I have him in
my power. I am king. I am king and ruler." "The same night,"
Acts 12 tells us, "Peter was sleeping between two soldiers, bound
with two chains; and the keepers before the door kept the prison."
Herod held the sword, Herod had power over the prison, but
one thing Herod overlooked. We read: "Prayer was made without
ceasing of the church unto God for him." Outside that prison
wall that night his congregation gathered in the home of one
of its members and prayed for Peter. The congregation prayed
for their pastor. That prayer was not in vain.

Suddenly, "Behold, the angel of the Lord came upon him,
and a light shined in the prison; and he smote Peter on the side
and raised him up, saying, Arise up quickly. And his chains
fell off from his hands. And the angel said unto him, Gird thyself,
and bind on thy sandals. And so he did. And he saith unto him,
Cast thy garment about thee, and follow me. And he went out,
and followed him" (Acts 12:7-9a). Peter was free. In a miraculous
way the Lord had delivered him out of prison and from the hand
of Herod. Peter was spared.

It was not so about twenty years later. Peter was again cast
into prison. Shortly thereafter, tradition tells us, he stretched
forth his hands on the cross and gave his life in the service of
the Lord. He was faithful unto death. By his death, as Jesus
had foretold, he "glorified God," a standing monument of God's
gracious love! Isn't it wonderful what God can do?

There are other rebuilt pillars in the church. Take *the apostle
Paul*. He too was once proud. The idol self was supreme in him.
But God graciously broke Paul's idol self and made him a new
chosen vessel. So on his third missionary journey, he could tell
the elders of Ephesus (Acts 20:22-24): "Behold, I go bound in
the spirit unto Jerusalem, not knowing the things that shall befall
me there: Save that the Holy Ghost witnesseth in every city,
saying that bonds and afflictions abide me. But none of these
things move me, neither count I my life dear unto myself, so
that I might finish my course with joy, and the ministry, which
I have received of the Lord Jesus, to testify the gospel of the
grace of God" (Acts 20:22-24). What a change! What courageous words!

A few days later he told the prophet Agabus and others at
Caesarea: "What mean ye to weep and to break mine heart?

For I am ready not to be bound only, but also to die at Jerusalem for the name of the Lord Jesus" (Acts 21:13). Proud and haughty Saul had become a humble and loyal servant of the Lord, Paul, a chosen vessel of God. A new spirit had taken possession of his heart.

That marvelous and iconoclastic work of the Lord *is still* going on today. Many men and women living in our age are faithfully serving the Lord. They are rebuilt vessels of God. Their names may not be known to us, but they are written in the Book of Life. They and we are cobuilders with God.

Let us thank God for this grace of having been chosen by Him as laborers together with Him in this greatest work of all ages, God's world-embracing rebuilding program. God has the blueprints. The Gospel, John 3:16, is His chief tool. Iconoclastic is His method. All must crumble before Him. All human efforts are blasted to pieces. Thereupon He takes those broken pieces, like the case of Peter in our text and millions of others in the onward march of the Christian church; He puts them all together again for God-pleasing service. He is the Builder and the Rebuilder. May He deign to take you, to take me, to take us all, dash the "idol self" to a thousand pieces, and then graciously reconstruct us for ever greater service in His kingdom!

Soli Deo gloria!

Ruled by Men or Governed by God

By HENRY A. LOEBER

(The Sixth Sunday After Trinity)

Then came to Jesus scribes and Pharisees, which were of Jerusalem, saying, Why do Thy disciples transgress the tradition of the elders? For they wash not their hands when they eat bread. But He answered and said unto them. Why do ye also transgress the commandments of God by your tradition? For God commanded, saying, Honor thy father and mother; and, He that curseth father or mother, let him die the death. But ye say, Whosoever shall say to his father or his mother, It is a gift, by whatsoever thou mightest be profited by me; and honor not his father or his mother, he shall be free. Thus have ye made the commandment of God of none effect by your tradition. Ye hypocrites, well did Esaias prophesy of you, saying, This people draweth nigh unto Me with their mouth, and honoreth Me with their lips; but their heart is far from Me. But in vain they do worship Me, teaching for doctrines the commandments of men. — *Matthew 15:1-9*

One of the most popular tourist attractions on the East Coast is the United Nations building located in New York City. Last year over 100,000 tourists saw the wonder and the beauty of this building. A rather inconspicuous little room is located near the main entranceway of the building. As you enter that room, you notice the expensive tapestries hanging on the wall and the drapes muffling the sound. It is a quiet room. It is a room for devotion. It is a chapel. In the very center of that room is a table, and on the table is a vase of flowers. You cannot but ask the question, Is this enough for Christian worship? There's no cross there. Out of deference to the Moslem block of nations, as well as to the communist groups, there is no reference whatsoever to our Lord Jesus Christ. As you stand in that chapel, you gain the impression that God is rather hazy and foggy and rather far removed. Christians, however, know their God in far better terms than that.

We are concerned with the true God, the Father, the Son, and the Holy Ghost, into whom we have been baptized and for whom we gather together in worship every Sunday. There's nothing remote about Him. If anyone would insinuate that we do not worship the true God, we would most certainly be insulted and respond with a hasty reply. However, history has shown that in every generation of Christianity, while men and women have known the true God and the Savior Jesus Christ and His redemptive work, yet there has always been some insincerity and a great deal of haziness in Christian worship. This morning, under the guidance of God's Holy Spirit, we wish to center our attention upon one of the problems that is involved in Christian worship as we consider the theme, Ruled by Men or Governed by God.

Worship in Christ's Day

The problem in worship revealed itself in Christ's day. It appears that there were some whom Christ described in these words: "In vain they do worship Me, teaching for doctrines the commandments of men." These were the scribes and the Pharisees, a group of men numbered among the elite religious class of the people. If anyone should have understood the Scriptures, it was these people. They made it their special function in life to study the traditions of the elders, to pore over the Scriptures, and to know the religious problems as well as the spiritual answers of their day. They had their fingers on all that touched religion. However, in their pursuit of religious knowledge they seem to have placed human reason above the very Law and the very rule of God. This was apparent, first of all, in the fact that they began to criticize others. They came to our Lord Jesus Christ, and they put it this way: "Why is it that your followers, in particular your disciples, do not ceremonially cleanse themselves by our traditional rite of washing before they eat a meal? This is certainly one of our laws and should be obeyed."

Our Lord Jesus did not deny that His disciples had disregarded this human tradition, but He replied with another question: "Why is it that you criticize when you yourselves in your traditions and in your laws overlook the rule of God Himself? For I have observed that some of you disregard the Fourth Commandment, which tells you to respect your elders and honor your parents, to provide for them in their advanced age. Some of you go so far as to say that your treasures and your wealth and what you have, this is something that is set aside for the Lord. It is a gift that is given to God, and therefore you do not have to take care of your elders. You do not have to face up to the responsibility of the Fourth Commandment. Moreover, after excusing yourselves from this responsibility, you squander your wealth and present nothing to God. This is one of your traditions, and this tradition of man overshadows the very spirit of the rule of God in your hearts."

Worship Centers in Christ

But the story doesn't end there. Jesus pointed out to these people that because they valued the human tradition of men more highly than the rule of God in their hearts, the note of insincerity and hypocrisy echoed throughout their worship life. "This people draweth nigh unto Me with their mouth and honoreth Me with their lips, but their heart is far from Me." "Not everyone that says unto Me, Lord, Lord, shall enter into the kingdom of heaven, but he that doeth the will of My Father which is in heaven." All worship is meaninglless that is practiced with the mouth and the tongue and the lips but in which the heart is not centered in the redemptive work of Christ. What God wants is the heart of the person. "A broken and a contrite heart, O God, Thou wilt not despise." (Ps. 51:17)

It is the heart of man for which Jesus looks. He has a rightful claim on man, for He came into this world not simply to cleanse hands before a meal, but to cleanse hearts for eternity, to remove the stain of sin that lies heavy upon the heart of man. To accomplish this, Jesus had to step from eternity into time, from heaven to earth. He had to take on a garment of humanness. He had to become as a lamb that was led to slaughter. As the Lamb he poured out His lifeblood on an altar called Calvary. This sacrifice was spoken of in the Old Testament worship, and it has become the very center of our worship under the New Covenant. We know that the blood of Jesus Christ, God's Son, cleanses us from all sin. But the problem of worship in Christ's day was that even among the scribes and Pharisees, even among the learned and the well educated, the traditions and the customs of the day loomed so large that they overshadowed this redemptive act of Christ. The rule of God was given second place in their hearts.

Worship Today

We say that happened long ago. It happened two thousand years ago in the days of Christ, and conditions were different then. Today we are an enlightened people and a greatly informed generation. However, a quick look around in the Christian church of today reveals that there are some people, some denominations that prevail in this very thing. There are some who insist that according to human tradition the Bible is not the Word of God. There are others who believe, in keeping with the traditions of the church, that it is an insult to human intelligence to assert that man cannot work himself into heaven. Still others tell us that our prayers should be directed to the mother of Christ. "In vain they do worship Me, teaching for doctrines the commandments of men."

Our Worship and the Inner Man

But the really important question is not: Can we find fault with others within the realm of the Christian church, but rather: What about our worship? Does the clear bell of sincerity ring true in our worship life? Abraham Lincoln was one of those unusual men who could plumb the depths of sincerity in people. On one occasion he visited a hospital during the Civil War. He talked with the soldiers who had been wounded, and then he stepped out into the corridor. As he was walking down the hall, a young man rounded the corner and without watching where he was going, he bumped into President Lincoln. He almost knocked him over. The young man didn't even pause to look up, but he said, "Why don't you watch where you're going?" President Lincoln replied, "Young man, what's wrong with you on the inside?" When we speak of sincerity in worship, we don't just refer to the outer man. On the outside we all look alike. We gather together, we fold our hands in prayer, we sing hymns, we listen and respond. We sit in the pews. We rise at certain points in the service, and we present an offering to God. We all look pretty much alike. Yet the Mr. Christian on the inside can be entirely different from the one on the outside. President Lincoln's question is one that we honestly should consider, "What is wrong with you on the inside?"

Tradition Replaces Rule of Christ

In other words, we are speaking of attitudes — attitudes that touch upon the customs and the traditions of our life and attitudes toward the rule of God in our heart. Perhaps you have found yourself in this situation on a given Sunday. You have had a rather tough week at work or in the house. You have had a great deal of problems, concerns, troubles, and perhaps a few heartaches. So on Sunday morning you reason thus with yourself. You say it has been a tough week. According to the customs and traditions of the world in which we live, a man must not only work but he must also rest if he is to be at his best. Thus you feel that for the particular Sunday in question it is your decision to rest and avoid church worship. The Third Commandment, which speaks of worship, doesn't fully and completely apply to your life on this Sunday, so you reason with yourself. If you have ever thought in such a manner, then at that moment the customs and the traditions of men have replaced the rule of God in your life.

The Scripture says, "Serve the Lord with gladness." Christians, however, at times say to themselves, I am a worshiper in the church. There are other people who are not as busy as I am. Let them build the Kingdom. I will worship, but I will not use my time or my talents. If you have ever reasoned thus with yourself, then the traditions of the world and the times have overtaken the rule of God in your heart.

The Two Kingdoms

Can you say that you have never at any time in your life come to terms with the world at Christ's expense? No one can say that he has never failed Christ, because not one of us is perfect. We have all sinned and fallen short of God's glory. Though we all are Christian, we are, at the same time, sinners. We live in a world of traditions, customs, and pressure, all of which weigh in upon us. In fact, these worldly pressures have a way of gaining access into the crevices of our personalities, of even permeating our hearts at the expense of the rule of God.

Paul, in his letter to the Romans, describes the dilemma of a Christian by pointing to two kingdoms. He says there is the rule of darkness over which Satan is the king. In the rule of darkness you find the traditions and the manners and the customs of the world. Then there is the rule of light in which Christ reigns supreme. Here you have the power of forgiveness, and the love of God shines over all. The strange situation, Paul points out, is that the Christian is in both worlds. He is both a saint and a sinner. We find that within us there is a veritable battle raging between the rule of God and the rule of darkness. It is our hope and desire that God wins this battle.

Christ is the key to that victory. When this Lord Jesus Christ, the Lamb whose blood was shed, reaches out for us, He not only conveys to us forgiveness, but in that very act He also strengthens us. Every time you and I bow the head to receive the words of absolution, "Thy sins be forgiven thee," and every time we partake of the body and blood of our Lord, the hand of God not only wipes away our sins, but in that very action He presents to us inner strength. This strength makes it possible for us to be changed creatures, to rise above the signs of the times, and to live our lives ever more completely dedicated to Him who loves us.

Our Response

In other words, we Christians must recognize that worship involves not just the outer man — the lips and the mouth. There is more to worship than occupying twenty inches of wood in a pew. Our worship is deeply affected by the behavior of the heart. That heart is cleansed and built up as we have contact with Christ in Word and sacrament. Therefore, as penitent sinners, forgiven by Christ, we should take advantage of every opportunity to hear His Word, to participate in His sacrament, that the inner man might be strengthened to resist the rule of darkness.

Many long years ago the loving eyes of Christ focused upon the scribes and the Pharisees in order that they be transformed from darkness to light. However, those men didn't even bother to take a second glance at the Savior. Today those same eyes are focusing on us. As we look into the eyes of Christ, we see hurt — hurt for our sin and iniquity, hurt for the many times the customs of the day have reigned supreme in our lives. We also see in those eyes pity — pity that we are so weak and so easily swayed by the world. But above all, we see in those eyes forgiveness. In the eyes of Christ we see ourselves as we really are — sinners. In those same eyes we see Christ as He really is — not a hazy, foggy, or remote God, but our personal Redeemer, our own Savior, our Rock, and our inner Fortress in whom there is everlasting strength. We respond to Him not only with the deep-rooted conviction of faith, but with a greater faithfulness in worship and devotion. We look forward to that day when those same eyes will focus on us and say, "Well done, good and faithful servant — enter thou into the joy of thy Lord."

Watch Your Heart!

By Leonard W. Koehler

(The Seventh Sunday After Trinity)

And He called the multitude and said unto them, Hear and understand. Not that which goeth into the mouth defileth a man, but that which cometh out of the mouth, this defileth a man. Then came His disciples and said unto Him, Knowest Thou that the Pharisees were offended after they heard this saying? But He answered and said, Every plant which My heavenly Father hath not planted shall be rooted up. Let them alone; they be blind leaders of the blind. And if the blind lead the blind, both shall fall into the ditch. Then answered Peter and said unto Him, Declare unto us this parable. And Jesus said, Are ye also yet without understanding? Do not ye yet understand that whatsoever entereth in at the mouth goeth into the belly and is cast out into tne draught? But those things which proceed out of the mouth come forth from the heart, and they defile the man. For out of the heart proceed evil thoughts, murders, adulteries, fornications, thefts, false witness, blasphemies. These are the things which defile a man, but to eat with unwashen hands defileth not a man. — *Matthew 15:10-20*

The heart is the most vital organ of the human body. Night and day, every day, it pumps blood through the veins and arteries of the body by its constant beating, which averages about 72 beats a minute and totals about 37 and a half million beats a year. It has been said that the work done by the heart in one day is equal to the energy needed for climbing about 250 flights of stairs.

Because your heart is such a vital organ, you should take care of it. Your doctor and your insurance agent are concerned about its condition, and so is your athletic director if you are in organized sports. In many types of employment men are required who have a sound, healthy heart.

The person who is most concerned, of course, is Jesus. He knows things about the human heart that the stethoscope, the microscope, and the cardiograph do not reveal. He knows that the hearts of men are spiritually sick with sin. He knows that "out of the heart proceed evil thoughts, murders, adulteries, fornications, thefts, false witness, blasphemies" (Matt. 15:19). These are the things which destroy not only the body but also the soul. "These are the things," Jesus says, "which defile a man." That's why He is concerned. He wants to cleanse the heart and save us from its follies. He wants to make it a temple of the Holy Ghost. He alone has the power to renew it spiritually and make it acceptable to God. Therefore on the basis of the text we say:

Watch Your Heart

I

There Is a Problem

What's wrong with my heart? That's the question a Pharisee might have asked Jesus. The Pharisees were not much concerned with the spiritual condition of the heart because no one could look into it anyway. Instead they laid much stress on outward things which people did notice, such as civic righteousness and the ceremonial laws of the church. They bathed and washed their clothes to counteract a ceremonial defilement. They abstained from eating foods which were considered unclean. They washed or sprinkled themselves on returning home from the marketplace. They would not eat without first washing their hands, lest they should defile their body by eating something considered unclean. They stressed the things that some people would call window dressing.

God Knows What the Problem Is

Jesus sees through the things which are nothing more than a veneer or cover-up. He recognized the fact that the regulated observance of outward cleanliness and adherence to ceremony on the part of the Pharisees received the wrong emphasis and often bordered on the ridiculous. That's why they were offended when Jesus said, "Not that which goeth into the mouth defileth a man, but that which cometh out of the mouth, this defileth a man" (v. 11), to wit, the cursing, lying, and unclean jesting of which many people in our day are guilty.

God always sees more than meets the eye. He searches the heart and understands all the imaginations of the thoughts. As far back as the Book of Genesis He said, "The imagination of man's heart is evil from his youth" (8:21). The fact that many people do not realize the sinful condition of their heart, or will not admit it, does not alter the fact. Scripture says, "I was shapen in iniquity, and in sin did my mother conceive me." (Ps. 51:5)

Men Cannot Solve the Problem

In many respects the Pharisees remind us of the social gospel advocates of our day who think that man is basically good and that there is nothing wrong with his heart. They believe that you can take a heathen or a degenerate, educate him, train him, dress him in respectable clothes, teach him to observe the rules of good society, and he becomes acceptable in the sight of God and man.

Others maintain that the heart is basically neither good nor evil. They maintain that if a man lives in a good environment, his deeds will be good; but if he lives in an evil environment, his deeds will be evil. Such reasoning ignores original sin, in which man is born. Man need not be exposed to sin or see and hear evil before he becomes capable of doing it. His wicked heart enables him to plan and execute evil schemes without any outside help.

Cain didn't need help to kill his brother Abel. Both were sons of Adam and Eve. They lived in the same environment and enjoyed the same advantages. Furthermore, there were no newspapers describing the lurid details of murder and the criminal's attempt to conceal his crime. There were no crime movies or detective magazines from which he could have taken ideas or suggestions. In fact, there was no precedent whatever for such a crime, but he committed it with all the savagery usually associated with a crime of passion and, as is characteristic of most murderers, he, too, thought he could conceal his evil deed. His sin did not originate somewhere outside him but deep down in the dark recesses of his sinful heart. The big difference between these two brothers was that one by God's grace had learned to rule over the natural passions of his heart while the other permitted them to rule over him. No doubt many a person, after seriously pondering on the crime committed by Cain, has said, "Thank God, I'm not like him." By nature, however, our heart is no better. It is just as sinful and corrupt. It harbors the same black ideas and is capable of carrying them out. And where can you find a franker or more humiliating appraisal of the human heart than that by Jeremiah, who says: "The heart is deceitful above all things and desperately wicked; who can know it?" (ch. 17:9). Therefore watch your heart!

Sin Is Our Problem

Let's not make the mistake of thinking that the text is merely describing the wicked heart of men such as Cain and Judas Iscariot. This is a description of your heart and mine too. If we did the sinful things that our heart desires and even devises, as far as the remnants of the sinful flesh are concerned, we would be in serious trouble. You would be ashamed, yes, terrified, if others could see your heart as it is. We might as well face it. Jesus means you and me and every man born into the world when He says: "Out of the heart proceed evil thoughts, murders, adulteries, fornications, thefts, false witness, blasphemies" (v. 19). These are the sins which flow from original sin, which has been correctly described as "the total corruption of our whole human nature."

Original sin is a worldwide problem. It is the cause of strife, injustice, rivalries, jealousies, fraud, suspicion, hate, and the like, which mar man's relationship with his fellowmen. That's why Joseph was sold into slavery by his own brothers. That's why tensions between nations sometimes reach the breaking point. That's why capital and labor often claw at each other and rival unions and political parties often break much more than the law of love.

Most serious of all is the breach which sin created between man and his God. Just as Adam and Eve hid from God in Eden and made excuses for themselves, so men today try to evade God; they feel uncomfortable when confronted with His truth and try to justify their sinful conduct. But the fact remains that sin brought God's curse down upon man. Familiar to you are the rumblings of His terrible words: "The wages of sin is death! . . . Ye shall be holy, for I, the Lord, your God, am holy! . . . The soul that sinneth, it shall die! . . . Cursed is everyone that continueth not in all things written in the Book of the Law to do them!"

Man's Effort at Solution

In every generation there have been philosophers, teachers, statesmen, who have looked for a solution to the problems created by the sinful ambitions of man. The Greek philosopher Plato, who lived more than 300 years before Christ, believed that where reason and self-discipline are practiced, virtue would replace vice. Basically it was the self-righteousness of the Pharisee. Plato, giant among philosophers that he is, never hit upon the law of love which Christ stressed again and again. It never once dawned on him that the love of one man for another and for all other men can accomplish vastly more than logic and reason.

· In our day socialism, the welfare state, the advocates of democracy, educators, scientists, and many others are trying to solve the problems of mankind, but they cannot find the solution because they are looking in the wrong places. Fallen men cannot save a fallen world. In the text Jesus puts it this way: "Every plant which My heavenly Father hath not planted shall be rooted up. Let them alone; they be blind leaders of the blind. And if the blind lead the blind, both shall fall into the ditch" (vv. 13, 14). Man's heart remains as it is, sinful and corrupt, in spite of all that moralists, educators, and philosophers have done and can do. Without the teachings of Jesus Christ to enlighten and guide them, and without the new life earned and given them by our Redeemer through His Holy Spirit, they are, sad to say, blind leaders of the blind. Both they and those who follow them are destined to end up in the ditch.

II

There Is a Solution

What can I do about my sinful heart? How can it be changed? Who can help me? Since "there is not a just man upon earth that doeth good and sinneth not" (Eccl. 7:20), since "we are all as an unclean thing, and all our righteousnesses are as filthy rags" (Is. 64:6), it's useless to depend on men for a solution. Man can do nothing to correct the sad state of his heart; but God can. God has done something about it. He has the solution.

The Solution Is Christ

God from eternity recognized the problem and decided on universal redemption through the atoning sacrifice of His Son, which was accomplished in due time by His innocent death on the cross. This precious Gospel of redemption God revealed to mankind from the very beginning. He told the parents of the human race that Christ, the woman's Seed, would bruise the serpent's head. He spoke of redemption as an accomplished fact when He

said through the prophet Isaiah: "Surely He hath borne our griefs
and carried our sorrows; yet we did esteem Him stricken, smitten
of God, and afflicted. But He was wounded for our transgressions,
He was bruised for our iniquities; the chastisement of our peace
was upon Him, and with His stripes we are healed" (53:4, 5). At
the time appointed by God those words went into fulfillment.
Jesus Christ, "Very God of Very God," came into the world in
the form of the lowly Son of man and, as was predicted, He shed
His holy blood and died on the cross as a sacrifice for the sins of
the world. This is redemption. Universal redemption it is called
because Christ died for all; not merely for some or for those who
are finally saved, but for all.

The Holy Ghost Offers Us God's Grace

Man with all his sin and pride does not want the redemption
of Christ. If he feels any concern about his soul's salvation, or
any need for God's favor, he wants to merit it and can't. For this
reason the work of the Holy Ghost is of the utmost importance.
By means of God's Law He shows us that we, left to our own
devices, are lost. He shows us that we cannot keep the Law and
that our only hope is Christ, who kept the Law for us. He calls
on men to repent, saying, "Rend your heart and not your garments" (Joel 2:13). He holds out to penitent sinners the promise:
"Though your sins be as scarlet, they shall be as white as snow;
though they be like crimson, they shall be as wool" (Is. 1:18).
There are dozens, yes, hundreds of gracious Gospel promises,
all of which direct sinners to forgiveness, life, and salvation
in Christ.

By God's grace you and I believe and put our trust in those
Gospel promises. As people who have been born again by water
and the Spirit, we realize that it's not what we eat or drink or
any outward ceremony that can cleanse the heart, but solely the
precious blood of Christ. In faith we have accepted forgiveness
as a gift of God's grace. We are no longer tormented by a guilty
conscience. We need no longer fear death and the punishment for
sin, because in Christ we are God's children and heirs of eternal
life. True, the desires of our heart and the will of our flesh will
assert themselves again and again, but they cannot have their way
as long as we obey the Holy Spirit, who speaks to us in the Word
and strengthens us for the struggle against evil.

Also in the Sacraments

In addition to the Word, God has given us the sacraments as
instituted by Christ. They also are means of grace because in
them God's grace in the redeeming blood of Jesus Christ is offered

and conveyed. First, there is Holy Baptism, which Scripture describes as "the washing of regeneration and renewing of the Holy Ghost, which He shed on us abundantly through Jesus Christ, our Savior" (Titus 3:5, 6). Baptism works faith and cleanses from sin. That's something which ceremony, logic, reason, philosophy, and good works cannot do. The blessings of Baptism are ours not just for a day or once in a lifetime, but every time we renew the vow to renounce the devil and to serve the one true God they are appropriated unto us anew.

The other sacrament Christ instituted for us is Holy Communion. Here, under the elements of bread and wine, Christ gives us His true body and blood for the forgiveness of sins. Through this salutary gift our faith is strengthened, and we can the better resist sin and temptation. Fasting and bodily preparation on the part of the believer are only outward disciplines. They neither add nor take away anything from the sacrament, just as the Pharisees added nothing to their righteousness by abstaining from certain foods because they were considered unclean. Luther ably stated a basic truth of Holy Communion when he said, "He is truly worthy and well prepared who has faith in these words, 'Given and shed for you for the remission of sins.' "

It is truly amazing when we stop to consider what God did in order to free us from Satan's domination and to cleanse us from sin. He gave us His Son and His Holy Spirit. He gave us His Word and the sacraments. All these are His free gifts without any merit or worthiness on our part. All He asks is that we accept them in humble faith. Truly amazing!

Our Response

"What shall I render unto the Lord for all His benefits toward me" (Ps. 116:12)? In the city of Jericho Jesus brought a publican by the name of Zacchaeus to repentance and faith. Zacchaeus was so grateful that he responded: "Behold, Lord, the half of my goods I give to the poor; and if I have taken anything from any man by false accusation, I restore him fourfold" (Luke 19:8). His cleansed heart responded immediately with good works, the fruits of faith.

There are ways in which we, too, can express our love and thanks to the Savior for cleansing us from sin and making us acceptable in God's sight. With the Holy Spirit's help we can be faithful witnesses of the Savior's redeeming love. Love for God and our fellowmen will prompt us to place more and more emphasis on spiritual things and less and less emphasis on material things. We can be Good Samaritans for the Savior in the homes of those who are in need or distress. Our love for the Bible, the church service, and the sacraments also are expressions of our love and thanks to Him from whom all blessings flow.

Of course, even the redeemed must be told: Watch your heart! It's so easy to forget God and to yield to the will of the flesh. That's why we must daily humble ourselves before God, confess our sins, and claim forgiveness. Then we find grace in the eyes of God. Then our heart will truly be a temple in which God Himself is pleased to dwell. King Asa, who reigned over Judah for 41 years, was by no means a perfect ruler or a perfect man, but he was a believer, and that's why Scripture pays him this tribute, "Asa's heart was perfect with the Lord all his days" (1 Kings 15:14). With the help of the Holy Ghost let us learn more and more to free our heart from worldly things and to fix it on the things that draw us closer to God. With the help of the Spirit we can learn to place not only our heart but our entire being into the service of our blessed Lord, who redeemed our life from destruction and rose from the dead that also we might live, body and soul, with Him in heavenly glory.

Christ Is the Righteous Judge of All

By CARL A. GAERTNER

(The Eighth Sunday After Trinity)

I can of Mine own self do nothing: as I hear, I judge, and My judgment is just; because I seek not Mine own will, but the will of the Father, which hath sent Me. If I bear witness of Myself, My witness is not true. There is another that beareth witness of Me, and I know that the witness which He witnesseth of Me is true. Ye sent unto John, and he bare witness unto the truth. But I receive not testimony from man; but these things I say, that ye might be saved. He was a burning and a shining light, and ye were willing for a season to rejoice in his light. But I have greater witness than that of John; for the works which the Father hath given Me to finish, the same works that I do, bear witness of Me, that the Father hath sent Me. And the Father Himself, which hath sent Me, hath borne witness of Me. Ye have neither heard His voice at any time, nor seen His shape. And ye have not His Word abiding in you; for whom He hath sent, Him ye believe not.

John 5:30-38

The other day, when we were discussing an obvious political development with a young man, he stated, "You better believe it." This rather quaint and provincial expression could be applied to many situations and facts which ought to be apparent to all.

As our Congress votes into law many kinds of new government programs, we better believe it, our national debt will have to be increased and our taxes will go higher to meet the cost.

When parents are indifferent to their responsibilities in rearing their children and are lax and inconsistent in disciplining them, you better believe it, they are paving the way for trouble and heartbreak for themselves and their children.

Only a fool would think today that the communists are not determined to conquer the world, and you better believe it.

As we study our text this morning, we want to say to you and to people everywhere — you better believe it — this truth:

Christ Is the Righteous Judge of All

I

As in the days of Christ, today also **people need to be confronted with this truth.** Though our Lord was forthright in what He had to say about Himself, most people did not believe Him. In this fifth chapter of John we have the report of Jesus' identification of Himself with the Father. He insisted that He was doing the works of the Father. He stated plainly that all judgment was committed to Him by the Father, and that He had the authority to execute judgment over all, indicating that some would come forth to the resurrection of life and some to the resurrection of damnation. Our text clearly shows that these claims and others made by Jesus were not accepted generally by the people who heard Him.

This is a continuing problem for people also in our generation. Religion of some sort is acceptable to many people today and Christ is acknowledged to have been an unusual personality. Most people would agree that He was an effective teacher and capable leader of men; indeed, a man of noble character with high ideals and superior ethics. At the same time many ignore the Scriptural teaching concerning Christ as the almighty Son of God, the Savior of sinners, and the Judge of the quick and the dead.

In some areas of the theological world it no longer is surprising to hear rationalists speak of our Lord as nothing more than a saving symbol, and we wonder about the content of faith of many people in the pews of our Christian congregations as well. In many respects we are a sentimental people, easily moved by our emotions. Frequently people get their sweet sentiments mixed up with the great truths of the Christian religion; they think of Jesus merely in His gentleness and compassion, going about doing good, and all the while they blot out of their minds the full image of Jesus Christ who, having completed His mission on the cross of Calvary, is the exalted Son of God, ruling over all in majesty and righteousness, until He shall return visibly to be the just Judge of all.

It is important for us all to face up to these great truths which Jesus spoke concerning Himself. Our Christian faith must be more

than a going along with the crowd. When we present Christ to
you as the Son of God, the Savior of sinners, and the righteous
Judge of all, we want to say in all earnestness — you better believe it! Your eternal destiny is involved in these issues; Christ in
our text gives convincing reasons why people should believe Him.

II

Surely Jesus wanted to help people in every way to accept
Him in faith and believe that the Father had sent Him. In our
text He again relates His entire activity to the Father and His
holy will. In fact when speaking of judgment He emphasizes that
in the role of Judge He does not act arbitrarily and independently,
seeking out His own will, but He does the will of the Father who
sent Him into the world.

After this plain statement, **our Lord supplies convincing evidence for His claims.** First of all, He directs their attention to
John the Baptist, who bore witness unto the truth concerning
Christ. And though this truth would stand without the witness
of man, Jesus brings to their remembrance this great voice crying
in the wilderness. Jesus knew that for a time John had made
a deep impression on Israel, for he was to them a burning and
shining light in which they had rejoiced for a season. His testimony to Christ was unmistakable. It was John the Baptist who
had told the world that Jesus was eternal, so great in His deity
that John was not worthy to loosen His shoe's latchet. In addition
to this John also explained publicly that Jesus as Judge had the
fan in His hand, separating the wheat from the chaff (Matt. 3:12).
This voice crying in the wilderness went all the way and pointed
to Jesus of Nazareth as the Lamb of God taking away the sin of
the world.

John's witness was wonderful, but Jesus, according to our
text, had even more telling testimony to support the truth about
Himself. He referred to the works which the Father had given
Him to finish. These people no doubt saw many of His miracles
and heard about others. How impressive it would have been for
them if there would have been a motion picture record of Jesus'
ministry in their midst. They had something far better, they had
the Lord in person and they should have believed Him. We do
not have a motion picture record of Jesus' works either, but we
also have something far better, we have the inspired Gospel accounts. From this we can learn Christ's convincing argument on
the basis of the works which the Father gave Him to finish.

Remember, for instance, how dramatically the Gospels report
that Jesus kept the Law of God perfectly as He lived among men.
This truly was unique. The devil could not lead Him into sin.

Every requirement of the Commandments was met. Even His bitter enemies could not prove one fault in Him. The Father had sent Him for this work of fulfilling the Law in our stead as we read in Galatians 4:4, 5: "When the fulness of the time was come, God sent forth His Son, made of a woman, made under the law, that we might receive the adoption of sons."

Probably the most tangible evidence for His Jewish contemporaries was the sensational series of miracles performed by Christ in their own communities. The lame were made to walk. The eyes of the blind were opened and the hearing of the deaf was restored. The sick were healed and the demons were driven out of the tortured bodies of the possessed. And there was more: even the forces of nature were subject to Him and He raised some from the dead. Here was evidence which they could not ignore and later at a council meeting the Jewish leaders plaintively asked "What do we? for this man doeth many miracles" (John 11:47). Also for us this is greater witness than the witness of John.

It is significant that Jesus in our text speaks about works which the Father gave Him to finish. The people hearing Him probably could not get the full significance of this, but we who have the full record of the Gospels see in this a reference to Christ's greatest work, namely the completion of God's gracious plan of salvation. This brings to our mind's eye His vicarious suffering and death, His resurrection and His glorious ascension. Nor should we forget His session at the right hand of God where He continues in His works as the Head of the church and rules over all as King of kings and Lord of lords.

In addition to all this there is to be one more convincing work of Christ which will erase all doubts as to His claims for Himself. We refer to His second coming in glory to judge the quick and the dead.

Does more need to be said to establish the great truths about Jesus Christ as Son of God, the Savior of sinners, and the righteous Judge of all? It should suffice, but Jesus has more to support Him. He now directs attention to the Father Himself.

Jesus states in our text that the Father bore witness of Him and at the same time frankly indicated to them that they did not know the Father, nor was His Word abiding in them. This witness of the Father is not only interesting but also tremendously significant.

Though the unbelieving people about Him did not hear the voice of the Father, He most certainly spoke emphatically in identifying Jesus of Nazareth as the One sent by the Father. We think of the voice sounding out of the cloud when Jesus was baptized: "This is My beloved Son in whom I am well pleased" (Matt. 3:17). Later, in the brilliant scene of the transfiguration of Christ on the mountain top, came this same voice in testimony for Christ: "This is My beloved Son, hear Him" (Luke 9:35). On another occasion some people thought it was thunder (John 12:29), but the Father had assured the Son directly that He would glorify His name again and Jesus explained: "This voice came not because of Me, but for your sakes." (John 12:30)

The support of the Father for the truth concerning Christ is substantiated when we examine such direct testimony as reported in the Gospel accounts, but there is much more evidence supplied by God through Moses and the prophets. All of the Old Testament promises of the Messiah, given in detail, fulfilled in the person, life, and work of Jesus Christ are convincing witness that Jesus of Nazareth is all that He claimed to be.

The evidence is all in and the people of His day should have received Him with joyful faith. If we can say that of them, then surely we should conclude that we better believe this truth that Jesus Christ is the Son of God, the Savior of sinners, and the righteous Judge of all. This is not merely a theoretical theological formulation, but an eternally valid reality.

III

However, let us not overlook the statement in our text where Jesus insists "My judgment is just." He is the Judge of all and **He is righteous in all His judgment.** No one will be able to accuse Christ of having made a mistake in His judging. He will not use a variable standard. On the basis of the Word which He has spoken will He judge rightly and justly.

This means: without exception He will bring His sentence of condemnation upon the guilty and will in all justice acquit the innocent.

Does this plain statement frighten you? After all we are conscious of transgressing the holy will of God. We confess that the Scriptural inclusion of all men under sin surely fits us. When we look at our own record of life on the basis of the Ten Commandments, and then remember that Christ is our righteous Judge, who must condemn the guilty, we tremble in fear.

However, we are afraid only until we remember in repentance and faith that this same Jesus is also our Savior who has cleansed us of all sins in His precious blood and covered us with His own righteousness; for He who knew no sin was made sin for us that we might be made the righteousness of God in Him (2 Cor. 5:21). When we, who have been baptized into Christ and who have put on Christ, stand in repentance and faith before our Judge, He will not condemn us, because in His righteousness we are innocent. That is divine justice. "He that believeth and is baptized shall be saved" (Mark 16:16). This we Christians believe, and we are not afraid of Christ, the righteous Judge of all.

Some people ought to be afraid, for such as do not repent of their sins and do not believe in Jesus Christ as their Savior are yet in their sins and will stand in their unbelief as guilty before the righteous Judge. For such there is no escape: "He that believeth not shall be damned" (Mark 16:16). If there is anyone in this church this morning who has not accepted the evidence of the Holy Scriptures concerning Jesus Christ and God's gracious plan of salvation for sinners in Him, permit me to say to such a person: the judgment and condemnation of Christ, the righteous Judge, is hanging over you like a dark, threatening cloud. Repent before it is too late, for today is the day of grace, now is the time of salvation for you.

Oh, that we all would be the children of God by faith in Christ Jesus! Believing the great truth that Jesus is the Son of God, the Savior of sinners, and the righteous Judge of all, we walk confidently through life, hastening to that great Day of judgment, rejoicing in the glorious hope of everlasting life, for He who is our righteous Judge is also our blessed Savior who has made us righteous before God, forgiving us all our sins.

Finding Christ

By EDGAR G. RUNGE

(The Ninth Sunday After Trinity)

Search the Scriptures, for in them ye think ye have eternal life, and they are they which testify of Me. And ye will not come to Me that ye might have life. I receive not honor from men. But I know you, that ye have not the love of God in you. I am come in My Father's name, and ye receive Me not. If another shall come in his own name, him ye will receive. How can ye believe, which receive honor one of another and seek not the honor that cometh from God only? Do not think that I will accuse you to the Father. There is one that accuseth you, even Moses, in whom ye trust. For had ye believed Moses, ye would have believed Me, for he wrote of Me. But if ye believe not his writings, how shall ye believe My words? — *John 5:39-47*

The Holy Bible is the most popular book in the world. The Bible is the most widely distributed book in the world. According to recent reports of the American Bible Society, the Bible, or portions of the Bible, have now been translated into about 1,200 different languages and dialects.

The influence of the Holy Bible upon mankind through the

years has been a tremendous influence for good. A great many oil paintings, painted by the gifted masters of the past centuries (Raphael, Rubens, Da Vinci), have had Bible characters and Bible stories as their theme. Many of these paintings today are almost priceless in value. In music the Bible has been the inspiration of many composers of great music, such as "The Messiah" by Handel, "The Crucifixion" by Sir John Stainer, and others. Poets have read the Bible for the purpose of word study. Writers and teachers have studied the Bible for its value in literary form, its rich phrases and word expressions. William Shakespeare quotes from the Bible in several of his plays.

Through the years the Bible has had a powerful influence upon society. The Bible gives womanhood its proper place in life. It has been a direct influence in the modern concepts of public education and democratic government. The Bible places the right value on the individual human being and his status before God. While heathenism and godless people place very little worth on the individual human life, the Bible places a high value on the individual soul — that it is worth more in the sight of God than all the treasures of the world!

The Bible is found in practically every home in America. In your home you perhaps have several copies of the Bible. You can buy a copy of the Bible in practically every department store in America. The Gideons have been placing Bibles into hotel and motel rooms for the benefit of travelers. However, the real richness of the Bible is Christ, the Savior of sinners. The contributions which the Bible has made to art, literature, music, education, and government are only by-products. The real purpose of the Bible is "to make us wise unto salvation" through Christ. The Bible directs us to Christ, the Savior, the only Hope of mankind; the Bible reveals the true Christ, His person and His will. While the Holy Bible itself is a great treasure, the prime jewel of priceless worth in this treasure is Jesus Christ. This is the point which Jesus stresses in the text.

I

This portion of the fifth chapter of John is the last part of one of Christ's sermons to the Jewish people. Jesus had healed a crippled man on the Sabbath. The Jews who witnessed this miracle brushed aside the great miracle itself and viciously attacked Christ because, they claimed, He had broken the Sabbath law and because, they said, He made Himself equal with God (v. 18). In fact, their hostile attitude toward Christ became so intense that they wanted to kill Christ.

And now Jesus gives these people a number of reasons why

they should have recognized Him as the true Messiah and why they should have accepted Him as the true Christ, sent from the Father, as the Savior of sinners. He reminds them of the witness of John the Baptist, in whom the people had placed a great deal of confidence. "Ye were willing for a season to rejoice in his light" (v. 35), Jesus says. "He bare witness unto the truth" (v. 33). For when Jesus came to John at the Jordan River, John said of Jesus, "Behold the Lamb of God, which taketh away the sin of the world." (John 1: 29)

Then Christ reminds the Jewish people of a witness greater than the witness of John — "I have greater witness than that of John; for the works which the Father hath given Me to finish, the same works that I do, bear witness of Me, that the Father hath sent Me" (v. 36). The miracles of Jesus, such as the one He had just performed on the impotent man, healing the sick, raising the dead, were even more decisive evidence than John's witness that He was the true Christ.

And now added to this is the witness of the Father. In v. 37 we read: "And the Father Himself, which hath sent Me, hath borne witness of Me." On the occasion of Christ's Baptism the voice of the Father had announced from heaven: "This is My beloved Son, in whom I am well pleased."

Now as a final argument that these people should have recognized Jesus as the true Savior, Jesus says to them: "Search the Scriptures, for in them ye think ye have eternal life, and they are they which testify of Me" (v. 39). Our Savior reminds these people that they should carefully examine "the Scriptures," that is, the Old Testament writings, and such a search would reveal plenty of evidence that He is the Christ, the Son of God. The word "search" implies a careful, diligent examination of something. This is the type of searching which miners engage in when they are searching for precious metals under the ground. This is a diligent and faithful investigation to find precious metal or precious stones. The Jewish people were familiar with the Old Testament. When a Jewish boy reached the age of 12, he had a fairly good knowledge of the Law and the Prophets. And the Pharisees certainly had searched through the books of the Law and were well acquainted not only with the Moral law but also with the ceremonial laws. The fact that they tried to keep all these laws so strictly was evidence of their knowledge of these laws.

But Jesus reminds them that in their searching of the Old Testament they should also have found the Savior — "they are they which testify of Me." A careful search of the prophetic writings in the Old Testament does clearly testify that Christ is the true

Messiah, the Savior. For example, the prophet Micah foretells Christ's birth (Micah 5:2), the prophet Isaiah foretells Christ's suffering, that He is to bear the punishment of the sins of all people (Isaiah 53), and Psalm 22 foretells accurately many details of the crucifixion of Christ. And had these people carefully studied the writings of Moses — and this is the climax of Christ's argument — they would know that Moses gives testimony to the fact that Christ is the true Savior and the Son of God. Jesus says: "There is one that accuseth you, even Moses, in whom you trust. For had ye believed Moses, ye would have believed Me, for he wrote of Me. But if ye believe not his writings, how shall ye believe My words?" (Vv. 45-47)

The Jews had a very high regard for Moses. Moses was held in the highest esteem. Every year at the Passover Festival the head of each Jewish family would relate, in detail, the deliverance of the Jewish people from slavery in Egypt under the leadership of Moses. Moses was a great hero to the Jewish people. And now Christ reminds these people around Him that Moses, "in whom ye trust," had written about Christ (Gen. 3:15; 12:3 [cf. John 8:56]; Deut. 18:15). But if they will not believe what Moses wrote about Christ, even though they regarded his writings so highly, then they certainly will not believe what Christ Himself was telling them about Himself!

II

It is a strange fact, isn't it, that these people in the days of Jesus did not recognize Christ and accept Christ as their Savior in the light of all the testimony which Moses, John the Baptist, God the Father, and Christ Himself give concerning Christ, the Son of God, the Savior. Perhaps you wonder how it was possible for these people to be so blind that they could not see the truth.

But isn't this same fact evident also today? In America today there are probably very few homes in which there is no Bible at all. Most homes in America have at least one copy of the Holy Scriptures. In spite of this, hardly half of the people in America sincerely believe that Christ is their personal Savior and Redeemer. Hardly half of the people in America are professing Christians. And less than these are regular worshipers in Christian churches on Sunday. Not only does the Old Testament give us testimony about Christ, but we today have also the New Testament as additional testimony. We have the historical facts of Christ's life; the gospels record many of Christ's sayings concerning Himself. We have the testimony of eyewitnesses who lived with Jesus on earth, we have the testimony of contemporary historians, we have the history and the growth of the New Testament Church, and finally we have God's own witness throughout the Holy Scriptures that

Christ is the Savior of sinners. So when Jesus invites us to believe in Him, He does not do so without witnesses. And yet, there are so many today who say, "I will not believe."

What is at the bottom of this rejection? Why do people turn their backs on Christ today? Jesus says that the people did not *want* to come to Him — "ye will not come to Me that ye might have life" (v. 40). While it is true that in many areas of the world people do not become followers of Jesus because of ignorance — "How shall they believe in Him of whom they have not heard?" — yet it is also true that many people in America, who have heard the Gospel, reject Christ because of their own stubbornness and pride. The human heart is no different today from what it was in Christ's day. People generally do not want to change their way of living even though God says He wants them to do it. When Jesus talked with Nicodemus about this problem, He said: "This is the condemnation, that light is come into the world and men loved darkness rather than light because their deeds were evil" (John 3:19). This is still true with people today. Many resist the efforts of the Holy Spirit to bring them to Christ because they love darkness rather than the light. They prefer to stay in bed on Sunday morning or read the Sunday paper rather than study God's Word in the Bible class and worship in the public service. They refuse to give up their pet sins. They do not want to change their way of life — not even for Christ!

At the bottom of this unwillingness to yield to the will of Christ is man's sinful pride. This was also true of the people to whom Christ was talking in the text. Had Jesus appeared in their midst with great pomp and ceremony, like a great earthly ruler, many would have followed Him, but not in the right way. But when Jesus asks people to put away their sinful pride and become as little children, become humble, and look at themselves honestly as God looks at them — sinful, unclean, in need of forgiveness — they are often unwilling to do so.

But this text also has its application for us Christians. Christ points out this important fact: We must find Christ in the Scriptures, we must find Jesus the Savior, we must find Jesus as our personal Savior in the Bible. In the first place, what are you doing with the Bible or Bibles you have at home? Are your Bibles mostly ornamental in your home? Is your Bible getting worn out, or is it almost as new as the day you bought it? Do you read it merely to be reading it, or are you "searching the Scriptures" as a miner diligently searches for a diamond or a ruby? The object of our search should be Christ, a better understanding of Christ, a closer association with Christ, and a search to do the will of Christ.

The Bereans are commended in the Bible for searching the Scriptures (Acts 17:11), and Timothy was praised for having learned the Scriptures as a child (2 Tim. 3:15); so God's blessing will flow into our lives as we search the Scriptures. It is important for us to know the books of the Bible in their proper order, and it is important that we teach our children the chief doctrines of the Bible through their Catechism instruction. It is a good thing to know many passages of the Bible from memory, but even more important than all this is that we find Christ, our Savior, in the Bible. "They are they which testify of Me." It is possible for one to be very familiar with the Bible and yet not find Christ in the Bible as one's personal Redeemer!

Therefore "search the Scriptures" — not only for what *you* want to find in them but also for what *God* wants you to find in them — that you, a lost sinner, have forgiveness and cleansing through your Savior Jesus Christ and that as Christ's people we should walk in the light and be living witnesses to His love for us.

When Is Our Worship Relevant and Acceptable?

By EDWIN E. PIEPLOW

(The Tenth Sunday After Trinity)

And Jesus went into the temple of God, and cast out all them that sold and bought in the temple, and overthrew the tables of the money-changers, and the seats of them that sold doves. And said unto them, it is written, My house shall be called the house of prayer; but ye have made it a den of thieves. And the blind and the lame came to Him in the temple, and He healed them. And when the chief priests and scribes saw the wonderful things that He did and the children crying in the temple and saying, Hosanna to the son of David, they were sore displeased and said unto Him, Hearest Thou what these say? And Jesus saith unto them, Yea; have ye never read, Out of the mouth of babes and sucklings Thou hast perfected praise? And He left them and went out of the city into Bethany, and He lodged there. Now in the morning as He returned into the city, He hungered. And when He saw a fig tree in the way, He came to it, and found nothing thereon, but leaves only, and said unto it, Let no fruit grow on thee henceforward forever. And presently the fig tree withered away. And when the disciples saw it, they marveled, saying, How soon is the fig tree withered away! Jesus answered and said unto them, Verily I say unto you, If ye have faith, and doubt not, ye shall not only do this which is done to the fig tree, but also if ye shall say unto this mountain, Be thou removed, and be thou cast into the sea, it shall be done. And all things whatsoever ye shall ask in prayer, believing, ye shall receive — *Matthew 21:12-22*

The invitation to worship rings clearly throughout the Holy Scriptures, but never so clearly as in Ps. 95:6: "Oh, come, let us worship and bow down; let us kneel before the Lord, our Maker!"

Luther is correct when he says that we always stand under the Law and under the judgment of God as isolated individuals.

Each of us must die for himself and stand in judgment by himself.
Adam and Eve both stood before God as individuals. In his book
The Great Divorce C. S. Lewis describes hell as an essentially
lonely place. All of us have felt this loneliness in our lives.

The first message of the Gospel, however, is that we are no
longer alone or by ourselves. Rather, by God's grace, we are in
fellowship with Christ through the forgiveness of sins. He takes
our sin upon Himself; He gives us His righteousness. We die alone,
but we die like many who have died with Christ. We are judged,
but Christ stands in the judgment with us. Peter and Matthew
are still individuals, but they are no longer lonely individuals,
because Christ is concerned about them. Jesus did truly place
the emphasis upon the individual.

Yet along with this there is the emphasis upon the group.
"Where two or three are gathered together in My name, there
am I in the midst of them," saith the Savior. Jesus speaks of His
followers as a "flock." "They were all with one accord in one
place," says Luke. "Not forsaking the assembling of ourselves
together, as the manner of some is," writes the author of Hebrews.
The invitation to worship is, then, an invitation to Christian
fellowship.

Our text confronts us with two kinds of worship. There is the
worship of the children who sang praises, the worship of the sick
who sang praises, and the worship of the sick who came to be
healed. But there is also the worship of the Pharisees, which is
condemned by Jesus in His cleansing of the temple and in His
cursing of the fig tree. This text, then, calls us to examine what
is actually going on in our worship.

When Is Our Worship Relevant and Acceptable?

I

When We Worship Jesus as the Savior
Who Has Authority to Forgive Sins

When Jesus entered the city of Jerusalem, He wept over it
because it did not know the day of its visitation. He wept over
the city because of its sin and the divine judgment which would
soon fall upon it. There was much that was not in keeping with
His divine will, although Jerusalem had been called the city of
God and of His people. However, it must be stated that there
were also things happening in the temple which were God-pleasing.
It was not that the temple was forsaken and empty and that the
sacrifices were not being made. Quite the contrary, the temple was
filled with people who purchased animals for the sacrifices. It was
not the buying and selling of the animals that brought down the

wrath of God upon the people but the attitude in which this
buying and selling took place. The attitude of the people and
the priests was under the judgment of God because the house of
God was being desecrated by men who were no longer holy, but
greedy. A man can be irreligious in church. There is no such
thing as the inviolability of the temple. Putting the worship service
under the roof of the temple does not change the essential nature
of the worshiper. All this can happen when the worshiper
does not accept Jesus as the Messiah who has authority to forgive sins. For a man who no longer recognizes or accepts what
Jesus has done will no longer know what he himself ought to do
or be doing.

The invitation to worship is also an invitation to active fellowship. It is an invitation to participation. Thus saith the psalmist:
"Let *us* worship and *bow down; let us kneel.*"

To bow down, to kneel, indicates that the true worshiper
is not just a spectator or an onlooker but also a participant in
a divine spiritual drama. "Let the redeemed of the Lord say so!"
The fellowship to which the redeemed belong is an active, creative
fellowship. In this sense the true worshiping church becomes the
true witnessing church. Those who truly participate in this worship
within the walls of His holy temple participate in the work which
goes on outside, "unto the uttermost parts of the earth."

The Pharisees rejected Jesus because He called them to this
active, creative fellowship. They wanted nothing to do with the
Friend of publicans and sinners because they themselves wanted
nothing to do with publicans and sinners. This active, creative
fellowship is a participating fellowship, and the Pharisees refused
to join in this activity. They refused to join the praises of Palm
Sunday. They were most chagrined at the hosannas which the
children sang. The Pharisees wanted nothing of the "I and Thou"
relationship. They did not need His prayers and His intercessions.
They rejected His call to follow Him, and they saw nothing in
His suffering and death for them.

Worship is essentially reciprocal, and only when this is realized
does the house of God become a Bethel in actual fact. We may
sum up the situation in two words — adoration and encounter.
As we draw near to God in the way which He has appointed, He
speaks to our hearts and lives. To worship God is to make Him
the supreme object of our esteem and delight, in public, private,
and in secret. Then worship becomes relevant and dynamic.

Worship in its truest sense is also an invitation to adoration
of the holy God. "Let us kneel before the Lord, our Maker." When
we kneel, we kneel before "the Lord, our Maker." We kneel

before the God who has created us, and this God now brings about His new creation in us. The lasting effect of true worship is an activity of God and not of us. It is God who lifts us up when we humble ourselves. God gives us altitude when we bow down. We find our true selves when we lose ourselves. God is not lost, *we* are lost, and God moves us out of ourselves and beyond ourselves. Sometimes we try to lift ourselves up by pride, the pride of race, of possession, of position, or of power. But that is not elevation, that is inflation. Even as the inflated dollar goes down in value, so does the inflated man. God gives us altitude through the forgiveness of sins. Jesus stands in the house of God with authority to forgive sins, but the Pharisees want nothing of it.

There are two parallel developments here. Matthew's Gospel makes it clear that the Pharisees did not deny Jesus' power to perform miracles, but they denied His power to forgive sins. They denied Him the right to affirm that He was the promised Messiah. They denied Him the right to be the friend of publicans and sinners. Throughout Old Testament history the worship of the Children of Israel was dedicated to preparing for the coming of the Messiah. But when Jesus the Messiah came, the whole structure of their worship collapsed. Why? "He came unto His own, but His own received Him not." The scribes and Pharisees, yea, the whole Jewish nation, would not accept Jesus as the Savior and the promised Messiah, and they insisted on their right to cut Him down to their own size. It was God's purpose to send Jesus Christ into the world, high and exalted as the Savior, the Son of God, the King of glory, and it was the intent of the Pharisees to bring Christ down to a mere prophet, a great teacher, a man on their own level.

With this emphasis on Christ by the Pharisees we now look at what is going on in the temple. The temple becomes the symbol of the entire life of Israel. It is a place where people are busy and actively worshiping God. *But it is not a house of prayer!* It is a den of thieves. There is a direct connection between the conversion of the temple into a place of "buying and selling" and the judgment of the Messiah who came to bring forgiveness of sins. For where there is forgiveness, there is no more need for buying and selling. In "housecleaning the temple," Christ condemns the worship which is not the worship of the holy God who forgives sins through Jesus Christ, Friend of publicans and sinners.

Therefore Christ goes into action. Behold His superhuman authority as He cleanses the temple. The Pharisees cower before Jesus. They tremble with fear in God's presence. They shrink from Him as before an irresistible force which beats them into submission. As whipped dogs they draw together into insignificance before the flash of Christ's eyes and slink away guilty and condemned. The thunder of His words showed Him to be the absolute Lord in the temple: "My house shall be called the house of prayer; but ye have made it a den of thieves."

Christ's zeal for the sanctity and purity of the temple is an appeal for unsullied religion and service rendered out of a pure heart. No combining of earthly interests with one's religion is acceptable, for the latter always suffers. There is no room for half-heartedness and indifference in God's service. There is no compromise with the forces of evil, which rob God of His glory and men of their forgiveness.

We may all take warning to guard our religion, our doctrines, and our worship from unwholesome influences; to keep our congregational life free from the commercialism and hypocrisy of our age. We can never represent Christ adequately to our age unless we worship Him as the Savior who has all power and authority to forgive sins. Then our worship will be relevant and acceptable in the sight of God.

II

When We Worship Christ as the Savior Who Has the Power to Give Us Healing

Our worship is relevant and acceptable when we worship Christ as the Savior who has power to give us healing.

There are people who find worship disappointing. They leave the house of God, saying, "I didn't get anything out of it. The worship service did not mean anything to me." What is it that makes worship worthwhile?

Our text emphasizes the Godward side of worship — where God speaks and draws near to us in His grace. The New Testament shows and the experiences of the church confirm that wherever the Word is faithfully expounded, Christ, the living Word, draws near, so that the most important question that a person can ask himself after a service is, "Did I meet Christ today?"

Temple healing immediately followed temple cleansing. "The blind and the lame came to Him in the temple." Here are three outstanding things of universal value: a temple, a healer, and people in need of healing.

Concerning the temple, there is no doubt as to its presence, its place, and its power. Churches and temples are to be found in every city and hamlet of our country. They are beautiful, they are efficient, they are the temples of God. There is no doubt as to the efficiency of the house of God. It is a house of prayer for all nations, the place of fellowship with our Lord; it is the place where His honor dwelleth. The house of God — the place where you were brought in infancy for Holy Baptism, the place where you were confirmed, the place where you brought your problems and got them solved. Here you raised your questions and found His answers. Here you brought your pains and had them eased; you brought your broken heart and had it healed. Therefore we sing:

> I love Thy kingdom, Lord,
> The house of Thine abode,
> The church our blest Redeemer saved
> With His own precious blood.
>
> I love Thy church, O God.
> Her walls before Thee stand,
> Dear as the apple of Thine eye
> And graven on Thy hand.

Christ's healing signifies that God is at work in His church. What takes place in the temple is a foreshadowing of what will take place on the day of the Resurrection. For Christ will change our vile bodies and fashion them after His own glorious body. In that day the redeemed will be free. Between now and then, through the forgiveness of sins, God brings into existence the true relationship between Himself and the sinful creature.

The Pharisees needed healing every bit as much as the lame and the blind. However, the Pharisees did not stay around for that healing. The blind and the lame came for healing grace. The Pharisees came to exalt themselves. The decisive question in our worship is not whether we are present in the house of God but *how* we are present. Is our worship adequate and relevant? Are we there as Pharisees, or are we there as blind and lame seeking healing from the divine Healer? Very often nothing happens to us in worship, because we do not come to be healed. We are not honest with ourselves or with God about our own needs and our own condition. We don't receive Christ as we ought to receive Him and as He comes to us in worship.

Jesus Christ is the divine Healer. When we say this, we are in no corridor of vague speculation. Christ heals men today as He healed men in ages past. At His touch physical ailments have disappeared. At His touch and word mental disorders have been cured. In His name healing has been carried into every continent. There is much on the stage and on the screen, and in the clinic, that sails under false colors and pretends to be divine healing in His name. Christ declares war on all such counterfeits. At the same time He declares that inexhaustible power is available in Him for the healing of men.

One of the most forceful aspects of this text is the singing of the children. In their praise Christ finds His supreme joy. Boys and girls caught the spirit in the message of the multitude that on the day before had sung "Hosanna to the Son of David!" These children, in the unfeigned sincerity of their heart, declare the Messiahship of Jesus and accord Him the homage and supplication which are due God alone. It must have been refreshing to Jesus to hear some people who were unquestionably sincere speak thus of Him. The Pharisees were so boastful and proud and so unreceptive to the grace and forgiveness of our Lord. Even His own disciples were to the very last so full of guile — expecting rewards but getting none. "Hosanna!" the children sang; it was so guileless and so genuine. They looked for no reward and received none. The children's praise is still the joy of Christian hearts.

When you place the children's singing against the hypocritical worship of the Pharisees, you see the truth through contrast. The priests and traitors are in guilty collusion. Over against them see the strange fraternity of suffering folk and children. On the one hand is an act of sacrilege which Jesus purged; on the other hand, Christ's healing mercy. The blind and the halt knew their need of God and were therefore more fortunate than the hale and rich traitors.

The children sang in faith. The children received the Savior as we must receive Him, as Savior and God. Children are not able to do anything in return for all the blessings that Jesus Christ gives them. However, they will respond with their praises! They give themselves in sincerity and truth. The Pharisees received from God, too, but it was their hope to give back to God something of which they were so proud: a catalog of self-styled virtues. Christ accepts the praise of these helpless children, but He does not accept the righteousness of the Pharisees. The Pharisees were in character. Such men are outraged by children singing hosannas to the Messiah. They thought it childish blasphemy and were blind to the real blasphemy of their own lives. Children joyfully worship Christ the Lord. What better testimony can be given to Him? He loved them and found strength in their love. Jesus calls attention to Ps. 8:2: "Out of the mouths of babes and sucklings Thou hast ordained strength because of Thine enemies, that Thou mightest still the enemy and the avenger." Children as well as adults should sing the praises of God. This is well pleasing unto the Lord. The theme of the Christian song should always be "Christ the Messiah, the Savior of the world." We represent Christ adequately and make our worship relevant and acceptable when we worship Christ as the Savior who has the power to give us healing for all our diseases, and when we sing our praises to Him as the children did in their "Hosannas to the Son of David!"

III

When We Worship as People Who Pray for God's Transforming Work in Our Lives

Our worship will finally be adequate and acceptable when we worship as those who pray for God's transforming work in our lives.

So many people are not ready to accept Christ's transforming work in their own lives. The Spirit of God is always at work in the Word and the sacraments to change our way of life and to make us new creatures in Christ, but many people are not willing to change. Such people want all the leaves of outward piety, and yet at the same time they rob themselves of all the fruit which God wills to supply them. Did Christ really curse that fig tree? The tree was growing along the side of the road. It belonged to no one in particular and was used by any passerby. There it stood where every passerby could see it. It was a symbol of deception. Every passerby expected to find fruit, but it had no fruit. This tree, then, was actually a deceiver. Did Jesus actually curse the fig tree? We have to identify God with the creation of the tree as well as the death of the tree. In effect what happened to the fig tree is what is happening to mankind all the time.

However, the most disturbing thing about the fig tree to us is that it points to a world under the judgment of God. The Pharisees were under the judgment of God. They refused to receive forgiveness; therefore they remained under the wrath of God. The real fruit would have been the acceptance of the Messiah, but Jesus did not find this acceptance. He did find it in the children who sang, "Hosanna to the Son of David, blessed is He who cometh in the name of the Lord!" "What doth the Lord require of thee but to do justly, to love mercy, and to walk humbly with thy God!" The Pharisees, who did justly, did not love mercy, and they did not walk humbly before God. They rejected the forgiveness of Jesus Christ, and they did not see themselves in need of forgiveness. On Palm Sunday they had rejected Christ as the Messiah, and on Monday Jesus interprets this rejection in the context of worship. He tells His disciples His house is the house of prayer. There was plenty of praying going on, but not the praying for God's transforming work in their lives. The Pharisees were on an exchange basis with God like the buying and selling in the temple. The Pharisees, when approached about forgiveness, said, "Yes, forgiveness, but I deserve forgiveness." This Jesus interpreted as thievery.

Jesus invites the disciples to pray in faith: "Verily I say unto you, If you have faith, and doubt not, ye shall not only do this which is done to the fig tree, but also if ye shall say unto this mountain, Be thou removed, and be thou cast into the sea, it shall be done. And all things whatsoever ye shall ask in prayer, believing, ye shall receive."

The Pharisee asked for something because he thought he had it coming to him. The Pharisees were looking for a Messiah who would give them what they thought they had coming to them; of course, they had a lot coming to them by all human standards of measurement. But not so by divine standards. The opposite of making the church a den of thieves is to make it a house of worship. The man who knows that his eternal existence rests in the grace of God through Jesus Christ rather than in what he has does not have to take any steps to secure his existence. The Pharisee had to get everything out of his brother because the Pharisee thought he had it coming to him. But the man who prays in faith is the kind of a man who will forgive his brother. The Pharisee who prays on the basis of what is coming to him has to take everything that is coming to him to be sure that he has something. The Pharisee who does not accept what God has done for him soon does not know what he ought to do for God or for his fellowman. If there be no rootage, there can be no fruitage. And the Pharisees had no roots, they did not accept the saving deeds of God. Therefore their worship was superficial, hypocritical, and shallow. They did not pray for the transforming power of God in their lives.

The bare essential for a God-pleasing discipleship is faith. Jesus tolerates nothing false, no mere outward show of piety; He demands inward purity and singleness of heart, which comes only by faith. These marks of discipleship reflect divine character, the divine character of His kingdom. Jesus is no earthly prince, but He is a heavenly King. So Jesus declares war on the temple, he declares war on the Pharisees, he declares war on the barren fig tree. We pray God that He may not declare war on us.

Therefore let us translate our faith into life, that the tree of our personal religion will bear the fruit of Christlike living. Then it shall never feel the ax of His consuming judgment. Remember that He said that His house was a house of prayer. He meant that the temple was set aside to be God's house. It was to be a place of sincere worship. It was a sacred and holy place, for God dwelt among His people in His holiness and majesty, coming to them with great grace and truth. What makes a church truly beautiful in God's eyes is that worshipers treasure the Gospel and recognize the scene of its proclamation as God's house. God's people should know that they are in the presence of God, where His Word is proclaimed, and that they are to conduct themselves accordingly.

If He came into our 20th-century temples, would Jesus find them houses of prayer or dens of thieves? If He searched the branches of our professed faith, would He find only leaves, or would He find thereon the fruits that He expects, the fruits of a poverty of spirit toward God and Christlike love toward our fellowmen? Would He find with us, too, a church that has been reduced to a business, a religion that is mere habit, a faith that ends with lip service? Would His final verdict be, "Well done, thou good and faithful servant," or would it be, "Let no fruit grow on thee henceforward forever"?

The condemnation of the fig tree and of the temple is the condemnation of all worship which has only the outward trappings of piety. Our worship is relevant and acceptable when we are true worshipers. Such true worshipers are those who have the right object of worship, that is, the true God, the Father, who sent His Son to be our Savior and who becomes the Father of those who believe in the Savior.

True worshipers are also those who worship in the right manner. Man should worship God not only with outward acts, performances, ceremonies, but with the *spirit,* soul, heart, and in truth — with all sincerity. True worshipers are those who give evidence of true worship by praying for God's transforming work in their lives.

May God keep us in the true knowledge of Him and our Savior, and let us ever in all sincerity of heart be devoted and consecrated to Him! Then we are true worshipers, and our worship will be relevant and acceptable.

Jesus Helps the Blind to See

By EWALD H. MUELLER

(The Eleventh Sunday After Trinity)

And as Jesus passed by, He saw a man which was blind from his birth. And His disciples asked Him, saying, Master, who did sin, this man or his parents, that he was born blind? Jesus answered, Neither hath this man sinned nor his parents, but that the works of God should be made manifest in him. I must work the works of Him that sent Me, while it is day, for the night cometh, when no man can work. As long as I am in the world, I am the Light of the world. When He had thus spoken, He spat on the ground and made clay of the spittle, and He anointed the eyes of the blind with the clay and said unto him, Go, wash in the Pool of Siloam (which is, by interpretation, Sent). He went his way therefore, and washed, and came seeing. — *John 9:1-7*

God knows what is in man. He knows all parts of man's nature, his emotions, his fears, his motives, his hopes and aspirations. He knows all about Adam and all about Eve. The evangelist John tells us, "But Jesus did not commit Himself unto them, because *He knew all men* and needed not that any should testify of man, for *He knew what was in man.*" (John 2:24, 25)

Jesus knows that man also loves the spectacular. He loves to be amused and entertained. He is an inveterate curiosity seeker. Jesus "knew what was in man," and to reveal His love, His power, His role as the true Messiah, He performed the miracle of healing spoken of in the text. The dramatic force of a miracle teaches us that

Jesus Helps the Blind to See

I

Jesus Changed the Life of the Man Born Blind

It was a desperately helpless man on whom Jesus worked this miracle of mercy. Born blind, he had experienced none of the normal joys of childhood. What he knew and experienced of life, he learned by other sensations: the senses of touch, taste, smell, sound. But his was a dark world. There were not even shadows, for all was darkness.

True, he had perhaps experienced the love of parents as a boy, but what of life and the future when they were gone? With few concerned for his welfare, he was undoubtedly left to his own resourcefulness to eke out an existence. Unable to be gainfully employed, he was at best an object of charity and pity; at worst, the butt of public scorn.

If blind men weep tears, you can be sure he wept many — and wept often. In the constant anguish of soul, he asked, "Why — why was I born blind?" This is the ultimate pain of the heart — not to know why. Anyone who is a parent knows how difficult it is to explain tragedy or illness to a child. The blind man's parents undoubtedly tried to explain, but knowing the futility of words to answer his queries, they tried to condition him to live in his world of darkness.

Is there a man alive who, measuring the disappointments and woes of life, has not felt the frustration of the seemingly unanswerable "Why"? Born in the midst of yesterday's problems, we grow up to find that they are still our heritage today.

Jesus knew what was in man. He knew every ache in the heart of the blind man, the emptiness of his life, the weariness of his lonely world of darkness. Quickly and without ostentation (another proof of Jesus' divinity) He mixed earth and saliva and made a poultice for the eyes of the blind man. "Keep it on your eyes," He said, "and go wash in the waters of Siloam." No mention is made in the text of this man's requesting Jesus' help. (How many needs God answers in the lives of men, even without prayer!) Our compassionate Savior, abounding in love, offers the simple imperative "Go, wash!" Compliance was a simple matter. Would he obey the directive, or would he disobey? The man born blind complied.

Compliance Means Help

Are we ready to conform to the will of God, or are we children of disobedience? If we are suffering an "impaired life," could it be from "impaired sight"? The Word of God richly provides light for the way, "yet men love darkness rather than light" (John 3:10). As surely as Jesus had compassion for this man, we know He has compassion for the multitude (Matt. 14:14). God would heal all men. Sin's dominion over the souls of men would incline them to think that disobedience is fashionable, a mark of true individualism. Yet blessed is he who will follow the example of the obedience of the man born blind. In faith he made his way to the Pool of Siloam. His sight was restored (v. 7). What abundant reason to thank God!

If you are suffering from impaired vision of things spiritual, apply corrective measures promptly. The Word of God can help you see clearly the truths that "make men free" (John 8:32). Through Jesus Christ, the Son of God, you are redeemed from sin. Sin makes the soul very myopic, or nearsighted. Satan appeals to the baseness of our natures by calling us to "live it up here and now." He obscures the real issues of life. What of the future, for example, for a young man who, in the spirit of the Prodigal Son, wastes the substance of his time, his talents, his strength, on riotous living? The reward of a life of profligacy and sin is shame, darkness, and death. What of the future for a young girl who, enchanted by the glamour of a freewheeling, whirlwind courtship, contracts a hasty marriage with a pseudosophisticated atheist? The sweet moments of romantic bliss soon give way to the anguished days and years of heartache.

What sorrow and pain are inflicted upon the world, the state, the community, the church, the household, yea, the individual, because men do not see or want to see what the Lord requires of them — "to do justly and to love mercy and to walk humbly with their God" (Micah 6:8). Lacking spiritual insights, men grope blindly through life. Haunted by fears, depressed in spirit, they shuffle through the darkness grasping at straws. Straining for some relief, men today are spending billions for tranquilizers and palliatives of every sort. Failing to square their lives and their consciences with God and his Word, they are as stumbling, fumbling fools. The tragedy of their lives might be characterized in the words "Eyes have they, but they see not." (Ps. 115:5)

The Blind Still Need Help

By nature man is spiritually blind, and not capable of discerning spiritual things. Man stubbornly resists the Light of the world. Jesus "came unto His own, and His own received Him not" (John 1:11). Jesus wept over Jerusalem for its rejection of the Gospel. It is true that the judgment of God as expressed in the words "Because thou hast rejected knowledge, I will also reject thee" (Hos. 4:6) applies to these people. If man stubbornly neglects the call of the Gospel, then surely the judgment of God will overtake him. But those that resist should not be regarded as helpless or hopeless.

Jesus worked this miracle of mercy on a *blind* man. The action of Christ is a specific directive to His church to be interested not only in those who see (our church members) that they may "see better" but also in those who are spiritually blind and ignorant of God's love in Christ. The church is under divine obligation to address these people. We must never regard the stubborn, recalcitrant scoffer living next door as helpless or hopeless. "Christ came not to call the righteous but sinners to repentance." (Mark 2:17)

Eyes That Need Cleansing

At this juncture you may have uttered a prayerful sigh of relief that you are not blind or were not born blind. You may also have thanked God that He has given you some spiritual insight concerning His Word. But have you seen *all* that God wants you to see, or are you seeing only those things that you want to see?

The Gospel comes with gracious promises of love and redemption. But it also moves and enables us to meet the obligations the Law imposes on us. Do you see your obligations to Christ, His Word, and His church? Christ "died for all, that they which live should not henceforth live unto themselves but unto Him which died for them and rose again" (2 Cor. 5:15). Have you seen your duty — and done it by remembering the powerful gift of God in Christ, who rose again that we should henceforth not live unto ourselves? Have you closed your eyes to the needs of men everywhere?

"Go, wash in the pool of Siloam!" Jesus said to the man born blind. His eyes needed cleansing. As our hands, hearts, and minds need cleansing, our eyes, too, need cleansing. It is easy to see the many needs in the kingdom of God. But man is inclined to close his eyes to these needs, or at least, turn his eyes in another direction. We pretend not to see, and like the priest and the Levite we "pass by on the other side." Although not physically blind as was this man or Bartimaeus, we yet have much reason to pray for release from spiritual blindness. We have need to ask for pardon of those things that we have neglected to do or done amiss. To this same Savior who wrought this miracle we ought to pray:

> Give me a faithful heart, Likeness to Thee,
> That each departing day Henceforth may see
> Some work of love begun, Some deed of kindness done,
> Some wand'rer sought and won, Something for Thee.

The immediate benefit of Christ's miracle was to change the life of the man born blind. But there were others present whose eyes were still blind to the truths of God, and these people, too, needed help.

II

Jesus Changes the Attitudes of the Spiritually Blind

Why This Suffering?

"Who did sin, this man or his parents, that he was born blind?" (V. 2.) "How cruel and crude of them," you say, "to imply that this long-endured infirmity was the result of some sin or indiscretion on the part of this man or his parents!" The inference is plain. Within themselves they argued, "They must have committed some horrible sin to be visited with such a severe judgment." How careless men are in their judgment of others! Knowing what was in their hearts, Jesus answers very simply: "Neither hath this man sinned, nor his parents." (V. 3)

We marvel at the patience of Jesus. The questions reveal the callous lovelessness of their mortal natures. As students of the Scriptures they should have known the Book of Job. In this book God clearly revealed that the greatest sufferers are not to be looked upon as the greatest sinners. They knew of the afflictions of the patriarchs and prophets. They knew of the trials that Israel had endured. Though they were somewhat religious they certainly revealed serious gaps in their spiritual training. Like many people, also Christians today, they had serious blind spots. Truths that were obvious they refused to accept or at least to apply in their lives. No wonder that Christ and the apostles wrote and spoke so often of charity and love. (1 Cor. 13:1-13)

If in the realm of personal experience the Pharisees had found that their sinful self-indulgence had violated God's commandments as well as common sense, and if as a result of such careless disregard they had experienced some suffering or afflictions, they justly reproached themselves. Jesus clearly reveals, however, that they had no right to pass judgment on others. "Neither had this man sinned, nor his parents, but that the works of God should be made manifest in him." (John 9:3)

What Is the Answer?

The Pharisees had their self-styled, preconceived notions of religious life. The self-righteous attitudes of the Pharisees had obscured so many spiritual truths. Not only did Jesus remove some blind spots, but in substance He was broadening their understanding of the nature of their problems and sufferings. As the Scripture reveals, our sufferings are not to be regarded as the punishment of sin unless, of course, self-inflicted. They are intended to reveal God's loving providence. (V. 3)

Christ's glory, His divinity, His power over all things, is revealed in this miracle. This man was not "born blind because of his own sin, or that of his parents, but to provide an opportunity to show the power of God" (Phillips). The power and glory of Christ are sometimes revealed through suffering — even death cannot negate the promises and power of the risen Christ.

The apostle Paul, who knew suffering indeed, triumphed in his newly found faith. Living above these sorrows, he professed: "I live; yet not I, but Christ liveth in me; and the life which I now live in the flesh I live by the faith of the Son of God, who loved me and gave Himself for me" (Gal. 2:20). Having endured hardships ("I suffered more abundantly," etc.) of every description for the sake of Christ and the Cross, he said: "The sufferings of this present time are not worthy to be compared with the glory which shall be revealed in us" (Rom. 8:18; cf. Rom. 8:38,39; Heb. 2:9-11). Our sufferings are marks of Christian discipleship.

The true child of God knows that the disciple is not above his Master. He knows "that we must through much tribulation enter into the kingdom of God" (Acts 14:22). Jesus said: "In the world ye shall have tribulation. But be of good cheer; I have overcome the world" (John 16:33). Troubled by the eternal "why," the Christian seeks his answer in the Word of God. His soul also reposes in faith on the words of Jesus "What I do thou knowest not now, but thou shalt know hereafter" (John 13:7). The unbeliever is often given to despair. The true child of God recalls the words "God is our Refuge and Strength, a very present Help in trouble; therefore will not we fear." (Psalm 46)

Peter's pride suffered a heavy blow when he sank into the sea, but Jesus rescued him. The widow of Nain thought that all was lost at the death of her son, but Jesus changed that for the better. If, in the economy of God, we are asked to bear hardship or suffering, these are intended to broaden the horizons of faith and spiritual understanding. O Lord,

> Should Thy mercy send me sorrow, toil, or woe,
> Or should pain attend me on my path below,
> Grant that I may never fail Thy hand to see.
> Grant that I may ever cast my care on Thee.

In all the miracles of Jesus, as in this one, Christ manifested forth His glory. He was revealed as the Son of God. "I must work the works of Him that sent Me, while it is day" (v. 4). There was a sense of urgency about what He did and when He did it. He was a master in the art of timing. He not only changed the life of the blind man but worked a change of heart on the witnesses to this miracle.

The Light That Conquers All Darkness

Christ as the Light of the world would dispel the darkness everywhere. At Christ's presentation in the temple, the aged Simeon took the infant Redeemer into his arms and declared Him to be a "Light to lighten the Gentiles and the Glory of His people Israel" (Luke 2: 32). In all of Jesus' life, in His public ministry, in His death and resurrection, He has demonstrated His right to the claim: "I am the Light of the world" (v. 5). Open the windows of your soul! Let in that glorious Light!

God has sovereignty over all His creatures. In His grace He wants to save *man*. He wants to help you. Do not fight against God. Do not frustrate His will. "While ye have light, believe in the Light, that ye may be the children of light" (John 12: 36). If you have been seeing only shadows, then face the Light of life. The shadows will be behind you. Blindness is a crippling affliction. Beware lest spiritual blindness cripple your life. Christ can spotlight the true values of life for you. Let the sunshine of His love offer perfect atonement for the darkness of sin. Come before His presence with thanksgiving. Follow Him, for He says, "He that followeth Me, shall not walk in darkness, but shall have the Light of life." (John 8: 12)

Twice Blessed with Sight

By REV. WALDEMAR A. ROOK

(The Twelfth Sunday After Trinity)

Then again called they the man that was blind and said unto him, Give God the praise. We know that this man is a sinner. He answered and said, Whether He be a sinner or no, I know not; one thing I know — that whereas I was blind, now I see. Then said they to him again, What did He to thee? How opened He thine eyes? He answered them, I have told you already, and ye did not hear. Wherefore would ye hear it again? Will ye also be His disciples? Then they reviled him and said, thou art His disciples, but we are Moses' disciples. We know that God spake unto Moses. As for this fellow, we know not from whence He is. The man answered and said unto them, Why herein is a marvelous thing, that ye know not from whence He is, and yet He hath opened mine eyes. Now we know that God heareth not sinners; but if any man be a worshiper of God and doeth His will, him He heareth. Since the world began was it not heard that any man opened the eyes of one that was born blind. If this man were not of God, He could do nothing. They answered and said unto him, Thou wast altogether born in sins, and dost thou teach us? And they cast him out. Jesus heard that they had cast him out, and when He had found him, He said unto him, Dost thou believe on the Son of God? He answered and said, Who is He, Lord, that I might believe on Him? And Jesus said unto him, Thou hast both seen Him, and it is He that talketh with thee. And he said, Lord, I believe. And he worshiped Him.

And Jesus said, For judgment I am come into this world, that they which see not might see and that they which see might be made blind. And some of the Pharisees which were with Him heard these words and said unto Him, Are we blind also? Jesus said unto them, If ye were blind, ye should have no sin. But now ye say, We see; therefore your sin remaineth. — *John 9:24-41*

God blesses some people with two kinds of sight. A Baltimore Lutheran pastor had come to know a famous ballplayer quite well. His career long behind him, the ballplayer now belonged to America's 350,000 blind people. However, patient research by the family doctor at length established the hope that an operation could restore the sight of the blind man. The operation was performed in due time. And so, as once again the pastor called on his friend, he was greeted with the cry: "Pastor, I can see." And the happy man proved it by reading a few paragraphs from a current magazine.

But that is not the end of the story. After some time the former star of the diamond became quite ill. Again the pastor was at his side with words of encouragement. However, it was apparent that this time no operation would restore the man's health, and he knew it! But imagine the surprise of the pastor when his friend suddenly burst out: "And now, pastor, let's talk about heaven."

But come to think about it, why should this have been a surprise? For here was a man who had received the gift of physical sight from his God. Now God had been especially good to him and given him "inner" sight through His holy Word. Each year some 75,000 people in our land receive the restoration of sight through corneal transplants and other dangerous and delicate operations, but none of these can receive spiritual sight. They cannot "see Jesus" unless God's Holy Spirit works within their hearts. . . . But here was a man who had received both his earthly and his heavenly sight through the miraculous workings of God's Holy Spirit. Oh, what a blessing!

Our Gospel for this day brings another such example to our attention. And because our age is steeped in spiritual blindness almost beyond belief, thousands do not know and do not understand, and what is worse, do not care, that they live in sin against the Almighty; thousands do not know the marvelous mercy of Jesus Christ, who died and rose again to redeem them from sin, and who paid the penalty of their guilt by His own precious and perfect sacrifice. And because thousands by their blind unbelief bind themselves to unhappiness, self-reproach, and a life of misery, and will remain so until they come to the Great Physician, and because we, too, often fail "to see" Jesus as we ought because of a lack of spiritual sight, it therefore will be more than worth our while to study closer the man:

Twice Blessed with Sight

Now the case history of this man reads like something taken from a medical journal. He had been born blind, which in that age before eye banks and Wilmer clinics and Seeing Eye dogs meant to be condemned to begging. Because of a question raised by His disciples Jesus is called into the case. He informs His disciples that this man was born blind not because either he or his parents had sinned but in order that the glory of God might become apparent through his pitiful plight. After all, does not God often send affliction in order that by a special revelation of power and grace to man from on high He himself might be magnified? . . . And so our Lord prepares a mixture of clay and spittle and applies this to the man's eyes. The ancients, long years before this, had somehow connected the use of saliva with a cure for the eyes. In this case, however, the cure is by a different means. Jesus instructs the man to wash in the Pool of Siloam. This he does and immediately receives his sight. How happy he must have been!

Now there follows one searching examination after another. One would have supposed that people would have been happy to see the former blind beggar fully restored. But if we think thus, we do not know human nature. Immediately his friends and neighbors begin to give him the third degree: "Who cured you?" The former blind man could only answer, "A man that is called Jesus." Next, because this thing had been done on the Sabbath, they bring him to the Pharisees for questioning. They in turn refer the matter to the parents. But the red tape doesn't end there. The parents refer the matter back to the Pharisees, stating their son is old enough to answer for himself . . . and he does.

At the risk of being thrown out of the temple, at least for 30 days, the man throws all the questions into one big category of uselessness and futility and replies: "One thing I know, whereas I was blind, now I see." . . . The meeting breaks up in confusion, but not until the man born blind accuses the Pharisees themselves of being really blind for not recognizing the Son of God by His miracles, whereupon he is thrown out of the temple.

Jesus, however, hears of the incident, finds the man, and asks whether or not he believes on the Son of God. "And He said, Lord, I believe. And he worshiped Him." (V. 38)

Seldom in all Scripture will you find a more dramatic incident.

This has all the elements of a real thriller for the movies. Some of the headings would surely strike a popular response: "Former Blind Man Accuses Pharisees of Blindness." Or this: "New Cure for Blindness." Or this: "Man Defies Medical Science and Sees." But we prefer the simpler "The Man Twice Blessed with Sight." And the more we read about him and study about Him, the more we come to like him. He had

I

Courage

Note this man's courage. His was not a cheap show or a play to the gallery. Remember, his insistence that it was Jesus who cured him, and his clever parrying of questions, would only get him one thing — excommunication! And furthermore one gets the rather uneasy feeling from the account of St. John that his parents were anything but examples of courage. We read: "They feared the Jews." And yet this man makes his profession loud and clear: "The man called Jesus made spittle and told me to wash." In effect, "He cured me."

One immediately comes to see that such courage is one of the crying needs of the hour, not only in our nation but also in our churches. Some time back a young man rather violently addressed the lecturer at an LSV school in the eastern part of our country: "But, pastor, you have no idea how hard it is to be Christian these days." He meant, it takes some courage to stand up for Christ. That it does! It isn't easy to find the raw, ready courage to speak for Christ and His cause, as did another Walther Leaguer. She had been working for a rather large chemical company on the East Coast. During the noon hour the girls of the office were wont to sit and discuss the usual things girls talk about at such times. Somehow the conversation turned to religion. Several girls volunteered they were having doubts. When this girl's turn came, she made the most of it. In her own words, "I told them." The pastor who had been listening in asked, "And what did you tell them?" Her answer came without missing a beat: "Why I told them Jesus is my Savior, and He died for me, and belief in Him is the only way to heaven." The pastor asked again, "And then what happened?" The girl replied, "They sat in stunned silence." You see, such things are not easy to say or to hear.

You do not really think that it is easy to go out into a world which is dedicated to enmity against the Cross and which delights in calling faith in Christ "a spot of foolishness" . . . you really do not think it is easy to go out into such a world and preach Christ Crucified as the only Hope of mankind. Furthermore, do not think for a minute that it is easy to go out into our complacent nation (so complacent that the Russian spaceman Titov can circle over our heads on a Sunday morning lacking only a bomb or two to wipe us off the face of the earth without warning, so complacent that we do not stop in our rounds of pleasures to pray, "May it never happen here") and confess Christ? Do you think it is easy to go out into such a world and announce, "Prepare for the Lord's Return"? It's hardly conceivable that our world, which does not pause and ponder because of the dangers threatening the body, will pause and give thought when we announce the dangers threatening the soul. Nor is it easy, in our world of materialism, false values, seeking after power, the lust of gain, and the worship of reason, to go out and announce: "Seek ye first the kingdom of God and His righteousness, and all these [other] things will be added to you." Nor is it easy in our age of double standards and divided loyalties, double-talk, and confusing terminology in things heavenly, to stand up and announce: "Thou shalt worship the Lord, Thy God, and Him only shalt thou serve." . . . "Please, no foreign altars in our churches." . . . "Except ye become as little children [in simple faith] ye shall not enter the kingdom of God." All this takes courage. . . . And the question is: Do we have it? That man born blind had it in abundance.

II

Shrewdness

Also note the shrewdness of that man. Somehow he is always able to shake off his questioners. And when they finally press him beyond his mental capacity and understanding, he simply tells them: "This I know, whereas I was blind, now I see." In effect, he was telling them he did not understand the process involved, but the simple fact was this: he could see. And facts speak for themselves. That's being smart.

God's people have not always, however, been known for their shrewdness and ability to get at the facts. Jesus, you will recall, once told a parable about an unjust steward. And although our Lord was not advising His people to follow the example of dishonesty set by the steward, He was concerned that His people follow the pattern of smart thinking set by the steward. So often our whole life is built up on things that can be seen, having a good time, belonging to organizations, and getting things. Men say these are the things that count. These are the things that supposedly make for progress and happiness. And all the while we know that God has made us for higher things, for eternal life in heaven, only we do not care to admit it. That is not being very shrewd. Neither do some of us weigh facts very carefully before we come to conclusions. There are people today who can't talk politics, or management, or labor, or race relations without seeing "red." We ought to know better. God gives these things that a Christian might employ them for the benefit of mankind, and he ought to busy himself about them and improve conditions about him, knowing the Gospel always prospers in the good climate of peace and good social conditions. We are not always shrewd either when it comes to our children, and especially when we maintain the old cliché that "children will choose their religion when they reach a mature age." God knows, and parents ought to know, that our children are like gardens. If good seed is not planted, the weeds will blow in and grow. Similarly, if children are not taught the will of God, by us, someone else will teach them the will of the world, the devil, and the way of the flesh. It is not shrewd of us to neglect the things pertaining to our salvation.

III
Faith

Also note the faith of this man. After Jesus had found the man and had identified himself as the Son of God, the blind man was quick to respond, "Lord, I believe." Of such stuff are the real heroes of faith made. Without any doubt, the men and women Christ needs in our day and age and in the hectic, trying days ahead, when Christians may again be called upon to shed their blood in the arenas, are not the indifferent, easygoing, quickly satisfied Pharisees mentioned in our text but men and women like the man born blind, who without fear and compromise respond to the Lord's questions with a "Lord, I believe."

This is the day and the age of scientific tabulations, exact predictions, and even calculated risks, and we have no quarrel with science in itself, for through it we have received the transistor radio, Salk polio vaccine, the Polaris missile, etc. But it is also true that the advances most enduring have really come to us through men and women of faith. One wonders how far Abraham would have traveled from the land of the Chaldees, and whether he would have become the father of God's people in faraway Palestine, if first he had consulted scientific findings. God himself in the Book of Hebrews, tells us how Abraham operated: "By faith Abraham, when he was called, went. . . ." One wonders, too, how Dr. Martin Luther would have fared and what kind of reformation would have resulted, had he at Worms first consulted a "table of calculated risks." Luther trusted his God, and thus he could say, "Here I stand." One wonders, too, how many young men would leave our seminaries and go into foreign countries if first they would consult the "exact predictions." There isn't anything very exact about preaching Christ in a foreign country, except the grace and the assurance of our Lord "Lo, I am with you alway, even unto the end of the world." Faith is the conquering force.

The beauty of it all is this: Although our Lord is not walking the pathways of this world as He did in the days of that blind man — and although He does not open eyes directly today as He did then — nonetheless, our Lord continually opens the eyes of the spiritually blind to see His love and mercy through the Gospel. Through the preaching of the Word, we come to know and understand ourselves as we are, poor lost sinners, and at the same time we come to see God's grace in Christ Jesus, which removes all our sins as far as the east is from the west. Through the preaching of the Gospel we come to arise from the gross darkness of this world and come instead to embrace Jesus with those wonderful words "Lord, I believe."

IV

Good Fortune

Note, moreover, the good fortune of the blind man. Jesus finds him! No, it wasn't that he went looking for Jesus but that Jesus went looking for him. And if there is anything that is characteristic of our Lord, it is this seeking and finding which our Lord constantly carries on, whether in the first or the 20th century. Pictures which show our Lord in the Garden of Gethsemane are beautiful, as are the pictures which show our Lord sitting in the temple and teaching. But the most beautiful picture of all is the one which shows our Lord seeking and searching, endlessly looking for, that one lost sheep, and having found it, bringing it home upon His shoulders with rejoicing.

The real lesson consists in this, that unless our Lord searches and seeks us likewise, we are hopelessly lost. By nature we do not seek to come to God; rather we resist Him at every turn. We are worse than a corpse, which is only capable of one action — decay. But by nature we war against our God, and that is worse; it condemns man to eternal ruin. Into this picture our Lord now steps with all His grace and mercy and kindness. Oh, we have not deserved it, but He comes and bears our sins on Calvary's cross. He dies that we might live. He pays the debt we owe. By imputation our sins are transferred to the bleeding back of our Lord, and we are declared righteous and innocent of all guilt. The Father is now our Friend. The moment we come a-running to Him crying like the prodigal: "Father, I have sinned against heaven and in Thy sight and am no longer worthy to be called Thy son. Make me as one of Thy hired servants" the Father replies: "Let us rejoice and be merry. This My son was dead and is alive, he was lost and is found." . . . That, too, is our good fortune!

V

Inner Sight

Again, note the inner sight of this blind man. After he has confessed his Lord aloud, we read, "And he worshiped Him." Could anything be more dramatic? Could anything prove his sincerity more convincingly? He saw his Lord with his newfound physical eyes, and He did indeed see in Jesus his Lord with his newfound spiritual sight.

Travelers to Puerto Rico love to tell of George Wally, who gives the blind the gift of inner vision. He teaches his pupils, all of whom are blind, to visualize the lines they draw. The process is called three-dimensional art. It is quite a dramatic moment when a pupil suddenly rises from the drawing board and cries *Veo*, "I see." What really has happened is that the pupil sees the lines with the mind, and the finished products often hang in the famous art galleries of the world.

Certain kinds of blindness cannot be cured no matter what the treatment might be. Yet it is possible for every man, woman, and child in this wide world of ours to cry out to our Lord "Veo." And it is possible for every child of God to prove the sincerity of that cry by worshiping and working for our Lord. In the final analysis the act of worship on the part of the blind man was really an act of gratitude. He had seen the King, and he would never be the same again. Now he really could see! "Veo." Recognition had flown over into power, and power into faith, and faith into action! Now he was a man twice blessed with sight.

"Extrasensory perception" has come to have meaning to us who are living in the new space age. Perhaps it is best explained by saying it refers to the ability to see more than meets the eye at first glance. Many people have that gift. And, it is safe to say, God's people need the gift of God's Holy Ghost in abundance as we enter a new age of exploration, new mission opportunities, and new fields of endeavor. The need is not only for physical sight but also for men "whose eyes have seen the King" and are concerned to do something about it. Pray God to give us the greater vision to come to know and understand the tremendous need existing to train young pastors and missionaries, and if need be, to equip them to go to the moon, bringing Christ to all nations. Pray God to open our eyes to see the crying needs which exist in almost every sphere of activity in our beloved church. A glance through the booklet *Know Your Synod*, with its vivid presentation of the needs existing in the areas of education for children and adults, in medical missions, in the program of tract distribution, among the Armed Services, and so many other spheres, can only move us to pray: "Lord, open our eyes and the eyes of our fellow Christians everywhere, so that we may meet these needs." The record of the human race is one of amazing blindness over against the heavenly vision. The crying need of the hour is, then, for men and women to be aroused and to hold up with Pentecostal fervor the light of eternity, so that the nations may come to see the Lord of lords and the King of kings. The blind can never lead the blind. They both shall fall into the pit. But the children of God, those who possess that special gift of the Holy Spirit, who can cry "Veo" and indeed have seen their Lord in His majesty and His mercy, they can direct men from disaster to the mansion above, there where there is eternal light, there where our Lord lives.

And thus we leave you even where we started — at the feet of our Lord and Savior. And where else should a man of God leave his people? We would leave you at the feet of Him who gives both physical and spiritual sight and with whom there is never the darkness of night. We would leave you at the feet of Him who has directed us to set our sights on the eternal goal and has promised never to fail us as we take that road. And if we but look closely and carefully, we shall see, oh, ever so dimly as yet, but the vision is there just the same — the souls of the ransomed and the redeemed on the eternal shores, offering praise and thanksgiving to the Lamb upon the throne. And this ought to cheer us onward.

And then there comes the time when earthly sight fails us and nothing can restore it. Familiar faces will be gone, and friends will fade away in a blur, but ahead will loom the eternal Christ, standing in the light of heaven's lamps, and we, too, shall then cry aloud: "*VEO.* . . . O Lord, I can see Thee, I can see Thee."

We Hear Christ Gladly

By ALFRED C. SELTZ

(The Thirteenth Sunday After Trinity)

And one of the scribes came, and having heard them reasoning together, and perceiving that He had answered them well, asked Him, Which is the first commandment of all? And Jesus answered him, The first of all the commandments is, Hear, O Israel: The Lord, our God, is one Lord; and thou shalt love the Lord, thy God, with all thy heart, and with all thy soul, and with all thy mind, and with all thy strength: this is the first commandment. And the second is like, namely this, Thou shalt love thy neighbor as thyself. There is none other commandment greater than these. And the scribe said unto Him, Well, Master, Thou hast said the truth; for there is one God; and there is none other but He; and to love Him with all the heart, and with all the understanding, and with all the soul, and with all the strength, and to love his neighbor as himself, is more than all whole burnt offerings and sacrifices. And

when Jesus saw that he answered discreetly, He said unto him, Thou
art not far from the kingdom of God. And no man after that durst ask
Him any question. And Jesus answered and said, while He taught in
the temple, How say the scribes that Christ is the Son of David? For
David himself said by the Holy Ghost, The Lord said to my Lord, Sit
Thou on My right hand, till I make Thine enemies Thy footstool. David
therefore himself calleth Him Lord; and whence is He then his Son?
And the common people heard him gladly. — *Mark 12:28-37*

"The common people heard Him gladly." These are the last
words of our text. They serve well as the first words of our
sermon.

What a meaningful statement: "The common people heard
Him gladly"! While the leaders of the people rejected Jesus and
warned the people against this "deceiver" (Matt. 27:63; John 7:12),
nevertheless "the common people heard Him gladly." The chief
priests and Pharisees consulted together and said, "If we let Him
thus alone, all men will believe on Him" (John 11:48). His enemies, too, saw that "the common people heard Him gladly."

Many common people hear Him gladly today. He still has a
way of "reaching" people, of reaching their hearts. Today our
Lord Jesus Christ is again speaking to us. Shall we not also be
counted among the common people who hear Him gladly?

We Hear Christ Gladly

I

Christ Tells Us God's Law and Our Sin

Sinful man, when hearing God's Law, cannot understand it
correctly. It is true, God once wrote His Law in man's heart.
As a part of His creation blessing, man had a clear and complete
knowledge of God's Law. Man knew right and wrong. He knew
what God wanted him to do and what God wanted him to avoid
doing. But after long and repeated sinning man no longer had a
clear knowledge of the Law. God therefore gave His Law to man
in a written form and made it public through Moses in the holy
Ten Commandments. The church of the Old Testament was in
the possession of the written Law. God told them to keep it in
their hearts and to teach it diligently to their children. And yet
there was a woeful lack of knowledge of the Law in Israel at
Christ's time. Religious leaders had added many rules and regulations of their own to God's Law. The Law of God was clear, but
men confused it by adding their own laws. Even the leading
churchmen did not know the real content of the Law. Because they
did not permit the Holy Spirit of God to guide their thinking they
could not see the Law of God clearly. Because they followed
their own erring hearts, they wondered, Which is the first commandment of all? Which is the great commandment?

Christ teaches God's Law plainly. When He told the inquiring scribe: "The first of all the commandments is, Hear, O Israel: The Lord, our God, is one Lord," and when He continued: "And thou shalt love the Lord, thy God, with all thy heart, and with all thy soul, and with all thy mind, and with all thy strength: this is the first commandment," the Lord Jesus really did not tell the scribe anything new. He merely put into clear focus in the confused discussions of the Israelites that Law which God first revealed at the creation and which He later gave in a written form through Moses. And when the Lord added: "And the second is like, namely this, Thou shalt love thy neighbor as thyself," He again quoted from the Old Testament book of Deuteronomy. The Lord had a way of speaking to the point and of teaching clearly. He added the brief explanation: "There is none other commandment greater than these." Never man spake as this Man! He spake the Word of God in truth. When Jesus teaches the holy Law of God to us today, His teaching still has the same clarifying and convincing effect. After Jesus has spoken to us, we wonder why we were ever confused about God's Law in the first place! With the scribe we reply: "Well, Master, Thou hast said the truth."

His teaching of the Law reveals our sin. Who of us loves the one true God alone? He is the one Lord who "in the beginning" created the heaven and the earth. He is the "God of Abraham, Isaac, and Jacob." He is the Triune God, Father, Son, and Holy Ghost, in whose name the whole work of the church is to be done. Who of us loves God with all his heart, with all his soul, with all his mind, and with all his strength? We use the phrase "I love you with all my heart" when speaking to a dear one. Strictly speaking, this should be said only to God. But do we really love Him with all our heart? Do we love Him with our inmost soul, with our mind and intelligence, with our total physical strength? Is it necessary to go to heathen lands to find the worship of idols? In our own country, is idolatry found only in Christ-rejecting sects? How common in our own lives are idols such as "our way of life," "our standard of living," "our Western civilization," "financial security," "our system of education," our pursuit of material comforts, our worldly entertainments, our eating and drinking, and the like! Often God doesn't even get a very prominent place in our hearts and lives, alongside of such idols! How much do we really love our neighbor? In every need we strive to take good care of ourselves. Do we strive to care for our needy neighbor as much? We do want to make sure of our own soul's salvation. Do we seek our neighbor's salvation as much? When the Lord Jesus teaches God's Law so clearly, He reveals and exposes to us our own great sins. God, have mercy!

We hear Christ's teaching of the Law gladly. The scribe of our text knew that Jesus had spoken well. He had listened attentively. He now agreed wholeheartedly. Jesus was pleased with the reception which this hearer accorded His Word, and He said to him: "Thou art not far from the kingdom of God." This scribe had probably heard Jesus' Word before this. The kind and loving manner of the Savior when He gave His clear instruction of the Law caused the beginnings of faith which were in this man's heart to assert themselves in a bold confession of acceptance and approval. He was "not far from the kingdom of God," was in fact already within the Holy Spirit's enlightening power. He truly appreciated and enjoyed Jesus' instruction and heard it gladly. — We, too, hear Christ's clear teaching of the Law gladly. We already know our sinful guilt in the sight of the holy God. We have already found refuge in the wounds of Christ, our Savior, and are already in His kingdom of grace. We realize that it is for our great blessing to hear the instruction of the Law of God by which we are kept in a true knowledge of our sins. We likewise hear the instruction of the Law gladly, for it shows to us the way on which we should walk. God's Word is a lamp unto our feet and a light unto our path. Even as the mariner looks intently to the lighthouse and sets the course of his ship accordingly, avoids hidden rock and treacherous shoal and steers safely into the haven, so we gladly hear the enlightenment of Jesus' instruction, take it to heart, follow its guiding. We hear Christ gladly!

II

He Tells Us God's Gospel and Our Salvation

In the Gospel He tells us that He is a man. It was agreed among the church leaders in Israel that the Christ who should come, the promised Messiah, would be the Son of David. Being a descendant of King David of old, the Christ would be a true human being. There was no disagreement about this. The Jewish leaders, however, were unwilling to accept Jesus of Nazareth as that promised Son of David. Jesus was indeed of the house and lineage of David. His birthplace was Bethlehem, the city of David. His legal father was Joseph, of the house of David. His mother was Mary, likewise of the house and family of King David. Before the scribes stood the Descendant of King David, who was human flesh and blood. How well He was known as a true human being! He walked among men and talked among men. He ate and slept with His disciples, for He became hungry and tired performing the many tasks of His calling. Of Him we confess that He is "true man, born of the Virgin Mary."

In the Gospel He tells us that He is the Lord. For the basis of this Gospel teaching Jesus again goes to a well-known Old Testament passage. It is granted that the promised Messiah is to be the Son of David, a true human. By inspiration of the Holy Ghost, David in Psalm 110 speaks of the promised Messiah as his Lord. There was no dispute about the authority of the Psalms. They were inspired by the Holy Ghost. Jesus knew that the people of Israel were in agreement with this truth. Therefore the Lord's testimony, which was based on an inspired word of the Old Testament Scripture, was irrefutable. It was evidently the Holy Spirit's teaching that the descendant of David who was promised to be the Messiah should also be the Lord. This is the claim which Jesus made concerning Himself. In effect He said to the hearers, I whom you know as the son of Joseph am indeed a human being of the house and lineage of David, but I am at the same time David's Lord. This was the undeniable conclusion to which what Jesus said had to lead His hearers. When the woman at Sychar's well spoke of the coming Messiah, Jesus said to her: "I that speak unto thee am He" (John 4:26). By His many miracles Jesus manifested forth His glory. He was the heavenly Father's beloved Son. The holy apostles taught that He is the eternal Son of God. Him the church ever confesses as "true God, begotten of the Father from eternity," and as our Lord. When the deity of Christ is denied, God is rejected. The inspired revelation of both the Old and the New Testament testifies of Jesus of Nazareth as the Lord.

In the Gospel He tells us that He is our Savior. David's Son, the eternal Son of God, would be victorious over all His enemies. He would have all His enemies under His feet. The grand climax of our Savior's redemptive work was His victory, evidenced in His glorious resurrection on Easter morning and in His triumphant ascension 40 days later. In the first Gospel promise, given to Adam and Eve in the Garden of Eden immediately after the fall into sin, God said that the woman's Seed would be bruised by the serpent, but that He would crush his power (Gen. 3:15). Satan and all his might would be utterly defeated. Preceding His final victory there would be His deep humiliation. His struggle against Satan and his power was a struggle unto death. He gave His life a ransom for many. By His holy suffering and death He paid the penalty of our guilt and suffered the punishment of our sins. Here in the words of Jesus are summarized what Dr. Martin Luther later formulated in the beautiful confession of faith: "I believe that Jesus Christ, true God, begotten of the Father from eternity, and also true man, born of the Virgin Mary, is my Lord; who has redeemed me, a lost and condemned creature, purchased and won me from all sins, from death, and from the power of the devil; not with gold or silver, but with His holy, precious blood and with

His innocent suffering and death." The stamp of verity and truth was placed on the teachings of His Gospel and upon His whole work of redemption when He rose from the dead on the third day. Man's enemies are defeated, mankind is redeemed, Jesus is the victorious Lord, Jesus is the all-sufficient Savior from sin. This is the Lord's message to us in His Gospel.

We gladly hear the Gospel of our salvation. When He made Himself known as David's Son and David's Lord, our Savior, the people were deeply impressed. This Man spoke with authority. What He said had upon it the stamp of truth. Here was He for whom God's people had waited for many centuries. Gladly the people heard Him. The message of His love was joyfully received. The message of the Gospel has the same penetrating appeal today. The common people can readily tell the difference between vapid religious generalities and the Gospel of Christ. Not the learned dissertations that give evidence of nothing more than deep human thought, not the profound reasoning of a supermind alone, but the sweet, comforting, uplifting presentation of the Gospel makes the deepest impression upon all. When the lowly sinner realizes that God truly loves him, that God gave His only Son to be his Savior, that the Savior has given Himself on the cross for his salvation — this is the Gospel that he loves to hear.

When heathen first hear this message, they ask, Why were we not told of this before? When Christians who have frequently heard the Gospel of God's love in Christ hear it anew, simply and sweetly presented in a children's Bible story, they thrill anew at the proclamation of God's love. When a mother tells her child the story of Jesus' love, she tells herself the same story over and over again, and she is warmed in her own heart by the love of her Savior as she tells of Him to others. The Christian minister, who in his preaching and teaching shares the Savior's redeeming love with his hearers, at the same time derives the benefits of this love himself. The aged grandmother who all her lifetime has heard the Gospel of Christ and who now hears her own grandson preaching the same old Gospel in one of his first sermons as a student, after the service tells him: "That's it! Preach the Gospel of Jesus, the Savior of sinners!" You could tell that she was speaking from her heart. The hospital patient, weak and wan, is prepared for her passage through the dark valley of the shadow of death by the same Gospel of her Savior, who loved her and gave Himself for her. Gladly we hear the Gospel of our salvation.

Do you, dear friend, hear Christ gladly and regularly? While we know that it is His will that we should gladly hear and learn His Word, yet we also know and confess that our hearing of Jesus and His Word often is not at all as wholehearted and as devoted as it ought to be. How frequently Satan succeeds in making us sluggish in the hearing of the Lord and His Word! How frequently we have neglected and even despised the Word of Jesus! We know that we enjoy the privilege of sharing the Gospel we have with others who need it but do not have it. Often we neglect this work of bringing Jesus' Word to others. Only by the mercy of God through the merits of Jesus, our dear Savior, do we receive forgiveness of our sins of neglect. May the same heavenly Father give us His Holy Spirit and fill us with greater love for the Word and with a more joyful readiness to hear Christ gladly.

> I heard the voice of Jesus say,
> "Behold, I freely give
> The living water; thirsty one,
> Stoop down and drink and live."
> I came to Jesus, and I drank
> Of that life-giving stream.
> My thirst was quenched, my soul revived,
> And now I live in Him.

The Conquest of the Heart

By ALFRED M. BULS

(The Fourteenth Sunday After Trinity)

And He went on from there and entered their synagog. And behold, there was a man with a withered hand. And they asked Him, "Is it lawful to heal on the Sabbath?" so that they might accuse Him. He said to them, "What man of you, if he has one sheep and it falls into a pit on the Sabbath, will not lay hold of it and lift it out? Of how much more value is a man than a sheep! So it is lawful to do good on the Sabbath." Then He said to the man, "Stretch out your hand." And the man stretched it out, and it was restored, whole like the other. But the Pharisees went out and took counsel against Him, how to destroy Him. Jesus, aware of this, withdrew from there. And many followed Him, and He healed them all, and ordered them not to make Him known. This was to fulfill what was spoken by the prophet Isaiah: "Behold My Servant whom I have chosen, My Beloved with whom My soul is well pleased. I will put My Spirit upon Him, and He shall proclaim justice to the Gentiles. He will not wrangle or cry aloud, nor will anyone hear His voice in the streets; He will not break a bruised reed or quench a smoldering wick, till He brings justice to victory, and in His name will the Gentiles hope." — *Matthew 12:9-21 RSV*

The Conquest of the Heart

A sham religion is worse than no religion. The person who claims no religion is likely to be open in his defiance of God. The man with a sham religion is led to a fanatical defense of a life that claims God's mark of acceptance. A raiding enemy band once captured a fortress. They massacred its defenders. Before leaving, however, they took the dead soldiers and propped them into the guard posts with guns ready. They cleaned up the debris of battle and raised the flag. They retreated to ambush. The fortress stood out as a haven of safety to the surrounding country-side. The enemy knew well that it was of no value but to deceive. It could only give false hopes and false claims. It would end in eventual defeat for those who trusted in it. In the Sabbath con-troversy between Jesus and the Pharisees we witness such a sham religion at work. If we look still deeper we recognize that the whole matter hinged on the condition of the heart rather than the claims of the lips. This was a conquest of the heart. Unless Christ was allowed entrance, the hearts would continue to serve Satan despite their religious sheen. When we are confronted by Christ there is bound to be a conquest of the heart.

Christ Knew Sin's Deadly Goal

Jesus' ministry was a minstry of rescue. He saw the pain, aimless living, hopeless future, the self-righteousness, and the pall of death that covered mankind. He came to confront sin. Jesus knew that the eventual goal of sin was eternal death, at work already in the lives of God's creation. He could not look upon the Pharisees on the one hand, or the man with the withered hand on the other, as simply another incident of life. "Is it lawful to heal on the Sabbath?" This was a seemingly honest and com-mendable question. But the heart that gave it birth was filled with evil. Sin is not a misdeed here or an omission there. Sin is man's heart alienated, apart from God. Here it puts on the claim of virtue. Its goal, even under this claim of virtue and especially in this claim, was defeat and eventual destruction of those under its power.

Jesus Met Sin's Resistance

It is always dangerous to question the claims of religious men. Faithful people of God will defend their God to the last. The defense of those who are self-righteous is a personal defense. The Pharisees were rigid in their observance of ritual and Law. Not satisfied with God's divine arrangement and completely mis-understanding His purpose, they added or subtracted from the Law of God as they saw fit. Jesus' ministry by its very nature was a threat to such "self-made" righteousness. They set a trap for Jesus. A man was brought to a place where he would meet Jesus on the Sabbath. Mark records the reaction of Jesus. "And He marveled because of their unbelief" (Mark 6:6). "He looked around at them with anger, grieved at their hardness of heart, and said to the man, 'Stretch our your hand!' " (Mark 3:5). The Father in heaven sent His Son to meet sin's resistance. He met it with calm. There is no strenuous denial of wrong or defense of action. Even here the Savior desired to give sight to spiritually blind eyes. He will do so for us today. Even the most devoted

Christian will have to fight the desire to bend God's will to his. He meets sin in our lives too. We should like to twist and excuse. We should like to have an explanation that removes the offense of His Gospel. In the conquest of the heart Christ will meet this sin in love.

Jesus Unmasked Sin's Deceit

The source of the intentions and desires of a man remain hidden to all but God. We must be content to accept the words and intentions at face value. Jesus, however, tore the mask of deceit from His accusers. He did not rant and rave and condemn. He set before them the inescapable truth. "What man of you, if he has one sheep and it falls into a pit on the Sabbath, will not lay hold of it and lift it out? Of how much more value is a man than a sheep!" The Pharisees had so remodeled the Sabbath that it would fit their religious claims. When a person is dedicated to a system which finally results in self-approval rather than in love to God they will always find it impossible to bear the words of God. What was the real purpose of the Sabbath? God had given it for the good of man. This was His eternal intention. The reaction of the Pharisees, who left in angry silence, indicates their defeat. Weird things take place in the church when men forget that God has called them to make known His praises for the eternal salvation of those about them. This is a good resting place for our thoughts as we measure our intentions, our defenses, and our feeling of purpose as participants in the family of God.

Jesus Served with Personal Sacrifice

The incident narrated in the text can be summarized in two words — "for man." This is, after all, a summary of Christ's ministry. It was this complete service that was given only at great personal cost and sacrifice. Jesus asked the man to hold out his hand, and He healed him. He pointed out the evil intent of the hearts of the Pharisees. "But the Pharisees went out and took counsel against Him, how to destroy Him." Jesus continued His service of love, but He did so in retirement. The Pharisees wrangled with vehemence to prove their point and defend their position. Jesus quietly but with resolution continued to "go about His Fathers' business." For the Savior this meant rejection. He was a marked man. It meant loneliness. It meant ridicule and persecution. "For even His brothers did not believe in Him" (John 7:5 RSV). It finally led to the sentence in the courtyard, to suffering, and to death. In contest for the hearts of men He paid the price of ransom. There was no personal consideration that would deter Him. He is the Servant, the Sacrifice, the Gift, for all of us. He had you in mind. He had His church in mind. He had the world in mind.

Jesus Served with Compassion

The Savior just could not "pass by on the other side." "He healed them all." "He will not break a bruised reed or quench a smoldering wick." While mighty men have fought bitterly to preserve their own small personal kingdom or to prove their own rights even at the cost of scheming, intrigue, and evil, Christ looked upon all this with compassion. In the middle of a culture that is bent on getting more for self this kind of compassion is easily quenched. After all, what can the "bruised reed" or the "smoldering wick" type of person add to our life? It is not only physical suffering for which the Lord has compassion, but He has compassion also for the despairing neighbor whose worries seem more than any man can bear. It is compassion for the man down the street who is being lured to unfaithfulness. It is compassion for the person tense with greed and the mind unable to turn from a course that will bring shipwreck to a marriage. It is compassion for those trying to find an excuse to exclude a brother of another color, or maybe compassion for the brother of another color. This is God's Servant, chosen, Spirit-filled, who brings to our darkness the brightness of God's magnificent love. This takes a conquest of the heart.

Jesus Served with Victory

Take this incident just as it stands and make it a story of its own. Would you consider Christ a smashing success? He withdrew. He asked the people not to make Him known. This is not the picture of a "headliner." We are sometimes so impatient with the speed with which the Holy Spirit works the conquest of the heart. We may experience this feeling as we desire greater spiritual gifts. We become impatient when we work with those who are lifeless and cold. But "There is salvation in no one else, for there is no other name under heaven given among men by which we must be saved" (Acts 4:12 RSV). Christ *does* set us free. He *does* bring the life and blessing of the Father. He *does* fan the flame of faith and binds up the broken reed in preparation for the great fulfillment of His coming. To Christ, who gives victory to the heart of man, be glory and honor!

Jesus Fills Our Heart with Hope

In the Gospel for this Sunday we recognize the ungrateful spirit of the nine lepers. In the lives of the Pharisees of our text and these lepers we recognize the works of the flesh proceeding from a heart empty of the power of God. We look around us and see this multiplied a hundred times. Many a person has turned cynical over it all. This is man! The answer is not to exhort to an act of thanksgiving or to convince the Pharisees to live in peaceful coexistence with Christ. The answer is in the conquest of the heart. Christ healed that man with the withered hand. No less will God meet our ills with forgiveness and fill us with the gifts of His Spirit. Only unbelief will look the other way and say that it cannot be done. God has acted, and in this action lies our hope.

Jesus Fills Us with Love

A rather obvious conclusion in Jesus' encounter with the Pharisees is their lack of love. Anyone who is in daily contact with the world will also note a shocking lack of love. For a good many people, love has no meaning unless it is attached to some personal benefit. Love, cradled in forgiveness and guided by mercy, branches out of the heart to which God has made Christ known. The Savior acted in love even to His enemies who wished to trap Him. He healed the man. He withdrew, not in cowardly fear but in order to fulfill a ministry set before Him by the Father. His hour of supreme love when He died on the cross had not yet come, but it would follow. When Christ has completed His conquest of the heart, it brings with it as a fruit of the Spirit, love, forgiveness, kindness and mercy.

Jesus Crowns Our Heart with Victory

When one talks about conquest the emphasis is usually upon the battered and defeated foe. This is not so in the conquest of the heart. "Behold My Servant whom I have chosen, My Beloved with whom My soul is well pleased. He will proclaim justice to the Gentiles . . . in His name will the Gentiles hope." The Pharisees had set up a religious dynasty. What poor soul on the street of Jerusalem or Bethlehem would dare to question their dictates? For all their pride and boast they were slaves of their flesh and their lust. God, in the conquest of our heart, sets us free from pride. He lifts us up so that all that we do in Christ's name is done in freedom. We bring our sacrifices and pay our vows as we serve Him with our heart, our life, and our work.

We need to forget, at least for a moment, being first in space, first in the eyes of men, first in acclaim, first in our own esteem, and seek rather to find a seat at the table of God's mercy and goodness. This is the victory that takes place when Christ claims your heart. He has done so in Baptism. He continues to claim you day by day as you look upon Him and confess Him as Savior and Lord. The day will come when the lame, the blind, the halt, the bruised reed and the smoldering wick, will sing continual Alleluias to the King of kings. That day will come because Christ has completed the conquest of the heart and offers eternal and final victory.

Charity Can Be Christian

By CHARLES R. BIRNER

(The Fifteenth Sunday After Trinity)

Then said He also to him that bade Him: When thou makest a dinner or a supper, call not thy friends, nor thy brethren, neither thy kinsmen, nor thy rich neighbors, lest they also bid thee again and a recompence be made thee. But when thou makest a feast, call the poor, the maimed, the lame, the blind; and thou shalt be blessed; for they cannot recompense thee; for thou shalt be recompensed at the resurrection of the just. And when one of them that sat at meat with Him heard these things, he said unto Him, Blessed is he that shall eat bread in the kingdom of God. — *Luke 14:12-15*

Everyone likes to be invited out to dinner. The joy increases when close friends extend the invitation. Jesus had these pleasures too. There were times when His invitations to dinner were exciting just in the anticipation of being with those whom He loved.

There were also other invitations. Luke records the day when one of the chief of the Pharisees held a banquet. Invitations went out to other Pharisees. On this particular occasion two guests were invited who did not fit into the picture very well. One of these was a man sick with dropsy. The other was Jesus.

Usually the conversation at the home of your host is pleasant and lively. Everyone has something to contribute. It is a source of joy and happiness. One would expect the conversation among the Pharisees to be a pleasure at this feast. Luke tells us that it is not the usual chit-chat but that Jesus uses this occasion to instruct the people whom He sees.

The sick man receives health from the Savior. The Pharisees undoubtedly wondered if He would heal because this was the Sabbath. Jesus then turns His attention to the guests as they seek out the most favorable places at the tables. From guests to the host — Jesus has some lesson for them all. They did not put Him out. They listened. Perhaps some learned.

Let us listen to Jesus speaking to the host. With the blessing of the Holy Spirit we shall learn that

Charity Can Be Christian

I

Charity Too Often Impractical

J. B. Phillips' translation quotes Jesus as saying: "When you give a dinner or supper party, don't invite your friends or your brothers or relations or wealthy neighbors, for the chances are they will invite you back, and you will be fully repaid. No, when you give a party, invite the poor, the lame, the crippled, and the blind."

Jesus has spoken. Everyone who listens to the words will undoubtedly think, "How impractical!" The custom of the Pharisees was to have a Sabbath feast to which the elite could be invited. This day must have been of some consequence because not only the notable religious people accepted the invitation but also the relatives and friends. Once all these people had gathered together, anyone could see that it would be impractical to invite others. How could a host possibly take people off the street and seat them next to the "religious" of the community! Think of the gossip this would create! How could a proper host deal with the poor who would want to eat more than their share! And the sick! What could be done with them?

Then, too, one had to consider the more serious aspects of the situation. What would the future hold? Once the guests acknowledged they would be present at the dinner the host could certainly look forward to invitations. He could be sure that the occasions would be known throughout the community. It would not hurt the prestige one bit to walk among the right people, to be known among the "religious," to be seen in the higher echelon.

You and I can almost hear the same thoughts among ourselves. How impractical it is to invite people who are in such a contrast to our own family.

"It isn't practical to hire people of different races. It creates tension." That is what the employer says. The owner of the local cafe reminds us that "it isn't practical to let all kinds of people eat in our restaurant. Other people will be offended." Many a businessman has complained: "If we hire a man with a prison record, we'll lose business, or we'll lose our good help."

Even in the home it is difficult to be "practical" about charity. A person of culture has difficulty when faced with the proposition of taking an abandoned child into the home for a few days or a few weeks. The average person cannot quite see any benefit in extending an invitation to those who live across the tracks or in the lower part of town. The home owner may not be able to ask the yardman to have dinner with him. The family man cannot face the responsibility that is thrust upon him when he is forced to deal with the community juvenile delinquents.

So many times the opportunity is ours to extend the hand of charity. But with the thought "It isn't practical" we are able to pass by and pretend we never heard the words of the Savior to His host. At times we are anxious to hear what the Savior has to say. On other occasions we are happy to hear His words. But these words spoken today would best be put off to another time.

See What Jesus Sees

That is, these words are best put off unless we can see what Jesus sees. Something compels the Savior to speak in this tone. Surely His words are not for the ears of the host alone. Let us try to look through the Savior's eyes; perhaps we can see what He sees.

Here is a man who desires honor. It is not enough that he is one of the chief of the Pharisees. He must have the praise of his fellowmen also. His ears will enjoy the comments that will attend such a lavish spread. Other Pharisees will have difficulty in holding the high standard he has set. Right now the honor is due to him and to him alone. Jesus can see his heart's desire — the sin of self-gratification.

The guests also hear the words of the Messiah. He had spoken to them just a minute before. The sound of His voice in their ears has not dimmed. Jesus sees these men crowding, vying, pushing, shoving, for the seats of honor. The latecomer must be satisfied with whatever position remains. What an honor it will be to be seen at the right hand of the host! Jesus sees the same desire in these men — the sin of self-gratification.

Each man thinks of himself more highly than he ought to think. Each Pharisee will have the opportunity to occupy the position of honor; for each one of these guests will eventually be host to those who are seated here. None can wait. Each wants the honor of this day.

The Problem Becomes Ours

Should Jesus occupy a seat in our midst, would He see the same attitude displayed by us? The average housewife explains to her budget-conscious husband: "But we owe them a dinner! And it really should be something special!" The sound is almost innocent. Accustomed as we are to doing good to those who have done good to us, the sin of self-gratification makes no mark in our thinking. The problems are the same faced by people in Jesus' day: Whom should we invite? Did we repay them in full? Did we outdo them a little? Did anyone get his feelings hurt? On and on it goes with little thought of charity.

Boy Scout-like we do our little deeds of kindness every day. Usually it is for the benefit of one we know will help us out later. The sound of Jesus' voice breaks through: "If ye do good to them which do good to you, what thank have ye? for sinners also do even the same." (Luke 6:33)

Spring and fall present our usual drives for clothing for the needy at home and in foreign countries. We can hardly wait to get the closets cleaned out. Thanksgiving and Christmas comes, and we have another opportunity to gather food and clothing for the poorer-than-we. It seems to help ease those conscience pangs a bit to do these things.

In a measure we forget the encouragement given by Jesus to "call the poor, the maimed, the lame, the blind." His exhortation is not for one day or for one season. Jesus gives these words of encouragement for every day of one's life.

Jesus is not against social activity in your home or in mine. He is not against our being kind to friends, neighbors, and relatives. These events we can still enjoy. But while all this is going on we are to keep in mind that our charity can be extended to everyone else. What we enjoy we should be able to have the poor, the maimed, the blind, and others enjoy with us. Jesus is saying charity can be and should be Christian.

Every person who listened to Jesus speak that day would have had some comment to make had he been given the time. Perhaps thoughts were racing through their minds. The Pharisees may have tried to excuse themselves in their own minds. They may have thought: "I'm glad I'm not the host. Jesus wouldn't mean me anyway. I've always invited others to my dinners. Besides, I'm a son of Abraham; I'm sure of getting into the kingdom of God."

Whether anyone felt this way or not is purely speculative. But one man gives us an idea how he felt when the Savior had spoken. Luke recorded those words for us. "Blessed is he that shall eat bread in the kingdom of God!" We'll put the best construction on his words. Here sits a man who has listened closely to the Savior's exhortation. He may be able to see in Jesus the Fulfillment of all Old Testament prophecy. He leaves us with the impression that he has a strong desire in his heart to be able to feast with Jesus in heaven. However anyone may feel about this man, his words are truth. That man who will be present at the feast in the kingdom of God will be a happy man!

II

Charity in Christ

If there is to be a lesson in God's Word for us this day, let it not be in words but in the person of Jesus. Jesus is speaking. Jesus knows of what He speaks. He is God. He brings God's will to men. He shows God's love to men. Let us look at Jesus as our Host.

Jesus would not speak in such a manner to His host if He did not hold such a position Himself. He is the Host for all men. It is His will that all men enjoy the feast He has prepared for them in heaven. The banquet is ready. The question is, "Whom shall He invite?"

If Jesus were to invite only those who were able to repay in some way, who would be able to offer Him a banquet such as He had prepared for men? If He invited only those who were without sin, who else could there be except the angels on high and God Himself.

Someone is to be invited. Men, created in God's image, could have been present at God's prepared feast but for their willful disobedience in the Garden of Eden. Should God now treat men as men treated Him? If the Almighty treated all men as they deserve, there would be no reason for you and me to make a spiritual pilgrimage each year to the little town of Bethlehem. It would be foolish to listen to any shepherds on a hillside or to follow any group of wise men traveling from the East. If God treated us as we deserved, there would have been no Christ Child wrapped in swaddling clothes and placed in a manger. Should men have received their due, no one would have been able to make meaningful a resolute walk to Jerusalem and beyond Jerusalem to the Garden of Gethsemane. Had God ignored the sinfulness of men and left men to their own devices, the names of all those who died by crucifixion on Golgotha would have faded in history. No resurrection would have emptied a tomb. No ascension would have been witnessed. No power would have come from God on high to begin His church. All of a sudden those words we learned so long ago — perhaps just recently — crowd into our mind: "We daily sin much and indeed deserve nothing but punishment."

Thanks be to God! You and I are listening to the voice of Jesus the Son of God. He *is* ignoring the sins of men. He extends His invitation to you and to me. He wants all of us to sit down at the feast in the kingdom of God. He comes to seek and to save the lost. His daily events among men show us His concern. One man cheats another, another, and another until it becomes hard for him to realize his wrong. Then Jesus confronts him to say: "Zacchaeus, hurry and come down from that tree, I am going to be your Guest today." This little tax collector heard Jesus say later, "Salvation has come to this house today" (Luke 19:9 Phillips). At Jacob's Well in Samaria a woman accepted the invitation of Jesus when He said, "But whosoever drinketh of the water that I shall give him shall never thirst; but the water that I shall give him shall be in him a well of water springing up into everlasting life" (John 4:14). Another woman came out of Canaan to plead for the life of her daughter only to hear Jesus say, "It is not meet to take the children's bread and to cast it to dogs" (Matt. 15:26). She continued to plead only for the crumbs. How thankful she must have been to hear the Lover of souls say, "O woman, great

is thy faith. Be it unto thee even as thou wilt" (Matt. 15:28).
To the chosen people of God Jesus spoke clearly, "I am the living
bread which came down from heaven. If any man eat of this bread,
he shall live forever; and the bread that I will give is My flesh,
which I will give for the life of the world. . . . Whosoever eateth
My flesh and drinketh My blood hath eternal life, and I will raise
him up at the Last Day" (John 6:51, 54). Jesus wanted these
people to eat of His feast by faith.

Think of all the people who received some gift from Jesus.
The blind had sight restored; those cripples could walk, jump, and
leap to His glory; those dead could sing His praise in their new
life! Do you think for one moment that these people remained
forever silent about the "feast" that was theirs? Study them. They
all had one thing in common. They would feast with Jesus in the
kingdom of God by faith. They would all say, "We believe and
are sure that Thou art that Christ, the Son of the living God."
(John 6:69)

It is this same Jesus who speaks to us today. He comforts
every sorrow; He forgives every sin; He invites every soul to
feast with Him in heaven. No matter how we fit into the picture,
whether we are maimed, halt, blind, whether we have committed
sins or omitted doing what should have been done, Jesus stands
as the Host inviting us to His feast.

In His Power We Accept

His invitation would go unheeded by everyone of us if it
were not for Jesus pouring out His Holy Spirit upon us. By Word
and Sacrament Jesus makes us willing to accept the invitation.
He makes us new men in the power of the Holy Ghost. What a
change! Today a man drives down the freeway suddenly to pull
off the highway because he has run out of gas. There is no possibility of getting to a service station. He can only wait or hitch
a ride to a phone. Another car pulls to a stop behind him. The
driver hops out, quickly finds the trouble, runs back to his car to
open the trunk and haul out a five-gallon can filled with precious
gas. He returns to his car and is ready to leave. "Wait a minute,
and I'll pay you," cries the first man. The benefactor replies:
"Sorry, you can't repay me. But if you will, fill the can and give
it to the first person you find that has run out of gas." That is
the action of the new man. He wants no pay. He works for and
in Christ. His charity has become Christian.

A young medical student is selling books to pay for another
year at school. At one home he cannot sell his books, but the
daughter says, "I can give you a drink of milk if you would like."
Years later a doctor looks upon the quiet form of a woman who
would have died but for his immediate surgery. "I can never

repay you for your kindness," she whispers. The doctor motions for her to be quiet, then replies, "It is all paid for by two glasses of milk." This is the action of the new man. He wants no repayment. His life is hid in Christ. His charity has become Christian.

The good mechanic knows that the spark and the fuel must be united under compression if there is to be power in the motor. With the Word and the Sacraments Jesus uses His Holy Spirit in our lives. With His supply of "spark," "fuel," and "pressure" we surge forward in power.

We could not be quiet about the change that has come over us. We could not hide for one minute the Savior, who has redeemed us. In Him we find the ability to love the enemy, to do good to those who hate us, to bless those who curse us, to pray for those who despitefully use us and persecute us. In Christ we can love the unlovable, invite those who seemingly are not invitable. You see Christ has made us extensions of Himself. We take over the task of host. We hold out the invitation to come and see. We want men to come to the Lord and be able to feast with Him in the kingdom of God. We recognize that all men are blood-bought souls whom the Lord wants with Him for eternity.

Whether there is repayment on earth or not is immaterial. The promise is given us by Jesus that we shall "be recompensed at the resurrection of the just." We shall have the thanks and praise given by our Father in heaven when on the Last Day we hear Him invite us to inherit the kingdom which He has prepared for us. It will be clear then that all these impractical invitations we have given will have been given in His name. We will have done all this for Jesus as our loving response to the Host who prepared His banquet for all sinners. Our charity will be Christian.

I Believe in a Life After Death

By L. K. MEYER

(The Sixteenth Sunday After Trinity)

Then came to Him certain of the Sadducees, which deny that there is any resurrection, and they ask Him, saying, Master, Moses wrote unto us, If any man's brother die, having a wife, and he die without children, that his brother should take his wife and raise up seed unto his brother. There were therefore seven brethren, and the first took a wife and died without children. And the second took her to wife, and he died childless. And the third took her, and in like manner the seven also. Therefore in the resurrection whose wife of them is she? for seven had her to wife? And Jesus, answering, said unto them, The children of this world marry and are given in marriage, but they which shall be accounted worthy to obtain that world and the resurrection from the dead neither marry or are given in marriage. Neither can they die any more, for they are equal unto the angels and are the children of God, being the children of the resurrection. Now that the dead are raised, even Moses showed at the burning bush when he called the Lord the God of Abraham and the God of Isaac and the God of Jacob. For He is not a God of the dead but of the living, for all live unto Him. Then certain of the scribes, answering, said, Master, Thou hast well said. And after that they durst not ask Him any questions at all. — *Luke 20:27-40*

Every Sunday Christians all over the world confess their faith in a life after death when they recite the words of the Apostles' or the Nicene Creed. We believe that at the moment of death the soul leaves the body and at once enters the glory and bliss of heaven. The body is laid to rest in the earth and decays. On the great Day of Judgment God will raise our body, which will be glorified, and soul and body together will live with God in glory everlasting. We all have recited these words many times, but are we fully convinced that this is actually what will happen?

A man who had attended a funeral service and committal at the cemetery approached the pastor with a puzzled look on his face. "Pastor," he said, "one thing has always puzzled me about a funeral service and the words of committal. In your sermon today you stated several times that we hoped the deceased is with the Lord, and in the committal service we state that the body is laid to rest 'in the hope of the resurrection to eternal life through our Lord Jesus Christ.' Pastor, is this only a hope? Aren't we sure of it?" Very kindly the pastor explained that ours is a faith based upon the sure Word of God. But since we cannot know whether anyone is a true believer we must speak of the hope of the resurrection to eternal life.

Perhaps you have been puzzled by similar questions regarding the life after death. With Job of old, men of all ages have asked: "If a man die, shall he live again?" (Job 14:14). The Sadducees in Jesus' day did not believe in a resurrection. Modern man, living for this world with its joys and pleasures, seems to think that an eternity of pleasure in heaven is only wishful thinking. After all, why be concerned about a life after death when this life has so much to offer? Our text answers these and other questions for us and gives us the comforting assurance that our faith is based on the infallible Word of God.

Our Confession of Faith: I Believe in a Life After Death

I

Why Such a Confession Is Necessary

Not all people believe in a life after death. We have the example of the Sadducees, who denied the resurrection of the dead. What kind of people were they? They were the intellectuals of

their day, many of them priests, wealthy, men of respected position.
Together with the scribes and Pharisees they were the religious
leaders at the time of Christ. Although there was a constant
and sometimes bitter rivalry between them, all three classes were
opponents of Jesus and tried on many occasions to entangle
Him in His teachings and thus discredit Him in the eyes of
the people. In the verses preceding our text Jesus had cleverly
avoided a question designed to trap Him and had told a parable
that put the finger of stinging condemnation on His questioners.
Now the Sadducees saw an opportunity to enhance their own
position over against their rivals, discredit Jesus, and make the
doctrine of the resurrection look ridiculous. So they came to
Him with a question based on the levirate law. According to
levirate law (Deut. 25:5-10), if a man died without children, his
brother was to marry his widow and raise up seed to his brother.
In the case they cited, this happened to seven brothers. Each
of them married the woman and died without children. So these
Sadducees now posed the question: "Therefore in the resurrection
whose wife of them is she?"

A Rebuke and an Answer

Jesus answers first with a stinging rebuke to these intellectuals.
"Ye do err," He said, "not knowing the Scriptures nor the power
of God" (Matt. 22:29; Mark 12:24). They must have felt this rebuke very keenly, for they were men supposedly well versed in
the Scriptures. Now Jesus proceeds to show them why such
a rebuke is in place. "The children of this world marry and are
given in marriage, but they which shall be accounted worthy to
obtain that world and the resurrection from the dead neither
marry or are given in marriage. Neither can they die any more,
for they are equal unto the angels and are the children of God,
being the children of the resurrection." They had made the
obvious mistake of imposing the laws designed for this world
upon the saints in heaven. People are born into the world, they
marry to perpetuate the human race, and then pass on in death.
But these are merely changes in time, belonging to this life, not
to eternity.

The State of the Blessed

Jesus now continues by stating who will inhabit "that world":
"they which shall be accounted worthy." He describes them as
being "the children of God" — "the children of the resurrection."
They are the ones who "have washed their robes and made them
white in the blood of the Lamb" (Rev. 7:14). They have no merit
of their own but trust alone in the merits of Christ, who gave
His life for them on the cross. Through His sacrifice they are

accounted worthy to stand before the throne of God. Jesus furthermore states the condition of those who are children of the resurrection and gives them a passing glimpse into their blessed state. The joy of marriage is not necessary in heaven because the joy of being with Christ is all the happiness they need. They cannot die, for they have entered eternal life, and God's promise of an everlasting bliss is fulfilled in them. Finally, they are equal to the angels. The joy and happiness which the children of God enjoy in heaven is in no way less than that which the angels enjoy. They will be in the presence of God continuously, and with the company of all the angelic hosts they will raise their voices and sing their praises to the Triune God.

Our World Today

Although the Sadducees have passed out of existence, we still have their kind with us, and they still seek to discredit the fact of the resurrection. We still have the scoffing unbelievers who ask, "How is it possible?" And they try to prove that the resurrection is impossible. How can the body that has turned to dust and ashes be raised again? What is the soul? Where is it? With such questions they try to make a Christian's faith in the resurrection look ridiculous. Or there are those who enjoy the pleasures of this life so much that they cannot conceive of any that would be greater. So they enjoy life to the fullest without giving any thought to eternity.

Our Christian Confession

As Christians we know that we are only strangers and pilgrims in this world, that the pleasures of life which we enjoy are given us by a gracious and merciful God. We look forward to the time when we shall leave this vale of tears and enter into the joy and happiness of heaven. There we shall have no worries or cares that are associated with this life, no sorrow or tears, no more death. Only unending joy and happiness will be the lot of those who, having been accounted worthy by the blood of Christ, will stand in the presence of God forever.

II

How Prove a Life After Death?

In His controversy with the Sadducees Jesus proves a resurrection and a life after death by quoting from the Scriptures. He could have used many different passages from the Old Testament Scriptures which prove a resurrection. Instead He chose a passage from the Pentateuch, which they supposedly knew and accepted. He cites the example of Moses at the burning bush

when God spoke to him: "I am the God of thy father, the God
of Abraham, the God of Isaac, and the God of Jacob" (Ex. 3:6).
From this statement Jesus proves that God is a God of the living.
The Patriarchs had died, but God referred to them as being alive.
Although their bodies had been placed into the ground and decayed,
they must be alive with God in heaven if He referred to them
as being alive. Implied is the fact that at the end of time their
bodies will be raised by the power of God, and they will live
with Him in heaven according to body and soul. Thus Jesus
answers His tormentors, and does it so conclusively that "after
that they durst not ask Him any questions at all."

Today's Proof

In order to discredit the resurrection and the life eternal
today's unbelievers point to the many different ways in which
people die. What about the people who die at sea and whose
remains are devoured by the fish? Can God raise them from the
dead? Or in extreme cases they challenge God to assemble and
restore the ashes of one who has been cremated and the ashes
scattered to the four winds. Foolish men! God is almighty, with
Him all things are possible. Jesus, God's Son, raised the dead
while here upon earth (cf. today's Gospel). He died and His body
was laid into the tomb in Joseph's Garden. But on the third day
He rose again. He "abolished death and brought life and immortality to light through the Gospel" (2 Tim. 1:10). Only those
who do not know or refuse to believe the Scriptures deny a resurrection and life eternal.

Our Comfort

Sooner or later each of us must die. What a comfort to know
that that is not the end! The God of Abraham, Isaac, and Jacob
is also our God, a God of the living. When we must accompany
the body of a loved one to its final resting place, as did the widow
of Nain, Jesus says to us, "Weep not." On the great Day of
Judgment, when the last trumpet sounds, God will call our mortal
bodies from their resting place. Body and soul will be reunited
and will be with Him in glory and bliss everlasting. Since Christ
rose from the dead, a place has been prepared for us in heaven.
Having become His own and living under Him in His kingdom
here in this life, we shall reign with Him in eternity.

Proper and Profitable Observance of the Lord's Day

By WALTER A. MAIER, JR.

(The Seventeenth Sunday After Trinity)

At that time Jesus went on the Sabbath day through the corn, and His disciples were ahungered and began to pluck the ears of corn and to eat. But when the Pharisees saw it, they said unto Him, Behold, Thy disciples do that which is not lawful to do upon the Sabbath day. But He said unto them, Have you not read what David did when he was ahungered, and they that were with him — how he entered into the house of God and did eat the showbread, which was not lawful for him to eat, neither for them which were with him, but only for the priests? Or have ye not read in the Law, how that on the Sabbath days the priests in the temple profane the Sabbath and are blameless? But I say unto you, That in this place is One greater than the temple. But if ye had known what this meaneth, I will have mercy and not sacrifice, ye would not have condemned the guiltless. For the Son of man is Lord even of the Sabbath day. — *Matthew 12:1-8*

Is it right or wrong to work on Sunday? Is it permissible to go to the movies? attend a swimming party? How about the opening of business houses on Sundays? How about something like trimming the lawn or weeding the garden at home? Would the Bible sanction a farmer's harvesting a crop on the Lord's Day? What may we, who are God's people, do, and what may we not do, on Sunday? Do any of the Old Testament Sabbath day restrictions pertain also to our New Testament observance of Sunday? We frequently find that there is confusion, and there are all kinds of ideas offered, on these subjects in Christian church circles. What answers would some of us give to these questions?

Since in all things you and I would do that which is pleasing to the Lord, it is important that we be perfectly clear on what God requires of us in the matter of Sunday observance. Our endeavor, then, will be to investigate this subject in the light of God's Word and to come to a definite understanding of what we Lutheran Christians believe, and why, regarding

Proper and Profitable Observance of the Lord's Day

in this mid-20th-century period in which we live. May God the Holy Spirit attend our meditation with His blessing!

I

Such Observance Is Rooted in an Understanding of How and Why the Lord's Day Came into Being

It will be particularly helpful to us to consider first of all how and why our Lord's Day came into being for the church.

For us the Lord's Day is Sunday. Originally, in the Old Testament era, the Sabbath, or Saturday, was designated as the day of the week sacred to the Lord and to be sanctified in a God-appointed manner by the people of Israel. The Third Commandment of the Decalog reads: "Remember the Sabbath day, to keep it holy. Six days shalt thou labor and do all thy work; but the seventh day is the Sabbath of the Lord, thy God. In it thou shalt not do any work, thou, nor thy son, nor thy daughter, thy manservant, nor thy maidservant, nor thy cattle, nor thy stranger that is within thy gates; for in six days the Lord made heaven and earth, the sea, and all that in them is, and rested the seventh day; wherefore the Lord blessed the Sabbath day and hallowed it" (Ex. 20:8-11). Severe punishments were meted out to the Jews who engaged in unnecessary labor on the Sabbath.

Why This Commandment?

Why did God give this Sabbath Commandment to Israel? Simply to compel the people to rest periodically and keep their bodies from wearing out prematurely? This may also have been a divine purpose, but there was a far more important one. Countless passages in both the Old Testament and the New Testament make it clear that the Sabbath ordinance was given primarily to afford the people an opportunity to attend to their spiritual needs. They were to sanctify, that is, to set aside as holy, the Sabbath, not that the day itself needed sanctification (God created it holy, sanctified the day from the beginning of creation) but that the people of God were to give special attention on that day to things that are holy, the sublime teachings of the Word of God.

A "holy convocation" of the people for worship was to take place on the Sabbath. Besides hearing the sacred Law read and expounded, they were to have opportunity at worship also to nourish their souls on the Bread and Water of life as presented in the Gospel. For the Old Testament church the Gospel consisted primarily in the assurance that God would one day send the people a Messiah, the Son of God Himself, who would redeem their race, and indeed all others, too, from ruin through a bitter experience of suffering and death. One of the great Jewish preachers, ancient Isaiah, had made this exceptionally clear when he prophesied of the coming Messiah: "Surely He hath borne our griefs and carried our sorrows. . . . But He was wounded for our transgressions, He was bruised for our iniquities. The chastisement of our peace was upon Him; and with His stripes we are healed. All we like sheep have gone astray; we have turned every one to his own way; and the Lord hath laid on Him the iniquity of us all." The faith which grasped the Old Testament Messianic Gospel promises saved the believing Israelites, just as our faith in Christ, who has come and poured out His lifeblood for us on the accursed tree of the cross on Calvary, has brought us cleansing from all sin, life and salvation.

Not that the people couldn't think of the wonderful truths of the Word throughout the other six days of the week; of course they could; in fact, they were so enjoined by their preachers. But on the Sabbath day they were afforded special leisure for prolonged undisturbed meditation; for further and formal instruction in the Scriptures; for the worship of their glorious God, Jehovah; and for the translation of their spiritual understanding of God's will into works of love performed for the benefit of family, friends, and neighbors. The Sabbath, then, had been established by God chiefly for the spiritual refreshment and strengthening of His people. Their observance of this holy day was to be for them a high point in each week's activity, a joyous experience to which they could eagerly look forward.

Fundamental Purpose Disregarded

Now it is true that this fundamental purpose underlying the Sabbatical regulations was not perceived as it should have been by all the Jewish people during various periods of Israelite history. A case in point is presented in our text. Sad to say, the Pharisees of Christ's day, the religious purists of the Hebrew nation, the enemies of Jesus, did not appreciate the basic divine intent concerning the Sabbath and Sabbath ordinances and were, as a consequence, bereft of the true spirit of Sabbath observance. "At that time," says our text, "Jesus went on the Sabbath day through the corn, and His disciples were ahungered and began to pluck the ears of corn and to eat." Some of the Pharisees, who had been dogging the tracks of Jesus in the hope of finding in something He would do or say grounds on which to incriminate the stainless Savior, immediately seized upon this procedure of the disciples and complained to Jesus: "Behold, Thy disciples do that which is not lawful to do upon the Sabbath day." (Jesus Himself had not taken any of the ears of grain.) In order to understand the disciples' action and also the Pharisees' indignant remonstrance, we need to be informed that it was perfectly permissible for the disciples to take of a farmer's grain growing in the field for the satisfaction of their hunger. Deut. 23:25 states: "When thou comest into the standing corn of thy neighbor, then thou mayest pluck the ears with thine hand." But the Pharisees regarded this plucking of grain from the field as a species of labor forbidden by the Sabbatical ordinance. The fact of the matter is that in formulating this judgment the Pharisees were manifestly guided by the regulations of the rabbis which had been developed as religious directives additional to (and going far beyond) the Law of God; the disciples' action was nowhere forbidden in the Old Testament Scriptures.

Jesus Exposes Misconceptions

Jesus immediately replies to the Pharisees' charge and rises to the defense of His disciples, but He does not choose to touch upon the fallacious assumption of the objectors. The Savior proceeds rather to expose His enemies' fundamental misconceptions concerning the Sabbath ordinances. He shows what these ordinances actually forbade, what they actually required, and for what purpose. To reprove their miserably censorious attitude, He lets their allegation stand for the moment.

"But He said unto them, Have ye not read what David did when he was ahungered, and they that were with him — how he entered into the house of God, and did eat the showbread, which was not lawful for him to eat, neither for them which were with him, but only for the priests?" Jesus refers to 1 Sam. 21, which contains the account of David's violation of an ordinance of the Ceremonial Law, at the time when he and his companions were fleeing for their lives from malevolent King Saul. Being famished upon arrival in the town of Nob, territory of Benjamin, he importuned the priest Ahimelech to let him and his party have as food the loaves of showbread which the ministering priests had recently removed from the display table in the tabernacle located at Nob — bread which was, according to Levitical ordinance, to be eaten by the priests only. Because of the fugitives' extremity Ahimelech acceded to David's request. Would any of the Pharisees dare criticize the act of David, their illustrious ancestor, whom they held in such high regard? They assuredly would not. Nor would Jesus find fault.

Higher Law of Laws

What fundamental principle of the divine will does Jesus bring to light in citing this account? Simply this: The regulations of the Ceremonial Law, which God had formulated as an adjunct to His Moral Law for the special training and education of the Israelite nation, were not to be absolutely binding upon the people. When human life and well-being (physical and spiritual) demanded it, the requirements of the Ceremonial Law were always to yield to those of a higher law, the law of love (the epitome of the Moral Law). Love compels the child of God under all circumstances to provide for the real needs of a neighbor to the limit of his capability.

The example offered by Jesus had to do with the Jewish

ceremonial regulation regarding the tabernacle showbread, but the Pharisees were probably ready to object: "How about the all-important Sabbath Commandment?" Jesus anticipates and refers His opponents to the ministrations of the Jewish priests in the temple. Concerning these rites He points out to the fastidious Pharisees a "shocking" fact, which evidently before this had escaped their notice. Through Moses the Lord had given Israel this instruction: "And on the Sabbath day two lambs of the first year without spot, and two tenth deals of flour for a meat offering, mingled with oil, and the drink offering thereof. This is the burnt offering of every Sabbath, beside the continual burnt offering, and his drink offering" (Num. 28:9, 10). First of all, to bring these sacrifices to the temple on the Sabbath day involved considerable labor for the Israelite worshipers. Then the priests were required by divine mandate, on the Sabbath day itself, to offer the sacrifices presented at the Lord's altar. This business of sacrificing involved strenuous activity: the slaughtering, dismembering, burning, of the sacrificial animals and the disposing of their remains. Would the Pharisees dare criticize the priests who entered upon these ministrations? They had better not. Though the priests "flout" the Sabbatical prohibition of work, in this temple service of theirs they are "blameless" before God, Jesus reminds His opponents. Here, in the delineation of exceptional and permissible Sabbath day activity, Scripture clearly interprets Scripture.

Spiritual Good Paramount

Of what basic principle of the divine will is this case again an illustration? Simply this: The spiritual good of the people was always of paramount importance to God. What was in their spiritual interest was finally to determine what might or might not be done also on the Sabbath. The Sabbath ordinance was not to be absolute; the higher law of love was — and under given circumstances might require — that the Sabbatical restrictions be set aside.

Now Jesus, as the Son of God, the "One Greater than the temple," tabernacle, priest, and Levitical precept; Jesus, as the "Lord even of the Sabbath day," the divine Originator of the Sabbath Commandment itself, who has perfect knowledge of the intent of the Sabbatical ordinance and the range of its applicability, makes fully authoritative pronouncement on the act of the disciples, for the benefit of the Pharisees. The Savior's followers have broken no divinely established law; they are altogether without blame. The disciples in thankfully accepting and eating for the nourishment of their bodies the food which the Lord had graciously provided indeed glorified God on the Jewish holy day.

If the Pharisees had only known their Scriptures better; if they had only realized how greatly the Lord God of Israel delighted in His people's showing love and mercy toward one another as opportunities presented themselves, they would never censoriously have taken the disciples to task for plucking grain on the Sabbath.

Pious Israelites received rich blessing through observing the Sabbath generation after generation down to the time of Christ. With the coming of Jesus and the completion of His mediatorial work, however, God abolished the Ceremonial Law for the people of his church. The early Christians, desiring on the one hand to indicate their independence from the Levitical Sabbath ordinance and on the other to perpetuate for themselves the blessings that had come to God's people through participation in the more important aspects of Sabbath day observance, selected Sunday — the day on which Christ rose from the dead and on which He poured out His Spirit on the infant New Testament church — in Christian liberty as their holy day. To our very own time Sunday has been set aside as the Lord's Day by followers of the Savior everywhere.

II
Such Observance Essentially Includes Participation in Public Worship of the Lord

In what, then, does proper and profitable observance of the Lord's Day in New Testament times consist? What similarities and differences are notable in the Christian celebration of Sunday and the Old Testament Jewish celebration of the Sabbath? With the Sabbath Commandment abolished for New Testament Christendom, there is no specific day of worship prescribed for the church. Nor do the external Sabbath day restrictions imposed upon Israel have any binding force for Christian people. The basic principles which underlay the divine establishment of the Old Testament Sabbath, and the Israelites' observance of these, however, continue to govern Christian Sunday observance in the New Testament era: (1) the ultimate purpose of Sunday observance is to provide God's people with special opportunity for the satisfaction of their spiritual needs, through divine worship; (2) the criteria of God's Word and the law of Christian love are to determine the propriety of all other extra-worship Sunday activities as well as activities throughout the remaining days of the week.

Essential to Proper Observance

We may conclude that the *essential* element of a proper observance of the Lord's Day today is participation in public, congregational worship. The requirement that God's people *sanc-*

tify their holy day by taking time out to assemble for worship is the original Third Commandment's one surviving implication that does go on having normative authority in the New Testament church. The writer to the Hebrews says that genuine Christians are to be such as are "not forsaking the assembling of ourselves together, as the manner of some is."

What is the profit of a church member's regular participation in Sunday worship? We would simply mention the following benefits, without elaborating upon them: (1) the good conscience that comes with the knowledge of having obeyed the will of God; (2) the growing understanding of the divine Word, as the result of listening to pulpit sermons; (3) the increase of the Holy Spirit's activity in, and operation through, us; (4) the privilege of receiving the soul-strengthening Sacrament of Holy Communion; (5) the opportunity to discharge in a measure the Great Commission's requirement to preach the Gospel to every creature, a responsibility which devolves upon all Christians, through the presentation of our offerings and joint prayers in behalf of missionary work throughout the world; (6) the encouragement to consistent, Christian living that comes through fellowship with a host of the people of God in His house; (7) consequent possession of the assurance that when we put God first in life, when we seek first His kingdom and righteousness, as we do by participating faithfully in public worship, all our basic physical and material needs through life will be graciously supplied by our heavenly Father. Many more benedictions could be enumerated.

Working on Sunday

Now back once again to a number of our questions relating to the Christian observance of Sunday. In the light of our discussion, these should not be difficult to answer now. Is it wrong to work on Sunday? No — some people have to, and this for the benefit of fellowmen; for instance, the pastor, the organist, the ushers, the custodian here at church on Sunday mornings; medical personnel in hospitals, employees of utility companies, workers in certain essential industries; operators of restaurants, drugstores, gas stations; the farmer with a field of waving grain that must be harvested before impending storm, and so on. However, all of God's people who must work regularly or occasionally on Sunday ought to make sure that they do not absent themselves from weekly public worship and deprive themselves of its benefits. If their jobs prevent them from coming to church altogether, then new jobs should be sought. — The opening of more and more business houses on Sunday for purposes of nonessential commercial transaction is hardly a wholesome trend on the American scene. Increasing numbers of store and sales personnel are thus deprived of the opportunity to attend divine worship.

On the other hand, the practice of abstaining from arduous physical or mental labor on Sundays, when this is possible, has much to commend it in our day of hustle, bustle, and tension. Such periods of rest allow our bodies and minds much-needed recuperation and refreshment and fit us for more able service through the week.

Sunday Recreation

What, then, about different forms of recreation on Sunday? We note from our text that after Sabbath worship Jesus and His disciples were out walking in the fields and, no doubt, enjoying nature, God's great out-of-doors, all about them. It may be generally stated that any recreational activity not inherently sinful and not giving offense to others may be engaged in to the glory of God. The all-important consideration is that nothing should be entered upon that will mar the spiritual impressions developed, dim the spiritual understandings cultivated, and weaken the spiritual life fortified during Sunday morning worship.

Sunday is a fine time for families to be and do things together; to visit friends or to call on the sick, the shut-ins, the underprivileged in congregation or community — to put into practice some of the good works which have been preached from the pulpit; to engage in acts of love and mercy, such as are supremely esteemed by the Lord Jesus and will insure His blessing in our lives. The mind, heart, and conscience enlightened by the faithful hearing of God's Word on Sunday mornings will have little difficulty in determining what constitutes proper and profitable observance of the Lord's Day during the extra-worship hours.

My beloved fellow believers, we have been redeemed from our sins, including our neglect of worship opportunities, by the precious blood of Jesus, who loved us and gave Himself for us, that we might be His own and serve Him through time to a blessed eternity. We were reborn by the Spirit of our God, whose mighty influence in our lives is mediated in ever-increasing measure through Word and Sacrament. Therefore let us now praise the Lord, the Almighty in heaven, for the gifts of Sunday: congregation, pastoral ministry, soul-strengthening Word and Sacrament. With joyful heart let us frequent the house of God on the Lord's Day and live out our years on earth in the love of Christ and to the glory of God, until, through our Savior's merits, we enter the eternal Sabbath rest of the blessed in heaven. God grant it to each one of us for Jesus' sake!

Important Prayer Pointers Presented by Our Lord

By Harold G. Parsch

(The Eighteenth Sunday After Trinity)

When thou prayest, thou shalt not be as the hypocrites are, for they love to pray standing in the synagogs and in the corners of the streets that they may be seen of men. Verily I say unto you, They have their reward. But thou, when thou prayest, enter into thy closet, and when thou hast shut thy door, pray to thy Father which is in secret, and thy Father which seeth in secret shall reward thee openly. But when ye pray, use not vain repetitions, as the heathen do, for they think they shall be heard for their much speaking. Be ye not therefore like unto them, for your Father knoweth what things ye have need of, before ye ask Him. After this manner therefore pray ye: Our Father which art in heaven, Hallowed be Thy name. Thy kingdom come. Thy will be done in earth as it is in heaven. Give us this day our daily bread. And forgive us our debts, as we forgive our debtors. And lead us not into temptation, but deliver us from evil. For Thine is the kingdom and the power and the glory forever. Amen. For if ye forgive men their trespasses, your heavenly Father will also forgive you; but if ye forgive not men their trespasses, neither will your Father forgive your trespasses.

Matthew 6:5-15

We are never too old to learn. This axiom applies also to our prayer life. We shall never reach the point where we can claim to have mastered the art of praying. This will become very clear to us as we listen intently to some

Important Prayer Pointers Presented by Our Lord

May the Holy Spirit alert and enlighten us as we sit at Jesus' feet for this instructive lesson.

I

The Proper Purpose in Praying

Our Lord begins His instruction on prayer by reminding us of the purpose of prayer. Being a very effective Teacher, He first of all presents the wrong purpose of prayer. In so doing He refers to the Pharisees of His day. They were regarded as experts in prayer. But they were deceiving the people and themselves, and the Lord saw through their sham. That is why He says: "When thou prayest, thou shalt not be as the hypocrites are, for they love to pray standing in the synagogs and in the corners of the streets that they may be seen of men" (v. 5). Did you hear this? The wrong purpose in praying: "that they may be seen of men!" Because the Pharisees wanted to impress the people, because they wanted to get a reputation for piety, they chose to pray where the traffic was the heaviest: in the most conspicuous spots in the church and at the main intersections of the city. But Jesus repudiates prayer which is for display purposes. Such prayer is hypocrisy.

This does not mean that prayer in public is wrong. A Christian is to pray everywhere. Sometimes, I fear, we are too ashamed to pray in public, too timid to confess our faith openly, too weak to let others know that we believe in praying.

But the point that Jesus is making is this, that the purpose of prayer is not to impress people but to implore God. Since prayer is a heart-to-heart talk with God, the best place for prayer is in private, where we are unhampered by the awareness of being watched by human eyes, where we can express our innermost agonies, emotions, and longings unhindered, where our full attention can be directed to Him who is "all ears" when our prayer is genuine. So please note: It is not necessary to be seen of men when we pray, but it is absolutely essential to have the attention of God. This is the point Jesus makes when He says: "But thou, when thou prayest, enter into thy closet, and when thou hast shut thy door, pray to thy Father which is in secret, and thy Father which seeth in secret shall reward thee openly." (V. 6)

Because the Pharisees had the wrong motive in praying, because they wanted to be seen by men, they tried to put themselves on display as long as possible, with the result that their prayers became very lengthy and mechanical. And again Jesus rebukes them, this time for their repetitious ramblings, saying: "But when ye pray, use not vain repetitions, as the heathen do, for they think that they shall be heard for their much speaking." (V. 7)

The effectiveness of prayer is not decided by the number of words we say. We do not improve our chances of being heard just because we pray longer. It is not a question of seeing who can hold out the longest — we or God: we in our asking or God in delaying His answer. It is not a question of trying to wear God down to the point where He will grant our request simply because He wants us to stop pestering Him. Nor is it necessary to inform God about our aches and fears and needs, as though He did not know. Everything that has happened to us has come to pass by His permission. God wants us to pray, not that He might be informed but that we might be reminded of our own inabilities and our need of Him from whom every blessing must flow. That is why Jesus adds the reminder "for your Father knoweth what things ye have need of, before ye ask Him." (V. 8)

It is easy to join Jesus in judging the Pharisees' wrong motives and habits in praying, but our Lord's prayer pointers certainly also throw the searchlight on our own praying. Is it genuine? Are we prone to fall into the same rut? As we participate in the worship of God Sunday after Sunday, are we not in danger of becoming mechanical at the various points in the service where the pastor invites us to join with the entire congregation in prayer: the collects, the sermon prayer, and the special intercessions. It certainly is not difficult to assume the posture of praying, especially here in the service where everybody is doing it, folding the hands, bowing our heads, and moving our lips. Any observer would conclude that we are praying. But would that also be the verdict of God? Do the prayers that are spoken in this service become the longing of our mind and heart? That is important! Merely to assume the outward posture of prayer, without throwing the thoughts of our mind and the desires of our heart into gear, will make our prayers no more genuine that were those of the Pharisees.

The danger of slipping into a mechanical mumbling of words is especially imminent every time we are asked to join the congregation in the Lord's Prayer. Someone has said that the Lord's Prayer is the most martyred of all prayers. The reason is that we say it so often. We can almost recite it in our sleep. We can even follow along while looking around to see who is in church and wondering how long it has been since we last saw them. But the solution does not lie in our saying it less frequently but in our praying it genuinely.

We certainly must feel sorry for our Roman Catholic friends who have been led to believe that God is interested in the arithmetic of prayer, the repetitious recitations of the rosary. Surely Jesus anticipated the errors of the Church of Rome also in the area of prayer when He said, "Use not vain repetitions" (v. 7). How often have our own prayers been thoughtless recitations! May God forgive us.

II

The Perfect Pattern for Praying

The Lord's Prayer

Having exposed and denounced the praying of the Pharisees as hypocritical and empty, yes, as repulsive to His heavenly Father, Jesus now proceeds to give an example of the content of genuine prayer. So that there can be no excuse for anyone, Jesus shows us how and for what we are to pray. In so doing He presents the prayer that has come to be known as the Lord's Prayer. Though the Lord's Prayer consists of only 66 words (vv. 9-13 KJV), it actually includes all our needs from time to eternity. That is why the Lord's Prayer is called the model prayer or the perfect prayer. I am now going to give you a very brief résumé of the Lord's Prayer. You of course understand that no sermon or even volume of sermons can exhaust the full meaning of this prayer of all prayers. Often each petition is the text or topic for an entire sermon. But since we are in the habit of reciting the Lord's Prayer in less than 30 seconds, it should prove a blessing to have the substance of its seven petitions in capsule form. This will give us an idea of some of the thoughts that should be engendered in our mind and some of the longings that should linger in our heart as we talk to God in this and other prayers.

The Introduction

In the introduction to the Lord's Prayer we address "our Father which art in heaven." The Pharisees wanted to convey the impression that prayer was hard work, as though God were most austere, almost impossible to approach, as though therefore only "professionals" could pray. But Jesus indicates that when prayer proceeds from a believing heart we can approach God as children approach their earthly father — with boldness and confidence. Knowing and believing that God has already taken care of our greatest needs, the needs of our soul, in sending His Son to become our Savior, we are invited to come to Him for anything and everything else that we need on our way to heaven. He can and will hear our requests.

The First Petition

The Spirit-instilled certainty that we are God's children through faith in Christ kindles within us the fervent desire to pray, "Hallowed be Thy name." Every true child of God wants to believe right and live right. The ability to do so must come not from within but from without, from our heavenly Father. False doctrine and ungodly living can only send us to hell. God is never honored by it. Yet we are constantly exposed to it and surrounded by it. As often as we observe it — and this is daily — this petition should become meaningful to us instead of mechanical.

The Second Petition

The realization that we could still lose our eternal inheritance should prompt us to pray, "Thy kingdom come." The falling away from the faith on the part of many is a sign of the last times. We certainly don't want to take any chances on becoming spiritually complacent. On the contrary, we want the Holy Spirit to keep on coming to us through the Word that we might remain in the kingdom of grace and finally come to the kingdom of glory. But more, as soon as we ourselves are on the way to heaven, we want others to join us. So this prayer at once becomes the prayer of a missionary. Every true Christian is a missionary, praying and witnessing and working and giving that others may join us in the kingdom of God. What a world-girdling prayer this becomes!

With it Jesus, as it were, puts our arms around the whole heathen world. Surely there are enough daily headlines to prompt us to express our Christian concern in a thousand different ways.

The Third Petition

The third petition always keeps us mindful of the fact that the going from here to heaven is not going to be smooth. True, it is our heavenly Father's first and foremost will that we might be saved. But there are other wills that are opposed to the will of our heavenly Father. There is the will of the devil, the will of the unbelieving world, and even the will of our own old Adam. Haven't you ever noticed it? How quickly our old Adam is ready to side in with the suggestions of the devil and the enticements of the world! Pray, brother, sister, pray! Pray especially amid the tense world conditions in which we live and move in this moment of history. Even if the whole world and all the inhabitants of hell should combine their forces to destroy the purposes of God, our prayer should always be: "Thy will be done on earth as it is in heaven." And when we pray this petition let us remember the promise of our heavenly Father that ultimately His counsel and will shall prevail.

The Fourth Petition

The fourth petition, "Give us this day our daily bread," is set right in the middle of the Lord's Prayer. Our Lord recognizes our need for the material things of life while passing through time on our way to eternity, and He wants us to confide in our heavenly Father with reference to all the wants and supports of life. This petition provides the answer to all the economic problems confronting the world, our nation, and our own households. Our heavenly Father still offers us the best financial and social security possible. "Seek ye first the kingdom of God and His righteousness, and all these things shall be added unto you" (Matt. 6:33). Isn't it true that many Christians, and even we ourselves, are mimicking the unbelieving world in our anxiety for things material? Oftentimes we act as if our heavenly Father were no longer interested or able to provide for us, His dear children. Perhaps if we were living in a country blessed far less with the abundance of things, we might be more inclined to pray this petition with far greater confidence.

The Fifth Petition

As we think of all the various items that we want our heavenly Father to provide, we suddenly realize that we sound like a disobedient child that comes to its parent with a request for a thousand different things. We are reminded of the fact that we are sinners, daily sinners, that we have no right to approach God with the attitude of a Pharisee, as though God owed it to us. No, never! We are totally undeserving. Before asking our heavenly Father for another thing, we must ask Him for the most important thing, the forgiveness of our sins. And this forgiveness is available only in Christ Jesus, who as our Substitute worked out the only righteousness which our heavenly Father will accept. And so this same Jesus taught us to pray, "Forgive us our debts, as we forgive our debtors." "As we forgive our debtors" — Jesus knew that a true appreciation of God's forgiveness toward us would move us to be forgiving toward our fellowmen.

The Sixth Petition

The sixth petition awakens us to the fact that we are constantly exposed to, and bombarded by, the forces of evil which would bring us to hell. Left to ourselves, we could never cope with these forces. That is why we need the help of our heavenly Father and must pray, "Lead us not into temptation." We know that He never intends our harm, and we also know that He has given us the means by which we can resist and conquer the forces that intend to lead us into misbelief, doubt, and despair. The prayer to overcome every type of temptation should lead us to use His Word, the sword of the Spirit, faithfully.

The Seventh Petition

There are many evils that can make life rough for us on our way to eternity, evils that can touch our body and our possessions and evils that can affect our spiritual well-being. But the greatest evil that can come to any human being is an evil end. The consequences of an evil end never end throughout the eons of eternity. The opposite of an evil end is a blessed end. A blessed end is an earthly end that finds us in the saving faith in Christ. No matter what God in His infinite wisdom permits to befall us throughout life, the most important hour is the final hour. Aware of the certainty of death and the uncertainty of death's hour should prompt us to pray this final petition with Christian watchfulness: "But deliver us from evil." The countdown continues day after day, night after night. The zero hour is bound to come, but with faith in Christ we know that the hour of death will usher us into the presence of Christ where no evil of any kind will ever touch us again. Do we see it clearly? Surely there is no day in which we can neglect to enfold our loved ones and ourselves in this prayer.

The Conclusion

The conclusion of the Lord's Prayer is a hymn of praise, a confession, acknowledging our heavenly Father's right to govern, to judge, and to glory with reference to anything that we ask and everything that He provides. Confident that this will be our conviction in the halls of heaven, we are ready even now to conclude our prayer with "Amen," meaning yes, it shall be so.

I trust that this résumé of the Lord's Prayer has given you an idea of the content of Christian prayer. Our Lord teaches us to put all of our physical and spiritual, temporal and eternal needs into a nutshell and place them into the lap of our heavenly Father. The Lord's Prayer should serve as a pattern for all our praying. And when you don't know what to ask or how to say it, pray the Lord's Prayer. Somewhere in the Lord's Prayer you will always find the petition that fits any particular situation in your life. May I also suggest that in your family devotions you restudy Luther's explanation with reference to the meaning of these petitions. Such a study will soon show that the Lord's Prayer is as relevant as the needs of today and will suggest a dozen different prayer subjects for every petition.

But we must hurry to the final point that Jesus makes in His lesson on prayer.

III

A Prerequisite in Praying

Whether we pray the Lord's Prayer or any other prayer, we must pray with a forgiving spirit. That is a prerequisite to praying the Lord's way. Jesus makes this very clear when He says: "For if ye forgive men their trespasses, your heavenly Father will also forgive you; but if ye forgive not men their trespasses, neither will your Father forgive your trespasses" (vv. 14, 15). The point is not this, that we earn God's forgiveness by forgiving others. No, never! There is only one way in which sins are forgiven, and that is through the merit and blood of Jesus Christ. The point that Jesus makes is this, that in forgiving our fellowmen we show that we have accepted God's forgiveness, that we are thoroughly and truly appreciative of His grace and mercy. We might say that when a Christian prays he is at peace vertically and horizontally — forgiven, he is forgiving: forgiven of God, he is forgiving toward his neighbor. Take the reverse: a person who carries a grudge and cultivates an unforgiving attitude toward his fellowman is blocking the forgiveness of God, indicating that he does not appreciate God's offer of forgiveness.

How important that we learn this lesson! There are people who will refrain from communing at the Lord's Table while living on "the outs" with someone. They should, but not for long. But sometimes these same people imagine that they can still pray, sing, worship, and praise God properly. What self-deception! The heart that lacks love is faithless, and without faith it is impossible to please God.

Only when we believe that we need the daily and complete forgiveness of all our sins, only when we are convinced of our own utter unworthiness, only when we believe that the blood of Jesus is sufficient to cleanse away our every guilt, only then will we be anxious to be reconciled with those whom we have offended or those who have offended us. Our efforts at reconciliation may or may not be successful. The genuineness of our prayer is not determined by our success or failure to be reconciled, but by the attitude of our heart, the forgiving disposition that we harbor toward others.

Surely by now every one of us should be ready to admit that there is still much that we can learn with reference to praying. As long as we live, we shall never reach perfection in the art of praying. We shall always have reason to say it again and again, "Lord, teach us to pray."

Two Perils of the Modern Church

By GEORGE H. SOMMERMEYER

(The Nineteenth Sunday After Trinity)

Do not lay up for yourselves treasures on earth, where moth and rust consume and where thieves break in and steal, but lay up for yourselves treasures in heaven, where neither moth nor rust consumes and where thieves do not break in and steal. For where your treasure is, there will your heart be also. The eye is the lamp of the body. So if your eye is sound, your whole body will be full of light; but if your eye is not sound, your whole body will be full of darkness. If then the light in you is darkness, how great is the darkness!
Matthew 6:19-23 RSV

We live in a country that looks favorably on religion. The problem of persecution which faced the church of the first century is not the problem of the church today — at least not in America. Our Government seeks to create a climate that is favorable toward the promotion of religion. At present over 62 percent of the population is enrolled in a church or synagog. At the beginning of the 19th century we had fewer church members than any of the nations which were called Christian. In the middle of the 20th century we have more church members than any nation of the world.

Church giving breaks new records every year. New and impressive church buildings are being erected at a steadily increasing pace. More religious literature is available in popular form and attractive style. Even Bible reading and Bible study are receiving increased attention in our churches and in many homes. Religion often gets into the articles of popular magazines as well as the conversation of ordinary people. As long as religion doesn't make too many demands on a man's own way of life, it grows increasingly popular.

But there is something strange about the recent upsurge of interest in religion. The country continues its plunge toward materialism. Crime statistics grow as rapidly as church statistics. Homes continue to break as rapidly as before. Church meetings spend more time discussing dollars than souls. Air conditioning, parking space, and outdoor lighting are major concerns on many agendas. The coolness and lack of concern for others which is so characteristic of our world is infecting more of our churches. There seems to be a secularization of the church which is growing as fast as the church itself.

We cannot discuss all the perils threatening the forward advance of Christ's church on earth, but we can underscore at least two of which Jesus spoke in the Sermon on the Mount almost two millenia ago. These perils are as much with us today (perhaps even more so) as they were with the people to whom Jesus spoke from the hillside long ago. The perils are: wrong treasures and impaired vision.

Two Perils Threatening the Church

I

Wrong Treasures

Jesus speaks clearly and precisely: "Do not lay up for yourselves treasures on earth, where moth and rust consume and where thieves break in and steal, but lay up for yourselves treasures in heaven, where neither moth nor rust consumes and where thieves do not break in and steal" (Matt. 6:19, 20). Our Lord well knew the weakness of human nature so prone to love the things of this world which it can see and touch rather than the things of eternity which can be perceived only by faith. We are so easily attached to the transient toys of time and so slow to be connected to the permanent foundations for eternity. It requires the long hard pull of God's Holy Spirit to lift our sights away from the things of the world up to the throne of God.

Many things which were treasured in one generation have little appeal for the next. Perhaps a few glimpses of life in America just 40 years ago will help show how rapidly man's values change.

At that time the war to "make the world safe for democracy" was recent history. American troops were home from the Rhineland, and the state of the nation had returned to what President Harding said was "normalcy." Heated taxicabs were the latest thing in transportation. Model T Fords sold for an all-time low of $260. Some of the popular makes which were the pride of their owners were Chalmers, Durant, Hudson, Oakland, Jordon, Marmon, Moon, Paige, Reo, Stutz, and Hupmobile. Airplanes were a dangerous novelty for daredevils. Homebrew bottling equipment and basement wine presses were common in many homes. But garbage disposals, freezers, dishwashers, automatic clothes washers and dryers were unheard of. Conventional work schedules in many industries were 63 hours a week. Life expectancy at birth was near 60 in contrast to today's 70 plus. Clothing and hair styles most desirable in the early 20s bring a chuckle or a laugh from the modern teen-ager who can't imagine why people ever dressed that way, or how they could ever wear their hair that way.

It doesn't take 40 years to show how futile it is to treasure earthly things. Like the child who is no longer interested in last year's toys, adults are continually shifting their attention from one thing to another. Automobiles, house furnishings, tools, sports equipment, clothing, home appliances, even the homes themselves, are treasured for a while and then disposed of. We just can't keep our attention fixed too long on any earthly things. Soon we know we have to give them up. How much more reasonable it is to fix our attention on things above where moth and rust do not consume and where thieves do not break through and steal. Of all the things in this world it is only the Word of God and the soul of man that abide forever.

Occasionally we read predictions of what the world will be like 40 years from now, soon after the year 2000. No one can say with certainty, but planners and scientists and industrialists are attempting some educated guesses. The trend toward more industrialization and more urbanization will continue. Life changes will take place so rapidly that man will be sorely tempted to treasure his own power over things more than God's eternal power over everything.

It is predicted that the Northeast Coast will be one big city from southern Maine to central Virginia. Most large cities will be doubled in size, while new urban centers will rise in areas now sparsely populated. Needs for water, wood, and metals will be doubled or tripled and more. But technology will keep pace with needs. The sea will not only supply fresh water, but even fuel and energy by thermonuclear fusion. All kinds of fantastic transportation systems will be devised, including a possible rocket belt with which a man could take a jump from his suburban home and land downtown at his office. Perhaps our boldest venture in the next 40 years will be into space. We are told that moon trips will be common. In fact some people are already trying to make reservations on space craft that will travel to the moon. The possibility of meeting other planetary people, also created in God's image, is no longer a total fantasy.

These challenging possibilities will bring increasingly strong bids for the hearts of men. We see it today in the glamorous appeal held before our young people to enter scientific fields as a life vocation rather than church vocations, social work, teaching, or other direct services to God and mankind. With all the exciting possibilities of harnessing and conquering things it is increasingly difficult to fix man's hearts on the love of God in Christ Jesus. Yet it is true that no power harnessed by man will ever move God off His throne in heaven. No rocket of man's making will ever transport his soul from earth to heaven. No discovery of man will ever shake the basic truths of the Christian religion.

God in His infinite wisdom and love made all things out of nothing. When the crown of His creation, man and woman, disobeyed and fell into sin, God provided a pathway for His prodigal creatures to return. Through the entrance of His Son into the world of creation, God provided a way for fallen man to come into the world of heaven and the angels. He wiped away the guilt of men's sins with one bold stroke of Jesus' holy precious blood. God was in Christ reconciling the world unto Himself. God has also entered the hearts of His fallen creatures with His Holy Spirit. The Spirit creates new life in men whose spirituality is dead. The Spirit changes our way of life, corrects our attitudes, and gives us a new set of values. He makes it possible to set our affections on things above where neither moth nor rust corrupts and thieves do not break through and steal. Without His power in us we could not follow the way that Jesus points in our text.

Even we who have the blessings of the Spirit in our hearts are in constant peril of losing them. The temptations to treasure earthly things abound. The switch of affections from the blessings which the Holy Spirit provides over to the attractions of this world is often a subtle and quiet procedure. Very few Christians would deliberately set out to be secularized. In fact they are usually unaware of what is happening to them. Many Christian congregations have experienced a strong temptation to treasure the wrong things while going through a building program. To build a church or an education unit as a place where the Holy Spirit might work in men's souls is a worthy challenge to any congregation. But the very nature of the project causes us to think in terms of contracts, building materials, room space, heat control, air conditioning, outdoor lighting, color schemes, and all manner of material things that man has developed from the resources God made available to him. A building project for a local congregation can be a tremendously spiritual experience, or it can be a temptation to get so wrapped up in the complicated material aspects of the building that we lose sight of the spiritual purpose for which the project was begun in the first place.

It seems that Jesus' warning is still in place: "For where your treasure is, there will your heart be also."

II
Impaired Vision

A second peril which is particularly strong in our time is impaired vision. There are so many obstacles to keep us from seeing clearly the things which pertain to the kingdom of God. When our eyes of faith are dimmed by the dust and clouds of 20th century living we are in danger of darkness. Jesus said: "The eye is the lamp of the body. So if your eye is sound, your whole body will be full of light; but if your eye is not sound, your whole body will be full of darkness. If then the light in you is darkness, how great is the darkness!"

Let's look at some of the things which keep us from seeing God clearly and knowing His will for our lives. For one thing there is the problem of language. God's message to man has not changed with the passing of years, but man has changed and language has changed. Words which were effective to communicate the Gospel in the days of the Reformation do not hold the attention of modern man. Church leaders are trying to put the Gospel in today's language, but it is simply imposible to put all the great mysteries of God in comic book and television jargon. The church speaks a language which it cannot give up completely without giving up the truth it conveys. Men must be taught to understand that language as they have been taught to understand medical and scientific terms they did not know a generation ago. If we were to give up all the language of the Bible, we should become enmeshed in the ways of the world instead of changing the world to conform to the will of God.

Many words have changed meaning. The word "faith" for example, means different things to different people. It might mean faith in man's capacity to produce, faith in light to turn on when one flips the switch, or a vague faith in God to help us out of trouble when we turn to Him in prayer. We must strive to see that people know the true meaning of faith. It is more than belief in

God's existence or acceptance of a doctrinal formula. One is not justified before God by perfunctory acceptance of a creed, but by the gift of God which causes him to wholly lean on the saving work of Jesus Christ and to trust the cleansing power of the Holy Spirit. Words like *forgiveness, salvation, justification,* and *redemption* — even *sin* and *grace* and *love* — must be clearly understood if man is to get a clear vision of God's mighty acts to save him from destruction. This problem of speaking the Gospel in clear terms is not one for the clergy alone, but for every Christian. "But you are a chosen race, a royal priesthood, a holy nation, God's own people, that you may declare the wonderful deeds of Him who called you out of darkness into His marvelous light." (1 Peter 2: 9 RSV)

Another factor that obscures man's vision today and leaves many in darkness is the failure to realize the need for God and His saving presence. Even in the church worship service how much real sense of God's presence is felt? How much do you feel the need for His sustaining grace every day, and how much do you seek it in Word and Sacrament? The need for God is often relegated to times of stress and pain rather than to a regular daily intake of His power and grace. If we do not realize the continual need for God's Spirit in our lives and if we do not regularly receive that power through Word and Sacrament, we who have opportunity for the light will still be filled with darkness. One of the real perils to our spiritual life is the feeling that we can get along quite well without God unless something goes wrong. Then we want to run to Him, like we do to the medicine chest, at the first sign of an ache or pain. This "gigantic aspirin tablet" view of God is stifling the spiritual growth of millions of Americans. It somehow makes God exist to come to the aid of man when man calls Him, rather than show that man exists for the glory and honor of God. We are tempted to ask, "How blind can one get?"

Let's identify one more cloud of smoke that impairs man's vision of the spiritual and the eternal. We might call it the merry-go-round of production and consumption of goods that so allures modern man he can see very little else. We live in a commercially dominated civilization. The great drive seems to be to produce more and more goods and help man find more and more ways to consume them. Particularly in the large cities man has become subservient to vast commercial interests that dictate policies, use land to serve economic goals, and destroy man's sense of worth and identity. In such a culture man is little more than a number, and the only things that seem to count are what he can produce and what he can be talked into consuming. In this kind of purposeless existence it is little wonder that so many ask, "What's the use?"

It is quite difficult for a man caught in this commercial whirl to see the relevance of our Lord's commands, "Believe on the Lord Jesus Christ," "Seek ye first the kingdom of God," and "Be ye witnesses unto Me."

If this analysis of some conditions prevailing today sounds a bit alarming it is meant to be so. We are living in perilous times! While certain circumstances are favorable to the preaching and teaching of the Gospel, there are dangers today more formidable than the dangers of persecution in the first three centuries. Let us pray fervently for the Spirit to keep our hearts pure and our vision clear. The way of life is still the way of the cross and suffering. We need an increase of God's grace and power to keep our total commitment to Christ. "If any man come after Me let him take up his cross and follow Me."

Help us, Lord, to treasure Thy way, and give us the vision to see it clearly.

Builders of the Temple of Life

By H. W. Hartenberger

(The Twentieth Sunday After Trinity)

Therefore whosoever heareth these sayings of Mine and doeth them, I will liken him unto a wise man which built his house upon a rock. And the rain descended, and the floods came, and the winds blew and beat upon that house, and it fell not, for it was founded upon a rock. And everyone that heareth these sayings of Mine and doeth them not shall be likened unto a foolish man which built his house upon the sand. And the rain descended, and the floods came, and the winds blew and beat upon that house, and it fell, and great was the fall of it. And it came to pass when Jesus had ended these sayings the people were astonished at His doctrine, for He taught them as one having authority and not as the scribes. — *Matthew 7:24-29*

The Sermon on the Mount — so named by Augustine in the fourth century — of which the text forms the concluding portion, is recorded in Matthew 5—7. This beautiful and familiar sermon appears to be a summary of several talks given by Jesus during a sojourn in Galilee, rather than a set discourse delivered in a single hour or day. Whether or not this supposition is correct, we do know that in the section before us the Lord summarized His remarks in a climactic admonition which offers practical applications to the daily lives of His followers.

Though known far and wide and cited frequently, Christ's Sermon on the Mount is misunderstood and falsely interpreted by many. There are those who call it the Creed of Christianity or the Gospel of the Kingdom or the Grand Charter of the Commonwealth of Heaven. However, the main theme of this hillside address is of a practical nature, emphasizing sanctification rather than justification, by God's grace alone, through faith in the Savior. Here the Lord Jesus does not dwell upon the free salvation of all men by the atoning power of His shed blood, but expounds the true meaning of the Law and teaches how to do the will of God more fully and perfectly. Luther comments: "Christ is saying nothing in this sermon about how we become Christians, but only about the works and fruit that no one can do unless he is already a Christian and in a state of grace" (Am. ed. 21, 291). The truth of this observation becomes evident as we scan the sermon's outline and note its contents: the Beatitudes, the call to be the salt and the light of the world, the description of the righteous and the hypocrites, the pointed statements concerning our treasures, judging others, prayer, the wide and narrow way, false prophets, etc. Although this great sermon contains rich material for dozens of separate sermons, we shall limit our discussion today to a consideration of the closing verses embodied in our text.

Unquestionably Jesus was the greatest Preacher and Teacher of all time. "He taught as one having authority and not as the scribes" (v. 29). The scribes repeated and elaborated on what had been said by others before them; our Lord brought a message direct from heaven. He spoke with authority out of His own divine consciousness as the Prophet greater than Moses. His preaching and teaching was simple, direct, compelling, purposeful. His frequent use of parables and illustrations from nature and daily life made His messages relevant. This fact stands out clearly also in the manner He concluded the Sermon on the Mount as noted in our text. There He, the "carpenter's son," stresses the hearing and doing of His words by picturing the wise and the foolish builder. The spiritual lesson we would draw from the text leads us to speak of

Builders of the Temple of Life

I

Many Erect This Important Structure on Shifting Sand

At some time or other in the course of his life almost every person wants to build something. The object he has in mind may be of simple construction, easily made, of little intrinsic value; yet from building it he may derive pleasure and satisfaction. For example, who among us during the happy days of childhood did not make mud pies, or whittle out a slingshot, or construct a crude wagon, or sculpture a snowman, or erect a birdhouse, or fashion a playhouse in the side of a hill or even in the crotches of a tree, or sew doll clothes? As we grew older we launched out on greater and more difficult construction projects, and we learned by doing.

To be sure, some learned faster and accomplished greater results than others, but the urge to create, to build and construct things, is pretty general with both young and old, as the many do-it-yourself books on the market will attest.

Constructing a house to live in calls for forethought, skill, and patient effort; building a *life* that reaches into eternity obviously requires much greater foresight, careful planning, divine guidance, fervent prayer, and consecrated effort.

One of the two builders in our parable is pictured as a thoughtless, careless, and foolish man. For one thing, the location he selected for his house was unwise, namely, low land near a stream of water. Moreover, it was a sandy spot. His greatest stupidity, however, was this, that he neglected to put down a deep, wide, firm foundation. In the hilly regions of Palestine most houses are built of masonry. Little or no wood is used in the building of walls, roofs, or floors. The weight of the building often makes it necessary to dig down 10, 20, or more feet to construct a strong foundation on solid rock. The foolish man in our story paid no attention to this requirement. Evidently he was unconcerned about the solidity of the foundation and the durability of the structure. Now, as long as there were no storms and floods, the house stood and probably looked as good as any other; but when the forces of nature were unleashed, the unstable sand and the inadequate foundation were no match for the elements. The house crumbled and fell, and great was the fall of it. Everything was a total loss: time, money, effort, material. Oh, what folly!

This part of the parable serves as a suitable background to illustrate a more vital truth, to teach a far more important lesson. This lesson has to do with the building of the house of our Christianity, the temple of life.

We are all building a temple of life. Whether we realize it or not, day after day the building of our life goes on. We cannot evade, we cannot avoid, the performance of this important task. Hence our supreme concern should be what kind of life structure we are building. Are we building our temple of life wisely, namely, on a firm, solid foundation of stone?

II

May We Wisely Build on an Enduring Foundation of Stone

In contrast with the foolish man who builds on sand, the wise man digs deep and erects his house on a secure foundation that can safely withstand the winds and storms, the rain and floods. How this may be done is stated in these words of our Lord: "Whosoever heareth these sayings of Mine and doeth them, I will liken him unto a wise man which built his house upon a rock. And the rain descended, and the floods came and beat upon that house, and it fell not, for it was founded upon a rock." "These sayings of Mine" are the teachings which Jesus had just inculcated in the Sermon on the Mount, but included also was everything that He had said and revealed at other times during His public ministry. Here, then, the Lord Jesus clearly indicates that He and His revealed Word are the one and only sure foundation on which can be built a temple of life that will last for time and eternity.

Many attempt to build their lives on other foundations: on human philosophies, speculations, and opinions; on intellectual pursuits and attainments; on the accumulation of money and goods; on earthly honor and fame; particularly also on their own imagined goodness and righteousness, efforts and merits. All such misguided people build on sand. The foundation in which they put their hopes and trust is insecure; it cannot remain firm and unshaken when the storms and floods of sorrow and trouble, trials and tribulations, temptations and afflictions, and finally death, release their fury against it.

If we are wise, we shall build our house, the temple of life, on a different foundation, a firm foundation that rests on Christ, the Rock of Ages. Concerning Him the great prophet Isaiah foretold: "Thus saith the Lord God, Behold I lay in Zion for a foundation a Stone, a tried Stone, a precious Cornerstone, a sure Foundation" (28:16). The apostle Paul says, "Other foundation can no man lay than that is laid, which is Jesus Christ" (1 Cor. 3:11). The same apostle assures the believers that they "are built upon the foundation of the apostles and prophets, Jesus Christ Himself being the chief Cornerstone" (Eph. 2:20). The Lord Jesus, our willing Substitute, Savior, and Redeemer, is the true Rock and Foundation on which all our hopes rest for time and eternity. He, and He alone, is "the Way, the Truth, and the Life," and no man can come unto the Father but by Him. Hence building the temple of life is not and cannot be a "do-it-yourself" accomplishment; all our own efforts and labors cannot remove from us our sin and guilt, no matter how earnestly we try. It is written: "Neither is there salvation in any other, for there is none other name under heaven given among men whereby we must be saved" (Acts 4:12). Therefore we confidently confess:

> My hope is built on nothing less
> Than Jesus' blood and righteousness;
> I dare not trust the sweetest frame,
> But wholly lean on Jesus' name.
> On Christ, the solid Rock, I stand;
> All other ground is sinking sand.

Again, we say and sing:

> Therefore my hope is in the Lord
> And not in mine own merit;
> It rests upon His faithful Word
> To them of contrite spirit
> That He is merciful and just;
> This is my comfort and my trust.
> His help I wait with patience.

May many of our fellowmen share our joy and sing:

> Christ is our Cornerstone,
> On Him alone we build;
> With His true saints alone
> The courts of heaven are filled.
> On His great love
> Our hopes we place
> Of present grace
> And joys above.

"Whosoever heareth these sayings of Mine *and doeth them,*" says Jesus, is a wise builder. We dare not overlook this solemn reminder that hearing alone is not enough in building our temple of life. "Knowing and doing" belong together. They must be like inseparable twins, for justification without sanctification is worthless and meaningless. "Faith without works is dead," St. James reminds us. Our Savior says, "Blessed are they that hear the Word of God and keep it." The mere hearing of the Word, no matter how diligently, thoughtfully, and reverently it may take place in public or in private, does not and cannot suffice. There must also be appropriate action. To hear, to accept, to believe, to trust, God's Word is certainly important and necessary for salvation; but it is equally true that God expects and requires us who call Him "Lord" to do His will, to serve and obey Him, to live our religion, to practice His precepts and teachings in our daily lives. The Lord Jesus, speaking by the mouth of the apostle James, urges us and all Christians to be "doers of the Word and not hearers only, deceiving your own selves" (1:22). Jesus Himself "came not to be ministered unto but to minister and to give His life a ransom for many" (Mark 10:45). He, our blessed Substitute and Savior, who sacrificed His life to effect the great work of redemption, calls upon us to do the will and work of the heavenly Father, to serve Him and our fellowmen, saying: "I have given you an example that ye should do as I have done to you" (John 13:15). Again, He declared, "I must work the works of Him that sent Me while it is day; the night cometh when no man can work" (John 9:14). The work we are to do for Jesus, particularly also the proclamation of the saving Gospel, is urgent. Moreover, while we live on earth, our service to God and man, which is basic for the building of our life, is never finished. In Tulsa, Okla., there is a magnificent church tower. A woman gave $100,000 that it might be built, stipulating only one condition to her gift. "Build it," said she, "so that to all future generations it shall appear unfinished." Similarly, as we build the structure of our life, let us remember that it is a great and important task which requires much "doing" and continuous effort under the blessing of God.

Will the building of the temple of our life be successful? Will it stand the test? We know that storms of adversity, trials, and tribulations will descend upon it, that the floodwaters of sorrow and trouble will threaten to overwhelm us as we experience the storms of life. Nor can death's coming be disputed or brushed aside. Are we ready and prepared to meet this challenge? Dare we hope that our temple of life will stand? Will the foundation of faith, on which our life's structure rests, be solid and secure? Yes, it will, if it is built on Christ, the Rock of Ages; if our entire life is centered in Him and His Word, which shall never pass away. Then the substructure, being wisely and firmly built on Christ, the sure Foundation, will unfailingly support the superstructure of our life despite all earthly storms and floods. On the Arctic Ocean icebergs are seen forcing their way steadily onward even in the face of a strong gale. Seemingly afloat on the surface, they really extend far below the surface, and it is the deep undercurrent in the ocean that bears them onward. So the life that rests on Christ and His "sayings" is directed in its onward course by a mighty power that overcomes all adverse winds and tides.

God grant that you and I may join every wise builder to say gratefully, confidently, and triumphantly:

> I know my faith is founded
> On Jesus Christ, my God and Lord!
> And this my faith confessing,
> Unmoved I stand upon His Word.
> Man's reason cannot fathom
> The truth of God profound;
> Who trusts her subtle wisdom
> Relies on shifting ground.
> God's Word is all-sufficient,
> It makes divinely sure,
> And trusting in its wisdom,
> My faith shall rest secure.

The Great Physician

By HERMAN SCHERER

(The Twenty-First Sunday After Trinity)

After this there was a feast of the Jews, and Jesus went up to Jerusalem. Now, there is at Jerusalem by the sheep market a pool, which is called in the Hebrew tongue Bethesda, having five porches. In these lay a great multitude of impotent folk, of blind, halt, withered, waiting for the moving of the water. For an angel went down at a certain season into the pool and troubled the water. Whosoever then first after the troubling of the water stepped in was made whole of whatsoever disease he had. And a certain man was there, which had an infirmity thirty and eight years. When Jesus saw him lie, and knew that he had been now a long time in that case, He saith unto him, Wilt thou be made whole? The impotent man answered Him, Sir, I have no man, when the water is troubled, to put me into the pool: but while I am coming, another steppeth down before me. Jesus saith unto him, Rise, take up thy bed and walk. And immediately the man was made whole and took up his bed and walked. — *John 5:1-9a*

Palestine now, as doubtless was the case in the days of the Lord, seems fairly overrun with those afflicted by one form or another of bodily ailment. They fairly throng the entrance ways to Jerusalem and the paths to Gethsemane and the Mount of Olives, living upon the sustenance that is granted them by many of the tourists and pilgrims who become overwhelmed with pity and sympathy for these poor unfortunates. Perhaps the scene at Bethesda will become even more real to us if we think of Zola's vivid description of the gathering of the sick from all over France at the grotto of Lourdes. We are told that "a perfect court of human woe rolled along the sloping pavement. No order was observed, ailments of all kinds were jumbled together . . . twisted trunks, twisted arms, necks askew, all the distortions of poor creatures whom nature had warped and broken . . . ."

Just so the scene at Bethesda. The five porches, crowded with the sick, waiting for the healing waters. "For an angel went down at a certain season into the pool and troubled the water; whosoever then first after the troubling of the water stepped in was made whole of whatever disease he had." Picture the scene. Everywhere disease stares you in the face. The patients are overwhelmed with a deep sadness, like a dark cloud hanging over the canopy of heaven . . . utterly helpless and seemingly having no cure for their disease.

Upon just such a scene comes Jesus, returning to Jerusalem for one of the annual feasts, after having ministered in Galilee for several months. And here once again Jesus reveals Himself as

The Great Physician

The Impotent Man

Let us concern ourselves for a moment with the peculiar situation in which one of these helpless souls at the Pool of Bethesda finds himself. For 38 years he had been dragging out an impotent existence. For 38 years he had suffered some incurable malady. How long he had waited by the waters is not stated. But the duration of his sickness emphatically shows us how hopeless was his case which every effort for 38 long years had failed to relieve. He was indeed in need of the Great Physician.

The Compassionate Physician

Notice first of all that Jesus saw this poor man before the poor man saw Jesus. Until Jesus came along, he was hopeless, absolutely powerless to help himself. He had probably given up all hope and saw no help anywhere, and then like a ray of light out of the darkness comes Jesus and immediately stops in compassion to help him. Although the word "compassion" is not used in our text, yet how else would one describe the attitude of Jesus as He stops before this helpless man? "Compassion." What a word! One of the biggest words in the Bible, and yet one that is all but forgotten in these days in which we live. Luke uses this word when speaking of the father who saw the prodigal coming and had compassion on him (Luke 15:20). The word embodies the meanings of love and sympathy and pity and a determination to help. It is also said of Jesus that when He saw the multitudes He had compassion on them, for they were as sheep without a shepherd. "Compassion" means to suffer along with. It suggests that our Lord felt the distress of this man as if He Himself had been so afflicted.

We Need the Great Physician

And that is just how Jesus feels for every one of us. And we are just as much in need of the Great Physician and His compassion as was the impotent man, aren't we? I am thinking now, not of any physical disease which may be ours, but of our moral and spiritual disease — the disease of sin, if you please — which tears our souls to tatters and tosses us about on the seas of restlessness and which, unless we are cleansed and healed, will keep us out of the kingdom of glory, that place of everlasting happiness and joy.

Our Moral Disease

We have evidence of this moral disease, which pervaded the entire strata of humanity throughout the ages, from the fall of Adam down to the present day. History will substantiate and confirm this statement only too well. Even while the world was yet an infant, comparatively speaking, man died because of the wickedness that saturated the entire world of that time. The end of the wicked by means of the Flood; the destruction of Sodom and Gomorrah with brimstone and fire from heaven; the adultery and heinous murder committed by King David; the murder of the infant children in Bethlehem by that infamous and bloodthirsty tyrant Herod the Great; the almost instant deaths of Ananias and Sapphira because they lied to the Holy Ghost — these are a few of the sure testimonies for the prevalence of sin during Old and New Testament times.

All Are Diseased

Is our generation less sinless, less wicked? You will find that all are included in this sweeping statement of the Bible "All have sinned and come short of the glory of God." Think of some of the sins and their horrors that you read about in your daily newspaper: a young teen-ager telling a policeman, "Sure, I tried to kill my mother? Why not? I wanted her to die." Think of the horror of a mother tying her little child to a bedpost and beating him to death. Think of the graft and bribery that is so frequently found in governmental circles. Our country leads the whole civilized world in crime. Our homes are being broken faster than ever before, many states permitting easy divorces. Indecencies among our people have increased 100 percent. People are getting drunk, not only on intoxicating beverages but also on pleasure and amusement and business.

Even many church people are not taking their religion seriously, but are just playing at being Christians. In fact someone has said, "There are so many church members today that you can hardly tell who are the Christians." Why, if all our sins were heaped together, they would build a purple mountain that would cast a shadow the length and breadth of our land. Are you and I innocent? Are we living righteous lives? Friend, look into your heart. Dwight L. Moody used to say that if we had to go about with a glass window over our hearts, we would all want that window to be stained glass, for our hearts are rotten to the core. Remember, "out of the heart proceed evil thoughts, murders, adulteries, fornications, thefts, false witness, blasphemy." Do you mean to tell me, pastor, that I am such an evil person? No, I don't mean to tell you at all. The searchlight of God's Word as it plays upon your thoughts and words and deeds will tell you this.

Where is healing for our sins? In the blood of Jesus Christ! When they crucified Him on Calvary they nailed His hands to a cross so that He died with arms outstretched in the very position of compassionate invitation, as if to say, "Sinner, come into My arms, and be safe forevermore."

Healing by Grace

When Jesus came upon this man at the Pool of Bethesda, Jesus approached him with the question, "Wilt thou be made whole?" And what was his answer? "Sir, I have no man when the water is troubled to put me into the pool, but while I am waiting another steppeth down before me." Jesus saith unto him, "Rise, take up thy bed, and walk." Notice here that Jesus did not touch the man; He used no other means than His life-giving word to confer the cure. One word from Jesus was powerful enough.

Jesus did it all and left nothing at all for this poor man to do himself. It was done for him, and there is not even a hint that he had anything whatsoever to do with his miraculous cure. He was not required to move a finger but merely to accept the help.

Salvation by Grace

In like manner our spiritual healing is all the Lord's doing. We have nothing at all to do with it. Our salvation is of the Lord, a salvation that was purchased at the cost of His own sacrificial death. The Bible tells us plainly, "For by grace are ye saved through faith, and that not of yourselves. It is the gift of God, not of works, lest any man should boast" (Eph. 2:8). Again: "Not by works of righteousness which we have done, but according to His mercy He saved us by the washing of regeneration and renewing of the Holy Ghost." (Titus 3:5)

God's Way vs. Man's Way

The moment any work of man is added to grace it is no more grace. God will not share the honor of salvation with any other, for salvation is of the Lord alone. Yet natural man wants to do something himself. That is why the gospel of Satan is so popular in the world. It appeals to a man's proud heart. If you do not know what the gospel of Satan is, let me tell you. Here it is. He says to man: "You are not so bad. You have within you certain good qualities which you only need to develop and cultivate. Why, there is a spark of the divine within you. If you do your very best to live a decent life you will get to heaven in the end. You do not need to come as a vile and hell-deserving sinner. God will recognize your sincerity and effort." That is the smooth-sounding gospel of Satan. That isn't what God says in His holy Word! God says: "There is none that doeth good, no, not one." "By the deeds of the Law shall no flesh be justified in My sight." "All have sinned and come short of the glory of God."

Although this is the consistent and unbroken testimony of Scripture, man is loath to accept it, for it denounces all man's own goodness and makes him a spiritual pauper before God. Man is too proud to admit that his estate is as bad as that. And so he continues on the way to perdition by trying to do his best, not knowing that his best is not good enough. It is a terrible blow to man's pride to tell him that he is so corrupt that without a miracle of grace he cannot be saved. Yet the Bible is clear on that point, and the old hymns of faith, based on the plain teachings of the Bible, all incorporate this idea. Listen:

> Just as I am without one plea,
> But that Thy blood was shed for me,
> And that Thou bidd'st me come to Thee,
> O Lamb of God, I come, I come.

Or this old favorite by Augustus Toplady:

> Rock of Ages, cleft for me,
> Let me hide myself in Thee;
> Let the water and the blood
> From Thy riven side which flowed,
> Be of sin the double cure,
> Cleanse me from its guilt and power.
>
> Not the labors of my hands
> Could fulfill Thy Law's demands;
> Could my zeal no respite know,
> Could my tears forever flow,
> All for sin could not atone;
> Thou must save, and Thou alone.

This is not popular theology any more these days, but it is still the only way of salvation.

Salvation by Grace Alone

Is this salvation yours? Are you sure of your spiritual healing through Christ, the Great Physician? Or do you still think that you must do something? I know that great churches have damned this blessed doctrine that we are saved by grace, and by grace alone. I know that human minds protest and deny and ridicule such a teaching. But as we approach the cross of our Savior we hear Him speak these wonderful words: "Verily, I say unto Thee, Today shalt thou be with Me in Paradise." To whom does He give this promise? A stainless life? A man whose life was holy and righteous and good? You know better. The dying Savior promised Paradise, heaven, salvation, spiritual healing, to a criminal. And this criminal died a few hours later without the opportunity of performing one good work. He was the penitent thief, saved by his faith in the pure grace of Christ. Crucified in the morning and glorified in the evening. At high noon a condemned sinner and at sunset a redeemed saint. So free, so sure, so unconditional, is the grace which God offers you through His Son.

Many years ago a wicked man lay dying of tuberculosis in a little frame hotel in a West Texas town. He had lived a terribly sinful life, yet in his dying hours he had turned to Jesus Christ by repentance and personal faith. One morning when an attendant delivered breakfast to the man's room he was found cold in death. However, just before he died that night he had written on a rough shoebox, in almost illegible hand, the words of an old Gospel hymn:

> I've tried in vain a thousand ways
> My fears to quell, my hopes to raise,
> But all I need, the Bible says, is Jesus.
> He lives, He reigns, He dies, He pleads,
> There's love in all His words and deeds.
> And all, yes, all, the guilty sinner needs,
> Is Jesus.

And every one of you needs Jesus. Let us know assuredly that Christ is the Great Physician, who alone can heal the sin-sick soul. A person who tries anything else except Christ and His remedy is simply taking patent medicine which is bound to fail. Oh, let Jesus, the Great Physician, heal your heart, cleanse your soul, and give you peace within! He will do it if by repentance and faith you turn to Him.

Giving Thanks for Your Salvation

After the poor impotent man at the Pool of Bethesda had received power from Christ to take up his bed and walk, John informs us, he was later found in the temple, undoubtedly giving thanks to God for his deliverance and then testifying to the Jews that it was Jesus who had healed him from his dreadful disease. Does this suggest something to you? Do you thank God for the manifold blessings He has poured out upon you? Do you thank Him especially for the redemption which is yours in Christ Jesus? Do you show your thanks by meeting Him in His Word, on the living pages of the Bible, as your eyes feast upon the printed Gospel? Do you show your thanks for your salvation by coming regularly to God's house to feed in His heavenly pastures and to worship Him with thanksgiving in your hearts? Do you thank Him by testifying to others what Jesus has done for you? You have been healed of your spiritual disease by the precious blood of Jesus. You know that Jesus alone can save. You know that your fellowmen are lost without Him. What are you doing about it? This poor impotent man made this sad confession to Jesus: "I have no man, when the water is troubled, to put me into the pool." Do you know of someone who has no man to tell him about the Savior? Of course, you do. But do you realize fully that God wants you to be that man? And then think of the perishing heathen who have never heard the Gospel of Christ for the salvation of their souls? What are you doing about that? Are you one of those professing Christians on the way to heaven utterly unconcerned about these sinners on their way to hell? Will you pray for your missionaries as they seek to reach souls with the saving Gospel? Will you bring your gifts to the Lord in increasing amounts so that He can have much more with which to send out more laborers to bring in the harvest? Do you want to be used by the Lord in this way? Oh, may God's Holy Spirit help you to bring Jesus, the Great Physician, to others and to bring others to Jesus, the Great Physician!

God's Chain Reaction of Love

By RICHARD R. CAEMMERER

(The Twenty-Second Sunday After Trinity)

And when He went forth to land, there met Him out of the city a certain man which had devils long time, and ware no clothes, neither abode in any house but in the tombs. When he saw Jesus, he cried out and fell down before Him, and with a loud voice said, What have I to do with Thee, Jesus, Thou Son of God Most High? I beseech Thee, torment me not. (For He had commanded the unclean spirit to come out of the man. For oftentimes it had caught him; and he was kept bound with chains and in fetters; and he brake the bands, and was driven of the devil into the wilderness.) And Jesus asked him, saying, What is thy name? And he said, Legion, because many devils were entered into him. And they besought Him that He would not command them to go out into the deep. And there was there an herd of many swine feeding on the mountain; and they besought Him that He would suffer them to enter into them. And He suffered them. Then went the devils out of the man and entered into the swine; and the herd ran violently down a steep place into the lake and were choked. When they that fed them saw what was done, they fled and went and told it in the city and in the country. Then they went out to see what was done; and came to Jesus and found the man out of whom the devils were departed, sitting at the feet of Jesus, clothed and in his right mind; and they were afraid. They also which saw it told them by what means he that was possessed of the devils was healed.

Then the whole multitude of the country of the Gadarenes round about besought Him to depart from them; for they were taken with great fear; and He went up into the ship and returned back again. Now the man out of whom the devils were departed besought Him that he might be with Him; but Jesus sent him away, saying, Return to thine own house, and show how great things God hath done unto thee. And he went his way and published throughout the whole city how great things Jesus had done unto him. — *Luke 8:27-39*

This story is really spectacular. A thousand devils infest a man and tear him to pieces. They are thrown out into a herd of swine which now jump into the sea. But let's not stop with these dramatics! Behind them is the story of a human being, a shameful and beaten one indeed, but still a human being. That is the story of how God in His Son loved that battered man. But the story isn't over. The man now becomes the agent for keeping that great act of God's love rolling on toward other people. There is the real drama of this story: God's love works like a chain reaction. As modern as the sound of that title is in this atomic age, so immediate and needful is this chain reaction of God's love in our own lives.

Count Yourself In

There's little sense to talking about this story unless we count ourselves in. Whenever Christians hear one of these great stories of Jesus' miracles, it's important that they find the part that they want to play. What part do we choose? Not the pigs, obviously. Not the people who went about complaining that they had lost their pigs. That leaves us two other choices. Would we like to play the role of Jesus? Certainly; He is the great Example of our lives. But in this story Jesus is doing good to a man, and is helping the man to do good to others. There's the part for us to play: the man whom Jesus helped, and to whom He now says, "Show how great things God hath done unto thee."

We probably shrink from playing this role because it looks like such a mean part. "He wore no clothes, neither lived in any house, but in the tombs." He was an outcast. We who can come to church this morning in our Sunday best don't think of ourselves at that level.

Furthermore, this man in the country of the Gadarenes was beset by devils. Today's listener to this story is apt to discount it and think that "the devils" is simply a sort of Biblical shorthand to describe all sorts of trouble. That makes sense, of course, for we have our troubles. We get old and full of aches and pains. We lose our money and our jobs. We get over the old sicknesses and become victims of new ones. We pay our taxes for complicated weapons of defense and worry that some madman may push the button that hurls death at us. Oh, yes, we have our devils too.

The other extreme, as we hear this story, is to say: "The devils rose up against Jesus in His time. But we don't seem to have them any more. So our trouble can't be as bad as this man's. I can't find myself in this story." Well, don't be too sure. Whatever these forces and powers were that infested the human race in Jesus' time, thoughtful people are quite sure that they have had their counterpart in our own age. A whole nation falls from its upright and cultured civilization into cruelty and gangsterism. "It's demonic," we say. This story tells of opponents of God and His Christ whom only Christ could master; beings which are under the direct control of the devil, the adversary of God. Do we face such opponents? Are we torn by them? Are we ready to admit that life, despite all its helps of health and education, government and security, brings forces to rip and tear us, forces too big for us?

Perhaps we aren't ready to say this at all. Perhaps we are quite satisfied with life. But then let's face it that the man among the tombs was a bit ahead of us. He was at the point when he knew his help was in a higher hand. If we belong to the worshipers of "the optional god" as Bishop Bayne calls him, the god whom you bring in when you need him and most of the time get along without, then we can expect very shortly that God will help us discover the emptiness of our power. He charges me to be the spokesman of His Word at this moment to repeat to our own age the sober word of Christ: "Except ye repent, ye shall all likewise perish."

God Does Great Things to You

We ponder our handicap and shortcoming only because God starts a chain reaction in us. Sooner or later we have to admit to ourselves and to other people that we are needy folk indeed. Saint Paul had to cry it out even when he was a great believer: "Who shall deliver me from the body of this death?" We go on serenely for a year or two, and then the roof falls in — misfortune, inconstancy, irresponsibility, weakness and shame, hopelessness. And then we are in splendid shape for God to make a difference.

The difference is that God loves. Already in the Introit this morning we heard the song, "If Thou, Lord, shouldest mark iniquities, O Lord, who shall stand? But there is forgiveness with Thee, that Thou mayest be feared" (Ps. 130: 4, 5). That's a good word for God's love: forgiveness. For it means that God comes to people who don't deserve it. We need His love because we are weak. But we have no claim on it because we have strayed so badly from Him and the purposes for which He made us. And yet God loves. "When we were yet sinners, Christ died for the ungodly." Christ has come to help. And His great work is finished. Do you remember how He said so on the cross?

In the story before us Christ helped too. The help seemed to cause more harm than good. Men lost their precious pigs. Today Christ comes to help with a Gospel, the word that God forgives sins because of Christ's cross. Men grumble and scream with objection. It takes away their precious self-respect. It conflicts with their standards of knowledge. They shriek: "Don't make us believe a thing like that!"

There was one big answer to the screamers in our story. "They found the man out of whom the devils were departed, sitting at the feet of Jesus, clothed and in his right mind; and they were afraid."

But we who have heard the story of Jesus' death and resurrection and have been given a share in them by Holy Baptism, and have been brought into the company of Christ's people, we are they who have found that "perfect love casts out fear."

True, the change in us isn't as spectacular — at least always — as the Gadarene's. We start out clothed. We haven't necessarily made fools of ourselves. The church is often pleased if it can point at reclaimed criminals or alcoholics as a sign of its power. That seems to leave many of us practicing Christians out. Yet, down under the surface, we are living our lives of attack from the devils too. Perhaps the public doesn't see the change, but people close to us do. This is what is after: that His great act of love to us in Jesus Christ, redeeming us from sin and death and putting us into the company of His people, becomes the next step in the chain reaction of love.

Get Busy Where You Are

When the Gadarene was healed, he wanted to follow Jesus. He wanted to very badly. He begged Jesus to let him go with Him.

We, too, discover that when God's love has taken hold of us, we want to do something for Jesus. And the bigger the help that we received and the more clearly we recognize how much we needed it, the more anxious we are to follow Jesus. Do you remember how Jesus analyzed the woman who had anointed His feet and dried them with her hair? "She loved much because she was forgiven much." That's the way it works. And actually — all of us have been forgiven a great deal.

This desire to love Jesus and to go with Him takes many forms. Some people want to enlist for full-time service in the church and become pastors or teachers, missionaries or deaconesses. That's a following that shows, and one that is very useful indeed. We professionals have to remind ourselves that we, too, need the forgiveness and the help every day anew and that our professional task must truly show that we have been helped.

In the story before us, however, Jesus was strangely unresponsive to the Gadarene's plea. "Jesus sent him away, saying, 'Return to thine own house, and show how great things God hath done unto thee.'" The story says that he told his whole town what had happened to him. The story spread like wildfire. When Jesus went back over the lake to the other side, He found that the news had gotten there. "The people gladly received Him, for they were all waiting for Him." That's how the chain reaction worked. Jesus loved a stricken man. The healed man showed others what had happened. And others were thus readied for the new word of God's love in Jesus.

Hence, whether we have some spectacular job for Christ, as we do this morning in worship, or in full-time service to the church, or in the many fields of help to the congregation, or whatever it may be, here is the first place where the chain reaction should set in: back home, in our family, among the people with whom we work, the people who "knew us when." One of the simplest tests of the Christian faith and witness is whether we are ready to talk about Jesus Christ to the people close to us in our own families. Many Christians do a better job toward strangers than toward their own dear ones. But the stranger doesn't know the great things God has done for us. He hasn't seen the change from surliness to kindliness; from selfishness to helpfulness; from apathy toward God to reverence for God. But the people who are near to us know the devils that bothered us once, and they will be mightily helped as they see what God can do to restore His own life and Spirit to the heart.

Many years ago several scientists huddled over a crude apparatus under an old stadium at the University of Chicago. They were about to test the first atomic reactor. They were quite sure that it would work. One thing perturbed them terribly: could they make it stop?

Well, here is one chain reaction that we don't have to worry about. We worry about this one if it does *stop*. Don't let it stop! Oh, how you have been loved by God! How wonderful that you know God to be your Father through Jesus Christ! What gifts of faith, of good words, of good actions, God has poured into you! Keep that chain reaction going! Men need God's love so badly. You and I are the people through whom it must reach them.

This Christ of Yours, Who Is He?

By CLEMONCE SABOURIN

(The Twenty-Third Sunday After Trinity)

After these things Jesus walked in Galilee; for He would not walk in Jewry, because the Jews sought to kill Him. Now the Jews' Feast of Tabernacles was at hand. His brethren therefore said unto Him, Depart hence and go into Judea, that Thy disciples also may see the works that Thou doest. For there is no man that doeth anything in secret, and he himself seeketh to be known openly. If Thou do these things, show Thyself to the world. For neither did His brethren believe in Him. Then Jesus said unto them, My time is not yet come, but your time is alway ready. The world cannot hate you; but Me it hateth, because I testify of it that the works thereof are evil. Go ye up unto this feast; I go not up yet unto this feast; for My time is not yet full come. When He had said these words unto them, He abode still in Galilee. But when His brethren were gone up, then went He also up unto the feast, not openly, but as it were in secret. Then the Jews sought Him at the feast and said, Where is He? And there was much murmuring among the people concerning Him; for some said, He is a good man; others said, Nay, but He deceived the people. Howbeit no man spoke openly of Him for fear of the Jews. — *John 7:1-13*

Only a few minutes ago, with Christians the world over, we confessed our faith in the Lord Jesus Christ, saying in the words of the Apostles' Creed, "And (I believe) in Jesus Christ, His only Son, our Lord, who was conceived by the Holy Ghost, born of the Virgin Mary; suffered under Pontius Pilate, was crucified, dead, and buried; He descended into hell; the third day He rose again from the dead; He ascended into heaven and sitteth on the right hand of God the Father Almighty; from thence He shall come to judge the quick and the dead."

In answer to the question, "What does this mean?" we respond with Lutherans the world over, "I believe that Jesus Christ, true God, begotten of the Father from eternity, and also true man, born of the Virgin Mary, is my Lord, who has redeemed me, a lost and condemned creature, purchased and won me from all sins, from death, and from the power of the devil; not with gold or silver, but with His holy, precious blood and with His innocent suffering and death, that I may be His own and live under Him in His kingdom, and serve Him in everlasting righteousness, innocence, and blessedness, even as He is risen from the dead, lives and reigns to all eternity. This is most certainly true."

This we believe and confess, and when someone, looking on from the outside, expresses doubt about the sincerity of our faith, we immediately become resentful. And yet, when in the depths of our own hearts we examine our faith in the light of our own thoughts and motives, words and actions, we may discover to our dismay that we have no reason to be offended when someone asks, Now really,

This Christ of Yours, Who Is He?

I

A King of Earthly Plenty?

His Brethren Did Not Believe in Him

Our text says, "And after these things Jesus walked in Galilee; for He would not walk in Jewry, because the Jews sought to kill Him. Now the Jews' Feast of Tabernacles was at hand. His brethren therefore said unto Him, Depart hence and go into Judea, that Thy disciples also may see the works that Thou doest. For there is no man that doeth anything in secret, and he himself seeketh to be known openly. If Thou do these things, show Thyself to the world." And then the holy writer adds significantly, "For neither did His brethren believe in Him."

Whether these brethren of Jesus were younger sons of Mary and Joseph, sons of Joseph by a former marriage, or cousins of Jesus through Cleophas, the brother of Joseph, is at this point immaterial. The point is that they did not really believe in Jesus, that is, they did not believe in Him as the Christ of God, the Redeemer of the world, and their personal Savior.

Perhaps a Man of Promise

It is evident from our text that these men had witnessed some of the great miracles which Jesus performed. It is possible that they had seen Him feed five thousand persons with five barley loaves and two small fish. The multitude was impressed by this, so greatly impressed that they wanted to take Jesus by force and make Him king, a bread-and-fish king, a king who could fill their stomachs and let them live a life of ease. Disappointed, He went off into a mountain, Himself alone.

Seemingly His brethren thought: True, He did reject a kingship. But was this rejection final? Would He accept a draft at a more favorable time? But even if He persistently refused to become a king, surely, with His unusual powers, He could become a great and influential figure, and if we have a hand in it, it would be all to our good.

Let's Promote Him

So these men went to Jesus with the suggestion that He attend the Feast of Tabernacles at Jerusalem. They said in substance: "You will never get anywhere here in the sticks. To gain acceptance you will have to do your great works where people can see you. If you are too timid to push yourself forward, you'd better let us promote you. . . . Now, there is no question about the place. It must be Jerusalem. As to the time, when is the crowd the greatest? . . . At the Feast of Tabernacles! . . . Near the holy city, at the confluence of pilgrims streaming in from all over the country, you can begin talking to the people and doing your wonderful works. Many of them have already heard of you. They will be expecting you! And by the time this growing river of humanity reaches the gates of Jerusalem, the stage will be set for a triumphal entry. In the face of the popular demand the opposition you have been experiencing at Jerusalem will wither like a vine that is cut at the roots. . . ." No doubt they added under their breath, "and we will be sitting pretty."

Jesus Declines

Jesus said to them: "My time is not yet come: but your time is always ready. The world cannot hate you; but Me it hateth, because I testify of it that the works thereof are evil." . . . It may be time to promote your materialistic ambitions, but it is not the time to complete the work which I came to do. The world will not hate you for your ambitious plans, because they are too much in line with the thinking of the world. . . . You see, His kingdom is not of this world. In due time He would enter the holy city, but riding on a beast of burden; for His purpose was not to enter earthly capitals with dazzling splendor, but to enter human hearts with love and forgiveness. His path to glory would be over the Way of Sorrows. The step to His throne, a cross!

Still Brothers Who Do Not Believe

Today, too, there are brothers who do not believe. We find them often among those who were baptized in infancy, confirmed in childhood, married in church, and retained on the membership rolls. They are "quotation-marks" Christians, people who are Christian only in culture and background. They are people who, finding themselves in a Christian area, take up Christianity as a worthwhile cause, a popular movement. You find them in "class" churches, where their membership enables them to rub elbows with the "ins." They are people who survey Christian physical assets — churches, schools, hospitals — and muse to themselves, "There must be gold in these imposing hills."

They are people who join church because they feel that it will enhance their business or professional reputation. Men who are ready to play ball with Christ if He will play ball with them. Men who want to deal with Christ on a this-for-that basis, pledging that they will do this for Christ if He does that for them.

At times such people bring into the church a great deal of know-how and enthusiasm: Let's get the show on the road . . . and it's got to be good! We've got to promote this thing. Organize, deputize, supervise. Budgets, pledges, goals. Keymen, pacesetters, reasonable expectations. Breakfast, luncheon, supper. Drive, drive, drive! Over the top! Victory dinner! Christ in concrete! . . . (And now, socially and businesswise, we who put this thing over ought to be sitting pretty.)

God forbid that we should disparage the efforts of our very active members or cast suspicion on those who honestly seek to do God's business in a businesslike way. But let us beware of false motives lest the Christ we serve is not the Christ of God. Glittering temples of glass and concrete are not necessarily the church of Christ. Frantic rounds of activity are not necessarily Christian service. *Things* do not constitute the kingdom of God. Christian service does not necessarily bring temporal prosperity. If the goal of our religious activity is material gain, if we serve a Christ who is a king of earthly plenty, we are serving a creature of our own imagination. For the Christ of God, who in this world had not where to lay His head, *may* bless us through riches, but He may also bless us through poverty. He *may* bless us through robust health, but He may also bless us through chronic illness. He *may* bless us through the esteem of men, but He may also bless us most when by men we are most despised. The truly Christian heart is the one that says, whatever the circumstances might be, O Jesus Christ, through whom alone we have forgiveness of sins and sonship with the Father, Thy will be done; and let my will conform to Thy will!

II

A Good Man?

The Anticipating Crowd

Our text says: "But when His brethren were gone up, then went He also up to the feast, not openly, but as it were in secret.

Then the Jews sought Him at the feast, and said, Where is He? And there was much murmuring among the people concerning Him; for some said, He is a good man."

In one respect at least the brethren were right. The people at the feast were expecting to see Jesus. He was the talk of the town. There was much speculation concerning Him. And, as usual, there were diverse opinions. Some believed Him to be a good *man*.

A Reasonable Opinion

Surely it is not difficult to understand why some people thought Jesus to be a good man. This is a reasonable opinion. He went about doing good. He healed the sick. He gave sight to the blind. He fed the hungry. He gave strength to the weak. He comforted the distressed. Never a man spake like this man. He knew how to meet His fellowmen at their point of need. In their opinion, one had to be willfully blind not to agree that this Christ was a *good* man.

Old Yet Ever New

This opinion held by some of the people at Jerusalem has been shared by men of recent generations. For instance, Ralph Waldo Emerson once said, "Jesus is the most perfect man of all men that have yet appeared." A good man.

Today, too, there are men who declare that Jesus was the greatest man who ever lived, a teacher without equal, a man so far in advance of his time that almost two thousand years later the word has not yet caught up with him. Look at his influence on art, music, literature. Look at his ideals of political life, his insistence on loyalty to the government, his cleavage between church and state. Look at his influence on education, on family life, on the struggle for human brotherhood. Surely this Christ was the greatest man who ever lived!

We Resent This

When men speak of Christ in terms like these, our hearts burn within us. We want to shout in reply, "Our Christ is the Incarnation of God, the Only-begotten of the Father. Our Christ is not only true man, but also true God. He is omnipotent, omniscient, omnipresent, sinless, eternal. He is our Savior, our Redeemer, our God!"

And Fall into the Same Trap

Yes, we confess the right faith, but let us examine our actions. Jesus says: "Thou shalt worship the Lord, thy God, and Him only shalt thou serve" (Matt. 4:10). Do we worship the Lord, our God, in private devotions and in public service? Do we do it regularly, or do we worship only when it is convenient to do so and time is hanging heavy on our hands? Do we *worship,* or do we "recite" our prayers and yawn our way through the Sunday morning service?

Jesus says: "Ye shall be witnesses of Me" (Acts 1:8). Do we seek opportunities to tell others of Jesus? Do we by word and deed declare whose we are and what God we serve? Or do we play or study or work with people from day to day without ever thinking of telling them what Jesus means to us?

Jesus says: "Go ye into all the world and preach the Gospel to every creature" (Mark 16:15). Do we really make it our business to see to it that the Gospel is preached to people far and near, or do we give for missions only after most of our wants have been supplied?

Listen, what do we do when Jesus speaks? If we hear His Word and take it lightly, then, although we confess the Christ of God with our lips, our real Christ is only a good man whose advice and suggestions we may take or leave according to our good pleasure. For if your Christ is the Christ of God, you have no choice but to listen while He is speaking and to strive with all your God-given strength to follow His every directive. "Blessed are they that hear the Word of God *and keep it.*" (Luke 11:28)

III

A Deceiver?

Some Believed This

Our text informs us that while some of the people said that Jesus was a good man, others said, "Nay; but He deceiveth the people." Jesus told His brethren: "The world hateth Me, because I testify of it that the works thereof are evil." This is the way Jesus spoke to some of them: "Woe unto you, scribes and Pharisees, hypocrites! for ye pay tithe of mint and anise and cummin, and have omitted the weightier matters of the Law, judgment, mercy, and faith. . . . Ye blind guides, which strain at a gnat and swallow a camel. . . . Ye make clean the outside of the platter, but within they are full of extortion and excess. . . . Ye are like unto whited sepulchers, which indeed appear beautiful outward, but are within full of dead men's bones." (Matt. 23)

You might well imagine what people like these thought of Jesus. It was to their interest to do everything in their power to convince the people that just the opposite was true. They were not the deceivers. . . . Jesus was! . . . Evidently they had a certain amount of success, for we find some of the people saying, "This Christ is a deceiver."

Some Act as Though They Believed It Today

Surely we detest the opinion expressed by these people. Jesus a deceiver? Did He not hurl the challenge into the face of the world: "Who of you convicteth Me of sin?" (John 8:46). To this day this challenge goes unanswered.

We know that we are saved by faith, and by faith alone. Yet the inevitable outflow of saving faith is a sanctified striving to do what God would have us do. Jesus said: "Herein is My Father glorified, that *ye bear much fruit;* so shall ye be My disciples" (John 15:8). Do we bear much fruit?

Let us take stock of ourselves: Jesus tells us that He would have all men to be saved and come to the knowledge of the truth. All men! Every creature! And this through the words and deeds of those who believe in Him. (Titus 2:11; 1 Tim. 2:4; Mark 15:16; Matt. 5:16; John 17:20)

Do we seek to bring all men to Jesus through our words and works? Of course, we say, but wait! Do you reach out to the humble and lowly and seek to bring them into your church, or do you seek your own kind and class? Do you reach out to people of another race and seek to bring them into your congregation? Or do you say that Jesus simply could not have meant that?

Jesus says: "A new commandment I give unto you, That ye love one another; as I have loved you, that ye also love one another. By this shall all men know that ye are My disciples, if ye have love one to another" (John 13:34, 35). Do we love one another? Do we show this love so that "all men may know"? Do we love and show our love for all His disciples — the rich and the poor, the learned and the unlearned? Or do we say that Jesus simply cannot expect that of us?

Jesus says: "Love your enemies, bless them that curse you, do good to them that hate you, and pray for them which despitefully use you and persecute you" (Matt. 5:44). Do we love our enemies? Do we even *try* to love them, praying all the while for the heart and mind of Christ? Do we strive to love the godless communists? Hateful Negroes (white people, Indians, Mexicans)? Or do we say that Jesus simply could not have meant that?

Jesus says: "Render unto Caesar the things that are Caesar's" (Matt. 22:15-22, the Gospel for today). The Christian ought to be a good citizen. Do we, acting within our democratic framework, seek to pass and uphold just laws and see to it that these laws apply equally to all — rich and poor, high and low, white and black? Do we, by using the legitimate techniques of democracy, seek to have unjust laws repealed and unjust customs changed? Or do we sit on our hands, plead for patience (as long as we are not the ones suffering from the injustice), and help spread the evil rumor that such groups as the sit-in demonstrators and freedom riders are either communists or communist inspired? (Or use other current example.)

The point is this: If we ignore the instructions Jesus has given and the example He has set, we are acting as though He were a liar and deceiver whose word could not be trusted. And if this is the manner in which we live, although we confess the Christ of God with our lips, our real Christ, the fictitious creature we are serving, is a liar and deceiver.

Repent Ye!

The events of our text took place about six months before the Lord Jesus Christ suffered and died for our sins and for the sins of the world. Even this late in the day, His brethren did not believe in Him. Later, however, we find these men among the faithful, helping to lead others to Christ.

Likewise may God grant *us* grace to reject forever the false Christ of our day — the Christ of Earthly Plenty, the Good Man, the Deceiver — and open our hearts completely to the Christ of God. For as many as receive Him, to them He gives power to become the sons of God, even to them that believe in His name (John 1:12). Then truly are we citizens of heaven and can look forward with confident hope to the coming of our Lord Jesus Christ, who shall change our vile bodies so that they will be like unto His glorious body. Then shall we be forever with the Lord. (Phil. 3:17-21, the Epistle for the day)

God's Assurance of Eternal Life

By PHILIP FRY

(The Twenty-Fourth Sunday After Trinity)

And it was at Jerusalem the Feast of the Dedication, and it was winter. And Jesus walked in the temple in Solomon's porch. Then came the Jews round about Him and said unto Him, How long dost Thou make us to doubt? If Thou be the Christ, tell us plainly. Jesus answered them, I told you, and ye believed not. The works that I do in My Father's name, they bear witness of Me. But ye believe not because ye are not of My sheep, as I said unto you. My sheep hear My voice, and I know them, and they follow Me. And I give unto them eternal life, and they shall never perish, neither shall any man pluck them out of My hand. My Father, which gave them Me, is greater than all, and no man is able to pluck them out of My Father's hand. I and My Father are one.

John 10:22-30

A young father had just bought $10,000 worth of life insurance. The agent had left the home. The husband told his wife, "It gives you a comfortable feeling." Their little boy heard the remark and asked wistfully, "Does life insurance mean you're not gonna die?" This set the father and mother thinking. They thought, studied, and searched the Scriptures until they found God's eternal life insurance, as the Savior Himself sets it forth in our text:

God's Assurance of Eternal Life

I

To Whom Given

The Lord Jesus came from Perea, east of the Jordan, to Jerusalem for the Feast of the Dedication, instituted by Judas Maccabaeus 165 B. C., in commemoration of the cleansing of the temple after its desecration through the sacrifices of the Gentiles. Because of the brilliant illuminations in the temple and in the homes it was also called the Festival of Lights. It began with Dec. 25 and continued for eight days, hence was celebrated in winter, a time of rain, when one could not stand without (Ezra 10:13). This explains why the Savior seeks out the portico on the east side of the temple court. This portico faced the valley of the Kidron and was a remnant of the old temple of Solomon, destroyed by Nebuchadnezzar 588 B. C.

Not to Those Who Are Not His Sheep

As soon as the people see Jesus in this archway they surround Him and demand that He remove their uncertainty regarding His person. The evangelist refers to them as the Jews, and the Savior's answer clearly indicates that they were His usual enemies, the scribes and Pharisees, the chief priests and the elders, who hounded Him at every possible opportunity. They pretend to be seriously concerned about His possible Messiaship. And they demand a clear-cut, straightforward answer: "If Thou be the Christ, tell us plainly" (v. 24). How foolish to play the hypocrite with Him who is the all-knowing God, who searches the very hearts of men and knows their every thought, even in advance! Obviouly their minds had been made up long ago that He was not the Messiah but an impostor worthy of death as a blasphemer. But they may have hoped to evoke a forthright self-incriminating statement from Him.

Some of them may also have used this opportunity to try to justify their unbelief and to "pass the buck" to Jesus by asking: "How long dost Thou make us to doubt?" (v. 24). This is the age-old habit of sinful man ever since Adam tried to blame Eve and God Himself for giving him "this woman."

Jesus, who in no uncertain terms had time and again testified of Himself as the Messiah, now tells them that their uncertainty or ignorance concerning Himself is certainly not His fault but their own. "I told you, and ye believed not" (v. 25). He had frequently told them who He was. He had also performed His miracles before their very eyes, and these miracles had proved that He was the Son of God. But they believed neither His words nor His works. "But ye believe not because ye are not of My sheep, as I said unto you" (v. 26). He had also previously informed them (most recently at the Feast of Tabernacles in the month of October, when He had given a description of His true sheep and had thus indirectly indicated that they did not belong in this category; therefore they did not believe but were groping in the blindness of Pharisaism).

The world is full of such people to this day. They reject Jesus and His Gospel because it is not to their liking. They neglect their souls and make all kinds of useless excuses, even trying to blame others. "I had too much religion when I was young." . . . "My husband (or my wife) doesn't believe in church. So to keep peace in the family I do not go either." . . . "There are too many hypocrites in the church." . . . "The church is too old-fashioned and out of date, too narrow-minded, too unfriendly," etc. But it is still the same old folly of blaming others for one's unbelief. The Savior's verdict "But ye believe not because ye are not of My sheep" still stands. And this can mean only one thing: Lost and condemned, you can expect nothing but everlasting death and eternal separation.

But to His Sheep

But to those who do belong to His fold, to those who do believe in Him, to those who are His sheep, He gives eternal life. "My sheep hear My voice, and I know them, and they follow Me. And I give unto them eternal life, and they shall never perish" (vv. 27, 28). This comforting and reassuring promise has refreshed many a weary Christian during his everyday struggle with the forces of evil and reassured many a dying saint as he passed through the valley of death.

"My sheep hear My voice." . . . They not only hear the Gospel message but also accept it. They believe in the Lord Jesus Christ, their Good Shepherd, as Savior and Redeemer. He even calls them by name, through the Gospel, proclaimed by His chosen shepherds here on earth. "He that heareth you, heareth Me" (Luke 10:16). And His sheep know His voice because He has clearly revealed Himself both by word and by deed.

"And they follow Me." They are not misled by hirelings; they will not follow a stranger (John 10:3-5). His sheep follow Him, their Good Shepherd, as He makes them lie down in green pastures and leads them beside the still waters. He feeds them with the bread of life and manna from heaven. He gives them to drink of the water of life. Thus He nourishes and sustains their faith. He protects them with His rod and equips them with His Word as an armor against all the assaults of evil. He guides and directs them with His staff. His Word is a lamp for their feet and a light upon their path. He anoints them with the oil of gladness by the wonderful workings of the Holy Spirit. And He fills their cup to overflowing with spiritual blessings of every possible description.

"And I give unto them eternal life" even here and now. All this because He is the Good Shepherd, who has laid down His life for the sheep. He has come into the world to seek and to save the lost. He has taken upon Himself the sins of us all. He has become our Substitute. In our stead He has paid the price of our sins by His innocent suffering and death and His holy precious blood as He suffered and died on the cross on Calvary's hill. No one took His life from Him. He had the power to lay it down and to take it up again. He did just this. Thus He was delivered for our offences and raised up again for our justification. He has conquered death and brought life and immortality to light. Therefore all they that believe in Him as Savior shall not perish but have everlasting life — here and throughout eternity.

It is not only a beautiful picture that the Savior paints of Himself as the Good Shepherd. Nor is it a mere resemblance of daily life in the Orient, where sheep actually do recognize the voices of their shepherds who actually do call them by name and where each sheep does follow his own shepherd after mingling with other sheep around the watering holes or in the common folds. But this is a truly descriptive reality and assurance of God for every believer.

II

Why Assured

The believers also frequently stray and act like sheep without a shepherd. The believers also fall short of the glory of God. The believers also are open to all kinds of temptations, and because of the weakness of their flesh they fall into all kinds of sins and feel driven to despair. Not only the young believers but also the strongest within the fold are aptly described as frail and trembling sheep by the poet in the confirmation hymn. All are in constant battle with the devil, the world, and the flesh. The sincerest believers, too, have the seed of sin embedded within them and the consequences of sin surrounding them on all sides. Even the best of them must confess, "The spirit, indeed, is willing, but the flesh is weak," and this applies particularly also when it comes to "departing this life and being with Christ." The flesh of even the staunchest Christian is averse to this departing. And so the believer by his own conscience and particularly by the wiles of the devil is made to fear and dread and tremble. The question "How can I be sure?" is not unknown to him.

Left to himself and his own devices he could never be sure of his salvation. In fact, the one thing he would be sure of is his perdition. The designation "sheep" is also most apt in this connection, for of all creatures none is more stupid and shortsighted than a sheep. With his eyes to the ground, he will follow tuft after tuft of grass until he has strayed from the flock, perhaps even into a thicket or over a cliff. How true also of the Christian, with his earthly and materialistic flesh! From experience Luther sings "Soon were our loss effected." Therefore with the publican we must plead: "God, be merciful to me, a sinner!"

Jesus Gives the Assurance

But here is the assurance "I give unto them eternal life" (v. 28). "By grace are ye saved through faith; and that not of yourselves. It is the gift of God, not of works, lest any man should boast" (Eph. 2:8, 9). It is the Savior, the Son of God Himself, who gives us the assurance. It is He who completed the work of our redemption and said: "It is finished"; He, who is the Way, the Truth, and the Life; He who knows whereof He speaks and whose Word can never be questioned or broken, it is this Good Shepherd who promises and assures us of our salvation.

"And they shall never perish." No matter how great the danger, how many the pitfalls, how numerous the temptations, His sheep shall never perish. The Good Shepherd will always rescue and uphold them, will always pour the healing oil, or balm of Gilead, into their wounds and sustain them with the power of His Word. Yea, "though devils all the world should fill, All eager to devour us, We tremble not, we fear no ill; They shall not overpower us." For "no man can pluck them out of My hand" reads the Savior's sure promise. . . . "This glorious promise and pledge has been given in order that we may trust in Him and not reject Him in doubt and unbelief. We shall build upon this Word as upon a firm rock, and he who builds shall realize the truth of his assurance." (Ylvisaker, *The Gospels,* p. 460)

On the basis of these words of Jesus, every believer exults: "I know in whom I have believed and am persuaded that He is able to keep that which I have committed unto Him against that Day" (2 Tim. 1:12). Again: "Who shall separate us from the love of Christ?" (Rom. 8:35). Again: "For I am persuaded, that neither death, nor life, nor angels, nor principalities, nor powers, nor things present, nor things to come, nor height, nor depth, nor any other creature, shall be able to separate us from the love of God, which is in Christ Jesus, our Lord." (Rom. 8:38, 39)

Of this assurance likewise speak the glorious hymns: "Who
Will Now Accuse Me?" (Bronson) and "If God Himself Be for
Me?" (Gerhardt). . . . And P. Leyser says very aptly: "Assured
of our salvation are we who know that our redemption rests with
Christ. But they who seek their salvation in the saints or in their
own works do well to ascertain what manner of assurance they
possess. The greater number doubt, some despair."

> In the eyes of the Jews the lowly hand of Jesus had no
> strength, and when they saw it shortly nailed to the cross, while
> the sheep that had been led by this hand were scattered in all
> directions, they could scoff and say: "How well do You hold
> them in Your mighty hand!" But His glory, hidden from the
> Jews, is, nevertheless, a true glory as of the Good Shepherd,
> and His hand is truly powerful enough to protect His sheep
> against all the strength of the enemy, because it is one with that
> of the omnipotent Father. (Besser)
>
> Truly, the sheep of Jesus are well taken care of by their
> Good Shepherd. They are in His almighty, benevolent hand;
> indeed, He has marked them in His hands from all eternity.
> And in His hands they are safe despite all enemies; even the
> gates of hell cannot pluck them out of His hands. With this
> assurance every Christian can and should comfort himself in
> every affliction and sorrow, especially also in the face of death,
> but only a Christian, who believes in Jesus, his Savior, who
> hears the Savior's voice, and who follows Him as a sheep.
> (George Mezger, *Homiletic Magazine* [Nov. 1913])

The Father Has Given Them to Him for the Express Purpose
of Eternal Salvation

The assurance of our Savior becomes more powerful still as
He adds: "My Father, which gave them Me, is greater than all,
and no man is able to pluck them out of My Father's hand" (vv.
29, 30). If any hostile power should be able to pluck the sheep out
of the hand of the Son, it must be able also to separate them from
the hand of the Father, and thus be more powerful than the Father,
who has given the sheep to the Son for the express purpose that
the sheep should obtain eternal life. But the Father's counsel of
love may in no wise be annulled, for He is over all.

> The Father has given Him His sheep, has given them to Him
> from eternity. It is the Father's will and good pleasure that
> the sheep should belong to Christ, that they should be and
> remain His sheep. He has from eternity elected them to faith
> and salvation. And the Father is greater than all. For He is
> the almighty God. No one and nothing is able to oppose His
> might no matter how big or mighty it may be. His will must
> prevail. And it is His will, His good pleasure, to give those
> whom He has given to His Son also the Kingdom, the eternal
> kingdom, eternal life. No one can pluck them out of the Father's
> hand, out of the hand of God. (G. Mezger)

The Savior concludes His discourse with the mighty assurance
"I and the Father are one" (v. 30). Christ, our Savior, who as true
man walked upon the earth, who took upon Himself the form of
a man, is also one with the Father, not only in the ethical sense,

as the new and old order of Arians and Socinians would have it, nor in power alone, but in essence, the one true God, coequal in power and majesty. As the sheep are in His hands; therefore they are in the hands of God, well preserved for time and eternity.

Most of us are well acquainted with the picture depicting the believer, in the midst of the stormy sea of life, clinging to the cross, embedded in a solid rock. Still more we love the picture that shows the believer clinging to the cross with one hand and with the other holding on to someone else. It is a beautiful picture, essentially true to fact. In our text our Savior assures us that nobody clings to Him in vain.

How long could the believer continue to cling to the cross of or by himself? How safe is the other one to whom he also clings? "With might of ours can nought be done. Soon were our loss effected." How easily the grip can slip! How soon weariness and exhaustion can overcome the clinging, gripping hand of man! But not so with the hand of God! His grip is firm; His hold is sure! There is no tiring, no slipping, no letting go, on His part. Nor is there any power in all the universe great enough to break His grip or hold. Nothing, and no one, can pluck or snatch us out of that hand! (1 Peter 1:5)

Not too many years ago the late King George VI of England was quoted around the world when in his Christmas message to the British Commonwealth he referred to an old writing, of unknown authorship, "Put your hand into the hand of God," and suggested that as the only safe way to venture forth into the unknown future of the new year.

Many of you, in a time of crisis or sickness, have also been reassured by your pastor that you have nothing to fear, that you are in good hands because you are in the hands of God! Such assurances are usually eagerly accepted, for man is constantly looking for security and reassurance — that is, as a general rule, for the body and for this life. Our greatest concern, however, must be our concern for the soul also and for the life that is to come.

Life insurance, total coverage, complete security, that is, the assurance of eternal life, is definitely ours because Jesus, our Savior, the Son of God, freely gives it to us by grace through His holy Word, whereby the Holy Ghost brings us to faith and keeps us in that faith. That is also our Savior's guarantee in our text: "My sheep hear My voice, and I know them, and they follow Me. And I give unto them eternal life, and they shall never perish, neither shall any man pluck them out of My hand. My Father, which gave them Me, is greater than all, and no man is able to pluck them out of My Father's hand. I and My Father are one."

Sermons for Special Occasions

"Good Tidings of Great Joy"

By Robert Howard Clausen

(Christmas Eve Sermon)

And there were in the same country shepherds abiding in the field, keeping watch over their flock by night. And, lo, the angel of the Lord came upon them, and the glory of the Lord shone round about them, and they were sore afraid. And the angel said unto them: Fear not; for, behold, I bring you good tidings of great joy which shall be to all people. For unto you is born this day in the city of David a Savior, which is Christ the Lord. — *Luke 2:8-11*

The Christmas story, with its quiet charm and simple language, presents a scene so lovingly described that our first reaction is to stand back and admire it and to wonder that so fragile and beautiful a thing should survive in our rough, materialistic world. But the Christmas story is stronger than it looks. It has such penetrating power that in all parts of the world men and women are affected by its spell and are brought in some degree under its influence. Time stands still, even if for a day, and the frenzied rush of human activity slows down. Good will and human kindness blossom in forgotten corners in the brief but temperate climate of this sacred season.

The story of Christmas, then, is not just something to be looked at and admired like any other pretty thing, but something to be stepped into and experienced, because in it we have wrapped up all human history, aspiration, endeavor, and every promise of hope and deliverance. Down through the ages, whenever it has been read and heard, it has brought

Good Tidings of Great Joy

Who are the persons connected with this glad announcement?

I

Caesar Augustus

At the very beginning of the Christmas Gospel, leading up to the announcement of good tidings, stands the name of Caesar Augustus. "And it came to pass in those days that there went out a decree from Caesar Augustus that all the world should be taxed (and this taxing was first made when Cyrenius was governor of Syria) (Luke 2:1, 2). Augustus is mentioned only in passing to establish the point in human history when the grand event of the Incarnation occurred. The reference to this Roman Caesar is quickly forgotten as the story moves on quickly to the amazing events of

Bethlehem. Yet in his day Augustus was a man to be reckoned with. He was the first to bear the title of Emperor when Rome changed from republic to monarchy. Under his scepter Rome entered upon a golden age of peace and prosperity. Culture and good government characterized his reign.

There is, of course, always the other side of the picture: the conquest and bloodshed required to establish empires, the oppression by the mighty, the sullen resentment of conquered peoples, the extortion and cruelty, the graft and injustice, found in all governments of all times.

Caesar Augustus represented the impersonal, frightening force of a government that by a decree could touch and change the lives of ordinary little people, could uproot them from their homes and businesses and families, could send them on long and wearying journeys, could interrupt their personal lives and pleasures, could order them to the place of their birth to be enrolled, all so that Caesar Augustus could know the number and extent of his empire and could the more systematically levy taxes for the financing of his imperial needs. Caesar Augustus stands for the powers of this world and all that they mean for good and bad to common people everywhere.

II

Joseph and Mary

Next in the Christmas Gospel we meet Joseph and Mary, some of the little people we have spoken about. We see them subject to the whims of a man they did not know and would never see, yet people who found for themselves a place and purpose in the plans and counsels of Almighty God. In their lives we find demonstrated what glory can result in human life when it is offered to God as a vessel to be filled with His goodness and love. What did they contribute to the "good tidings of great joy"?

Mary had been given the startling news that in her virginity she would bear a son. She had been told that the Holy Ghost would come upon her and that the power of the Highest would overshadow her and that the holy child to be born of her would be called the Son of God. To this momentous revelation her response was humble, obedient, and complete: "Behold, the handmaid of the Lord. Be it unto me according to Thy word." This pious Jewish maiden yielded her soul and body to the Holy Spirit, and she became the earthly mother of the Son of God.

Joseph also, strong and silent, showed a faith submissive to the will of God. He became the stalwart guardian of Mary and the infant Jesus. If he was not a father according to the flesh, he certainly was a father to the Christ Child in loyal and tender spirit, shepherding his little family through dark, dangerous, and difficult months, later guiding them to Egypt and back until they were safely established in Nazareth.

Alongside Caesar Augustus, Joseph seems small and insignificant from the world's point of view, yet his life was expanded to its fullest and greatest capacity because he became a willing and true instrument in the hands of a loving God.

"And Joseph also went up from Galilee, out of the city of Nazareth, into Judea, unto the city of David, which is called Bethlehem (because he was of the house and lineage of David), to be taxed with Mary, his espoused wife, being great with child. And so it was that while they were there the days were accomplished that she should be delivered. And she brought forth her firstborn Son, and wrapped Him in swaddling clothes, and laid Him in a manger because there was no room for them in the inn." (Luke 2:4-7)

III

The Shepherds

At this point in the story we come upon the shepherds, symbolic of mankind at its daily work, still feeling the edge of sin's curse. "In the sweat of thy face shalt thou eat bread." Mankind, lost without work and yet burdened with it, for with work at its best there will come days which seem rude, monotonous, and oppressive, when the hours with their sameness are sapped of their joy of living; when endless tomorrows stretch out with little hope of variety or relief.

"And there were in the same country shepherds abiding in the field, keeping watch over their flocks by night." (Luke 2:8)

The shepherds are all humankind, going through their daily duties and hoping inwardly for a different, brighter world of peace and personal fulfillment.

IV

The Angels

Suddenly, in this night of mankind's watching and waiting, we are greeted by the angels, and the scene takes on a new dimension. The confining curtains of earth are thrown aside, and we are confronted by the reality of heaven and the bright beings who inhabit that blessed realm.

And, lo, the angel of the Lord came upon them, and the glory of the Lord shone round about them, and they were sore afraid. And the angel said unto them: Fear not; for, behold, I bring you good tidings of great joy which shall be to all people. For unto you is born this day in the city of David a Savior, which is Christ the Lord. And this shall be a sign unto you: Ye shall find the Babe wrapped in swaddling clothes and lying in a manger. (Luke 2:9-12)

The angels are the ministers of God who do His pleasure, and their presence here affirms the fact that this event is of God's doing. These are the spirit beings of the invisible creation, reminding us that though there is a part of the creation which we cannot see, its existence is real and its promise is sure.

V

The Christ

All these events found their cause and purpose in the other figure in the story, the infant Jesus, the "Babe lying in a manger," seemingly the smallest and the least, the frailest and the feeblest of all who populate the Christmas Gospel, and yet immeasurably the greatest, for He is Immanuel, God with us. Because of Him God used Caesar Augustus to send Mary to Bethlehem; because of Him Mary was highly favored among women; because of Him the shepherds heard good tidings of great joy, so that their lives were nevermore the same; because of Him the hosts of heaven burst forth in their hymn of praise: "Glory to God in the highest, and on earth peace, good will toward men."

This was a peace achieved in spite of human sin and rebelliousness, for God set His beloved Son down in the middle of it, to feel its pain, to endure its curse, to suffer its punishment, and thereby to break its power forever. Jesus Christ, the Child of Bethlehem, is God's Word of love for sinful people such as you and I, a love which did not falter but which remained true and unswerving up to and through the agony of the cross. The eternal meaning of the cross is summed up in two terse verses from the New and Old Testaments: "But God commendeth His love toward us in that while we were yet sinners Christ died for us" (Rom. 5:8), and "The Lord hath laid on Him the iniquity of us all" (Is. 53:6). The shadow of the cross falls over the manger, and the Child of Bethlehem is to be the Savior of Calvary.

VI

You and I

This is where the good tidings relate to us as you and I step into the Christmas story to feel its dynamic power gripping us and saving us today.

Caesar Augustus is no more, but what he stood for is still with us . . . worldly pomp and power, national ambition, pride in greatness, injustice, oppression, and the sword of war. We sometimes feel helpless under the impersonal forces which touch our lives and affect our plans. But let us remember that God is greater than they all. God used Caesar Augustus to bring the prophecies of centuries to fulfillment so that His Son, the promised Savior, would be born at Bethlehem. Caesar Augustus is gone; Cyrenius, governor of Syria, is gone, but Christ remains, and His birth has meant the transformation of history and of countless human lives. His death has meant our reconciliation to God. His resurrection tells us that God's plans will never be defeated by the designs of men. His ascension assures us that His kingdom fills heaven and earth and that, safe in His love, our eternal happiness is secure.

Observing Mary and Joseph we are heartened at the thought that our lives, small and obscure in the world's passing parade as they may seem to be, can have an infinite worth to God and can be used to His glory to further the mighty purposes of His kingdom.

God gave Jesus in the flesh to Mary. We hold Christ by faith and have Him as surely as Mary held Him in her arms. Our response to Christ in faith is the working of God the Holy Spirit. As new people of God, redeemed, restored, forgiven, our lives become vessels filled with God's love and goodness. This we in turn are to pour out in forgiveness, compassion, and works of Christian love in the sin-stricken world around us. God says to us, "I want thee for My very own to do My works through thee." May our reply be given in this same responsive spirit: "Be it unto me according to Thy word."

Like the shepherds we are caught in the treadmill of our daily tasks; sometimes we seem to be tiny cogs to be dismissed and replaced at will. Life seems cold, the night seems dark, the way seems lonely. What a joy to be assured that this world and what it offers is not the completion of our lives! What a joy to be told that there is a Savior by whom we are delivered from sin and death! What a joy to find that here, day by day, in our ordinary duties, we can live as sons and daughters of God! The angels have declared it, and as they have come from God, so we shall one day go to Him.

As we have explored the events and people connected with the "good tidings of great joy," we see that the Bethlehem scene is not to be framed and admired as a beautiful relic of a lovely moment in the past. The Christmas Gospel, with its joyful news, is to be relived at its every announcement.

The world and its Caesars? "This is the victory which overcometh the world, even our faith." (1 John 5:4)

Our weakness and inferiority? "My grace is sufficient for thee, for My strength is made perfect in weakness." (2 Cor. 12:9)

Monotony, weariness, heartsickness? "Set your affection on things above, not on things on the earth, for ye are dead, and your life is hid with Christ in God." (Col. 3:2, 3)

Longing for a greater reality? Remember the angels and the promise, "Beloved, now are we the sons of God, and it doth not yet appear what we shall be; but we know that when He shall appear we shall be like Him, for we shall see Him as He is." (1 John 3:2)

And Christ the Savior, who is the Good News for all people everywhere, is still with us, still the eternal Expression of God's love, Jesus Christ, the same yesterday, today, and forever. His blood cleanses us from all sin, and in Him alone we find forgiveness and life everlasting.

Believe the good tidings. Worship the Christ. The words about Him are true. He will be your great Joy and your living Peace.

No Lasting City

By ROBERT C. SELTZ

(New Year's Eve)

For the bodies of those animals whose blood is brought into the sanctuary by the high priest as a sacrifice for sin are burned outside the camp. So Jesus also suffered outside the gate in order to sanctify the people through His own blood. Therefore let us go forth to Him outside the camp, bearing abuse for Him. For here we have no lasting city, but we seek the city which is to come. Through Him, then, let us continually offer up a sacrifice of praise to God, that is, the fruit of lips that acknowledge His name. — *Hebrews 13:11-15 RSV*

Tonight many of you are thinking serious thoughts. You are aware of the incessant forward march of time and of the fleeting nature of your life. It hardly seems possible that another year, a rather large segment of your life, has so quickly rushed into the past. We are all closer to the time when we shall leave this world and enter another.

Recently a man was telling me about the many moves he had made from one city to another in the last few years. The firm that employed him was involved in the rapidly changing picture of our country's defense program. Company operations required frequent and sudden moves on the part of many employees. "My family and I," he said, "have had to learn how to live in one city and at the same time prepare mentally to move on to another." Could not his statement be made by every one of you tonight, and that with a deeper meaning? You and I must live in this world while at the same time preparing to move on to another. "For here we have no lasting city, but we seek the city which is to come," says the text.

It is good that on this eve of the new year you have come to the house of the Lord to be with God's people and to set your faces again in the direction of that holy city which is to come, which was founded and established and built by Him who was named Jesus Christ. It would be good if tonight you and I would resolve that in the new year, above everything else, we will seek that "home of the future," that palace and kingdom which abides forever.

Life Terminates

"Here we have no lasting city." This is true in the first place so far as our life on earth is concerned. Eventually it runs out. During this holiday season the earthly pilgrimage of many people will come to an abrupt end on the highways. Recently a traffic expert estimated that about 500,000 people will die on the nation's highways during the next 10 years. But even those who do not lose their lives accidentally must still affirm with the sacred writers: "My days are swifter than a weaver's shuttle" (Job 7:6). "What is your life? It is even a vapor that appeareth for a little time and then vanisheth away" (James 4:14). "Our days on the earth are as a shadow" (1 Chron. 29:15). "For all flesh is as grass. . . . The grass withereth, and the flower thereof falleth away." (1 Peter 1:24)

Is this a dark and hopeless picture? It isn't if you realize that your present life must come to an end before you can enter fully into that richer life which is found in God's eternal city.

Much of the time, however, you and I want to hold on to this life and everything in it. Often it appears as if we would be satisfied to build only a city here and now, even though it be one which will not last. We want to hold on to what we've got. Sometimes we almost stop looking for that city which is to come, where our Lord Jesus Christ has prepared a place for us.

Institutions Will Come to an End

Secondly, our social and domestic way of life is not permanent. You have adopted certain standards and hopes, plans and dreams, for your life. You have devised a philosophy of life. You are searching for stability and security and strength. You hope to find these in your home, your family, and in other social institutions, all of which are good. But you and I must realize that even all these things are not a "lasting city." The woman who seeks security only in her home and her family should remember that these are not permanent. The man who bases his confidence for the future in his government's social welfare program should recall that governments have a way of collapsing. Even the church's organizational and institutional structures will ultimately come to an end.

But all this will be replaced by greater things in the eternal city, which is to come. You will enjoy perfect security; you will have deeper and more satisfying relationships with God and with His people. The church of Christ will be triumphant, with no need for plants and structures such as we need now. For you there will be a greater way of life by far than you enjoy now.

Seek the Lasting City

As we enter the new year let's resolve that we will seek the eternal kingdom and dwelling place of God and that all the rest of our concerns will derive their focus from this. Let's resolve that we will beware of excessive straining and working and overworking simply in order to maintain our temporary earth-bound way of life no matter what.

Christ Shows the Way

You and I could never make our way to God's eternal city without help. After World War II the press informed us that one of our bombers crash-landed in the desert of northern Africa. Not realizing how far inland the site of their crash was, the crew tried to walk the distance to the northern coast. But it was too far. Since no one discovered them and came to their rescue, they perished. Our predicament is similar. We can't make it to our eternal destination without help. Sometimes we think we can, and so we start out going our own way, trusting in our own wisdom, stamina, and effort. But our destination is far beyond our reach. Unless someone shows us the way and helps us reach it, we'll never make it. We will perish.

But someone does help. That someone is He who was named Jesus by the angel before He was conceived in the womb. It is this Jesus who makes it possible for you and me to reach the city to come. He walked the dusty paths of Palestine doing the good that we cannot do, fulfilling the righteousness that we cannot fulfill. Later He was lifted up on a cross of suffering. He poured out His blood as the price for our rescue. Our selfishness and rebellion, our guilt and alienation from God, all this Christ took upon Himself in order to gain for us entrance into the holy city of God.

The text illustrates Christ's redemptive sacrifice with a ritual used under the old covenant. Certain animals were slain, and their blood was brought into the sanctuary by the high priest as a sacrifice for sin. This was a type, or symbol, of the future Messiah. The bodies of these animals were then taken outside the camp of the Israelites and burned. Calling this to mind, the writer of the text says: "So Jesus also suffered outside the gate in order to sanctify the people through His own blood." Jesus is the Antitype, or Fulfillment, of the Old Testament ritual. He was taken "outside the camp" of Jerusalem and crucified. He was slain so that

He might do what the angel said — save His people from their sins. By this Gospel He wishes to draw you to Himself so that He can make you as white as snow even though your sins are like scarlet. And thus He prepares you for life in His abiding city, which is to come. Will you respond to His love? Or will you insist on striving for these things which will not last?

A Present Reality

You may wonder whether this wonderful, eternal city is something that is only in the distant future. I believe that you have already begun to enter it. If you have responded to God's love in Christ, if you have given yourself to God with full confidence in His deliverance and grace, then you are already in the suburbs of His everlasting city. You have already entered the anteroom of heaven. You enjoy a foretaste of its blessings, and you experience the joy of God's presence. Even now you eat the heavenly food of God's Word and Christ's Holy Supper, in which He gives you His body and blood as a pledge of forgiveness and life eternal. Is this not a beginning of that which the text says is going to come?

Textual Guidelines

What can we do in the year ahead in order to seek the permanent things of God's kingdom? A lengthy list of things to do would only confuse. The text offers a single but comprehensive suggestion: "Through Him [Jesus] let us continually offer up a sacrifice of praise to God." It says *continually* and *sacrifice*. These are challenging words which imply a total commitment. And the phrase "sacrifice of praise to God" includes our every response and service to Him. One such response, according to the text, is "lips that acknowledge His name," the name of Jesus. What better sacrifice is there than to acknowledge with faith the name of Christ, trusting in Him from the heart?

Earlier in the text another sacrifice of praise was mentioned. This we should not overlook. The writer suggested that since Jesus had suffered for us, we should go to Him "outside the camp" and bear abuse for Him. Jesus was taken outside the gate of Jerusalem and crucified. He was despised and abused. Our abuse and sin were heaped upon Him. Will you now be willing to go out to Him, to Calvary, to the foot of the cross? Will you be unashamed to claim this despised Man as your God and Savior, to acknowledge His name before a world which still despises Him? If so, you may find yourself bearing some of His abuse. The world often reproaches those who seriously bear the name and the faith of Christ. In the year which we now enter will you also offer this sacrifice of praise? Those who do will find in the eternal city something that lasts forever, "If you are reproached for the name of Christ, you are blessed because the Spirit of glory and of God rests upon you." (1 Peter 4:14 RSV)

Here we have no lasting city. Therefore in the new year turn your hopes and expectations more toward that city which is to come. Seek first the kingdom of God and His righteousness, and let God add all other things to you as He will and as He has promised. Let not the next 12 months be another year of putting off God but rather a year of God's putting on you the seal of His love through Jesus Christ. May it be a year of blessing for each of you, of peace in the world, and of grace for our congregation and the universal church of Christ. My new year's wish for you is recorded at the end of this chapter. It reads: "Now the God of peace that brought again from the dead our Lord Jesus, that Great Shepherd of the sheep, through the blood of the everlasting covenant, make you perfect in every good work to do His will, working in you that which is well pleasing in His sight, through Jesus Christ, to whom be glory forever and ever. Amen." (Heb. 13:20, 21)

"This Is the Day Which the Lord Hath Made"

By NORMAN BRANDT

(Sermon for New Year's Day)

This is the day which the Lord hath made; we will rejoice and be glad in it. — *Psalm 118:24*

"Happy New Year!" we are saying to one another. New calendars with fresh pages grace our desks. The new year seems to give us a new lease on life. We are likely to think of January 1 as something fresh and new, and we ought to. But the text we have chosen this morning points up that not only the first page of the year is a new gift from God, but this is true of *every* day God will give us in the year before us. If we open our eyes on January 2, or February 2, or August 2, or any day, we can say of that day, "This is the day which the Lord hath made; we will rejoice and be glad in it." For the believer the trademark of God is written across every new day. For three reasons may we say with the psalmist

This Is the Day Which the Lord Hath Made

I

God Has Made *Today* Filled with Blessings

God would have us rejoice and be glad in this day with its blessings. We can rejoice. The day began for most of us with a night of rest and refreshment. Then there was breakfast, not of crumbs or of some dry roots, as it was the lot of some of our brothers and sisters in the world to have. We had toast with *butter* on it, and more. Luther, in his explanation of the First Article of our Creed, points up how God daily and richly provides us "with all that we need to support this body and life."

Today God is at work in your body and mine, making life possible. He has pipe lines and blood vessels and capillaries that are at work in each of us today. If these pipe lines of life in your body were placed end to end, you could start out here in Wisconsin, go across the state of Minnesota, across South Dakota to the West Coast, out across the Pacific, finally to the coast of China — a total of more than 12,000 miles. These life-giving pipe lines are at work *today* in your body. In the period we call today, God will allow your heart to beat a hundred thousand times. Yes, "This is the day which the Lord hath made."

He made it possible for us again *today* to open our eyes on a world of beauty. *Today* the sun shines forth in beauty. Tonight bright stars will stud the sky. The psalmist says, "The heavens declare the glory of God." They remind us that God is at work *daily,* telling us of His glory, saying, "Day unto day uttereth speech, and night unto night showeth knowledge" (Ps. 19:2). If today we had opened our eyes on steel-gray skies or looked out on showers of rain or snow, we could nevertheless say that this day is God's. I recall a kind old lady who used to greet me as I was coming in out of the rain, whether the rain was pouring down or gently falling, by saying, "Isn't this a lovely rain?" We need to pray, not only, as we do in one of our worship services, "O Lord, open Thou my lips," but also, "O Lord, open Thou our eyes so that we can see the day as a blessing from Thee."

In his explanation of the Third Article of the Creed, Luther reminds us also that God is at work in every *today* when he says that in the Christian church "God *daily* and richly forgives all sins to me and all believers." In one of the great spirituals we say of Jesus, "Nobody works like Him." He who died for us has been at work *today,* blessing us and all of His children with the forgiveness of our sins, purchased for us with His blood. Need we remind ourselves how much we need this blessing? Think only of the two great commandments bidding us to love God with all our heart, soul, and mind and our neighbor as ourselves. How we have failed in loving God that way and in being concerned for those about us in the way the commandments prescribe! And that is a sin. And the risen Christ lives today to bless us with this forgiveness. In v. 14 of the psalm of our text the psalmist says, "The Lord is my Strength and Song, and is become my

Salvation." Blessed daily by this salvation, he had reason to say, "This is the day which the Lord hath made." V. 22 he says, "The Stone which the builders refused is become the Headstone of the Corner." Jesus had to be "refused," had to be rejected, had to suffer, so that *today* God's forgiveness could be coming through to each of us.

Jeremiah knew this forgiveness, knew this *daily* grace of God, and could therefore say, ". . . the Lord's mercies . . . are new *every morning*" (Lam. 3:22, 23). So we attribute glory to our God, a glory which not only was "in the beginning" and "ever shall be" but also is *now,* that is, *today.*

But some of you may be saying: "Pastor, you don't know the problems in my life. How can I call this the day which the Lord hath made?" While none of us is without problems, everyone of us has countless blessings. Each of us needs to pray, "Lord, if I cannot have what I like, help me like what I have." You remember how He said it through St. Paul: "And we know that all things work together for good to them that love God . . ." (Rom. 8:28). When martyrs were led to the stake during the Reformation, which verse was so often found on their lips? Here it is: "This is the day which the Lord hath made; we will rejoice and be glad in it." They could say this, for the day in the dark valley of the shadow of death is also, in Christ, the day that leads to eternal life.

II

God Has Made *Today* to Be Lived One Day at a Time

Not only because God filled each today with blessings we can say "This is the day which the Lord hath made," but also because, under God, each day can be lived as one day at a time. There can be no real rejoicing in the *today* if we attempt to cram other days into it.

There is great danger that we will try to live in the yesterdays of life. Yesterday's sin and last year's wrongs can haunt and shroud every *today* of this new year if we fail to take seriously the atoning sacrifice of Christ. It is possible to begin each day with a clean slate because this Christ obtained eternal redemption for us and now "daily forgives sins to me and all believers." St. Paul says in his Letter to the Philippians that we can forget "those things which are behind," because he knew that his Savior, who died for him and rose again, was continually blotting out the sins that are past. So we know we are heard when we pray:

> When the morning wakens,
> Then may I arise
> Pure and fresh and sinless
> In Thy holy eyes.

During the new year there is again the danger of our failing to see each *today* as "the day which the Lord hath made" and of attempting to live in the yesterdays by looking back nostalgically to the "good old days." "The good day," God would tell us, "is *today*." Our Savior reminds us that when we put our hands to the plow in His kingdom, we are not to be looking back. How often we hurt our work for the Lord in our home, in our community, in our church, by looking back and saying, "If only so-and-so were here again, things would be different!" "If things were like they used to be, I'd be willing to work and help." But God would have us see our job, our task in His kingdom, in the todays of life.

If there is danger in living in the yesterdays of life, there is also danger in living tomorrow before it comes. He would have us say, "This is the day which the Lord hath made; we will rejoice and be glad in it." This is the day — shut out tomorrow in terms of worry or care. This is the day — "Do not be anxious about tomorrow, for tomorrow will be anxious for itself. Let the day's own trouble be sufficient for the day" (Matt. 6:34 RSV). How we spoil and soil the day by filling it with the sin of worry, of lack of faith in our God, who knows every tomorrow.

III

God Has Given Us *Today* with Its Uniqueness of Opportunity

If the *today* in our lives is the "day which the Lord hath made" because of its blessings and because He has made it possible to live one day at a time, it is also "the day which the Lord hath made," in the third place, *because of its uniqueness of opportunity.* We are prone to think of a day as "just an average day," as "just another day." But the day is always unique, is always critical. Each day that God gives us during the new year will be a golden coin that He places in the hands of our life. There will be no other day like it. He says: "Redeem the time"; each day is precious. Use the day! See its uniqueness! Exploit its opportunities. You pass by this day but once in your life's journey. There is no other day exactly like this January 1. Luther reminds us of the critical nature of each *today* in our lives. Under Holy Baptism in our Catechism he tells us that Baptism "signifies that the old Adam in us should, by *daily* contrition and repentance, be drowned and die with all sins and evil lusts and, again, a new man *daily* come forth and arise who shall live before God in righteousness and purity forever." The divine day is always the current day.

God would have us repent of our sins *today*. He would have us work in His kingdom *today*. When we fail to see this uniqueness and divine quality in each day, we are apt to say, with the materialist in Jesus' parable, "Soul, take thine ease." But you recall that the Lord labeled this man a fool and said, "This night shall thy soul be required of thee." *Today* each of us is in the "valley of decision," in the presence of God-given opportunity or God-appointed judgment. "Now is the *day* of salvation." *Now* is the accepted time.

In every *today* of this new year there will be needy people about us. Some of these will be without Christ. Some will have few friends. Some will be crushed by sin. When their paths meet ours there will be "divine moments" in the day, God-given moments of opportunity. The days will bring across our paths some who are "difficult" because life has been difficult with them. Some may even be mean. Many will not know the meaning of forgiveness. Our moments of meeting in days and hours and situations now unknown will truly be golden moments, not only for us but, under God, also for them. *Today* is the time to "forgive if we have ought against any." *Today* he would remind us to agree with our adversary *quickly* "while thou art in the way with him." *Today* "let not the sun go down upon your wrath." Each *today* carries with it opportunities for the work of His Spirit — for repentance, for new life; opportunities for new worship, for new love, for new forgiveness, for new witness, for new sacrifices. And it is so because God's mercies in Christ are new to us each morning.

May we carry this verse of the 118th Psalm with us into the new year — into each day that God gives. Let this verse be for us a daily sermon. When we open our eyes each morning, may we also open our lips and lift our thoughts toward God, with these words: "This is the day which the Lord hath made; we will rejoice and be glad in it."

The Birthday of Abraham Lincoln

By Armin W. Born

When Abraham Lincoln died on the Saturday before Easter in the year 1865, his Secretary of War, Edwin Stanton, said, "Now he belongs to the ages." If Mr. Stanton felt already in his lifetime — and he had at one time been Lincoln's enemy — that this man would belong to the ages, then he must have sensed something of the durable quality of his life and words, of his attitude toward his fellowmen and of his anchorage in the belief in an eternal God. We speak of the Bible as being the Rock of Ages, and to this speaker it appears that this statement, "Now he belongs to the ages," would not have been possible if Lincoln had not been conversant with and guided by the Rock of Ages, the eternal Word of our God.

It goes without saying that we would not bring the life of Abraham Lincoln into the pulpit if he did not have some relevancy, some connection with God's everlasting Word and our blessed Bible — if it did not give us something that could help build Christ's kingdom. In our own country the government has a benign attitude toward the church, which it permits to operate tax free because government believes the church is of great blessing and does many things that the government otherwise ought to do and would have to do. Important state ordinances demand or allow freedom of conscience and freedom of worship, freedom of speech, and above all, separation of church and state. When we have men in the life of the country who uphold these important constitutional arrangements by which the church can operate and do its work to the glory of God and the saving of souls, we certainly cannot be faulted for calling attention to such men, who gave us these boons of liberty. In fact, they ought to be honored and remembered, and we ought to pray God that He would continue to give us such leaders.

In stark contrast, for instance, with such men like Abraham Lincoln or George Washington or Daniel Webster or any other Christian men who have filled the highest office of our country, we think today of communistic tyrants under whose heel the church has to go underground, people are forbidden to worship, and things are deliberately done to undermine the Christian faith. Certainly we ought to think of the vast difference between our country and such countries, and we ought eternally to be grateful we have been spared the horrors of such — not only civic — but religious and ecclesiastical tyranny.

It is not foreign to the Bible that men in high places in the government were honored — especially if they were God-fearing men. Such a man, for instance, was King David, who was a king but also in many ways a spiritual leader (although the actual leadership of the church was in the hand of the high priest). In the days of King David, the church operated as a church but the king himself was a loyal member of that church, and therefore he planned and worked also as a very important layman. He worked in perfecting the worship. He planned to build a great temple to the glory of God, which was built and dedicated by another great king, his son Solomon. David prepared many of the great psalms of praise and other psalms which were used by the sons of Korah in the temple worship. We can make similar assertions for men like Moses and Joshua. We think today of the difficulties that our own Lord Jesus Christ had in building the Kingdom because of the problems raised by a hostile Roman government. The church itself had become so formal that it was almost a tyranny.

Looking at our own country, we remember today that in Kentucky in the year 1809 on February 12, God permitted a man to be born, who, by his statesmanship, his great leadership, his high sense of morality, his tremendous love for the downtrodden and the lowly, and above all, a man who by his own convictions came to believe that no man ought to toil and work in the sweat of his brow as a slave for taskmasters and that such an arrangement, such a social order in a country claiming to be Christian, was in direct violation of the very finest and the best that man ought to ask or expect of Christian people.

When we look at Abraham Lincoln today, a fact which strikes us is that in the entire Lincoln family, which came to Massachusetts, emigrated to Virginia, and then went to Kentucky, no ancestor was distinguished. Historians have been searching but they have searched in vain for evidences of greatness that might have been inherited by Abraham Lincoln.

We Christians, however, have a definite answer for this. We are sure that Abraham Lincoln became the great man that he was (and he showed it throughout the great bleeding years of the Civil War of our country) in this that his thinking, his attitudes, his character, were formed by reading good basic literature, including the Bible. We know Abraham Lincoln became steeped in the phraseology of the King James version. Throughout his great speeches, both before the country and during the Civil War, and in his many brief but telling letters, there are constant references to Scripture and constant quotations of Bible passages. In his speeches before smaller groups, especially church groups, he was as much at home in the Bible as any of those who came to him. We consider today

Abraham Lincoln: Man for the Ages

It is not our purpose today to talk about him as a great leader, to speak about his saving of the Union, or to talk about his Cooper Union speech. (Although there again his Christian attitudes came to the fore when he closed that president-making oration by saying, "Let us dare to do our duty as we understand it! Let us have faith to the end that right makes might.")

Was He a Christian?

There has been some question raised whether Abraham Lincoln was a Christian in the sense that you and I use the word. In other words, did he believe in the atonement of our Lord and Savior Jesus Christ on the cross of Calvary? To this question there cannot and will not be a firm answer. Undoubtedly, towards the end of his life Abraham Lincoln came to believe in Jesus as the Redeemer. He speaks of Him on several occasions as the "Savior." Prior to this, however, in his formative years in Illinois and then in the first years in the White House (although he often refers to God and he quotes the Bible, and he believes in the infinite wisdom of God, and he prays to God over and over again, and he directs people to believe the Bible, and he will never say a single word against the Bible nor will he ever make fun of the Bible), it is nonetheless true that he never did join a church in a formal way, although he always went to church. He went to church when he was in Springfield. He went to the famous church on New York Avenue in Washington, D. C., where his pew is still being shown. All of his boys were baptized. He felt much closer to God and to heaven when his son, Edward Baker Lincoln, died in Springfield, Ill. He comforted his wife in the death of their son, Willie, in 1862 by assuring her that he was in heaven. There are articles, as those appearing in the *Lutheran Chaplain* recently, which very definitely claim that Lincoln, in spite of the fact that he did not formally join a church, had as much Christian conviction as Christians in general have. And we also believe that if he had had a formal religious training, especially on the basis of the church year, perhaps he might not have been found in a theater on Good Friday.

It might also be claimed that at no time in the history of the Christian church did as many pastors change their sermons as when the news flashed across the country on that Saturday before Easter that Abraham Lincoln had died.

Abraham Lincoln lived in a time when people generally accepted the Scriptural doctrines as we have them today. It was not yet the day of evolution. It was not the day of rampant rationalism, or of liberalism as we know it today. The pastors did not try to explain the Bible away but quoted the Bible as a firm authority for all that it said. Throughout the rank and file of all Lincoln's generals, leaders, officers and men in the army, people bowed before the authority of Holy Scriptures. And Abraham Lincoln, when he ran up against any opposition to this position, always took the side of the Bible; he always said that we should accept it. He told one of his co-workers: "accept all that you can of this Bible on the basis of your reason and what you cannot, on the basis of *faith*."

Christian Kindness

As the Bible shows the love of God for sinful mankind in the sacrifice of His Son Jesus so Lincoln could learn kindness

and love to others from reading the example of God in the
Scriptures. Lincoln showed very great kindness to both of his
mothers; deep heartache came over him when both his mother
and his sister died in the pioneer woods of Indiana. Later we see
in him constant solicitude for his stepmother, Sarah Bush Lincoln,
who did so much to help him, and of whom he undoubtedly said,
"All that I am, I owe to my angel mother." His tremendous
concern for his illiterate relatives that continued to plague him
during his incumbency of the presidency, the fact that he never
forgot a kindness, that he is known as "honest Abe," that he was
willing to pay out a complete indemnity to the Southern slave
holders for their losses in slaves — reveal an almost fabulous attitude of kindness and a lack of hatred. As a matter of fact,
Mr. Warren of Fort Wayne, Ind., maintains that Lincoln just was
not capable of carrying ill will or ill feeling towards anybody.
He was willing, for instance, to defend and prove Jack Armstrong
innocent just because the mother of this boy had in former years
taken care of him. His generals were discomfited by the fact that
he found it practically impossible to sign an order for execution,
especially if people came and pleaded for the life of their loved
ones. In so many instances of this nature, we see how deeply
embedded were the great injunctions of the Holy Scriptures that
we should love our fellowmen and be kind and tender-hearted
and forgiving to others. As a matter of fact, those who write of
the character and the life of Abraham Lincoln today go out of
their way to emphasize that perhaps never in the history of man
was there anyone as thoughtful, as kind and forgiving, as tender-
hearted and patient toward others as Abraham Lincoln. Whatever
accolades are showered on him in this matter, one thing is sure,
he learned these qualities by reading his Bible.

Christian Utterances

And now let us look at a few of the great utterances in which
we see this Bible-lore appearing. In his letter to Mrs. Bixby
he says, "I pray that our heavenly Father may assuage the
anguish of your bereavement and leave you only the cherished
memory of the loved and lost."

When in the fall of 1863 he dedicated the cemetery at Gettys-
burg and began that famous speech by saying, "Four score and
seven years ago," what was that, my friends, but only the echo
of his constant reading of the Ninetieth Psalm, "The days of
our years are threescore years and ten; and if by reason of
strength they be fourscore years, yet is their strength labor
and sorrow"?

When he took affectionate farewell of the people from the

rear platform of a train coach at Springfield early in 1861, he said, "Commending you to Him who can both go with me and stay with you. . . ." What a beautiful way of stating the omnipresence of our God!

In his second inaugural address on the steps of the Capitol in Washington just a few days before he was laid low by an assassin's bullet (people have called it a sermon rather than a speech), he said that even if the war should have to last so long that every drop of blood drawn by the lash would have to be paid for by another drawn by the sword, even so it must still be said that the judgments of the Lord are righteous altogether. He closed that famous address by saying, "With malice towards none, with charity for all, let us bind up the wounds of the nation." He was thinking of the orphan and of the widow and of the people whose homes dotting the entire countryside were saddened by vacant chairs. He was thinking of what the country owed these people. This great humanitarian attitude filled his soul from day to day. He was never hardened by the war; on that day when he came out on the balcony to talk to the crowd celebrating the final victory of Lee surrendering at Appomattox, in deference to those men who had fought for what they thought right, Lincoln asked the band to play "Dixie." He said, "We are not going to look upon these people any differently but as boys that have run away for a while and now, having learned their lesson, are to be welcomed back home."

He wrote March 15, 1865, which is just about one month before he died, "Men are not being flattered by being shown there has been a difference of purpose between the Almighty and themselves. To deny it, however, in this case is to deny that there is a God governing the world. This is a truth which I thought needed to be told."

To further establish his beliefs, we quote his letter to Eliza P. Gurney:

My Esteemed Friend:

I have not forgotten — probably never shall forget — the very impressive occasion when yourself and friends visited me on a Sabbath forenoon nearly two years ago. Nor has your kind letter, written nearly a year later, ever been forgotten. In all it has been your purpose to strengthen my reliance on God. I am much indebted to the good Christian people of the country for their constant prayers and consolations; and to no one of them more than to yourself. The purposes of the Almighty are perfect, and must prevail, though we erring mortals may fail to accurately perceive them in advance. We hoped for a happy termination of this terrible war long before this; but God knows best, and has ruled otherwise. We shall yet acknowledge His wisdom, and our error therein. Meanwhile we must work earnestly in the best lights He gives us, trusting that so working still conduces to the great ends He ordains. Surely He intends some great good to follow this mighty convulsion, which no mortal could make, and no mortal could stay. Your people, the Friends, have had, and are having, a very great trial. On principle and faith opposed to both war and oppression, they can only practically oppose oppression by war. In this hard dilemma some have chosen one horn, and some the other. For those appealing to me on conscientious grounds, I have done, and shall do, the best I could and can, in my own conscience, under my oath to the Law. That you believe this I doubt not; and, believing it, I shall receive for our country and myself your earnest prayers to our Father in heaven.

Your sincere friend,

A. Lincoln.

This was submitted to the Secretary of War, Edwin Stanton: "On principle I dislike an oath which requires a man to swear he has not done wrong. It rejects the Christian principle of forgiveness on terms of repentance. I think it is enough if a man does no wrong thereafter." Here, my friends, we have a definite statement by Abraham Lincoln that he recognized that God forgives when we repent. Certainly he also applied this doctrine to himself. (Those who do not repent deserve God's punishment and condemnation, as Scripture plainly teaches.)

Christian Thanksgiving

In closing, we want to say, let us not forget that, although we like to think of our national Thanksgiving day at the end of November as being founded by the Pilgrim Fathers and this in itself is not historically incorrect, the real observance of Thanksgiving comes from the heart and pen of Abraham Lincoln. In the year 1861 in spite of all the ravages of war, he called upon all the people of our country, both the North and the South, to think of the multitudinous blessings of God, and he asked everyone to repair to their respective churches and there give thanks for the blessings of the Almighty. Many people today neglect this day. It has become for us a day of football and turkey. We take for granted all of God's blessings which have come to us since the years of Abraham Lincoln, the healing of the wounds in the South, the building of a great nation now unified, the solution of the political problem as to states' rights and the centrality of the federal government. . . . And though the Blue and the Grey sleep in cemeteries from one end of the country to the other, and though thousands upon thousands of boys died and bled for our rights, I say, even though people forget these things, forget Memorial Day, and forget what it cost others to give us the priceless liberties that you and I have today, we know that Abraham Lincoln in his day did not forget, and that he constantly reminded his fellow citizens of the benign influences of God's Word in our lives and of the importance of religion and faith and church, and above all, loyalty to the Bible which he used in his own life. The little devotional book which he carried around has been recently found and has become an absorbing item to all those interested in Lincolniana.

I say, whenever we celebrate Thanksgiving, perhaps we ought, besides thanking God for all His blessings in our country and for the cross of the Lord Jesus Christ and salvation through His eternal blood, we ought also to think that it was this President of the United States who, although he was also a sinner who had his faults, wanted us to thank God for all His blessings.

The Birthday of George Washington

By Armin W. Born

George Washington was laid to rest in December 1799. The memorial funeral service was held in Zion Lutheran Church, Philadelphia. Many dignitaries were present, including members of the Senate and House of Representatives, the Supreme Court, generals of the army, as well as other prominent persons. A Lutheran pastor conducted the service and it was on this occasion that General Lighthorse Harry Lee, father of Robert E. Lee, referred to Washington as "First in war, first in peace, and first in the hearts of his countrymen."

When we as Christian people gather to hear words relative to this first President and the man known as the "father of our country," we do so only in the perspective and the relevance of his life and leadership to our own happiness as Christians in the Christian church. Since George Washington is indeed correctly called the father of our country, and since we as Christian people enjoy unlimited blessings because of many of the principles which he first enunciated or at least supported and since he was party to the concept of liberty and democracy and freedom of worship and of conscience and the blessed Scriptural principle of the separation of church and state, I say, since this is all true, we do well to pause and to thank God that He led men of the stature and the ability, the statesmanship, and the Christianity of George Washington, in the progress and the beauty, the blossoming and the impact of the Christian church as we know it today in our land.

Whereas, in many another country the life of the church was stymied, the easy flow of doctrine impeded, the open proclamation of the eternal love of God in our Lord and Savior Jesus Christ was dammed up by political and civic leaders, whose religious concepts were contrary to Scripture, but who, with the power of the sword, were able to impose their will upon their people — I say in contrast to that, we had here an entirely different type of leader. Washington steadfastly adhered to the view that an enlightened people could govern themselves through their own representatives. He believed that people of different religious faiths could live side by side and still be joined together in common civic purposes.

I say, then, it is not wrong for us to pause (as does indeed our entire country and the many, many states which have declared the date of George Washington's birth a legal holiday), to think about a few of the religious and Christian actions and concepts of George Washington, and then to thank God that He gave him to our country. Thank God for all those blessings which through Washington and his contemporaries formed the concept of our country's government. We indeed thank God for all the blessings which have come down to us now through those five generations since his time.

The Birthday of Washington: a Christian View

George Washington: a Penitent Sinner

Let us first ask a question: Was George Washington a Christian? By Christian we mean, did he believe in the God of the Bible? Did he accept the words of the Bible? Did he believe that Jesus was his Savior?

That he was a sinner, we know right well. There are men who today write books debunking the great leaders of a yesteryear; they think that by so doing, they do people a great service. As an example of such debunking, W. E. Woodward in his revealing biography of George Washington, writes: "For these reasons I decided to write a biography in which I would treat Washington as a human being, one of exceptional ability, of course, but not without faults or failings. That is the spirit that runs through my book." We can say to Mr. Woodward that we know full well that George Washington was a sinner, because there is not a man upon earth who is not a sinner, "for all have sinned and come short of the glory of God."

We might also say for his information that George Washington would have been one of the first to admit his sinfulness. He was a fairly regular churchgoer, and he had his arguments with the parish pastor of his day, but it seems to us that the most revealing answer to the question which we proposed above is that when his survivors were gathered to hear his last will and testament, the first words which they heard from the heart of this man were: "My beloved, I sincerely trust to meet you all again in heaven, through the merits of my Lord and Savior Jesus Christ." These are words that sound just a little different from the statements of contemporary deists of that day. They show greater faith in the truth of Scripture and the Saviorhood of our Lord than perhaps men like Benjamin Franklin and others enunciated. We therefore believe, on the basis of his last will and testament, that he believed in the Saviorhood of Christ and that we, too, someday shall, by God's grace and mercy, meet Washington in the realms of heaven above.

George Washington — a Praying Man

Nor should we forget that when all seemed to be lost, and when the British invading armies had driven the colonial militia out of Philadelphia to nearby Valley Forge, Washington was struggling manfully to maintain an army intact through the bitter winter — praying in the snow for God's benediction and God's protection and God's abiding sustenance. We therefore honor George Washington also as a praying man, who believed in the economy and the providence and the dispensation of God; he is unlike many leaders of today who never mention God nor believe that the destinies of people and of nations are in the hand of Him who created us, redeemed us, and sanctified us. We much rather today think of him as one who did pray to God and he stands therefore as a glorious example to all of us that we, too, should remember to be instant in prayer for the welfare of our country and that we should lift up holy hands, praying for kings and governors and for "all that are in authority, that we might lead a quiet and peaceable life in all godliness and honesty."

Let me quote at this time also the prayer which appears in some of our own church prayer books, the prayer of George Washington for the United States: "Almighty God, we make our earnest prayer that Thou wilt keep the United States in Thy holy protection, that Thou would'st incline the hearts of the citizens to cultivate a spirit of subordination and obedience to government and entertain a brotherly affection and love for one another, and for their fellow citizens of the United States at large, and finally, that Thou wilt most graciously be pleased to dispose us all to do justice, to love mercy, and to demean ourselves with that charity, humility, and pacific temper of mind, which were the characteristics of the divine author of our blessed religion, without a humble imitation of whose example in these things we can never hope to be a happy nation. Grant our supplication, we beseech Thee, through Jesus Christ, our Lord. Amen."

George Washington — Kind and Considerate

There is the story of his kindness and consideration for others. Whenever he had his headquarters in the homes of citizens, he was solicitous of their welfare, although there might be temporary inconvenience to the owners. In fact, the story is told that one night when he was in a home where the mother was sick and lying in bed, he retired to an adjoining room in order to lay out his plans and to work on his papers, while some of his staff members were in the living room and indulging in loud talk and laughter. George Washington was displeased. We are told that he left his room, tiptoed across the living room where the men were, picked up a book at the opposite end, and, indicating that it was the book he wanted, went back to his room, tiptoeing again, by which he demonstrated to these men that he wanted them to be quiet for the sake of the sick mother in the home. It is said that the officers in shame became quiet and respectful because of this noble act and gesture by George Washington.

Here it appears we have a little story of thoughtfulness for the comforts, the rights, and the happiness of others. Compare this to some of the things that have gone on in our own day when the military have come into homes and ordered people to leave in 20 minutes, and not to take along anything but what they could carry; people have been dispossessed and forced to make the long, long trek into exile because of the ruthless decisions of powerful military leaders. Think of the brutality, the bestiality, and the cruelty that invading armies have inflicted upon the populace, or the demands made upon citizens for the sake of the military with utter disregard for citizen rights and comforts and the dignity of the human individual.

George Washington never lost sight of the dignity of the human individual. For these traits we today honor him and we would say to ourselves that we should learn to respect the dignity of the human soul. We live in an age in which the rush for material things, in which the emphasis upon pleasure, in which the desire for career and education and progress and power . . . somehow has left us cold and hard and calloused to the true beauties of the human soul, which have to do with love and temperance and patience and kindness. These were the great characteristics, or rather the great qualities, which the Lord Jesus wanted you and me to have and to use, on the basis of the fact that we were to recognize that we are all sinful, that in the sight of God no man is better than another man, that we have all come short of the glory of God, and finally, that we have all been redeemed by the same blood of the same Savior, the one and only-begotten Son of the Father.

George Washington — Humble and Helpful

When we, therefore, in foolish pride insist on our rights in our own little domain, when we, because of imagined self-importance, think that some kind of work is beneath our dignity, let us remember the example of Washington's humility. Perhaps you have read the famous story which tells that as a general, with his coat covering the insignia of his rank, Washington was riding past a detail where a corporal was commanding his men to lift a heavy log beyond their capacity. He was shouting at them and commanding them to "heave ho." Since they could not do it, George Washington dismounted quickly, walked over, and with his strong and tall body, gave the log a quick push, and it went into its place. Turning to the corporal, he asked him why he had not helped his men. The man said, "Sir, do you not see that I am a corporal?" George Washington humbly opened his coat and said, "Yes, sir, I see you are a corporal, but I wish for you to see that I am the general."

If this story is true, and we believe it is true, we have here another classic example of the humble obedience and willingness to help his fellowman which filled the heart of this great leader of our country.

Since Washington's Time

Since that day, many years have passed. The country which he helped to found and of which you and I are citizens, has gone through many years of growth, heartache, progress, and problems. Some 62 years after the death of George Washington, the country was torn by a great Civil War. Based on moral issues, the questions then revolved around the Bible and about God's will. Since that day our country has grown in industry and might. Contrary to the advice of George Washington that we should not be entangled in foreign commitments, the world has so shrunk by communication and transportation and travel and speed that in our jet-propulsion age, it is impossible for our country to be completely aloof from other countries. Since his day we have fought with four different European countries. God has continued to give us the victory.

In our day people stream by the millions to church Sunday after Sunday. It is a shame that millions of others do not. But had George Washington been able to envisage the blessings and the beauty of our great farmlands, of our teeming cities, of our many factories, of our great system of education with all its universities, and had he been able to catch a vision of the countryside and the villages and the towns and the cities, where church-spire after church-spire points heavenward — if he could have seen the luxury and the miracle of a world on wheels, the miracle of our television sets through which we can all travel to Washington today and see what our representatives in government do for us or do not do for us, if he could have imagined that after the lapse of two centuries the Constitution of the United States would still be intact (and guarded in a most precious manner by our citizens), and that amendment after amendment has been added to make it still more democratic and still more effective for the happiness of our people, he would indeed have rejoiced over the fruits of his labors.

However, all of these things happened under the guidance and the provision of God. It was He who set these things in motion. It was He who so guarded and guided our country that it did not fall apart, but rather became a mighty factor in opening the airways to the proclamation of the Gospel of our Lord Jesus Christ. God has so guided our country since the days of George Washington that we are a blessing to countless millions of people through such organizations as World Relief and through the hundreds and thousands of missionaries that go out of Christian churches into other countries proclaiming the blessed message of the Gospel of the Lord Jesus Christ. Religious freedom has given churches a great and a wonderful opportunity to grow and to work. It is through God's providence that many are cared for and protected by our country. We are the envy of countless millions of people because of the blessings which have come to us — a people that has to this day not completely forgotten the Lord God. Many, many Scripture passages tell us that a nation that will honor its God will receive the blessings of the Lord from on high, that "righteousness exalteth a nation" and that if we remain true to Him, He will bring us into a land of flowing milk and honey. I say, all these great prophecies have been fulfilled right here in our own country as a result of pioneering mothers with a child in one hand and a Bible in the other and of fathers who, when they came into a new area, immediately built a church as well as their homes.

In spite of American sins which today cry to high heaven, in spite of the laxity and the spiritual complacency, in spite of the refusal of countless peoples to remember their Creator and their Lord, in spite of the wastefulness and the sinful pleasures and the immorality that goes on in our country — because of these pioneer Christian men, and because of their dedication to the church, and because of God's promises of which Luther says "He promises grace and blessing to all that keep His commandments," we today still have the priceless boon of liberty, we still have freedom of worship, we still have the open Bible, we still have democracy, we still have separation of church and state.

Thanksgiving and Supplication

Dear friends, on the occasion of Washington's birthday — without giving undue adulation or prominence to this man (because he was still just a man saved by the blood of Christ) — it nonetheless behooves us to think of that miraculous guidance that God gave to the founding fathers of our country; down deep in our hearts there should breathe forth some kind of prayer, some voice of gratitude, some thought of marveling over God's ways.

And then, turning from the father of our country, our thoughts move to our own fathers in our homes, to the church fathers, and above all to our Father which is in heaven. We, too, in the dark hours of concern that not everything may be well with our country, should kneel in the snow of our fears, with men like George Washington, and implore God to continue His hand of benediction upon our people and upon our country, that He might continue unto us the blessings of the Word of God proclaimed in our churches. Yea, "Praise to the Lord, the Almighty, the King of Creation! O my soul, praise Him for He is thy health and salvation."

By the Cross of Christ We Conquer Sin

By RUDOLPH F. REHMER

(Ash Wednesday)

And almost all things are by the Law purged with blood, and without shedding of blood is no remission. It was therefore necessary that the patterns of things in the heavens should be purified with these, but the heavenly things themselves with better sacrifices than these. For Christ is not entered into the holy places made with hands, which are the figures of the true, but into heaven itself, now to appear in the presence of God for us. Nor yet that He should offer Himself often, as the high priest entereth into the Holy Place every year with blood of others, for then must He often have suffered since the foundation of the world. But now once in the end of the world hath He appeared to put away sin by the sacrifice of Himself. — *Hebrews 9:22-26*

"Jesus, I will ponder now on Thy holy Passion." This is the resolution of the church of Jesus Christ as it enters the sacred season of Lent. Though Lent originally came from the Anglo-Saxon word *Lencten*, meaning "springtime," it soon became associated in Christian usage with that momentous act of God, the crucifixion of our Lord Jesus Christ, which again brought springtime to the hearts and souls of men.

The 40 days of Lent have been variously interpreted. Some link them with the 40 days of Jesus' temptation in the wilderness. Others prefer to take the 40 as the number of hours that Jesus was dead, from sundown on Good Friday to sunrise on Easter morning. These 40 hours were then extended to 40 days of prayer and meditation to give Christians more time and opportunity to contemplate Jesus' death and its meaning for their lives.

This is the dedicated objective of every Christian at the beginning of Lent, to raise the cross anew in his life, to center his thinking more completely upon the death of Jesus Christ, and to learn to appreciate its meaning for him more fully.

Without a doubt the primary meaning of Christ's cross is that through it sin is conquered and that through the cross and Christ's sacrificial death upon it we can conquer sin in our own lives. May we, then, during this Lenten season earnestly fix our eyes upon the cross and ponder the central truth of the Christian faith — that Christ died for our sins. May the Holy Spirit engrave it upon our minds and hearts that

By the Cross of Christ We Conquer Sin

I
The Cross Required the Shedding of Blood

The crucifixion of our Lord Jesus Christ brought about His death, a death which Scripture consistently terms a sacrificial death. Crucifixion, as a form of punishment, was indeed the cruelest form of death. Introduced by the Phoenicians, it was extended in its cruelty by the Romans. Though the Jewish Maccabean King Jannaeus did crucify some 800 persons in Jerusalem at one time in the days before the Roman rule, this was a small number compared with the crucifixions which took place under the Romans. Historians say that during the last siege of Jerusalem, about A. D. 70, for example, hundred of crosses arose daily till there seemed to be neither sufficient room for them nor sufficient wood to fashion them.

Death by crucifixion was a bloody death. When we sing in our Lenten hymns, "Glory be to Jesus, Who in bitter pains Poured for me the lifeblood From His sacred veins," and "Come hither now and ponder, 'Twill fill thy soul with wonder, Blood streams from every pore," these are not merely poetic figures of speech. With nails driven through hands and feet, the crucified one bled profusely, so that very often death resulted from bleeding to death. There is no denying that Jesus' death was a bloody death.

II
The Shedding of Blood Was Necessary
for the Atonement of Sins

The author of the Epistle to the Hebrews states very emphatically in our text: "Indeed, under the Law almost everything is purified with blood, and without the shedding of blood there is no forgiveness of sins" (RSV). In the Old Testament blood was considered a sign of life. In Deut. 12 the Lord through Moses sets forth requirements for His chosen people as they are about to possess the Promised Land. He commands: ". . . thou shalt eat in thy gates whatsoever thy soul lusteth after. . . . Only be sure that thou eat not the blood, for the blood is the life, and thou mayest not eat the life with the flesh." (Deut. 12:21-23)

As blood was considered to contain the very essence of physical life, the shedding of blood was deemed essential for spiritual life, for atonement of sin. The writer of the Epistle to the Hebrews therefore clearly shows how in Old Testament times the blood of bulls and of goats sanctified to the purifying of the flesh. In fact, this is the backdrop of the whole epistle, the sacrificial system of the Old Testament. Against this backdrop the author sets the sacrifice of Jesus upon the cross to point out how once "at the end of the age He hath appeared to put away sin by the sacrifice of Himself."

The sacrificial system of the Jews was a very involved one. It included primarily sacrifices of goats, bulls, heifers, and sheep for the expiation of sin. When Aaron received the breastplate of judgment containing the Urim and Thummim, he also received the directions regarding the blood sacrifices he and his sons were to make for the sins of the people (Ex. 28-30). But Aaron and his successors needed always to purify themselves first with blood. So when they were ordered to take two rams for offerings, the blood of one was to be put on the tip of the right ear of Aaron, and upon the tip of the right ear of his sons, and upon the thumb of their right hand, and upon the great toe of their right foot, and upon their garments. Such rituals were to be performed often. In fact, the command of the Lord was, "Thou shalt offer every day a bullock for a sin offering for atonement. . . . The one lamb thou shalt offer in the morning, and the other lamb thou shalt offer at even." (Ex. 29:36, 39)

The climax of these bloody sacrifices of atonement was reached on the Great Day of Atonement, when the High Priest would enter the Holy of holies, within the veil which separated the Holy Place from the Most Holy Place, to sprinkle blood upon the ark of the covenant. The numerous sacrifices of the day and the week of the atonement are described in Lev. 16 and Num. 29. By reading them we get the picture of the vast amount of blood which was shed for sin offerings, for the atonement of the sins of the priests and of the people.

"It was necessary," explains our text, "that the pattern of things in the heavens be purified with these, but the heavenly

things themselves with better sacrifices than these." Here the King
James translation is a bit cumbersome. The thought is brought out
more clearly by the New English Bible: "If, then, these sacrifices
cleanse the copies of heavenly things, those heavenly things themselves require better sacrifices to cleanse them." Yes, the sprinkling
of the blood on the altar, the cleansing of the garments, the bloody
sacrifices — all these were but copies of the great sacrifice of Christ
on Calvary's cross, to which we lift our eyes and hearts in faith
and adoration.

Through Christ's sacrifice on the cross and the shedding of His
blood He has made a new covenant with us. Just as blood was
necessary for expiation of sin in the old covenant, blood was also
the means for the making of a new covenant. The Old Testament
precedent of blood to ratify and verify a covenant we find illus-
trated in Gen. 15, where Abram's covenant with the Lord was
sealed through the offering of various animals. The new covenant,
which God Himself made with us, the spiritual heirs of Abraham,
needed also to be ratified with blood, the lifeblood of Jesus Christ,
our Lord.

Christ's sacrifice is a better sacrifice than those of the Old
Testament. The transcendent superiority of His sacrifice lies in
this, that He sacrificed Himself and that He was and is God's
only-begotten Son, the very Paschal Lamb of God. His sacrifice
was the one to which all the Old Testament sacrifices pointed. His
was the original; all the other sacrifices of expiation by means of
the blood of animals were only copies of that original. As aspiring
artists today spend hours in art galleries like the Louvre of Paris
and the Uffizi gallery of Florence seeking to copy the originals,
like Da Vinci's "Mona Lisa" and Dürer's "Adoration of the Magi,"
and cannot duplicate them, for there is but one original, so the
sacrifice of bulls and goats and heifers could not replace the original sacrifice. It was this original that was conceived in the counsels of the Holy Trinity. Christ's death on the hill of Calvary was to
be the climax, the one Great Day of Atonement, when "He Himself
bare our sins in His own body on the tree that we, being dead to
sins, should live unto righteousness." Let us reflect often during
this Lententide on the blessed fact that "the blood of Jesus Christ,
His [God's] Son, cleanses us from all sin."

III

Christ's Sacrifice on the Cross Conquered Sin
for All Time

When Jesus died upon the cross of Calvary, all sins and transgressions of mankind of the past, the present, and of future ages
were atoned for, and there is now no longer any need for additional

sacrifices of expiation. The veil which Christ entered once was not a curtain of thick cloth, but a creation of God Himself, His own human body. As we hold firmly to the atonement, we must just as firmly hold the truth of the incarnation, "that God was in Christ, reconciling the world unto Himself." Christ's human nature was not generated in the usual manner, but "He was conceived by the Holy Ghost" and then born of the Virgin Mary. In the veil of His flesh He performed His priestly duties, which included implicit obedience to the Father's will and then suffering and dying on the cross. And with His perfectly sanctified flesh ("for He did no sin, neither was guile found in His mouth") He has now entered into the very presence of God to continue His priestly duties. No more does He need to bring sacrifice. That priestly function has been completed for all time. "But as it is, He has appeared once for all at the end of the age to put away sin by the sacrifice of Himself" (v. 26 RSV). Now having shed His blood, He presents this sacrifice of His blood before God as the constant token and seal of the forgiveness of our sins. "Christ is not entered into the holy places made with hands . . . but into heaven itself, now to appear in the presence of God for us." (V. 24)

"He ever liveth to make intercession for us." Before the bar of God's justice we have an advocate, a lawyer, Jesus Christ, the Righteous." As we place our full reliance and trust in Him, His blood avails for us. We must then never act or pretend that the "sacrifices" we make for Jesus in Lent or at any other time have any merit for the forgiveness of sins. It remains forever true, whether the time is Lent or not, that "all our righteousnesses are as filthy rags." We had nothing to do with Christ's coming into the veil of His flesh; we had nothing to do with His making that one great sacrifice at the end of the age; we had nothing to do with it, except that out of love for us and all men God planned it, God executed it, and God sealed it with the blood of His Son. Quite properly we ask in the Christian questions of the Catechism, "What was it that moved Him to die and to make satisfaction for your sins?" and then answer, "His great love to His Father and to me and other sinners, as it is written in John 14, Rom. 5, Gal. 2, and Eph. 5."

Once and for all, purely out of love, Christ hath put away sin by the sacrifice of Himself. Contrition, sorrow, repentance for sin, we can and should have. A new and deeper appreciation of God's love as it shines through the cross may prompt us to bring Lenten self-denial offerings, prompt us to resolving to worship Christ, with God's help, more frequently in midweek Lenten services, in private devotions at home, or in an open church, or stir us to be more concerned for those who have not yet embraced Him in faith; but these can never be substituted for the real and enduring sacrifice. Jesus alone could bring to God a ransom for us. He offered up the sacrifice once when He offered up Himself (Heb. 9:27), and now "He ever liveth to make intercession for us." (Heb. 9:25)

IV

Through the Cross There Is a Continuous Conquest of Sin in Our Lives

As we in the Lenten season in particular focus our eyes upon the cross, the altar of sacrifice of "the Lamb slain from the foundations of the world," we shall also want to fix our eyes on that cross to draw from Christ the power for our constant fight against sin. Daily we must declare war against "the lust of the flesh, and the lust of the eyes, and the pride of life" in ourselves. With all his wiles does Satan try to convince us that we can improve ourselves and that it is old fashioned to believe that "there is power in the blood." Only through a strong faith, nourished and built up by His Spirit through Word and Sacrament, can we confront the Evil One with the evidence how the cross works mightily in us to combat the sins of every day.

In the year A. D. 312 the Roman emperor Constantine had his outnumbered forces stationed at the Mulvian bridge about 10 miles outside Rome. On the other side of the Tiber River were the forces of Maxentius, the rival emperor. Constantine, well aware that Maxentius had the famed praetorian guards on his side, sought divine help. But being a worshiper of Mithra, the Persian sun god, he was minded to seek her help. However, on the evening before the battle, as the legend goes, he saw a cross above the sun as it was setting in the west. In letters of light the cross bore the inscription *In hoc signo vinces,* "In this sign conquer." On the next day, Oct. 28, 312, the furious battle took place. The praetorian guards were overcome. Maxentius himself was drowned in the Tiber. And from that time Constantine had emblazoned on his shield and on the shields of his soldiers the sign of the cross. He issued the famous edict of Milan, which made the Christian religion a legitimate religion in the Roman empire. Constantine himself is said to have been baptized.

"In this sign conquer." For us these words are not legendary. They are fact. Through the cross we can conquer, not the cavalry of a national enemy but the fiery darts of the Wicked One. In the cross we have the symbol of victory, and through Christ, who strengtheneth us, we can receive the power to conquer every sin, great or small, known or unknown, revolting to us or dear to our natural self.

The very purpose of our existence, of our life and being, is "to be crucified with Christ" and have "the body of our sins put away." Having died with Christ, we are also to live with Him and to live in Him. Once in the end of the age Christ suffered that our sins could be put away and that henceforth our life might be hid with Him in God. As we, then, in this holy and blessed season of Lent come near the cross, may we find in it not just the cruel instrument of torture and death where Christ with His blood paid for our sins, but may we find in it the source of life, of joy, of strength that we may live for Him. As J. S. Whale writes: "Just as long ago we sinners crucified Him, slaying our sacrificial Victim; and just as He took His surrendered and outpoured life through the Veil of His broken flesh into the holy presence of the Father, and atoned for us: so we come now, pleading that eternal sacrifice and participating in it with adoring gratitude. And because Christ-in-His-Church thus offers to the Father the Church-in-Himself, we offer and present ourselves, our souls and bodies, to be a reasonable holy and living sacrifice. He makes the offering. He accepts the offering. He receives us." * Therefore in this Lenten season and always let us praise Him with believing hearts and sing:

There is a fountain filled with blood
Drawn from Immanuel's veins,
And sinners plunged beneath that flood
Lose all their guilty stains.

Dear dying Lamb, Thy precious blood
Shall never lose its power
Till all the ransomed Church of God
Be saved to sin no more,
Be saved to sin no more.

The Large Upper Room

By HENRY W. BRILL

(Maundy Thursday)

Then came the day of Unleavened Bread, when the passover must be killed. And He sent Peter and John, saying, Go and prepare us the passover that we may eat. And they said unto Him, Where wilt Thou that we prepare? And He said unto them, Behold, when ye are entered into the city, there shall a man meet you, bearing a pitcher of water; follow him into the house where he entereth in. And ye shall say unto the goodman of the house, The Master saith unto thee, Where is the guestchamber where I shall eat the passover with My disciples? And he shall shew you a large upper room furnished. There make ready. And they went, and found as He had said unto them, and they made ready the passover.

* Quoted by permission of the publishers, The Syndics of the Cambridge University Press, from J. S. Whale's *Victor and Victim*, p. 59.

And when the hour was come, He sat down and the twelve apostles with Him. And He said unto them, With desire I have desired to eat this passover with you before I suffer, for I say unto you, I will not any more eat thereof until it be fulfilled in the kingdom of God. And He took the cup, and gave thanks, and said, Take this, and divide it among yourselves; for I say unto you, I will not drink of the fruit of the vine until the kingdom of God shall come.

And he took bread, and gave thanks, and brake it, and gave unto them, saying, This is My body, which is given for you. This do in remembrance of Me. Likewise also the cup after supper, saying, This cup is the new testament in My blood, which is shed for you.

Luke 22:7-20

St. Luke describes the Upper Room as being "large," and large it is. In its significance it reaches way back 1,500 years into the Old Testament, to the night when the Children of Israel first ate the passover in the land of Egypt. It reaches forward to this Maundy Thursday of the year 1963 and to us. We who have gathered here to commemorate the institution of the Lord's Supper and to partake of it are in the Upper Room. But it does not stop with this day or with us. It reaches out to the end of time, and beyond time into eternity. It is truly a *large* Upper Room.

The Large Upper Room

I

The Upper Room of the Old Testament Passover

Everything in the Upper Room can be characterized by the word "deliverance." As they had done for years and centuries, the faithful of Israel gathered in groups of ten or more on this particular Thursday evening in the spring of the year 30 to commemorate the deliverance of their forefathers from the slavery of Egypt. However, from the very beginning the Passover was also a type of the far greater deliverance from the slavery of sin to be accomplished by the Messiah, "the Lamb of God, which taketh away the sin of the world." (John 1:29)

As Peter and John ascended the temple steps in the afternoon of the first Maundy Thursday with the paschal lamb to be sacrificed for the feast, they must have thought less about a deliverance accomplished 1,500 years previous than about the impending happenings which Jesus had been impressing upon them and which seemed so intimately related to this Passover. The fact that they had found the man with the pitcher of water and the "large upper room furnished," just as the Lord had told them, not only impressed upon them again the omniscience and deity of Christ but also reminded them that what He had told them about His suffering and death would surely come to pass. Their inward conflict between their desire for deliverance by Christ and their natural aversion to the whole thought of the sacrifice of Himself prevented them from thinking clearly on the subject. Nevertheless, they must have known, although hazily, that the slain lamb they were carrying to the Upper Room for the Passover Feast was a type of a wonderful deliverance soon to be accomplished.

The hour for the Passover meal had arrived. The sacrificial lamb had been roasted according to the Law. Jesus and His 12 disciples were reclining upon pillows around the low table in the Upper Room. Before the first cup of wine was passed to open the feast, the Lord said, "With desire I have desired to eat this passover with you before I suffer." His Savior heart was burning to accomplish the deliverance which the Passover lamb prefigured. This would be the last Passover, the last supper. On the morrow Christ, the real paschal Lamb, would hang on the cross until He could say, "It is finished" (John 19:30). Then there would be no more need of Passover lambs in the Old Testament sense, to prefigure the real Passover Lamb. Then the faith of God's children would no longer rest on promise but on fulfillment, on completed redemption.

II

The Upper Room of the New Testament Sacrament

The transition from the old to the new was so natural, so normal. The blending of the Old Testament Passover into the New Testament Sacrament of the Lord's Supper was so smooth that there hardly seems a paragraph break in St. Luke's record of it. Really, in a sense, they are one and the same concept of the faithful gathered about the Lamb sacrificed for the deliverance of God's people.

And yet there is an enormous difference. The Old Testament Passover lamb, which the faithful sacrificed and ate, could never in itself take away sins. It could only typify and foreshadow. But the Lamb of God sacrificed on the cross, whose body and blood we eat and drink in the Lord's Supper, is the very Lamb of God, whose blood "cleanseth us from all sin." (1 John 1:7)

At the close of the Passover meal, while wine and unleavened bread were still on the table, Jesus stressed that this was His last Passover and indicated that all Passovers would now cease. Then He "took bread, and gave thanks, and brake it, and gave unto them, saying, This is My body, which is given for you. This do in remembrance of Me. Likewise also the cup after supper, saying, This cup is the new testament in My blood, which is shed for you." With these simple words the Upper Room was transformed from a place of promise into a place of fulfillment. "This is My body, which is given for you. . . . This is the new testament in My blood,

which is shed for you." The disciples were now no longer eating
the flesh of a symbolical, figurative lamb, but they were eating the
flesh and drinking the blood of the Lamb of God, given and shed for
them for the remission of their sins. Thus the Upper Room became
for them the place where God pours down all His saving love in
a unique manner. He not only told them, "Thine iniquity is taken
away, and thy sin is purged," as He once told Isaiah (Is. 6:3), but
also gave them the very body and blood by which all sin is taken
away and is purged.

"This do in remembrance of Me." The Upper Room was not
to be closed after the first Maundy Thursday. The disciples were
to do this, and continue to do it, until the end of their lives. Nor
was it to be closed after the age of the apostles. The Bible makes
it clear that the faithful are to continue to show the Lord's death
through the celebration of this sacrament till Christ comes at the
end of the world (1 Cor. 11:26). The Upper Room is open to us,
and we gather there frequently about the Table of the Lord.

It is a large Upper Room, and you and I are in it tonight.
We came here as sinners needing forgiveness, as captives needing
deliverance. A term which well describes our spiritual problem
is the term "captivity." By nature all of us are captives, prisoners,
and that which holds us bound is our own sin. Conscious of our
many sins, we feel ourselves pressed into the dark corner of our
spiritual prison cell, hounded captives. In our sin and sorrow we
yearn for deliverance. And here in the Upper Room we find our
Deliverer. Our Lord and Savior fought our battle for us to His
very death on the Cross, and He was completely victorious. He gave
His body and shed His blood in atonement for our guilt. He delivered us from all our sin, from death, and from the power of the
devil. This Deliverer is here with us as surely as He was in the
Upper Room the night He was betrayed. As we approach the
Lord's Table, He gives the bread into our mouth, and He presses
the cup to our lips, saying to us: "This is My body, which is given
for you. . . . This cup is the new testament in My blood, which
is shed for you." And as we eat and drink, we participate in the
new covenant which God made with sinners through Christ,
whereby He forgives our iniquities and remembers our sins no
more (Jer. 31:34). Oh, blessed, indeed, are our experiences at the
table of Christ in the Upper Room!

III

The Upper Room of Glory

The Upper Room, as St. Luke describes it, is large. It reaches
not only to the end of time but through it into eternity. At the
beginning of the last Passover Jesus told His disciples: "I will not

any more eat thereof until it be fulfilled in the kingdom of God. . . . I will not drink of the fruit of the vine until the kingdom of God shall come." Here our Lord looked beyond the last Passover, beyond the better feast of His body and blood, beyond all the experiences of the faithful at the table of the Upper Room, unto the end of the world, looked into eternity itself, and assured His disciples and us that He would feast with us again in the glory and perfect joys of heaven.

This is the eternal climax of everything that was foreshadowed in the Old Testament Passover and offered and dispensed in the New Testament sacrament. In the Book of Revelation Jesus calls it the marriage supper of the Lamb (Rev. 19:9). The heavenly Bridegroom, who nourishes His bride (the church), while she is on earth, with His own body and blood, given and shed for her for the remission of sins, will finally and forever feast with her in the halls of paradise.

> In mansions fair and spacious
> Will God the feast prepare
> And, ever kind and gracious,
> Bid us its riches share.
> There bliss that knows no measure
> From springs of love shall flow,
> And never-changing pleasure
> His bounty will bestow.

This is always the great hope of the faithful. Amid all the sins and sorrows, the temptations and troubles, the disturbances and disappointments, the perils and pains, the trials and tears of this present life, we yearn for ultimate deliverance. Although it is true that all things are ours in Christ Jesus here and now, we are still pilgrims wandering in a strange land of sin and imperfection, longing for home. Each time we gather in the Upper Room on earth to feed our souls with the body and the blood, not only does our joy over our present deliverance grow, but also our longing for our final deliverance increases.

In the final consummation of the Savior's grace the light of heaven will flood the Upper Room with all its perfect brilliance. Seeing Jesus face to face, we shall join all the saints in light in the endless marriage feast of the Lamb.

The Upper Room is large. In it the Old Testament believers ate their Passover of remembrance and hope. In it we gather with the whole New Testament church on earth to eat and drink the body and blood given and shed for us. In it we shall feast forever with our Lord and Savior in glory.

Christ the Conqueror of Death

By F. Dean Lueking

(Good Friday)

Since therefore the children share in flesh and blood, He Himself likewise partook of the same nature, that through death He might destroy him who has the power of death, that is, the devil, and deliver all those who through fear of death were subject to lifelong bondage.

Hebrews 2:14, 15 RSV

A great challenge awaits us this Good Friday. It is to grasp something of the infinitely great meaning and blessing which have come to us because Jesus Christ endured the death of crucifixion upon a hill of execution so many years ago. For most of us that story is not new. But all of us must now return to that familiar account and see it not merely as a story of how death cruelly cut down a blameless man. We must understand that in the death of Jesus Christ the sting and power of death itself is forever conquered. He liberates us from bondage to death so that our lives might be free for joyous service to Him.

As Man Views Death

On our own we human beings take a definite and rather obvious view of the meaning of death. In human parlance death is a word which describes the end of physical life. It is something we speak of as yet in the future so far as we are concerned. Death is the opposite to life. It is where life is not. It is shrouded in mystery. Death is, in Hamlet's word, "that undiscovered country from whose bourn no traveler doth return." Death has nothing in common with life. Thus we place our cemeteries outside our town gates, away from the activity of life. And though the embalmer's art attempts to restore lifelikeness to the lifeless corpse, the glow and touch of life that once animated the body is delivered by death into the clutch of an enemy against whom we are helpless.

Death, as man views it, is a vast and ominous prospect. Men have thought hard and long about this mysterious fact of death, and these thoughts have evoked some classical interpretations of its meaning. In some of the great monuments of human literature death is the relentless protagonist whose inevitable victory nonetheless entices something heroic out of the human spirit. For the classic tragedies all point to the noble struggle of man against death as the sign that his very struggle against the impossible is the seal of human greatness at its peak. But beyond this praise of man as the rebel against his sure destiny is the melancholy awareness that it is always death that writes the last word on the last page of every book of human life.

As the Bible Reveals the Meaning of Death

But the Biblical view of death pentrates far deeper than our human associations with the term. True, the Scriptures tell us of men whose lives were brought short by death. But the Biblical view of death pries open a vastly greater dimension of meaning. Death is not only that which waits at the end of life. Death is that demonic power which also surrounds life and enslaves it at every point. The author of the Letter to the Hebrews speaks of the power of death to subject men to lifelong bondage through fear (2:15). Luther's hymn emphasizes the same truth: "In the midst of earthly life Snares of death surround us." The Biblical meaning of death can be compared to a man who is told of a debt he owes. And as he reads each clause of the terms of his debt, he discovers to his horror that his debt is not only something to be paid from this time forward but also something that is retroactive! Death signifies a condition of life. It describes a whole way of being. Death means life apart from God.

Death Is the Tool of Satan

Yet still another word about the Biblical teaching of death must be added. Human beings view death as an ominous and impersonal course of fate and destiny. God reveals death to be the outrigger of evil and rebellion made personal. The text speaks of "him who has the power of death, that is, the devil." Death ought to be capitalized, then, for it refers to the personal sway and rule which the devil holds upon life. This is not to say that being a finite creature is in itself evil. If this were the case, then it would have been impossible for the Son of God to "share in flesh and blood" (2:14). No, the power of Satan's tyrannical rule through death is the fretful anxiety which descends upon us at the realization of death. You know many stories of wealthy people who have begged doctors with their fortunes to prolong life, yet the fear of death cannot be bought off. Closer to home, you must recognize in your own life the tremendous force which the awareness of death exerts upon you. Why is it that we squeeze each day of life so selfishly? It is because of the realization that this means one day closer to the end. Thus the philosophy of so many is "life must be lived to the hilt while the living is good." Do you see what is meant by the textual phrase "lifelong bondage"? Do you understand the subtle tyranny of Satan's grip upon life through the fear of death? This is what it means to be a sinner: to live under the illusion that we are free when distant from God, free to be our own master. The truth is that we are under bondage, and the relentless hold which is upon us is made real by the fact that there is an end with us. Death is sin's final wage. (Rom. 6:23)

The Deliverance Christ Has Won for Us

Now the great and joyous message which this Holy Week
proclaims is that our Lord Jesus Christ has broken the grip of
death over life and delivered us. In a single sentence our text
states this great truth. The good news concerning the death of
Jesus Christ is this, that God has vanquished the prince of darkness by the cross and resurrection of His beloved Son. Our
heavenly Father has not abandoned us to the plight of lifelong
bondage under the satanic fear of death. In the work of the Son
at the cross the old tyranny is broken. The climax of the Savior's
mission to this world lies in His triumphant word while hanging
upon the cross: "It is finished." The former sway of death and
fear is finished. Because Christ has conquered death, we have
been delivered from the dominion of darkness and transferred to
life under His own loving rule. (Col. 1:13)

Christ's View of His Own Death

When we look carefully at the full picture of our Lord's last
days upon earth as the four gospels portray it, we gain a striking
and impressive insight concerning Christ's own view of His impending death. As the events of His earthly ministry led through
mounting conflicts and crises, He could have avoided the cross
simply by retiring to some remote area far removed from the
danger which awaited Him in Jerusalem. But He resisted this
temptation. He knew that it was necessary that the Son of man
"suffer many things from the elders and chief priests and scribes,
and be killed, and on the third day be raised" (Matt. 16:21). Thus
He set His face steadfastly toward Jerusalem (Luke 9:51). He
did so, however, not with a stoic resignation to blind fate. Nor
did He merely seek a martyr's crown for the sake of etching His
name indelibly upon the pages of human history as one more
struggler for the right.

No, the startling truth is that the Lord Christ went freely to
the cross, trusting completely in His Father's will that "He, for
whom and by whom all things exist, in bringing many sons to glory,
should make the Pioneer of their salvation perfect through suffering" (Heb. 2:10). And so Jesus says of His own death: "No one
takes My life from Me, but I lay it down of My own accord.
I have power to lay it down, and I have power to take it again;
this charge I have received from My Father" (John 10:18). Jesus
is by no means, then, a helpless leaf driven to destruction by the
winds of circumstance. Standing before Caiaphas, or Herod, or
Pontius Pilate, He is calm and composed while it is His enemies
who are engulfed in a delirium of panic and rage. And while He
hangs upon the cross, His words reveal not only the anguish of

One who bears the full weight of divine wrath upon the sins of the whole world but also a tender concern for those who torment Him. If ever the powers of evil would have appeared to have triumphed, it was at the cross. But just the opposite is true! The Evil One was vanquished through the death and resurrection of Jesus Christ. "Through death He broke the rule of him who held us in lifelong bondage."

The Fruits of Christ's Victory

We come to this Good Friday service of worship not to lament the tragic death of a heroic young Galilean; we gather here around the Word of Him who has "tasted death for everyone" (Heb. 2:9). His death has altered the destiny of every one of us both for time and for eternity. Because He is the risen Lord, He bids us to lift up our hearts in rejoicing because through His death He has done for us what we were helpless to do for ourselves. He has vanquished the paralyzing power of Satan over us. He frees us from bondage to fear because of the guilt of our sins and brings us peace and power for renewed living through His Gospel. It is because of this that we can rejoice this Good Friday: our death, our guilt, our sin lie behind us, not ahead of us. This is true because Jesus Christ is our Lord. In the power of His Holy Spirit He liberates us from our last and great enemy — death.

The person who knows this truth about his own death is in a position to know the fullest and grandest truth about his own life. Because our Redeemer has removed the sting and power of death, we are invited to share with Him in the fruits of His victory. Through your Baptism you have been joined with Christ in His death and raised to newness of life! Never let the staggering fact that death no longer rules you grow dim and powerless in your life. Never let the great gladness of God's gift of His life to us through Christ sag and founder upon the bare skeleton of an intellectual system. Rather see your whole life as an opportunity to share the gift which God has shared with us all because of what took place on that first Good Friday. There will come times when all the luster and joy of Christ's victory fades from our minds and hearts. Such moments come when severe illness, heartache, business reverses, and other sudden calamities overtake us. It is especially at such times that you will need to recall what God intends to do within us through the death of His Son. It is deliverance that He grants. That deliverance comes again and again to us by the good news that our sins are forgiven.

Another point of emphasis concerning the fruits of Christ's victory over death concerns our own natural reluctance to face the final moment of our life upon earth. No man relishes the

thought of his death. The thought of parting with the familiar
faces and scenes of this world sends a shudder to the depths of
the bravest men. But inevitable as that fear of death is, Christ
has made it unnecessary for every man who trusts Him as the
Good Shepherd, who leads through the valley of the shadow.
More than a century ago the Danish Christian Soeren Kierkegaard
wrote of the prospect of death in a manner that indicates the
incomparable blessing of Christ's victory over death:

> When the deathbed is prepared for you, and when you have
> gone to bed, never more to rise, and they only wait for you
> to turn to the other side to die, and the stillness grows about
> you — when gradually the nearer friends go away, and the still-
> ness grows because only the dearest remain, while death comes
> nearer you; then when the dearest go softly away, and the
> stillness grows, because only your own family remain, and
> when the last one for the last time has bent over you, and turns
> away, and now you turn to the side of death: there yet remains
> One by that side, He the last at the deathbed, who was the first
> to conquer Death through His love for you.*

And so the Christ who is the Life of all the living, and the
Death of death our foe, delivers us through His death into His
kingdom of life. He who has stood by us throughout each moment
of our earthly pilgrimage shall not fail us at the last moment.
Because He has gone on into death before us, He returns to take
our hand and bid our anxious heart to be at peace.

Motherhood and Faith

By HARRY N. HUXHOLD

(Mother's Day)

Samuel was ministering before the Lord, a boy girded with a linen
ephod. And his mother used to make for him a little robe and take it
to him each year, when she went up with her husband to offer her
yearly sacrifice. Then Eli would bless Elkanah and his wife and say,
"The Lord give you children by this woman for the loan which she
lent to the Lord"; so then they would return to their home. And the
Lord visited Hannah, and she conceived and bore three sons and two
daughters. And the boy Samuel grew in the presence of the Lord.
1 Samuel 2:18-21 RSV

IN THE NAME OF JESUS. An old Spanish proverb reads:
"An ounce of mother is worth a pound of clergy." This suggests
the truth that the mother exerts more influence in shaping the
lives and destinies of her children than any other person. She is
in position to teach and exemplify Christian precepts and faith

---

* Soeren Kierkegaard, *Works of Love*, translated by David F.
Swenson and Lillian M. Swenson (Princeton University Press), pp.
121, 122. (Used by permission.)

to a much larger degree than any other representatives of the church. The mother is the first and foremost representative of God's love to her children. The Christian heart of a mother is God's fullest vessel for pouring out His love upon a new generation. We can easily become sentimental about mother love unless we see the role of mother in its profound relationship with God. The story of Hannah provides insight into the relationship between a pious mother and God. The story is a good example of

Motherhood and Faith

I

It is quite clear from the story of Hannah that she came to a sense of the meaning of motherhood through faith. The story pictures her as praying fervently that God would bless her with a child. In her prayers she promises that if God would bless her with a son she would dedicate him to His service. Through these prayers for God's blessing, Hannah came to understand the relationship between the Fatherhood of God and the parenthood of man. She, who had been childless for many years, who had been the rebuke of other women, was burdened with the desire to be mother. In spite of her hopes, she remained barren. In her emptiness she encountered the great truth which all mothers, too, must face: that the birth of a child is possible only because of the divine miracle of birth itself. Maternity and paternity are regulated only within the creative will of God. In prayer Hannah so penetrated the truth of His mysterious will. In prayer she attempted to regulate her lot with the way of God. Because of her faith in God, in whom rests the power of life, she petitioned Him that she might taste the sweetness of motherhood.

Finally God answered her prayer in the affirmative. She was blessed with a son. For Hannah, then, motherhood was the answer to prayer. Her son was a gift of the Lord. She named him "Samuel" — asked of God. Her entire behavior after the birth of her son radiates her awareness that the infant was a gracious gift of God. Her husband, Elkanah, makes a special offering of thanksgiving to the Lord. The story relates that she prepared diligently for the early date in which she would bring Samuel to the house of the Lord at Shiloh to dedicate him for service to God in remembrance of her vow.

The purpose of the story of Hannah is to make us conscious of the fact that Samuel was a rare child and that his birth bordered on the miraculous by virtue of the faith of Hannah. However, the faith of Hannah is not unique. The heavenly Father must be besieged regularly by the prayers of a myriad of Hannahs who come before His throne of grace for the gift of a child. Undoubtedly, many a holy vow has been made between the delicate creatures and the almighty Creator in whispered prayers. If the endless parades of interviews, letters, and phone calls to an adoption agency are any indication of the genuine desire of Christian people for parenthood, then heaven must be swamped with the earnest prayers of Hannahs every day. However those prayers are answered, they are the exercises of faith in which the Hannahs learn that they are the vessels of God's creative acts which He in His wisdom chooses to use or not to use in His own time.

When the Lord did grant a son to Hannah and Elkanah, their reactions were exemplary. If they had any pride in that hour, it was not evident in this story. They reacted in thankfulness and obligation. These are the ingredients of good parenthood. The mother who has felt within her own body the palpitations of another life, has nourished with her own bloodstream the child of her prayers, and has entered the valley of the shadow of death to bring it to life, can choose two directions. She may demand that the fruit of her body live the rest of its life in thankfulness to her. Or she may thank God eternally that He has called her to bring forth life that He has redeemed to His child. She may force the child to live in constant obligation to her. Or she may feel the obligation to devote her life to teaching the child to live unto God.

The story indicates that thankfulness to God for His gift and obligation to use the gift to God's glory completely dominated the life of Hannah. We are left to imagine how tenderly she must have prepared him for the day she would present him at the house of the Lord. One can almost see her humming hymns, a lullaby to the baby, explaining the meaning of his name to the infant, teaching him his first prayers, telling him the story of the heavenly Father and His chosen and redeemed people. Then when he had finally outgrown his infancy, she takes him up to the house of the Lord at Shiloh. She worships with the young lad there and sings an excellent song of praise much like the song of Mary, the mother of our Lord. After the worship service she takes him to the home of the priest Eli, kisses him good-by, and with a final embrace leaves him to the care of the priest. But she does not forget him. Each day she prays for him as he grows under the tutorage of the priest. Each year she makes for him with her nimble fingers a new robe and takes it to him. What joyous occasions those were for a mother and son! A happy meeting in which they could exchange the news of the year and Hannah could be overwhelmed with the added inches and wisdom of her Samuel. Upon her parting, Eli would give his annual blessing to Elkanah and Hannah: "The Lord give you children by this woman for the loan which she lent to the Lord." And Hannah was blessed with three more sons and two daughters.

One does not find it easy in the 20th century to tell mothers that no vocation in life matches the high calling that Hannah found in her motherhood through faith. In an age that has invented varieties of reasons for wooing mothers out of their homes, an age that has thrust them into competition with men, an age that has made the name "housewife" a drab and uninteresting name, we must in some way find the secret of restoring the faith, the joys, the adventure, the pleasure, and the status of being *mother*. Somehow we have been deluded into believing that if we are to give glory and dignity to the role of mother, we must cover up all of the commonplace and monotonous routine that is required of motherhood. This could well be an evasion of that to which God has called mothers through their role as mothers.

Dr. Martin Luther in a sermon "On the Visitation of Mary to Elizabeth" comments on Mary's reaction upon her return home. He says, "See how purely she leaves all to God, and claims for herself no works or reputation. She behaves just as she did before any of this was hers — seeks no greater honor, is not puffed up, vaunts not herself, calls out to no one that she is the mother of God, but goes into the house and acts just as before — milks cows, cooks, scrubs the kettles, and sweeps the house like any housemaid or housemother in the most menial tasks, as if none of these overwhelming gifts and graces were hers" (*The Martin Luther Christmas Book*, by Roland H. Bainton [Philadephia: The Westminster Press, 1948], page 29). So is the service of our mothers to their children unspectacular. As Mary bore in her body the gift of God's Son, so they bear Him in their hearts. And because they have Him in their hearts, they may have the joy in knowing that in faith they have the freedom to serve their children in love.

Most certainly it does not fall to all our Christian mothers to lend their sons and daughters to the Lord in the manner in which Hannah or Mary did. However, it is for all Christian mothers to be motivated with the same faith as possessed Hannah; that their children are gifts of the Lord, who must be raised to His honor and His glory. If the ministry of motherhood is a ministry of care and prayer, of love and sacrifice, of attention and protection for their children as was the motherhood of Hannah, there is no vocation, no profession, no calling on earth that is so well-pleasing unto God.

Obviously there is much in contemporary life that blocks the spiritual efforts of mothers. The constant hammering of headlines at the prospect that she shall have to send her sons to war, the

insistent wooing of her children from her footstool by school and
community activities, and the consistent infiltration of worldliness
into the common order of living create mountains of difficulties
and heartaches for the mother to surmount. For these reasons the
Christian mothers of our time need love, prayers, and cooperation
of husbands and children as they have never had before. But the
mother herself must by her prayers and faith work in the role
of mother as one who stands always in the presence of the redeeming God. By her faith our Lord shall equip her to make her
arms and her hands the cradle of His love.

II

Evidence of the faith that enveloped the motherhood of Hannah rested within the person of Samuel. The description of the
boy Samuel ministering before the Lord and attending the tabernacle in the robe his mother made for him reflects the aura of
love, faith, and care that his mother bestowed upon him. One is
made to feel that his mother clearly fitted him for the great role
he played in the destiny of God's chosen people, Israel. Samuel
himself grew to be the hope of Israel.

Samuel entered upon his young and tender years of service to
Israel at a time when the people knew some dark hours. Israel had
experienced great doom. The nation was defeated in battle, the
ark of the covenant had been taken away, and the people had lived
under the domination of the Philistines. Then God raised Samuel
to a role of spiritual leadership that was to lead the people out
of their darkness. By Samuel's faithful teaching and also by his
piety and devout example God brought the people of faithlessness
back to faith. Through Samuel's leadership God turned the tide
in the political affairs of Israel. During the time of his leadership
the ark of the covenant was returned, peace prevailed between the
Philistines and the Israelites, and the Philistines learned to fear
the God of Israel. By his own great faith Samuel was able
to restore to the Children of Israel the conviction that they
were a chosen people of the redeeming God, in whose history
Jehovah acted with purpose and love unknown to their idolatrous
neighbors.

In order to maintain this role of spiritual leadership, Samuel
was to his people a prophet, a deliverer, and a judge. As a prophet
he continually reminded his people of the role which God played
in their Messianic history. As a deliverer he continually reminded
the people of God's great redeeming promise. As a judge he
ruled his people in accordance with God's rule. In all this he
behaved as one who believed implicitly the prayer which Hannah
prayed: "My hearts exults in the Lord; my strength is exalted

in the Lord. My mouth derides my enemies, because I rejoice in Thy salvation."

The record of the career of this great spiritual statesman is recorded in the First Book of Samuel. It is quite significant that the record of that book prefaces it with the story of Hannah, leaving the impression that the history of the Children of Israel would have been quite different had not God employed a pious mother to bring her son in faith to Shiloh.

So it is through all of history. Great leaders and champions have appeared upon the scene of life, not merely wearing the garments woven by their mothers, but also personalities of faith woven by their mothers. On the other hand, the blackest pages of history tells the story of mothers too. How different the dark hour of history might be if the champions of evil had not been weaned on selfishness but had rather inherited the faith of Christian mothers.

But history cannot be rewritten. The story of man is and always will be the history of the conflict between the deliberate forces of evil and the active love of God which He has revealed in Jesus Christ. It is in the suffering, death, and resurrection of our Lord Jesus Christ that the Christian mother draws the power to do battle with those forces that threaten her ability to love and forgive. As the demand for forgiveness, patience, and grace arise in her household, as her husband and children test her patience and provoke her, as her family daily stands in need of her love, she is driven to the God of mercy and grace for His help. And in Jesus Christ God gives the pledge that He does not fail her. And as she brings the tokens of God's love in grace and forgiveness to her family, God's work is fulfilled in her, and her family is restored as His family. Thus as the faith of the Christian mother is expressed in her children, they will have good reason to thank and praise God and "arise up and call her blessed." (Prov. 31:28)

Why Upset About Victory?

By MAX G. BECK

(Armed Services Day)

And the victory that day was turned into mourning unto all the people; for the people heard say that day how the king was grieved for his son. — 2 Samuel 19:2

Normally there is not much reason to grieve when we attain some athletic achievement. To win in bowling, to be star pitcher of the softball or baseball team, to score the extra point or touchdown against that formidable, ancient rival calls for a rejoicing more than anything else. You don't ordinarily walk about with a long face, visibly upset, over this type of accomplishment.

Generally there has been no substitute for victory. And when victory has come, it has touched our sensibilities so that we have rejoiced.

Our church has won great victories. There have been times, of course, when those who make up the body of the church have been confused as to what constitutes victory and have, while gaining the upper hand, squandered the advantages obtained. But the church can look back upon its history and be pleased because of its many successful bouts with its enemies.

And the Christian military serviceman, chaplain and layman, can generally be pleased with his victories. He has overcome many problems along the way, has furthered the cause of his God, has avoided pitfalls along which others have fallen, has raised the cross of Christ to new heights in countries all over the world and yet the words of our text strike us right between the eyes when it says that victory for King David over his renegade son rather than being a cause for rejoicing became mourning for all his people.

We can easily see why someone can be upset over death, particularly if the death is that of a member of the family. Blood still flows thicker than water and we often are prone to ignore or pass over difficulties especially at death. But there are certainly other reasons fully obvious, fully pertinent, fully upsetting that make us pause today as we consider the topic:

Why Upset About Victory?

I. There are many reasons why Christians don't have to be upset, but can rejoice over the church's victories.

II. The causes for mourning or upset in spite of victory are certainly present.

III. God faithfully through His mercies gives us cause to rejoice in Christ's victories for us.

I

Reasons to Rejoice

Even as David had reason to rejoice because of the crushing of the rebellion of his son, so today we rejoice over the church's victories. We think specifically of the many victories for the church that the Christian military servicemen and servicewomen have notched since the great buildup and the great dispersion of the pre-World War II and the World War II era.

In many areas of the world, our Lutheran Church has established a foothold or has strengthened a tottering or almost failing establishment principally because some conscientious servicemen or servicewomen wouldn't take "no" for an answer. They insisted that their church be strengthened; they insisted that their church gain a foothold and sometimes even now the full potentialities of the work haven't been fully realized.

We think how work in the Philippine Islands was fostered through the Lutheran Service Center; while one never knows exactly how much benefit can be attributed to a single factor, much of the Philippine missionary work received impetus from the many dedicated Christians who were service personnel and who gave of their time and efforts.

We look at the list of our Lutheran churches in Hawaii and note that six churches now preach God's Word when in the early days of World War II the service center alone was the rallying point for the Lutheran Christians. Many a non-Lutheran was brought to his Savior in this and other centers in England, France, Hong Kong, Panama, and in any service center in the States you may wish to mention, because some chaplain together with members of his flock thought that the time was ripe to let the world know what God was doing through His Lutheran Church. Victories for Christ and the church! Certainly nothing to be upset about.

The matter of accessions to the church by baptism is a matter of record as is also the confirmations and the marriages performed by Lutheran chaplains. Many of these had a hand in bringing people closer to their Maker. Not so well documented are the many hours spent by Lutheran chaplains, servicemen and servicewomen, Army, Navy, Air Force, Marines, and Coast Guard: teaching the background for the Christian faith, living a life of example for the strengthening of Christian faith, showing in many cases to the nonbeliever, the non-Christian, and the non-Lutheran what loyalty could mean to the increase of God's kingdom. Victories for these there is ordinarily no cause to mourn.

We think of the victories of our service personnel among orphanages, the halt, the lame, and the blind. We have seen whole orphanages taken over by our chapel funds; we have seen whole areas rehabilitated by conscientious servicemen. And who knows how many of our Christians in foreign lands: Australia, Brazil, Argentina, or Africa were strengthened in their resolves and their high purposes, because the Lutheran chaplain was able to lend the prestige of his position as a called servant of the Word to his relations with that struggling parish. Many had been disheartened or discouraged by some event only to be encouraged and buoyed up through the work or association with the Christian servicemen who came to their midst. Many a struggling group came to the

attention of the proper authorities through these means, and the
kingdom of God was aided thereby. Surely the causes for rejoicing
over the victories of the church were present in many of these
situations.

II

There Are Causes for Mourning

While there are a myriad of reasons for rejoicing over our
church's military victories, the more discerning man would say
that there is often reason to be upset at the time of victory.

David and Absolom

Absalom, David's Son, had gathered a group about himself and
had rebelled against his father, the king. David hadn't wanted to
kill his son. He had asked that Absalom be spared (2 Samuel
18:12). But the exigencies of war had placed Absalom in the position where he had been hunted, cut down, and had met his God in
the midst of an oak when David's commander, Joab, had thrust
three darts through Absalom's heart.

The plot had unfolded some time before. Absalom had killed
his brother Amnon, who had previously violated their sister,
Tamar. When the opportunity had presented itself, Absalom had
gotten rid of Amnon, for one of the deadly seeds of disaster,
"hatred," had entered into Absalom's heart. (2 Kings 13:22)

Hatred

Most people can understand the complications caused by
murder. Absalom certainly knew what he could expect if he
were found guilty of killing his brother. But all too often the
warnings of 1 John 3:15 are ignored: "Whosoever hateth his
brother is a murderer." Hatred is murder and perhaps Absalom's
life was doomed when he permitted the deadly poison to enter
into his life.

A Christian cannot take much satisfaction from the fact that
he has never been before the bar of justice for murder — when
and if he is guilty of hatred. Perhaps the commandant of the
Marine Corps knew whereof he spoke when he said that the Marine
Corps didn't teach its members "hatred." Even as we exult over
our accomplishments we bow before the Lord above in humbleness
in request for forgiveness for bitter hatred engendered in our
hearts.

Lust for Power

We may also conclude that Absalom's lust for power was
a cause of his ultimate death and a reason why there was mourning by the people in spite of David's victory. Power is a corrupting factor in the church anyway you look at it. We have often

been involved or associated with some "church victory" such as was mentioned before, not necessarily because we've desired the work of the church to be enhanced, or because we've believed that "to God belongs the glory" but because we've been cunning frauds. We have stepped on others on the way up the ladder, and self-righteously we have assured ourselves that the work of the church has been our motivation, when without doubt our self-gain has been a substantial factor.

As Christians we mourn over such church victories because they have the appearance of a generous spirit, but in the eyes of God they are definite failures that bring disaster.

Double Dealing

Absalom was a clever man. He would sit beside the road leading to the gate and whenever he learned of any controversy that the man wanted the king to judge, he would inform the man that the king had not thought enough to appoint anyone to judge the affair. However, if he, Absalom, were king, he would certainly deal justly with the man who had the problem. In fact, he often pre-judged the case before him, telling the supplicant that he certainly had a good case. By double dealing he accomplished much. But by his double dealing he was sowing the seeds of his own ruin.

Double dealing of course is something that none of us claims as one of his virtues. What someone else finds to be this sin, we often consider to be shrewd dealing. Only God knows how many times leaders in our churches have feathered their own nests while giving the appearance of honesty. And it is the type of situation that lasts terribly long after the deed has been done. It is the type of problem that anyone or everyone in the church can become involved with even while furthering the church's desires, and this type brings mourning in spite of victory.

It is not always noticed by the individual but here we may well pay attention to the statement, "Be not deceived, God is not mocked." (Gal. 6:6)

We Make Ourselves Miserable

In spite of victory over the rebellion David and the people mourned for him who had had such great potential to be a loving son. We often work hard at making ourselves miserable. The difficulties we face are real but they wouldn't have to be either so serious or so much of a problem if we ourselves didn't work so hard causing damage.

The young man or woman learning early lessons in life make every effort to convince people (who often times could not care less), that he or she is smarter than his or her parents and pastor. He insists that he lives in a more sophisticated age that is not bothered by morals that are the victories of times past. Maybe husband or wife have mismanaged their marriage. They have started to follow a path from which there is no turning. Perhaps our thinking has been corroded to the point where we Christians want to do things we know are not the things we should do. The difference between what we do and what we should do is a lot greater than it ought to be.

III
God Gives Us the Cause to Rejoice

Maybe we need something to pull us up short. Maybe the non-ordinary fact of the many reasons for grieving over our victories can draw us closer again to the mercies of Christ our Savior. That they are new every morning is a certainty in which we can trust. But taking hold of them for ourselves is the growing problem in our lives.

How can we correlate Christ's mercies with our problems? It is not always easy, that's true. But the everlasting truth: "Him that cometh to Me, I will in no wise cast out" (John 6:37), is a promise that has been available to us for many, many years. It may be difficult to see the cross of Christ light up when there appears to be so much darkness about, but light up it does for the penitent individual.

Our victories and the victories of the church don't have to bring sorrow but they can be sources of rejoicing without the complications caused by mourning. It is not a simple process, 'tis true. But God, who gave to our forefathers many different glimpses of the truth in words of the prophets, has now, at the end of the present age, given us the Truth in the Son. . . . This Son, Radiance of the glory of God, flawless Expression of the nature of God, Himself the Upholding Principle of all that is, effected in person the reconciliation between God and man (Heb. 1:1, 2 Phillips). This is our satisfaction.

The Joy of the Ascension
By ARNOLD T. WANGERIN
(Ascension Day)

Then He led them out as far as Bethany, and lifting up His hands He blessed them. While He blessed them, He parted from them. And they returned to Jerusalem with great joy and were continually in the temple blessing God. — *Luke 24:50-53 RSV*

Nobody likes to say good-bye to those he loves. I think most of us have had some dealings with life's inevitable separations.

We feel keenly the pain of parting with friends and those whom we love, especially when we know we shall not see them soon again, perhaps even never again in this world.

That is why it's puzzling to watch the behavior of the disciples after Jesus ascended into heaven. They loved Him dearly. When He had announced on the night in which He was betrayed that He was about to leave them, they were heartbroken.

But what a difference when Jesus ascended before their eyes and then vanished out of their sight. Our text tells us, "They returned to Jerusalem with great joy and were continually in the temple blessing God." They knew He was gone, that He would not appear to them again. And still they shed no tears. Quite the opposite, their hearts throbbed with joy.

We are all happy at Christmastime, for this is the festival of Jesus' coming to us. We are all happy at Eastertime, for this is the festival of Jesus' coming back to us from the grave. But can we be happy at Ascensiontime, when Jesus clearly went away? — The first disciples were happy, and once we catch their vision we, too, shall mark this as one of the happiest days of the year. And "The Joy of the Ascension" will be not only a sermon topic but a powerful force in our lives.

I

The Joy of a God "Touched with the Feeling of Our Infirmities"

Because man is a creature of senses, it is necessary for him to have constant contact with things he can see and touch and feel and understand. As soon as a subject enters into the realm of the incomprehensible he becomes afraid, and to cover his fear he becomes rebellious and defiant.

Now God, who is infinite and eternal, certainly is incomprehensible. He commands our reverence and submission. But His very grandeur tempts us to doubt whether He really understands us. In the heat of life's day with its stress and pain we want to be absolutely sure He understands us, that He knows what our infirmities are like. We want someone on the throne who knows what it means to be tempted, tried, and troubled. How can we confide in Him if He is not like us?

This is one of the things the atoning work of Christ and the Ascension does for us. It assures us of God's loving understanding. There is not an ounce of our fear that Jesus has not felt. Not an ache or a tear or a temptation that He has not shared. During His life on earth He walked each step of our pilgrim way right down to the end of the last bitter mile. And this same Jesus is the ascended Son of God. He has returned to the Father to pre-

pare a place for us, not just as God, but as the God-man. And as
He now rules over all things we know that He deals with us
in perfect understanding.

When we see the ascended Jesus sitting in majesty on high,
all our doubts and fears about God's sympathetic understanding
for us disappear. We can understand why the apostles returned
to their tasks with great joy.

II

The Joy of a God Who Can Be Approached

Man instinctively seeks God and communion with Him. This
is something that is inborn in all men. But most men never learn
how God can be approached. Not only does God seem distant
from us, but we know also that there is something radically wrong
between us. We are not on speaking terms with Him. We have
offended Him. Conscience thunders our guilt, and nothing will
silence it. Our sins have separated us from God, and we grope
for a way back to Him.

In the Old Testament this fact was clearly portrayed to Israel
in the tabernacle, or as it is also called, the place of meeting.
The people in general were kept outside the building, away from
the presence of God. The priests in general were permitted entry
to the tabernacle, but only up to a certain point, the veil, before
which they burnt the incense of prayer. It was only the high
priest, and he only once a year, who was permitted to enter
into the holy of holies, the innermost room where God manifested
Himself in the cloud of glory. And it was only through the person
of the priest that the people had access to God.

The author of the Letter to the Hebrews writes about this in
connection with the Ascension. He explains that now Jesus has
gone into a tabernacle not made with hands, heaven itself. He
has entered there on our behalf. He has made the one great sacrifice which pays the debt of all our sins. He has given His own
life as a sin offering, and the Father has accepted this as complete
payment for all sins. By His Spirit He moves us to believe and
accept this. Because of Jesus and because of His blood shed once
and for all, we may draw near with a true heart into the holy
of holies of heaven. In Christ we have access to God. We are
not held to some outer court. We may come directly to the
throne of mercy because our sins are forgiven in His blood.

Each of us personally approaches God in the privateness of
his own feelings. No one can completely obstruct our way to Him.
Only we ourselves can block our path to God when we set up a wall
of unconfessed sin. Whenever we come to Him in humble faith
and penitence, we find Him waiting to receive us. — This, too, is
one of the joys of the ascension of our Lord.

III

The Joy of a God Who Is with Us

While Jesus was on earth, in His state of humiliation, He was limited by all our human limitations. He hungered and thirsted, He became fatigued, and He suffered pain. The divine powers which always were His were concealed, as it were, beneath His humanity, and showed forth only in occasional rays of divine glory during His miracles.

We rarely think of it, but it is true that while Jesus was here on earth visibly, according to His human nature He could be at only one place at a time. If a person wanted help from Him, he would either go and find Him or else send word to Him. Even after His resurrection and before the Ascension, Christ did not show Himself at different places simultaneously.

The Ascension changed all that. Now Jesus is no longer restricted to one place at a time. Just before He ascended and withdrew His visible presence from the world, He said to His disciples, "Lo, I am with you alway." Actually He now is closer to His followers than He ever was when He walked this earth.

Think what that means. Because Christ is everywhere, Christians can all worship in His presence at the same time. Because He is everywhere, you and I can pray to Him in our homes, in our autos, at our work, and we know that He is with us to hear us. We can also hear His living voice speaking to us in the Scriptures. Because He is everywhere we can find strength in temptation, courage in hardships, comfort in sorrows, and most blessed of all, pardon for our sins — everywhere. — This, too, is a joy of the Ascension.

IV

The Joy of a God Whom We Shall See Again

Jesus had frequently spoken of His return to earth at some future, undetermined date. When He ascended into heaven this promise was renewed by special angel messengers of God. Right on the mount of the Ascension the angels explained, "This Jesus, who was taken up from you into heaven, will come in the same way as you saw Him go into heaven."

The One who is to come will not be a new person, not a new way in which God will show Himself. He will be the same One who dwelt here in the flesh. As he left in person, He will return in person. As He left in His glorified body, He will return in His glorified body. As He left in the sight of men, He will return in the sight of men. The only difference will be that at the Ascension there was but a handful that saw Him; at His return every eye will see Him.

The joy of the Ascension reminds us that here Jesus was despised and rejected; then He shall be seen victorious over all His foes. Here He was crowned with thorns; then He shall be crowned with glory. Here He was humiliated and put to death on a cross; then He shall be honored and adored.

With that prospect in view the disciples went back to Jerusalem. From there they pushed out to the far corners of the world in His name. — Can you begin to see also this joy of the Ascension? Do you begin to share in the vision? Do you see in Christ's ascending also His descending on the Great Day?

V

The Joy of a God with Whom We Shall Dwell

In the gathering gloom of the night before the cross Jesus had said to the Eleven, "I go and prepare a place for you. I will come again and will take you to Myself that where I am you may be also." (John 14:3 RSV)

The Ascension leaves no doubt whatsoever as to this reunion. It is not an impersonal condition, not some shadowy existence in a disembodied state. Our reunion with Christ, and through Christ with one another will be in the Father's house, it will be in the body, and it will never end.

How can we who are imperfect be caught up into perfect union with Christ? The Ascension and Christ's redeeming work preceding it gives the answer. It was no soul, no disembodied spirit, but the glorified God-man who ascended from Olivet. He preceded us into the Father's house, heaven. He is our Forerunner, preparing for our safe and sure arrival. When the days of cross-bearing are over, we shall be with Christ in His glory forever.

Ascension Day is a day of joy. We sing on this day, *Te Deum Laudamus,* "Thee, God, We Praise." For the joy of the Ascension has touched us on all sides. It clarifies for us the fact that our God is a God "who is touched by our infirmities." He is a God who can be approached. He is a God who is with us here on earth. He is a God whom we shall see again. He is a God who is preparing for the Great Day when we shall dwell with Him forever.

Oh, grant, dear Lord, this grace to me,
Recalling Thine ascension,
That I may ever walk with Thee,
Adorning Thy redemption;
And then, when all my days shall cease,
Let me depart in joy and peace
In answer to my pleading.

Remember — Worship

By R. C. HOHENSTEIN

(Memorial Day)

All the ends of the world shall remember and turn unto the Lord, and all the kindreds of the nations shall worship before Him.

Psalm 22:27

In the calendar of our country, this weekend commemorates the occasion known as Decoration Day, or Memorial Day, the 30th of May having been designated in 1868 by a General Logan as the day to decorate the graves of our heroic dead. This day, originally established for the purpose of decorating the graves of those who died in the war between the states, otherwise known as the Civil War, has in the course of time been expanded to include the graves of all those who have given their lives in time of national emergency and crisis for our nation and for the cause that we all espouse: liberty, freedom, and the pursuit of happiness. As we think on these things, we would go beyond just the mere decorating of graves with little American flags; we would go also deeper into the background of the cause and why we must have such a thing as Memorial Day. This is not just, shall we say, a patriotic occasion, but also, in its deeper significance, a spiritual and a religious occasion. To lead us and guide us in our meditation for today, I would read to you one verse of Psalm 22, verse 27: "All the ends of the world shall remember and turn unto the Lord, and all the kindreds of the nations shall worship before Him." Would that this statement were literally true today: that all the nations had already turned unto the Lord and that the people from all the ends of the world and to the ends of the earth would now worship Him in spirit and in truth! That is a goal toward which we work. It is a picture toward which we move. It is a hope; it is a prayer, which we hold and which is held before our eyes, which leads us on and gives us courage to go forth. Today, then, let us pick out the two significant words of our text and think on them:

Remember — Worship

I

Remember

Today above all we remember. We remember our God; the God who has made us; the God who has redeemed us; the God who in His love has sanctified us and made us His own through faith. As Christians on this occasion we also remember others. There are some 1,064,000 known graves of our military dead in the national cemeteries of our own country and in plots set aside all over the world. We think today, not only of the 1,064,000 American flags that will flutter in the breeze, but we think of those whose remains lie under those flags and who gave their lives for a cause in which they believed, and for a country which they loved. We remember still others — the many whose graves are unknown and whose identities are unrecalled. I personally think in this connection of funeral services that were a daily occasion in the Red Hill Cemetery behind Pearl Harbor for months after World War II began. Many of these graves could be identified with names. Others of these graves contained parts of dozens of humans, the identity of none being known. On occasions such as this, we remember also others whose graves are marked only by a small "X" on a chart of the high seas and an entry in a ship's log. I think of those whose mortal remains I personally consigned to the deep during World War II in various parts of the vast Pacific Ocean. But behind all these there are yet others that we must not forget — their loved ones who stayed behind: their parents, their wives, their sweethearts, and their children. These, too, were called upon to make great sacrifice, not only a sacrifice in anxiety and in wonder and in separation, but a sacrifice of carrying on and living on for the cause that took the lives of their loved ones. So we remember all these and others today, and thank God for them.

We remember them not merely as a mental exercise or as an annual patriotic ceremony or ritual, but we remember them because of the cause for which they died, the reason, and the purpose behind it. Let us not go so far as to say that these were all willing and anxious and zealous volunteers. I know many people in World War II put on the uniform and were what they were because of the exigencies and the circumstances which surrounded them. They were willing to live and to suffer and to die, although they were not anxious to do it; they were willing though, and in a sense glad if it would only mean that the freedoms and the liberties that we as Americans know would be preserved for them, for theirs, and for those to come after. Those liberties we would remember, for they have been bought with a price — a great price: sacrifice, suffering, and sealed by death. Think on these things today — these liberties.

We would remember, not only as something that we do sitting still with head bowed and eyes misty, but we would do it as a thing of action. For if our memory and recollection of these things this day do not stir us to action, then we have wasted the morning and have missed an opportunity, and tomorrow will become bleaker in prospect as a result. Let us, therefore, remember well. In order to do this, let us remember in *worship*.

II

Worship

That's the second thought for this morning — *worship.* "All the kindreds of the earth shall worship before Thee." That is not, as I said, literally true. But may it be true of us, that today we voluntarily and lovingly worship, as we remember. And on this holy occasion, let us remember again whom we worship. Not just some vague, indefinable, unseeable Source or Force, but rather the Holy God of the Scriptures: the Father, the Son, and the Holy Ghost. For it is the Father, who in His love and in His holy wisdom created this world and all the unfathomable things about it. Only little by little is man moving forward in his research and his understanding of the vast knowledge that is contained in this universe. But don't forget that the sum total of this information and this knowledge is all God's. For it is a product of His holy mind, the result of His creation. This is the God who hath made us and hath formed us in so wonderful and wondrous a fashion and who hath loved us, even though we at times turn our back upon Him in acts and words of unholiness and unrighteousness. This is the God who loved us to the extent that He gave His only-begotten Son Jesus Christ, that He might on this earth take our form and be fashioned like unto us for a time; that He might keep for us the whole will and Law of God; that He might then voluntarily and lovingly take that holy and perfectly sinless life and give it into death for our sakes and for our redemption; and that He might on and after Easter say to us, "Whosoever believeth on Me shall not perish but have everlasting life." This is God the Son who loved us on His own behalf, that He voluntarily did all this for us.

We would also worship today the Spirit of God, who is known to us as the Sanctifier; who through His activity and His action within our hearts through Word and sacrament has made it possible for us to appropriate individually those things that I have just described; that we may now personally experience the joy and the happiness and the peace of knowing that Christ has redeemed us and made us again a forgiven son and daughter of God. We know this through the Spirit, who tells us that He would make of us His holy temple. This is the Triune God who would live within us, live through us, and become real to others because of us. Him we worship.

But again, as we remember, so also our worship is not only a mental exercise or a spiritual one but is something that must become real and active if it is to be of any value beyond ourselves. For we worship not only in words here in His house.

This is indeed the starting place, but it is not the ending place. For we who love the God of peace and the God of freedom and who know the peace and the freedom of life and faith in that God, we would serve Him and dedicate to Him these redeemed and sanctified lives of ours.

How shall this be done? By dedicating these lives in service to our fellowmen and to those principles on which our nation was founded, and which through the years have proved to be good for all men everywhere. Peace with and in God brings a desire and a yearning for peace with our fellowmen, whom we too, as God, must love — not only those who love us; for if God had acted on that principle, we would in this hour be without hope. But it was because God loved us who hated Him that we today have the peace that is ours in Christ.

So it is part of our Christian religion to love not only our friends, but as our Savior tells us, "Love your enemies! Bless them that curse you. Do good to them that hate you, and pray for them which despitefully use you and persecute you" (Matt. 5:44). This is the Christian way; this is really the American way — that we would worship our God by living for those whom He loves, our fellowmen.

Yet how shall we do it? There are so many opportunities, and we so frequently blunder and muff them! I think of the land from which I have so recently come, Japan. This is a land where we have had and still have many opportunities for good and for peace. But the Japanese people that I have gotten to know thought of Americans as all being Christians. The two in their minds went together. So when Americans came to their country in 1945 and stayed thereafter, they thought that this was Christianity in action. And, brother, what they saw in many instances wasn't good. And just exactly what they have seen and what they have experienced in other cases has not only turned them against our country and our people, but also against the Christian religion. There is still an opportunity in Japan, and there are opportunities in all the world of this kind. But we must be real; we must be genuine in our worship and service of God when we are in those places where it may appear that He is not looking or watching.

Today we hear and read much about the Peace Corps which is being supported by our President. This can be a great thing. This can also be a horrible failure, depending on those and the spirit of those who implement it and go forth. Will they be again a group of "ugly Americans," or will they truly reflect the best of America and the best of Christianity?

So we remember, so we worship, so we pray, and so we hope this day. You and I have never known what it means to be without the Christian Gospel or the benefits of Christian influence; to be without freedom to do within reason what we wanted to do. We have never known what it means to live under an occupation force unfriendly toward us and ill-disposed toward all those things which we hold near and dear and sacred. Sometimes I believe we get the idea that we are invincible; that the America we know must always win in war and always win in its diplomatic debates. We cannot look upon the history of the last eighteen years with any degree of realism and still come up with the conclusion that we must inevitably gain some marked advantage after every diplomatic conference with allies or potential enemies.

Let it be said that God does not need America or Americans to spread His Word or serve His cause. He had others doing this very thing long before America was ever discovered. The people who brought the Gospel here, in many cases, now need that it be brought back to their homelands. Will that day come also for these beloved United States that we say we love, and for which these thousands and hundreds of thousands have lived and died? It need not be so if we will but *remember* and *worship* in truth, in dedication, and with complete self-commitment — not only for our own sake, for that is at the bottom of the list — but rather, first of all, to the glory of God in Jesus Christ. Then to the welfare of our fellowmen, in the memory of those who have given themselves for these principles of freedom! To God, and in the honor and memory of these others, let us devote ourselves really and truly to the cause of peace. Then this Memorial Day will have served a good purpose to God's glory and humanity's welfare. In Jesus' name may God grant it.

Symbols of Freedom

By HENRY C. WOLK, JR.

(Flag Day 1963)

We will rejoice in Thy salvation, and in the name of our God we will set up our banners. — *Psalm 20:5 a*

In 1877, one hundred years after the Continental Congress adopted the flag of the United States as the national emblem, Congress requested that it be flown from all public buildings. Flag Day was thus observed for the first time. It is now observed each June 14 by Presidential proclamation. Though it is not considered an official national holiday, many religious and patriotic groups and individuals throughout the nation plan special celebrations and observances in order to emphasize the continuing importance of loyal and patriotic citizenship.

We should be extremely grateful for the varied and rich contributions made in the interest of our national welfare by all patriotic Americans. We shall emphasize today, however, that the citizens who utilize the dynamic resources of our holy Christian faith will bring to their citizenship a quality, a fervor, a dedication, and a blessing which are uniquely essential to personal as well as national welfare. The Christian faith teaches us, and God's Word and the sacraments also enable us, in the most effective manner to "render . . . unto Caesar the things which are Caesar's, and unto God the things that are God's" (Matt. 22:21). Reminded constantly of our dual citizenship (on earth and in heaven) and of our responsibilities both to state and church, the Christian sings with the psalmist: "We will rejoice in Thy salvation, and in the name of our God we will set up our banners."

It is appropriate, therefore, that we observe Flag Day as a congregation of American citizens by reminding ourselves of the profound meaning of the two symbols of freedom, the flag and the cross.

I

The Flag

Loyal Citizenship

Loyal citizens treasure the flag as the symbol of American freedom. "I pledge allegiance to the flag of the United States of America." Millions of Americans have taken this pledge with deep emotion and sincerity. They prove their loyalty as they share the daily responsibilities of good citizenship. They obey the laws, pay their taxes, fight the wars, support their government, share the responsibilities for our schools, churches, and communities. They register and vote. They keep abreast of the news, read the editorials, write letters to the editor and to their Congressmen. They pray regularly for the President and for all who are in authority. Such devoted citizenship not only reflects credit upon our flag and upon our nation but is essential if our liberty is to be preserved.

Deviations to the Right or Left

However, there have been misguided citizens who have misused and degraded the flag of our country. Students of the American scene have noted the activities of fanatical flag-wavers who periodically make spurious appeals in the name of religion and patriotism for their insidious political movements. While masquerading under the banner of freedom, the American flag, they have attempted to sow seeds of disloyalty and discontent in their treasonable efforts to destroy democratic process and ideals. Some of these self-styled patriots are extremely nationalistic, and fanatical salesmen of their shortsighted and provincial Americanism. Some isolationists may be devout Christians and sincere patriots, firmly convinced that our country should not be involved in foreign affairs. Some are old-fashioned isolationists in modern garb, who have not yet learned that this is "one world" whether they like it or not, and that no nation can rightly or safely isolate itself from cooperative efforts in the area of international relationships and responsibilities.

In contrast to these Rightists there is a group of individuals who aspire to be "citizens of the world," whose internationalism not only transcends but has virtually abolished their national loyalty. These political dreamers do not realize, perhaps, that they are in fact tied to their country — not only by a debt of gratitude for blessings already received but also by very practical necessities like citizenship papers; police, fire, and military protection; money, and many other essential government services and facilities without which a large society cannot function. International vagabonds, no matter how sincere, are no asset to any nation. In order to achieve their political objectives, these "citizens of the world" will have to work and vote and pay taxes and utilize existing political and legislative institutions along with their fellow Americans. Freedom is not free. Its cost is not only eternal vigilance; it also includes personal sacrifice and national loyalty — sometimes in terms of toil and sweat, tears and blood. Flag Day should remind all citizens of these truths.

Patriotic Ceremonies

We are grateful to God today because the flag is so precious a symbol of freedom for the vast majority of Americans. A most stirring moment in the daily life of every military man (and in the memory of every veteran) is the Retreat Ceremony, when the flag is lowered from the mast at the close of day. Traffic ceases, silence prevails. Pedestrians salute as "Retreat" is sounded by the bugler, and the National Anthem is played by the band. When the last note drifts off into the distance, the ceremony is completed and traffic resumes. A daily moment of patriotic prayer, rededication, and reminiscence has been experienced.

Another meaningful patriotic observance treasured by Americans is the recitation at public gatherings of the Pledge of Allegiance: "I pledge allegiance to the flag of the United States of America, and to the republic for which it stands; one nation, under God, indivisible, with liberty and justice for all."

The Scope of the Pledge to the Flag

Perhaps the words of the pledge are sometimes said thoughtlessly (as we sometimes recite our prayers); nevertheless the concise content of the pledge is most profound and significant. With these beautiful words loyal citizens pledge their undying loyalty to our *flag,* to our *republic,* to our *nation,* and to our *God.* Will you notice how the stated objects of our loyalty progress in order of importance from the lesser to the greater? We pledge loyalty first to the flag (which is our national symbol), then to the republic (which is our form of government), then to the nation (which means our fellow citizens), and then, of greatest importance, to our God. These are the glorious objects of the citizens' loyalty.

Significance of Our Flag

Yes, the American flag is our national symbol of freedom, of liberty and justice for all. It stands for all the blessings which we have received as a heritage from our founding fathers and later statesmen, from the Declaration of Independence, the Constitution with its Bill of Rights, and from other freedom documents. It stands for the hosts of freedom's pioneers and freedom's defenders in every profession and lawful occupation by which Americans have contributed to the establishment and development of our democratic society. The flag stands for our history, our traditions, our laws, our ideals, and our aspirations. It stands for our rights and our privileges, as well as for our responsibilities as citizens. It stands for the freedom and dignity of the individual, for the freedom of speech, press, worship, and assembly; for the right to life, liberty, and the pursuit of happiness. It stands for the costs of freedom already paid and for the price yet to be paid for its maintenance and development. It stands for the security of U. S. citizens; for benevolence to all people, especially in time of disaster; for the defense of the weak against the strong; for this nation's gratitude for national heroes, known and unknown, who have paid the price of freedom on the battlefield and in other vital activities of government service.

Our flag also symbolizes the hope for freedom and peace far beyond our national borders. The United States Government has taken the initiative in establishing and strengthening international organizations and alliances like the United Nations, NATO, SEATO, and others. It has spoken and continues to speak not only of coexistence, but of a world in which all nations, great and small, may live together cooperatively and peacefully. Our armed forces have not been used as an aggressive threat, but as a deterrent to would-be aggressors. Nations which desire peace and pursue it sincerely have nothing to fear from America's armed might. She is a mighty arsenal — but she is the arsenal of freedom . . . and peace is her military objective. The American flag symbolizes and represents these lofty ideals and concepts.

The Christian's Resolve

In time of war and in time of peace American citizens have uttered the prayerful resolve: "We will rejoice in Thy salvation, and in the name of our God we will set up our banners." This conviction and resolution is a sound guarantee that American citizens under God will never forsake the principles of freedom which have resulted in such manifold blessings for our nation and for the world.

II

The Cross

As we proceed to discuss the cross as a symbol of freedom, we sense that we are approaching the "crux" of the freedom problem, that we are now pausing to view the very heart and center of the conflict between freedom and slavery — the battle engaged in by our Lord and Savior Jesus Christ against the forces of sin, death, and hell, the most significant incident in history, the victory by which freedom and eternal salvation were won for all men everywhere.

The Promise of the Cross

Generally speaking, the world today recognizes the cross as a symbol of healing and salvation. When displayed on churches, on hospitals, on vehicles, on uniforms, it is an emblem of charity, an offer of assistance, a sign of hope. The instrument of execution has become the symbol of life.

The cross, however, is not a guarantee of physical health or of material prosperity. Neither does it promise political or social equality or world peace. It addresses itself rather to a more basic and vital issue, namely, the relationship between a man and his God. It is concerned with the spiritual slavery and bondage into which every child is born and from which each person can emerge, but only by the power of His cross.

The cross is more powerful than nuclear explosions. It is more powerful than miracle drugs. It is more powerful than the most dynamic philosophy. It can accomplish that which is impossible for humans to accomplish: the forgiveness of the sins of the whole world, including yours and mine. Its effects are not ephemeral, fleeting, and transitory, but eternal. The blessings it confers are effective under any political regime, any social circumstance, any physical condition. Regardless of the status or condition of men, the message of the cross offers freedom, forgiveness, life and salvation to all mankind.

The Message of the Cross

The message of the cross proclaims that the eternal Son of God visited this planet in person to "seek and to save that which was lost." He left the glory of His heavenly habitation to walk humbly among men as one of them. He came in fulfillment of prophecy, but chiefly in order to fulfill His love for the fallen human race. He came not to condemn, but to save. He came to accomplish for us those things required of us by God but impossible for us to render because of our sin-infected nature. He therefore came as a representative man and fulfilled in our behalf all of God's moral requirements. And He accomplished more than that. By His suffering and death, including His banishment from the Father, He paid the uttermost farthing required as man's penalty for disobedience and lack of love. He assumed upon His spotless soul the entire burden of mankind's accumulated guilt, and with this torturing burden He climbed Mount Calvary to die. The world's most innocent man became the world's greatest criminal, having voluntarily assumed the total moral indebtedness of mankind to God. He shed His blood, and gave His life of priceless worth as the Son of God, in final and complete payment for the sins of the world. He was then raised from the dead on the third day "for our justification," in proof of His victory as mankind's Redeemer, and in order that we might receive Him into our lives by Word and sacrament as our living Savior. The symbol of the cross proclaims this saving Gospel to all men, inviting them to believe it, to be transformed by it, and to find in it eternal peace with God.

The cross stands for this glorious message. It stands for Christ Himself, for the entire Christian faith with all its blessings, privileges, and opportunities. It stands for the Christian church, the fellowship of the redeemed, with its glorious history and traditions, its apostles, martyrs, missionaries, pastors, teachers, and every faithful follower.

The power of the cross has changed our natural status: Christians have become the adopted children of God, reinstated members of His family; we have become citizens of heaven, heirs of God, and coheirs with Christ. We have received direct commissions in the Church Militant and have been directed to proclaim this Gospel to every creature. The cross is the banner of the army of God, and as soldiers of His cross we are set on the spiritual conquest of the world for Christ.

The flag is a national symbol, but the cross is universal. The flag is not an imperialistic emblem, it does not represent aggressive thirst for conquest. But the cross proclaims that God desires to reign in every human heart, that He seeks the love and the obedience and the worship of all nations and all races.

The Banner of the Church Militant

On a day of patriotic observance it is especially appropriate to speak of the Church Militant. We were taught this concept even as children, as we sang: "Onward Christian soldiers, Marching as to war, With the cross of Jesus Going on before." Perhaps it was one of your favorite hymns as a child. You responded to the challenge to join forces with fellow Christians, to fight against sin, to learn self-discipline and self-sacrifice, and to set up the banner of salvation in lands where Jesus was not yet known. Since that time many of us have learned much about the army of God and have served faithfully for many years. We know that the Christian churches are the arsenals of heaven; that Word and sacraments are God's invincible weapons; that the schools and homes of the church are its training academies; that although the Command Post is in the King's capitol, He is with us in the midst of conflict by His power and by His Spirit; that our supply lines are always open to His storeroom of grace, and that through prayer we are in instantaneous contact with Him from any location. What a glorious privilege it is to serve Him militantly now, knowing that we shall serve Him triumphantly forever!

Our Comprehensive Pledge

It is proper for us to pledge our allegiance to the two significant symbols of freedom — the flag and the cross. Each in its own sphere requires and deserves our loyalty. As we have pledged loyalty to the flag and our nation, let us for the sake of our nation and for the eternal welfare of all mankind also pledge our allegiance to the cross, the symbol of our salvation, to our church, to the people of Christ wherever they are found, and to the Triune God, for

> By STRIPES is healing wrought, and STARS
> Point ever to a central Sun;
> He flies the conquering flag, whose scars,
> Transfigured, speak of Victory won.
> (Alfred Gurney, 1843—1898)

By the power of this faith we are enabled to join in the psalmist's fervent resolve: "We will rejoice in Thy salvation, and in the name of our God we will set up our banners."

Dependent Independence

By ARTHUR CARL PIEPKORN

(For July 4)

"Are you not like the Ethiopians to Me, O people of Israel?" says the Lord. "Did I not bring up Israel from the land of Egypt, and the Philistines from Caphthor and the Syrians from Kir?" — *Amos 9:7 RSV*

The God who made the world and everything in it . . . made from one every nation of men to live on all the face of the earth, having determined allotted periods and the boundaries of their habitation, that they should seek God, in the hope that they might feel after Him and find Him. — *Acts 17:24, 26, 27 RSV*

On June 7, 1776, not quite 14 months after the battles of Lexington and Concord had begun the American Revolution, Richard Henry Lee offered a resolution in the Continental Congress "that these United Colonies are and of right ought to be free and independent States." The Congress appointed a committee of five to formulate a declaration of independence. The committee in turn designated Thomas Jefferson to draft the document. On July 2 the Congress passed a resolution asserting the independence of the United Colonies and claiming for them the power "to make war, conclude peace, establish commerce and to do all other acts and things which other States may rightfully do." In a letter written the next day John Adams called it the greatest question "which ever was debated in America" and went on to voice the opinion that "a greater, perhaps, never was or will be decided among men." July 4, 1776, however, is the date that appears on "the Unanimous Declaration of the thirteen united States of America" and that is the date we keep as Independence Day.

Within the halls of the Continental Congress the decision was unanimous, but not outside. The political situation was fraught with ambiguities. In a sense the Declaration of Independence was the assertion on North American soil of the rights that Englishmen had vindicated for themselves through centuries of struggle with governmental tyranny. Even in England the cause of American independence has the support of influential figures. At the same time, while about one third of the colonists — among them Lutherans like Peter Gabriel Muhlenberg and his congregation in Woodstock, Va. — were solidly committed to the cause of independence even if it meant war, another third of the colonists — among them Lutherans again — were equally committed Loyalists. Their ranks produced (in the words of a recruiting broadside published in 1777 in Philadelphia) the "intrepid able-bodied Heroes" who were "willing to serve His Majesty King George the Third in Defence of their Country, Laws, and Constitution against the arbitrary Usurpations of a tyrannical Congress" in the Loyalist battalions and regiments. At the war's end not a few among them preferred permanent exile in Canada under the Union Jack to life in the United States under the Stars and Stripes.

How narrow the margin was between defeat and victory, how many problems harassed the infant nation, how dismal its prospects were, how slow unity was in coming — these are commonplaces of our historical knowledge. As we look back on those dark decades we have no difficulty in understanding why the reverse of the Great Seal of the United States, depicted on our one-dollar bills, has over the pyramid, which it labels a "new order of the ages," the triangle-and-eye that symbolizes God, along with the legend *Annuit coeptis*, "He" — that is, God — "has smiled on our undertakings."

The Sacred Scriptures, completed more than 17 centuries earlier, had of course nothing to say about these events specifically. Those who try to find in the oracles of Daniel and in the visions of the Revelation of St. John the Divine explicit prophecies of our nation succeed only by an intolerable twisting of the sacred record.

Nevertheless, that God's hand was in the creation of the American nation and in its subsequent history we cannot doubt, for our texts tell us that God's hand is in the creation of every nation. Amos, the author of our first text, had to remind his fellow Israelites in the eighth century before Christ that God was as much concerned about the Ethiopians in Africa as about the chosen people. Furthermore, he pointed out, God had not only brought the ancestors of the Israelites up out of Egypt. The same God, he insisted, had also brought the Philistine enemies of the Israelites out of their ancestral island of Caphthor, or Crete, just as He had brought the Syrian enemies of the Israelites out of their ancient homeland in the Caucasus, Kir. Similarly, in our second text, St. Paul, in his address to the Athenians gathered to hear him in the court of the Areopagus, reminded them that God had made all the nations of the world out of one original race of men and that all the epochs of every nation's history and all the boundaries of all their territories were fixed by His divine hand.

Thus, while the annual recurrence of the Fourth of July provides us with an occasion to observe Independence Day, the Sacred Scriptures remind us that as Christians we are to celebrate a —

Dependent Independence

While we may remember with joy the achievement of our nation's independence from the alien domination of the kings of the House of Hanover, we must never forget our nation is still under the rule of the King of kings. Hence Independence Day is for the Christian citizenry of America —

I

A Call to Contrition

By making man the way he is, God created government as
a principle. Our race could not survive a generation if all its
members were compelled to lead solitary existences. Ultimately
even the family unit would be too small a unit for the perpetuation
of humankind and human culture. Larger associations of individuals are in God's design inescapably necessary. Every concrete
expression of this divinely constituted principle of government
shares in the character of the principle itself. The governmental
authorities — including our own national state — that exist are expressions of the divine will that human beings should live together
under government.

At the same time God has nowhere given us any blueprints
for the form that a government must or should take. This He has
left to the wisdom and the freedom of choice with which He endowed human beings. He has not commanded men to create either
democracies or republics or aristocracies or constitutional monar-
chies or authoritarian dictatorships. Christians have prayed the
Fourth Petition of the Our Father under every kind of political constitution that the world has seen, and God has heard their prayer.
There is no divine norm against which concrete political institutions are to be measured. The divinely willed purposes of impartial
justice, of personal integrity, and of social morality can at least
in theory be achieved under many different forms of political
organization. To this extent Alexander Pope could justify his
couplet:

> For forms of government let fools contest;
> Whate'er is best adminster'd is best.

At the same time, in a world where as a result of the Fall
man's political judgment is fallible, no form of government is perfect. No national state is or can be the realization of the kingdom
of God on earth. The dream that William Blake puts on the lips
of John Milton: to build Jerusalem in England's green and pleasant
land, is destined to frustration not only on the soil of Britain
but everywhere. No human political program can be identified
as wholly embodying the will of God, and no human political
achievement is exempt from divine judgment. The theories of
government embodied in laws and in constitutions — including
our own — reflect the fallibility and the limitations of the men
who constructed them, and the day-by-day administration of the
laws and the policies — including those of our nation — that statesmen and politicians devise, always reflect at some point their archi-
tects' weaknesses, if not their prejudices, their ambitions, and
their selfishness.

If we had any doubt of this, we should merely have to catalog the political institutions and the laws that we ourselves regard as inadequate or even destructive. Or we might ask ourselves, What promises of any given candidate for whom you voted in the last election actually decided you to vote for him? Was your reaction to these promises wholly disinterested, wholly unselfish, wholly uncolored by a primary concern for your own welfare or the welfare of a group with whom you identified yourself? Or we might ask ourselves, What was the motive that prompted the last letter or telegram of protest or of commendation that you sent to one of your political representatives or to a newspaper editor? Or, What was it that determined your last request for exemption from some provision or some penalty of the law? Did you ask with a purely altruistic concern for the common good and for the requirements of strict justice, or did selfish interest play a perceptible role? Our representatives in government are not likely to be much different from what we ourselves are.

Approaching the problem from another angle, it is unlikely that many or even any of those to whom I am preaching at this moment are influential elected officials of the Federal Government. But some of you at least may be *employees* of government, and a considerable proportion of the men in this congregation are certain by virtue of their military service to have been a part of the executive arm of the government. What these past and present employees of government do and did from day to day is a pretty fair measure of what the government is and was, since a government is never a theoretical idea but always something that becomes concrete in the people who made and execute its policies.

Thus Independence Day becomes a call to contrition — contrition: because we have too often blinded ourselves to these facts; because we have too often forgotten that behind the masks of human activity in the political life of our nation God was at work; because we have claimed for our American political system an absolute value that no human political system can claim; because we have contributed to the failures of American politics by our own laziness and our lack of interest in day-by-day political matters, by our desire for special privileges for ourselves and the groups to which we have belonged to the disadvantage of others, and by attempting to have the policies of government molded and administered for our selfish profit; because we have been unwilling to concede the right of equal justice under the law; ultimately, through our attitudes the institutions of justice are perverted into instruments of injustice.

Genuine contrition, let us remind ourselves, means an admission of *our* failure. It requires us to renounce the easy way of justifying, or rationalizing, the things we have done wrong. It involves seeing that, even though these offenses are apparently far removed from the obvious violations of the Ten Commandments that we have learned to avoid, they are still violations of God's will and require the forgiveness that He offers us in Christ.

II

A Call to Gratitude

Independence Day is a call for gratitude as well as contrition. In spite of our individual and corporate failures God still lets us celebrate Independence Day. The good government that we enjoy is His gift, the gift of a good God. His goodness we who are His own in Christ find incontestably revealed in His once-for-all action for us men and for our salvation in the incarnation, the life, the death, and the rising to life again of our Lord and Savior Jesus Christ. We find His goodness personally attested by His action in putting us into the family that is His church through Holy Baptism, and in nourishing and sustaining us through the Word of the Gospel preached to us, through the absolution that is pronounced upon us by His called and ordained servants, and through the pardoning body and blood of His Son in the Holy Eucharist.

With a kind of favor that is parallel to that with which He has made us His children by adoption and grace, this good God has given us as Americans political gifts that claim parallel gratitude. For most of these gifts *we* cannot — not even the oldest and wisest among us — claim credit. None of us, for instance, helped to devise our Constitution or the Bill of Rights. We did not shed our blood to achieve our national independence in the Revolution or to preserve our national unity in the War Between the States. We did not go to jail with John Peter Zenger or die with Elijah P. Lovejoy to secure the freedom of the press. We did not buy at the price of our suffering the right to speak freely, to assemble freely, or to worship God according to the dictates of our individual consciences. We did not devise the economic and social system that gives Americans an average standard of living unsurpassed anywhere in the world; that over the span of generations has provided an increasing degree of educational opportunity and social mobility; and that has thus insured that the contributions that an individual makes to our society and the rewards that he receives from it will reflect his own abilities rather than merely his inherited wealth and status.

We did not stock our 50 states with the natural resources that not even the intemperate prodigality of our past or the reckless wastefulness of our present have been able to exhaust. None of us invented the traditions of law and justice under which we live.

None of us called into being the 185 million other Americans without whose cooperative activity the puny efforts of one or even many of us would be doomed to failure. Independence Day is a good occasion for recalling gratefully these and all the other political benefits that we owe to the goodness of God.

III
A Call to Constructive and Positive Action

Gratitude, if it is genuine, will inevitably find reflection in positive and constructive action. Patriotism of the right kind is one of the moral virtues that the new obedience which is the result or our faith will foster and strengthen. Here, too, there is a direct link between our churchmanship and our citizenship. In its important Article XVI on civil affairs and political government the Augsburg Confession asserts that "the Gospel does not destroy political or domestic institutions, but rather commands that we preserve them as divine ordinances and that we exercise love in these ordinances." The love that we are to exercise is the love that we have learned from God in His giving of His Son for our redemption. Our Christianity will reveal itself in our life as citizens.

It is conventional in a sermon like this to observe the fact that a nation's Christians, simply by being Christians, are a stabilizing and conserving factor of the first order, and to stress that Christians are bound to pray for their government. They are conscientiously to obey all laws and ordinances that do not require them to commit sin in carrying them out. They are to vote intelligently, to respect the representatives of government with whom they come into contact, and to be honest about paying their taxes.

Such an exhortation is perfectly in order. A Christian who intentionally fails to intercede for his government, a Christian who deliberately flouts any law, a Christian who pointedly refuses to exercise as intelligently as he can his right to vote, a Christian who by design acts or speaks contemptuously with reference to the persons in whom the principle of government finds concrete embodiment, a Christian who is wittingly dishonest in reporting or paying his taxes, such a Christian is doing wrong, and by persisting in his wrongdoing without repentance he can banish the Holy Spirit from his heart and kill the life of faith within his breast just as completely as he can by persisting without repentance in any other kind of wrongdoing.

But these observations fail to touch certain obligations that are peculiarly ours as *American* Christians. Because ours is a government of the people, by the people, and for the people,

Americans are not merely the objects of government, not merely the governed; they are the ones who do the governing as well. The elected officials as well as the appointees and employees of government in our land are not the source of governmental power but merely its executors. Every law and every executive policy is finally, in our political theory, an expression of the will of the people.

Hence what God says in the Sacred Scriptures to the kings and the princes and the rulers of the Biblical world applies in principle to us. In the United States we the people are the king and the princes and the rulers, and the Government — from the Chief Executive in the White House through all the stages of governor and mayor and county supervisor down to the policeman on the beat and the stenographer in the Internal Revenue office — are quite literally the people who do our work for us. Each of us therefore has a responsibility to be interested in every phase of our Government, to keep himself informed, to use all the legitimate means available to him to correct abuses, and according to his ability and vocation, to take an active part in the Government.

In October 1961 a study conference on the Christian World Mission brought together in St. Louis County, Missouri, 53 leaders of The Lutheran Church — Missouri Synod, executives, administrators, parish pastors, theologians, teachers, laymen, and laywomen. One of the six study groups of the conference concerned itself with the relationship of church and state as it affects the Christian world mission. Out of the concern of the members of this group for the spread of the Gospel in the world came some important observations that we can take to heart. The group called upon Christians to undergird the "nongovernmental agencies that render essential philanthropic services" with their "voluntary personal and financial assistance," to communicate "their concerns to their elected and appointed representatives," and to be "ready to render public service of all kinds as circumstances and their talents permit." The group advocated for our church "a comprehensive educational program designed to educate our people more fully" in this whole area with a view to giving "guidance on how to secure information about issues, how to reach one's own intelligent decisions, and how to communicate one's convictions effectively to those who make the ultimate decisions." The group urged the creation of "a climate which encourages capable young people to follow [those] professions and occupations and to accept positions through which they can render effective public service (including the various kinds of civil service, the foreign service, the military services and the Peace Corps), the law, medicine, social service, public philanthropy, education, and the mass communications media occupations." The group called on Christians to "discourage the attitude that political activity is the proper province only of the selfish, the venal, and the power-hungry."

If we are to carry out these suggestions, it will mean a reorientation of some of our inherited thinking. We cannot any longer look on politics as a dirty business in which a Christian cannot participate without peril to his eternal salvation. If anywhere politics is that dirty a business, part of the fault lies in the fact that Christians have evaded their responsibility. The 16th century had to reassure Christian princes that theirs was a God-pleasing condition of life; be assured that responsible political activity by Christians in 20th-century America rests on exactly the same Biblical basis. An American Christian can with a good conscience prepare himself for a career in government as an elected official or as an employee. Every Christian in America has a responsibility actively to do what he can to insure, for instance, that justice is impartially administered; that public educational and public employment opportunities are available to all on a basis of individual ability; that the basic rights which any citizen enjoys are the full possession of every citizen without discrimination on the basis of race or religion or color; that God's gifts of art and the expressions of culture which have always depended on government patronage are adequately supported; that the principle which regards a public office as a public trust takes precedence over the cynical maxim that to the victor belong the spoils; and that the power of our Government is not invoked or applied on the local, national, or international level in the interest of injustice and exploitation.

This general responsibility imposes upon the influential Christian a special obligation. (By an "influential Christian" understand a person whom God has put in a position of responsible leadership.) The Christian in government has an obvious obligation which does not come into consideration at this point. Less obvious possibly but just as binding is the obligation of the Christian leader in other spheres — the educator in nonpublic schools, the spokesman for management or labor, the executive of the trade union or the industrial concern, the youth leader, and above all, the parent. He must give a consistent, positive, planned, and programmatic witness in precept and practical example to the principles of Christian patriotism.

So far we have spoken of government in terms of the natural purpose of man in this age. Because creation is God's work and government is part of God's plan for His human creation, we are not to downgrade or despise this aspect of our life in this world. But this aspect of our lives does not exhaust God's purpose. God fosters the natural purpose of man not only for itself but also in the interest of His supernatural purposes; He preserves the life of this world in order by a new creation to populate the world to come. The same God who made man a political being has also, in St. Augustine's famous words, made man for Himself and the human heart is restless until it has found its rest in conversion to Him. God fixed the epochs of human history and the limits of national territory, St. Paul says in our second text, in order that men might seek God and, it might be, touch Him. God is active in the political world of our America with the same purpose. Because we are to cooperate with God in our new life as Christians, an awareness of this second (but not secondary) purpose must pervade our political activity also.

It is not jingoistic provincialism that leads us to regard the relation of church and state in America as in many ways a most desirable one. Within this relation the Christian church, including our own denomination, has witnessed the blessing of God on its outreach in our country at a time when the influence of the church has declined sharply in other parts of the Christian West.

Our primary task as *churchmen* is to work with God for the accomplishment of that second — but, we repeat, not secondary — purpose. Through us God tells all men that He loves them. Through us God declares that in stooping down to take our humanity into His Godhead His Son has become the blood brother of every human being. Through us God asserts that through His life of perfect obedience and His sacrificial death on the cross He has conquered sin and death and delivered mankind. Through us God affirms that through Holy Baptism and Holy Communion He makes men participants in this deliverance and in His holy community unites them to Himself.

On the other hand, our primary task as Christian *citizens* is to work with God for the preservation of the world and of the American nation, in which His church is currently carrying His ministry of reconciliation.

God invites us to participate in the fulfillment of our prayers in both spheres. When we pray by His Son's direction "Hallowed be Thy name, Thy kingdom come, Thy will be done," God calls us to the task of mission that these petitions might find their fulfillment in part through our witness. When in the fourth petition of the Our Father we pray for "good government" He calls us to partnership with Him in achieving that end. Independence Day, when we as American Christians recall our dependent independence, is a good day to rededicate ourselves to our tasks in both spheres — in contrition, in gratitude, and in constructive action.

Blessed Daily Work

By John Daniel

(Labor Day)

Do not labor for the food which perishes, but for the food which endures to eternal life, which the Son of Man will give to you; for on Him has God the Father set His seal. — *John 6:27 RSV*

The Sunday before Labor Day is a good time to dip into the well of God's Word to refresh ourselves with Christian knowledge and Christlike motivation for our life and labors. The will and way of God regarding work is clearly told by precept and examples in Holy Writ. The sacred Scriptures are able to make us wise unto salvation and perfect us in every good work, for in them we are told much about the work of God and the works of men, the labor of love of our Lord and Savior Jesus Christ, and the labors of faith of the early Christian disciples.

With vacation days now only a memory for most of us, we will again join the back-to-work movement to fulfill the challenge and promise of the psalmist: "You shall eat the fruit of the labor of your hands; you shall be happy, and it shall be well with you" (Ps. 128: 1 RSV). Let us therefore meditate on the blessings of our daily work.

I

Our Daily Work Will Be Blessed
When It Is God-directed

When God is our Partner and Master in our work, there is a surety of success no matter what our calling. All work is holy if it is directed by God. Working as fellow workers with God, we can creatively perform the tasks assigned to us by our calling and vocation. The patriarchs and prophets and the saints and apostles of old worked hard to earn their daily bread. Jacob, Moses, and David were shepherds, while Rebecca, Leah, and Rachel tended their gardens and families. Isaac and Elisha put their hands to the plow, while Paul was a tentmaker and Peter a fisherman. From the great kings David and Solomon to the lowly service of Mary and Martha, God has directed the lives and labors of His own in the channels of His grace and mercy.

Jesus said to men and women who worked hard only for material gain and possessions, "Do not labor for the food which perishes." There is labor which is done from wrong motives and for improper ends. As a result, not all who work are happy with their labor, with the fruits of their work, or with their lot in life. Some do not have the material means they need even though they work hard. Others do not want to work and suffer want, for "if any would

not work, neither should he eat." Others waste what they earn
by faithful work and complain about their misfortune. Still others,
though they labor hard and long in all fidelity, remain poor materially because they are poor spiritually. These never appreciate
what God has done for them in creation and continues to give them
in His merciful providence. They do not know the riches of the
spiritual blessings of His Son Jesus Christ. They do not labor for
the glory of God or the welfare of their fellowman. Some descend
to the level of animals, rooting and grubbing in sinful occupations
which demean man and tempt his body and soul away from God.
"They eat the bread of wickedness and drink the wine of violence" (Prov. 4:17). There is no satisfaction for such workers or
security for their families. Their homes are centers of sin and
strife. There is no profit in such work which leaves out God. "Unless the Lord builds the house, those who build it labor in vain"
(Ps. 127:1 RSV). The end result of godless labor is described by
the prophet Haggai, "You have sown much and harvested little;
you eat, but you never have enough; you drink, but you never
have your fill; you clothe yourselves, but no one is warm; and he
who earns wages earns wages to put them into a bag with holes"
(Hag. 1:6 RSV). Thus, work for sinful, selfish, useless, or merely
utilitarian ends is not blessed work.

We must, under God, work for the food which is eternal. This
is the work which Jesus did according to the will of His heavenly
Father in every respect, at all times, in constant dependence of
God His Father. He said that both He and His Father worked in
the truest sense in the creative and redemptive work for the world.
And God expects us to work with all our might and energy, whatever our hands find to be done, in this world of His. "The earth is
the Lord's and the fullness thereof, the world and those who
dwell therein" (Ps. 24:1). Jesus asked the men and women of
His day to continue instant in prayer but also to work, by giving
directions to those whom He called how they were to be about
their heavenly Father's business. His example, from Joseph's
carpenter shop to the cross of Calvary, inspired others to cease-
less holy activity.

Because much of our work is not purposeful and prayerful,
but unholy and unguided by God, it does not have the adventure or
the blessings we rightfully should seek in our work and vocation.
God will not bless the mere activist who works to keep busy and
shows himself very energetic before men. Only the work of God
will endure. Only when we combine heavenly prayers with earthly
work will we be able to work for the food which does not perish.
Indeed, our earthly work will have the hallmark of heavenly
benediction.

II

Our Daily Work Will Be Blessed if Done in Loving Obedience and Trust in God

This will lead us to work in loving and trusting obedience to God. A notable instance of this is given us in the Gospel of Luke (5:1-11), which tells us of the call of Peter, the great fisherman, after Jesus had shown him by a miracle the blessings of obedience to God and love of his heavenly Father. Peter and his companions had labored all night, fishing just offshore in the shallows, but they caught nothing. The experienced fishermen knew that this was the place and time for fishing. However, when they saw Jesus, who requisitioned their boat for a pulpit, from which He taught the people, they were moved by His sermon to love and obey. Although they knew Jesus but imperfectly, they evidenced what many of us lack in our work — a loving, obedient, and trusting heart toward the Master. Jesus spoke as one having authority, and Peter, as big, bold, and burly as he was, obeyed. "At Your word I will let down the nets." He went out into the deepest section of the lake in the daytime, against his own judgment and experience, enclosed a great shoal of fish so that their nets broke and they could only with difficulty and the help of their companions bring both ships filled to the brim to shore.

The word of Jesus must be for us the guide for all our work. The love of Jesus should lead us to venture into any task He commands with trust and confidence. Then we shall have direction for our work which no mortal can give, and though His word and way may conflict with that of men, we will obey. All labor is thus sanctified for the Christian by Christ, who came to work the works of His Father in heaven and to minister to men. We must also be sure that in our work we are doing the Father's will as called children of God. We must be satisfied, if we can ever be fully satisfied here on earth, with the guiding love of God, which governs and guards our every step and endeavor at work or at home and in all things commends us to His fatherly care and commands us to depend on His providence. (Cp. 2 Kings 4:1-7)

Beyond this there is no way of success or blessing in our life and labor. To obey is better than sacrifice. To follow His Word and to do His will in love — to love God with our whole heart, soul, and mind, and in this love to labor for the food and bread, the meat and drink, the house and home which He alone can give and bless to us; to seek the living waters of life which He can send to us and the bread of life which He will multiply for us, is the end and aim of our work. For then we shall have the food which will endure to eternal life. Then our daily work will be

profitable for our body and soul, useful to others and eternally
beneficial. All who heard the Word of Jesus and sought His kingdom and His righteousness never suffered real want. When they
were hungry, Jesus fed them; when they were thirsty, He poured
for them the water of life (cp. John 6:5-13). They sought first the
kingdom of God and the righteousness of God, and all these things
were given them.

The multitudes who obeyed Jesus left all their earthly possessions behind them and followed Jesus. Their work now became,
as for the Big Fisher of Men, for Levi-Matthew the tax collector
or for the other pilgrims on the way a liturgy *(leiturgia)*, a blessed
and obedient service *(diakonia)*, and for some even martyrdom,
obedience to death *(martyria)*. The love of Christ and obedient
service to God and men showed that they were new creatures,
ministers of the grace and mercy of God to their fellowmen.

How were they able to do this work of eternity?

III

Our Daily Work Will Be Blessed if Done
by Faith in Christ Through God's Grace

When we have done all the good work we are capable of doing,
and expended all our holy energy and zeal in prayerful service
and humble obedience and love of God and in the service of man,
we are and remain unworthy servants. We must confess that the
good we wanted to do we did not do and the evils we wanted not
to do we did in the weakness of our sinful flesh. This is not the
view or the way of business and labor and industry in the world.
They all expect rewards, payments, and compensations even though
they are imperfect in their work and management of their businesses.

Only in the economy of God do we find the teaching of grace-
rewards and the compensation of faith. This blessed doctrine that
God by His grace gives us what we have not deserved and blesses
us with riches we have not earned is the heart of the Christian
Gospel. For some people this is a paradox or a contradiction. How
can we labor for the food which endures to eternal life if God
gives it to us by grace?

We must remember that in Jesus, who lived the perfect life
and died for us, we have a full salvation, complete payment for all
our debts to God. Our redemption is done, finished, accomplished.
Now by the grace of God we are given the message of God's loving
sacrifice. The seed of this Gospel is planted into our hearts by
God so that we can begin to comprehend that we are not our own,
but that we are bought with a price, we are redeemed from sin

and the bondage and slavery of death by Christ to God. We are God's own! God has declared us righteous in His sight through Christ. This is the operation of God, the work of God in us. Our meanest and vilest sins are covered by the blood of Jesus. All our inadequacies and failings are made up by the life and labor, the suffering and death, the resurrection and exaltation of our Christ. God gives us the reward of His gracious presence. His face shines and beams upon us, and His hands continue to bless us for the sake of Jesus Christ, our Savior. He forgives us our sins daily by grace in Word and sacrament. We believe this. But even this faith is a gift of God for the sake of the Son of Man, by the work of the Holy Spirit. Faith comes by hearing, and hearing of the Word of God creates faith.

Here then, we find all our answers to questions about bread and work, food and labor, meat and drink, house and home.

The multitude who followed Jesus and were fed by His gracious hand also wondered, as did the disciples, where they would get the bread to feed so many. How and where could they buy it? Jesus found it, prayed over the loaves and fishes, blessed and multiplied. How little faith they had! They had heard the blessed and blessing words from His holy lips. They should have depended on Him in full faith. But like many of us, they did not.

Jesus chided them for coming after Him only because they were breadseekers. But there were some men and women of faith among them. These perseveringly followed Jesus around the lake and now asked Him about the works of God. Jesus said: "This is the work of God, that ye believe on Him whom He hath sent" (John 6:29). Faith was to be the God-wrought work in them, and faith in Christ was to be the gift which the Son of Man was to give them. Faith was not a virtue, a meritorious work or an infused grace, but an activity of God which overlay every other work and action of man, by the power of Gospel, which is the power of God to salvation to everyone that believes.

Faith in Christ was the motivating power in the light of which God was loved, feared, and trusted as God. In the light of faith men could know and revere His name; honor, hear, and obey His Word.

This faith was and is the rule for the carpenter, a plumbline for the mason, a gauge for the plumber, a scale for the business-man, a coin for the banker, a measure for the merchant, a guide for the mariner, a chart for the astronomer, a compass for the explorer, inspiration for the writer, a calm for the distressed, a balm for the sick, a scalpel for the physician, the hope of mothers, the seed for farmers, strength for soldiers, and comfort for all the lost. Faith in God and His Christ is the final measure of a man. It is the last best hope of us all. For without faith it is impossible to please God. Whatever is not of faith is sin. And this is the victory that overcomes the world, all the sin in our bodies, and the materialistic matrix of our society — even our faith. Truly then, in all our work and play, every day in every way we must grow in faith and trust in our Savior, that we might find blessings in all our activity and accomplishments for God and His redeemed children on earth.

As we pray, "Give us this day our daily bread," we trustingly depend upon God to provide all the needs and wants of this life by His mercy and grace and goodness, and then we work at His direction, in loving obedience and trust and in firm faith in the God who sent His Christ and called us out of darkness into His marvellous light. To pray and work, to believe and praise Him who has promised to be with us till the end of time is to know and have, to hold and enjoy the Bread of Life, the eternal food which will not be taken away from us as long as we believe in Him, but will nourish us for all eternity.

And when all our striving and our labor is past and done, we shall yet find the greatest blessing in this incarnate and glorified Bread of Life at the very last. For on Him, the Son of God and the Son of Man, has God the Father set His seal.

Stand Fast in Your Christ-given Liberty

By GILBERT T. OTTE

(Reformation)

Stand fast therefore in the liberty wherewith Christ hath made us free, and be not entangled again with the yoke of bondage.
Galatians 5:1

A little prayer book appeared on the book market in recent years containing as its gem of devotion this personal plea: "O Lord, revive Thy church, beginning with me!" For a long time we have felt the need of such a personal petition by every member of our church. Not long ago someone passed out some tracts after our services containing a scathing criticism of our Lutheran Church, calling upon pastors and people to repent of their neglected duties and to rise to new spiritual life. It is salutary for us to have someone give us a "going-over" so that we learn to see ourselves as others see us. Reformation is generally most unpopular where it is most needed.

If Dr. Martin Luther could come back today and check up on the church body that bears his name, would not his clarion voice speak out against his brethren, calling them to carry out a real reformation, a personal reformation of heart and soul and life? We rejoice indeed in the heritage of liberty that is ours since his reformation of the medieval church. We trace in that religious movement of his day the genesis of the rights of man, of modern democracy, of social and political freedom. Liberty of conscience, liberty of the human mind to enlarge and to expand its store of knowledge, liberty of free speech and worship, liberty of church and of state in their relationship toward each other: these and many more benefits we enjoy in this 20th and perhaps last century of the world we rightly ascribe to the Reformation.

But what should move us to special thankfulness is the liberty wherewith Christ has made us free and which has become our prize possession due to Luther's restoration of the Gospel. Let us consider a few features of this freedom as we commemorate this anniversary of the Reformation of the church. On the basis of this stirring text I issue this appeal to you

Stand Fast in Your Lutheran Liberty

I

In This Liberty Go Directly to the Holy Bible for the Truth That Can Save Your Souls

"Stand fast therefore in the liberty wherewith Christ hath made us free, and be not entangled again with the yoke of bondage." St. Paul was greatly concerned about the Christians in the province of Galatia in Asia Minor to whom he had preached the Gospel of redemption from sin by the blood of the cross of Christ. False Christians had invaded this church, sowing the seed of confusion of Law and Gospel. They were demanding of the Galatians the observance of all the ceremonial laws of the Old Testament at the same time that they were accepting the New Testament Gospel of the Savior Jesus Christ. But St. Paul, deeply concerned about the salvation of their souls, pointed out that Christ Himself had abrogated those Old Testament ceremonial ordinances concerning circumcision, sacrifices, the observance of the Sabbath and of Holy Days commanded only to the Jews until Christ had come. To revive observance of those Old Testament ceremonial laws would amount to a denial of the advent of Christ and of the validity of His redemption. It would split men's trust between Christ and their own works, and thus deny the basic truth that men are justified before God not by their own merit but by faith in the Savior Jesus Christ. St. Paul seemed to be pleading: "God open your eyes to know the Gospel truth and give you courage to contend for it!"

Direct Access to the Truth

Stand fast in your liberty to go directly to the Holy Scriptures for the divine truth that can save your souls. Our Lord Jesus Christ Himself directed us: "Search the Scriptures, for in them ye think ye have eternal life; and they are they which testify of Me" (John 5:39). Yes, Christ came into this world to redeem us from sin by the sacrifice of Himself, and because of that finished redemption God forgives us all our sins, is fully reconciled to us, acknowledges us as His dear children and sure heirs of heaven. This message of salvation is recorded in the Bible, and God does not want it hidden but made known. He wants it heard, read, learned, believed, lived. It is the "power of God unto salvation to everyone that believeth" (Rom. 1:16). "All Scripture is written by inspiration of God" (2 Tim. 3:15). The Christians at Berea were commended for receiving the Word with all readiness of mind and for searching the Scriptures daily whether those things were so. All right-minded Christians know that God would have His Word, the Holy Scriptures, used firsthand by all of his children. Luther gave the Bible back to the people to enable them to come to know and to believe the saving truth. But the Roman papacy for centuries had been doing the contrary, had been withholding the Bible from circulation among the laity as though it were dangerous. One pope condemned Bible societies for printing and distributing the Bible, and one cardinal went so far as to say it would be better for the church if there were no Bible. In its stead they declared that God set priests and the bishops as the source of doctrine. Of them the laity could inquire as to the Bible's contents. Yes, they went so far as to claim infallibility for the pope, demanding that all Christians give him unquestioning obedience. But what a mass of contradictions, of confusing inconsistencies, these so-called infallible popes have piled up on the consciences of their deluded subjects! What a yoke of bondage the whole complicated system of Romanism has become in its utter departure from the simplicity of the Gospel, which the original Christians of the apostolic age believed and confessed! And what fools men are to barter away their liberty in Christ for the bondage of the Antichrist.

The Fact Situation

Papists deftly seek to cover up their unjustifiable suppression of Bible reading by the laity by declaring Scripture a dark and difficult book easily misunderstood; and they point to the many divisions of Protestantism supposedly caused by everybody's interpreting Scripture as he pleases. But does God want blind obedience for men or does He want a faith which is honest personal conviction born out of direct use of His Holy Word? Does not God (Psalm 1) call the man blessed whose delight is in the Law of the Lord and who meditates in His Law day and night? That supposed "unity" of the Roman Catholic Church is not all that it appears to be. History bears out the fact that there was rivalry among different orders of monks, that an order like the Jesuits was fostered by one pope, dissolved by another, and revived by a third. About 90 years ago, when the doctrine of the infallibility of the pope was about to be made church law, many of the Roman Catholic clergy as well as laity protested against the idea and withdrew from the Roman Church. Others, fearing excommunication, submitted, but not because they were convinced. A unity that rests on hypocrisy is not the unity God wants for His church. Blind obedience and slavish submission, throttling and gagging open-minded inquiry as to whether everything taught in the church tallies with the truth revealed by God in Holy Writ — is this living in the light? Is this standing fast in the liberty wherewith Christ has set us free? Is this continuing in His Word, being His disciples indeed, knowing the truth that is able to set us free?

Let's Look at the Record

Some superficial people say: "What does it matter whether we get the truth from the Bible directly or secondhand through the priest?" Need I tell a Lutheran congregation that the papacy designedly padlocks the Bible to its laity because papal teaching does not stem from the Bible as a Bible-reading laity might readily discover? No one has been able to prove up to this day — over 400 years after the Reformation! — that there is one statement in our Unaltered Augsburg Confession or in Luther's Small Catechism which is contrary to the Bible. Rome dare not make such a claim for her decrees. Her own leaders admitted centuries ago that she stands *outside* the Scriptures while we stand *within* them!

Stand fast in your precious liberty to go directly to God's Word for the truth on which you must stake your eternal destiny. Use your Bible, use your church services, use your Bible classes and study groups, use your family devotions faithfully to grow in your mastery of the Bible, to nourish your faith, your spiritual life, your hope for eternal salvation, on the unchanging Word.

Stand fast in your Christ-given liberty,

II

In Your Deliverance from an Evil Conscience by the Gospel of Full Pardon in Christ

There is no worse bondage than that of being guilty in the sight of God. Yet all men are by nature and by their own doing in such bondage. "All have sinned and come short of the glory of God" (Rom. 3:23). Death and its fearful consequences loom up as the result of such sinning. To this conscience bears witness, and from that voice within his own bosom man cannot run away. How desperately men have tried to settle the score, make atonemen for the evil they've done, free themselves from the insistent accusations of their own consciences! Only Christ can set us free from this woe. Do you dread facing the divine Judge, to whom every day and every night of your life is an open book? Do you look for refuge from His impending wrath? Here is that refuge in the Gospel of His Son Jesus Christ! *He* made good for all of your sins. He gave Himself upon the cross into death to redeem you. To every penitent believer, drawing nigh unto Him, He says, "Be of good cheer; thy sins are forgiven thee." This sweet Gospel of the adequacy of Christ to supply salvation St. Paul sets forth in clearest terms. Oh, what a precious liberty, what a deliverance from fear and an evil conscience, is this truth, that because of Christ, because of *His* fulfilling all the commandments for us, because of *His* suffering all the punishment for our sins, God is fully and forever reconciled to us! Jesus Christ has redeemed me that I may be His own!

Yet Romanism thinks it honors God by deliberately decimating His clear and sure Gospel, by denying that Christ has by His one Self-sacrifice "perfected forever them that are sanctified" (Heb. 10:14); where remission of sins is "there is no more offering for sin" (10:18). But ever new sacrifices, penances, masses, atonements for sin, are offered by a priest in the Roman Church, and these alone are set forth as valid to absolve from sin!

Oh, what has become of Christ's word on the cross "It is finished"! "Christ *has* redeemed us from the curse of the Law, being made a curse for us. The blood of Jesus Christ, His Son, cleanseth us from all sin. He that believeth on the Son hath everlasting life and shall not come into condemnation but is passed from death unto life." Oh, glorious Gospel liberty from the agony of Roman uncertainty! Who would give it up and entangle himself again with the yoke of bondage?

Stand fast in your Christ-given liberty

III

To Serve God Not from Fear but from Love

In Galatians St. Paul shows what true religion is. Its motive power is the love of Christ. Its spirit is not that of fear but of faith working by love. It brings forth the fruits of the Spirit. It permeates every area of daily life. It makes man a new creature in Christ.

Love Is the Fulcrum

The trusting believer, who has come to Jesus at the foot of the cross, receives the Spirit of Christ and begins to love the Savior, proving that love by shunning whatever displeases God and by doing what is Christlike. But when men are held back from Christ as their loving Redeemer, they do not absorb the true motive and mainspring for leading a Christian life; they must be driven to do good. That is why the papacy has had to develop new laws and ordinances, fasting and alms and other regulations to which men outwardly conform but often with rebellious hearts. To urge them on, special merits, indulgences, and rewards are promised. They are thus treated as slaves, hired workingmen, not as God's loving children; for what child that truly loves his father does things to please him only for reward?

Oh "stand fast in the liberty wherewith Christ has made us free." We are children of God, whom we love and whom we serve voluntarily, without thought of special prizes or honors or awards. "We love Him because He first loved us" (2 Cor. 5). Stand fast in your Christ-given liberty

IV

To Pray Directly to God

This is our glorious privilege that we can worship God in spirit and in truth. Christ our Savior has taught us how to pray in the "Our Father," to call upon Him directly as our Father, knowing ourselves to be His dear children. "Ye have not received the spirit of bondage again to fear, but ye have received the Spirit of adoption, whereby we cry, Abba, Father." Did not our blessed Lord expressly teach us: "Whatsoever ye shall ask the Father in My name He will give it you"?

The One Way to God

We take Christ at His word. We go directly to God with all our prayers and to Him only. Is it in keeping with homage to Christ to disregard His direction: "Thou, when thou prayest . . . pray to thy Father"? Long ago Holy Scripture settled the question of by-passing Christ and addressing prayers or petitions for intercession to saints: "Doubtless Thou art our Father, though Abraham be ignorant of us and Israel acknowledge us not. Thou, O Lord, art our Father, our Redeemer; Thy name is from everlasting" (Is. 63: 16). What warrant is there in Holy Scripture for intercessions in our behalf by the Virgin Mother Mary? How can alleged champions of the truth blind themselves to the clear testimony of Scripture that rules out all intercessors but Christ? "There is one God and *one Mediator* between God and men, the man Christ

Jesus, who gave Himself a ransom for all" (1 Tim. 2:5). "If any man sin we have an Advocate with the Father, Jesus Christ, the Righteous; and He is the Propitiation for our sins, and not for ours only but also for the sins of the whole world" (1 John 2:2). It is God who answers prayer. To Him should all flesh come. Christ is "the Way, the Truth, and the Life: no man cometh unto the Father *but by Him*" (John 14:6). Stand fast in your Christian liberty

V

Because It Frees You From the Fear of Death

Thanks to the Gospel of our full salvation in Christ we know God aright, not as a tyrant to dread but as a Father to love, reconciled to us by His Son, our only Mediator and Redeemer. Now that we are Christ's own His promises to us will be fulfilled: "Because I live ye shall live also." "My sheep hear My voice, and I know them, and they follow Me, and they shall never perish, neither shall any man pluck them out of My hand" (John 10:27 f.). "Blessed are the dead which die in the Lord from henceforth; yea, saith the Spirit, that they may rest from their labors, and their works do follow them." (Rev. 14:13)

Like the first Christians whose faith in the full forgiveness of their sins was wholly set on Christ, and whose hope for life everlasting was wholly founded on Him, we can approach death with fearless defiance, saying: "O death, where is thy sting? O grave, where is thy victory? The sting of death is sin, and the strength of sin is the Law. But thanks be to God, which giveth us the victory through our Lord Jesus Christ!" (1 Cor. 15:55 f.). Armed with these assurances we can walk into the valley of the shadow of death and fear no evil. Christ is with us, before us, beside us. He has overcome death and brought life and immortality to light.

Oh, perilous papacy that would rob us of this confidence and this comfort, that would plunge us into endless despair! O foolish ex-Lutherans who gave up glorious freedom from fear and superstition and ignorance to become entangled in the yoke of popery's bondage! Strange the slave once set free who chooses to go back to ball and chain, to the lashes of the tyrant's whip! The Reformation cost our fathers in Christ much blood, tears, and sweat. Let it not be in vain! Cling to it ever as your most precious heritage!

Help God Move His Left Hand!

By ROBERT K. MENZEL

(Election Day)

(No single text is supplied for this sermon for Election Day, since none of the Holy Writers speak to the specific subject of democratic institutions, such as free elections. The sermon, however, is based broadly on Scriptural truth, particularly Luther's application of Law and Gospel to the church-state question.)

We are speaking of the hands of God. However, since He is Spirit, God has no hands. When Scripture speaks of the "hand of God," it uses figurative language. It uses picture language. When we make things or move them around, we use our hands. We cannot think of God making things or moving them about without hands. So we speak of God's hands: "He has the whole wide world in His hands," we say. By the hand of His power He preserves the world. God is ceaselessly active upholding and controlling the universe which He made with His hands. God is no absentee landlord. Neither is He the hired handyman whom we may summon to satisfy our latest whim. In an orderly way God is active in keeping this world in shape as long as He wishes. In this work of keeping the world going God wants to make use of our hands also. On this day nearest to Election Day we invite:

Help God Move His Left Hand!

Among the many contributions Dr. Martin Luther made to our Western world his clear distinction between the role of the church over against the state has been most helpful. In pointing out that the functions of each must be kept separate Luther thought of the church as the right hand of God and of the state as the left.

I

God Moves in the World with His Left Hand

Before we can understand what Luther meant by "the left hand of God," we must understand what he meant by the "right hand of God." *The task of the left hand of God is seen in contrast to the work of His right hand.*

God is using His right hand when the good news of our salvation through Jesus Christ is proclaimed. The right hand of God was busy in the teaching, miracles, death, and resurrection of God's "right-hand Man," Jesus Christ. It is at the right hand of God the Father that Christ is now active. At the right hand He is Lord over all, "given a name which is above every other." Although we do not deserve it, by His "marvelous loving-kindness

... He saves by His right hand them which put their trust in Him"
(Ps. 17:7; cp. also Ps. 20:6; 48:10; 60:5). On the Last Day the
Savior-Judge will gather the "sheep" at His right hand to hear the
welcome words "Inherit the kingdom prepared for you." Then
they will take their places at His "right hand," where there shall
be "pleasures forevermore." (Ps. 16:11)

With His right hand God establishes His kingdom of grace.
Where the pastor speaks the Word of grace, there is God's hand.
As a teacher tells of Christ, the right hand of God is active.
In Baptism the right hand of God places the pearl of salvation
into the water, and the hand of faith picks it out. His right hand
lays the wafer of the sacrament on the tongue and lifts the cup
of blessing to the lips. The right hand of God is stretched forth
in love to save and heal.

We help God's right hand move out into the world when we
bring others the good news of salvation through Christ. In our
world and in our day God is counting on us to help move His
right hand out into the places where people need Him. Through
us He wants to touch the eyes of the spiritually blind. Through
us He wants to place His fingers on the tongues of those who
do not know how to speak His name. Through us He wants to
touch the biers of those who are "dead in trespasses and sins."

Lawful Authority — The Left Hand of God

God also reaches with His *left* hand into the world He created.
In this way Luther described the functions of the state to distinguish it from the functions of the church. While the right hand
of God holds the Gospel, His left holds the Law. Whenever men
do not respond in faith to the sword of the Spirit (which is the
Word of God), God will be Lord by wielding the sword of power
with His left hand. In the church God rules by grace; in the
world by law. As God makes use of human instruments, fallible
men, to move His right hand through the Gospel, so also He
makes use of human agents to keep order by law in the world.
This is what the apostle wants to tell us when he wrote (Romans 13) that the authority (all authority) comes from God.
God is the Author of law and order. He gives men conscience and
reason to make just laws. Through these lawful governments
God keeps order in the world He created. Proper authority is
the left hand of God.

"The whole structure of authority in the world is God's
work. . . . For it is not the intention of rulers to discourage what
is good, but to prevent what is bad. . . . (The officer of the government) is a servant whom God has appointed for your welfare."
(Paraphrase of Rom. 13 by Clinton D. Morrison, *The Powers That*

Be, SCM Press, p. 107.) As God's left hand civil government holds a sword of law and force, and will use it, if need be, to bring lawbreakers to justice and to protect the law-abiding citizen. Whenever we do a charitable deed, Jesus urges us not to let the left hand know what the right is doing. However, God's left hand knows very well what His right is doing. God wants to establish His kingdom of grace through the Gospel. Law, the tool of God's left hand, is the means God has given to preserve the world so that the Gospel can be proclaimed in the world. So also when God uses His left hand, we can see the love of God moving out into the world.

Both God's left hand and His right enfold the Christian. The believer lives under the care of both hands. In the church we live under His right hand in a "kingdom not of this world," and with our "citizenship in heaven" (Phil. 3:20). At the same time, in the world we are under the left hand of God, under the authority of municipal, state, and federal governments. But we do not live a split personality existence. Both hands are God's hands. God is Lord of both church and state. Between these two arms we have a perspective from which to see both church and state as servants of God's purpose. In the kingdom of God we walk by faith. In the kingdom of the world we walk by love. We see civic duty as a sacred calling. God, who has moved us by His right hand, calls each of us to help His left hand move out into the world. In the realm where His left hand operates, God challenges the believer to carry out his responsibilities. Many possibilities immediately come to mind as to how we may respond to the call to help the left hand of God move out into the world. However, today we shall endeavor to see how our concerns apply to the coming election.

II

How Can We Help God's Left Hand Move into the World?

There are few countries outside the United States and Canada where there is such a variety of opportunities for people to right wrongs and help their neighbors. In a democratic society such as ours we are free to express our opinions, organize groups to implement them, and to cast our ballots in free and secret elections. Christians, *as Christians* and not merely as patriotic citizens, have a stake in the maintenance and development of our democratic institutions. The ballot rates high on the list of devices which help the left hand of God move in the world. We want to look at the way in which the vote of the Christian helps God's left hand move. If good government is the work of God through us, His servants, His left hand, then several considerations force themselves on us:

"My Vote Won't Count Anyway!"

The Christian will never stay away from the polls (except for good reason). The Christian who doesn't vote actually slows down the movement of the left hand of God. Of the 33 percent of the people of voting age who did not vote in the 1960 presidential election, about one third failed to vote because of plain indifference. "Politics is dirty business; it is all crooked," some mistakenly say. Others complain, "Why should I vote? One vote more or less doesn't matter."

In his famous "Cross of Gold" speech in 1896 William Jennings Bryan said, "When I find a man who is not willing to bear his share of the burdens of government which protects him, I find a man who is unworthy to enjoy the blessings of a government like ours."

One vote can have crucial significance, even when nearly 69 million people go to the polls as they did in the 1960 presidential election. President Kennedy was edged into the White House with a plurality of only 118,000 out of nearly 69 million votes. A Congressman from a county in California was sent to Washington by a majority of — just one vote.

The Christian who does not vote is, in effect, "resigning from the human race." He is shrugging off his part in the nation's problems, mistakes, and lost opportunities. Failure to vote means to withdraw from the involvement which Christian faith demands. The nonvoter says, "God, get someone else to help move Your left hand; move it without me." It is God who binds us together in the corporate life of the community; here He throws us together so that we may serve each other as He served us.

The Hon. Herbert Freise, a Washington State Senator and Lutheran layman, was asked, "Why is it necessary for the Christian citizen to vote in order to express his Christian faith in action?" He replied,

> A Christian has a dual citizenship — he is a citizen of his nation and also a citizen of the kingdom of God. This is evident from our Lord's words: "Render unto Caesar the things that are Caesar's and unto God the things that are God's." Not only does the Christian exercise his faith by *obeying* the laws of the government, but also by *participating* in it. In our democratic way of life it is important that a Christian participate in his government to a maximum degree, since the actions of the government are our actions. We are responsible for our government. And participation in our government begins with voting, the act whereby we express our will and help determine what course of action our government should take and what character it shall have.

The Christian's share in carrying the burdens of the state begins in precinct work and continues in the privacy of the ballot box. God's left hand is at work there.

Champion Human Rights

The Christian who helps the left hand of God move will be a champion of human rights. Many are the blights and scars on our beloved land. As we encourage our people to cast their votes for freedom and justice, we must never forget that over two million Americans of voting age are deprived of this expression of liberty by illiteracy, poll taxes, and other pressures. Still others do not have the right to learn in proportion to their abilities because of the color of their skin or the place of their birth. Others cannot work where they like or live where they please because they belong to some unpopular minority group. A great theologian (Thomas Aquinas) said centuries ago, "Patiently to endure wrongs done to yourself is a mark of perfection. But patience over against the wrongs done to others is a sign of imperfection; in fact, it is sin." The Christian voter will want to help the left hand of God move in the direction of those whose "inalienable rights" to "life, liberty, and the pursuit of happiness" are but slogans in the Declaration of Independence.

The Hand of Love Marks the "X"

The Christian who helps the left hand of God move will show his *love for people* as he casts his ballot.

Nearly every state ballot includes numerous "propositions" which are presented to the voters for approval. These include measures on social welfare benefits, unemployment compensation, old-age pensions, matters of public health, and other far-reaching measures. The follower of Christ, who has heard Him say, "Inasmuch as you have helped the least of My brethren," will feel that he has a vital stake in legislation which may act to harm or benefit his fellowman. The hand that marks "X" on the ballot, or pushes the lever on the voting machine, is impelled by the love of Christ. The Christian will be concerned about the community's work in clearing crime-breeding slums, feeding the hungry, settling refugees, protecting children, providing for the sick and aged, conserving health, and promoting peace.

The Christian need not fear that the so-called welfare state will push out the practice of Christian love. Christ-motivated love is very inventive. Christian love will never perish for the lack of places to get exercise. There will always be ample opportunity for us to show our love to our neighbor. And that demonstration of love to our neighbor can begin in the voting booth.

Be Well Informed

The Christian who helps the left hand of God move in the world will be well informed.

Have you ever gone to the polls and placed an X after the

ELECTION DAY

name of candidates about whom you knew little or nothing? How
many measures have you rejected because your tax rate would
be increased, without analyzing whether the measure is a good
one or not? Several years ago in a Western state a candidate who
was an alleged communist succeeded in accumulating several
hundred thousand votes for superintendent of education, simply
because her name appeared first on the ballot.

The word of Jesus has application here: "We must be as harmless as doves, but as wise as serpents." The uninformed use of the
ballot may do more harm than good. A poorly informed voter
might as well stay at home. A poor vote may be more damaging
than none at all. The Christian who wishes to help move the left
hand of God will be well informed, able to grasp the realities in
which faith must make its important decisions.

Be Critical of People and Events

The Christian who wants to help move the left hand of God
will use his vote to stand in criticism of people and events.

Men make use of their reason to make laws. Sometimes men
make foolish laws. The Christian is also to use his "reason and
all his senses," which he acknowledges as the gracious creation of
God. Being a child of God, the mind and reason of the Christian
is enlightened by God's Word. But since the Christian remains
a sinner, even his reason does not always function without error.
Since governments are run and laws are made by human beings,
the laws will be less than perfect. There will be "loopholes" in
the law. Special interests will often get their way, while the desires of less-organized or smaller groups will be overlooked. Certain individuals will seek and receive special privilege.

For these reasons we must uphold the freedom of our press,
even when they publish things with which we disagree. We must
permit every view to be expressed publicly, even those views which
are unpopular. However, criticism must always be expressed
humbly, and in a way which gives demonstration of the love of
Christ in our hearts. And we recall that that is a love which extends even to our enemies. The Christian will surely not engage
in the muckraking and mudslinging that seems to take place in
every major campaign. The ultimate tool of criticism is the ballot.
We do not return to office the weak or poor public servant.

In Conclusion: "Toward a Tranquil and Quiet Life . . ."

St. Paul gives us a remarkable insight as he writes to Timothy
(1 Tim. 2:1-7): "I urge that petitions . . . be offered for all men;
for sovereigns and all in high office. . . ." Timothy had no chance
to help the left hand of God move by means of free elections. The

most he could do was to pray for "all in high office." Today we
can do that and something more about those for whom we pray.
We can put them into office at the polls. And we can remove them
by not voting for them next time.

Then the apostle goes on: ". . . in order that we may lead
a tranquil and quiet life in full observance of religion and high
standards of morality. Such a prayer is right and approved by
God, our Savior, whose will it is that all men should find salvation
and come to know the truth." Here the right hand of God moves
in again. God's left hand, St. Paul is telling us, works through the
government of our land *in order that* we may have the tranquility
and peace to enjoy the outstretched right hand of God which brings
us every spiritual blessing — salvation through "the one Mediator
between God and men . . . Christ Jesus, who sacrificed Himself
to win freedom for all mankind." (New English Bible)

May God give us the insight and the strength to help Him
move His powerful left hand through our votes on election day,
in order that His gracious right hand may move freely and that
the "Gospel may have free course and be preached to the joy and
edifying of Christ's holy people."

Let Us Give Thanks!

By Walter E. Kraemer

(Thanksgiving Day)

Oh, give thanks unto the Lord, for He is good; for His mercy
endureth forever. — *Psalm 136:1*

The theme for the sermon today is inescapable: "Thanksgiving."

This reverses the pastor's usual process in the preparation of
a sermon. Instead of the theme and sermon rising out of the
selected or appointed Bible passages, the Festival of Thanksgiving
sends him to Scripture to find a text to fit the subject. His difficulty,
then, will not be to find one, but to make a selection out of an
abundance of Scripture verses. Even in the limited concordance
included in many Bibles he will find the word "thanks," and its close
relatives, almost 100 times. Using cross references from these
passages would probably exhaust most of the Bible.

This is revealing and significant. The record of God's revela-
tion to man is saturated with a response of praise and thanksgiving.
The morning stars sang together at the creation of the world.
Bethlehem's angels sang in full chorus at the gift to man of the
Christ Child. The choirs of eternity in Revelation chant the praises
of Him who stands in the center of the triumphant church (cf. *The*

Lutheran Hymnal, Number 35, "Songs of Praise the Angels Sang").
The Bible is a book of praise to God for His glory and goodness.
The history of the church of God is a story of victory. The life of
every Christian is a song of thanksgiving.

Dip anywhere into the stream of the water of life, and you
come up with a cup of gratitude brimming over. And so we offer
as our text one of the most familiar and best-loved Bible passages
for our celebration of this day: "Oh, give thanks unto the Lord,
for He is good; for His mercy endureth forever." Today then,
let us, too, give thanks unto the Lord. But how? And for what?

I

Negative Thanksgiving

As with everything else, there is a wrong way of giving thanks.

There is, for example, the giving of thanks for the fact that our
troubles during the past year were no worse than they were.
A Chinese proverb is said to read: "I complained that I had no
shoes till I met a man who had no feet." This is an approach to
the act of thanksgiving and to God that has much more of Oriental
fatalism in it than of Christian providence. It springs more from
a sense of being lucky than of being blessed. It sees God or the
gods as enemies who cannot be trusted and who must be outwitted
or circumvented. You give thanks to the extent that you succeeded
in doing so. A young missionary in India was startled when he
tried to be friendly and complimented a mother on her healthy-
looking child. Instead of beaming modestly as expected, the mother,
frightened, covered the child's face with her *sari* and fled the room.
Such a compliment was in her mind an invitation to the "evil
eye" of some god to harm her by harming something she had revealed as precious.

Surely the greater sufferings of our millions of fellowmen will
always call forth our Christian sympathy, but they dare never
become subtle evidences that somehow or other we stand in better
with God in our lesser troubles and therefore have this status to
be thankful for. We would then be thanking Him solely for His
justice and fairness, in the manner of the Pharisee, and not for
His mercy and long-suffering, as did the publican.

Somewhat similar to this negative way of giving thanks is the
approach that decides to see only the blessings received and to
close the eyes to the afflictions endured or the troubles borne. This
would be unrealistic and not quite honest, and Christianity and
Christians are always honestly realistic. Our Lord did not so close
His eyes to the misery around Him or try to shun or avoid it. And
surely He was fully aware of the evil done and yet to be done

to Him personally. He, and the Scriptures that testify of Him, knew and faced the fact that "man is born to trouble as the sparks fly upward." Christ saw clearly the pain and sorrow men bore, and He reached out in sympathy to heal and to comfort. He preached neither stoicism ("Grin and bear it") nor Pollyanna sentimentalism ("This is the best of all possible worlds"). He did not reproduce the symphony of God with the thunder of the kettledrums silenced and only the flutes sweetly singing. Trouble, like sin and born of sin, is a basic part of life — also of the Christian life — and must be taken into account even in an act of thanksgiving. And so today we cannot forget that the past year brought with it for each one of us greater or lesser days of anxiety, bewilderment, and doubt. These, too, must somehow or other be included in our remembrance as we assemble on this Thanksgiving Day, and even be made part of our reason for the celebration of this day. We shall come back to this problem, but let us first outline the larger frame within which our thanksgiving as Christians will be set. We are here for a

II

Positive Thanksgiving

Our text urges us to "give thanks unto the Lord, for He is good." Change that last word ever so slightly and enlarge its meaning. Listen to it then: "Oh, give thanks unto the Lord, for He is *GOD*." In the English language, "God" and "good" both come from the same ancient word. God is good, and the highest good is God. Jesus said to the rich young ruler, "Why callest thou Me good? There is none good but one; that is, God" (Matt. 19:17). And when you so read or speak our text, you have reached as high as you can in your thanksgiving — and as wide. We thank Him for all that He is and all that He has done and for all that we are and have received.

First of all we thank God for God, whose enduring mercy has supplied us constant *support* for life. We do well to remember this.

Our American Thanksgiving Day has largely supplanted an older church festival, the Festival of Harvest. When most of the people of the church lived close to the soil, the need for such a remembrance was obvious and persistent. But as the church moves increasingly away from the source of its support to the pavements of the city and the neighborhood stores, the celebration becomes the more necessary. A Sunday school teacher had this brought home to her when she asked her class whence all that we needed to live came, and she got the answer, "The supermarket." All the people who stand between the ultimate source and the meal on our table or the clothes on our back or the roof over our head — all these "middlemen" serve only to bring us these gifts. The giver still remains God. Man may manipulate and improve and multiply the production of food and clothing and shelter — and for this growing skill and control we also have God to thank — but the primary cause remains the gift of God's sun and rain, seedtime and harvest, germination and growth. Oh, give thanks unto the Lord, for He is God, who, knowing that we have need of all these things, He again granted them to us in unmerited abundance.

We thank God for God, secondly, because His enduring mercy has supplied us constant *strength* for life. Food, clothing, shelter — these things support life, but they are not all of life. Man is more than animal, and his life is more than food and raiment. He needs length and breadth and depth in living lest life become meaningless and aimless and empty and his spirit die within him. These needs, too, God knows and supplies, and for them, too, we have come today to thank Him.

Now there are many things that go to enrich life. There is a deep hunger for beauty in man, and we are grateful today for all those artists who have satisfied this hunger with literature and music, art and architecture. There is also the abiding excitement in the use of our bodies which Browning called

> . . . the wild joys of living! the leaping from rock up to rock.
> . . . the cool silver shock
> Of the plunge in a pool's living water, the hunt of the bear. . . .

And when we grow too old to participate, we enjoy watching others demonstrate skill, strength, and endurance. We give thanks for sports. Despite what the soiled hands of men have done to them, let us give thanks also for the convenience and joy we have had in the telephone, the radio, the TV, the daily newspaper, and our magazines. In short, we should remember with gratitude God's blessing on all efforts of man to win victories over "distance, darkness, and disease."

But so close at hand, so taken for granted, and therefore so often overlooked is God's gift of companionship. "God," said David, "setteth the solitary in families." We underestimate this strength in life until it is cut off or reduced by bereavement. Each one of us stands in the center of ever-widening circles of fellowship. We are members of a family. Large or small as it may be now, it goes back through ancestors to include millions who have helped to make us, and it goes forward through descendants whom we are now fashioning. We are members of a community, of a state, a nation, and ultimately of all mankind. In their strength we find strength; in their needs we find our opportunity to serve the Christ.

"Solitary confinement," ostracism, a "ship-wrecked-on-a-desert-island" kind of life is an ultimate woe that can break the strongest man. Today we pause and look around at family, friends, acquaintances. They give our lives continuity and strength. In them we find cause for thanks and praise to the enduring mercy of God.

But most precious for us is the fellowship of the saints, the holy Christian church. The Old Testament constantly refers back to history and tells again how God interrupted it with His wondrous and mighty acts; and how by them He preserved the family of the elect. The 136th Psalm, which our text introduces, thanks God for deliverance from Egypt's bondage; the protection in the wilderness wanderings; the conquest of evil kings. All this is part of history — our history. We have sprung from a people for whom God did not hesitate to break into time to give support and strength. Ours is the great heritage of a "cloud of witnesses" eager to testify to the good God we worship. They are unseen and glorified; we are here present and still mortal; but we are both made one in the family whose Father is God. This fellowship is ours today and ours to share with our world and our descendants. Here we are not in solitude, no strangers or foreigners, but fellow citizens with the saints and of the household of God. Let us give thanks unto the Lord, for He is God, and we are His children, supported and strengthened in weal and woe, for time and eternity, in life and death.

And yet more. Beyond support and strength we thank God today because in His enduring mercy He has *sanctified* life, has made it holy and given us sinners that second title of saints.

The theologian-philosophers have given our era a new name. It is no longer to be called the Century of Progress or of Science. They insist we name it the Age of Anxiety. The combination of fear and guilt arising from known deeds of evil or clear threats of danger are terrible enough, but when, like a character in a novel by Kafka, man walks ignorant of his crime and toward a nameless doom, then there is added to anxiety the terror of the unknown and unknowable. Then there is literally "no place to hide." This, they say, is the modern sickness unto death. The grief of poverty is the lack of wealth. The grief of illness is the lack of health. The grief of bereavement is the lack of the loved one. But the ultimate grief of anxiety is the lack of God. We have not lost Him, for we have known Him in the fact and face of our Lord Jesus Christ. And to know Him is eternal life.

Let us give thanks unto the Lord, for He is God, and we have heard His voice raised in wrath. We know that it is from Him we flee and that it is the guilt and burden of our transgressions of His law that makes our hearts restless and afraid. The afflictions we have had this past year are but the obverse side of His love chastening those He pitieth as a father his children. It was for our good that we were afflicted.

But finally let us give thanks unto the Lord, for He is God, whose mercy endured even to the gift of His only Son, His unspeakable gift that alone is able to deliver us from the bondage of death. "Once He came in blessing, All our ills redressing," and now there is a place to hide:

> Rock of Ages, cleft for me,
> Let me hide myself in Thee.

We have much to be thankful for, and so today let us give thanks — not as fatalists or Pharisees, but as children of faith in His enduring mercy that supports, strengthens, and sanctifies life, yesterday, today, and forever.

"Oh, give thanks unto the Lord, for He is good; for His mercy endureth forever." And in that angels and archangels, cherubim and seraphim, saints and martyrs join to say "Amen and Amen!"

Witnessing for Jesus: Every Christian a Witness

By PAUL J. FOUST

(Mission Sermon)

Ye shall be witnesses unto Me both in Jerusalem and in all Judea and in Samaria and unto the uttermost part of the earth. — *Acts 1:8*

When the Lord Jesus had completed His enormous assignment of earning heaven for the world, He was very much concerned that this redemption, which had cost His life, should not be left undelivered. And He knew full well that the only people He could bank on to deliver it were those who had tasted and experienced "the peace of God which passeth all understanding." Those who were "walking in the light" had discovered that the Christian life was something which no one could afford to turn down; these had hearts that were filled with faith and also honestly wanted to share Him with others.

Now Jesus knew that His work of redemption had required much more than human power. He knew that only the "blood of Jesus Christ, God's Son, could cleanse us from all sin." He knew equally well that although it sounded easy to give away this blood-bought redemption (since it was something that people need more than they need anything else), yet it was actually going to require the power of God to do this, too, because in spite of their need, people as they are by nature do not want the pardon of Jesus. Sin has so clouded their minds and robbed them of their vision that instead of getting right with God, they try to run from Him and avoid Him and make all kinds of excuses as to why they cannot take His pardon even though it had cost the life of the Son of God and even though it is to their eternal advantage!

No wonder Jesus had to bolster their courage by assuring them, "Ye shall receive power after that the Holy Ghost is come upon you!" This was planned to take care of their weak-kneed feeling of inadequacy when that little band of disciples faced a teeming world full of people all trying to run away from God. The power of God would go to work right beside them, the power which they had seen in action for three solid years, the power which knew no limitations. And while the world of unbelief may laugh at this promise of Jesus, yet the thousands of Christians, who are marching in the army of Christ in every continent of the world, are evidence enough that the power of God has been functioning wherever there have been witnesses of Jesus bearing the torch of the Gospel.

When we who are His 20th-century witnesses become tongue-tied and no longer function as the early disciples did, it is apparent that we have forgotten His promise of power. You can talk about being afraid, but I really don't know what we are afraid of when the Almighty is right beside us. It would seem rather that we would be afraid *not* to witness! Or some talk about being ashamed. But it would seem rather that we should be proud to represent Him who built this world and supplies every single need, who was not ashamed to die for you and me, and whose principles are honorable rather than shameful. If Satan has clouded your mind so that shame and fear takes over where faith and courage ought to be, then he has functioned well as the archdeceiver and has hidden from you the Savior's promise, "Ye shall receive power."

This morning I pray that the Holy Spirit may possess your heart in an abundant measure and build within you the kind of loyal Christian faith which cannot be silenced; which will result in every day of your life being devoted to:

Witnessing for Jesus: Every Christian a Witness

Now to guide you in your life's witness, I have chosen a text which gives you God's blueprint for this function, which forms the very purpose of your earthly existence. For you know that God has not left you in this world to mark time. In fact, if this is all you're doing, then it would be better for you that He would move you into heaven today! But God left you here, after you became His child, to be a walking example of His Gospel, to lead others to Calvary and to eternal life with God.

When Jesus handed His blueprint to His first disciples, His
directions were not at all unclear. In fact He mapped out an inch-
by-inch program for witnessing. His orders were to start right in
Jerusalem, then to branch out into surrounding Judea, then go to
Samaria to the people of another race, and finally they were not to
rest until it has been delivered to the last soul on earth!

Now we in our 20th century can come up with lots of fancy
evangelism programs, but we will never top the one Jesus designed.
It worked pretty well in those early centuries, and it could be
working just as well today if every Christian would use it! *But
this is the real jinx!* For some strange reason there are too many
people who want the pardon of Jesus to cleanse their own soul,
who want a cozy nook in heaven for themselves, but who claim
a strange exemption when it comes to sharing these eternal blessings with others. But is there any Christian within the range of
this message who has ever been excused from being a witness for
Jesus? When a little five-year-old child can clasp the hand of
a playmate and bring him to Sunday school; when a 90-year-old
lady can call on the telephone and urge others to visit her church;
when a man with a speech impediment can plead with his friends
to take Jesus into their lives; when invalids can tell the story of
Jesus to those who pass their bedside, is there really anyone here
this morning who has a valid alibi as to why he or she cannot be
a witness for Jesus?

I

Witness In Your Home

Now the Savior did more than pinpoint individuals to dis-
tribute His pardon. He left no room for questions. He even told
them where to go in their witnessing. The first step was to be
taken right at home; right in their own Jerusalem! There were
plenty of souls there without a Savior. This ought to be a significant directive to us in our 20th-century evangelism program.
The most fertile place for any of you to witness for Jesus is in
your own home. And if you don't witness where you spend the
greatest amount of time and where you have the greatest influence,
then I don't know how you expect to witness anywhere else! There
are souls within your home who need to be drawn closer to Jesus,
and there may be souls who have never experienced the blessings
of a Christian life. Many a child has led a parent to the Savior
and vice versa; many a wife has brought eternal life to a husband.
Let there be no doubt in your home that Jesus is the Savior of your
soul and the Lord of your life. Let your whole family know that
you have found pardon on Calvary and that you want nothing
more than that their souls should be washed by the same blood

of Jesus and their lives filled with the same Spirit of God. You see, you ought to be concerned that your family will spend not only this life together but also the next! And you know perfectly well that unless their souls are cleansed by the blood of Jesus, they will never see heaven. Go, then, and be a witness in your own Jerusalem.

II
Witness in Your Community

Jesus proceeds further in the text and instructs the disciples that they were not to be satisfied to stop in Jerusalem; they were to reach out into their community of Judea. I hear people say sometimes that religion is a private thing and that they just don't pry into other people's business and "talk church." But it's strange how we talk about everything else. We talk about baseball, politics, crime, farming, and marriage. In fact, you name the subject which is private in our 20th century! Why, then, should the God who is the Author of everything I am and have be private and His plan of salvation for a world of people be kept quiet? This sounds more like Satan's philosophy than God's! As a matter of fact, just wait till you stand in front of the open casket of your next-door neighbor, or your partner at work, and you'll wish then that you had just once invited them to church, or just once, at least, had a heart-to-heart talk with them about getting ready for eternity! You could at least have explained to them what Jesus went through to purchase pardon for them. Then if they turned it down — at least you delivered the message! The fact is that if you will only witness, you'll discover that God keeps His part of the bargain; His power goes with you. Go and be a witness in your Judea.

III
Witness in Your World

The next part of Jesus' directive must have really jarred those nationalistic Jews. Jesus said, "Go into Samaria!" "Imagine," they must have murmured, "offering pardon to people who aren't Jews!" But let's not smile at the disciples for their strange attitude. Our 20th-century Christians haven't quite learned yet either that Jesus died for all. "Samaria and the uttermost part of the earth" is a little far from our lives too. Do you doubt this? Just check how many people in our congregations would close the door to those who are of the wrong color or tradition. Check the mission side of the offering envelopes, and see how many are empty on the side that says, "Into all the world." Can we really say that these people are serious about Jesus' directive "Into Samaria and unto the uttermost part of the earth?" Well what about *you*? You may

not be able to go there yourself, but there are boys graduating
from our seminaries who are anxious to go for you if your
mission offerings will only feed them while they witness for you
and for Christ. Jesus says to *you*, "Go into Samaria and all the
world"! Are these missionaries all over the world *your* workers?
Or aren't you supporting them?

Go to Calvary

I am very sure that the thing which made those early disciples
such valiant witnesses for Jesus was the fact that they saw Him
purchase pardon at the price of His life. How could they now allow
this pardon to go unused? If any of you have not been the kind
of witnesses you should have been in your home, your community,
or your world, then you had better take a trip back to Calvary and
see again what Jesus paid for the souls of men, and for your soul.
If He could buy redemption with His life, can you not use your life
to give it away? When you can say by the Spirit of God, "He died
for me," you cannot but add, "And I will live for Him."

Bear in mind that He only asks you to witness! He doesn't
ask you to turn hearts or manufacture Christian faith. This is His
business. You are only to sow the seed; the growth is in God's
category. But He tells you to sow even if you are sowing on
cement. Penetrating the hardened hearts is a work of His almighty
Spirit. You go and tell the story of Jesus, and let God do the rest!

Will You Hoard it or Share It?

There is a story told of a man who was given two million
dollars. One million was to be put into his right pocket, and this
he could use for the necessities of his life. The other million was
to be put into his left pocket, and this was to be given away to
others who had needs. But as the story goes, he lived a full life,
spent most of his million, and finally died. And sealed into his
casket in his left pocket was one million dollars. He had selfishly
hoarded it all, deprived many people of much happiness, and the
million rotted! In a similar way God has placed into the pockets of
the soul of every Christian much more than two million dollars —
pardon for a whole eternity! The one portion is for your eternal
needs; enough that every day's mistakes are paid for by God's Son.
But in the other pocket of your soul is a "million in pardon" to give
away. When your casket is closed, will it still be there, or will
there be eternal souls to whom you have delivered what Jesus
bought with His life?

This is why my Savior went to Calvary for you and me, washed
us clean with His blood, made us His eternal children. May we be
witnesses unto Him!

Glorifying God, Who Blesses His Church

By ALFRED W. KOEHLER

(Mission Sunday)

I have planted, Apollos watered; but God gave the increase.

1 Corinthians 3:6

Today we are assembled to encourage one another in doing the great work which we Christians are privileged to do during our sojourn on earth. This work is Kingdom work. It is life's most important work for God's children. It involves our real purpose for living and should affect every area of our life.

In our text the apostle Paul is speaking of himself and of Apollos as workers in the Lord's kingdom, specifically as ministers of the Gospel. He states that he planted and that Apollos watered. Yet the basic principle of being workers in God's kingdom applies not only to those who occupy the office of the public ministry, but to all Christians everywhere. *All* Christians are to be laborers together with God.

God and Man Working Together

When we speak of the Christian church and of work in the Christian church, we are thinking of both God and man. According to God's plan and arrangement a cooperative effort is to be maintained in His kingdom work. Under God the Christian has work to do. God also is active in Kingdom work. Man does the planting and watering; God gives the increase. Man labors for the Lord, but success depends on God. Let us this day look at man's work in the kingdom of the Lord and at God's work in the kingdom, as God and man labor together in a common cause.

Man's Work in the Kingdom

1. *Man's work is varied.* Paul speaks of "planting" and of "watering." He is referring to the variety of work in the kingdom. As in agriculture, so in God's kingdom there are many types of work to be done, and not one of us is capable of doing every type of work. We do not all have equal abilities, and therefore none of us can do the variety of work demanded in the kingdom. Neither have we all the same opportunities in life to serve in the various fields of service. Each of us differs also in that respect. But there is some spiritual work suited to each of us. If Christians do nothing, it is not because of lack of ability or of opportunity, but only because they want to do nothing. Let each of us realize that there is a place for work in God's kingdom for every child of God, for you and for me.

2. *Man's work is important.* In agriculture planting and wa-

tering are important. So is the harvesting. Without the one the
other could not result. In life we often make the mistake of
attaching more importance to the glamorous work, to the work
which attracts attention, to the work which catches the public eye.
So we are apt to conclude that certain types of work in the Lord's
kingdom are unimportant, because they do not attract much attention, if any, and do not appear large and significant. Again, to
other work we attach importance. Let us never think that any
work in the Lord's kingdom is unimportant. All work for the
Lord is important. The parent who teaches his child the Word
of the Lord and guides him on the Christian path of life is doing
important work in the Lord's kingdom. The Christian who speaks
to the unchurched about his need of Christ in life is doing important work in the Lord's kingdom, even though such testimony
may never be known to any other person. The Christian child
who sings praises to God in the junior choir is doing important
work in God's kingdom. The pastor in the church, the officers
and elders of a Christian congregation are doing important work
in God's kingdom when they perform the duties of their office.
When you admonish a backsliding member and encourage him to
participate faithfully in the work of God, you are doing important
work in God's kingdom. So I could refer to singing in the choir,
doing administrative work in the church, ushering at the services, etc. All work for the Lord is important. It is just as wrong
to downgrade the importance of any church work as it is to regard
it too highly.

3. *Man's work is honorable.* In agriculture all phases of work
are honorable, whether it be tilling, planting, watering, weeding,
or harvesting. In God's kingdom there is nothing but honorable
work. We are workers together with God, and that makes the
Christian worker one of God's nobility.

4. *Man's work is limited.* Each worker in God's kingdom can
do only so much. We all are limited by our abilities and by our
opportunities. We are limited also regarding the eventual success
of our labors in the kingdom. Some may be five-talent people,
while others are two-talent people. Some people are in positions
of greater opportunities than others. And as to the result and
success, we also are limited. We may preach and teach, bear witness for Christ and confess our faith, but we cannot convict and
convince man's heart. We may invite and warn, but we cannot
convert. We cannot produce spiritual results; neither does God
hold us to do so. We are not responsible for spiritual results. Our
responsibility is limited by our abilities and by our opportunities;
but let us not underestimate them. Let none of us say there is
nothing for us to do. Let none of us hide his candle under a bushel.

Let none of us think there is no place of work for us. We may be limited, but none of us is bereft of ability and opportunity.

5. *Man does not work independently.* In God's kingdom we are not to "go it alone," choosing our own methods and plans to achieve our own desired results. We cannot do kingdom work apart from God. First of all, God has made us laborers in the kingdom by calling us out of darkness into His marvelous light. He has called us into the vineyard of the kingdom. Furthermore, our abilities and opportunities come from God. None of us should take credit for his abilities, and it is God who guides us to our specific place of influence and labor. Furthermore, in doing kingdom work we are using the seed of the Word, and this also comes from God. We are doing the work which is God's. Let us ever bear in mind that God supplies us with whatever we need to work for Him. And let us be diligent in asking God in prayer for these gifts. Every Christian is qualified as a worker in God's kingdom for some phase of work.

6. *Man's work will be rewarded.* Two verses after our text Paul says: "Every man shall receive his own reward according to his own labor" (1 Cor. 3:8). God does not forget the work His children have done or are doing for Him in His kingdom. He will reward graciously. The reward is not according to the success, which God promises, but is based on the faithful application and use of our abilities and of our opportunities in life. While success usually follows faithful labor, the Lord places the emphasis on the faithfulness with which His children apply themselves in the cause of the Lord. The parable of the laborers in the vineyard (Matt. 20: 1-16) points up the fact that there is a reward and that the reward is one of grace, which means it is undeserved and that it is given freely out of love by the Lord. These gracious rewards may come here in time, sometimes apparent — sometimes not, and will surely be given on the Day of Judgment. While we know that these rewards are undeserved, we should nevertheless let them be an incentive to be faithful laborers in the Lord's kingdom.

God's Work in the Kingdom

Without God all work for the Lord is of no avail. It is He who blesses the efforts of His children. "But God gave the increase," says Paul. In the verse following our text Paul says: "So then neither is he that planteth anything, neither he that watereth; but God that giveth the increase." That means: As to the success, neither the planter nor the one who waters is significant, but only God. As far as success is concerned, man is insignificant.

1. *God's work is all-important.* All blessings come from God. There is no other way to arrive at them. This holds true in agri-

culture. Of what value would be the planting of the seed and the watering of the soil, if God would not permit the seed to germinate and grow? So in the kingdom of the Lord it is God who blesses. "Except the Lord build the house, they labor in vain that build it. Except the Lord keep the city, the watchman waketh but in vain" (Ps. 127:1). So God urges us to pray: "Thy kingdom come." Recognizing the all-importance of God in kingdom work should inspire us to a willingness and a readiness to use our abilities and opportunities. It should incite us to greater faithfulness in doing kingdom work.

2. *God's work is marvelous.* There is a great mystery involved in the development and growth of the seed which is placed into the ground. Too often we take things for granted and expect things to happen because we are accustomed to them. If only we were more aware of the many mysteries which are involved in God's creation, we would be more grateful for the blessings of God and would walk more humbly on this earth. As God empowers the seed to germinate in the ground and to sprout forth, so by His miraculous power He convicts man and persuades the human heart to repent of sin and to trust in His plan of salvation in Christ Jesus. By means of the Law the Lord shows man how sinful he is, how insufficient, yea filthy, is his vaunted righteousness, and how desperately he is in need of a Savior. By means of the great revelation of Christ and His redemptive work in behalf of sinful man God assures man of a complete atonement with God, wiping clean the slate inscribed with the sin and evil of his life. God in Christ assures us of forgiveness, of His sustaining grace and love, and of the hope of heaven. Truly, "if any man be in Christ, he is a new creature" (2 Cor. 5:17). It is a miracle of God when a sinner is turned from his wicked self-righteous way to become a child of God and to trust in the redemptive work of Christ for strength in his life and hope in his death. Yes, "we are *God's* workmanship, created in Christ Jesus unto good works" (Eph. 2:10). "Turn *Thou* me, and I shall be turned; for Thou art the Lord, my God." (Jer. 31:18)

To Whom Does the Glory Belong?

In view of the relative importance of man's work and God's work in the Lord's kingdom, to whom does the glory belong? The unequivocal answer is: TO GOD ALONE.

1. *God is our Creator.* "Of Him and through Him and to Him are all things; to whom be glory forever" (Rom. 11:36). Our faculties, abilities, resources, and materials to live the Christian life and to labor for the Lord are from God. So the glory belongs to Him.

2. *God is our Redeemer.* God has removed the mountain of sin which separated us from Him through the redemptive work of Christ. Christ in the fullness of time humbled Himself, assumed the human nature, and lived under the Law to redeem them that were under the Law, that we might become the sons of God. "That God in all things may be glorified through Jesus Christ" (1 Peter 4:11). "Ye are not your own; ye are bought with a price; therefore glorify God in your body and in your spirit, which are God's" (1 Cor. 6:19, 20). God deserves to be glorified because He has redeemed us for heaven and eternal life.

What Does It Mean to Glorify God?

To glorify God means to live according to God's purpose in life, that we reverence His will, that we recommend His service, that we utter His praise. God's purpose of life should be evident in our life, showing itself by a true spirit of gratitude to Him and by a life of obedience to His will. We are to be "the light of the world and the salt of the earth." If God is to be glorified in our life, it must be according to the divine intent. "This is the will of God, even your sanctification" (1 Thess. 4:3); this means that God wants us to live according to His will, which is outlined for us in the Ten Commandments. To live the Christian life is God's will regarding us, and it should please us also to live according to God's will.

The principle of glorifying God applies to all areas of our life. It applies to everyday living. It extends to all things, even to the most ordinary and trivial. Paul says in 1 Cor. 10:31: "Whether therefore ye eat or drink, or whatsoever ye do, do all to the glory of God." No interest of life is so wide, no relationship to people or things is so sacred, no occupation is so exclusive, as not to come under this principle. Glorifying God gives dignity to all functions of human life. It is a rule for every part of life. It applies to small things as well as to the great. It saves anything from becoming insignificant by giving it the supreme significance, namely, to do all things to the glory of God.

That kind of life fulfills the purpose for our being on earth. It is beneficial to us because it delivers us from miserable and debasing self-seeking. To live for God is to rise above the murky atmosphere of earth into the serenest air of heaven. This kind of life is also a personally satisfying life, because it is in accord with the will of God, and we never need to be ashamed of that kind of life. It is joy-bringing too, because of the joy of expectation of God's gracious reward here in time and hereafter in eternity.

Conclusion

As we once again are reminded of our high calling in Christ
Jesus, being laborers together with God, let these words of the
apostle Paul urge us to greater efforts and to more diligent and
faithful use of our abilities in the interest of God's kingdom:
"Therefore, my beloved brethren, be ye steadfast, unmovable, always abounding in the work of the Lord, forasmuch as ye know
that your labor is not in vain in the Lord." (1 Cor. 15:58)

Our Stewardship Relation to God

By ARNOLD F. MEYER

(Stewardship)

For we are His workmanship, created in Christ Jesus unto good
works, which God hath before ordained that we should walk in them.
Ephesians 2:10

For many years we have thought of the teaching in our elementary schools in terms of the "three R's": reading, 'riting, and
'rithmetic. This is as it should be. These primary skills are basic
and essential for living in this modern world. How difficult it
would be to get along without them! How hard it would be to
make our way in this world without being able to read, without
the ability to write, or without the fundamental knowledge of
addition, subtraction, division, and multiplication.

Quite recently, however, some emphasis has been given to
another skill, the skill of living. A prominent educator, superintendent of the public school system in one of our larger cities,
called attention to it in a newspaper article in which he spoke
of the social relationship, the skill of living with one another. This
he called the "fourth R."

We, too, believe in the importance of the "fourth R." However, the scope should go even farther. There is, to be sure, a
horizontal relationship which we do well to ponder, understand,
and cultivate. But there is also a vertical relationship on the part
of believing people between themselves and God. This is the
R of our relationship to God, which must precede the right relationship to one another.

A little girl walked out of the school door one day, but
immediately came back and said: "Teacher, I've lost my steeple."
She then proceeded to explain that she could not see the steeple
that gave her a sense of direction to find her way home. The
teacher told her that she had walked out of the wrong door.
She took her to the other door. The little girl saw her steeple and

walked home rejoicing. Many people have lost their steeple, children as well as adults. They have lost their sense of direction because they fail to comprehend fully their relationship to God.

This relationship has many phases, the relationship of children to their heavenly Father, the relationship of sinners who have been "redeemed, restored, and forgiven" toward Him who redeemed and restored them, and many others. On the basis of the text before us we consider:

Our Stewardship Relationship to God

I

What Is This Relationship?

The verse which we read to you from Paul's Letter to the Ephesians contains a beautiful statement of the relationship between the Christian and God. It says: "We are created in Christ Jesus." Of course, this is picture language, but the picture is very clear. All of us are acquainted with the Biblical narrative about the first creation. God said: "Let Us make man in Our image, after Our likeness" (Gen. 1:26). "And the Lord God formed man of the dust of the ground and breathed into his nostrils the breath of life; and man became a living soul" (Gen. 2:7). It is a very familiar story, which you have read repeatedly. You will find further details of it in the first two chapters of the Bible.

Alas, something terrible happened to that first creation. God had created man in His own image. He had equipped him with perfect knowledge of God and endowed him with righteousness and holiness. That which God had created, the devil proceeded to wreck. And sad to say, the creation of man was ruined. And this ruination had its lasting effect on the children of Adam and Eve and all their descendants. This is the meaning behind the words of St. Paul to the Romans: "By one man sin entered into the world and death by sin; and so death passed upon all men for that all have sinned." (Rom. 5:12)

What a tragedy! The divine image was gone. Man was indeed sold under sin and subject to eternal damnation. But God in His great mercy would not let go. He sent His own Son to become the Rescuer, the Redeemer, the Savior. This is the beautiful story of love and sacrifice on the part of God who gave His Son into death for the reconciliation of the world. In order to accomplish this, the Son of God had to become the Son of Man. First man had been like God, now God came in the likeness of man so that man might once more become a child of God.

This is usually referred to as the great plan of redemption. To continue the picture language, Paul speaks of it as a second creation, a creation in Christ Jesus. When Jesus died on the cross, He completed this second creation.

Many years ago a large number of railroad workers were employed in the building of a road of rails across the American continent. They finally met at a small place in the territory of Utah called Promontory. There they drove a golden spike into the last rail to signify that the iron road across the whole country was now an accomplished fact. The cross of Jesus Christ is much more than this golden spike. Christ and His redemption is the complete way back to God and heaven. When Jesus on the cross triumphantly cried: "It is finished!" He had forever restored the way by which the wayward heart of man may return to the ever-living and ever-loving heart of God.

By His suffering and death Christ brought forth this new creation. It is different from the old creation in one important point. While it was prepared and is intended for all mankind, it actually becomes an active creation only in the lives of those who accept Jesus Christ as their personal Savior.

This new creation finds its fulfillment in the Christian church, concerning which we sing in one of our favorite hymns:

> The church's one foundation
> Is Jesus Christ, her Lord;
> She is His new creation
> By water and the Word.

Our personal creation in Christ Jesus began for most of us on the day when we were baptized. On that day we were received into the holy Christian church, the communion of saints. We were graciously created anew as St. Paul wrote to Titus: "Not by works of righteousness which we have done, but according to His mercy He saved us by the washing of regeneration and renewing of the Holy Ghost, which He shed on us abundantly through Jesus Christ, our Savior" (Titus 3:5, 6). At that time we were baptized into Christ. We put on Christ. We became new creatures. "Therefore if any man be in Christ, he is a new creature. Old things are passed away; behold, all things are become new." (2 Cor. 5:17)

It is because of the new creation in Christ Jesus, usually referred to as the redemption, that St. Paul could write so confidently to the Ephesians in the verses immediately preceding our text: "By grace are ye saved, through faith; and that not of yourselves: it is the gift of God; not of works, lest any man should boast." (Eph. 2:8, 9)

This, then, is the new relationship which Christians enjoy, having been redeemed by grace through faith. They are creatures of redemption, children of God, "God's workmanship," as our text calls it.

II
What Is the Purpose of This Relationship?

The word which is translated in our King James Version as "workmanship" is the same as the Greek word from which we have such English words as "poem" and "poetry." Hence we can say that we are God's creation, His poetry, His composition. God is the Creator, we are His creation; He is the Poet, we are His poetry; He is the Composer, we are His composition.

We all know that great masterworks are not composed to be stored away in a vault. The intention is that they be performed and played on various musical instruments, by bands and orchestras. Choral compositions are to be living works sung by voices and choirs. Poems, likewise, are not written to be buried in libraries and to gather dust on bookshelves. They are to be read, used, and enjoyed. In the same spirit, we as God's poetry are not merely intended to *be* something, but to *do* something. We are "created unto good works."

When God created our first parents, He had a definite purpose in mind. He created them for partnership and fellowship with Himself. The basic element of this fellowship was sharing. He shared His knowledge, His love, His ability so that He might share the work and responsibility with man. He put him in charge with such directives as "have dominion," "replenish the earth," "subdue it." He placed Adam and Eve in the Garden of Eden "to dress it and keep it." Man was to be God's partner, God's steward.

Even after the fall into sin this purpose of God was not disrupted. It took on new meaning for those who accepted the promise of the Savior who was to come and believed in Him. This is very evident when we consider the partnership which God established with Noah in the building of the ark. The Book of Genesis tells of the wonderful partnership which God had with Abraham. On many occasions God talked with Abraham, even taking him into His confidence in discussing His concern and His plans about the destruction of Sodom and Gomorrah. He called many people in the Old Testament to Himself in a blessed partnership.

Then finally there came the fulfillment of the promise. A Savior was born. He lived and died and rose again. Concerning Him St. Paul writes: "In whom we have redemption through His blood, even the forgiveness of sins." (Col. 1:14)

Like the first creation, this redemption had in it the purpose of fellowship and partnership with God. This is unmistakable. Read closely the Biblical record of the 40 days after Easter, and you will see clearly what Jesus had in mind for all of those to whom He said: "Follow Me." Here are some of the great com-

missions which Jesus gave His followers: "All power is given unto
Me in heaven and in earth. Go ye therefore and teach all nations,
baptizing them in the name of the Father and of the Son and of
the Holy Ghost, teaching them to observe all things whatsoever
I have commanded you; and, lo, I am with you alway, even unto
the end of the world." (Matt. 28:18-20)

"Go ye into all the world, and preach the Gospel to every
creature." (Mark 16:15)

"Thus it is written, and thus it behooved Christ to suffer, and
to rise from the dead the third day, and that repentance and remission of sins should be preached in His name among all nations,
beginning at Jerusalem. And ye are witnesses of these things."
(Luke 24:46-48)

"Then the same day at evening, being the first day of the
week, when the doors were shut where the disciples were assembled for fear of the Jews, came Jesus and stood in the midst
and saith unto them, Peace be unto you. And when He had so
said, He showed unto them His hands and His side. . . . Then
said Jesus to them again, Peace be unto you; as My Father hath
sent Me, even so send I you." (John 20:19-21)

"But ye shall receive power, after that the Holy Ghost is
come upon you; and ye shall be witnesses unto Me both in Jerusalem and in all Judea and in Samaria, and unto the uttermost
part of the earth." (Acts 1:8)

All of these sayings and commands of Jesus as well as numerous others put the responsibility of partnership and stewardship
squarely on the shoulders of all those who have been created in
Christ Jesus. If you claim to be one of His new creatures, and as
a Christian you surely do, then you are His workmanship, one of
His poems. You are not ready to be placed purposelessly on the
shelf, but you are ready to do and to dare, yes, even to die if need
be, for you were "created in Christ Jesus unto good works."

III

How Does This Relationship Affect Our Work and Our Life?

Every person who has been made a new creature in Christ
Jesus will want to spend his life in the service of his new Creator.
This is called Christian sanctification. We also speak of it as the
total stewardship life. It is the life of dedication to follow daily,
diligently, and consistently in the footsteps of Him who said:
"I must work the works of Him that sent Me while it is day. The
night cometh when no man can work." (John 9:4)

The text before us speaks of such works in this way, "created
unto good works, which God has before ordained (prepared) that

we should walk in them." Which are these good works which God has prepared for us to do? You do not have to look very long in the Scriptures to see the many opportunities for service which God makes available to those who love Him.

On the first day of Pentecost there were many people gathered together in a certain upper room. Then Peter opened his mouth and began to speak, confessing his Savior. Today God also has prepared opportunities for us to speak of our faith to others. We, too, should open our mouth and begin to speak, thus performing the good work of personal witnessing. Throughout the world there are still millions upon millions who do not have the right relationship to God because they do not know Jesus, "the Lamb of God, which taketh away the sin of the world." We are to see to it that they hear. These and many other opportunities for good works abound all around us.

God has not only placed us in the midst of opportunities, He has also generously and purposefully endowed us with the physical, mental, spiritual, and material resources that are required for such works. In His wonderful first creation "He has made me and all creatures. He has given me my body and soul, eyes, ears, and all my members, my reason and all my senses," as we confess with Luther in the words of the explanation of the First Article of the Apostles' Creed.

This creation God accomplished with a purpose in mind: "unto good works." He has preserved us alive unto this very day and hour with a purpose in mind: "unto good works." He endowed us with clothing and shoes, meat and drink, house and home, fields, cattle, and all our goods with a purpose in mind: "unto good works." He redeemed us, lost and condemned creatures, with His holy, precious blood and His innocent suffering and death with a purpose in mind: "that I might be His own and live under Him in His kingdom and serve Him," as Luther explains it with such clarity in the Second Article of the Apostles' Creed. Finally, the Holy Ghost called us by the Gospel, enlightened us with His gifts, sanctified and kept us in the true faith with a purpose in mind: "unto good works."

Of all the good works that a Christian can and should do in his blessed relationship to God and his partnership with Christ, there is none that is quite so far-reaching as the work of bringing people to the cross of Christ and bringing the Christ of the cross to people. This is the greatest good work that we can do for anyone, namely, to lead the wayward, lost, and condemned sinners to the foot of the cross and to invite them in the name of Jesus to lift up eyes of faith to that cross. There are far too many people who are satisfied that they themselves are able by the grace of

God to *lean* on that cross, but they fail to see that they are to *lift up* that cross for others to see and to believe. They forget that they were created in Christ Jesus especially also for this particular good work.

In closing, let us make this stewardship relationship that we have to God even more meaningful and personal by inserting the personal pronoun into the text and reciting it in the first person: "I am His workmanship, created in Christ Jesus unto good works, which God has before ordained that I should walk in them."

God grant that you and I and many others like us, who have experienced this wondrous grace and power by being created in Christ Jesus, may daily recognize this extraordinary relationship which is ours through faith in Christ. May our daily prayer be that this bond of fellowship in Christ and partnership with Him may ever become stronger and firmer as we pray:

> Savior, I long to walk
> Closer with Thee;
> Led by Thy guiding hand,
> Ever to be
> Constantly near Thy side,
> Quickened and purified,
> Living for Him who died
> Freely for me.

Education for Eternity

By SAMUEL J. ROTH

(School Sermon)

Grow in grace and in the knowledge of our Lord and Savior Jesus Christ. To Him be glory both now and forever. Amen. — *2 Peter 3:18*

Have you heard the little nursery rhyme lately:

> Mary, Mary, quite contrary,
> How does your garden grow?

Mary's answer was phrased for the ears of children. But any gardener here today knows that she should have answered: "By loving care and consistent weeding."

Suppose we phrase a question of our own:

> Parent, parent, quite concerned,
> How do your children grow?

Children will grow naturally, as long as we give them three meals a day. They will also grow in knowledge and in attitudes and in characteristics of behavior. But if we want them to grow the *right* way, it takes loving, watchful care and constant attention and guidance.

Any parent who is worth his salt wants his child well trained for this life. We want our children equipped with the knowledge that they need to earn a living. We want them to be able to read so that they can enjoy the treasures of literature that our civilization has produced. We want them to have a knowledge of history so they appreciate their heritage. We want them to understand the sciences so they know what is going on around them. We want them to learn to put thoughts down on paper so they can communicate with others.

We want them to be *growing* in these skills. We know that such growth doesn't just happen by itself; children have to be taught and directed and guided. We establish schools for this purpose, and we employ teachers.

We also do a good portion of the training ourselves; we know that children learn in our homes. As parents we keep a check on them in their schoolwork too; we work with them sometimes, we inquire about their homework, we keep in touch with the teachers and inquire about their progress.

But as *Christian* parents we are concerned about more than growth just in these skills of making a living and being alert citizens. We ask ourselves:

> Parents, parents, quite concerned,
> How do your children grow . . . in faith?

How do your children grow in understanding God's Word? How do your children grow in Christian character? How do your children grow *in grace and in the knowledge of their Lord and Savior Jesus Christ?*

And once again the answer comes, "By loving, watchful care and constant attention and guidance."

This kind of growth demands no less attention than growth in the ability to read and write and figure. As a matter of fact, it is our *first* concern. "What is a man profited if he shall gain the whole world and lose his own soul?"

This kind of growth means daily instruction in God's Word. It means consistent, steady influence from Christian teachers. It means patient guidance to lead the children to see things as God sees them. It means careful discipline which is exercised in love.

Education for Eternity

Another way of putting it is this: we want our children to have an "education for eternity." We want them to be prepared not only for this life but also for the life to come. We want them not to set their sights on the treasures of this earth, but to know that their real treasure lies with God. We want them to see themselves as God's creatures born to live eternally, and we want to train them to live for that God who has made them and redeemed them!

Educating for eternity means not simply saying, "Look ahead to heaven," although that is certainly an important part of their education; but it means also saying, "This is what the God of eternity has given you on earth; let us serve Him with our whole heart."

That kind of education is not a one- or two-hour-a-week job to be done by the church and the Sunday school. That is a 24-hour-a-day task to be done by us as parents together with the church. And it is to that end that we have established a Christian day school, where we can provide education not only for time but also for eternity.

Is It Important?

None of us, I am sure, has to be convinced of the importance of Christian education, or "education for eternity." We know that we live in a world in which material values are often prized entirely out of proportion to their true worth. The frightening thing is that we find ourselves adopting this same set of values, even though we know it is all wrong.

Some time ago a television columnist wrote in regard to the ratings by which the popularity of television shows are measured: "No one believes in them. They are unscientific, unsound, unreliable. Nobody believes in them; but everybody uses them!"

That, it strikes me, is the way it is with us very often when it comes to the standards of this world. No one here today would say that money is the measure of success of a man. Not one of us would say that the size of a man's salary check, the model of his car (or boat), the cut of his clothes, and the price of the furnishings in his home are the standards by which we should measure success or happiness. Not one of us believes in these things — and yet, to a greater or lesser degree, every one of us operates with these standards and lives by them.

"The world" has a way of squirming and squeezing into our Christian lives. It has a very willing ally in our own flesh; and these two forces, slyly but ably aided by Satan, strive to crowd our religion into a neat little compartment which is well insulated from our life as we live it day by day. They are content to have us pull our religion out of its compartment occasionally, perhaps once a week, or when we find some drastic need for it. But, slowly and patiently, they nourish the idea that it has no real relation to the honest-to-goodness realities of living, the real live facts of science that we learn by investigation, the hard-nosed business of making a living in a world of men and money and machines.

Our Religion Is Relevant

But this propaganda of the world is a lie. We know, and our children must know, that our relationship to God is the most important factor in all of our living. The most important happening in all of history is this, that God sent Jesus Christ to make us one with Him again, though our sins have separated us! The most important literature in all the world is the Holy Bible, where God gives us a record of His mighty deeds in Christ, and where He tells us furthermore how we might live to serve Him and glorify Him.

Our life is divinely planned. God still rules the world today, just as He has guided the events of the world in all past centuries. We cannot teach our children about the world without teaching about Him! We dare not teach them how to live without taking His will into account! It is wrong to give them a goal and purpose in life without giving them at the same time a knowledge of their final goal in heaven!

To educate a child only for time is like handing over a high-powered automobile to a youngster after only a very elementary instruction in how to make it run. We teach him how to start the car, how to shift gears (if that is necessary), how to "step on the gas." But we do not tell him the rules of the road, the importance of safety, the tremendous responsibility which a driver has — nor do we give him a road map or any directions as to where to go and why. He may get along all right for a few blocks, but eventually he will become lost (at best) or will crash (at worst).

We must do far more with our children, too, than teach them how to make a living and "get along" in life. We must give them direction, purpose, spiritual understanding. The "why" and "where" must be taught *along with* the "how."

The Need for Thoroughness

While it is easy to see the importance of the Christian element in our education, what sometimes escapes us is the need for *thoroughness* in Christian training. Somehow we often feel that Christian education does not take too much effort. It is a simple matter. It can be handled in a few hours per week. But never was any idea farther from the truth!

It is certainly true that a man can become a Christian after hearing the Gospel just once and believing that Jesus Christ is his Savior. And if a child learns about Jesus from its parents or others, that child can certainly be a child of God.

But the apostle says here, "*Grow* in grace and in the knowledge of our Lord and Savior, Jesus Christ." Applying God's Word and will to our daily lives so that we live more and more in a way

that pleases Him — this is an increasingly difficult task in a world
like ours. There are so many, many influences upon our children that tend to draw them away from thoughts of God. Holy
Scripture is a great treasure-store, and even in a lifetime of study
we glean only fragments of the wealth to be gained there.

No wonder God has told parents, "These things which I command thee this day shall be in thine heart, and thou shalt teach
them diligently unto thy children." No wonder Jesus said, "Teach
them to observe *all* things whatsoever I have commanded you."
No wonder St. Paul wrote with such evident gratitude that Timothy had "from a child . . . known the Holy Scriptures, which are
able to make thee wise unto salvation through faith which is in
Christ Jesus." For "all Scripture is given by inspiration of God
and is profitable for doctrine (teaching), for reproof, for cor-
rection, for instruction (training) in righteousness, that the man of
God may be perfect (complete, mature), thoroughly furnished unto
all good works."

Home, Church, and School

These words of God emphasize the need for careful home
training, first of all. We know how much the example of parents,
the home influence, means in regard to giving our children the
proper aim in life, the proper attitudes and behavior patterns.
Nothing can take the place of the home in this process.

God's words also emphasize the need for regular Sunday
school and church attendance, where the children will hear Bible
stories and get the indispensable experiences of worship.

But what about the school experiences of our children? Every
child spends about one thousand hours each year in school —
hours, as we know, in which the children are developing mentally and socially.

In reading, science, health, history, they accumulate information. Is God regarded as central as they accumulate this information, or is He excluded? Our children develop attitudes
toward people, toward things, toward institutions, in the school.
Are they being led to look at people and things from God's viewpoint? Are they applying God's standards, or is He necessarily left
out? In the school our children are developing patterns of
behavior, as they are influenced by teachers, friends and play-
mates, and the heroes the children choose to imitate. Are those
influences geared to the will of God?

To put it simply, we believe that Jesus needs to be present in
our schools just as He needs to be present in our homes, if we are
to give our children the best and most thorough Christian education! And for those formative years we cannot provide anything
less than the best!

That is why we value the Lutheran elementary school so highly. It makes possible the most *thorough* Christian education, and the most *consistent*. Children learn that religion is a part of their everyday lives, not something that deserves just an hour or two of consideration each week. It's not like the poppy seeds on a loaf of bread which stick on the outside and fall off when you handle it, but it's like the yeast which permeates the bread and makes something happen inside.

What About Public Schools?

We Lutherans believe wholeheartedly in the public school system. It is a bulwark of democracy in our country, and absolutely necessary thing if we are to have intelligent citizens who can govern themselves. Our public schools are served by many well-qualified teachers who are sincere and dedicated to the cause of helping children acquire a good education. Many of the teachers, moreover, are sincere and dedicated Christians.

But our laws must provide for the separation of church and state, and therefore Christ cannot be brought into the classroom. Public schools cannot offer a Christian education. That would be contrary to our laws.

Recently a school in our land was threatened with a denial of the use of tax funds because the officials of the school insisted on using the historic McGuffey's reader, a textbook widely used in the earlier days of our country's school system. The reader may not be used, said the Government, not only because its teaching methods are outdated, but because it contains religious teachings. Years ago people felt that it was a good idea when teaching reading to use material which was religious in nature, in order to help the children in a twofold way. This can no longer be done in tax-supported schools; the Government was quite right in its case.

Worship is forbidden in public schools, and religious instruction is not in place there. But these are the very things we want for our children! We believe each day should begin with devotion, and the first period should be dedicated to a study of God's Word and way. We believe the Bible should govern and pervade all the instructions and textbooks of other subjects as well.

For this reason we maintain our own school and support the public school system as well, as American citizens. Is it worth it? With all our hearts we answer, "Yes!" It is worth every cent that we as parents and we as a congregation invest, for it is enabling our children to grow in grace and in the knowledge of their Lord and Savior Jesus Christ. He is our priceless Treasure. How much better to do without a few material things — for instance, to have fewer clothes, fewer home furnishings — and to be rich in Him!

In this connection it is well to note that church schools in America antedate the public school systems by over two hundred years. The first public school was organized in Massachusetts as recently as 1839. Before that year all education of the elementary, secondary, collegiate, and postgraduate levels was in the hands of the church.

Gradually, and in many cases by necessity, the state has taken over the task of education. But the need for Christian education has never diminished. We are thankful that the forefathers of our Synod provided immediately for church-sponsored schools and also established the training institutions necessary for providing teachers for those schools. That, in so many cases, was at least one reason why other church schools went by the board: the lack of church-related teacher-training institutions.

We operate our schools, then, not in opposition to the public school system, but in cooperation with it.

One Couple's Viewpoint

One Christian father and mother have written down some of their thoughts on why they send their children to a Lutheran elementary school. Let me read a portion of their letter.

"Most parents want to give their children every opportunity to become happy, well-adjusted, successful adults. My wife and I surely feel that way about our five youngsters. But we feel even more strongly about another point: we want our children above all else to be sincere and faithful Christians.

"We know that this is an age of insecurity, fear, and hysteria — of hot and cold wars and a race for supremacy on earth and in outer space. And we also know that the real way to happiness and mental stability does not lie in tranquilizing pills or any type of mental hypnosis. Rather it lies in a firm-rooted knowledge of the Word of God and His plan for our salvation and in a flourishing faith in Jesus Christ as our loving Redeemer and Friend.

"This is the kind of knowledge and faith we want our children to have too. In other words, we want to educate and prepare our children for this life, and yet we also want to be certain they are prepared for life eternal.

"Our Lutheran congregation, by the grace of God, helped us solve this problem by giving the best possible education to our children. It has done so through the elementary school which it operates. My wife and I send our youngsters to the Lutheran elementary school.

"I have the God-given responsibility to bring up my children as Christians. Therefore I want to teach my children all I can about God and His Word. I want to help them build Christian character and lead Christian lives. I know that Christian habits started early and practiced frequently will aid and influence my children throughout their lives.

"That's why I appreciate the opportunity of having them in a Christian elementary school. Here I can be sure that Christ will not be forgotten for those 25 hours each week and those 36 weeks each year. I am grateful that in our school religion is made an integral part of the educational program and that the Christian attitude permeates every aspect of each subject.

"Each year I realize more and more how our Lutheran school aids me in carrying out my own responsibility. It supports and extends the training my wife and I give our children, and it is a powerful adjunct to what they learn every week in Sunday school and church. It means a lot to me to know that the office of teacher, which the children learn to respect and often idolize, is filled by sincere, dedicated Christians.

"Because I have experienced in my own family the benefits of a Christian home and school working together, I now support my congregation more enthusiastically than ever before in its endeavor to further its school. I thank God for the help I am receiving in bringing up my children 'in the nurture and admonition of the Lord.' "

These are the words of Christian parents. Their Christian school is a blessing to them; it is a blessing to their children. It is a blessing to the congregation, for it trains solid, well-grounded leaders for the church. It is a blessing to the nation, for it trains Christian citizens, who know that "blessed is the nation whose God is the Lord."

Parents, parents, quite concerned,
How do your children grow?

May God enable us, through our Christian homes, through our Christian school, to say, "They grow in grace and in the knowledge of their Lord and Savior Jesus Christ."

Abide with Us

By A. Karl Boehmke

(Wedding Address)

They drew nigh unto the village whither they went, and He made as though He would have gone further. But they constrained Him, saying, Abide with us; for it is toward evening, and the day is far spent. And He went in to tarry with them. — *Luke 24:28f*

Ronald and Joan, this is a supremely happy time for you. For months you have been getting ready for this day. In a certain sense you have been preparing for it all your lives. Now your wedding day is here in all its glory.

Your many friends have come to share the joy of the occasion with you. Your families are here, hearts bursting with happiness and pride. There is another Guest among us, more important than any other — it is the Lord Jesus. He has come to bid you the blessing of Heaven and to bestow on you the promise of His unfailing mercy. Ask Him to stay with you as you begin your new home. Make this your constant prayer and motto across the years:

Abide with Us, Lord Jesus!

I

Your Home with Christ Will Be Bound in Love

Blessing at Emmaus

It was in the glow of just such a golden afternoon as this. Two disciples were making their way to their home in the suburbs of Jerusalem. With them walked a divine companion whom they did not recognize. Yet their hearts burned with a new fire of hope as He spoke to them of God's plan fulfilled for His Son and for them. At the door of their home they paused, while the traveler announced He must go on. Then it was that they pleaded (anxious that their newfound hope and understanding might continue), "Abide with us, for it is toward evening, and the day is far spent." And blessing of blessings, "He went in to tarry with them."

Blessing at Your Home

Today it will be your joy to found a new home. Husband and wife, you will be joined together to search out the treasures that life holds in store. Soon you will make your way to your own little house in the suburbs. At the threshold you will pause, then step across into the world of wedded life of which you have dreamed and for which you have planned.

In that moment the Lord Jesus will stand with you. So much will depend on your awareness of His presence. So much will depend on your invitation of faith and hope, as you turn to Him to plead, "Abide with us." So much good beyond your fondest expectations lies in store if only you will fervently pray that He may stay with you.

Danger in Selfishness

Learning to live together in a new home is a glorious adventure. Day by day two lives once lived apart are drawn close to each other in a thousand ways. Two souls are merged to live each for the other. In the flushed beauty of the wedding hour this would seem to be the simplest undertaking in the world. Yet the cooler light of human experience reminds us otherwise. We have witnessed the tragedy of some who have anticipated happiness in marriage and found bitterness and heartache instead.

Satan conspires against every home. Our human heart would not have us put the other person first; it tells us to live to our own interest. We are much in need of the Helper and Savior. In your home (as others in their homes) you will need the Lord Jesus to help you deal with selfishness. You will need Him if you are to be filled with the love of God and true devotion to each other.

Christ Brings Newness of Life

How important, then, that you pray, "Abide with us, Lord Jesus! Come and bless us with Thy renewing grace." How important that you live under the daily remembrance of His cross and with the strength of His resurrection! He will help you walk in newness of life. He will help you build a home dedicated to the purposes of God. Strengthen first your allegiance to Him, and you will find yourselves drawn together in a companionship ever richer, deeper, and more precious.

II
Your Home with Christ Will Meet Life's Challenges
His Strength in Adversity

I am sure that today you must wonder what the many years ahead hold in store. You will walk together and share whatever life shall bring. Some days, no doubt, there will be blue skies — with the sun shining as brightly as at this moment. Other days, I suppose, will bring grayer skies and gathering clouds. Trouble, sickness, accident, may break as a storm over you. Where is the home forever exempt from these? Out of the tempest of adversity the Lord calls men and women fit for His kingdom. In times of trouble some homes grow weak and crumble. Not so the home where Christ is a constant Guest! How important that you pray, whatever the cast of your sky: "Abide with us, Lord Jesus. Help us conquer adversity and fear. Stand by us in every hour of need." Then He will assure you of His mercy, saying, "I will never leave thee nor forsake thee." "Lo, I am with you always." "My grace is sufficient for thee." Adversity shared in faith within the Christian home will not harm you, but bring a blessing more precious than the human heart can imagine.

His Steadfastness in Success

You will walk together and share whatever life shall bring. Across the years, we may well suppose, there will come days of success — times when the good fortunes of life will smile sweetly on your labors. How will your home fare then? Here, too, some families falter and fail. Overpowered by worldly prosperity, they lose their first love and stability. Only homes built on foundations of the Spirit can stand up to the temptations of success. So you will need to pray again: "Abide with us, Lord Jesus. Help us seek first the things of Thy kingdom. Help us be thankful people and follow humble ways." Then He will speak good counsel to your family endeavors: "Take My yoke upon you, and learn of Me, for I am meek and lowly in heart." "The works that I do shall ye do also." With Him you will find the true success in life and the peace that passes human understanding.

I know that during the days of your courtship you have delighted to work together in the church. You have found each other mutually attractive in your labors for Christ. Therein lies promise of even greater love. Continue in His work, whatever other demands may be made upon you. "Abide with us with Thy good Spirit, Lord Christ. Guide us, inspire us, to use our family in the building of Thy church in earth and heaven."

III

Your Home in Christ will Reflect the Hope of Heaven

For it is to the ultimate glory of heaven that you also look today. From the altar of God's house and the threshold of your first home you can look clear across with eyes of faith to the home of perfect fellowship and service with your Lord. Nothing that you may hope or strive for in this world will ever count apart from the hope of God's eternal presence. You will want your home here always to be a forecast of heaven. You will want your words and actions to reveal the hope that is in you as people meant to live with God. It is our hope and prayer that such may always be the glory of your marriage.

Husband and wife we shall call you now — bound in time by the love of Him who is God's perfect revelation of love — and bound to all eternity by the promise of His unfailing mercy.

> Abide, O dearest Jesus, among us with Thy love;
> Grant steadfastness, and help us to reach
> our home above.

Love One Another in Christ

By A. KARL BOEHMKE

(Wedding Address)

A new commandment I give to you, that you love one another; even as I have loved you, that you also love one another. By this all men will know that you are My disciples, if you have love for one another. — John 13:34f. RSV

Albert and Mary, this is a time of unforgettable joy and excitement. I have seen your beautiful gifts — the remembrances of this day — the linens, the glassware, the silver. These are objects which will grow more precious to you as time goes by. Across the years they will bring back in memory the events of this your wedding day.

There is still one gift to come. It is more precious than all the others. It has been your possession already; still it comes to you new on this day when you begin your married life. The Lord Jesus Himself brings you this gift from the treasure house of Heaven's grace. It is the gift of His commandment — a special, gracious commandment that will be to you both promise and guide for the future. "A new commandment I give to you," He says, "that you love one another; even as I have loved you, that you also love one another. By this all men will know that you are My disciples, if you have love for one another." To this we all add our own prayerful wish for your great happiness, saying,

Love One Another in Christ!

I

Jesus Comes with Cleansing, Redeeming Love

Love of Man and Maid

Every home has need of love. With that, I am sure all will agree. What is more thrilling and ennobling than the love of a man for a maid, and of a maid for a man? Here is an emotion deep and powerful as the sea. Love will make a man leave his father and mother, from whom he has sprung, and cleave to his wife. It will make him climb the highest mountain, run the swiftest race that he may woo her and win her, claim her and keep her. It will make him labor early and late to build a home, rear his children, and provide for their wants. Love will impel a maiden to give herself, her beauty, her tenderness, to the one she calls her own. It will make her toil, plan, and tend her family in sickness and health, in prosperity and adversity. Such is the glory and strength which love brings to humankind.

Christ's Redeeming Love

But when our Lord says, "Love one another," He has something in mind beyond this affection. He is speaking of love more wonderful still — a love which fulfills and redeems that emotion which we have just described. He points to a love that makes up where the other falls short, a love that fulfills when the other fails. He speaks of the love that goes deep into the springs of the spirit. It is the love that comes from the heart of God, enters into the life of man through the revelation of His Son, and remains to bless by the power of His Holy Spirit. *"I have loved you,"* says our Lord, in this fuller, deeper, redeeming sense.

"I have loved you at Bethlehem when I came among the family of men to share your plight of sin. I have loved you in the streets of Galilee, as I laid My hands on the sick, spoke hope to the hearts of the poor, proclaimed the promise of salvation to the lost. I have loved you at Calvary, as I battled the powers of Satan to free your hearts again from their bondage. Always I have sought not My own good but yours. I have pleased not Myself but you, to whom the Father sent Me."

This is redeeming love. This is His strong and cleansing love. "Christ loved the church and gave Himself up for her that He might sanctify her, having cleansed her by the washing of water with the Word" (Eph. 5:25 RSV). This is God's wonderful gift to you. None other is so precious. This is the promise of redemption He brings you as you begin your new home.

II

He Bids You Love as He Has Loved You

His Command of Love

Now with such a promise He also gives His commandment. "Love one another," He says. This will be your response to My gift. Show the same devotion in your family that I have shown for you. I will make it possible by My Word and Spirit for you to do this.

Forgiveness

"I have forgiven you — you must learn to forgive one another. When in the day-to-day duties you trespass one against the other in word or deed, My Spirit will bring you the will to forgive from humble and sincere hearts. This is My way for your home. Some families may find themselves powerless to forgive, but so long as My gift of redemption is with you, you will remember and be able to forgive.

Sacrifice

"I have sacrificed for you — you must learn to sacrifice for one another. Your human heart will make demands for itself, but I will teach you to seek the good of the other from sincere and generous hearts. This is My way for you. Others may not find it in themselves to sacrifice, but My gift of redemption will make you able. Thus your home will have my cleansing, purifying Spirit at work to bless you in every undertaking.

A Larger Service

"Nor will your love stop at the walls of your house. You will learn to reach out in My name also to other families who are in need — in your community, in your church, across the whole world. You will come to realize more keenly the dire plight of God's children, the multitudes of hungry, homeless, brokenhearted, and wretched persons. Through your home I will reach out to help these, too. My love will be seen in your love. This is the larger reason that you are joined togther, that you may be My workers in a needy world, serving those in want for My sake. This is My new commandment. Because you belong to Me, your home has the highest of goals. I am expecting much of you. The more you realize the extent of My gift to you, the more you will open your hearts to show My love to all men."

III
He Will Win Others Through Your Love

Such thoughts of grace and guidance the Lord brings to you today. There is also a final promise: *"By this all men will know that you are My disciples,* if you have love for one another." When people observe that Christ is at work in your home, they will be led to consider and to seek Him, too. This is among the greatest of blessings, for it will add the element of hope to all that you do.

Do you remember the old song "People Will Say We're in Love"? This is true — especially in the deeper sense of love that we have been talking of. People will see it; they will sense it. Through your home you will be saying something about Christ to them, convincing them of their need for His love. The light of Christian faith and service that you kindle in your window will become a beacon of hope to others. "Let your light so shine before men that they may see your good works and give glory to your Father who is in heaven" (Matt. 5:16 RSV). "By this all men will know that you are My disciples, if you have love for one another."

All this is the gift that the Lord Jesus brings to you today. In a moment you will come to His altar to speak your vows of faithfulness. May deep joy fill your hearts, and may the peace of the Savior be with you now and always.

The Lord Is with You

By ROBERT L. DOROW

(Funeral)

Sermon for the funeral in an unexpected death of a young husband and father

The Lord is with thee — *Judges 6:12*

"Boast not thyself of tomorrow, for thou knowest not what a day may bring forth." The truth of these words from the Book of Proverbs faces us squarely and painfully this afternoon. What happened Sunday morning in the home of this family has been a reminder to everyone of us here this afternoon what a difference a day can make. As each one of us heard the news, we may all have said within ourselves, "I just can't believe it. I just saw him the other day or the other week. He was so young." It is hard for us to believe, and yet all of us have had to accept the truth of it. This afternoon I am going to ask you to accept another truth, a truth that in the light of what has happened is hard for us even as Christians to believe about God in a situation like this, namely, that He is truly with us in this tragedy and already has the plan and the answers how He will lead this family through this period of great distress and provide a way for them not only to find comfort, but also to find help in the many-sided perplexity which is theirs particularly. The message from God's Word to us today is

The Lord Is with You

I

We Find It Difficult to Believe This Truth of God's Presence in Tragedy

"The Lord is with you." These words were spoken to a man many years ago who had great difficulty believing it, because it didn't look that way to him. The man's name was Gideon. In the chapter from which this text is taken we are told that the angel of the Lord, a term used in the Old Testament for the Son of God, visited this man while he was busy threshing grain in a secret place to keep it from a tribe of marauding bedouins, called the Midianites, who had overrun the land and plundered it. For a period of seven years Gideon and his countrymen had to live like refugees in their own land, struggling desperately to stay alive. These Midianites had descended upon the land like a plague and all but snuffed out any hope that the people had of ever recovering the land which they had taken possession of through the instrumentality of God. Before the scourge things had looked very promising in this so-called land of promise. There were in the pages of their history mighty evidences of God's presence which went all the way back to the time of their release from bondage in Egypt to their rapid establishment in the new land. However, in the light of what had now taken place, it seemed that God had withdrawn His hand from their affairs and that He was leaving them to be ground again to dust from which they had been taken. When Gideon heard the greeting, "The Lord is with you," from this person whom he did not know, it sounded almost like mockery to him. This was a common greeting with meaning in the past, but this greeting seemed to be very much out of place now because there was nothing outwardly to support it, the people felt. Gideon's reply to this greeting was this, "If the Lord is with us, why then has this evil befallen us?"

Humanly speaking, the words, "The Lord is with you" could seem to be out of place and like Gideon we could find it difficult to believe this truth. We are perhaps more apt to say with him, "If the Lord is with us, why then has this evil befallen us?" Before Sunday morning these words certainly had meaning to this family, we would agree, but how about now? In the life of this family there were rich evidences of God's presence. In almost ten years of married life, God had richly blessed this family. God had given them four children, concrete evidence of His goodness. With thanksgiving they had received these blessings, and under God were working together for a home that served the Lord. Just this year a second child was enrolled in the Christian day school. The family was growing up, and the father was happily adjusted at his new place of work after about nine years as a police officer in which no evil befell him, in an occupation where men are exposed to dangers that the average citizen does not face. Yes, even as recently as last Saturday this family could speak confidently how the Lord was with them. Mr. N. was back to work and feeling fine. He had come home from the hospital where he had been told that although he had a heart condition, to all appearances it was something that perhaps in one case out of a thousand caused death at this stage. What a happy report and reassurance that the Lord was with them. Then came Sunday, and he was gone. What about this truth now?

II

God Reveals His Presence to Us in Christ

In the case of Gideon, the Lord made it very plain to him that the statement was not a hollow greeting, but the truth, in spite of all outward appearances. He revealed His presence to Gideon in a most miraculous manner. Gideon asked for a sign, and he received one. According to the report of our text, Gideon asked this stranger, whom he had met, to remain until he could return with a present for him. Gideon perhaps still supposed this stranger to be a mere traveler to whom he would accord the hospitality of a present to send him on his way. When he brought the present the stranger commanded him to place the dish on a rock. The stranger stretched forth the staff that was in his hand, and the entire present was consumed by fire. The angel of the Lord departed and Gideon knew then that the Lord had indeed been with him. From that time forward, moreover, the Lord revealed His plan unto Gideon to save the people of Israel from their plight and how He was going to use Gideon to be His instrument in this rescue. Unbeknown to Gideon and the others in the land during the depths of their distress, during the depths of their uncertainty about God and the future, God had already planned what He would do. When it appeared that God was not busy in their behalf and only punishing them for their sins, it was nevertheless true that He was busy. In time this plan of God was unfolded and His hand was seen again. What seemed like a hopeless situation at the moment turned out to be one in which God demonstrated His love, power, and endless mercy.

Friends, what the Word here tells us concerning Gideon and the people of Israel is also intended for our learning, especially in this hour of distress. In spite of all appearances to the contrary, the truth remains that the Lord is with us in this tragedy. We too would believe this, but in our weakness we too would see a sign. In a most miraculous manner God has revealed His presence to us in the revelation of His Son Jesus Christ. The manger, the cross, and the open tomb are evidence that God is with us always because Christ our Emmanuel has been with us. Christ, indeed, took on human flesh, kept God's Law perfectly for us, and died our death on the cross. In His resurrection Christ has displayed His victory over death itself and brought life and immortality to light. There is only one whom God utterly forsook and that is Christ *for us*. In Christ nothing can separate us from the love of God. It is to Christ and His work for us that God asks us to turn again today and to see in it the unshakable truth of His presence and His love for us in our greatest distress as sinners and thus to remember that what has happened will never contradict what has happened in Christ Jesus. By the grace of God your husband and loved one knew and believed these truths concerning God's love in Christ. In the endless mercy of God Mr. N. is in the presence of God, and in His presence there is fullness of joy and at His right hand there are pleasures forevermore. He is with the Lord, and the Lord is with you. Even as Gideon was to believe this truth so God would have you to believe it. Here lies comfort in this distress, and nothing must shake and nothing will shake you if you continue to allow God to reveal Himself to you in Christ.

What is more, that which is unknown to us in this distress concerning the future of this family without husband and father is known to God. In the same unsearchable wisdom with which He planned to take your loved one from you at this time, He already knows far better than we what this means for this family. Time will reveal His plan even as the fullness of time has revealed His great plan for our salvation. Even as our thoughts concerning His presence in this sorrow can go awry, so also our thoughts concerning His power can go awry where we fail to trust Him. Like a mountain when a person stands at the face of it and tries to look up and sees only mountain, so also your great sorrow appears to you today. But even as a person sees the mountain in its true perspective as he looks at it from a distance, so also with the passing of time God will show you even this sorrow in its true perspective through His grace as the time passes. As the psalmist says, "The Lord never slumbers or sleeps." May God give to you, the wife and mother, that picture of Himself in your loneliness so that you will remember that He is watching over you and is ever busy also in your interest and that of your young family.

In closing, let me say to all of you who sympathize with this family that your expression of love and kindness can continue to show itself. The widows and fatherless are to be objects of our consideration. May God lead you to His throne in their behalf and lead you to them in acts of love. Isn't God also looking to us to be His instruments in this distress? The Lord is with us. May we ever be found with the Lord here in time and hereafter in eternity through our Lord Jesus Christ.

When God Calls

By ROBERT L. DOROW

(Funeral for an Aged Christian)

Get thee out of thy country, and from thy kindred, and from thy father's house, unto a land that I will show thee. — *Genesis 12:1*

When a child of God dies, we use the expression "The Lord called for him or her." This is a very apt way of putting it, because the death of the child of God is a call from Almighty God. As we are about to lay to rest the body of our departed sister in Christ, who was called somewhat unexpectedly, it is to the Word of God that we turn for comfort and direction. What happens when God calls is what we learn anew today. On the basis of this text we would show you that His call is a purposeful one, that is intended as a blessing for those who obey His voice. May the Holy Spirit testify to the same to your inner self even now as we consider together the theme:

When God Calls

I

God Calls His Own to Inherit a Blessing

God calls. This is in itself a solid indication of His nearness to His creatures even though fallen. God calls. This is a solid indication of His concern for man as man. God calls. Here is a solid indication that God desires to speak with man. In the words of our text we have the contents of God's call to Abraham, the Old Testament patriarch, which explains that Abraham was to inherit the promised land of Canaan in keeping with God's plan for His people. Abraham, as the Biblical narrative explains, lived in the land of Mesopotamia. At the age of seventy-five, God stepped into that life, and His intervention was a gracious intervention. Abraham was to come into possession of an inheritance which God Himself would provide. There was divine purpose to this call. It was intended to bring a blessing. God made that truth visually evident by pointing him to the stars. It was going to involve a change, a disruption of his present life, to bring it to fruition. It was going to mean leaving the place of his birth, his friends and relatives. Things had been going along from day to day, year in and year out, in their accustomed manner, but now God stepped in and changed all that. Who of us, however, would say that this transfer with God's thinking behind it was not a wonderful move? Surely, it was a wonderful blessing of God to Abraham. When God led him to Canaan, when Abraham arrived, he could behold with his own eyes what he went to inherit on promise. But how about his friends and relatives, those who stayed behind? Not only would they miss him, but unless they were made to see and believed God's promise of the inheritance, their hearts would have remained sorrowful.

It is important for you, the immediate family and relatives together with us her friends, to understand and believe God's promise of an eternal inheritance if we are to be comforted at the departure of a loved one. God called your departed mother and wife. It was a call of grace. At the age of seventy-six God stepped into her life, and His call was a gracious intervention. There was divine purpose to that call. It was intended to bring a blessing. Mrs. N. was called to inherit, to come into possession of, the eternal inheritance. God promised this to her a long time ago when she came to faith in her Lord and Savior Jesus Christ, whose suffering and death procured it and whose resurrection proclaimed it. It was hers by faith during her lifetime. It is hers now by sight. Her eyes may now behold what she went to inherit on promise. As recently as the day that she left to possess it, God held out this promise to her again visibly in the Sacrament of the Lord's Supper which she received only a short time before she departed. It was perhaps the last meal which she had below, the meal of forgiveness.

It meant a change, a transfer from this land to the heavenly Canaan, in order to receive the possession. It meant leaving behind relatives and friends. The accustomed manner of life was changed, but who of us would say that this transfer with God's wisdom ordaining and executing it was not a wonderful move? God blessed the departed sister in Christ in her earthly life with a family, 50 years of wedded life, and a number of personal joys. However, who could have wished her a greater blessing than the eternal inheritance of heaven through our Lord Jesus Christ, who earned this crown which no man deserves because of sin? Think of the land which she went to possess! It is God's abode!

II
Let Us Obey His Call

When God called Abraham to inherit the land, Abraham obeyed this call in faith. It was his faith in the promise of God that led him to the acquisition of the inheritance. Abraham did not question the promises of God. God had spoken, and He followed. Of himself, he would never have gone and he would never have possessed, either. He could have thought of a number of reasons why not to go. He could have doubted whether or not it was a blessing, because as yet he could not see the land. It was, however, through these selfsame promises that God worked that kind of faith in him that made all doubt cease and make all misgivings seem wrong. Abraham's faith is mentioned in the New Testament also as an example of what it means to believe God's promises. How the greatness of God actually stands out here! God not only gave him great and glorious promises and led him to them, but He also gave him the faith so that these promises were not in vain. From beginning to end it was the work of God and to Him belongs all the glory. Purely out of God's grace the call came to him, and the possession.

When God called Mrs. N. to inherit the eternal blessing already as a child, she believed those promises as they unfold for us in the person of Jesus Christ. With the same affirmative nod with which she indicated her desire for the Lord's Supper the other day as a pledge and seal of the forgiveness of sins, so also with the same affirmative nod of faith she accepted the merits of Christ for her salvation in her lifetime. The promise of eternal life and an eternal inheritance, which does not fade away, rests firmly but solely on the work of Jesus Christ on Calvary. It was her faith in Him and in Him alone that enables us to speak positively about her death, and with all the comfort which this fact brings. God not only gave her great and glorious promises, He also gave her the faith to make those promises her very own. She could have doubted them as some do. Like many she could have passed up what God had to offer in Christ, but by the grace of God she did not. They were dear to her in life and in death. She clung to them in hope. How the greatness of God stands out here as well. God was at work in her life, and to Him also today we give glory and thanks for what He has done, and our love to Him grows more fervent and intense. He did not fail her in life or in death.

Yes, God calls. Let us also obey His voice. His call comes to you in His Word and He calls to you particularly in your sorrow. His call is one of concern. He desires to speak with you. He wants to assure you by His message of the Gospel of His unfailing love to you as well. He wants to remove all doubt of His love by showing you the love which moved Him to give His dearest, His Son, into death. I can recall the doctor speaking to you in the hallway of the hospital about your mother and wife and asking you to trust his judgment in the matter, and I can remember hearing you say, "Well, you know best about these things." Your divine Physician speaks to you also today and explains that He has made His decision with divine judgment and asks you to trust His divine action. May He also hear you say in true faith and humble obedience to His wisdom, "Lord, you know best about all things." With that kind of faith in Him you too will gain strength to keep His promises before you as a source of abiding comfort and hope. May this moment of grief only help to make the importance of God and His power stand out to you in your weakened condition.

To all of us will one day come the call of God; may God grant to all of us the obedience of faith in His Son Jesus Christ always, so that we too may inherit the promised land of heaven as our possession. "You can save your words, because nothing you say will bring back my daughter," a grief-stricken man said to his pastor and headed for the door. "How do you know that she would want to come back?" the pastor replied. The consideration of these words turned the tide in that man's sorrow. As you consider the facts about the heavenly home, you will rejoice that your wife and mother is with her Lord Jesus Christ and with faith's anticipation look forward to reunion under greater joys than you experienced together here below. May God's protective arm shield you in your loneliness, and may the cross of your Lord Jesus Christ send you solace and peace with its story of deliverance from all which would separate us from Him in time and eternity. Thus may we ever understand what happens when God calls.

Special Series

THE WORD IS THE LAMB

A FOUR-SERMON ADVENT SERIES

By Enno Klammer

I

The Word Was God

(The First Sunday in Advent)

In the beginning was the Word, and the Word was with God, and the Word was God. The same was in the beginning with God. All things were made by Him, and without Him was not anything made that was made. In Him was life, and the life was the light of men. And the light shineth in darkness, and the darkness comprehended it not. — *John 1:1-5*

Men are generally willing to accept the fact that Jesus was a human being. The Jews acknowledged the fact that a man by the name of Jesus really lived. The Mohammedans list Jesus as one of their great prophets. History records that such a man lived. Liberal theologians today recognize Jesus at least as a great man. Most men today will generally admit that Jesus was a good man, indeed, that He was the best of men. But one thing that men are not so willing to admit and accept is this, that Jesus is actually God. The only place that tells us conclusively that that is so, is God's holy Word. John opens his entire Gospel account with a ringing declaration that Jesus was and is God. On the basis of John's inspired words, we too see that

The Word Was God

John begins his narration with these words: "In the beginning was the Word, and the Word was with God, and the Word was God." He uses a term to identify Jesus which is quite foreign to us at first. He says that Jesus is the Word. At first glance this strange term doesn't mean much to us, but when we study further, we see what John means by it. "Word" is used in human language to identify certain parts of speech. We have such words as nouns, pronouns, adjectives, adverbs, verbs, and the like. A word is simply the visible or audible symbol for a thing. It is the way we write things down to preserve them. It is more permanent than the spoken language. When we talk, the sound of our voices soon dies away. But when we write things down in words, then our ideas are recorded for future generations and are more or less permanent. Our words can be reconstructed again. Our words can be made into sounds again. A word, then, is a permanent expression of an idea.

When we apply this to spiritual things, we recall that God had an idea. His idea was that man should not die everlastingly. Instead, man should be saved from his sin. To record that idea and to make that idea permanent so that men can grasp that idea, God used His Word. The Word, then, is the expression of God's love. Our study of the Bible tells us that only Jesus is the real expression of God's love to sinful man. Therefore Jesus is that Word. This Word, says John, was in the beginning. It existed from eternity. It was not created. It was always there. And that is exactly what God tells us in other parts of Scripture. Even before He had laid the foundations of the heavens and the earth, God had provided the means whereby man could be saved from the sin that God knew he would commit. Even before the earth was created, the Word existed, and therefore Jesus existed. Since only God existed before the creation of the world, therefore Jesus is God.

John becomes more specific in speaking of Jesus as God. He tells us that all things were made by Him, that is, by this Word, and without Him was not anything made that was made. When we look to the opening verses of the Bible, we see in Gen. 1:1: "In the beginning God created the heaven and the earth." We put Gen. 1:1 and John 1:1 together, and we come to the only possible conclusion, namely, that Jesus is God and that Jesus was active in the creation of the heavens and the earth. This same idea is revealed to us in other parts of Scripture also. In Heb. 1:10 we read in reference to Jesus, the High Priest: "And Thou, Lord, in the beginning hast laid the foundation of the earth, and the heavens are the works of Thine hands." The same thought is expressed by the apostle Paul in two of his letters, in Col. 1:16 and in Rom. 11:36. Without a doubt, Jesus was instrumental in the creation of this temporal universe. This points us to the doctrine of the Trinity. On the basis of the Bible we know that there is one God, but that there are three Persons in the Trinity. In our imperfect human thought and reasoning powers we generally ascribe to the Father the creation and preservation of the world, to the Son the redemption of the world, and to the Holy Ghost the sanctification of the world. But we cannot divide God. Each Person of the Trinity was active in all events of the world, even though we separate these activities so that our weak human reason can understand them to some extent.

This leads us to the second part of our contention that Jesus is God. Not only was Christ active in the creation of the world, but He was active as the Redeemer of the world and is active today as the Sanctifier of the world. John tells us in our text, "In Him was life, and the life was the light of men." Again we stumble over a word in this text. What is meant by "life"? The simple word "life" means that a being has vitality, that a being is animate. Applying this idea to Jesus Christ, and judging from what John says in a later part of his Gospel account, in John 5:26, we see that Jesus Christ is a being who has life in Himself. Hear what John says in the fifth chapter: "For as the Father hath life in Himself, so hath He given to the Son to have life in Himself." Jesus therefore is a Being in His own right, though He is God. He is the Second Person of the Godhead. But the word "life" has a higher meaning even than this. Again God tells us through the apostle John what is meant by this word. In his First Epistle, John tells us: "And this is the record, that God hath given to us eternal life, and this life is in His Son" (1 John 5:11). Jesus, as the Second Person of the Trinity, is the means whereby we can come to the life that is of real value. He did this by giving up His own life for us so that we do not now have to give up our lives. "He died for all that they which live should not henceforth live unto themselves but unto Him which died for them and rose again." (2 Cor. 5:15)

John continues this account of Jesus' divinity by stating that that life was the light of men. Why do we use a light? Why do we take a lantern or a flashlight into the night? We do it so that we might see. We take a light so that we might not lose our way or stumble or bump into objects in the darkness. And so Jesus is the Light of men. He comes so that men might see. He comes so that men might understand. He comes so that men might not lose the way. He comes to show men how they might be saved. He Himself says, "I am the Light of the world; he that followeth Me shall not walk in darkness, but shall have the light of life." (John 8:12)

John's record of the life of Christ is a realistic one. He admits what has happened. He tells us that Jesus, the Light of the world and the Light of men, shone into the darkness. Jesus came into a world which was dark with sin. He came into a world where men are disobedient and willful. He came into a world which wanted nothing to do with Him but which needed Him so desperately. He came to those who were sick with sin, as He Himself says, "They that are whole have no need of the physician. I came not to call the righteous but sinners to repentance" (Mark 2:17). This is the wonderful story of the Gospel, that Jesus came into the world which needed Him most.

But we mourn with Jesus over the unbelief of men as He Himself mourned over the city of Jerusalem. "The darkness comprehended it not" (v. 5). When Jesus was talking to Nicodemus late at night, He told him what the trouble was in the world. He said, "This is the condemnation, that light is come into the world, and men loved darkness rather than light, because their deeds were evil" (John 3:19). In Paul's First Letter to the Corinthians we read and learn why this is so. Paul explains it this way: "The natural man receiveth not the things of the Spirit of God, for they are foolishness unto him; neither can he know them, because they are spiritually discerned" (1 Cor. 2:14). Man simply does not want God's way of salvation, because God's way gives glory to God and not to man, and man is full of pride and wants to take credit for his own abilities. What a tragedy! The darkness did not appropriate the Light of life unto itself.

This plain and brutal statement which John makes about the world should prompt us to reconsider our own acceptance of Christ. It should lead us into a sincere appreciation for all that God has done for us. It should cause us to flee again into the loving arms of God. It should drive away every thought of our own abilities. It should cleanse our hearts by leading us into the grace of God. We should therefore receive Jesus Christ, the God who was made man, as our Creator, Redeemer, and Sanctifier. Having received Him, we should then also honor, praise, and obey Him. Consider again what John has to say about Jesus as Creator. "All things were made by Him, and without Him was not anything made that was made." He made you and me also. He is your Creator and my Creator. As the preexistent Word of God He has created me and all things and still preserves me. For that reason it is my duty to thank and praise, to serve and obey Him, as Luther points out in the explanation to our creed.

A greater reason for such thanks and praise is also given in our text. When John says, "In Him was life, and the life was the light of men," he recalls to us the astounding fact that Jesus Christ is our Redeemer. He could be our Redeemer only because He is God, and because this God became man. The incarnation of the Son of God is tremendously important for us. Only through this incarnation — "God becoming man" — could there have been a perfect man who could keep the Law of God perfectly in our stead. Only through the incarnation could there be a man who could die for the sins of other people instead of for his own sins. Only through the incarnation could there be a man who could be raised from the dead again as a sure guarantee that God had accepted the sacrifice made by that man. Only because that man who died and rose again was God — or, let us reverse the statement — only because God became man, could there be a Redeemer. Joy beyond compare! He has redeemed you!

By creating life in you, He enables you to live the real life both here in time and hereafter in eternity. What is your life if you try to live it without Christ? Psalm 90 tells us. If God wills it, your life is threescore years and ten. You might live to be 70, but even if you do, says the psalm, "yet is their strength labor and sorrow." Labor and sorrow! That's all you get out of life unless you live with Jesus in your heart. But those who accept that life which God has prepared for them in Jesus Christ receive eternal life with Christ. They also live with Christ here on earth. No, He never says that you won't have troubles, but when you live with Christ, you share your burdens with Him, and Christ takes your burdens upon Himself.

When burdens are shared, the load becomes lighter for each party. When two men carry a 100-pound sack of grain, each man carries only 50 pounds. When two people share their sorrows, each one assumes half the burden of sorrow. When you and Jesus join in an undertaking, Jesus takes more than half. He takes all the burden. The contrary is true of joys. When one man is happy by himself, there is only his own happiness. When he shares his happiness with another man, he keeps all his own happiness, and the second man gets as much as the first. When you share your joys, they increase. That is how we respond to the love of God in Christ. We share our sorrows and our joys with our fellowman. That is all that Jesus ever asks us to do while we are here on earth. That is the only commandment that He has really given us, that we love one another.

In retrospect we see that Jesus is really and truly God, for He is the Word who created the world, He is the Savior who has brought light and life to men, even though they reject Him. We accept Him for what He is, because God has revealed this to us in the Gospel according to St. John. We can praise Him with the hymn writer:

O Word of God incarnate,
O Wisdom from on high,
O Truth unchanged, unchanging,
O Light of our dark sky,
We praise Thee for the radiance
That from the hallowed page,
A lantern to our footsteps,
Shines on from age to age.

II

The Word Was Made Flesh

(The Second Sunday in Advent)

There was a man sent from God whose name was John. The same came for a witness, to bear witness of the Light, that all men through Him might believe. He was not that Light, but was sent to bear witness of that Light. That was the true Light, which lighteth every man that cometh into the world. He was in the world, and the world was made by Him, and the world knew Him not. He came into His own, and His own received Him not. But as many as received Him, to them gave He power to become the sons of God, even to them that believe on His name; which were born, not of blood, nor of the will of the flesh, nor of the will of man, but of God. And the Word was made flesh and dwelt among us (and we beheld His glory, the glory as of the Only-begotten of the Father), full of grace and truth. — *John 1:6-14*

The early Christian church was persecuted at times for what seems to us to be an odd reason. It was accused of eating and drinking human flesh, for those who spied on the Christians reported that they had heard them say, "Take, eat; this is My body; drink ye all of it, this is My blood." To us such an outrageous claim sounds odd indeed. But there is an idea prevalent in the world today that the Christian church preaches a theology of blood. The claim is made that the Christian church is in reality a pagan society, for it teaches that God demanded the sacrifice of a human being to satisfy His anger and wrath. It is our purpose to study this charge and to see what God Himself says about the necessity for the death of a man. On the basis of this second part of the first chapter of John's Gospel account, we learn of the necessity for the incarnation of the Son of God and study the theme

The Word Was Made Flesh

Is there any truth to the charge that God is not living up to His promises when He demands the death penalty? Is there any truth to the idea that God must be a kind and benevolent grand-fatherly type of being who forgives and forgets the little misdemeanors of His children? Well, what kind of God would He be if He did not demand justice? What difference would it make if He did not threaten to punish? We must remember that it was not God who brought sin and death into the world, but it was man himself. God had made man perfect and good. Man was the one who disobeyed. Paul tells us, "By man came death" (1 Cor. 15:21). Paul also tells us: "As by one man sin entered into the world, and death by sin, and so death passed upon all men, for that all have sinned" (Rom. 5:12). Again, we read that "the wages of sin is death" (Rom. 6:23). God tells us: "The soul that sinneth, it shall die" (Ezek. 18:4). You see, God tells us quite plainly and clearly that death is the natural and inevitable result of sin, even as He had told Adam and Eve when He gave them that one commandment: to abstain from eating of the tree of the knowledge of good and evil.

God's first law states that any man who sins must pay for his sin. That law holds true even in human courts. But should that sinning soul be forced to pay that debt, then there is no longer any hope for that soul, for it is eternally dead. God's justice would be satisfied, but God's love demanded that something more be done for man. When Paul had said, "Since by man came death," he continued his statement by adding, "by man came also the resurrection of the dead. For as in Adam all die, even so in Christ shall all be made alive" (1 Cor. 15:21, 22). This is God's plan of salvation. Whereas in the Old Testament the priests had to make a special sacrifice for their own sins before they could make a sacrifice for the sins of the people, God sent a new priest into the world who did not have to make a sacrifice for His own sins first. God sent a man into the world who had no sin, so that whatever sacrifice He made would be counted for the sins of other people. The only kind of man who could do that would be God Himself who became man. Only God is sinless, and yet God had to become man so that He could die a human death. That is the reason for the incarnation. That is the reason for the birth of Christ as a human being. And that is the reason we still celebrate Christmas to this day. God became man.

The fact that God became man is revealed to us in the narrations of the Gospel writers, even though many in the world reject that God-man and reject the account which the apostles have written for us. But that same Jesus Christ who is the Redeemer of the world is in truth a man, just as you and I are human beings. All we have to do is read the account as it has been preserved for us. We read in Matthew and Luke that Jesus was born. Even His ancestors are enumerated for us so that there can be no doubt. The story of His birth of Mary, and of Mary and Joseph as His earthly parents, is well known even to the smallest of schoolchildren. We read that Jesus grew up like an ordinary human being. We read that Jesus needed food and drink. He wore clothing like anyone else. He walked. He talked. He prayed. He slept. He suffered. He died. There can be no doubt that this Jesus was in fact a true man. There can be no doubt that the Word became flesh.

John had begun his Gospel account by stating that the Word was God; he repeats that idea in verse 10 of the text. "He was in the world, and the world was made by Him, and the world knew Him not." Strange, isn't it, that the creature does not recognize his Creator? Strange, isn't it, that though the world was made by Him, yet the world knew Him not? The world did not wish to accept Him and acknowledge Him for what He really was. The world did not want to submit to His authority, nor did the world want to accept the love which He displayed for it when He laid down His life on the cross.

But surely, we say, the Jewish people should have accepted

Him. He was born into their midst. He was of the house of David.
He was born in their city of Bethlehem. He was the One who had
been prophesied long before. Certainly His own should have
received Him. But what does John record for us? John tells us
in a sad voice, "He came unto His own, and His own received
Him not" (John 1:11). Not even the Jews, who had the advantage
of being the chosen nation; not even the Jews, who had the advantage of 2,000 years of Scripture to teach them; not even the Jews,
to whom the promise had been given, accepted Him for what He
really was, the Light of the world and the Savior of mankind.

There were a few. There were a few, says John. In the very
last verse of the text John shows us the hope that still exists. He
says, "WE beheld His glory." Thank God for that. Thank God that
there was someone who believed, for had there been none, there
might not now be any record of His coming. "We beheld His glory,
the glory as of the Only-begotten of the Father," says John. That
glory is revealed to us by the fact that Jesus Christ is also the
Creator of the world, as mentioned in the sermon last week. That
glory is His by virtue of the fact that Jesus Christ Himself is
God, to whom alone belong honor and glory. His glory is the
glory as of the Only-begotten of the Father.

That glory is His because He illumines, He lights up, the
whole world. John dwells on this point at some length (vv. 7, 9).
He speaks of the Light, through whom all men might be saved.
He tells of the fact that He was the true Light, the genuine article,
which lighteth every man that cometh into the world. Jesus Christ
is not some false prophet. He is not a false God. He is not a false
aspirant for divine honor and glory. John tells us that He is the
genuine thing. He is not an imitation, but He Himself is the very
Light of the world.

His glory is full of grace and truth, John goes on to say. What
do we mean by grace? Grace is something that is not earned.
It is free. Grace is that which God has done, not man. Grace is
a gift, not of works. Grace is the act of God whereby He has made
it possible for man to be saved — something which man himself
could not do. The word which is translated "grace" is similar in
meaning to the "love of God." That's what His glory consists of.
His glory is the undeserved love of God brought down to men.

Let us emphasize the words of John again. We beheld His
glory. John is speaking of those who actually saw Jesus in person. He is speaking of those who not only saw the Lord Jesus
physically but also accepted Him for what He really is, the Light
of the world that illumines every man who enters into the world.
John is here speaking of himself and the other apostles. We apostles, he says, observed His glory and believed that this One was

in truth the Son of the living God. It was not their merit that they had the privilege of seeing Jesus and knowing Him as their Savior. John puts that thought out of the way very quickly. He says that this knowledge came not by a blood relationship, nor by human birth or choice, but by a new birth. This new life was born in them by the will of God (v. 13). This new life came into existence in every person who received Him. "To them gave He power to become the sons of God" (v. 12). This is accepted by the individual through faith, for John tells us plainly that He gave such power "to them that believe on His name." (V. 12)

Do you want to see the glory of Jesus, the glory as of the Only-begotten of the Father, full of grace and truth? Surely you do! It's easy too. You have been chosen of God to hear the message of the Gospel. It is preached to you regularly. It is available to you in various forms. You can read the Gospel. You can hear the Gospel. You can see the Gospel in the sacraments. To you comes the statement, "The Light was in the world." To you John says, "That was the true Light, which lighteth every man that cometh into the world." All you have to do is accept this word of truth, which God presents to you. All you have to do is believe that Jesus Christ, true God, has become true man for the forgiveness of your sins. Then there comes to you the assurance which John voices in this portion of our text, "As many as received Him, to them gave He power to become the sons of God, even to them that believed on His name." Accept the Lord Jesus Christ now, while you may. Take Him into your hearts and minds and souls. Let Him fill up that heart which by nature is filled with sin. Let Him bring comfort, hope, and strength, where before there was but weakness, anxiety, and fear.

Do Christians teach a blood theology? Perhaps in the eyes of the world we do. But we preach nothing more than what God Himself has commanded us to preach. We believe nothing but what God Himself in His holy Word has asked us to believe. We preach only that God chose to send His only Son into the world in the form and nature of a human being so that He could take upon His own shoulders the burden of sin with which each one of us was loaded down. We preach only that Jesus satisfied the justice of God by dying for all mankind. We preach only that those who believe and accept this pure and simple Gospel statement are made the sons of God. If that is a blood theology, then let it be a blood theology. We are glad for what God has done for us. The Word was made flesh, and we beheld His glory, the **glory as of the Only-**begotten of the Father, full of grace and truth.

III

He Hath Declared Him

(The Third Sunday in Advent)

John bare witness of Him and cried, saying, This was He of whom
I spake, He that cometh after me is preferred before me; for He was
before me. And of His fullness have all we received, and grace for grace.
For the Law was given by Moses, but grace and truth came by Jesus
Christ. No man hath seen God at any time; the only-begotten Son,
which is in the bosom of the Father, He hath declared Him.
John 1:15-18

In our previous Advent worship services we have seen from
the study of the first chapter of John's Gospel account that Jesus
was true God. We have also seen that Jesus was true man. In the
text before us now we see the practical application of these truths.
Why was it necessary for Him to be both true God and true man?
What does this mean for us? We see that only by being both
divine and human could Jesus reveal the true fullness of God's
nature to men. Therefore we study this text under the heading

He Hath Declared Him

It doesn't take a genius to know that there is a God. Only
the fool denies that God exists. Every normal person with reasonable intelligence has to admit, whether he wants to or not, that
there is some kind of God who has planned the universe and has
set it in operation. We call this the natural knowledge of God.
But no man can by nature know the true character and nature
of God, simply because no man has ever seen God (v. 18). You
immediately reply that Moses saw God, but the Bible tells us
otherwise. God told Moses that he could not look upon the face
of God and live, for that is not allowed to sinful and mortal man
(Ex. 33:20). Paul writes the same thing. He says, "Whom no
man hath seen nor can see" (1 Tim. 6:16). Our own text tells us
in v. 18 that "no man hath seen God at any time." Isn't it pre-
sumptuous then for men to claim that they can reveal something
that they haven't seen? Isn't it a mockery of our intelligence
when people assert that they can reveal God to us by their own
resources? God denies this claim in His Bible.

Not even Moses, who had stood in the presence of God, could
reveal the fullness of God to men. It is true, he did stand in God's
presence, but as Exodus 33 tells us, he was not allowed to see God.
The second reason Moses is unable to reveal God to us is told us
in our text. John writes, "For the Law was given through Moses."
The Law was given, and the Law is only half of God's nature.
God's justice was revealed in particular when He gave the Ten

Commandments on two tables of stone to Moses on Mount Sinai. The entire fifth chapter of Romans treats this difference between Moses and the Law on the one hand and Jesus and God's grace on the other hand. I don't mean to say that the Old Testament Hebrews were saved by the Law. Not by any means. They, too, were saved by faith in the covenant of grace. The covenant had been established by God in the days of Abraham many years before. However, this is true, that God delivered the Law to Moses primarily, and the Law brings with it the knowledge and conviction of sin.

One would expect that surely John, of all men, could reveal the true nature of God to men, for he himself was the immediate forerunner of Jesus, the Savior. But what does John the Baptist say of himself? He himself admits that he *"knew Him not"* (v. 33). He himself says that the identity of Jesus had to be revealed to him. He himself describes how it was only the fact that the Holy Spirit descended upon Jesus in the form of a dove that revealed to John who this man Jesus was. John was incapable of revealing the fullness of God to men, because he himself stood in need of revelation. Therefore by relying on our own devices and by relying on the wisdom of men alone we would have been sorely disappointed. Men cannot know the fullness of God's nature. That has to be revealed to us.

Only Jesus can reveal the Father to us. We can pick out a number of reasons for this. The first reason is that which the evangelist John gives us in this chapter. Jesus is and was eternal and was from eternity. John the Baptist freely and forthrightly explains this to the people who went to hear him. He says, "This was He of whom I spake, He that cometh after me is preferred before me, for He was before me." We know that John was conceived and born about six months before Jesus was conceived and born, so that John cannot be talking about the sequence of natural events. When John the Baptist talks about Jesus as being "before" him, he is then referring to the same thing that the evangelist tells us in the very first verse of this chapter, "In the beginning was the Word." This Word was already in existence at the beginning of time. In other words, this Jesus was from eternity. He Himself had no beginning. He was God, even as John tells us in those same opening verses: "And the Word was with God, and the Word was God."

Another reason why Jesus can reveal God to us is this: Jesus is well acquainted with God. Jesus knows the Father intimately, because He Himself is God. And Jesus is the *only* one who can reveal God to men, because our text tells us that Jesus is the Only-begotten of the Father. There is no other one who has that same knowledge that Jesus has. And how do we know that He is so intimately acquainted with the true nature of God? Our text tells us that too. We read, "The only-begotten Son, which is in the bosom of the Father, He hath declared Him." The Bible says, "Who *is* in the bosom of the Father." Jesus did not lose His knowledge of God when He became man, for He at the same time remained true God. He is at the same time both here and there. His divine-human nature enables Him to be on earth and in the bosom of the Father at the same time. That is why the writer uses the present tense "is," to show that even while He was man, Jesus was God and retained all His divine properties.

But had He not come down to earth, we would still be ignorant and untaught. That is the value of the incarnation to us. That is the reason why His becoming human is so important. God doesn't speak man's language. It is unknown whether God speaks a language at all. We do not know and will not know until we get to heaven. Sometimes God chose to appear in the form of a man or to send His angels to earth to communicate with men; but God, by Himself, chose not to reveal Himself to men except through man — through that man Jesus Christ, who spoke men's language. Why did God have to become man? Not only so that He could die as a man, but also that He could talk with men and reveal Himself to men.

What did Jesus say? It wasn't only what He *said*, but it was also what He *did*, that reveals God's fullness to us. Jesus showed us the whole nature of God's grace to men by His life and by His words. In fact, Jesus is the very manifestation of the grace of God. Our text says that "grace and truth came by Jesus Christ." We can translate that a little more completely by saying, "grace and truth came into existence through Jesus Christ." The Law was given through Moses, and we know what the Law does. The Law condemns men, because men are unable to keep it. *Before Christ*, or shall we say, before the promise of Christ, *there was no such thing as grace.* There was only the heavy burden of the Law which said, "Thou shalt" and "Thou shalt not." There was only that awful feeling in man that he hadn't kept his bargain. There was only the depressing knowledge that he owed an incalculable debt which he could not pay. That was God's justice and God's wrath, and that was only one half of God's true nature. Then came Christ by promise and by the flesh. Then came grace. Then came the knowledge that man didn't have to pay for his own sins. Then came the relieving fact that man was the recipient of a free gift. Then came the forgiveness of God through Jesus Christ. Then came Jesus Christ Himself, who not only said that God was loving and would forgive every sinner who accepted the atonement, but who actually paid the price of our debt for us. You know what that price was. The price was our life. That was the price that Jesus paid — His own life. He Himself died so that men need not die. All that man has to do is to rely on Jesus' work of salvation. That is the second half of God's true nature. God is not only a God of justice and wrath, but He is also a God of love. That was what Jesus declared unto us.

John tells us that we all have received all of God's love. John puts it this way, "And of His fullness have all we received, and grace for grace." That last expression tells us in a measure just how wonderful this event really is. It's not simply that there is a set limit of love which God has appointed for every person. No! There is enough grace, there is enough love, that should we empty out one heartful of love, our heart would immediately be showered with another heartful of love, and another, and another. There is a limitless supply of God's love. Not all the world can contain it. It is as if we were to try to pour the ocean into the sand bucket of the little child playing on the beach. The water would keep on overflowing the edges of the bucket for ages and ages to come. It is as if we were to try to haul the mountains in a toy truck which a boy might get for Christmas. The mountains would keep on loading the truck for aeons and aeons. That's the way God's grace is. It showers us and covers us completely and fully, and it keeps on showering over us. We are drowned in a sea of God's love. That's what Jesus revealed to us about God. It is impossible to get this knowledge of God in any other way than to accept God's promise and believe the Word and actions of Jesus Christ Himself.

What does it all mean? What is its significance for us? Is it really such an important thing that Jesus Christ became man and assumed our flesh? Is there any need for such a question? Thank God that He did. Thank God that God became man, for it is only through the birth of Jesus Christ that all this is possible. Thank God that Jesus revealed the fullness of God's grace in His life, in His death, in His words, and in His actions. Accept Jesus as your own Savior. Repent! Clean out your heart by confessing your own sins and your inability to merit anything of God's grace. Prepare yourselves mentally and spiritually for the coming of the newborn Babe of Bethlehem, so that when He comes into your memories and into your hearts and souls again on Christmas, you can fill up your hearts with the love of God and the joy of the knowledge that you are indeed the sons of God and heirs of salvation. Even so, come, Lord Jesus.

IV

Limited Man and Limitless Lamb

(The Fourth Sunday in Advent)

And this is the record of John, when the Jews sent priests and
Levites from Jerusalem to ask him, Who art thou? And he confessed,
and denied not, but confessed, I am not the Christ. And they asked him,
What then? Art thou Elias? And he saith, I am not. Art thou that
prophet? And he answered, No. Then said they unto him, Who art
thou? that we may give an answer to them that sent us. What sayest
thou of thyself? He said, I am the voice of one crying in the wilderness,
Make straight the way of the Lord, as said the prophet Esaias. And
they which were sent were of the Pharisees. And they asked him and
said unto him, Why baptizest thou then if thou be not that Christ nor
Elias neither that prophet? John answered them, saying, I baptize with
water; but there standeth One among you whom ye know not; He it is
who, coming after me, is preferred before me, whose shoe's latchet
I am not worthy to unloose. These things were done in Bethabara,
beyond Jordan, where John was baptizing. The next day John seeth
Jesus coming unto him and saith, Behold the Lamb of God, which taketh
away the sin of the world. — *John 1:19-29*

"Who are you?" When someone asks us that question, we are
ready to reply by giving him our name. We may, if necessary, give
some pertinent information about ourselves, such as our address,
our place of work, present age, telephone number, whether we are
married, how many children in the family, and the like. The people
who asked this question of John the Baptist were interested in
a very specific answer. They were sent by the priests and Levites
to examine John. That was their job. They were entrusted with
the business of safeguarding the religious exercises of the people.
And so they came to John as they came to every preacher on the
horizon, with the question, "Who are you?" Let us hear from John
himself that he was a man who knew his limitations.

John gave a very simple and forthright answer to the question
which was addressed to him. He said, "I am not the Christ." Many
another man would not have said that. Many another man, given
the chance, would have capitalized on the situation by saying,
"Yes, I am Christ. Follow me. Be my disciples. I will deliver you."
Jesus Himself later warned His disciples and us against just such
impostors. They are nothing more than false prophets. They are
fakes. They will not deliver anyone. They will only be blind
leaders of the blind, and both shall fall into the ditch of despair,
despondency, and damnation.

John's answer would much rather coincide with the answer
which Peter gave as spokesman for the entire band of the disciples.
When Jesus asked them, "Who do men say that I am?" His disciples gave the answers which are reflected in the questions addressed to John in our text. They told Jesus that some people

thought He was Elias, some thought He was that prophet, and some that He was John the Baptist brought to life again. Thereupon Jesus asked His disciples, "But who do you say that I am?" Peter's answer is the same one John would have given. He said, "Thou art the Christ, the Son of the living God."

"Art thou Elias? I am not." Enoch, Elias, and Jesus are the only men of whom the Bible says that they ascended into heaven bodily. There was an opinion held by many of the rabbis of Jesus' day that Elias would be made to come down to earth again and to precede the coming of the Messiah. That opinion was founded on the Old Testament prophecy that Elijah would really come to preach to the people and to prepare the way for the coming of the Messiah (Mal. 4:5, 6). But John disclaims that honor. He simply says that he is not Elias returned to earth. Jesus, however, does give that name to John when He says that "Elias has come already and they knew him not" (Matt. 17:12). Jesus calls John the Baptist by the name Elias, because John the Baptist preached the same thing that Elias had preached in his own day. As Elias had preached repentance and a return to the Lord, even so did John preach repentance, "for the kingdom of heaven is at hand." On that score we can say that John the Baptist was indeed Elias, even though he was not Elias brought back to life again.

His questioners reach back into the pages of Old Testament Scripture once more to inquire of him who he was. "Art thou that prophet?" God had told of the coming of a "prophet" already in the Book of Deuteronomy. There He tells the children of Israel through Moses: "The Lord, thy God, will raise up unto thee a Prophet from the midst of thee, of thy brethren, like unto me; unto Him shall ye hearken" (Deut. 18:15). The term used in this prophecy and in the question addressed to John is a term which applies only to Jesus both in its prophecy and in its fulfillment. Only to Jesus, that is, to God, should we hearken. That the term is also used of Jesus in the fulfillment is shown us in several places in the New Testament (John 6:14 and 7:40), where the people who saw Jesus' miracles and heard the wisdom of His preaching acknowledge that He was in truth "that Prophet." But John says, "No, I am not that prophet."

His inquisitors have exhausted their resources. Finally they despairingly ask, "Well, who are you then? so that we can take an answer back to those who sent us in the first place." John concedes to them and tells them quite plainly. But he doesn't make up his own answer. He quotes his answer from the Bible itself. He says, basing his reply on the prophecy of Isaiah, "I am the voice of one crying in the wilderness, Make straight the way of the Lord" (Is. 40:3). Read the chapter from which those words come.

Read Isaiah 40 for a clear statement of the reason for John's existence. Read it for the comforting Gospel you will find there. John's advent was clearly foretold in the Old Testament, and here, in this chapter of the New Testament, we see clearly the fulfillment of that prophecy. We notice also that John understood his position in the plan of salvation as God had prepared it. He does not identify himself as John. He simply calls himself a voice. He does not put on airs. He simply says that he is crying in the wilderness, both literally the wilderness along the Jordan and figuratively the wilderness of sin in men's hearts.

But John becomes even more plain in stating his limitations. He does not boast of his job. He does not brag of his position as the forerunner of Christ. He simply says, "I am not worthy to loose the straps of His sandals." It was customary in the days of Jesus for a host to provide a second pair of shoes or slippers for his guests as they entered the house. The job of taking off the street shoes of the guests and washing their feet for them was considered one of the lowest jobs of a servant. John uses this is an illustration. He effaces himself before Christ so much that he says he is not even worthy of that job.

But see how great a work he has done. Though he himself claimed no honor and glory, God chose this rough man, John, to be the forerunner of the Messiah. God Himself appointed John to announce the coming of the greatest man that ever lived, the God-man Himself. John was like a diamond which lies among the stones or gravel. The undiscerning eye cannot notice its real worth, but the diamond is there nonetheless. People may think that the stone is worthless, but there is one who can detect its real value. So was John. Clad in rough garments, living a hermit's life, traveling up and down the Jordan, he appeared to be quite harmless to the leaders and quite ineffectual among the people. But God had chosen him for a special task. That task was to proclaim the coming of Christ as Savior.

John pointed away from himself toward Jesus. Speaking of Jesus, he said, "He it is who, coming after me, is preferred before me." In the natural sequence of events John came before Jesus. But in the work and in the characters of the two there was no doubt. Jesus is the most important Person in the history of the world. Even the unbelieving world recognizes this in part, for the Western world dates its calendar from the time of His birth. Jesus' work is the most important work that was ever done in this world, for it is only through the work of salvation which Jesus performed for all men and for us that men can have peace with God. The birth, the life, the death, and the resurrection of Jesus is the decisive point in the history of the world. It reconciled man to God. It made sons of God out of the sons of men. It made saints out of sinners.

This Jesus shall baptize with the Holy Ghost and with fire. John indeed baptized. He did not deny that. But he only claimed that his baptism had to be given to him. He only claimed that his was a baptism of water. He only claimed that God had commissioned him to baptize. Jesus Himself (in Matt. 21:25) acknowledges the validity of John's baptism.

But Jesus baptized with the Holy Ghost and with fire. This is a prefiguration of the first Pentecost Day, and it tells us of the real power of Jesus. He did not baptize by commission. He needed not to have someone else give Him authority to baptize. He baptized according to His own authority. His baptism was a complete outpouring of the Holy Spirit. He Himself shed the wisdom of the Spirit upon His believing followers. He it was who revealed the mysteries of God to His disciples so that later they could say without contradiction that they were the "stewards of the mysteries of God." (1 Cor. 4:1)

John's testimony concerning Jesus also contains an indictment against the people of his day, and especially against the chief priests and Levites who had come to question him. He tells them, "He is standing among you, and you do not know Him." That was not the fault of Jesus, nor was it the fault of John. At this point in the story of John's ministry and the story of Jesus' life, John had been preaching for some time along the Jordan, telling them about the Messiah who was soon to come. Was it his fault that the leaders did not listen to him? Jesus rarely walked incognito. He rarely tried to hide His identity. Jesus walked openly, teaching and preaching to the people, and working the miracles which He did with the express purpose of leading people to accept Him as true God in the flesh.

It was the people who refused to recognize Him. It was the priests and the Levites and the Pharisees who refused to accept Him as the Messiah. It was the stubbornness of their own minds which prompted them to reject him. It was, perhaps, the fear of losing their positions of leadership which led them to deny His authority and finally led them to kill Him in the hope of ridding themselves of that troublesome man whom we, by faith, have come to know as Jesus our Savior.

Those denials did not prohibit John from continuing his proclamation — nor did they frighten him into delaying it. Our text goes on immediately, as John's testimony went on immediately. "The next day John seeth Jesus coming unto him and saith, Behold the Lamb of God, which taketh away the sin of the world" (v. 29). This, too, is part of John's forthright testimony of Jesus. In fact, this is the meat of it. By knowing his own limitations, John could properly point to Jesus. That expression "Lamb of God" is filled with meaning. It took his people back to their days of slavery in Egypt, to the first Passover when God delivered them by the blood of the lamb (Ex. 12:3 ff.). It took them back to the prophecy of Isaiah, who spoke of the "lamb brought to the slaughter, and as a sheep before her shearers is dumb, so He [Christ] openeth not His mouth" (Is. 53:7). It pointed them beyond the moment of Christ's death to the victory of "the Lamb that had been slain" (Rev. 5:6). This simple expression, "Lamb of God," pointed them away from John the Baptist to their Savior "which taketh away the sin of the world" by His dying as their Substitute. It showed them their own limitations, which had caused God to exercise His limitless love by sending that Savior.

Yes, John knew his limits. He taught his people their limits. He teaches us our limits. When our heart asks us the question, "Just who do you think you are?" let none of us try to answer, "I am my own Christ, my own savior." Our conscience tells us otherwise as it accuses us of our sin. Let none of us try to answer, "I am Elias or that prophet," for we do not preach repentance to ourselves — God does that. Let none of us even assume the role of a John the Baptist as a voice crying in the wilderness, for what shall we cry unless the Lord gives us His word? Here is what John tells us, and here is what we should do. Look to Jesus and cling to Jesus and point to Jesus as your Savior, your "Lamb of God" who takes away *your* sins. Know your limits. But know also the limitless love of God for you. This "limited" John was exalted by Jesus, who said: "Among those that are born of women there is not a greater prophet than John the Baptist" (Luke 7:28). But we, who are limited by our sins and frailties, are by our faith exalted above John, as Jesus states, "He that is least *in* the kingdom of God is greater than he." (Luke 7:28)

This, then, is our preparation for Christmas. We worship Jesus as true God who became true man to redeem us from our sins by His own death. As we know our limits, we glory in the Lamb of God whose love knows no limits.

> Come, Thou precious Ransom, come,
> Only Hope for sinful mortals!
> Come, O Savior of the world!
> Open are to Thee all portals.
> Come, Thy beauty let us see;
> Anxiously we wait for Thee.

Even so, come, Lord Jesus.

FOUR MIDWEEK ADVENT CANDLES

By Karl V. Grotheer

(Unless otherwise indicated, all Scripture references are taken from the RSV)

I

The Prophecy Candle

All this took place to fulfill what the Lord had spoken by the prophet: "Behold, a virgin shall conceive and bear a son, and His name shall be called Emmanuel" (which means, God with us).
Matthew 1:22, 23

Class prophecies! Each year another group reaches the plateau of confirmation and graduation. Each class presents boys and girls of vision, calculated dreams, and plans for the future.

In a reflective mood the pastor remembers that Scott never became a professional baseball player. Douglas forgot about becoming an engineer and even quit high school because of his determination to work in order to buy an automobile. Judith was married right after high school graduation, and this ended her ambition of becoming a teacher. Peter wanted to be a missionary but was diverted into a business enterprise. Many a person carries within his breast the remembrance of some shattered dream.

With God it was decidedly different. A promise was made. The Father would be revealed through His Son. There was the long night of waiting, but a night illumined with stars of prophecies — brilliant and mysterious.

As we begin another Advent season we light the first candle, known as the Prophecy Candle. The climax of the text is:

Immanuel, God with Us

I

God with Us Through the Word

During the long night of waiting a brilliant star appeared when the Holy Spirit moved Isaiah to prophesy: "Behold, a virgin shall conceive and bear a son, and shall call His name Immanuel" (Is. 7:14). Then St. Matthew, in the time of fulfillment, makes it his special assignment to point out to his fellow Jews: "All this took place to fulfill what the Lord had spoken by the prophet: 'Behold, a virgin shall conceived and bear a son, and His name shall be called Emmanuel' (which means, God with us)."

Advent is a period of the church year when the faithful prepare for a rightful commemoration of the coming of the Word — the holy Incarnation. St. John beautifully expresses the truth of

Advent and Christmas as he writes: "In the beginning was the Word, and the Word was with God, and the Word was God. . . . And the Word became flesh and dwelt among us, full of grace and truth; we have beheld His glory, glory as of the only Son from the Father." (John 1:1, 14)

God with us through the Word! What validity for the true Mass of Christ — known to us as Christmas! The Word, Christ, was with the Father from the beginning. The Word, Christ, was God. And when Jesus was born of the blessed Virgin Mary, then God Himself became as one of us, of the flesh, the "God with us."

To know God we must know Christ, for Christ is the Sent-one of the Father. Through Christ the Father reveals His purpose and will. God wills that all should be saved. God swears that He has no pleasure in the death of the wicked. Our gracious Father planned the great redemption before the world was even formed and molded. Much time elapsed. Agonizing ages passed. But then it happened!

> When all was still, and it was midnight, Thy almighty Word, O Lord, descended from the royal throne. (Introit for the Sunday after Christmas)

II
God with Us in the Church

The Christ Child came to be not only the Savior of the world but also the Bridegroom of the church. In the kingdom of grace Christ rules over the church, which is His particular project of love. He was born in order to die; He died for His bride, the church.

As entrance is made through the portals of another church year the bride enters into another year of grace. The church is the company of all believers in Christ. And when Christ established the New Testament church He entrusted its ministry with the rich treasure trove of the audible and visible Word. The remission of sins, which by His sacrifice Christ achieved for us, is conveyed to us through Word and Sacrament.

It is a transcending thought, a sublime truth, that as we enter another year of grace the Son of God, the incarnate Word, will accompany us. The richness and fullness of God's forgiving love will never be withdrawn. God with us in the church! God always present in every form of worship and the blessed Sacrament!

III
God with Us in the World

Much of the world is on the anxious seat. Contending ideologies are causing constant brush fires that may momentarily burst into a world conflict. President Kennedy's stirring words on draft schedules and assignment of duty chilled many a heart and home. Stark terror and unrestricted destruction could envelop the world.

In such dark hours, even in the midst of raining death and destruction, our Immanuel will not forsake us. He is God with us not only in Holy Baptism on some peaceful Sunday, not only in a particular, miraculous way at the altar and the Communion rail, but also in the silent chamber, the lonely vigil, on the battlefield, and in the city of destruction.

As you light the first candle of Advent think of the sages of old foretelling the coming of the world Messiah! Think of the holy night when Christ was born of the blessed Virgin Mary in fulfillment of the Father's promise to redeem the world! Think of the high and noble privilege of being members of the body of Christ through a faith kindled and sustained by Word and Sacrament! Think of God's never-failing love and presence even in the dark hour of night and storm of war! Immanuel, God *is* with us!

II
The Bethlehem Candle

And you, O Bethlehem, in the land of Judah, are by no means least among the rulers of Judah; for from you shall come a ruler who will govern My people Israel. — *Matthew 2:6*

The second Advent candle bespeaks preparation. It is termed the Bethlehem candle.

Many thoughts crowd the mind of the faithful during this busy season. It is of the utmost importance that our hearts be attuned to John the Baptizer's admonition to repent because of the presence of the kingdom of God.

Even as frantic efforts are made to lay in a supply of Christmas baking, to check off names on the shopping list, and to decorate the home with an evergreen, sprigs of green, ribbons, and candles, so efforts should be made to be at all midweek Advent vespers and to receive the body and blood of our Lord in the Sacrament.

The blessed Virgin Mary, together with Joseph, made a trip to Bethlehem. It was a long and tedious journey. But it was necessary as preparation for the great event of that first Christmas.

Our text projects the thought of

The Coming of the King
I
He Did Come

When the Wise Men came to the royal city of Jerusalem they inquired: "Where is He who has been born king of the Jews? For

we have seen His star in the East and have come to worship Him."
King Herod was troubled and assembled the church leaders for information as to where Christ should be born. To their credit it
must be said that they knew the Old Testament prophecy of Micah
5:2, which read: "But you, O Bethlehem Ephratah, who are little
to be among the clans of Judah, from you shall come forth for Me
One who is to be Ruler in Israel, whose origin is from of old, from
ancient days."

The King of Israel, the promised Messiah, was to come from
a small, insignificant town by the name of Bethlehem. Micah adds
"Ephratah" to Bethlehem in order to distinguish it from another
Bethlehem in Zebulon.

The development of the coming of the Messiah is a fascinating
study of the towering wisdom of God. The first promise in Gen. 3:15
is rather vague. The next reference assigns the Messiah to the
Shemitic division of mankind. Next we learn that He is to be of
the seed of Abraham, the father of the Jewish race. The image
becomes clearer when the tribe of Judah is declared to be God's
choice for the Redeemer. The mystery keeps unfolding when King
David's is selected as the family. Then the very town is announced
where the King is to be born.

And when the world was dead ripe for the coming of the King
we read what transpired in the Christmas Gospel:

> And Joseph also went up from Galilee, from the city of Naz-
> areth, to Judea, to the city of David, which is called Bethlehem,
> because he was of the house and lineage of David, to be enrolled
> with Mary, his betrothed, who was with child. And while they
> were there, the time came for her to be delivered. And she
> gave birth to her firstborn Son, and wrapped Him in swaddling
> cloths, and laid Him in a manger, because there was no place
> for them in the inn. — *Luke 2:4-7*

Yes, the King did come!

II

Why Did He Come?

It is always a thrill to celebrate Christmas — even in a secular
fashion. After all, there are the dress-up occasions, the parties, the
dinners, and the sentimental songs. A festive air reigns throughout
the season. Christmas is also a popular time for young people to
become engaged.

All these legitimate and external features of "the season to
be jolly" could easily distract a person from the true significance of
the birth of Christ. It is not too difficult to imagine how thousands
upon thousands of people religiously follow protocol in all the
details of distribution and exchange of gifts, the Christmas card list,
the tree with a few extra ornaments, and the dinners for this-and-

that group, and never find time to make the spiritual journey to Bethlehem in order to sing "Glory to God in the Highest" for His unspeakable Gift.

Why did the King come? No better answer can be provided than the word of the angel to Joseph: "Joseph, son of David, do not fear to take Mary, your wife, for that which is conceived in her is of the Holy Spirit; she will bear a son, and you shall call His name Jesus, *for He will save His people from their sins."* (Matt. 1:20b, 21)

Man was in trouble. He lived in open rebellion against God. There was no one who could show any righteousness befitting the holy majesty of God. All efforts of man to make even an approach to the Father remained futile and vain. In this hopeless scene God gave the promise of His Son. The coming of the King was not ordained in order to evoke excitement over pageantry and pomp, or to be a show and spectacle of power and might. The coming of the King was a coming in love, out of love, for a loveless people. The King came in order personally to save His people. The King willingly yielded His frame to the temporal authority of His day in order to be offered upon the altar of the cross and thus fulfill God's eternal purpose of redeeming the world and offering all sinners the adoption as children of the heavenly King.

This is the true joy of Christmas — a joy which has the undertones of the slashing of the scourge, the hammering of the nails, and the cry of anguish.

We hail our King and bow down in holy reverence. We pray for God's Holy Spirit to grant repentance and faith. The King comes to save us!

As you light the second candle of Advent, think and plan your spiritual journey to the little town of Bethlehem. Think of the great salvation God prepared through the Child of Bethlehem. Believe in Him, and remain a loyal son and daughter of the King.

III

The Shepherds' Candle

Oh, come, let us worship and bow down, let us kneel before the Lord, our Maker! For He is our God, and we are the people of His pasture and the sheep of His hand — *Psalm 95:6, 7*

The Christmas Eve midnight Eucharist was over. Many had communed on that most holy night, and the pastor was weary but happy. His wife had presented him with Bach's *Christmas Oratorio.* In the magic light of the Christmas tree the pastor listened with silent rapture to the famous "Hirtenmusik" — shepherds' music —

for the second day of the festival. Immediately after the entrancing pastoral music a mighty chorus sings the chorale:

> Break forth, O bright and rosy Morn,
> Till earth with splendor blazes;
> Ye shepherds, consternation scorn,
> And hear the angels' praises.
> This Child that lies a helpless boy
> Shall yet become your endless joy,
> Shall frustrate hell's endeavor,
> And reign in peace forever.

The pastor was transported in spirit to that great night of which St. Luke writes: "And in that region there were shepherds out in the field, keeping watch over their flock by night. And an angel of the Lord appeared to them, and the glory of the Lord shone around them, and they were filled with fear. And the angel said to them, Be not afraid; for behold, I bring you good news of a great joy which will come to all the people; for to you is born this day in the city of David a Savior, who is Christ the Lord." (Luke 2: 8-11)

The third candle of Advent is known as the shepherds' candle. We consider

The Chief Shepherd and His Flock

I

The Need to Worship the Chief Shepherd

We often wonder why a great many people even bother about the observance of the Feast of the Holy Nativity. The number of people who undergo all the ritual of celebrating Christmas *minus* the invitation to "worship . . . the Lord, our Maker," must be staggering. We realize, of course, that the merriment of the season, the excitement of giving and anticipating gifts, throws an aura of glitter and glamor around the various functions and activities of the season. But since the significance of Christ's birth is hazy and irrelevant to them, and since the response to worship is completely absent, the observance of Christmas is actually nothing more or less than an annual pagan rite.

The general disappointment becomes particularized when our own parishioners follow suit. We remember only too well how members would crowd the church for the Christmas Eve children's service and then vanish from sight until well in January. The fact that their church voted to have a midnight Holy Communion on Christmas Eve, a number of services on Christmas Day, vespers on Sylvester Eve, festival services on the Circumcision and Name of Jesus, on the Epiphany of our Lord, besides the usual Sunday services, does not seem to affect them in the least.

Christmas is the Feast of the Father. The text speaks of "the Lord, our Maker!" We attribute the work of creation to the Father. But let emphasis always be made that it was the Father who planned our redemption and gave us His Son to be our Savior. Likewise it is the Father's will and wish that all men should believe in the Son and thus be saved.

God must be worshiped. His holiness demands it; His love inspires it. His hunger for His children must be satisfied. The celebration of Christmas must always be highlighted by faithful and adoring worship by all the grateful children of God.

II

The Need of Undershepherds for the Flock

Somehow the thought keeps pushing us that the blessed season of Christmas could be much happier if the need for sufficient pastors, missionaries, and teachers could be supplied. Many more people could be reached, particularly in foreign areas. Even the dogged encroachment of pagan celebrations of Christmas in our own land could be somewhat stemmed if more undershepherds of Christ were available.

To the credit of our church it must be said that ambitious yet reasonable projections are annually made to make the story of the Father's love more accessible and available to more people. Plans and methods are carefully studied and proposed. With what result? The church is becoming more indebted with the years. Heartrending cutbacks are made. Thousands of redeemed people, for whom Christ has shed His blood, are denied the genuine joy of Christmas. Why? Because our parishes refuse to supply men and material to make such joy possible.

God give us men! God give us the best and most highly gifted people possible for full-time service to our Chief Shepherd!

III

The Need of Assistants to the Undershepherd

The text states, "And we are the people of His pasture and the sheep of His hand." (V. 7 b)

The third candle has been named the shepherds' candle because of sharing experience. "And the shepherds returned, glorifying and praising God for all they had heard and seen, as it had been told them." (Luke 2:20)

The whole event and purpose of Christmas would fall flat on its face unless a God-pleasing reaction and response took place in answer to God letting "the skies pour down righteousness." (Introit for the Fourth Sunday in Advent)

God needs your face to express the joy of Christian living to others. God needs your hands to be busy with the affairs of the local parish, thus sparing the pastor "waiting at tables" and enabling him to be concerned with strictly pastoral activities. God needs the feet of many members to do the errands, calls, and visitations, thus exercising and fulfilling their functions as priests and kings.

Inestimable are the services and opportunities to glorify the Chief Shepherd and to be of valuable aid in assisting the called ministers of Christ.

In lighting the third candle of Advent remember to kneel and bow down in deepest reverence before the Christ Child. And then remember, like the shepherds of old, to bring others to the manger.

IV

The Angels' Candle

When the Son of man comes in His glory, and all the angels with Him, then He will sit on His glorious throne. — *Matthew 25:31*

An old love ballad contains these words: "You may not be an angel, because angels are so few." This statement is both right and wrong. Granted, not even a lovely Christian girl is an angel, but the spirits of God number millions.

I will never forget a story related to our seminary class by the sainted Dr. L. Fuerbringer with reference to the doctrine of angels. A blinding blizzard raged for days across the terrain of one of our northern states. The snow piled into high drifts and barriers. As a result a poor family living in an outlying area was completely marooned and faced with starvation. The God-fearing father gathered his family together and offered a fervent prayer to God for help and food. Some time later a mysterious man astride a strong horse made his appearance in the yard and delivered a bountiful supply of bread and food. And just as suddenly he disappeared. The family had never met this stranger, and never heard of him again. They came to the firm belief that God had sent his angel in the garb of a horseman in order to provide for His children.

The world, naturally, would scoff at such an "immature" belief; even our own people would be inclined to doubt. But let it be said that faith really can remove mountains, whereas doubt never will.

Our concluding consideration for this midweek Advent series is:

The Angels of God and the Final Advent

I

Angels Are the Ministers of God

Fascinating and appropriate is a discussion on angels in this blessed season of Advent and the coming Christmastide. The Gospel narrative is replete with accounts of angel appearances. St. Luke, the "beloved physician," opens the portals to the whole sequence of events leading up to the birth of Christ. The Gospel relates that an angel appeared on the right side of the temple altar as Zacharias was functioning as God's priest. He received the startling announcement that his wife, Elizabeth, would bear a son who would become the great Advent prophet and herald for the coming of the Messiah. Six months later the same angel of light, Gabriel, became God's instrument to make the earth-shaking announcement that the world Savior was about to appear. The angel said to the young maiden: "Do not be afraid, Mary, for you have found favor with God. And behold, you will conceive in your womb and bear a son, and you shall call His name Jesus. He will be great, and will be called the Son of the Most High . . . and of His kingdom there will be no end" (Luke 1:30-33). The Holy Spirit would come upon the blessed Virgin Mary, and the result would be that the true God, Jesus Christ, would also be true man! A divine mystery, a staggering miracle — but a sublime truth!

On Christmas Eve an angel of the Lord appeared to the shepherds keeping watch over their flock outside Bethlehem. This messenger of God preached the first Christmas sermon: "For to you is born this day in the city of David a Savior, who is Christ the Lord" (Luke 2:11). And then the heavenly host "of angels, bending near the earth to touch their harps of gold," sang *Gloria in excelsis Deo.*

An angel of the Lord appeared to Joseph and warned him to take the Christ Child to Egypt and to remain there until bloody Herod's death.

Angels appeared to Jesus after He was tempted for 40 days and 40 nights and ministered to Him; an angel from heaven strengthened Jesus in the depth of His agony in the Garden of Gethsemane.

Two angels accompanied our blessed Lord on the Day of Ascension, saying, "This Jesus, who was taken up from you into heaven, will come in the same way as you saw Him go into heaven." (Acts 1:11b)

And now our text declares: "When the Son of man comes in His glory, and all the angels with Him. . . ." (V. 31a)

All the accounts and references of the Word of God concerning angels teach us that angels are spirits who do God's bidding. Angels are always presented in a serving and ministering capacity. Scripture, for our deep and abiding comfort, also assures us that angels serve God's people and watch over our children. Blessed Martin Luther incorporates this gem in both his Morning and his Evening Prayer: "Let Thy holy angel be with me that the wicked foe may have no power over me."

The fact that angels are holy, that they are mighty, and that they are of great number is of great significance and joy. The greatest comfort, however, is that angels of God ministered to Jesus and that they also serve me, for I am united with Christ through faith in Him. We are all the children of God through Christ, who redeemed us with His precious blood. It is a privilege to know that redeemed sinners are accorded a bodyguard by God. The day will come when we shall become acquainted with these mighty ministers of God.

II

The Second Coming of Christ — Advent Completed

The entire tone and emphasis of Advent should be the overriding truth of Christ's final coming to judge the quick and the dead. It is impossible to twist historic facts and create a mood whereby we think of Advent merely as Christ's coming in the flesh when that already occurred over 1,900 years ago. True, we can celebrate and observe the anniversary of the holy Incarnation. We will praise God for "so great a salvation."

However, it is obvious that the coming of Christ, the theme for every Advent as long as the earth stands, has to do with the *final,* or *second,* coming of Christ. This season should heighten and sharpen our hunger to be with Christ forevermore. We repent of our sins and make confession of them to God and to our fellowmen. We pray that the Christ who came to Bethlehem, who paid the supreme sacrifice for sin on Calvary, who rose on Easter and then returned to His Father, will forgive us our great debt.

As we pursue our calling and render Christian service in devotion and gratitude to our great Redeemer, the Advent Lord will send the angel of death in the hour of our departure and place His eternal claim upon us.

Then, as the final moment, known only to God, breaks upon this world, the Advent King, in a blinding display of power and dazzling glory, will sit upon His throne to judge all mankind.

It will be a devastating experience for the unbelievers. They will be separated from God in all eternity.

It will be a blessed experience for believers, who together with angels and archangels will raise a mighty chorus: "Blessing, and honor, and glory, and power, be unto Him that sitteth upon the throne and unto the Lamb forever and ever." (Rev. 5:13b KJ)

As you light the angels' candle of Advent, think of God's love through Christ and His holy angels who serve you. Think of the final Advent. Lift up your head, for *your* redemption draws near.